83653

D1378523

Learning Resources Center
Collin County Community College District
SPRING CREEK CAMPUS
Plano, Texas 75074

Social Science
Reference Sources

Social Science
Reference Sources

A PRACTICAL GUIDE

THIRD EDITION

Tze-chung Li

GREENWOOD PRESS
Westport, Connecticut • London

Library of Congress Cataloging-in-Publication Data

Li, Tze-chung, 1927–
    Social science reference sources : a practical guide / Tze-chung
Li.—3rd ed.
        p.   cm.
    Includes bibliographical references and indexes.
    ISBN 0–313–30483–1 (alk. paper)
    1. Social sciences—Bibliography.   2. Social sciences—Bibliography
of bibliographies.   3. Social sciences—Reference books—
Bibliography.   I. Title.
    Z7161.A1L5   2000
    [H61]
    016.3—dc21   99–31574

British Library Cataloguing in Publication Data is available.

Library of Congress Catalog Card Number: 99–31574
ISBN: 0–313–30483–1

First published in 2000

Greenwood Press, 88 Post Road West, Westport, CT 06881
An imprint of Greenwood Publishing Group, Inc.
www.greenwood.com

Printed in the United States of America

The paper used in this book complies with the
Permanent Paper Standard issued by the National
Information Standards Organization (Z39.48–1984).

10 9 8 7 6 5 4 3 2 1

To Dorothy In-lan, and
Lily and Rose

Contents

Preface to the Third Edition

This book is intended as a guide to basic, important reference sources in the social sciences. It is a substantial revision of the earlier, second edition, with major changes as follows:

1. The third edition is confined to reference sources. Chapters that appeared in the second edition on the nature of the social sciences, bibliographical needs of social scientists, and unpublished materials and sections on periodicals have either been deleted or incorporated into other chapters.

2. Most titles with imprints before 1980, ceased serial publications, and all sections of additional reference sources in the second edition are generally excluded. The second edition may be retained for many titles not listed in the third edition.

3. A large number of digital products are selected for inclusion. Web sites alone number well over 200 and are listed separately for reference.

4. New to this edition is a unique selected listing of periodicals that provide reference sources of information such as bibliographies, indexes, abstracts, research in progress, theses, directories, and rankings and ratings (Chapter 6).

5. Titles are described and, if necessary, their histories and relationship to other titles are given. Some publishers, vendors, agencies, and organizations are noted for their activities, functions, and products cited in the book.

6. Brief descriptions of the features and search methods of online vendors such as Dialog, Lexis-Nexis, Ovid, Questel-Orbit, Westlaw, and Wilsonline are provided.

The book consists of two parts: "Social Sciences in General" and "Subdisciplines of the Social Sciences." Part 1 contains seven chapters on reference sources in an electronic age, research resources, access to sources, sources of information, statistical sources, periodicals, and government publications. The ten chapters in Part 2 deal with cultural anthropology, business, economics, education, geography, history, law, political science, psychology, and sociology respectively. Reference sources are broadly divided into access to sources and sources of information.

The new edition contains approximately 1,600 source entries. For each entry, the print version title is listed first. If the title is available in digital format, it will be labeled at the end of the title as "print & digital." If the title is only available in digital format, it is so labeled or provided with a URL.

The general cut-off date for inclusion was December 1998. However, many titles published in 1999 are included. Web sites were visited up to December 1998; a few were revisited as recently as July 1999.

Entries are listed in alphabetical order under each heading and subheading; some are arranged according to their contents and features. For each entry, titles/names, author(s), place of publication, publisher, date of publication, pagination, and ISBN or ISSN number are given when available. Each entry is assigned an alphanumeric code for quick reference, but the letters I and O are not used, to avoid possible confusion with the numbers 1 and 0.

Acknowledgments

The author is grateful to Dominican University for allowing generous use of online databases and for material support and to De Paul University Library, Dominican University Library, John Marshall Law School Library, New York Public Library, Oak Park Public Library, University of Chicago Library, and University of Illinois in Chicago Library for using their facilities and resources. Thanks also are due to Cynthia R. Letteri for her assistance in proofreading and to Janice Nichols, who helped compile the name and title index.

Abbreviations of Institutions and Terms

AAA	American Anthropological Association
AACSB	American Assembly of Collegiate Schools of Business
AAG	Association of American Geographers
ABA	American Bar Association
ACT	American College Test
AFL	American Federation of Labor
AHA	American Historical Association
AMEX	American Stock Exchange
APA	American Psychological Association
ARL	Association of Research Libraries
ARPANET	Advanced Research Projects Agency Network
ASA	American Sociological Association
ASCII	American Standard Code for Information Interchange
ASDP	Asian Studies Development Program
BALLOTS	Bibliographic Automation of Large Library Operations Using a Time-Sharing System
BEA	Bureau of Economic Analysis
Blaise	The British Library's Automated Information Service

BLDSC	British Library Document Supply Centre
BLS	Bureau of Labor Statistics
BNA	Bureau of National Affairs
BRS	Bibliographic Retrieval Services
CARL	Colorado Alliance of Research Libraries
CCH	Commerce Clearing House
CD-I	Compact Disc—Interactive
CD-R	Compact Disc—Rewritable
CD-ROM	Compact Disc—Read Only Memory
CD-WORM	Compact Disc—Write Once, Read Many Times
CEO	Chief Executive Officer
CIA	Central Intelligence Agency
CIO	Congress of Industrial Organizations
CIS	Congressional Information Service
CMSA	Consolidated Metropolitan Statistical Areas
CRB	Commodity Research Bureau
CSWE	Council on Social Work Education
CTI	Computers in Teaching Initiative
DUNS	Data Universal Numbering System
DVD	Digital Video Disc
EDRS	ERIC Document Reproduction Service
EIU	Economist Intelligence Unit
ERIC	Educational Resources Information Center
FINIS	Financial Industry Information Service
FIPS	State and City Federal Information Processing Standards
FTP	File Transfer Protocol
GDP	Gross Domestic Product
GIS	Geographic Information Systems
Gopher	Go-fer
GPO	Government Printing Offce
HMO	Health Maintenance Organization

HRAF	Human Relations Area Files
HTML	Hyper Text Markup Language
Http	Hypertext Transfer Protocol
IAC	Information Access Company
IBIS	Illinois Bibliographic Information Service
ICD	International Classification of Diseases
ICJ	International Court of Justice
ICPSR	Inter-university Consortium for Political and Social Research
ICSE	International Classification by Status in Employment
IFLA	International Federation of Library Associations and Institutions
IFSW	International Federation of Social Workers
ILCSO	Illinois Library Computer Systems Organization
IP	Internet Protocol
ISBN	International Standard Book Number
ISI	Institute for Scientific Information
ISIC	International Standard Industrial Classification of All Economic Activities
ISO	International Organization for Standardization
ISSN	International Standard Serial Number
KWIC	Keyword-in-Context
LC	Library of Congress
LIS	Library and Information Science
LOCIS	Library of Congress Information System
MBA	Master of Business Administration
Milnet	Mlitary Network of Unclassified Data
MSA	Metropolitan Statistical Areas
NAICS	North American Industrial Classification System
NARS	National Archives and Records Service
NASDAQ	National Association of Securities Dealers Automated Quotations system

NASS	National Agricultural Statistics Service
NASW	National Association of Social Workers
NBS	British Library National Bibliographic Service
NCAS	National Center for American Statistics
NCES	National Center for Education Statistics
NCHS	National Center for Health Statistics
NCJRS	National Criminal Justice Reference Service
NCLIS	National Commission on Library and Information Science
NICEM	National Information Center for Educational Media
NOTIS	Northwestern Online Total Integrated System
NYPL	New York Public Library
NYSE	New York Stock Exchange
OCLC	Online Computer Library Center
OLC	Ohio Library Council
OMB	Office of Management and Budget
OPAC	Online Public Access Catalog
OPLIN	Ohio Public Library Information Network
ORBIT	On-Line Retrieval of Bibliographic Information Timeshared
OTC	Over-the-Counter
PAIS	Public Affairs Information Service
PDF	Portable Document Format
PMSA	Primary Metropolitan Statistical Areas
PPO	Preferred Provider Organization
RLG	Research Libraries Group
RLIN	Research Libraries Information Network
ROTC	Reserve Officer's Training Corps
S&P	Standard and Poor's
SAT	Scholastic Aptitude Test
SCED	International Standard Classification of Education
SDI	Selective dissemination of information
SEC	Securities and Exchange Commission

SIC	Standard Industrial Classification
SPIndex	Subject Profile Index
SuDoc	Superintendent of Documents
TQM	Total Quality Management
UMI	University Microfilms International
UN	United Nations
UNESCO	United Nations Educational, Scientific and Cultural Organization
UNSCOM	United Nations Special Commission
URL	Uniform Resource Locator
USGS	United States Geological Survey
Veronica	Very Easy Rodent-Oriented Net-wide Index of Computerized Archies
WAIS	Wide Area Information Servers
WKS	White Knight Systems
WLN	Western Library Network
WWW	World Wide Web

Part I

Social Sciences in General

Chapter 1

Reference Sources
in an Electronic Age

Over the last decades, there has appeared an imposing array of technical
achievements in digital information services: online databases in the 1970s,
CD-ROMs in the 1980s, and multimedia and the Internet in the 1990s.
The traditional library has emerged into a digital library. A digital library
stores, preserves, retrieves, and disseminates materials in digital format and
provides a gateway to materials in digital format outside the library.

The rapid development of digital information services has had serious
impacts on the storage, retrieval, and use of resources. Access to resources
is no longer geographically limited to the library where resources are physically housed. A computer search of a million records takes only a few
seconds. The most useful feature of a file in digital format, known as a
database, is its ability to provide multiple access points and a multidimen-
sional approach. Users can direct the computer to match terms and retrieve
only those documents in which a match occurs. Resources can be used by
numerous people at the same time. Information can be located through the
author, title, subject, source, language, date of publication, document type,
and/or any other access point structured. For instance, it is practically im-
possible to find how many males and females are listed in print biographical
sources. Using Dialog's File 234 (*Marquis Who's Who*) or File 236 (*American Men and Women of Science*), a searcher may find through the sex field
the number of males and females listed as biographees. Also, in *Newsearch*
(Dialog File 211), a user may use the article type field to locate editorials,
biographies, illustrations, and so on. A user may also find ratings and rankings in some databases by sorting the data retrieved. None of these searches
can be performed in print hard copies. Additionally, many databases have
no print counterparts. Online searching is the only means to obtain infor-

mation from these resources. With the emergence of the Internet, resources are available worldwide.

Both the Internet and online database vendors, such as Dialog and Ovid (noted later), are huge databases. For the convenience of discussion, this chapter deals with online databases and the Internet in separate sections.

DIRECTORIES

The following are two Gale Research directories, or databases of databases:

> *Gale Directory of Online, Portable, and Internet Databases*. Detroit: Gale Research. Print & digital. (A1)
> *Gale Directory of Databases*. Detroit: Gale Research. Annual with semiannual updates. ISSN 10668934. Print & digital. (A2)

Gale Directory of Online, Portable, and Internet Databases, marketed through Dialog (File 230) and in the GaleNet Web noted later, consists of the print version of *Cyberhound's Guide to Internet Databases* (Gwen Turecki, ed., Detroit: Gale Research, 1996, 1,062 p., ISBN 0787609358) (A3) and *Gale Directory of Databases*, noted next. *Cyberhound's Guide* (formerly the *Gale Guide to Internet Databases*) contains 2,750 domestic and international databases arranged in alphabetical order. For each database, it provides (1) access and retrieval information, (2) descriptive information, and (3) ratings information. Also included are a bibliography listing more than 70 Internet guides and reference sources, subject directories, and an Internet glossary. There are five indexes: Host/Provider Index, Alternate Format Index, White Pages listing contacts of databases, a subject index, and a master index. The Alternate Format Index lists other formats, such as CD-ROM, diskette, magnetic tape, online vendors, and print.

Gale Directory of Databases is published in two volumes: Volume 1, Online Databases and Gale Directory of Databases, and Volume 2, CD-ROM, Diskette, Magnetic Tape, Handheld, and Batch Access Database Products, and part of the online version *Gale Directory of Online, Portable, and Internet Databases* and *Gale's Ready Reference Shelf Online* (noted in Chapter 4) and CD-ROM products. Its online database is marketed via DataStar (File GDDB). The online database is also expanded to *Gale Expanded Directory* (A4), marketed through Dialog (File 230). It contains more than 10,000 publicly available databases, including CD-ROM, and over 3,000 databases on the Internet.

ONLINE DATABASES

A database contains machine-readable records for the purpose of information storage and retrieval. A typical database entry contains a bibliographic citation with or without an abstract or in some cases full text or only an index. All databases may be broadly classified into two categories: (1) access to sources of information, such as indexes and abstracts, and (2) sources of information, providing users direct information, such as numeric, statistical, census data, and full-text, without referring to other sources. A large number of databases have print, microform, and CD-ROM counterparts. Others are available online only.

Each record in a database is divided by fields. Most fields are searchable. An online database features free-text search, that is, any word or phrase in the text can be searched as a subject. Search of words can be coordinated by using logical and positional operators. For precision and relevance of result, search can be conducted by index terms or controlled vocabularies.

Not many libraries can afford to acquire, maintain, and process databases. They must rely on externally available databases by functioning as an interface or a broker between the users and online database services. In recent years, end-user databases have gained popularity. Users can use these database services directly bypassing an intermediary.

Several online searching vendors actively publicize and promote their services and market their services to the public. The following are some vendors of databases:

Dialog. Mountain View, CA: Dialog Corp. (A5)

FirstSearch. Dublin, OH: OCLC. (A6)

Lexis-Nexis. Dayton, OH: Lexis-Nexis. (A7)

Ovid. New York: Ovid Technologies. (A8)

Questel-Orbit. McLean, VA: Questel-Orbit. (A9)

Wilsonline. Bronx, NY: H. W. Wilson. (A10)

Dialog, developed at the Lockheed Palo Alto Research Laboratory, had its initial application early in 1967 when a Dialog terminal was installed at the NASA Ames Research Center in Moffett, California. It began operation to the public in 1972 with a single database. It is now the largest vendor, marketing over 600 databases.

Dialog's databases are broadly classified into twelve subject categories: Business; News; Law and Government; Patents, Trademarks, and Copyrights; Medicine, Biosciences, and Health Care Industry; Agriculture, Food Science, and Food Industry; Drugs and Pharmaceutical Industry; Chemistry and Chemical Industry; Science, Technology, and Engineering; Energy and Environment; Social Sciences and Humanities; and General Reference. There are over 150 databases in the social sciences and related fields.

Dialog can be connected via telephone, telecommunications, and the Internet (telnet dialog.com; http://www.dialog.com). In 1997, Dialog constructed its Web site, *Dialog Web and Dialog Web Select*. Both sites will be noted later. There are two types of indexes for command searching: (1) Basic Index for searching by subject and (2) Additional Index for searching by non-subject, such as author, journal, date, and language. The Basic Index consists of, in most files, words from titles, words assigned as subject terms, and words from abstracts.

The user may limit the search by a variety of fields such as language, date, or journals, save the search statement and have it repeated in other databases, sort the search results, conduct one search of a number of databases, rank the search result, target the search, and retrieve images. One feature of Dialog is its result format, the REPORT format, by which the user may retrieve data from a number of databases and make a report form that can be exported to spreadsheets and other programs. Another feature of Dialog is its image retrieval. But in image retrieval, except in the Web as noted later, Dialog's program, DialogLink, must be used.

Dialog's companion, DataStar (A11), developed in 1984, provides access to over 300 databases. It emphasizes European databases and includes a number of databases in the United States as well. DataStar offers worldwide business and technical information with emphasis on Europe. European news, European Union legislative development, trade, country and market reports, and industry information are well covered. Each file in DataStar is designed in general by four letters. Many databases are available in both DataStar and Dialog. DataStar uses dot-dot commands, similar to Ovid's, and menu search on the Web. It can be accessed via telephone, telecommunications, and the Internet (telnet datastar.com; http://www.datastarweb.com).

FirstSearch is a menu-driven database. It displays a menu in every step of searching. FirstSearch has the following features: (1) There is no need to enter Boolean logical operators and positional operators, because the system formulates searched words into a search statement. (2) When FirstSearch is connected, it puts the user into search mode. (3) Even though it is a menu-driven database, a user must grasp a few commands. First-Search can be accessed via telephone, telecommunications, and the Internet (telnet firstsearch.oclc.org; http://www.ref.oclc.org:2000). OCLC provides a Passport program that helps users connect with one of its three systems: EPIC, PRISM, and FirstSearch.

FirstSearch contains some 30 databases. One of its databases is *World-cat*, its flagship database and the largest, most current union catalog, updated daily. It contains over 30 million records of any type of materials cataloged by OCLC member libraries, including manuscripts written as early as the eleventh century. Another database updated daily, ARTICLE-FIRST, contains nearly 12,500 journals in science, technology, medicine, social science, business, the humanities, and popular culture from 1980 to the present.

FirstSearch provides three main search options: subject, author, and title with samples. In addition, it gives "hints" and "actions" for further selection. FirstSearch, like other OCLC databases online, such as EPIC and PRISM, uses the Z39.58 standard command language.

Started as the first full-text legal database, Lexis expanded in 1979 to add Nexis for news, business, and government. Lexis-Nexis is available on the Internet, CD-ROM, and online. It contains some 24,000 sources, including over 18,000 news and business sources and 4,800 legal sources. All files are organized into 184 libraries. Over 20 libraries are in news, business, and government.

Lexis-Nexis can be accessed via dial-up and the Internet (http://www.lexis-nexis.com). In dial-up access, the user may use Windows, DOS, or Macintosh commands. In DOS, most dot commands can be performed by function keys, but some dot commands must be used if no function keys are available. Searching is conducted through levels: library, file (group or individual), and words or phrases. Boolean logical operators, proximity, truncation, an online thesaurus, fields (called segments in Lexis-Nexis), and savings can be used for searching.

Lexis-Nexis will also be noted in the chapters on business and law. Among legal databases, Lexis-Nexis and Westlaw, noted in Chapter 14, are two giants, and natural language searching is available in both.

Ovid continues Bibliographic Retrieval Services (BRS), which began operation in 1976. BRS was acquired by Pergamon in 1989 and by CDP in 1995. CDP marketed it as CDP Plus Online and later changed to Ovid. Ovid now has over 80 databases with strength in science and technology; fewer than 20 databases are in the social sciences and general reference. Ovid can be connected via telephone, telecommunications, and the Internet (telnet ovid.com; http://gateway.ovid.com).

Once Ovid is connected, three choices are available for use: Ovid (Ovid Technologies) full-screen interface (menu), Ovid Colleague (BRS menu-based interface), and Ovid Online (BRS native interface—"dot-dot" mode). In Ovid, commands are preceded by two dots. As compared with its predecessor, BRS, Ovid has omitted many BRS features and simplified command search. Ovid does not make a distinction between subject and non-subject searches. To narrow the retrieval of data, the user must qualify searches by field.

Ovid puts the user automatically in search mode. The user may start the search in general without using any command, limit the search by fields, repeat the search strategy, and sort the search result. The menu search has two search modes: basic and advanced. It also displays the databases for choosing. There are some databases in the social sciences, such as *ABI/ INFORM, ERIC, Harvard Business Review/Online, PsycINFO, Sociological Abstracts*, and a few H. W. Wilson abstracts.

Questel-Orbit (On-Line Retrieval of Bibliographic Information Time-shared), developed by the System Development Corporation, an outgrowth of RAND's System Development Division, became commercially available in 1973. It was acquired by Pergamon in 1988. Orbit is now Questel-Orbit of France Telecom Group. Over 70 databases are currently marketed through Orbit, with an emphasis on intellectual property, science and technology, patents and trademarks, business, and news. Questel provides in-depth European business news. However, not many databases are available in the social sciences and humanities, except in business.

Orbit can be accessed via telephone, telecommunications, and the Internet (telnet orbit.com). Its QPAT-US (A12) for U.S. patent information for over 20 years is available on the Web (http://www.qpat.com). The Orbit system defaults to search mode; the use of the search command is optional. Similar to Dialog, it uses two approaches of searching: (1) the subject term or the Basic Index search and (2) subject-implicit and other types of search. The Basic Index is constructed, in most files, from words in abstracts, words assigned as index terms, single words from the index terms, and words from titles. The subject-implicit and other searches vary with databases, including author, journal, language, update, and specified period of coverage or publication search. Free-text, Boolean, proximity, field, and controlled vocabulary searching are available. Questel-Orbit provides PowerIndex, a master online index, and PowerSearch, to search in multiple files.

Questel-Orbit's search result is one of the best. It can print fields of documents in a sequence specified by the user. Questel-Orbit also developed the Imagination program, a window-based communication software package that enables the user to retrieve images and to download data to be transferred into a word-processing format, has multitasking capability for downloading and searching at the same time, and provides Automatic Search Session Viewer to view an entire search session.

Wilsonline, offered by the H. W. Wilson Company, contains primarily indexes and abstracts, some with full-text, of the H. W. Wilson family. Wilsonline has more than 30 databases, including *Education Index Abstracts, Education Index, Humanities Abstracts, Humanities Index, Index to Legal Periodicals, Social Sciences Abstracts*, and *Social Sciences Index*. The coverage of Wilsonline, however, extends to recent years only. Some of the Wilson databases are also marketed through Dialog, Ovid, OCLC, ProQuest, and SilverPlatter.

Wilsonline can be accessed via telephone, telecommunications, and the Internet (telnet wline.hwwilson.com; http://www.hwwilson.com). Wilsonline uses two approaches in searching: (1) the basic access point search and (2) additional access point search. The basic access point search includes author, title, and subject search. Additional access point search includes search of publisher name, languages, journal title, year of publication, and ranging. Wilsonline defaults to search mode. With exceptions, the user does not need to enter a search command. It may be noted that Wilsonline is the first vendor to have developed a single search of multiple databases. It also features a catalog card format result.

According to a survey of the use of digital information by members of the Association of Research Libraries (ARL), Dialog led all vendors among mediated online services in 1997, with 94.9 percent of the responses to the survey, whereas among the end-user online services, FirstSearch ranked highest, with 84.2 percent, followed by Lexis-Nexis, with 64.9 percent.[1] The survey also reveals that end-user online searching continues to grow in popularity and that new end-user services for libraries will compete with FirstSearch, including Information Access Company's Search Bank and ProQuest, noted later, and others.[2]

OPTICAL DISCS

An optical disc is a high-density platter for writing or reading through a laser-emitted beam. Its forms consist of CD-ROM (compact disc—read only memory), CD-WORM (compact disc—write once, read many times), CD-R (compact disc—rewritable), and CD-I (compact disc—interactive). CD-R is considered the mainstream of optical technology.[3] Digital Video Disc (DVD) is another development of information technology that will likely replace library collections of VHS videotape.[4] Practically all major indexes, abstracts, American encyclopedias, and many full-texts are produced on CD-ROM. All major American encyclopedias are produced on CD-ROM. *Microsoft's Bookshelf* (A13) represents one of the early electronic multimedia on CD-ROM. It consists of such books as *American Heritage Dictionary, Roget's Thesaurus, Columbia Dictionary of Quotations, Concise Columbia Encyclopedia, Hammond Atlas, The People's Chronology*, and *The World Almanac*. Other multimedia publications include Microsoft's *Encarta, Compton's Interactive Encyclopedia, World Book Multimedia Encyclopedia*, and *Grolier Multimedia Encyclopedia*. Concept search is also available in some of them, such as *Compton's* "ideal search" and *Grolier's* "word search." In a concept search, which differs from a free-text search, the system interprets the user's concept of words used for the search. To search "dogs" as animals will not retrieve "hot dogs."

One advantage of the optical disc is that, because it is run by a computer, multiple access points to documents are provided. Major producers of CD-ROMs for information storage and retrieval include Bowker, Dialog, H. W. Wilson, LaserQuest, LaserSearch, Marcive, OCLC, Ovid Technologies, and SilverPlatter. Dialog markets its *OnDisc CD-ROM* (A14) on a number of subjects, some of which are noted in Part 2. Ondisc provides three choices for searching: Dialog commands, menu, and link to online.

THE INTERNET

The Internet, a widely used network, began as ARPANET (Advanced Research Projects Agency Network), which the Department of Defense initiated in 1969 to link researchers with remote computer centers.[5] By 1983, ARPANET had split into two: the ARPANET and the Milnet (Military Network of Unclassified Data). Interconnection between the experimental networks was called DARPA Internet, or simply the Internet.

The Internet provides electronic mail, electronic publications, and electronic reference, such as WAIS (Wide Area Information Servers). Since the 1980s, the Internet has gained rapid popularity. According to "The 1996 National Survey of Public Libraries and the Internet: Progress and Issues" of NCLIS (National Commission on Library and Information Science), net connections in libraries grew a staggering 113 percent in 1995, and 44.6 percent of our nation's public libraries were linked to the information superhighway, with at least one net connection, more than double the previous year's figure of 20.9 percent.[6] Sites on the Internet can be linked, a very useful feature.

Components of the Internet

Internet services may be broadly classified into three categories: (1) Communication Services, such as e-mail and Usenet newsgroups; (2) Connection Services, Telnet; and (3) Data-Access Services, including FTP (File Transfer Protocol), Gopher (Go-fer), WAIS (Wide Area Information Servers), and WWW (World Wide Web).[7]

E-mail

E-mail is the most widely used component of the Internet. An e-mail address consists of three parts: user, @, and the host's address. The host's address can be either the domain name or the Internet Protocol (IP) number. The domain name system assigns names to different groups with responsibilities of giving subsets of names. Domains are identified as follows: .com for commercial, .edu for educational, .gov for governmental, .mil for military, .org for organizations, .net for networks, and .int for international. In addition, an e-mail address outside the United States includes a two-letter country code at the end. Addresses may also be represented by IP numbers.

Telnet

Telnet is used for connection services. It may be considered as a gateway to other computers. Telneting OPAC (Online Public Access Catalog) is a widely used service. Vendors of online databases can be connected via the

Internet, as noted earlier. The address for Telnet consists of the database and/or host and domain. For example, using Telnet to connect to Dialog, enter telnet dialog.com.

Data-Access Services

Data-access services consist of FTP, Gopher, WAIS, and WWW. FTP is used to transfer data archives. Used in association with FTP is Archie, an index to FTP archives. Gopher, developed at the University of Minnesota, is a menu-driven program to access resources provided by other gopher servers. Veronica (Very Easy Rodent-Oriented Net-wide Index of Computerized Archies) is an indexing service to all Gophers. WAIS provides subject search for information. WWW (World Wide Web, W3, or simply the Web), developed at the European Laboratory for Particle Physics in Switzerland, known as CERN, provides access to text and graphics. The Web is an information delivery tool for retrieving hypertext and hypermedia documents from a host server. It consists of three components: transfer protocol, locator, and host server.[8] The transfer protocol is http (Hypertext Transfer Protocol) for accessing and linking hypertext documents, graphics, and sound. The locator is the URL (Uniform Resource Locator), loaded in the host computer. To use a Web site, enter http://www.host server/path/—that is, to access, using hypertext transfer protocol followed by a colon and two slashes, the host server name and file divided by a slash. For example, http://www.ala.org/alaorg/oa/uslis.html/ is using http protocol to access the American Library Association server, its organization category, a subcategory (Office of Accreditation), and the file of Accredited LIS Master's Program—United States, written in hypertext mark language.

The use of browser software is necessary to surf the Internet. A number of browsers for Microsoft Windows are available, such as *Explorer, Mosaic, Cello, Netscape, EINet's WinWeb,* and *InternetWorks Lite.*[9] *Mosaic, Netscape,* and *Explorer* are popular browsers.

Mosaic, developed by the National Center for Supercomputing Applications at the University of Illinois in 1993, "takes the Internet by storm; WWW proliferates at a 341,634% annual growth rate of service traffic."[10] *Netscape* is an enhanced version of *Mosaic.* One of *Netscape*'s features is its speedy retrieval of textual information first.[11] *Explorer* is Microsoft's product.

Guides

There is no shortage of guides and directories to the Internet. Guides and directories are kinds of bibliography. Definitions of bibliography will be noted in Chapter 3. Since 1993, *College and Research Libraries News* has published a series of Internet resources on a variety of subjects, such as

Latin American studies, psychology, government information, women's studies, distance education, anthropology, law, and education.[12] These lists are classified by broad topics and within topics by service category, such as Gopher and the World Wide Web. *American Libraries* has as a regular feature "Internet Librarian." *Library Journal*, noted in Chapter 3, publishes as regular features the columns "Internet" and "Web Watch."

The following volumes are useful Internet guides and directories.

> *The Internet Compendium: Subject Guides to Social Sciences and Law Resources*. Louis Rosenfeld, Joseph Janes, and Martha Vander Kolk. New York: Neal-Schuman Publishers, 1995. 424 p. ISBN 1555702201. (A15)
>
> *The Online Student: Making the Grade on the Internet*. Randy Reddick and Elliot King. New York: Harcourt Brace College Publishers, 1996. 317 p. ISBN 0155031899. (A16)
>
> *Reference and Collection Development on the Internet: A How-To-Do-It Manual*. Elizabeth Thomsen. New York: Neal-Schuman Publishers, 1996. 175 p. ISBN 1555702430 (A17).

The Internet Compendium is one of a three-volume set. (The other two volumes deal with humanities resources and health and science resources.) It is both a guide and a directory, consisting of three parts. Part I, "How to Use This Book," has four chapters dealing with Internet addresses, clients and servers, tools and resources for navigating, and communicating with individuals and groups. All important aspects of the Internet are well covered. It explains domains, e-mail, URL, Gopher, finger, netfind, listservs, FTP, Telnet, WWW, and so on.

Part II, "Beyond This Book: Next Steps," contains five chapters. It deals with how to find and make use of Internet resources. Access to Archie, Veronica, WAIS, and so on are described. The main body of the book is Part III, "Subject-Oriented Guides." It consists of seventeen chapters on a variety of subjects. Although the subtitle specifies the social sciences, business, and law, content is not confined to these subjects but includes Internet sites in the humanities and science and technology as well. The chapter on government covers the humanities, physical and applied sciences, biology, chemistry, health and medicine, and physics. In the chapter on operation research/management science, non–social science topics are listed.

With a few exceptions, each chapter of the *Internet Compendium* contains an introduction and a table of contents. But there are no consistencies. Some chapters are provided with an index, others not. The chapter tables of contents differ from one another in arrangement. Some list contents by subject, others by format, and still others by a combination of format and subject. For each site, in general, a brief description, a URL, and if needed a login and password are given. The information contained in the volume is also "electronically available via the Internet from the Clearinghouse for Subject-Oriented Internet Resource Guides" (Introduction). The Index contains "Recommended Resources" and a subject index.

Intended for the academic community, *The Online Student* consists of fifteen chapters on Internet resources, which can be broadly classified into two parts: Part one, consisting of the first ten chapters, introduces the Internet and the components of the Internet (e.g., e-mail, WWW, Gopher, Telnet, FTP, Usenet, Muds, and so on), and research strategies and Internet behavior. Part two, the remaining five chapters, deals with Internet resources in the humanities, the social sciences, business, the sciences, and miscellaneous areas (entertainment, recreation, food, travel, and so on). Illustrations and addresses of selected sites on the Internet are provided. The book has two appendixes: Glossary and Index. It is a good guide to the use of the Internet.

Reference and Collection Development on the Internet contains eight chapters, divided into three parts and two appendixes. The first two chapters in part one deal with the history of the Internet and Internet basics. Part two consists of six chapters on Internet protocols, special resources such as library catalogs, databases, and electronic books, and FAQ (Frequently Asked Questions) files. The two appendixes constitute the third part.

The second part is the core of this book, presenting concisely how to connect and how to use e-mail, Gopher, WWW, and so on. Chapter 5 is specially devoted to one Usenet newsgroup, the Rabberatti. Chapter 8 provides access examples to a number of databases, such as the United States Postal Service for its zip code directory, Subway Route Finder, U.S. Gazetteer, and Decisions of the U.S. Supreme Court.

The two appendixes are (I) the Virtual Vertical File and (II) the List of Lists. The former is a listing of files on the Web arranged alphabetically by subject, from Adoption, African-Americans to Science. The latter provides booklists available through gophers and the Web sites, also arranged alphabetically by subject.

Search Engines

There are many searching tools with which to find information on the Web. *2ask* (http://www.2ask.com) (A18), developed by @tlasNet, Inc., provides search engines, named *Cyber-Gadgets*, to the databases on the Internet in some fifteen languages and links to a number of Web search engines, including *Excite, Harvest, InfoSeek, LinkStar, Lycos, Open Text, SavvySearch, Spry Internet, WebCrawler, WWW Web, Yahoo!* and *Yellow Pages*. The following are some search engines:

> *Alta Vista.* Palo Alto, CA: Digital Equipment Corp. http://altavista. digital.com (A19)

HotBot. San Francisco, CA: Wired Digital, Inc. http://www.hotbot.com (A20)
InfoSeek. Sunnyvale, CA: Infoseek Corp. http://www.infoseek.com (A21)
Lycos. Waltham, MA: Lycos, Inc. http://www.lycos.com (A22)
Northern Light. Cambridge, MA: Northern Light Technology. http://www.nlsearch.com (A23)
Open Text. Waterloo, ON, Canada: Open Text Corp. http://www.opentext.com (A24)
Yahoo! South Clara, CA: Yahoo, Inc. http://www.yahoo.com (A25)

AltaVista claims to be the largest Web index, indexing 30 million pages on over 270,000 servers and 3 million articles from 14,000 Usenet news groups. It provides simple search and advanced search. Greg R. Notess, using a single, nontruncated keyword search, compared *AltaVista* with *Inktomi, InfoSeek, Open Text, Lycos, Excite*, and *WebCrawler* and stated that search in *AltaVista* has a much higher number of hits with two to six times the number of hits found by the second-ranking search engine.[13]

A search result of *Altavista* lists up to ten best matches of the search terms first and indicates the approximate total number of matches. For each item listed, it gives name or title, brief note, author or person in charge, URL, size, and date indexed.

The home page of *Hotbot* displays a number of topics for searching. Its directory consists of fourteen categories, including business and money, computers and Internet, health, news and media, reference, regional, science and technology, and society. The category of "society" lists countries, government-related organizations, related categories, and site recommendations. Related categories and site recommendations are helpful to information seekers. Under "international," Hotbot provides related categories such as science and technology, social sciences, political science, international relations, society, law, areas of practice, international law, politics, and global governance. Recommended sites for international information include Social Democratic Parties Around the World, and WWW Virtual Library: United Nations and other international organizations. Search can be conducted with words, date range, and language. Search can also be qualified by media types or technologies, such as image, audio, *Shockwave, Java, Acrobat*, and so on, by location/domain and by page depth, such as any page, top page, and so on.

InfoSeek displays a menu of six choices: Infoseek Guide, New Search, Big Yellow, World News, Fast Facts, and the *i*Zone. Some topics are self-explanatory. The main menu for New Search lists eleven popular topics: arts and entertainment, business and finance, computers and Internet, education, government and politics, health and medicine, living, news, reference, science and technology, and travel. For searching a subject, the user has the choice of searching all Web pages or searching only selected topics. Search results are provided together with related topics. Big Yellow is the

Yellow Pages Business and Shopping Directory, consisting of such categories as Shopping Adviser, Explore the Net, Web Business Guide, How to Advertise, and Mail Box. Fast Facts offers quick reference to e-mail addresses, stock quotes, bank and market rates, company directories, and street maps, and it also provides references at other Web sites, such as directories, dictionaries, a thesaurus, and historical and scientific references. The *i*Zone provides the latest information on Computer and Internet, Home Living, New Sports, and Business and Finance, and lists career opportunities.

Lycos, "Catalog of the Internet," provides a2z Directory Search by Subject and Point News and Web Reviews. It lists sixteen subjects for browsing: Arts/Humanities, Business/Finance, Computers, Education, Entertainment, Government, Health/Medicine, Internet, Just for Kids, News/Info, Science/Tech, Shopping, Social Issues, Sports, Road Less Traveled, and the World. For each subject searched, Lycos provides postings of the search research and displays the first ten items. For each item, it gives name or title, brief note, author, URL, and size.

Northern Light, named afer a clipper ship built in 1851 for its speed and groundbreaking technology, contains two categories of search: search the entire World Wide Web and search the Special Collection. The Special Collection consists of two million articles in over 3,400 journals, books, magazines, databases and news wires. A user may search any or all of them. The Special Collection is broadly classified into sixteen categories, including social science subjects, such as business and investing, education, government, law and politics, and social sciences in general. Each category is further divided into subcategories; in Business and Investing, there are eighteen subcategories, such as Accounting and Taxation, Advertising, Marketing and Sales, Banking and Finance, Consumer Information, Economics, International Business, Management, and Non-profit Organizations. A listing of publications in a particular category can be viewed. In Accounting and Taxation, there are over 60 publications in alphabetical order, and most publications are briefly annotated.

Northern Light organizes each search result and creates a custom search folder for focused results. There are four types of custom search folders: subject, type, source, and language (English, German, French, Spanish). *Northern Light* has a policy of "Pay Only for What You Use." Article summaries are free. Documents are delivered on the screen for a price ranging from $1.00 to $4.00 per article. If an item is not what is needed, a refund will be made, with a no-questions-asked, money-back guarantee.

When *Opentext* is invoked, a main menu displays several choices, such as What's Hot!, About Open Text, Products & Services, Search the Web, Livelink Intranet, Livelink Commons, and Other Languages. Opentext's LiveLink enables Boolean and proximity searching, phrase searching, and field searching and offers a relevance ranking for searches, audits corporate servers, and provides detailed statistics.[14] The Open Text Corporation provides free access to its indexing.

For each search, *Opentext* provides the number of pages that contain the terms searched and lists the first ten items. For each item, it gives name or title, score (the highest first), size, URL, author or person in charge, brief note, and referral to Visit the Page, See Matches on the Page, and Find Similar Pages.

Perhaps the most popular search service is *Yahoo!* It is a classification system in which information is arranged by category and subcategory. As such, *Yahoo!* is considered a directory, not a search engine.[15] *Yahoo!*'s main menu displays fourteen categories in alphabetical order, such as art, business and economy, education, government, reference, social science, society and culture, and so on. If the category of education is chosen, it displays a list of nearly 40 subcategories, from Adult and Continuing Education, Alternative, College Entrance, Courses, Databases to Journals, Libraries, Online Teaching and Learning, and Vocational Schools, with the number of files in parentheses. The Databases category contains eight databases, including *AskERIC* and *ERIC*, both noted in Chapter 11.

All these are single search engines. *Metasearch*, which may be called the search engine of search engines, is designed to search information in a number of search engines simultaneously. Five *Metasearch* engines were selected as the best performers by Judi Repman and Randal D. Carlson.[16] They are: *ByteSearch* (http://bytesearch.com) (A26), *Mamma* (http://www.mamma.com) (A27), *MetaCrawler* (http://www.go2net.com/search.html) (A28), *ProFusion* (http://www.profusion.com) (A29), *SavvySearch* (http://www.savvysearch.com) (A30). Of the five, according to the authors, *SavvySearch* features search breadth and *ProFusion* search options.

A searcher who is familiar with online databases such as *Dialog* and *Ovid* is frustrated by the lack of detailed field search in search engines. A review of the field searching capabilities of five search engines (*Altavista, Infoseek, Lycos, Yahoo! and Hotbot*), suggests that field search in the Web is not so advanced as traditional search in online databases.[17] According to Randolph E. Hock, *Hotbot* and *Altavista* have the most field search capabilities.[18]

Although many search engines have been developed, coverage of Web sites is limited. According to "Search Engine Features Chart," *AltaVista, Excite, HotBot,* and *Northern Light* are the four search engines with the largest size in terms of pages indexed.[19] In a study of six search engines, Stave Lawrence and C. Lee Giles reported that based on an estimated indexable Web of 310 million pages, the individual engines cover from 3 to 34 percent of the indexable Web. The two engines with the largest coverage were found to be *HotBot* and *AltaVista*, followed by *Northern Light, Excite, Infoseek,* and *Lycos*.[20]

Web Sites

Web sites are most popular in retrieving data. Web sites of libraries, institutions, companies, factories, retailers, newspapers, and resources are numerous. Many OPAC (Online Public Access Catalog) and library resources can be directly connected on the Web. Some OPACs will be mentioned in Chapter 2. Vendors of databases that use command languages have moved toward menu search, particularly on the Web, for end-users. End-users can directly use online services, with no mediating assistance. Vendors of databases noted earlier are also on the Web:

> *DialogClassic*. Mountain View, CA: Dialog Corp. http://www.dialog-classic.com (A31)
>
> *DialogSelect*. Mountain View, CA: Dialog Corp. http://www.dialog-select.com (A32)
>
> *DialogWeb*. Mountain View, CA: Dialog Corp. http://www.dialogweb.com (A33)
>
> *FirstSearch*. Dublin, OH: OCLC. http://www.ref.oclc.org:2000 (A34)
>
> *Lexis-Nexis*. Dayton, OH: Lexis-Nexis. http://www.lexis.com (A35)
>
> *Ovid*. New York: Ovid Technologies. http://gateway.ovid.com (A36)
>
> *WilsonWeb*. Bronx, NY: H. W. Wilson. http://wilsonweb.hwwilson.com (A37)

DialogWeb and *DialogSelect* were developed in 1997. *DialogWeb* is a Dialog version on the Web. However, a few files and commands are not available on the Web.[21] All databases on the two Web sites are classified into twelve topics, such as news and media, business and finance, intellectual property, government and regulations, social sciences, and reference. The topic is further divided with databases for search. For instance, Reference is divided into Books, Book Reviews, and Dissertations; Conference Proceedings and Events; Demographic Data; Directories, Foundations and Grants; People; U.S. Government Publications; and so on. A user may use either basic Dialog commands or guided search to conduct searching. DialogWeb also adds Bluesheet and other features, such as the Help menu.

On the other hand, *DialogSelect* is menu driven. It includes over 250 databases in a single Web site, providing news, company profiles, research articles, patents, and other materials. These databases are classified, as in DialogWeb, into twelve topics, such as news and media, business and finance, government and regulations, and social sciences. The social sciences topic includes *Social SciSearch, Sociological Abstracts*, and *Social Sciences Abstracts*.

In 1998, Dialog introduced a new Web access, *DialogClassic*, as the original Dialog command retrieval system. It does not have the added features of *DialogWeb*, such as Bluesheets and the Help menu, but its operation is much faster than that of *DialogWeb*.

FirstSearch on the Web displays a database area consisting of fourteen categories, which are: all areas, Arts and Humanities, Business and Economics, Conferences and Proceedings, Consumer Affairs and People, Education, Engineering and Technology, General and Reference, General Science, Life Sciences, Medicine and Health Science, News and Current Events, Public Affairs and Government, and Social Sciences.

Lexis-Nexis on the Web, also noted in Chapters 9 and 14, provides Lexis-Nexis Xchange, Business including Xchange for business, and Government for searching legal, business, and government information. Click Xchange for legal information. As noted earlier, all sources in Lexis-Nexis are organized by libraries. The Web site provides shortcuts to the following topics: News—last 90 days; Federal and State Cases; Federal Cases and American Law Reports; Supreme Court briefs; Supreme Court Oral Arguments; U.S. Code Service; *Federal Register* and *Code of Federal Regulations; Congressional Record*; State Cases and American Law Reports; All State Cases; Secondary Sources; Law Reviews; Career; *Martindale-Hubbell*; Judicial Clerkship Directory; and *NALP Directory of Legal Employers*. The user may use Boolean and proximity or Freestyle (natural language) search. Search can also be qualified by dates.

Ovid on the Web is structured by menu, providing two search modes: basic and advanced. "Dot-dot" commands are not available. It also displays the databases for choosing. Databases in the social sciences include *ABI/Inform, ERIC, Harvard Business Review/Online, PsycInfo, Sociological Abstracts*, and a few H. W. Wilson abstracts.

WilsonWeb classifies all databases into the following: full text databases, abstracts databases, indexing only databases, and other databases. Searches can be performed by entering keywords and phrases, proximity operators, words truncated, and subject. A user may also limit the search by fields, such as title, author, corporate author, source, series titles, descriptor, publisher, and reviewer.

In addition, other general Web sites related to the social sciences are noted as follows:

Dialog@CARL. http://dialog.carl.org (A38)

GaleNet. http://www.galenet.com (A39)

InfoTrac SearchBank. http://www.searchbank.com (A40)

ProQuest. http://www.umi.com (A41)

Dialog@CARL, designed by CARL, complements Classic Dialog for end-users. It includes some 300 databases from Dialog and the Research Libraries Group's RLIN Bibliographic Database and CitaDel files, noted respectively in Chapters 2 and 3. D@C provides graphic Web application and character-based Web application.

GaleNet consists of the following databases: *Associations Unlimited, Biography and Genealogy Master Index, Brands and Their Companies, Gale Business Resources, Gale Database of Publications and Broadcast Media, Gale Directory of Databases*, and a number of databases in the DISCovering series. Some are noted earlier, and others are mentioned in the following chapters.

InfoTrac SearchBank, developed from *InfoTrac*, provides access to primarily periodical articles. *InfoTrac* (A42) consists of CD-ROM products and *InfoTrac SearchBank*. Over 30 databases on CD-ROM cover academic journals, business and industry journals, legal journals, general interest magazines, newspaper articles, and government publications. *InfoTrac* databases may be broadly classified into a number of categories: the Business & Technology category of fifteen databases including the well-known *F & S Index*; the Academic & Interdisciplinary category of five databases including *Academic ASAP, LegalTrac*, and *Government Publications Index*; and the General Reference category of some ten databases including *Magazine Index* and *Academic Index*. These two indexes and other databases are mentioned in later chapters.

There are two methods of searching: EasyTrac and PowerTrac. In EasyTrac, a user simply enters a word or words to retrieve information. The PowerTrac is an enhanced method of searching that includes citation list, index browsing, proximity operators, range operators, and restoration marks.

Some 20 databases are now available in *SearchBank*, such as *Books in Print, Business and Company ASAP, Expanded Business File ASAP, General Reference Center (Magazine Index), General Reference Center University Microfilm International (UMI), Investment, ISI Current Contents, ISI Current Contents—This Week, LegalTrac, PAIS International, PsycInfo*, and *Sociological Abstracts*.

ProQuest enables a user to search for information in thousands of published journals, periodicals, dissertations, newspapers, and magazines in UMI's archives. Three types of databases are offered: Abstract and Index for nearly 5,000 periodicals, Full-Text, and Full Image for nearly 2,000 periodicals. One of the features is a search of all databases. By category, in General Reference, are listed *Dissertation Abstracts, Newspaper Abstracts, Periodical Abstracts/General Periodical Abstracts Online, Source One Full Text/Magazine Express, The New York Times*, and *Full-Text Newspapers*. Four databases are in the business category: *ABI/Info/Business Periodicals Online, Accounting & Tax, Banking Information Source*, and *Business Dateline*. The category of the social sciences includes *Education Index/Full Text* and *Social Sciences Index/Full Text*.

Boolean logical operators, truncation, word and phrase searching, and field searching can be conducted. When it is invoked, the system displays a search form and provides Search Assistant, which gives a listing of fields and operators.

The availability of resources in digital format makes resources readily accessible anywhere at anytime and by any person. In an age of global information availability and universality of information access, the whole world is a repository of resources. The development of collection resources has a new challenge. To this topic, we turn next, in Chapter 2.

NOTES

1. Carol Tenopir and Lisa Ennis, "The Digital Reference World of Academic Libraries," *Online* 22, no. 4 (1998): 22–28.

2. Ibid., 24.

3. Deborah Jessop, "A Survey of Recent Advances in Optical and Multimedia Information Technologies," *CD-ROM Librarian* 17, no. 2 (1997): 53–59.

4. Ibid.

5. Tracy Laquey, *Internet Companion* (Reading, MA: Addison-Wesley, 1993), pp. 3–6.

6. *Library Journal* 121, no. 17 (1996): 242.

7. Eric Richard, "Anatomy of the World-Wide Web," *Internet World* 6, no. 4 (1995): 28–30.

8. Ibid.

9. Greg R. Notess, "Comparing Web Browsers: Mosaic, Cello, Netscape, WinWeb and InternetWorks Life," *Online* 19, no. 2 (1995): 36–42; Mark Sheehan, "Pulling the Internet Together with Mosaic," *Online* 19 no. 2 (1995): 16.

10. Ibid.

11. Greg R. Notess, "Searching the Web with Alta Vista," *Database* 13, no. 3 (1996): 86–89.

12. Ibid.

13. For instance, *College and Research Libraries News* 54, no. 7 (1993): 299, 395–96; 54, no. 9 (1993): 510–11; 54, no. 11 (1993): 635–37; 55, no. 3 (1994): 139–41, 143; 55, no. 5 (1994): 256–58; 56, no. 3 (1995): 153–57, and recently, "Internet Resources: Genealogy," by Thomas Jay Kemp, 60, no. 6 (1999): 442–55.

14. "World Wide Web Search Engines: Open Text, Harvest, 2ask," *Online Libraries and Microcomputers* 14, nos. 6–7 (1996): 1–5.

15. Deborah Lynne Wiley, "Beyond Information Retrieval: Ways to Provide Content in Context," *Database* 21, no. 4 (1998): 20.

16. Judi Repman and Randal D. Carlson, "Surviving the Storm: Using Meta-search Engines Effectively," *Computers in Libraries* 19, no. 5 (1999): 50–55.

17. Randolph E. Hock, "How to Do Field Searching in Web Search Engines: A Field Trip," *Online* 22, no. 3 (1998): 19–22.

18. Ibid.

19. As of June 17, 1998. See http://www.searchenginewatch.com/webmasters/feature.html.

20. Steve Lawrence and C. Lee Giles, "Searching the World Wide Web," *Science* 280, no. 5360 (1998): 98–100.

21. Refer to two views on DialogWeb: Alice Klingener, "DIALOG Web—Finally It's Arrived," *Online* 21, no. 5 (1997): 18–24; Susan M. Klopper, "Testing, Stretching, Pushing, and Pulling the DIALOG Web," *Online* 21, no. 5 (1997): 26–32.

Chapter 2

Research Resources
in the Social Sciences

One of the main functions of a research library is to build collections to meet the need for research. Levels of building collections vary. The Research Libraries Group sets up levels on a scale from 0 to 5: 0, Out of Scope; 1, Minimal Level; 2, Basic Information Level; 3, Instructional Support Level; 4, Research Level; and 5, Comprehensive Level.[1]

The development of research resources has been controlled traditionally by two distinctive yet mutually related principles, the principle of local self-sufficiency and the principle of sharing resources.[2] A research library must be self-sufficient to support studies and research. When self-sufficiency is not attainable, the library should be able to provide access to resources outside its own collections.

QUANTITATIVE AND QUALITATIVE MEASUREMENT OF RESOURCES

There is an assumption that the larger the collection, the more likely the library is to be able to satisfy the information needs of users. But how large a collection is considered sufficient, what are the standards by which to judge the quantity, and to what extent does quantity imply quality? The controversy over qualitative and quantitative measurement of library resources has raged for a long time. Despite opposition to quantitative measurement, it appears that quantitative evaluation is by far the most practical means to test the strength of library holdings. In general, the absolute size of the collection, the growth rate of the collection, and expenditure on the collection fall into the category of quantitative measurement. The absolute size of the collection denotes the number of items below which a library is assumed to be unable to function effectively.[3]

The assumption of a close relationship between quantity and quality is by no means conclusive, just as enrollment alone is not the sole factor for evaluating the quality of an institution. In qualitative measurement, librarians must know the subject field and must be well acquainted with its reference sources to evaluate collections. These questions should be asked: whether or not the resources are sufficient to support curriculum requirements or to meet the needs of users, whether or not the resources include materials needed for research in depth, and whether or not the collections consist of the basic, current, and significant titles. Meeting the needs of users is another key factor in building collections.

SELF-SUFFICIENCY AND SHARING RESOURCES

Self-Sufficiency

Guidelines for Building Research Resources

There are several guidelines for building research resources:

1. It is necessary to know your community—its program interest, course requirements, curriculum stress, and study and research levels. The social science collection should be built to be consistent with the degree of library services and users needs.

2. One problem facing most librarians in selection of materials is the "unknown." Librarians should keep abreast of the concepts and development of the social sciences and gain subject knowledge in the subdisciplines of the social sciences.

3. The collection should be built to meet the needs of users. As Arthur Curley and Dorothy Broderick state, "librarians remain constantly sensitive to the needs of the community and respond accordingly."[4] A librarian may use various means to discover the needs of users, including such methods as user surveys, interviews, questionnaires, and citation studies.

4. A proper balance should be maintained between "demand" theory and "value" theory in the selection process. No library can afford to provide any book in any subject for anybody.[5] Oscar Handlin commented that "the academic research library should focus on tightly defined areas of interest that somehow relate to the university's work and aspirations."[6]

5. One must know one's own collection, such as its strengths and weaknesses, the collection levels, and the availability of different media. The field of the social sciences is interdisciplinary. Not only materials in other subject fields but also popular books should be considered for selection.

6. Attention must be given to the factor of continuity in the social science literature, the constantly changing subject field, recent developments

and progress, and new experiments. The library collection should not be limited solely to current needs, but should be envisioned to meet future needs. Serials, characterized by their recency in coverage, are absolutely essential to research.

7. Criteria for evaluating materials are many, including the reputation of publishers, the author's status, and the purpose and scope of the book and its clarity of expression and objectivity of presentation. It is necessary to rely upon value judgments (one's own examination or consultation with subject specialists); reviews by others; reference tools such as standard guides, bibliographies, and publishers releases and catalogs; and, for comparison, holding lists of other libraries.

Methods of Selection

In selection, which is both an art and a science, the following ten methods are frequently mentioned:

1. To consult the specialists. In academic libraries, the faculty plays an important, sometimes dominant, role in building up collections. There is a risk, however, that overdependence on specialists may result in the unbalanced development of holdings.

2. To check the standard lists. This method appears to be the most popular one. *Books for College Libraries*, noted in Chapter 3, and *Magazines for Libraries*, noted in Chapter 6, represent some of the standard lists upon which librarians may rely to select books and periodicals.

3. To check general bibliographies, such as the *National Union Catalog* and the *New Serials Titles*, noted in Chapter 6. Andrew D. Osborn considers the *New Serials Titles* the number-one selection tool for all libraries that intend to build up their serials collection substantially.[7]

4. To check indexing and abstracting services for selection of periodicals. If the title is not indexed or abstracted, it is probably not the first choice, except for new titles. Various bibliographies give notations on indexing and abstracting services, such as *The Serials Directory* and *Ulrich's*, both noted in Chapter 6.

5. To check periodicals for current information on books and periodicals. Such information is provided in quite a few periodicals, such as the *Library Journal*, noted in Chapter 3.

6. To compare holding lists of other libraries. This method is particularly useful for cooperative acquisitions. Duplicates or infrequently used materials and items of marginal interest should be avoided, if they are available at other cooperating libraries.

7. To refer to publishers' releases and advertisements. They are the most up-to-date sources. Librarians should use them to keep aware of new titles and to request sample copies, if available, for evaluation.

8. To use value judgment. Choice is based on reviews or personal examination of the materials.

9. To conduct library-use counting. This method is based on the demand theory and is particularly useful to determine whether books in some subject categories should be acquired or whether a subscription to a periodical should be continued.

10. To count reference citations. The method of reference citation counting is used to discover the use pattern and to identify a core number of the most productive or frequently cited items. The importance of a book or a periodical can generally be ascertained if it has been frequently cited in the literature.

A combination of two or more of these methods should be used for selection. Any selection undoubtedly involves some degree of personal choice. On the other hand, one should also realize the weaknesses of value judgments of others. Ratings do not necessarily reflect objectivity and accuracy.

Sharing Resources

The means of sharing resources are many, among which interlibrary loan and photocopying services have long been used. The Illinois Library Computer Systems Organization (ILCSO) with 45 member libraries, a statewide cooperative organization, provides the online service, ILLINET Online, that enables participating institutions to share library resources through interlibrary loan. It is one of the largest library systems in the United States, following OCLC and RLIN,[8] both noted later. Beginning the fall of 1998, ILLINET Online is available on the Internet (http://pac.ilcso.uiuc.edu or telnet:pac.ilcso.uius.edu).

The creation of the Center for Research Libraries in Chicago exemplifies another form of sharing resources. The cooperating libraries are jointly building research resources to be mutually shared. The center was incorporated in 1949 by ten universities as the Mid-West Inter-Library Center, a nonprofit corporation with the primary purpose of increasing the library research resources available to cooperating institutions in the Midwest. The name was changed in May 1960 to indicate that the center's services were not confined to the Midwest but extended to all libraries without geographic limitation.

The Center's basic purpose is to accept and house for common use infrequently used materials for its members. The purpose is achieved in two ways: by the cooperative housing of infrequently used materials deposited in the center by its members and by the direct acquisition of infrequently used materials of interest to its members but which none has. The Center has provided facilities for research and greater economy in cooperatively housing materials and sharing them to avoid unnecessary duplication.

Its collection components are classified into "Categories of Materials" and "Areas of the World."[9] Categories of Materials includes Russian Academy of Sciences publications, archival materials, foreign doctoral dissertations, foreign newspapers, U.S. ethnic newspapers, U.S. general circulation newspapers, general periodicals, and U.S. State documents. Areas of the World consists of Africana, East Asian materials, South Asian materials, and Southeast Asian materials. There are over eighty subjects, including African Studies, Anthropology, Black Studies, Business, China, Dissertations, Government Publications, Law, Literature in various countries, U.S. History and World War II and Aftermath, with stress on the social sciences and the humanities.[10]

The Center's online public access catalog, CRLCATALOG (B1), of over 465,000 bibliographic and authority records of the center's cataloged collections is accessible through the Internet. The user can telnet to crlcatalog.uchicago.edu and enter "guest" at the log-in prompt and "guest" at the password prompt. Search can be conducted through author, title or series title, words in the title or series, OCLC bibliographic record number, CRL call number, ISSN or ISBN, or subject.

Another form of sharing resources is collaborative collection development or coordinating cooperative collection development, a program evolved from cooperative acquisition.[11] Participating libraries reach an agreement to build, separately, research resources in a designated subject area or format to be shared by others. Cooperative acquisition has a long history. The once-famous Farmington Plan from 1948 to 1972 was intended to acquire at least one copy of every new foreign publication of research interest and to make it available on loan to other libraries.

In 1974 a Research Libraries Group (RLG) was formed by four major research libraries in the East (Columbia, Harvard, Yale, and the New York Public Library).[12] In spite of Harvard's later withdrawal, the group has grown steadily; it has selected Stanford University's automated bibliographical system for bibliographical control, now known as RLIN. One of the group's purposes is to develop a multifaceted program of shared collection development. The tool for coordinated collecting activities is the *RLG Conspectus*. The *RLG Conspectus* is also available online in RLIN and can be searched by subject, class, collection level, and institution.[13]

The RLG's arrangement has served as a model for collaborative collection development among other libraries. For instance, quite a number of law schools have formed consortia for sharing resources collaboratively built.[14] In the Legal Information Network of New York, an agreement has been reached for shared collection development whereby Columbia Law School collects English legal treatises in even editions, state administrative material, and foreign law publications, whereas it is the New York University Law School's responsibility to collect English legal treaties in odd editions, official state advance sheets, and United States documents.[15]

Widespread networking among libraries contributes to another type of sharing resources. A number of databases are available in the network to be shared by participating libraries. OPLIN (Ohio Public Library Information Network) (B2) was initiated by the Ohio Library Council (OLC), the state library association, in early 1994.[16] It became operational in 1995. Now nearly 700 libraries, or 83 percent of Ohio's public libraries, are connected to OPLIN, such as *EBSCOhost MasterFILE 1000*: indexing and abstracting service on 3,100 titles with full-text titles of 1,087; *SIRS Researcher*: full-text articles from over 1,200 newspapers, magazines, journals, and government publications on social science issues; *SIRS Discover*: full-text articles for school children; Electric Library: full-text of over 800 newspapers and magazines and eighteen reference books; and *HANNAH Online*: full-text of Ohio House and Senate bills introduced or passed from 1987 to the present.

In Illinois, the Illinois Bibliographic Information Service (IBIS) (B3) is a collection of databases accessible through participating libraries. Databases are organized by broad subject into six areas: (1) Art, History, Literature, and Other Humanities; (2) Business; (3) Education, Psychology, and Other Social Sciences; (4) Health, Medicine, and Other Life Sciences; (5) Science and Engineering; and (6) Multiple subject area searches. In Area 3, Education, Psychology, and Other Social Sciences, a number of databases are accessible, including *ERIC, PsycInfo*, and *Social Sciences Index*.

It must be noted that resource sharing is by no means a complete solution to collection development.[17] Each library has its well-defined area to serve to fulfill its mission. To acquire sufficient funds for collection development is a necessity. It has been suggested that resource sharing should never be relied upon beyond the RLG's instructional support level, a level of collection adequate to support undergraduate and most graduate instruction or sustained independent study.[18]

Online databases marketed through vendors or on the Internet may be considered in a broad sense a means of sharing resources. In general, a library does not own such a database but shares access to it with many others. With the rapid development of full-text resources in digital format, many resources are hosted in universally accessible Web sites. One example is

The Internet Public Library. Ann Arbor, MI: University of Michigan, School of Information. http://www.ipl.org (B4)

The Internet Public Library, founded in 1995, contains three groups of sources: Divisions, Rooms, and Services. In the Division group, there are Reference, Youth, Teen, MOO, and About the Library. The Reference category provides: General Reference Associations; Arts and Humanities; Business and Economics; Computers and Internet; Education; Entertainment and Leisure; Health and Medical Sciences; Law, Government and Political Science; Science and Technology; and Social Sciences. The Business and

Economics category links to general business Web sites, such as Hoover's Online. It also leads a reader to subsections of Business and Economics. The Reading Room has 2,000 full-text books. The MOO (Multi-user Object Oriented environment) provides live reference services. The Library also provides LISTSERV and FAQ.

One of its interesting files is POTUS (Presidents of the United States) (B5). The file provides background information, election results, cabinet members, presidency, and other facts about presidents. It also links to other sites.

The new technological achievements that expand library resources beyond the physical walls of the library have changed the meaning of traditional collection development and resource sharing. It does not matter whether the library has the resources on its premises. Resource delivery becomes the library's main function. The availability of electronic information delivery makes the library simply a gateway to information.

DELIVERY OF RESOURCES

All vendors of databases noted in Chapter 1 provide document delivery services. FirstSearch, for instance, has three types of document delivery: fax, rush mail, and mail. Its ARTICLEFIRST, updated daily, contains nearly 12,500 journals in science, technology, medicine, social science, business, the humanities, and popular culture from 1980 to the present. A subset of ARTICLEFIRST is FASTDOC, which contains about 200,000 records with a high percentage of citations for online view and delivery. In addition, the agencies listed here provide electronic delivery of resources:

> *UnCover*. Denver, CO: CARL Corp. http://unweb.carl.org (B6)
> *Personal Journal*. New York: Dow Jones Business Information Services. http://www./wsj.com (B7)

UnCover, a subsidiary of CARL, began table-of-contents and document delivery services in 1988. Uncover has access to almost seven million citations over 17,000 periodical titles, with 5,000 citations added daily. Uncover can be accessed through some libraries' OPACs and the Internet.

Personal Journal provides personalized daily news briefs download of selected features from *The Wall Street Journal*.[19] News items are selected from a list of 3,500 companies and 43 regular columns and quotes on up to 25 stocks and mutual funds.

LIBRARY CATALOGS

The best place to locate research resources is the major library catalogs.

Printed Catalogs

Comprehensive though not current is a series of printed catalogs from the Library of Congress. These published catalogs in their early stage listed titles represented by the Library of Congress printed cards and later became the National Union Catalog with holding locations. The following titles may be mentioned:

> *National Union Catalog, Pre-1956 Imprints: A Cumulative Author List Representing Library of Congress Cards and Titles Reported by Other American Libraries.* London: Mansell, 1968–1984. 754 vols. (B8)
>
> *National Union Catalog: A Cumulative Author List*, 1956–1982. Washington, DC: Library of Congress. Monthly with quarterly and 5/year cumulations. (B9)
>
> *National Union Catalog. Books*, 1983– . Washington, DC: Library of Congress. Monthly in microfiche. ISSN 07347650. (B10)
>
> *LC MARC.* Washington, DC: Library of Congress, 1968– . Weekly. Digital. (B11)
>
> *REMARC*, pre-1980. Etobicoke, ON, Canada: ISM Library Information Services. Digital. (B12)

The Library of Congress catalogs provide an immense depository of literature output.[20] The *Pre-1956 Imprints* supersedes all published Library of Congress catalogs. *National Union Catalog: A Cumulative Author List*, 1956–1982, no longer published in hard copy, is continued by the microform version of *National Union Catalog. Books*. The significance of the *National Union Catalog* has diminished, since the availability of many OPACs, the online union catalogs noted below, and online databases.

The digital format of the Library of Congress catalog is available on CD-ROM, as *CDMARC* (B13) and online as *LC MARC* (*Library of Congress MAchine Readable Cataloging*) that contains 2.5 million records of monographs as of November 1998 in English and in other languages since 1973. It is marketed by a few vendors, including Dialog (Dialog File 426). Prior to 1968, refer to *REMARC* (*Retrospective MAchine Readable Cataloging*), a companion to *LC MARC*. It is a huge file. Dialog divides it into five files (File 421–425) that contain over 4.2 million records cataloged by the Library of Congress, but not included in *LC MARC*.

Digital Catalog

Online Public Access Catalogs

Many OPACs (Online Public Access Catalogs) can be accessed through Gopher, Telnet, or WWW. Both the Library of Congress and the British Library have made available their online public access catalogs on the Web.

Library of Congress Catalog. Washington, DC: Library of Congress. http://
lcweb.loc.gov (B14)
British Library's OPAC. Boston Spa, England: British Library, National Bibliographic Service. http://opac97.bl.uk (B15)

The Library of Congress Catalog is part of the Library of Congress (LC)
Web site. The main menu displays the following choices: American Memory, noted in Chapter 13, Thomas for legislative information, noted in
Chapter 14, Catalog, Copyright, Exhibitions, Global Legal Information,
Library Services, Library of Congress Information System (LOCIS), LC
Marvel (Gopher), Access to Catalogs at Other Libraries, and Public FTP
sites. New on the Web is the 1997 *Library of Congress Information Bulletin* (http://www.loc.gov/loc/lcib) (B16). The LIB Web also links to pre-
1997 issues from the Library's text-based site (gopher://marvel.loc.gov: 70/
11/loc/pubs/lib/).
For the Library of Congress catalog, the site provides the Z39.50 Gateway. Z39.50 is an American standard protocol for computer transmission
of data approved by the National Information Standards Organization
(NINO) in 1988. The Z39.50 Gateway gives two choices for searching: LC
Catalog and Other Catalogs. LC Catalog has two forms of searching capability: (1) Title or Personal Name only—limited to books and name au-
thority files, and (2) Supporting More Complex Searches. LC MARVEL
(Gopher) is easier to use than the Z39.50 Gateway.
For searching other library catalogs, the site links to state libraries, li-
brary agencies, and commissions in all 50 states and foreign countries. For
each site, if available, the library system being used is also given, such as
DRUMS, GEAN, INN OPAC, and NOTIS.
OPAC97, a part of the British Library National Bibliographic Service
(NBS), is designed to locate materials in the Reference and Document sup-
ply collections of the British Library. The British Library currently provides
such services as Blaise Line and Web, Current Serials Received, Gabriel,
Inside, and OPAC97. Blaise (The British Library's Automated Information
Service) Line or Blaise Web contains 21 databases of over 18 million bib-
liographic records. Blaise Web (http://www.bl.uk/services/bsds/nbs/blaise/)
(B17) provides links to the Document Supply Centre to order materials.
Current Serials Received provides access to over 62,000 serials currently
received by the British Library Document Supply Centre (BLDSC). Gabriel
Web (http://www.bl.uk/gabriel/) (B18) serves as a gateway to Europe's national libraries. Inside (http://www.bl.uk/online/inside/) (B19) enables the
user to search, order and receive delivery of articles and is a good source
for locating conference proceedings, noted in Chapter 3.
OPAC97 displays two choices of searching: Reference Collection and
Document Supply Collection. Reference Collection consists of humanities
and social sciences (1975–   ), science, technology and business (1975–   ),

music (1980–   ), combined reference collections (1975–   ), and other reference material (to 1975 only). Document Supply Collections is classified by format including books and reports (1980–   ), journal/serials (1700–   ), conferences (1800–   ), and combined document supply material.

Online Union Catalogs

In addition to the catalogs mentioned, OCLC, RLIN, WLN, and COPAC are the major online union catalogs providing millions of records held by participating libraries.

> OCLC. Dublin, OH: OCLC. http://www.oclc.org (B20)
> RLIN. Mountain View, CA: Research Libraries Group. http://www.rlg.org (B21)
> WLN. Lacey, WA: WLN. http://www.wln.org (B22)
> COPAC. Manchester, England: University of Manchester, Manchester Information Datasets and Associated Services (MIDAS). http://www.copac.ac.uk/copac (B23)

OCLC, RLIN, and WLN are the major online union catalogs providing a wealth of information on a variety of materials. OCLC (Online Computer Library Center, formerly Ohio College Library Center), founded in 1967, consists of several systems, such as cataloguing, interlibrary loan, local library system, acquisitions, serials control, and databases. The OCLC database contains millions of bibliographical records in eight formats and innumerable location symbols. The eight formats are books, serials, sound recordings, musical scores, audiovisual media, maps, archives and manuscripts, and machine-readable data files.

Since 1990, OCLC has offered, in addition to cataloging, reference services in EPIC, PRISM, and FirstSearch, which feature the use of Boolean logical operators and subject keyword, term, and phrase searching to its database. EPIC and FirstSearch will be merged into the OCLC FirstSearch in 1999. OCLC is the largest online union catalog. It serves over 3,000 libraries in more than 60 countries worldwide.

OCLC's Web site displays services as access services, collection and technical services, reference services, and resource sharing. Its collection and technical services provide collection management, cataloging, and authorities services. Reference services include OCLC FirstSearch service, OCLC Electronic Collections Online, OCLC EPIC service, and OCLC ContentsAlert service. OCLC resource sharing services refer primarily to interlibrary loan. OCLC's flagship is WorldCat, which contains millions of records held in numerous libraries worldwide, as noted in the preceding chapter.

RLIN (Research Libraries Information Network), formerly BALLOTS

(Bibliographic Automation of Large Library Operations Using a Time-Sharing System), began as an automated cataloguing project at the Stanford University Libraries in 1972. It is one of the services of RLG (Research Libraries Group), a not-for-profit membership corporation of institutions. The RLG databases consist of RLIN Bibliographic Files, RLIN Specialized Files, and CitaDel Article Citation Files. The RLIN Bibliographic Files contain 82 million records in over 365 languages as of March 1998. They are searchable through the RLIN, Eureka, and Zephyr, a Z39.50 server.

In RLIN, records can be searched through personal names, title words in any order, conference titles, corporate names, subject phrases and subject words, and many other fields. Search can also be conducted through Boolean operators and truncations and can be limited by language, place, date of publication, and holding library. RLIN's JACKPHY Plus enables searching and inputting Japanese, Arabic, Chinese, Korean, Persian, Hebrew, Yiddish, and Cyrillic scripts. Eureka, a searching software launched in 1993, has telnet (eureka-info.rlg.org) and Web-based (http://eureka.rlg.org) versions. Zephyr provides a Z39.50 server for searching RLIN Bibliographic, the English Short Title Catalogue (ESTC), and CitaDel.

WLN, formerly known as Western Library Network and Washington Library Network, is a nonprofit corporation since 1976. Its primary function is to integrate catalogs, acquisitions, local holdings, and interlibrary loan with the bibliographic subsystem as the core system. The bibliographic subsystem consists of five major files: Bibliographic, Authority, Working, Waiting, and Summary Holdings.

WLN provides library resources and links to library-related subjects, libraries (Alaska, Idaho, Montana, Oregon, Washington and libraries elsewhere), books and readings, and library and information organizations. Searching can be conducted through keyword, Boolean operators, title, truncation, and other fields. There are also sort options, such as format, date, title, author, and chronology (earliest date first). It has been reported that OCLC plans to merge with WLN.

COPAC is a newcomer, launched in 1996, a national online public access catalogue in the UK and Ireland. It was developed from the CURL (Consortium of University Research Libraries) database. Some twenty research libraries are CURL members. COPAC contains 9 million MARC records in CURL members. There are three types of search: author/title, periodical, and subject. Search can also be limited by publication date, language, or library. Two formats of displaying records are available: brief records and full record. COPAC also provides links to CURL libraries.

Of particular interest to users of library catalogs in the social sciences is G. K. Hall's annual series, *Bibliographic Guides* (B24). The series, beginning in the early 1970s, is a computer processing and photocomposition text listing works in all languages and in all forms, catalogued primarily by the New York Public Library (NYPL) and the Library of Congress. It provides complete Library of Congress cataloging information for each title, as well as ISBN number and identification of NYPL holdings. The series is basically a library holding list geared to the use of large research and university libraries. There are nineteen subject areas currently published, with some fourteen bibliographies in the social sciences, including black studies, business and economics, education, law, maps and atlases, North American history, psychology, Latin-American studies, Soviet and East European studies, East Asian studies, and anthropology. One million entries are added annually. Some titles of the *Bibliographic Guides* are produced on CD-ROM, such as *Black Studies on Disc* and *Anthropology Bibliography on Disc*, noted in Chapter 8.

INFORMATION ABOUT RESEARCH RESOURCES

Social science research is largely university based. This is evident in the number of listings in the *Research Centers Directory* mentioned later. The best research resources are generally found in leading institutions of higher learning. Reference sources for library holdings include:

> *Subject Collections: A Guide to Special Book Collections and Subject Emphasis as Reported by University, College, Public, and Special Libraries and Museums in the United States and Canada.* 7th ed. Lee Ash and William G. Miller, comps. New York: Bowker, 1993. 2 vols. ISBN 0835231437. (B25)
>
> *Directory of Special Libraries and Information Centers*, ed. 1– , 1963– . Irregular. Detroit: Gale Research. ISSN 0731633X. Print & digital. (B26)
>
> *Government Research Directory*, ed. 1– , 1980– . Detroit: Gale Research. Irregular. ISSN 08823766. Print & digital. (B27)
>
> *Research Centers and Services Directory*. Detroit: Gale Research. Semi-annual. Digital. (B28)
>
> *Research Centers Directory*, ed. 1– , 1956– . Detroit: Gale Research. Biennial. ISSN 02782731. Print & digital. (B29)
>
> *Research Institutions and Learned Societies*. Joseph C. Kifer, ed.-in-chief. Westport, CT: Greenwood Press, 1982. 551 p. (Encyclopedia of American Institution Series). ISBN 0313220611. (B30)
>
> *World Directory of Social Science Institutions*. UNESCO, Social and Human Sciences Documentation Centre. 5th ed. Paris: UNESCO, 1990. 1,211 p. ISBN 9230025526. (B31)

Subject Collections is a description of resources arranged by subject and within each subject alphabetically by place and then by the name of the library. Like its former editions, this one does not list college and university archives and small local history and genealogy collections. For each entry are given, if available, personal name collections, manuscripts and collections other than books, manuscripts, and published catalogs. Compilation of resources was primarily dependent upon replies to questionnaires. Although other sources are used for inclusion, such as news releases, only 75 percent of questionnaires were returned. According to compilers, it "contains 65,818 entries cataloging collections held within 5,882 institutions. Of these, 13,266 entries are entirely new, including information from 879 libraries not included in the sixth edition" (Introduction). *Subject Collections* complements the *National Union Catalog of Manuscript Collections* noted in the next chapter.

For information on research institutions and their facilities and services, Gale has published a number of directories with international, national, and state coverage. The following items are directories of particular importance:

The twenty-third edition of the *Directory of Special Libraries and Information Centers* (1998, 2 vols., ISBN 0787620947) consists of listings in alphabetical order in two parts in volume 1: A–M and N–Z. The term "special libraries" is broadly construed to include divisions, departments, and branches of academic and public libraries. "More than 23,600 special libraries, research libraries, information centers, archives, and data centers research libraries, maintained by government agencies, business, industry, newspapers, educational institutions, nonprofit organizations, and societies in the fields of science and engineering, medicine, law, art, religion, the social sciences, and humanities" (subtitle). It has an international coverage, but focuses primarily on the United States and Canada. Each entry contains over 30 items of information, such as name, address, phone, e-mail, URL, founded, staff, subject, special collections, holdings, subscriptions, services, automated operations, OPAC, electronic resources, publications, special catalogs, and special indexes. There are seven appendixes and a subject index. Appendixes include Networks and Consortia, Regional and Subregional Libraries for the Blind and Physically Handicapped, Patent and Trademark Depository Libraries, Regional Government Depository Libraries, United Nations Depository Libraries, World Bank Depository Libraries, and European Community Depository Libraries. Volume 2 contains geographic and personnel indexes. It is also available on CD-ROM as part of *Gale's Ready Reference Shelf* and online via GaleNet.

The *Directory* is rearranged to become the *Subject Directory of Special Libraries and Information Centers*, 1985– (irregular, ISSN 0731633X) (B32), in four volumes: (1) Business and Law Libraries, including military and transportation libraries; (2) Social Sciences, Humanities, and Education Libraries, including area/ethnic, art, audiovisual, geography/map, history, music, publishing, rare book, religion/theology, theaters, and urban/regional planning libraries; (3) Health Sciences Libraries, including all aspects of basic and applied medical sciences; and (4) Science and Engineering Libraries, including agriculture, environment/conservation, and food sciences libraries. Within each category, the libraries are alphabetically arranged. The *Directory* and the *Subject Directory* contain the same information arranged differently.

The ninth edition of *Government Research Directory* (1996–1997, Jacqueline K. Barrett and Monica M. Hubbard, eds., 1996, 1,038 p., ISBN 0810349418) is "a descriptive guide to more than 4,200 U.S. and Canadian government research and development centers, institutes, laboratories, bureaus, test facilities, experiment stations, data collection and analysis centers, and grants management and research coordinating offices in agriculture, commerce, education, energy, engineering, environment, the humanities, medicine, military science, and basic and applied sciences" (title page). It is arranged into chapters by departments and agencies grouped into three categories: Legislative, Judicial, and Executive Offices; Independent Agencies; and Government of Canada. Each entry gives agency/research names, acronym, address, phone and fax numbers, head of unit, organizational notes, research activities and fields, special resources, publications, and services. There are three indexes: subject, geographic, and master. It is also available on CD-ROM and on Galenet.

A companion is the *Research Centers Directory* (1999 24th edition, 1998, 2 vols., ISBN 0787621951), which lists over 14,000 university-related and other nonprofit research organizations in the United States and Canada, including research institutes, centers, foundations, laboratories, bureaus, experiment stations and similar research facilities, activities, and organizations, in various subject fields. Research centers are grouped into seventeen sections under five broad categories: life sciences, physical sciences and engineering, private and public policy and affairs, social and cultural studies, and multidisciplinary and research coordinating centers. In addition to general directory information—such as name, address, and telephone number, fax number, and home page—of particular value is its information on volume of research, research contact, field of research, special resources, publications and services, meetings/educational activities, other services (clinical, consulting, technical, and other public services), and the library. There are four indexes: subject index, geographic index, personal name index, and master index. The master index is arranged by research center name and by principal keywords within the center name. The directory is part of Gale's *Ready Reference Shelf*, a CD-ROM product. All Gale Research publications noted here are included in the GaleNet Web, noted in Chapter 1.

These two directories, together with *International Research Centers Directory* and *Research Services Directory*, form the database of the *Research Centers and Services Directory*, marketed through Dialog (File 115). The database contains some 30,000 organizations conducting researach worldwide.

Research Institutions and Learned Societies contains historical sketches of 164 "nongovernmental, not for profit organizations aiding the promotion or performance of basic research and the advancement of knowledge" (Preface). With a few exceptions, all institutions and learned societies are in the United States, arranged in alphabetical order. In general, no address is given.

The *World Directory*, formerly *World Index of Social Science Institutions*, 1970–1976, a bilingual looseleaf card index accompanying the *International Social Science Journal*, 1949– (Oxford, England: Blackwell, quarterly, ISSN 00208701) (B33), is a second volume issued in the World Social Sciences Information Service Series, the first being the *World List of Social Science Periodicals*, mentioned in Chapter 6. The fifth edition of *World Directory* briefly describes 2,088 active social science institutions, international and national, in 199 countries. Institutions specializing in peace or human rights research included in other UNESCO publications are not listed. It contains four sections. Section 1 is an alphabetical index to official names and acronyms of institutions. Section 2 gives full details of each institution in 20 items, including country of location, name of institution, address and cable address, creation date, present head, size of staff, senior researchers, parent organization, relationship with intergovernmental organizations, type of organization, subject coverage, geographical area coverage, activity, method of data processing, publication, titles of journals, titles of bulletins, titles of recent research projects, titles of recent research publications, and annotation. The *World Directory* complements *Research Centers Directory* and other directories of research centers and institutions.

NOTES

1. Nancy E. Gwinn and Paul H. Mosher, "Coordinating Collection Development: The RLG Conspectus," *College and Research Libraries* 44, no. 2 (1983): 129, 139–40.

2. Verner W. Clapp, *The Future of the Research Library* (Urbana: University of Illinois Press, 1964), pp. 4ff.

3. F. W. Lancaster, *The Measurement and Evaluation of Library Services* (Washington, DC: Information Resources Press, 1977), p. 165.

4. Arthur Curley and Dorothy Broderick, *Building Library Collections*, 6th ed. (Metuchen, NJ: Scarecrow Press, 1985), p. 43.

5. Pauline Atherton Cochrane, Oscar Handlin, Hendrik Edelman, and William Herbster, "Research Library Collections in a Changing Universe: Four Points of View," *College and Research Libraries* 45, no. 3 (1984): 214–24.

6. Ibid.

7. Andrew D. Osborn, *Serial Publications: Their Place and Treatment in Libraries*, 2nd ed. (Chicago: American Library Association, 1980), pp. 77–78.

8. Gay N. Dannelly, "Coordinating Cooperative Collection Development: A National Perspective," *Library Acquisitions: Practice and Theory* 9 (1985): 308.

9. The Center for Research Libraries, *Handbook 1996* (Chicago: Center for Research Libraries, 1996), p. v.

10. Ibid.

11. For a summary of a conference on the topic, refer to Gay Dannelly, "Coordinating Cooperative Collection Development: A National Perspective," *Library Acquisitions: Practice and Theory* 9 (1985): 307–15. For collaborative collection development among Chicago-area law schools, see also In-lan Wang Li, "Collaborative Collection Development," paper presented at the Library Cooperation and Development Seminar, August 17–18, 1986, Taipei, Taiwan.

12. David H. Stam, "Collaborative Collection Development: Progress, Problems, and Potential," *Collection Building* 7 (1985): 3–9.

13. Gwinn and Mosher, "Coordinating Collection Development," p. 133.

14. Margaret A. Goldblatt and Bernard D. Reams, Jr., "Cooperative Acquisitions among Law Libraries: A Review," *Law Library Journal* 477 (1984/1985): 648–65.

15. Ibid.

16. Meribah Mansfield, "Ohio's OPLIN: The Future of Library Service?" *Library Journal* 122, no. 16 (1997): 44–47.

17. Jay K. Lucker, "Library Resources and Bibliographic Control," *College and Research Libraries* 42 (1979): 141–53.

18. Gwinn and Mosher, "Coordinating Collection Development," p. 140.

Chapter 3

Access to Sources

Reference sources are traditionally organized by document type, such as guides, bibliographies, indexes, abstracts, encyclopedias, dictionaries, and handbooks. They fall into two broad categories: access to sources and sources of information. This pattern of organization is generally followed in this book. It must be noted, however, that since with the emergence of the Internet, most Web sites in subject fields contain all document types or many of them, the traditional division of reference sources into two categories has become less distinctive. In particular, many indexes and abstracts contain full-text materials; as they have diminished their identities as simply indexes or abstracts, they themselves are sources of information.

GUIDES

A guide is a kind of bibliography. Definitions of bibliography vary. It is suggested that a bibliography, properly so called, must be comprehensive and not selective.[1] According to this view, a mere list of authors and titles issued by a bookseller or publisher or a library catalog is not a bibliography, because it does not aim at comprehensiveness. In this book, the term "bibliography" is used in a broad sense. Any listing of records of human communications arranged by a certain logical scheme is a bibliography. A bibliography includes guides, library catalogs, publishers' lists, directories, union lists, indexes, abstracts, or any list of printed or nonprinted works.

It may be noted that when the term "guide" is used in connection with "bibliography," it means more than a mere list of works. A guide introduces the materials in a systematic presentation of the subject content to aid in the use of these materials. In order to be called a guide, the work must possess certain characteristics: (1) It should evaluate the work and state the relationship among works of comparable nature. Its treatment is usually critical. (2) It should introduce the reader to the subject field and to its subdisciplines. Its content is by nature selective. (3) Like a tour guide, it should lead the reader to various parts of a discipline; it helps the reader study the subject. (4) It should indicate to the reader the availability of sources of information and the way to use them. But the term "guide" has long been used loosely. In practice, the distinction between "guide" and "bibliography" is lost, and people use the two terms interchangeably. In this book, the term "guide" is used, but the choice of a reference as a guide or a bibliography is subjective.

The following are two guides in the social sciences:

> *Sources of Information in the Social Sciences: A Guide to the Literature.* 3rd ed. William H. Webb and Associates. Chicago: American Library Association, 1986. 777 p. ISBN 083890405X. (C1)
>
> *The Social Sciences: A Cross-Disciplinary Guide to Select Sources.* 2nd ed. Nancy L. Herron, ed. Englewood, CO: Libraries Unlimited, 1996. 323 p. ISBN 1563083094. (C2)

The Webb book deals with social science literature and eight subdisciplines: history, geography, economics and business administration, sociology, anthropology, psychology, education, and political science. Twenty authors contributed nine chapters. Each chapter has two parts: survey of the field and survey of the reference works. Webb has substantially revised and enlarged the earlier work by Carl M. White. Over 8,000 citations are included, in contrast to 4,500 citations in the second edition, with noticeable expansion in history, geography, anthropology, and political science. The surveys of the reference works are listings of over 3,400 citations of reference sources, an invaluable guide to social science sources of information.

In contrast to Webb, the Herron book confines itself to reference sources. It contains 1,030 sources in twelve chapters, grouped into four parts. Part 1 is a chapter on general social science sources. Part 2, "Literature of the Established Disciplines of the Social Sciences," has seven chapters on political science, economics, business, history, law and legal issues, anthropology, and sociology respectively. Part 3, "Literature of the Emerging Disciplines of the Social Sciences—Those with a Social Origin or Those Having Acquired a Social Aspect," comprises two chapters, one each for education and psychology. There are two chapters on geography and communication in Part 4, "Literature of the Disciplines Related to the Social Sciences—Those with Recognized Social Implications." Each chapter consists of an introduction to the subject or discipline and an annotated listing of selected sources. The second edition lists over 200 new titles more than the first edition, and it features many electronic sources or Internet sources in most chapters.

An old standby, though aging, is *A Reader's Guide to the Social Sciences*, edited by Bert F. Hoselitz, rev. ed. (New York: Free Press, 1970, 425 p.) (C3). It is a collection of essays on geography, political science, economics, sociology, anthropology, and psychology. Each essay introduces the reader to the discipline, its significant production, and the development and trends within the discipline. The inclusion of over 100 pages of "Bibliography and Author Index" (pp. 319–425) is a valuable feature. Its first edition (Free Press, 1959, 250 p.) may be retained for titles not listed in the second edition and for a good, concise essay, "The Social Sciences in the Last Two Hundred Years" (pp. 7–25).

BIBLIOGRAPHIES OF BIBLIOGRAPHIES

> *Bibliographic Index: A Cumulative Bibliography of Bibliographies*, 1937–   .
> New York: H. W. Wilson, 1938–   . 3/year with cumulations. ISSN
> 00061255. Print & digital. (C4)
> *A World Bibliography of Bibliographies and of Bibliographical Catalogues,
> Calendars, Abstracts, Digests, Indexes, and the Like*. 4th ed. Theodore
> Besterman. Lausanne: Societas Bibliographica, 1965–1966. 5 vols.
> (C5)

Bibliographic Index indexes current bibliographies separately published as books and pamphlets and those published as parts of books, pamphlets, and periodical articles in English, other Germanic languages, and the Romance languages. It regularly examines some 2,800 periodicals for bibliographies. Arrangement is alphabetical by subject. There were 6-, 4-, and 3-year cumulations from volumes 1 to 8. Annual cumulations have been published since Volume 9. *Bibliographic Index* is less comprehensive than Besterman, *World Bibliography of Bibliographies*, yet it complements the latter in its currency, seriality, and inclusion of "concealed" bibliographies. *Bibliographic Index* is one of the indexing/abstracting services of the H. W. Wilson Company. It may be noted that all H. W. Wilson's indexes and abstracts, except *Readers' Guide Abstracts Select Edition* (CD-ROM version only), are produced in four formats: hardcopy, CD-ROM as *Wilsondisc*, tape, and online as *Wilsonline*. Fairly recently, these items are on the Web, as noted in Chapter 1. *Bibliographic Index* in digital format covers the period from 1984. Other Wilson indexes and abstracts will be mentioned later in this chapter and elsewhere in other chapters.

A World Bibliography of Bibliographies (or Besterman, by author's name) records 117,187 bibliographies in over 50 languages, arranged under more than 15,000 headings and subheadings. It is limited to "the separately published work," which is defined, with exceptions, as a work having separate pagination.

A supplement to Besterman is *A World Bibliography of Bibliographies, 1964–1974: A List of Works Represented by Library of Congress Printed Cards, A Decennial Supplement to Theodore Besterman, A World Bibliography of Bibliographies*, compiled by Alice F. Toomey (Totowa, NJ: Rowman and Littlefield, 1977. 2 vols. ISBN 0874719992) (C6). Toomey's work is a subject bibliography of reproduced Library of Congress printed cards. Its coverage of bibliographies in foreign countries is far from complete, and it lacks the fine indexes of Besterman.

BIBLIOGRAPHIES

General

For reference sources, the two bibliographies listed here provide a good coverage of the social sciences:

> *Guide to Reference Books*. 11th ed. Robert Balay, ed. Chicago: American Library Association, 1996. 2,020 p. ISBN: 0838906699. (C7)
> *American Reference Books Annual*, 1970–   . Bohdan S. Wynar, ed. Littleton, CO: Libraries Unlimited. Annual. ISSN 00659959. (C8)

Well-known by the names of the authors in its earlier editions as "Mudge," "Winchell" and "Sheehy," *Guide to Reference Books* has achieved over the years a celebrated status in reference works. Balay retains practically the same arrangement of the previous editions divided into five sections: A. General Reference Works; B. Humanities; C. Social and Behavioral Sciences; D. History and Area Studies; and E. Science, Technology and Medicine. The book consists of some 15,500 titles, of which Section C and Section D list over 6,100 titles. "The largest single section continues to be Literature, followed by Bibliography, Language Dictionaries, Economics and Business, and Political Science, but the disciplines with the largest number of entries is still History and Area Studies" (Foreword). The eleventh edition includes a number in machine-readable form flagged by a bullet. It has a dictionary index.

American Reference Books Annual (ARBA) is current and limited to works published or distributed in the United States and Canada. Some foreign titles in the English language from Great Britain, Australia, and India are also included. It has limited coverage of government publications; they are generally included in *Government Reference Books*, noted in Chapter 7. *ARBA* reviews in general all reference books published during a single year. Reviews are classified into four parts: General Reference Works, Social Sciences, Humanities, and Science and Technology. Appended are two indexes: author/title and subject. Since its publication, more than 50,000 titles have been reviewed.

A number of periodicals carry reviews of reference sources. *Choice* (Chicago: Association of College and Research Libraries, 1964– , monthly, ISSN 00094978) (C10) and *Booklist* (Chicago: American Library Association, 1905– , semimonthly, ISSN 00067385) (C11) publish reviews of reference sources. A part of *Booklist*, its "Reference Books Bulletin," is exclusively devoted to reviewing reference sources. Both *Choice* and *Booklist* can be accessed on the Internet: http://www.ala.org/acrl/choice/home.html and http://www.ala.org/booklist, respectively. An annual review of reference books has appeared in the May issue of *American Libraries*, 1907– (Chicago: American Library Association, semimonthly; monthly July and August, ISSN 00029769; http://www.ala.org/alonline) (C12). Titles of recent years' "Outstanding Reference Sources" are listed on the Web (http://www.ala.org/refsource.html) (C13).

The *Library Journal*, 1876– . (New York: Bowker, semimonthly; monthly, July and August, ISSN 03630277; http://www.bookwire.com/lj-digital) (C14) also publishes an annual listing of reference books, generally in the April issue. A regular feature of the *Wilson Library Bulletin*, 1914–1995 (New York: H. W. Wilson, monthly, September–June, ISSN 00435651) (C15) is "Current Reference Books," exclusively devoted to reviewing reference sources. Since the demise of *Wilson Library Bulletin*, "Current Reference Books" was retained as "Rettig on Reference" in the company's Web site (http://www.hwwilson.com). At present, it is available from Gale Research's Web site (http://www.Thomson.com/gale/rettig/rettig.html) (C16).

The "Sources" column in *Reference & User Services Quarterly* (formerly *RQ*), 1960– (Chicago: American Library Association, quarterly, ISSN 10949054) (C17) regularly reviews databases and reference books. *College and Research Libraries*, 1939– (Chicago: American Library Association, bimonthly, ISSN 00100870) (C18) has a regular section, "Selected Reference Books," an informal updating of Balay, noted earlier.

Subfield

The best-known bibliographies in the social sciences are:

> *A London Bibliography of the Social Sciences* (London: London School of Economics and Political Science, 1931–1932. 4 vols.; and its *Supplement*, 1st–24th, 1929/1931–1989. London: British Library of Political and Economic Sciences, 1934–1965; Cassell, 1970–1990. ISSN 0076051X. (C19)
>
> *International Bibliography of the Social Sciences*, 1951– . London: Routledge, 1952– . Annual. Print & digital. (C20)

The *London Bibliography* was compiled as a union catalog on the basis of the holdings of seven libraries and special collections. Beginning with the Third Supplement, volume 7, it became the catalog of the British Library of Political and Economic Science and the Edward Fry Library of International Law and an annual with its Ninth Supplement. Arranged by subject, it records books, pamphlets, and documents in many languages with brief information on author, title, paging, date, location, and information as to bibliography. The demise of *London Bibliography* makes *International Bibliography*, noted next, the only comprehensive bibliography in the social sciences.

The publication of the *International Bibliography of the Social Sciences* (IBSS) is the general programme of the International Committee for Social Sciences Documentation, formed in 1950 with UNESCO's support, to promote all bibliographical and documentary work of interest to the social sciences. The bibliography consists of four parts:

> *International Bibliography of Sociology. Bibliographie Internationale de Sociologie,* 1951– .
> *International Bibliography of Economics. Bibliographie Internationale de Science Economique,* 1952– .
> *International Bibliography of Political Science. Bibliographie des Sciences Sociales,* 1953– .
> *International Bibliography of Social and Cultural Anthropology. Bibliographie Internationale d'Anthropologie Sociale et Culturelle,* 1955– .

The aim of the bibliographies is to record the most useful publications, excluding newspaper articles and unpublished works, concerned with each discipline in all countries and in all languages. Each of the various bibliographies is a classified listing, in uniform format, style, and arrangement, of books, research reports, microform, periodical articles, and official government publications. Some 100,000 articles from over 2,500 journals and 20,000 books are regularly scanned for inclusion in the four parts. *IBSS* is also available on CD-ROM and on the *BIDS-IBIS* Web, noted in the following list.

Some disciplines such as psychology, demography, and law are deliberately excluded from listing, either because of their complexity or because bibliographies already in existence in the fields have satisfied their requirements. *Psychological Abstracts, Population Index,* and *Index to Legal Periodicals,* all noted in the following chapters, should be consulted for these areas.

There are a number of bibliographies on the Internet. But their coverage is quite extensive, not limited to bibliographies. Below are some representative titles:

BIDS-IBSS. Essex, England: University of Essex. http://libwww.essex.ac.uk (C21)

BUBL (BUlleltin Board for Libraries). Glasgow, England: Strathclyde University, Andersonian Library. http://www.bubl.ac.uk/BUBL (C22)

Social Science Information Gateway (SOSIG). Bristol, England: University of Bristol, Institute for Learning and Research Technology. http://sosig.ac.uk (C23)

Social Science Ready Reference. Pennsylvania: Mansfield University. http://www.mnsfld.edu/~library/mu-scref.html (C24)

BIDS-IBSS (International Bibliography of the Social Sciences) is one of the databases maintained at the University of Essex. Other useful databases include *UnCover*, contents pages of journals from various publishers, guide to archival repositories, and *BUBL (Bulletin Board for Libraries)* and *SOSIG*, both noted below.

BUBL provides services for the higher education community such as *BUBL* LINK, a catalogue of selected Internet resources; *BUBL* Search; *BUBL* UK, the UK home page; *BUBL* Archives, LIS (Library and Information Science), journals, Internet development; *BUBL* Journals, abstracts, full text, hundreds of titles; and *BUBL* News, events, surveys, and so on. *BUBL* LINK provides selected Internet resources on academic subjects in eight areas: general reference; humanities; language, literature, and culture; social sciences; engineering and technology; health sciences; mathematics and computing; and physical sciences. A search of political science, a subarea of the social sciences, will link to a number of Web sites including *IBSS* noted earlier and *SOSIG* noted next. A user may also browse subjects by Dewey class.

BUBL Search consists of two categories: "Search *BUBL*" and "Search the Internet." Search *BUBL* searches *BUBL* LINK, *BUBL* Journals, and *BUBL* Archives. Search the Internet contains search by subject, search by country, search for people or organizations, and general search services. For instance, search by country searches Internet services by country or area such as UK, Europe, Africa, Asia, Oceania, and North and Central America. General search services provide a selected list of search programs, metasearch programs, and directories of search programs.

BUBL Archive contains thousands of files grouped into six categories: LIS Archives; Journal Archive; Subject Archive; Internet Archive; Mail Archive; and About the *BUBL* Archive. The category of Subject Archive includes in the social sciences archives of economics, accounting, and management; education; history and archaeology; law, politics, and government; and psychiatry and psychology. Contents, abstracts, or full text of 250 journals and newspapers are contained in *BUBL* Archive in two categories: journals held by *BUBL* and journals held elsewhere. *BUBL*

Journals also list major journal services, journal publishers, and electronic journal projects.

SOSIG, a project funded by the UK government, is run at the Centre for Computing in the Social Sciences at the University of Bristol. It provides access to over 1,000 social science networked sources. Its main menu offers basically the following choices: Search *SOSIG*, World Resources, UK Resources, Latest Additions, and Add New Resource. It also links to *BUBL*, Social Statistics Briefing Room (U.S. White House), noted in Chapter 5, and statistics sources. In the Search *SOSIG* mode, one or more terms may be entered for searching records of networked resources. Boolean logical operators, AND, OR, and NOT, and truncation can be used to narrow or broaden the search. Its World Resources provides access, in alphabetical order, to a variety of subjects, including accountancy, anthropology, business and industrial management, demography, development studies, disability issues, economics, education, environmental issues, ethnology, feminism, geography, law, military science, politics, psychology, sociology, and statistics.

Social Science Ready Reference at the Mansfield University displays two categories for searching: Starting Points and Reference Sources. Starting Points lists eight databases: (1) COOMBSWEB Social Science Server (Australian National University) provides access to most of the world's best social science resources; (2) H-Net (Humanities Online) consists of Discussion Lists, Review; (3) Project (reviews of books, videos, and software) and Job Guide; (4) Social Science Data Archives (Swedish Social Science Data Service) provides world's best Internet social science resources; (5) Social Sciences Data Center and Geographic Information Systems Lab (University of Virginia Library) provides access to demographic, political, and Geo-Spatial information; (6) Social Science Data Collection (University of California—San Diego) indexes social science studies and provides Social Science Links and links to Data Sources; (7) *Social Science Information Gateway (SOSIG)* (University of Bristol), noted earlier; and (8) Social Studies Sources provides sources and links to History, Geography, and Politics and Government.

Its Reference Resources lists databases in law, demography, economics, Gallup, psychology, and sociology, including Bureau of Justice Statistics, Census and Demographics, Clearinghouse for Social Sciences Subject-oriented Bibliographies, Economics and Numeric Data, Emotional Support Guide (University of Michigan), Gallup Organization, ICPSR [Interuniversity Consortium for Political and Social Research] Homepage (University of Michigan), Library Sources in Anthropology (University of Maryland), National Criminal Justice Reference Service (NCJRS), Post-Traumatic Stress, Psychology Electronic Journal and Periodicals (Hanover College), Psychology Software Catalog (University of York, UK), Social and

Economic Development Bibliography (University of Pennsylvania). The system provides links to other databases. For instance, it links to the Interuniversity Consortium for Political and Social Research (ICPSR), noted later.

PROCEEDINGS

There are a few sources from which meeting proceedings can be located. Below are bibliographies of proceedings, all with international coverage:

> *Index to Social Sciences and Humanities Proceedings*, 1979– . Philadelphia: Institute for Scientific Information. Quarterly with annual cumulation. ISSN 01910574. Print & digital. (C25)
> *Directory of Published Proceedings. Series SSH: Social Sciences/Humanities*, v. 1– ; 1968– . Harrison, NY: InterDok. Quarterly with 4-year cumulation. ISSN 00123307. Print & digital. (C26)
> *Inside Conference*. London: The British Library. http://www.bl.uk (C27)

The *Proceedings* is currently produced in four formats: print, online, magnetic tape, and CD-ROM. The print version indexes more than 24,000 papers of over 3,600 conference proceedings a year, updated quarterly with an annual cumulation. It contains seven sections: (1) bibliographic citations to proceedings, (2) subject index, (3) key word index, (4) sponsor index, (5) author/editor index, (6) meeting location index, and (7) corporate index. The online database since 1978 is marketed by DIMDI. The magnetic tape version, *ISSHP Search*, updated weekly, and CD-ROM, updated quarterly, have the same annual coverage since 1990. The digital version has more coverage than the print version, indexing 200,000 papers of over 24,000 conference proceedings.

It may be noted that the *Proceedings* is one of ISI's bibliographic products and services. ISI publishes bibliographical product services of over 6,000 journals, books, and conference proceedings in a variety of formats. There are in general six formats at present: Internet and Intranet, online, magnetic tape, CD-ROM, diskette, and print. The products and services include Current Awareness Products and Services, Reference Update, Focus On, Alerting Services, Document Solution, Journal Citation Reports, and Research Services Products. Not all products and services are available in the social sciences. Some of ISI's products and services in the social sciences are mentioned elsewhere in this chapter.

The *Directory of Published Proceedings, Series SSH* lists proceedings in chronological sequence by conference year and month, with indexes to editor, location, and subject/sponsor, and an acronym listing. A main record consists of date of conference, accession number, location of conference, name of conference and/or title of publication, conference number, conference acronym or initials, conference theme, sponsor, title of publication if needed, series or serial information, editor, publisher, distributor, and so on. A companion volume is the *Directory of Published Proceedings, Series SEMT: Science, Engineering, Medicine, Technology*, v. 1– , 1965– (Harrison, NY: InterDok, 10/year with annual and 2- and 5-year cumulated indexes. ISSN 00123293) (C28). Both directories are available online marketed through DataStar (File DOPP) and on the Web (http://www.interdok.com). InterDok also provides the Proceedings Acquisitions Service for users to procure proceedings.

Inside Conference, a service provided by the British Library, noted in Chapter 2, is also marketed via Dialog (File 65). The database, updated weekly, contains conference papers in all fields received by the British Library since 1983. Over 500,000 citations from more than 15,000 proceedings are added annually.

UNPUBLISHED MATERIALS

Unpublished materials are elusive, and little systematic control of them has been attained. There is no current published guide to unpublished materials. *Harvard Guide to American History*, noted in Chapter 13, has a chapter on unpublished primary sources that deals with archives and manuscript collections and provides some directory information on regional, presidential, and state archives (v. 1, pp. 94–108). There is also a two-page note on bibliographical guides to manuscripts in the Hamer *Guide*, noted later.

Three types of unpublished materials will be discussed: archives and manuscripts, theses and dissertations, and research in progress.

Archives and Manuscripts

Guide to the National Archives of the United States. U.S. National Archives and Records Service. Washington, DC: GPO, 1995. 3 vols. Print & digital. (C29)

A Guide to Archives and Manuscripts in the United States. Philip M. Hamer, comp. for the United States National Historical Publications Commission. New Haven, CT: Yale University Press, 1961. 775 p. (C30)

Directory of Archives and Manuscript Repositories in the United States. 2nd ed. National Historical Publications and Records Commission. Phoenix, AZ: Oryx Press, 1988. 853 p. ISBN 0897744756. (C31)

The National Union Catalog of Manuscript Collections (NUCMC), 1959–1993. Washington, DC: Library of Congress. Annual. ISSN 00900044. Print & digital. (C32)

ArchivesUSA: Integrated Collection and Repository Information. Alexandria, VA: Chadwyck-Healey. http://archives.chadwyck.com (C33)

ICPSR. Ann Arbor, MI: University of Michigan, Institute for Social Research. http://www.icpsr.umich.edu (C34)

NUCMC Cataloging. Washington, DC: Library of Congress. http://lcweb.loc.gov/coll/nucmc/nucmc.html (C35)

Repositories of Primary Sources. University of Idaho. http://www.uidaho.edu/special-collections/Other/Repositories.html (C36)

The *Guide* by NARS controls archives and describes official records of the U.S. government regardless of where they are located, including as of October 1, 1994, "over 1.7 million cubic feet of textual records; approximately 300,000 rolls of microfilm; 2.2 million maps and charts; 2.8 million architectural and engineering plans; 9.2 million aerial photographs; 123,000 motion picture reels; 33,000 video recordings; 178,000 sound recordings; 7,000 computer data sets; and 7.4 million still pictures" (Introduction). The book is divided into six parts: (1) U.S. Government— General, including government under the Articles of Confederation; (2) Legislative Branch; (3) Judicial Branch; (4) Executive Branch; (5) Records of or relating to other governments, including the District of Columbia; and (6) Other holdings. Descriptions of presidential and other personal papers and historical manuscripts in the custody of presidential libraries are, however, excluded. Unless otherwise indicated, all records described in the *Guide* are located in the National Archives Building. There is an index, though this is limited to organizational units, names, and functions or broad subjects mentioned in the text and is, therefore, not a general subject guide to the specific contents of records.

For each record group are given, in general, a brief history and a concise statement of the major functions of the agency or agencies that created the records, general description of the records as to their type, purpose, content, chronological span, quantity, and restrictions of access or use of records. At the end of many statements, is indicated a list of published finding aids. The Guide is also available on the National Archives and Records Service's Web (http://www.nara.gov) (C37).

The Hamer's *Guide* lists the archival and manuscript holdings of some 1,300 depositories in the 50 states of the United States, the District of Columbia, Puerto Rico, and the Canal Zone, arranged alphabetically by state or other major governmental units and thereunder by cities and towns. For each depository, there is usually a general statement about its field of interest. The size of holdings and groups of papers considered to be of special interest are indicated. The materials in each depository are grouped by category or type with papers of individuals identified. At the end of the entry for each depository is a reference to printed sources. Its index was considered not sufficiently specific and complete.[2] The *Guide* is not a union catalog or a complete listing; it merely characterizes the nature of the holdings by indicating the subject areas in which the repository collects and major collections. Readers should also be aware of its limitations. First, it is a guide to large groups of collections, excluding numerous smaller ones. Second, it includes only materials in a public or quasi public repository that regularly admits researchers. Private collections are not listed. Third, it does not include material one might reasonably expect to find, such as county records in county courthouses. Finally, collections consisting entirely of photocopies and transcripts of original manuscripts located in the United States are generally excluded.

An updated version of Hamer's *Guide* is the *Directory of Archives and Manuscript Repositories in the United States*. Its arrangement is similar, but more detailed and more appealing in format. It gives full entries for 4,225 repositories and abbreviated entries of 335 institutions listed in Hamer's *Guide* and NUCMC. For each institution, full treatment includes directory information, days and hours of service, user fees, access, copying facilities, materials solicited, and holdings. The *Directory* complements both Hamer's *Guide* and NUCMC. It is not a replacement for Hamer's *Guide*, which should be used for institutions listed in the *Directory* without holding information, particularly for those institutions that are not found in the *Directory*. As indicated in the first edition, published in 1978, the base date of A.D. 1450 was set to exclude classical and medieval manuscripts. There are a repositories index and a subject index.

In 1962, the first volume of *The National Union Catalog of Manuscript Collections*, heralded as the NUCMC (pronounced NUCMOC) revolution in archival methods, was published.[3] Each volume covers a period of one to three years and includes an index that cumulates into three- or four-year indexes. It describes manuscript collections including oral history interview transcripts and sound recordings housed in American repositories that are regularly open to scholars. Entries are arranged in sequence by the Library of Congress printed cards. Specific information about the collections is readily accessible by using the name index, subject index, and repository index at the end of the volume.

The last print version was published in 1994. The printed volumes, 1–29 (1959–1993), list 72,300 collections located in 1,406 repositories with over one million references to subjects and personal, family, corporate, and geographic names. The print version is now taken over by NUCMC Online Cataloging from 1986/1987 ongoing via the Library of Congress Web. The Library of Congress also provides a NUCMC Z39.50 Gateway to RLIN.

ArchivesUSA contains the complete NUCMC print version on CD-ROM and the Internet. As of July 1998, there are 109,744 collection records, including over 44,400 National Inventory of Documentary Sources records and over 4,800 repositories with 1,100 links to their home pages. Two indexes were published: *Index to Personal Names in the National Union*

Catalog of Manuscript Collections, 1959–1984 (2 vols., 1988) (C38), and *Index to Subjects and Corporate Names in the National Union Catalog of Manuscript Collections, 1959–1984* (3 vols., 1994) (C39).

The University of Idaho in its *Repositories of Primary Sources* also offers "a listing of over 3,000 websites describing holdings of manuscripts, archives, rare books, historical photographs, and other primary sources for the research scholar" (home page). The database is organized by regions into Western United States and Canada; Eastern United States and Canada: States and Provinces; Latin America and the Caribbean; Europe; Asia and the Pacific; Africa and the Near East; and Additional lists. There are two indexes: State, Province, Country Index and Integrated Index/List. Repositories are arranged under each country, state, and province.

Also listed is a source for data archives. Data archives are primarily materials in a form for machine processing. With the proliferation of databases on the Internet, there is little distinction between data archives and archives in a general sense. The U.S. National Archives and Records Administration, noted earlier, is a large repository of data archives. ICPSR is another large repository of data archives. Created in 1962, ICPSR aims at acquiring and preserving social science data, providing open and equitable access to these data, and promoting effective data use. It contains ICPSR data archives and other data archives, including data on education, data on aging, criminal justice data, data on substance abuse and mental health, and series data. ICPSR data archives are organized by subject into eighteen categories, such as Census Enumerations; Community, Urban Studies; Conflict, Aggression, Violence; Economics Behavior, Attitudes; Education; Elites and Leadership; Geography and Environment; Government Structures, Policies; International Systems; Legal Systems; and Social Indicators.

Theses and Dissertations

Many theses and dissertations never appear in print. Bibliographical control of doctoral dissertations excels. Doctoral dissertations are listed in many places. One of the familiar sources is the academic journals, mentioned in Chapter 6.

A number of bibliographies of doctoral dissertations have appeared as separate publications. An earlier bibliography, *A List of American Doctoral Dissertations Printed in 1912–1938*, was compiled by the Library of Congress (Washington, DC: GPO, 1913–1940, 26 vols.) (C40). It is limited to printed dissertations in full text or in abstract. A comprehensive coverage of doctoral dissertations began in 1934 with the publication of *Doctoral Dissertations Accepted by American Universities, 1933/34–1954/55*, compiled for the Association of Research Libraries (New York: H. W. Wilson, 1934–1946, nos. 1–22) (C41). Among bibliographies, the following are of particular importance:

American Doctoral Dissertations, 1955/56–   . Compiled for the Association
of Research Libraries. Ann Arbor, MI: University Microfilms International. Annual. (C42)

Dissertation Abstracts International, 1938–   . Ann Arbor, MI: University
Microfilms International. Monthly. Print & digital. (C43)

Masters Abstracts International, 1962–   . Ann Arbor, MI: University Microfilms International. Quarterly. ISSN 08989095. Print & digital. (C44)

Master's Theses Directories, 1952–   . Cedar Falls, IA: Master's Theses Directories. Annual. ISBN 10725903. (C45)

American Doctoral Dissertations (ADD), formerly *Index to American
Doctoral Dissertations, 1955/56–1963/64)*, continues *Doctoral Dissertations Accepted by American Universities*. It is a list classified by nearly 80
subjects and over 180 subsubjects of all doctoral dissertations accepted by
American and Canadian universities and colleges. Earlier issues were published as number 13 of each volume of *Dissertation Abstracts* (now *Dissertation Abstracts International*). Since the 1965/66 issue, *American
Doctoral Dissertations* has been published separately. Its earlier features,
such as statistical data on doctoral degrees grouped by broad subjects, listings of abstracting dissertations by degree-conferring institutions, and information on lending and preservation of doctoral dissertations, have been
dropped since the 1983/84 volume.

Dissertation Abstracts International (DAI) (formerly *Microfilm Abstracts*, vols. 1–11, 1938–1951; *Dissertation Abstracts*, vols. 12–29, 1952–
1969) is a list, by broad general subject, of abstracts of doctoral dissertations submitted to the publisher by cooperating institutions. Current volumes have three sections: (1) the humanities and social sciences, (2) science
and engineering, and (3) European abstracts.

Through the National Research Council, the National Science Foundation maintains a doctoral record file claimed to list 99 percent of doctoral
dissertations produced in the United States and Canada, from the earliest
one to the present. However, the file has not been available for public use
since the promulgation of the Privacy Act of 1974.

Masters Abstracts International (MAI), formerly *Masters Abstracts: Abstracts of Selected Masters Theses on Microfilm* (1962–1986), includes master's theses in the humanities, social sciences, the sciences, and engineering.
Items are arranged by subject, with author-prepared abstracts. The two
directories, *DAI* and *MAI*, are also available as *Dissertation Abstracts Online* (C46), marketed through the publisher in its ProQuest and online vendors, such as Dialog (File 35), DataStar (File DISS), Ovid (File DISS), and
FirstSearch. It is a comprehensive bibliography of dissertations and theses
from 1861 to the present, with British and European dissertations added
since January 1988. The database contains over 1.2 million doctoral and
masters theses, updated monthly, with an annual addition of more than

40,000 titles. Its CD-ROM version is entitled *Dissertation Abstracts on Disc*, updated quarterly, a University Microfilms International (UMI) product.

Master's Theses Directories contains two former directories: education and the arts and social sciences. It is a classified listing of master's theses. The thirty-seventh issue (1988, 397 p.) lists over 4,200 thesis titles as reported by the awarding institutions in the United States and Canada.

RESEARCH IN PROGRESS

Of all types of unpublished material, research in progress is the most difficult to locate. Some research in progress can be found in *Grants Index*, noted in Chapter 4. *Federal Research in Progress*, provided by National Technical Information Service (Dialog File 265, 266) (C47), lists federally funded research projects but is limited to the fields of physical sciences, engineering, and life sciences. The best source for locating research in progress in the social sciences is the academic journals, noted in Chapter 6. But, even journal coverage of research in progress is fragmentary.

REVIEWS

In the information flow, book reviews and reviews of literature are regarded as scholarly communication and a means for quality control of new knowledge and for collection development. According to Ylva Lindholm-Romantschuk,[4] a scholarly book review serves the following purposes. First, it is to announce the publication of a scholarly work, a new addition to the body of knowledge. Second, it evaluates the scholarly merits of the book. Third, it serves a gatekeeping function, that is, to accept or reject the innovation the author has put for evaluation. Fourth, it serves as a forum for disciplinary discourse. Finally, the disciplinary background of the reviewer is the lens through which the reviewer looks at and evaluates the work at hand. Academic book reviewing is a vital part of the scholarly communication system and an integral part of the peer review process.[5]

Reviews of literature will be mentioned in chapters on subdisciplines of the social sciences. For book reviews in the social sciences in general, the *Social Sciences Index* and the *Humanities Index*, both noted later, are two indispensable tools for book reviews listed in their book review sections. Other listings of reviews may be found in general review indexes and abstracts, such as *Book Review Digest* and *Book Review Index*. Michael D. G. Spencer points out, however, that standard indexing and abstracting services often omit book reviews and he regards the *Social Science Citation Index* and *Arts & Humanities Citation Index* as highly superior tools for identifying book reviews.[6] The following is a comprehensive listing of book reviews:

Combined Retrospective Index to Book Reviews in Scholarly Journals, 1886–1974. Evan Ira Farber, ed. Arlington, VA: Carrollton Press, 1979–1982. 15 vols. ISBN 0840380167X. (C48)

It consists of twelve volumes of author index and three volumes of title index, providing access to more than one million book reviews that appeared in 459 scholarly journals in history, political science, and sociology.

INDEXES AND ABSTRACTS

An index is a systematically arranged list of works giving sufficient bibliographic description about each item to enable it to be identified and traced. An abstract gives a summary of an item in addition to a bibliographic description. It serves the same purpose as an index, but a reader can read the summary and get the information without referring further to the source. In a broad sense, any device used for the purpose of tracing and identifying an item is an index. Thus, the library card catalog is an index. But traditionally, an index refers to a means of providing access to parts of a work. It is a key to the contents. As such, an index is usually used as the aid to periodical literature.

Indexing and abstracting services are one of the three basic means to help readers use periodical literature. The other two, directories and union lists, are discussed in the chapter on periodicals. There are four types of indexing and abstracting services: (1) indexing and abstracting service, (2) current awareness service, (3) citation indexing service, and (4) selective dissemination of information service.

An index to periodicals has distinct features as compared with an index to a book. A book is a one-shot deal; once the book is indexed, the job is done. This is not so in periodicals. A periodical is published continuously, and it contains a number of independent articles, often dealing with widely divergent topics and always by many authors. An index to a periodical should adhere to certain rules to ensure uniformity and consistency among the various issues being indexed and for the future issues. The subject headings once chosen must be strictly followed, and the items should be correctly classified under the subject.[7]

One of the problems of indexing and abstracting services is the time lag. Since the arrangement of indexes and abstracts is involved in editing, the delay is unavoidable. One means to solve the problem of time lag is the employment of words instead of chosen concepts as subject headings for indexing. Keywords or essential words can be extracted from the title, abstract, or text as subject headings. Such an approach, also called natural language indexing, may reduce time lag to a certain extent. It has problems, too. First, the word indexed does not necessarily relate to the content of an item. Second, to retrieve an item under the indexed word will miss items on the same subject but indexed under different words. A user must refer to synonyms, related terms, and abbreviations to ensure complete searching. Last but not least, indexing a word with a broader meaning may not include an item that is indexed under the word with a narrow meaning, or vice versa.

In recent years, the abstracting service has gained its momentum and will eventually replace indexing services. Some of H. W. Wilson Company's indexes are also available in abstracts. They include *Readers' Guide Abstract, Readers' Guide Abstracts Select Edition, Wilson Humanities Abstracts, Wilson Social Sciences Abstracts,* and abstracts in other subject fields. The other trend is moving towards full-text. A number of Wilson's abstracts include full-text.

The current awareness service is the other method for rapid dissemination of information. The service can take many forms. Theoretically, any attempt to notify a reader speedily of new materials that may be of interest to him can be considered a current awareness service. Display of new books and of newly arrived periodicals, routing materials, and notification of works on slips and cards are all current awareness services. In a formal sense, it refers to (1) advance publication of titles (not available in the social sciences) and (2) contents reproduction. In contents reproduction, no scanning and editing work is necessary. It is relatively inexpensive for the same reasons, and some clerical work, such as typing and filing, can be eliminated.

Another approach to access to materials is the citation indexing service. It lists cited articles, each of which is accompanied by a list of citing articles. The citing article is a source, and the cited article is a reference.[8] The theory is that when a scientist cites an earlier work in his research paper, he specifies a conceptual, that is subject, relationship between the two papers.[9] A scientist will follow from one article to related articles and forward in time to the latest article published on the subject in which he is interested. In addition to retrieving information, citation indexes can be used to evaluate authors, to conduct market research, and to identify most cited works.[10]

The selective dissemination of information service, frequently referred to as SDI, offers an individualized service. An interest profile of individuals is maintained. Notices of publications are sent to each person, geared to his or her interests and needs. The SDI is generally a machine-operated system. Every time the selected database is updated, searching on a requested subject will be automatically performed and the result sent to the user.

For listings of indexes and abstracts, one may consult directories of periodicals and other reference sources mentioned in Chapter 6.

Indexes

General

The general, interdisciplinary indexes and abstracts are a good place to find articles in the social sciences. Three representative titles may be noted:

> *Readers' Guide to Periodical Literature*, 1901– . New York: H. W. Wilson, 1905– . Semimonthly (Monthly February, July, and August) ISSN 00340464. Print & digital. (C49)
> *Magazine Index*, 1959– . Belmont, CA: Information Access Company, 1977. Microform & digital. Monthly. (C50)
> *Academic Index*, 1985– . Belmont, CA: Information Access Company, 1987– . Monthly updates. Digital. (C51)

Readers' Guide (RG) is a cumulative index in three formats: (1) permanent cumulated volumes; (2) annual volume, until superseded by a new permanent volume; and (3) semimonthly and monthly, by cumulative index. *RG* indexes U.S. general and nontechnical periodicals in the social sciences, humanities, and natural and applied sciences. Its abridged version for school and small public libraries is *Abridged Readers' Guide to Periodical Literature* (1935– . New York: H. W. Wilson, monthly except June-August, with annual and biennial cumulations, ISSN 0001334X) (C52). The *Readers' Guide Abstracts* began publication in 1988 (New York: H. W. Wilson, monthly except June and July, with semiannual cumulation, ISSN 08991553) (C53). It abstracts approximately 25,000 articles annually. It is also available online on Wilsonline and marketed through Dialog (File 141) and FirstSearch.

Both *Magazine Index* and *Academic Index* are subject indexes to periodicals of general interest. *Magazine Index* indexes cover to cover more than 450 periodicals from the United States and Canada on current affairs, business, education, consumer information, government relations, public relations, social sciences, and other subjects. Some 1,000 records are added each month. The full-texts of articles in some 100 periodicals are provided. A full-text database of *Magazine Index* is *Magazine ASPS* (Belmont, CA: Information Access Company, 1984– , monthly) (C54). Some 2,500 records are added each month. Its online version, *IAC Magazine Database* or *Magazine ASAP* (C55), is marketed through Dialog (File 47), DataStar (File MAGS), and Ovid (File MAGS). All Information Access Company databases are updated daily in *IAC Newsearch* (current 45 days) (C56), marketed through Dialog (File 211). At the end of a month, data will be transferred to various databases.

Academic Index, on InfoTrac II, is a CD-ROM subject index to 375 periodicals plus *The New York Times*. Its coverage includes the social sciences, humanities, education, natural science, and current events. It indexes periodicals of the current year and three previous years of the 200 most popular magazines. Approximately 30 percent of the periodicals are indexed in Magazine Index. Academic Index is also marketed via Ovid (File ACAD).

Subfield

> *Social Sciences Index*, 1974– . New York: H. W. Wilson. Quarterly with annual cumulation. ISSN 00944920. Print & digital. (C57)
>
> *Humanities Index*, 1974– . New York: H. W. Wilson. Quarterly with annual cumulation. ISSN 00955981. Print & digital. (C58)
>
> *PAIS International in Print*, 1991– . New York: Public Affairs Information Service. Monthly and annual cumulation. ISSN 10514015. Print & digital. (C59)

The *Social Sciences Index* and the *Humanities Index* were originally published in 1916, with the same plan as *Readers' Guide to Periodical Literature*, noted earlier, under the title *Readers' Guide to Periodical Literature Supplement*. With the publication of the third cumulative volumes 8 to 11 for the period 1920–1923, the name of the index was changed to *International Index to Periodicals*. In June 1965, its name was again changed to the *Social Sciences and Humanities Index*. Beginning in June 1974, it was divided into the current two indexes.

Social Sciences Index (*SSI*) indexes more than 400 English-language periodicals. Fields covered include anthropology, area studies, business, communication, community health and medical care, criminal justice and criminology, current affairs, economics, family studies, geography, gerontology, international relations, law, media studies, minority studies, planning and public administration, policy science, political science, psychiatry, psychology, social work and public welfare, sociology, urban studies, and women's studies.

Humanities Index (*HI*) indexes 350 English-language periodicals. Fields covered include archaeology, area studies, art, classical studies, dance, drama, film, folklore, history, journalism and communication, language, literature, music, performing arts, philosophy, religion and theology, and women's studies. For the social science literature, the two indexes complement each other. Both indexes have a separate listing of book reviews. The digital format of *SSI* and *HI* on CD-ROM is Wilsondisc, online database is Wilsonline, and on the Web is WilsonWeb. It may be noted that other H. W. Wilson's indexes should be consulted for a wide coverage of social science sources, such as *Business Periodicals Index, Education Index*, and *Index to Legal Periodicals*, mentioned in the chapters on business, education, and law respectively.

PAIS International in Print is an index merging the previous two print indexes: *Public Affairs Information Service Bulletin* (1915–1990), known as PAIS by its publisher, and *Public Affairs Information Foreign Language Index* (1972–1990). *PAIS International in Print* is one of the best indexing services in the social sciences because of its currency and extensiveness. It is a subject list of "latest books, pamphlets, government publications, reports of public and private agencies, and periodical articles relating to business, economic, and social conditions, public administration, and international relations in English throughout the world" (title cover). It is also a good source for locating foreign government documents, bibliographies, and directories; it is particularly valuable in locating publications of international conferences and obscure agencies.

PAIS is also available online as *PAIS: International* (C60) marketed through Dialog (File 49), Ovid (PAIS), DataStar (PAIS), and FirstSearch, and on CD-ROM, called *PAIS on CD-ROM* (C61), or *PAIS International*. PAIS provides the Document Delivery Service. Copies of indexed items can be ordered from PAIS or through Information on Demand (IOD) or Dialog. Beginning in 1996, it offers *PAIS Select Full-text CD-ROM* (C62), two CD-ROM discs per year, in the fall and the winter. It contains documents in English only. Each document contains a full bibliographic description, PAIS subject headings, full text, and charts and graphs. Selected items come from many sources, such as *Africa Report, The Brookings Review, The Economist, Foreign Policy Bulletin*, and *Weekly Compilation of Presidential Documents*.

Abstracts

> *Applied Social Sciences Index and Abstracts*, 1987– . London: Library Association Publications. Bimonthly with annual cumulation. ISSN 09502238. Print & digital. (C63)
> *Wilson Humanities Abstracts*, 1994– . H. W. Wilson, 1995– . Print & digital. (C64)
> *Wilson Social Sciences Abstracts*, 1994– . H. W. Wilson, 1995– . Print & digital. (C65)

The most comprehensive abstract service is *Social Science Abstracts: A Comprehensive Abstracting and Indexing Journal of the World's Periodical Literature in the Social Sciences* (New York: Social Science Abstracts, Columbia University, 1929–1933. 5 vols.) (C66), which abstracted more than 70,000 articles in over 4,000 journals during its existence. It was, unfortunately, shortlived. There had been no comprehensive abstracting service in the social sciences for over half a century, until *Applied Social Sciences Index and Abstracts (ASSIA)* appeared. Though not as extensive as the *Social Science Abstracts*, the abstracting service is a much needed addition. *ASSIA* abstracts and indexes over 630 English language journals and newspapers from the United Kingdom, United States, "Old Commonwealth," Europe, and other countries, with a predominant coverage of journals and newspapers in the United Kingdom and in North America, constituting 85 percent of the total. Subject coverage is broad, including cultural anthropology, communication, criminology, education, ethnic studies, family, geriatrics, health, housing, immigration, industrial relations, legal issues, nursing, political science, psychology, sociology, urban planning, women's studies and humanities, such as religion. Each issue consists of four sections: Abstracts Sequence, the main index, containing main records arranged alphabetically by topic; Author Index; Subject Index, indexing terms other than the lead term; and Source (Journal) Index. The main record consists of abstract or record number, main subject heading, title of the article, author(s), title of the periodical, the volume and/or issue, pagination, and the abstract of an average of 50 words. *ASSIA* is also available on CD-ROM as *ASSIA Plus* (C67), and online as *ASSIA: Applied Social Sciences Index & Abstracts* (C68), marketed via Dialog (File 232) and DataStar (File ASSI).

Both *Wilson Humanities Abstracts* and *Wilson Social Sciences Abstracts* have the same coverage as their index counterparts. Abstracts range from 50 to 150 words each. Both abstracts are also available on CD-ROM, online database, and magnetic tape. In 1997, Wilson made available *Humanities Abstracts Full Text*, marketed through Dialog (File 436) (C69), 1995 forward. Full-text articles from more than 90 journals are included.

CONTENTS REPRODUCTION

General

> *Current Contents: Arts & Hamanities*, 1979– . Philadelphia: Institute for Scientific Information. Biweekly. ISSN 01633155. Print & digital. (C70)
>
> *Current Contents: Social and Behavioral Sciences*, 1969– . Philadelphia: Institute for Scientific Information. Weekly. ISSN 0590384X. Print & digital. (C71)
>
> *EBSCO Alert*. http://eadmin.epnet.com/ealert (C72)
>
> *Periodical Contents Index. (PCI Web)* http://pci.chadwyck.com (C73)
>
> *UNCOVER/REVEAL*. http://www.carl.org/reveal (C74)

Current Contents: Arts & Humanities (AH) and *Current Contents: Social and Behavioral Sciences (SBS)* are two of seven multidisciplinary editions of contents reproduction. *SBS* is produced in six formats (Internet, online, magnetic tape, CD-ROM, diskette, and print) with weekly update indexes for some 1,500 journals. It covers anthropology, archaeology, communication, economics, education, environmental studies, geography and development, law, library and information sciences, management, political science and public administration, psychiatry, psychology, public health and health care science, rehabilitation, social work and social policy, and sociology.

AH is produced in five formats (Internet, online, magnetic tape, CD-ROM, and print) with biweekly update indexes of some 1,100 journals. It covers disciplines in or related to the social sciences, such as archaeology, Asian studies, history, and philosophy.

In both *SBS* and *AH*, the tables of contents are reproduced as soon as the journals are published and sometimes before subscribers receive them. They are arranged broadly by subject. Four indexes are provided for each: the Journal Index, the Title Word Index, Author Index and Address Directory, and Publishers Address Directory. These two *Current Contents* complement each other. Some 20 periodicals are covered in both.

All editions of *Current Contents* are available on the Web as *Current Contents Connect* (http://connect.isihost.com) (C75). The online database, *Current Contents Search* (C76) is marketed via Dialog (File 440), Ovid (File CCALL or individual files as BEHA and ARTS), DataStar (Files CBIB and CTOC), SearchBank, and FirstSearch. The database covers all editions. For social science sources, the search has to be qualified by subfiles of *Current Contents: Arts and Humanities* and *Current Contents: Social and Behavioral Sciences*. In the diskette and CD-ROM, additional features include author abstracts and library holdings tags (in CD-ROM). CD-ROM is available from Ovid, SilverPlatter, and Digital: CC Search.

EBSCO Alert provides contents reproduction and SDI services. A subscriber may have access to a table of contents (TOC) of approximately 13,000 journal titles, and set up a profile of interest containing up to 25 journal titles and 7 keyword SDI strategies. Each week, the subscriber receives via e-mail new TOCs that match the subscriber's profile selection. Delivery of documents is also available from *EBSCO* Document Services.

Periodical Contents Index (PCI Web) provides contents of over 2,000 journals in the humanities and social sciences, from their first issue to 1990/1991. It is international in coverage in English, French, German, Italian, Spanish, and other Western languages. It adds more than one million more articles each year. According to the producer, it will grow to 3,500 journals and 15 million articles.

PCI Web can be searched by journal title or journal subject. All journals are classified into 23 subject areas. Subjects in the social sciences include anthropology and ethnology, archaeology and ancient civilizations, area studies, black studies, economics and business studies, education, geography, history, Jewish studies, law, library and information science, political science and public administration, psychology, social sciences, and women's studies. *PCI Web* is for subscribing institutions only. It is also marketed via FirstSearch.

UnCover is a subsidiary of CARL (Colorado Alliance of Research Libraries). The Alliance began in 1974 as a consortium of research libraries for the purpose of regional resource sharing and was incorporated as a nonprofit in 1981. CARL began the *UnCover* table-of-contents database and document delivery service in 1988. *UnCover* was officially formed in 1993. This is a content reproduction and delivery service. *Uncover* is able to have access to almost 7 million citations over 17,000 periodical titles, with 5,000 citations added daily. Uncover can be accessed through some libraries' OPACs and the Internet. *Uncover/Reveal* provides the journal tables of contents and topical alerting service as well.

Other databases also provide contents reproduction, such as FirstSearch. Contents reproduction can also be found in periodicals as noted in Chapter 6.

Subfield

> *International Current Awareness Service*, 1990– . London: Routledge. Monthly. (C77)

International Current Awareness Services (ICAS) consists of four parts as follows:

> *Anthropology and Related Disciplines* (ISSN 0960511) covers anthropology, applied anthropology, area studies, development studies, ethnography, and social and cultural anthropology.
> *Economics and Related Disciplines* (ISSN 0960152X) covers economics, econometrics, economic history, labour economics, development economics, statistical and mathematical sciences.
> *Political Science and Related Disciplines* (ISSN 09601538) covers political science, political thought, government, public administration, international relations and contemporary history.
> *Sociology and Related Disciplines* (ISSN 09601546) covers sociology, criminology, human geography, industrial relations, law and society, social administration, social and industrial psychology, social policy, and women and society.

The four parts contain literature in 30 languages from over 60 countries. Over 120,000 materials are surveyed for inclusion each year. Its compilation is based on the collection of the British Library of Political and Economic Science, the Institute of Commonwealth Studies, the School of Oriental and African Studies, University College, and other special libraries in London. Each issue has two sections: (1) Journals and Monographs, a content reproduction service. Most contents are listed fully under the journal and monograph title. English language title translation and any summaries in English are accompanied with each item. (2) Subject and Placename indexes. ICAS is published side by side with the *International Bibliography of the Social Sciences* as the latter's complement.

CITATION INDEXES

> *Social Sciences Citation Index*, 1972–   . Philadelphia: Institute for Scientific Information. 3/year with annual and quinquennial cumulations. ISSN 00913707. Print & digital. (C78)
> *Arts & Humanities Citation Index*, 1976–   . Philadelphia: Institute for Scientific Information. 3/year with annual and quinquennial cumulations. ISSN 01628445. Print & digital. (C79)

Social Sciences Citation Index (SSCI) and *Arts & Humanities Citation Index (A&HCI)* are two of the three multidiscipline citation indexes. (The other multidisciplinary citation index is *Science Citation Index.*) *SSCI* with weekly update in the Internet, online, and magnetic tape, monthly update in CD-ROM with abstracts, quarterly update in CD-ROM, and triennially in print, with multiyear cumulations indexes over 1,700 social sciences journals and over 5,600 other journals that have items on the social sciences. It covers anthropology, business, communication, criminology and penology, economics, education, environmental studies, family studies, geography, geriatrics and gerontology, health policy and services, history, industrial relations and labor, information science and library science, language and linguistics, law, philosophy, political science, psychiatry, psychology, public health, social issues, social work, sociology, substance abuse, urban studies, and women's studies.

A&HCI, with weekly update on the Internet, online, and for magnetic tape, triennially in CD-ROM, and semiannually in print with multiyear cumulations, indexes over 1,100 arts and humanities journals and over 7,000 other journals that have items on arts and humanities. It covers social sciences topics, such as archaeology, Asian studies, folklore, and history.

All ISI's citation indexes are arranged in the same pattern. Each of the two citation indexes just listed consists of three parts.[11] (1) The Source Index provides a complete author index to the articles indexed and bibliographic description of each article listed. (2) The Citation Index gives cited author and his work in chronological order followed by a listing of citing papers. Citing papers are always those published during the period being indexed, while cited works vary in forms including both published and unpublished materials. (3) The Permuterm Subject Index is an alphabetical list of significant words extracted from the titles of all source items indexed. Each significant word from a title is paired with every other significant word in the title. These permuted pairs are arranged alphabetically in two-level indexing entries and are linked to the names of the authors who used them in the titles of their works.

SSCI and A&HCI are available online, entitled Social SciSearch (C80) and Arts & Humanities Search (C81) respectively, marketed through Dialog (File 7 and File 439), DataStar (File SSCI and AHCI), Ovid (Files SSCI and AHCI), and FirstSearch (File Arts & Humanities Search. The CD-ROM version features a journal holding utility program by which a librarian can identify and tag library holdings.

SELECTIVE DISSEMINATION OF INFORMATION

Since the introduction of online databases in the 1970s, all major database vendors offer selective dissemination of information (SDI), such as Dialog, Ovid, and Questel-Orbit. The Institute for Scientific Information provides four kinds of alerting services: Journal Tracker, for delivery of table of contents and author abstracts, up to 25 journals; Corporate Alert, for delivery of table of contents and author abstracts, as many as the user needs; Discovery Agent, a Web-based service enabling the user to create, manage, and revise a personal profile for document delivery; and Personal Alert for delivery of author names, journal titles, articles, and keywords relevant to the user's selected topics. Alerts are delivered via e-mail.

AREA STUDIES

There is no consensus on the position of area studies in the social sciences. Some consider that the field relates to history. The traditional division of history among ancient, medieval, and modern becomes less important when historians tend to study it by area. Area studies deal with all aspects of life in a country or a larger area. Their approach is interdisciplinary.

In this book, reference sources in area studies are noted in the following pages and elsewhere in other chapters. Some representative bibliographic sources of area studies are listed here. It must be noted that bibliographies may also be found in Web sites for area studies, noted in Chapter 4.

African Studies

A Current Bibliography on African Affairs, 1962– . Farmingdale, NY: Baywood. Quarterly. ISSN 00113255. (C82)

African Studies, 19th Century– . Baltimore: National Information Services Corporation. http://www.nisc.com (C83)

Quite a few bibliographies have been published on African studies. *A Current Bibliography on African Affairs* features articles and book reviews, but over two-thirds of its contents are devoted to a bibliographical section, a classified bibliography with most entries annotated. Volume 28, 1987–1988, provides over 2,100 entries of books and periodical articles, with extensive coverage of current books, articles, and papers in African studies.

African Studies is a huge database of databases containing over 280,000 records drawn from a number of databases, some of which are listed here: (1) Library Catalogue of the African Studies Centre (ASC), Lieden, 1988– . (2) Africa Institute, Pretoria, 1981– . (3) The Southern African Database, Sardius, 1961–1997. (4) School of Oriental and African Studies (SOPAS) Library Catalogue: Africa, 1989– . (5) NAMLIT, 19th century– . (Namibia collections in Europe). (6) The Kille Campbell Africana Library Catalogue, University of Natal, 19th century– . (7) Business and Industry, Africa, 1994– (drawn from Business and Industry database, noted in Chapter 9. (8) APEX '97: The African Periodicals Exhibit Catalogue, African Academy of Sciences in Kenya. (9) Bibliography on Contemporary African Politics and Development, 1981–1992, University of California at Los Angeles. (10) International Library of African Music (ILAM), Rhodes University. (11) Database of Swiss Theses and Dissertations, 1897–1996).

The database is one of several databases in BiblioLine by the National Information Services Corporation (NISC). Nearly 40 databases are offered in BiblioLine, including those mentioned in this chapter and in Chapter 17. In BiblioLine, any word or phrase in the text can be searched. The user can also use Boolean, proximity, wildcard, and range operators for searching. BiblioLine also features in each database listings of its related database titles, CD-ROM titles, and links to other databases.

One related database is *South African Studies*, 1987– . It contains over 467,000 records, including theses and current research. The database consists of a number of databases, some of which are listed here: (1) *Index to South African Periodicals*, South African State Library, 1987– . (2) South African National Bibliography, South African State Library, 1988– . (3) Investor's Guide, updated quarterly, with detailed information on over 600 companies listed on the Johannesburg Stock Exchange. (4) National English Literary Museum (NLM) indexes. (5) Index to South African Theses and Dissertations, University of Potchefstroom Library, early 1900s– . (6) Centre for Rural Legal Studies Database, 1987– .

Asian Studies

ASDP Syllabus and Bibliography Collection Online. Honolulu, University of Hawaii. http://lama.kcc.hawaii.edu/asdp/index.html (C84)
Bibliography of Asian Studies, 1956– . Ann Arbor, MI: Association for Asian Studies, 1957– . Annual. ISSN 00677159. (C85)

ASDP (Asian Studies Development Program), a joint national program of the East West Center, University of Hawaii, and the Library of Kapiolani Community College, created *ASDP Syllabus and Bibliography* in 1995 to make the materials accessible worldwide. The materials are organized into 32 categories, from Accounting and Anthropology to Sociology and Women's Studies. One of the categories is Bibliographies. Titles in Bibliographies are organized in general according to the main categories and further divided by region and country. Most titles are not annotated.

The *Bibliography of Asian Studies* (formerly *Far Eastern Bibliography*, 1936–1953) was published as part of the *Journal of Asian Studies*, noted in Chapter 7, from 1956 to 1969. Since 1970, it has been a separate publication. The bibliography is an unannotated comprehensive listing of Western-language monographs, articles, parts of composite works, and doctoral dissertations pertaining to Asia, with the heaviest emphasis on history, the humanities, and the social sciences. It is arranged by region, country, and a hierarchy of subjects. The 1991 *Bibliography* (Ann A. Shulman, ed., 1997, 732 p.) contains 37,000 entries. The main problem with the *Bibliography of Asian Studies* is its time lag.

Latin American Studies

> *Bibliographic Guide to Latin American Studies*, 1981–   . Boston: G. K. Hall. Annual. ISSN 01625314. (C86)
> *Handbook of Latin American Studies*, 1945–   . Austin, TX: University of Texas Press. Annual. (C87)
> *HAPI: Hispanic American Periodicals Index*, 1970/74–   . Los Angeles: University of California Latin American Center Publications, 1975–   . Annual. ISSN 02708558. (C88)
> *Latin American Studies*, 1970–   . Baltimore: National Information Services Corporation. http://www.nisc.com (C89)

Bibliographic Guide to Latin American Studies is basically a subject catalog of the collection of the University of Texas, with additional entries from the Library of Congress. The bibliography serves as a supplement to the *Catalog of the Latin American Collection of the University of Texas at Austin* (Boston: G. K. Hall, 1969, 31 vols.) (C90).

The *Handbook of Latin-American Studies* provides bibliographical coverage of the significant materials in various languages in the social sciences and humanities concerned with Latin America. The growing amount of materials led in 1964 to the division of the handbook into two parts, the humanities and the social sciences, published in alternate years. *Handbook Number 54: Humanities* (Dolores Moyano Martin, ed., 1995, 936 p., ISBN 0292751907) contains over 5,500 entries in art, history, literature, music, philosophy, and electronic sources, whereas *Handbook Number 55: Social*

Sciences (Dolores Moyano Martin, ed., 1997, 928 p., ISBN 0292752113) contains over 5,200 entries in anthropology, economics, geography, government and politics, international relations, sociology, and electronic sources.

The *Handbook* is the largest annotated bibliography of its kind. In 1997, it was made available on the Web (http://locweb.loc.gov), as *HLAS Online* (C91), updated monthly with prepublication sources. *HLAS* is also available on CD-ROM produced by the Foundation MAPFRE.

More current is the annual *HAPI*, a multilanguage index to some 250 journals published throughout the world. The 1995 annual (Barbara G. Valk, comp., 1996, 652 p., ISBN 0879034033) lists sources by subject, book review, and author. Arrangement is by subject, based on the *HAPI Thesaurus and Name Authority* 1970–1989, and its updates, compiled by Barbara G. Valk (C91). *HAPI* is also available online through UCLA's Latin American Center and the Research Libraries Group's CitaDel Citation and on CD-ROM produced by the National Information Services Corporation.

Latin American Studies is available on the Internet and CD-ROM. The CD-ROM version consists of two volumes: Volume I, Multidisciplinary, 1970– , and Volume II, Current Affairs, Business and Law, 1986– . These two volumes contain nearly 900,000 records. It covers anthropology, arts and archaeology, banking, business, education, foreign relations, geography, history, human rights, industry, legislation, marketing, politics and government, public administration, refugees, religion, refugees, sociology, and women's rights. The database is based on two products: *Hispanic American Periodicals Index (HAPI)* and the Nettie Lee Benson Latin American Collection at the University of Texas at Austin.

Middle East Studies

> *The Middle East Abstracts and Index*, 1978– . Seattle, WA: Reference Corporation. Annual. (C92)

It covers archaeology, art, business, current affairs, economic development, education, history, language, literature, politics and government, and sociology. The 1998 volume (Volume 21, James Joseph Sanchez, ed., 1998, 5 parts) contains periodical articles, newspaper articles, monographs, and government documents, classified into the following parts: A, Near East; B, Israel-Palatine; C, Central Area-Inner Asia; D, Maghreb-Sahel-Horn; and E, selected topics.

Slavic Studies

> *The American Bibliography of Slavic and East European Studies*, 1967– . London: M. E. Sharpe. Annual. ISSN 00943770. (C93)

Slavic Studies: A Guide to Bibliographies, Encyclopedias, and Handbooks.
Murlin Croucher, comp. & ed. Wilmington, DE: Scholarly Resources,
1993. 2 vols. ISBN 0842023747. (C94)

The *Bibliography* for 1993 (Patt Leonard and Rebecca Routh, comps.
and eds., 1996, 602 p., ISBN 156324750X), sponsored by the American
Association for the Advancement of Slavic Studies, is an index to English-
language and selected foreign-language materials published in the United
States and Canada and publications produced by American Institutions
abroad (Preface). It contains over 6,200 entries of books, periodical articles,
government and research reports, dissertations and book reviews, primarily
in the humanities and the social sciences, relating to Eastern and East-
Central Europe and the former Soviet Union, including Albania, Armenia,
Azerbaijan, Belarus, Bulgaria, the Czech Republic, Lithuania, Moldova, Poland, Romania, the Russian Federation, Slovakia, Tajikistan, Turkmenis-
tan, Ukraine, Uzbekistan, and the former Yugoslavia. It is a classified
bibliography but not annotated. There are three indexes: author, title, and
subject. For European publications on Slavic studies, refer to the *European
Bibliography of Slavic and East European Studies*.

Slavic Studies is a classified, annotated bibliography arranged by topic
and countries. Volume 1 covers area studies, Eastern Europe and the Bal-
kans, Bulgaria, Czechoslovakia, and Poland. Volume 2 covers the Soviet
Union, former Yugoslavia, and general references. Two indexes are provided: author and title.

NOTES

1. Roy Stokes, *Bibliographical Control and Service* (New York: London House
and Maxwell, 1965), p. 30; Roy Stokes, *The Function of Bibliography* (London:
Deutsch, 1969), p. 45.

2. *Booklist* 58, no. 2 (1961): 41–48.

3. Frank G. Burke, "Automation in Bibliographical Control of Archives and
Manuscript Collections," in Dagman Horna Perman, ed., *Bibliography and the
Historian* (Santa Barbara, CA: ABC-Clio, 1968), p. 96.

4. Ylva Lindholm-Romantschuk, *Scholarly Book Reviewing in the Social Sciences and Humanities: The Flow of Ideas within and among Disciplines* (Westport,
CT: Greenwood Press, 1998), pp. 40–42.

5. Ibid., p. 40.

6. Michael D. G. Spencer, "Thoroughness of Book Review Indexing: A First
Appraisal," *RQ* 27 (1986): 188–99.

7. Robert L. Collison, *Indexes and Indexing* (London: Ernest Benn, 1972),
pp. 125–27.

8. Morton V. Malin, "The Science Citation Index: A New Concept in Indexing," *Library Trends*, 16 (1968): 376.

9. Eugene Garfield and Irving H. Sher, "ASCA (Automatic Subject Citation Alert)," *American Behavioral Scientist* 12, no. 5 (1967): 19.

10. Melvin Meinstock, "Citation Indexes," *Encyclopedia of Library and Information Science*, vol. 5 (New York: Marcel Dekker, 1971), pp. 36–37; Eugene Garfield, "The 100 Most-Cited Books in CompuMath Citation Index, 1976–1980," *Current Contents* 34 (August 24, 1984): 3–6.

11. Eugene Garfield, "How to Use Science Citation Index (SCI)," *Current Contents* 9 (February 1983): 5–14; Meinstock, "Citation Indexes," 27–30.

Chapter 4

Sources of Information

ENCYCLOPEDIAS

General

An encyclopedia may be defined as a work that contains significant information on all branches of human knowledge. Well-known large general encyclopedias such as the *New Encyclopaedia Britannica* and the *Encyclopedia Americana* should be consulted for topics in the social sciences. In the *Encyclopedia Americana* (New York: Grolier, 30 vols.) (D1), articles are arranged alphabetically with a good, detailed index. It emphasizes American history, geography, and biographies.

In contrast to encyclopedias' familiar arrangement of articles in alphabetical sequence, the fifteenth edition of the *New Encyclopaedia Britannica* (D2), published since 1974, provides an innovative structure of three parts: Propaedia, a one-volume outline of knowledge and guide to the *Britannica*; Micropaedia, twelve volumes of ready reference, with short articles arranged in an alphabetical order; and Macropaedia, seventeen volumes of knowledge in depth, consisting of longer articles also arranged alphabetically. In 1985, a two-volume index was published. The index is well designed and remarkably compiled to make use of the encyclopaedia more convenient.

One feature of larger American encyclopedias is their continuous revision. Editorial staffs constantly review subjects and plan revisions. Revisions are seen in every printing. For previous printings, encyclopedias are brought up-to-date by annual supplements. *Americana Annual: An Encyclopedia of Events*, 1923–   (D3), and *Britannica Book of the Year*, 1928– (D4), record events for the previous years to supplement *Encyclopedia*

Americana and *Encyclopaedia Britannica* respectively. Beginning in 1985, *Britannica Book of the Year* added "Britannica World Data" in two parts. Part 1 is the "Nations of the World," comprising single country statistical summaries. Part 2, "Comparative National Statistics," provides comparative country data. Since country data change rapidly, the annual update is a most welcome enhancement. Both the Americana and the Britannica are available in CD-ROM, and the Britannica is the first major encyclopedia on the Web as Britannica Online (http://www.eb.com) (D5). The Web version consists of *Encyclopaedia Britannica, Britannica Book of the Year, Merriam-Webster's Collegiate Dictionary*, and links to selected Web sites. The *Americana* is also on the Web as one of the Grolier Online's Encyclopedia Family (http://go.grolier.com) (D6). When it is connected, *Grolier Multimedia Encyclopedia* and *Encyclopedia Americana* are displayed for choosing.

Subfield

Encyclopedias in the social sciences are:

Encyclopedia of the Social Sciences. E. R. A. Seligman, ed.-in-chief; Alvin Johnson, asso. ed. New York: Macmillan, 1930–1935. 15 vols. (D7)

International Encyclopedia of the Social Sciences. David L. Sills, ed. New York: Macmillan and Free Press, 1968. 17 vols. (D8)

International Eycyclopedia of the Social Sciences Biographical Supplement, v. 18. New York: Free Press, 1979. 820 p. ISBN 0028955102. (D9)

The Macmillan Book of Social Science Quotations: Who Said What, When, and Where. David L. Sills and Robert K. Merton, eds. New York: Macmillan, 1991. 437 p. ISBN 0028973976. (D10)

The Social Science Encyclopedia. 2nd ed. Adam Kuper and Jessica Kuper, eds. London: Routledge, 1996. 923 p. ISBN 0415108292. (D11)

Survey of Social Science. Frank N. Magill, ed. Pasadena, CA: Salem Press, 1991–1995. (D12)

The *Encyclopedia of the Social Sciences (ESS)* is arranged by topic, except in the first and last volumes. An extended introduction in the first volume consists of two parts: (1) the meaning of the social sciences and development of social thought and institutions and (2) the status of the social sciences in various countries with emphasis on Europe. At the end are three indexes: classified and schematic subject, dictionary subject, and contributors.

The *International Encyclopedia of the Social Sciences (IESS)* aims to reflect and encourage the rapid development of the social sciences throughout the world. Alvin Johnson remarked that "an encyclopedia, particularly one of the social sciences, should remain a historical document of its time and that each generation should have an encyclopedia—new from the ground up."[1] The *IESS* is a completely new reference work, designed to complement, rather than supplant its predecessor, the *ESS*.[2]

The majority of the topical articles in the *IESS* are devoted to the concepts, theories, methods, and emphasized regularities that characterize the social sciences today. Topics such as collective security, developmental psychology, information retrieval, motivation, policy science, and simulation that had not formed an accepted theory, concept, or method in the social sciences during the 1930s are well treated in the *IESS*. Historical and descriptive materials are, however, included only for illustrative purposes. Many articles in the *ESS* have been brought up to date and some have substantially expanded, such as those in psychology and statistics. David L. Sills, *IESS* editor, compared major disciplinary relevance on sample pages of the two encyclopedias and found that 54 out of the 85 articles in the *ESS* sample do not have counterparts in the *IESS*; 41 out of the 79 articles in the *IESS* sample do not have counterparts in the *ESS*.[3] It must be noted that there are articles in the *ESS* either not found in the *IESS* or only superficially touched on in the *IESS*, as for instance, the articles on the commune of Paris, impeachment, inquisition, income tax, and the Social Christian movement. Readers will miss many historical accounts of events, institutions, and people not contained in the *IESS*.

Readers may also note that the *IESS* has fewer but longer biographies—some 600 articles on both deceased and living persons born after 1890, as compared with the 4,000 biographies of deceased persons that comprise one-fifth of the entire contents of the *ESS*. Its *Biographical Supplement* lists 215 biographies of deceased social scientists and those living who were born no later than December 31, 1908, but Ernest Becker, born in 1924, who did not meet the age criterion, was included. The supplement is preceded by an alphabetical list and classification of biographies. An *IESS* by-product is the *International Encyclopedia of Statistics*, noted in the next chapter.

In *The Macmillan Book of Social Science Quotations*, quotations are arranged by author in alphabetical order with a summary of the source for each. For a complete source, refer to "Bibliography" (pp. 261–328). It has a detailed subject index. Authors are also listed in the index. Many quotations are cross-referenced. Some authors have more quotations. Authors with over twenty quotations include William James, John Maynard Keynes, John Locke, Bronislaw Malinowski, Karl Marx, Adam Smith, and Alfred Weber. Sigmund Freud has 43 quotations. It is also published as Volume 19 of *International Encyclopedia of the Social Sciences*.

The work by Kuper and Kuper contains some 600 entries dealing with theories, issues and methods, and biographies. In the second edition, 50 percent are new or have been completely rewritten, 40 percent have been substantially revised, and only about 10 percent have been retained in their original form (editorial preface). Entries are arranged in alphabetical order, all signed, and ended with References and/or Further Reading. Its "Entries listed by discipline and subject" lists 20 broad subjects, including anthropology, business studies, demography, economics, education, family and kinship, feminism, geography, government, history, law, linguistics, philosophy, and others. The length of entries varies. Many entries are divided by subtopics.

The *Survey of Social Science* consists of four parts:

> *Survey of Social Science: Economic Series*. Frank N. Magill, ed. Pasadena, CA: Salem Press, 1991. 5 vols. ISBN 0893567256.
>
> *Survey of Social Science: Sociology Series*. Frank N. Magill, ed. Pasadena, CA: Salem Press, 1994. 5 vols. ISBN 0893567396.
>
> *Survey of Social Science: Psychology Series*. Frank N. Magill, ed. Pasadena, CA: Salem Press, 1993. 6 vols. ISBN 0893567329.
>
> *Survey of Social Science: Government and Politics Series*. Frank N. Magill, ed. Pasadena, CA: Salem Press, 1995. 5 vols. ISBN: 0893567329.

All parts in the series are arranged in a similar pattern, and all list articles by topics in alphabetical order. The series is suited to nonspecialists. The parts will be mentioned in chapters in Part 2.

DICTIONARIES

General

General unabridged dictionaries have good coverage of terms used in the social sciences. Most of the social science terms can be found, for instance, in *Webster's Third New International Dictionary of the English Language* (1961, reissued, Springfield, MA: Merriam-Webster, 1981, 2,662 p., ISBN 0877792011) (D13). Its definitions are fuller and better than those found in many subject dictionaries. Yet, it is estimated that over one-third of social science terms are not listed in *Webster's Third*.[4] There is a dictionary of dictionaries:

> *Dictionary of Dictionaries*. 2nd ed. Thomas Kabdebo and Neil Armstrong, assisted by Elaín Ô. Síocháin. London: Bowker-Saur, 1997. 418 p. ISBN 1857391039. (D14)

This book has a broad scope not limited to words. As its introduction states, "[t]he terms of this dictionary are what have been considered to be the most helpful categories, namely the wide *variety of dictionaries*, in terms of their topics or subjects." It contains dictionaries, encyclopedias, biographies, library catalogs, and genealogies.

Works are arranged under 1,389 subject entries in alphabetical order, from "abbreviations" to "Zulu." Again, subject entries have a broad scope not limited to subject headings. The Introduction indicates the scope of "listing dictionaries by the name of the principal language, the main topic, or subject, or by their 'household name.' " Some titles are entered as topics, such as *ENCARTA, Encyclopedia Americana, Encyclopaedia Britannica, Dictionary of National Biography, Lloyd's Register, Marquis Who's Who,* and *New Dictionary of National Biography.*

A typical entry includes a description, significant titles, and citations. According to authors, 400 new headings have been added, and the book includes some 8,000 sources. Many descriptions are useful and up to date. The book is extensive in coverage. Selection of titles is generally sound.

Subfield

The following dictionaries in the social sciences are recommended:

A *Dictionary of the Social Sciences.* Julius Gould and William L. Kolb, eds. New York: Free Press, 1964. 761 p. (D15)
A *Dictionary of Social Science Methods.* P. McC. Miller and M. J. Wilson. New York: John Wiley, 1983. 124 p. ISBN 71900354. (D16)

Although published over 30 years ago, A *Dictionary of the Social Sciences* remains one of the best subfield dictionaries. It comprises signed articles by 273 social scientists that define close to 1,000 basic terms and concepts in political science, social anthropology, economics, social psychology, and sociology. An attempt was made to exclude those terms whose meanings have been adequately defined in a standard dictionary. Most entries are divided into sections. Section A sets out the core meaning of the terms. Section B gives a historical background of the meaning and/or more detailed discussion. In the longer entries, there are sections labeled C, D, E, and more that provide historical or analytical discussion.

The volume is more than a dictionary; it has encyclopedic treatment, though editors modestly stated that it was not their aim to produce an encyclopedia. The inclusion of significant literary productions and their contributions and the bibliographical references in most of the articles enhance its value as a reference work. Readers must note, however, that since the dictionary deals with key concepts most widely used in the various social science disciplines, its coverage is limited. Other subfield dictionaries in the social sciences should be used.

Of limited coverage is the Miller and Wilson dictionary. The work is exclusively devoted to empirical methods of inquiry in the social sciences. Terms are well defined, and it includes a substantial number of statistical models. The length of entries varies from one paragraph to as long as three pages (on forecasting).

DIRECTORIES

A directory is a work for locating, identifying, or obtaining information about a person or organization or both. Actually, it is a list of persons or organizations, or a combination of both. Directories may be grouped into four types: (1) general directories for locating names and addresses not limited to a particular profession, trade, or subject; (2) professional directories listing members of a profession; (3) institutional directories, listing primarily organizations, societies, institutions, foundations, government agencies, and the like; and (4) trade directories for locating information on manufacturers, companies, industries, and other business organizations and services. Most directories provide information about persons. In this regard, the distinction between directories and biographical sources is superficial. However, works that deal with primarily biographical sources will be mentioned in the next section.

General

> *Directories in Print.* ed. 1– , 1980– . Detroit: Gale Research. Biennial. ISSN 02755580. Print & digital. (D17)

Directories in Print, formerly *Directory of Directories*, is an outgrowth of *Directory Information Service*, 1974– (current title: *Directories in Print Supplement*, ISSN 18162569) (D18), which now serves as a supplement between editions. The seventeenth edition of the *Directory* (Dawn Conzett DesJardins, ed., 1998, 2 vols., ISBN 0787615137) is a descriptive guide to print and nonprint directories, buyer's guides, rosters, and other address lists of all kinds. Volume 1 contains 15,456 entries arranged in 26 broad subjects. Each entry provides 29 elements of information, including title, publisher/compiler, address and phone and fax, e-mail, URL(s), covers, language(s), arrangement, indexes, pages, frequency, editor(s), accepts advertising, circulation, price, ISSN, orders to, and so on. Volume 2 consists of three indexes: alternate formats, subject, and title and keyword. The directory is also available on CD-ROM and the Web, noted below.

Subfield

Organizations

> *Encyclopedia of Associations*, ed. 1– , 1965– . Detroit: Gale Research. Annual. ISSN 00710202. Print & digital. (D19)
> *Encyclopedia of Associations: International Organizations*, 1989– . Detroit: Gale Research. Annual. ISSN 10410023. (D20)
> *Encyclopedia of Associations: Regional, State and Local Organizations*, ed.

1, 1988–1989– . Detroit: Gale Research. 7 vols. ISSN 08942846.
Print & digital. (D21)
Gale'S Ready Reference Shelf. Detroit: Gale Research. Digital. (D22)
Yearbook of International Organizations, ed. 1– , 1948– . Union of International Associations. München: Saur. Irregular. ISSN 08843814.
(D23)

The subtitle of the *Encyclopedia of Associations* varies. The 34th edition (1999, 2 vols., 3 parts, ISBN 0787622257) is "a guide to nearly 23,000 national organizations, including: trade, business, environmental and agricultural, legal, engineering, and technological, natural and social sciences, educational, cultural, social welfare . . ." (subtitle). Volume 1, National Organizations of the United States, consists of three parts. Parts 1 and 2 provide descriptive listing of organizations. Part 3 is a name and keyword index. Volume 2 is a Geographical and Executive Index. There are two updates between editions.

Companions of the encyclopedia include international organizations and regional organizations. Both are compiled on the same pattern. The former is a listing of multinational and binational nonprofit membership organizations. The latter is the seven-volume listing for regional, state, and local organizations. The seven volumes cover Northwestern, Middle Atlantic, South Eastern, Great Lakes, South West and South Central, Western, and Northwestern and Great Plains, arranged geographically by state and city. All these Gale's publications belong to the *Encyclopedia of Associations Series* and are part of Gale's "Associations Unlimited" available on the Web, noted in Chapter 1. The Web site contains some 440,000 U.S. national, regional, state, and local and international nonprofit membership organizations. They are also available on CD-ROM and online. The online database is available on GaleNet, and marketed through Dialog (File 114). The database, updated semiannually, consists of national, international, and regional associations.

Readers may also find Gale's publications on the Web. *Directories in Print* is one of the publications in *Gale Database of Publications and Broadcast Media,* noted in Chapter 6. The database, updated semiannually, consists of *Gale Directory of Publications and Broadcast Media,* noted in Chapter 6, *Directories in Print,* and *Newsletters in Print.* It is also marketed through Dialog (File 469).

The *Encyclopedia of Associations* constitutes a part of the database *Gale's Ready Reference Shelf.* The *Reference Shelf* version provides access to over 276,000 associations, products, publishers, databases, directories, and so on. In addition to association encyclopedias, it includes *Publishers Directory, Gale Directory Publications and Broadcast Media, Directories in Print, Directory of Special Libraries and Information Centers,* and *Research Centers and Services Directory.* The encyclopedia and many other

Gale publications are also available in GaleNet, a Gale Web site noted in Chapter 1.

The 35th edition of the *Yearbook of International Organizations*, for 1998–1999 consists of four volumes. Volume 1 is the basic volume, Organization Descriptions and Cross-References. Each entry includes, if complete, organization name, main address, secondary addresses, founded, aims, structure, languages, staff, finance, activities, events, publications, information services, members, consultative status, IGO relations, NGO relations, and date. There are seven appendixes: Contents of Organization Descriptions, Types of Organization, Statistics, Continuity, Editorial Policy, Related Reference Works, and the United Nations. The other three volumes are: Volume 2, Country Directory of Secretariats and Membership; Volume 3, Subject Directory and Index; and Volume 4, National Organization Bibliography and Resources.

Foundations

Foundations may be found in the directories listed previously. The following are some directories devoted to foundations:

> *The Foundation Directory*, ed. 1– , 1960– . New York: Foundation Center. Annual. ISSN 00718092. Print & digital. (D24)
>
> *Foundations*. Harold M. Keele and Joseph C. Kiger, eds.-in-chief. Westport, CT: Greenwood Press, 1984, 516 p. ISBN 0313225567. (D25)
>
> *Guide to U.S. Foundations, Their Trustees, Officers, and Donors*, 1975– . New York: Foundation Center. ISSN 1071202X. (D26)
>
> *The International Foundation Directory*, 1974– . London: Europa. Irregular. (D27)
>
> *National Directory of Corporate Giving: A Guide to Corporate Giving Programs and Corporate Foundations*. 4th ed. Victoria Hall, ed. New York: Foundation Center, 1995. 1,092 p. ISBN 0879546468. Print & digital. (D28)

The 20th edition of *The Foundation Directory*, published in 1998 (Elizabeth H. Rich, ed., 2,260 p., ISBN 0879547650), lists 8,642 private or community foundations arranged alphabetically by state. These foundations, according to the publisher, held more than $247 billion in combined assets (88.8 percent of all foundation assets) and awarded more than $12.4 billion in grants (90 percent of total foundation giving). A complete entry includes foundation name and address, date of establishment, donor(s), foundation type, financial data, purpose and activities, fields of interest, international interests, limitations, publication, application information, officers, board of governors, number of staff, EIN, and selected grants.

A foundation is defined by the *Directory* as a nongovernmental, nonprofit organization, with its own funds (usually from a single source, either an individual, family, or corporation) and program managed by its own trustees and directors, which was established to maintain or aid educational, social, charitable, religious, or other activities serving the common welfare primarily by making grants to other nonprofit organizations. For inclusion in the directory an organization must meet this definition and have reported assets of $2 million or more or have made total contributions of $200,000 or more in the year of record. Foundations whose assets are over $1 million but less than $2 million or have an annual giving of over $50,000 but less than $200,000 are listed in a companion volume, *The Foundation Directory, Part 2* (Elizabeth H. Rich, ed., 1998, 998 p., ISBN 0879547634) (D29). It lists 4,926 midsized foundations that hold assets from $1 million and less than $2 million or with annual grant programs from $50,000 and less than $200,000.

The *Directory* also contains twelve statistical tables, three appendixes, and seven indexes. Appendixes include A, "Edition 19 Foundations not Included in Edition 20"; B, "Private Operating Foundations Excluded from *The Foundation Directory*"; and C, "Private Non-Operating Foundations not Included in *The Foundation Directory*." The seven indexes are: Index to Donors, Officers, Trustees; Geographic Index; International Giving Index; Types of Support Index; Subject Index; Foundations New to the Edition; and Foundation Name Index.

A supplement is published between editions. The 1998 *Foundation Directory Supplement* (Jeffrey A. Falkenstein and Margaret Mary Feczko, eds., 1998, 749 p., ISBN 0879547642) (D30), an update to both *The Foundation Directory* and *The Foundation Directory, Part 2*, lists 2,882 foundations "that have reported substantial changes in personnel, name, address, program interests, limitations, application procedures or other areas by the midpoint of the yearly *Directory* cycle" ("How to Use the Foundation Directory Supplement"). It has six indexes: Index to Donors, Officers, Trustees; Geographic Index; International Giving Index; Types of Support Index; Subject Index; and Foundation Name Index.

For foundations not listed in the *Directory* and its companion volume, consult the *Guide to U.S. Foundations* (formerly *National Data Book*). The 1998 edition (1998, 2 vols., ISBN 0879547677) in Volume 1 contains 42,071 entries arranged by state, including 36,885 private foundations, 1,969 corporate foundations, 2,323 grant-making operating foundations, and 411 community foundations that awarded grants of one dollar or more from 1994 to 1997 (Introduction). More than 28,000 foundations are not covered in any other reference source. Each entry includes if available address, contact person, telephone number, financial data, geographic limitations, publications, application information, and a complete listing of trustees, officers, and donors. At the beginning of the volume is a "Bibliography of State and Local Guides to U.S. Foundations," compiled by

Sarah Collins. Volume 2, Indexes, consists of two sections: An Index of Trustees, Officers, and Donors and a Foundation Name Index.

National Directory of Corporate Giving lists 2,256 companies making contributions to nonprofit organizations. There are 391 foundations, and 193 corporate giving programs are new. There are 67 basic data elements included in an entry, if available. These data elements are grouped into three categories: company general description, direct corporate giving program, and foundation. Data elements include company name, company address, giving statement, program name, contact person, purpose and activities, fields of interest, type of support, application limitation, foundation name, contact person, assets, grants made directly to or on behalf of individuals, application information, and so on. Seven indexes are provided: Officers, Donors, and Trustees; Geographic; International Giving; Types of Support; Subject; Types of Business; and Corporation, Corporate Giving Program, and Corporate Foundation.

In addition, the Center produces other resources, including *The Foundation 1000* (formerly *Source Book Profiles*) and three databases: *Foundation Directory, National Directory of Corporate Giving*, and *Foundation Grants Index*. These databases are marketed through Dialog (File 26 and File 27). Dialog File 26, *Foundation Directory*, for current year, contains both *Foundation Directory* and *Corporate Giving*. File 27, 1973 forward, is the online counterpart of *Foundation Grants Index*, noted later, and *Foundation News*. The 1997/1998 *Foundation 1000* (Francine Jones, ed., 1997, 2,922 p., ISBN 0879547219) (D31) lists the 1,000 largest foundations in the United States. According to the publisher, these foundations account for 47 percent of all foundation grant dollars awarded in a giving year. Each entry includes name and address, telephone number, contact, purpose, limitations, support areas, program areas, financial data, officers, governing board, program staff, number of staff, sponsoring company, background, publications, subject area, recipient type, population group, and sample grants. There are five indexes: Index to Donors, Officers, Trustees, Staff; Index of Subjects; Index of Types of Support; Geographic Index; and International Giving Index.

In July 1996, the Foundation Center released its database on CD-ROM. The CD-ROM provides information on over 43,000 U.S. foundations and corporate givers, and the names of almost 180,000 trustees, officers, and donors who make the funding decisions. It also contains descriptions of more than 115,000 grants of $10,000 or more awarded by over 1,000 of the largest foundations. Search mode includes browse, a basic grantmaker search mode, and an advanced search mode.

The International Foundation Directory follows the definition of *The Foundation Directory*, listing "non-governmental, non-profit organization having a principal fund by its own for the purpose of maintaining or aiding social, educational, charitable, religious, or other activities serving the common welfare" (Introduction). It includes foundations having an international activity arranged by country. Each entry provides name, founding year, activities, publications, finance, personnel (trustees, board of directors, officers, and so on), address, and telephone. There are a Selected Bibliography and two indexes: foundation and main activities.

Foundations belongs to the series of *The Greenwood Encyclopedia of American Institutions*, which provides "concise histories of major voluntary groups and non-profit organizations that have played significant roles in American civic, cultural, political, and economic life from colonial to the present" (Foreword). Directories in the series include *Labor Unions, Political Parties and Civil Action Groups*, and so on, mentioned elsewhere in the book. The one listed here presents brief histories of 230 foundations.

Grants

> *Directory of Research Grants*, 1975– . Phoenix, AZ: Oryx Press. Annual. ISSN 01467336. Print & digital. (D32)
> *The Foundation Grants Index*, 1970/71– . New York: Foundation Center. Annual. Print & digital. ISSN 00901601. (D33)
> *Foundation Grants to Individuals*, ed. 1– , 1977– . New York: Foundation Center. Biennial. (D34)
> *The Grants Register*, 1969/70– . New York: St. James Press. Biennial. ISSN 00725471. (D35)

The twenty-second, 1998 edition of *Directory of Research Grants* (1997, 1,204 p. ISBN 0897749480) provides information on 6,000 grant, contract, and fellowship support programs available from federal and state governments, private foundations, associations, and corporations for research, training, and innovative efforts, arranged by academic discipline. Each entry gives the grant name, brief description, requirements, funding amount, application/renewal date, contact, and sponsor. Before the main listing, there are Internet World Wide Web sites and "A Guide to Proposal Planning and Writing" by Lynn E. Miner. Four indexes are provided: subject, sponsoring organizations, grants by program type, and geographic. It has, however, limited coverage of foreign grant programs. The *Directory*'s database is also marketed through Dialog's CD-ROM as *Grants Database* (D36) and online as *Grants* (File 85) (D37). The database consists of the *Directory, Directory of Biomedical and Health Care Grants*, and *Directory of Grants in the Humanities*. Grants Database is also available on the Internet as GrantsSelect (http://www.oryxpress.com) (D38).

The Foundation Center's annual, *The Foundation Grants Index* (26th, 1998 edition, 1997, 2,416 p., ISBN 0879547243) is a cumulative listing of foundation grants reported in 1996. It lists more than 78,000 grants of

$10,000 or more by a total of 1,010 funders. According to the *Index*, these foundations represent only 2.5 percent of the total number of active grant making foundations, but their giving accounts for more than half of total grant dollars awarded by all U.S. foundations in 1996. The Index consists of seven sections: 1, Grants; 2, Recipient Name Index; 3, Subject Index; 4, Type of Support/Geographic Index; 5, Recipient Categories Index; 6, Index to Grants by Foundations; and 7, Foundations (addresses and limitations).

Grants are arranged by major subject fields with grants listed alphabetically by state and by foundation name. "A typical grant record includes name and location, the recipient, the amount awarded, the date of authorization, a description of the grant, the source of data, and the grant identification number" ("How to Use the Foundation Grants Index"). The grants included are also entered into the center's computerized foundation grants data bank. It is a part of the database marketed through Dialog (File 27) noted earlier.

A very useful reference to individual grant seekers is *Foundation Grants to Individuals*. Its tenth edition (1997, 858 p., ISBN 0879547138) lists 2,475 grants by foundations that give in general at least $2,000 annually. Grants are arranged by eight categories: Education Support, General Welfare, Arts and Cultural Support, International Applicants, By Nomination Only, Research and Professional Support, Restricted to Company Employees, and Restricted to Graduate or Students of Specific Schools. Each category provides a brief description, nature, scope, and limitations. There are an appendix of foundations, in Edition 9 but not listed in Edition 10, a bibliography of funding for individuals; and six indexes: Geographic Focus, Company Employee Grants, Specific School, Types of Support, Subject, and Foundation Name.

An international coverage of grants is the *Grants Register*, which provides information on grants for nationals of the United States and Canada, the United Kingdom and Ireland, Australia and New Zealand, South Africa, and the developing countries. The sixteenth edition (1997, 730 p., ISBN 031217585X) contains five sections: 1, Subject and Eligibility Guide to Awards; 2, The Grants Register, listing 2,850 awards by awarding organizations in alphabetical order; 3, Index of Awards; 4, Index of Discontinued Awards; and 5, Index of Awarding Organizations. Each entry of award provides subject area, eligibility, purpose, type, number of awards offered, frequency, value, length of study, country of study, application procedure, and closing date. It has a subject index and an index of awards and awarding bodies.

CONGRESSES AND MEETINGS

International Congress Calendar 1960/61– . Brussels: Union of International Associations. Quarterly. Annual. ISSN 05386349. (D39)

MInd: The Meetings Index Series SSH: Social Sciences/Humanities. Harrison,
NY: Interdok, 1988– . Quarterly. (D40)
World Meetings: Social & Behavioral Sciences, Human Services, and Management, 1971– . New York: Macmillan. Quarterly. ISSN
01946161. (D41)

The *International Congress Calendar* lists future meetings arranged in five basic sections: chronological, geographical, "last minute" meetings, international organization title index, and an analytical index of organizations and themes of meetings. The *Calendar* is the best source of information about the future meetings of the organizations listed in the *Yearbook of International Organizations*, noted earlier. More than 7,000 meeting events are listed.

MInd is devoted to the social sciences and humanities. It "classifies and indexes forthcoming meetings (congresses, conferences, courses, symposia, seminars, summer schools and similar meetings) to be held on a worldwide bases" (Preface). Entries are arranged by keyword. There are three indexes (sponsor, location, and date) and a contact list. Its companion volume is *MInd: The Meetings Index Series SEMT: Science/Engineering/Medicine/Technology*, 1984– , a bimonthly (D42).

Another source for worldwide meetings in the social sciences is *World Meetings: Social and Behavioral Science, Human Services, and Management* (title varies), a companion to the three other directories: *World Meetings: United States and Canada*, vol. 1– , 1963– (New York: Macmillan, quarterly, ISSN 00438693) (D43); *World Meetings: Outside United States and Canada*, vol. 1– , 1968– (New York: Macmillan, quarterly, ISSN 00438677) (D44); and *World Meetings: Medicine*, vol. 1– , 1978– (New York: Macmillan, quarterly, ISSN 01612875) (D45). It is a two-year registry of future meetings consisting of a subject index, a date index, a deadline index, a location index, a main entry section, and a sponsor directory and index. The main entry, arranged by quarter of the two-year period, consists of eight subsections for each entry: (1) registry number, title, location, and date of meeting, (2) sponsor, (3) general information, (4) content, (5) attendance, (6) deadlines, (7) publications, and (8) exhibits.

Directories are the primary sources of information on organizations and individuals. Yet other forms of materials provide equal information. There is a wealth of information on organizations and individuals in encyclopedias, dictionaries, almanacs, handbooks, guides, bibliographies, and indexes.

BIOGRAPHIES

Although biographies are the major sources for biographical information, other types of works also supply information on individuals, such as encyclopedias, dictionaries, handbooks, and yearbooks. Much biographical information is found in general encyclopedias. The *Columbia Encyclopedia* (5th ed., Barbara A. Chernow and George A. Vallasi, eds., New York: Columbia University Press, 1993, 3,048 p., ISBN 039562438X) (D46) is noted for its coverage of biographical information. The two encyclopedias of the social sciences and the *Supplement* mentioned earlier give about 4,600 biographies. In addition, newspaper and periodical indexes and membership lists of professional associations are also good sources for locating information about persons.

General

Indexes

> *Biography and Genealogy Master Index.* 2nd ed. Miranda C. Herbert and Barbara McNeil, eds. Detroit: Gale Research, c1980 [1981]. 8 vols. ISBN 0810310945. Annual supplements and 5-year cumulations. Print & digital. (D47)
>
> *Biography Index: A Cumulative Index to Biographical Material in Books and Magazines.* New York: Wilson, 1947– . Quarterly with annual and 3-year cumulations. ISSN 00063053. Print & digital. (D48)
>
> *World Biographical Index.* Munchen: Saur Electronic Publishing, 1997. (D49)

A quarter of a century after *A Dictionary of Universal Biography of All Ages and of All Peoples* (2nd ed. Albert Montefiore Hyamson. New York: Dutton, 1951, 679 p.) (D50) was published, the emergence of *Biography and Genealogy Master Index* is a welcome addition. It is compiled under the similar principle as Hyamson's *Dictionary*. The *Master Index*, formerly *Biographical Dictionaries Master Index*, gives name, date of birth and death if available, and source or sources with date of publication, but no nationality and profession as given in Hyamson. It is an index of international coverage to more than 3,000,000 biographical sketches from some 630 current and retrospective biographical directories.

The *Master Index* is supplemented by a five-year cumulation and annual supplements. Three five-year cumulations have been published: *Biography and Genealogy Master Index 1981–1985 Cumulation* (1985, 5 vols., ISBN 0810315068) (D51) indexes more than 2,250,000 biographical sketches in current and retrospective biographical dictionaries; *Biography and Genealogy Master Index 1986–1990 Cumulation* (1990, 3 vols., ISBN 0810348039) (D52) indexes more than 1,890,000 biographical sketches in 250 current and retrospective biographical dictionaries; and *Biography and Genealogy Master Index 1991–1995* (1995, 3 vols., ISBN 0810355167) (D53) indexes more than 2,270,000 biographical sketches in 320 current and retrospective biographical dictionaries. *Biography and Genealogy Master Index* is also available in microfiche as Bio-Base (D54), online as *Biography Master Index* (D55) marketed through Dialog (File 287), and on the Internet, GaleNet, noted earlier.

Biography Index indexes all types of biographical material including critical material of biographical significance, autobiography, letters, diaries, memoirs, journals, genealogies, fiction, drama, poetry, and pictorial works from over 2,700 periodicals indexed in the Wilson indexes, over 1,800 current books in the English language, obituaries from *The New York Times*, and other biographical materials. In the main or "name" alphabet are given full name, dates, nationality if other than American, and occupation or profession with notations on bibliographies, portraits, and other illustrations. There is a checklist of the composite books analyzed, with works of collective biography designated by a star and juvenile marked by a pyramid. *Biography Index* is characterized by its comprehensiveness and currency for whatever persons, living and dead, are mentioned in the sources. The index by profession and occupation is very useful. *Biography Index* is also available on CD-ROM (Wilsondisc), online (Wilsonline), tape, and on the Web.

World Biographical Index, an index to *World Bibliographical Archive,* noted later, is limited currently to five languages: English, French, German, Italian, and Spanish. It provides eleven fields for searching, and fields can be combined. The eleven fields are name, gender, period, birth year, death year, year cited, occupation, occupational classification, archive, source, and country. Wildcards and Boolean logical and relational operators can be used. It is on CD-ROM and the Web (http://www.saur.de). Its CD-ROM Manual provides clear explanation of how to use the index. It complements Gale's *Biography and Genealogy Master Index,* noted earlier.

Biographies

Biographies of social scientists can be found in both general biographies, such as *Who's Who in America* (New Providence, NJ: Marquis Who's Who, 1899– , annual, ISSN 00839396, print & digital) (D56) and *Current Biography* (New York: H. W. Wilson, 1940– , monthly, except December. ISSN 00113344) (D57). The following are representative titles of biographies:

> *Bowker Biographical Directory.* New Providence, NJ: R. R. Bowker. Biennial/triennial. Digital. (D58)
>
> *Marquis Who's Who.* New Providence, NJ: Marquis Who's Who. Annual. Digital. (D59)
>
> *World Bibliographical Archive,* 1982– . Munchen: Saur. Microfiche. (D60)

Bowker's Biographical Directory consists of three print counterparts: *American Men and Women of Science*, noted earlier, *Who's Who in American Art*, and *Who's Who in American Politics*, noted in the chapter on political science. The database is marketed through DIALOG (File 236).

Who's Who in America, noted earlier, is included in *Marquis Who's Who* marketed through Dialog (File 234). *Marquis Who's Who* contains over 750,000 biographical sketches from eighteen separate who's who publications, including *Who's Who in America*, *Who's Who in American Law*, *Who's Who in American Education*, and Who's *Who in Finance and Industry*. The database offers many features in searching. One search covers all who's who publications, and the database provides many access points. By using online searching, you can find out birthplace, how many biographees were born in a particular country, and how many female or male biographies are listed. Dialog File 234 consists of profiles of men and women in such fields as business, industry, finance, education, and law. It is also available on CD-ROM as *The Complete Marquis Who's Who on CD-ROM* (D61).

World Biographical Archive is a monumental work expected to be completed by 2000. According to the publisher, if completed, it will consist of the following separate biographical archives:

African Biographical Archive

American Biographical Archive

American Biographical Archive Series II

Australasian Biographical Archive

Arab-Islamic Biographical Archive

Baltic Biographical Archive

Biographical Archive of the Benelus Countries

Biographical Archive of the Classical World

British Biographical Archive

British Biographical Archive Series II

Chinese Biographical Archive

Czech and Slovakian Biographical Archive

French Biographical Archive

French Biographical Archive Series II

German Biographical Archive

German Biographical Archive Series II

Greek Biographical Archive

Hungarian Biographical Archive

Indian Biographical Archive

Italian Biographical Archive

Italian Biographical Archive Series II

Japanese Biographical Archive

Jewish Biographical Archive

Korean Biographical Archive

Polish Biographical Archive

Russian Biographical Archive

Scandinavian Biographical Archive

South-East Asian Biographical Archive

South-East European Biographical Archive

Spanish, Portuguese and Latin-American Biographical Archive

Spanish, Portuguese and Latin-American Biographical Archive Series II

Turkish Biographical Archive

Biographical data have been gathered for the world archive from many sources, including biographies, almanacs, handbooks, memoirs, and newspaper articles. The archive will be the most extensive coverage of biographies ever published. For instance, *American Biographical Archive* is a compilation of 367 original biographical reference works covering 280,000 individuals from the earliest period of American history through to the early twentieth century. *World Biographical Archive* is, however, limited to retrospective information. Each archive has its own index. Its master index is *World Biographical Index*, noted earlier.

Subfield

Volume 18 of the *International Encyclopedia of the Social Sciences*, noted before, is an excellent source for biographies in the social sciences. Other biographies in the social sciences include the following:

> *American Men and Women of Science: The Social and Behavioral Sciences.*
> 13th ed. New York: Bowker, 1978. 1,545 p. ISBN 0835210189.
> (D62)
> *Directory of American Scholars: A Biographical Directory*, 1942– . New
> York: Bowker. Irregular. ISSN 00705150. (D63)

American Men and Women of Science and *Directory of American Scholars* have a similar arrangement and similar criteria for inclusion. One of the requirements for inclusion is an earned doctorate. Each volume has a geographic index. *American Men and Women of Science* lists 24,000 names in twelve areas: administration and management, area studies, business, communications and information science, community and urban studies, economics, environmental studies, futurists, international studies, political science, psychology, and sociology. There are a discipline index to the twelve areas and a geographic index.

The eighth edition of *Directory of American Scholars* (1982, 4 vols., ISBN 0835214761) "profiles over 37,500 United States and Canadian scholars currently active in teaching, research and publishing; 3800 appear for the first time" (Preface). The four volumes are (1) History; (2) English, Speech and Drama; (3) Foreign Languages, Linguistics and Philology; and (4) Philosophy, Religion, and Law. The criteria for inclusion include a doctoral degree, publication of scholarly works, and a position of scholarly achievement. Each entry in general consists of primary discipline(s), vital statistics, education, honorary degrees, professional experience, membership, honors and awards, research interest, publications, and mailing address. It has a name index.

HANDBOOKS, YEARBOOKS, AND THE LIKE

A yearbook may be defined as a yearly publication that gives trends and current developments in a specific area of human knowledge. The best-known type of yearbook is the encyclopedia supplement. Frequently mentioned yearbooks in the social sciences are the following:

General

> *Europa World Year Book*, 1926– . London: Europa. Annual. ISSN 09562273. (D64)
>
> *Statesman's Yearbook: Statistical and Historical Annual of the State of the World*, 1864– . New York: St. Martin's Press. Annual. ISSN 00814601. (D65)
>
> *Worldmark Encyclopedia of the Nations.* 8th ed. Detroit: Gale Research, 1995. 5 vols. ISBN 0810398931. (D66)
>
> *World Quality of Life Indicators.* Timothy S. O'Donnell. Santa Barbara, CA: ABC-CLIO, 1991. 199 p. ISBN 0874766577. (D67)

In both *Europa* (formerly *Europa Year Book: A World Survey*) and *Statesman's Yearbook*, countries are arranged in one alphabetical list. *Europa* is a "political and economic guide to all the countries" (Foreword). The 39th edition (1998, 2 vols., ISBN 1857430417) consists of two parts: (1) 1,650 international organizations, including essays of more than 50 major international and regional organizations, and (2) countries arranged in alphabetical order, from Afghanistan to Zimbabwe. Each country has three sections, which are further divided into many subsections. For instance, the three sections and subsections for the United States are as follows: the first section, "Introductory Survey," includes location, climate, language, religion, flag, capital; recent history; government; defense; economic affairs; social welfare; education; public holidays, and weights and measures. The second section, "Statistical Survey," consists of area and population, agriculture, forestry, fishing, mining, industry, finance, external trade, transport, tourism, communications media, and education. The third section is a directory that presents the Constitution, the executive, legislature, independent agencies, state governments, political organizations, diplomatic representation (embassies in the United States), judicial system, religion, the press, publishers, broadcasting and communications, finance, trade and industry, transport, and tourism.

Statesman's Yearbook is both a statistical compendium and a concise description of the governments of the world, about their politics, industry, diplomacy, and economics. The 1998–1999 135th edition (Barry Turner ed., 1998, 1,815 p., ISBN 0312215886) consists of two parts: (1) international organizations and (2) countries of the world A–Z. For each country, information includes, with some variations, history, territory and population, constitution, government, economy, natural resources, industry and trade, communications, social institutions, diplomatic representations, and further reading. The book concludes with currency rates, weights and measures, conversion of units, abbreviations, maritime limits, and a place and international organization index. A companion volume is the *Statesman's Yearbook World Gazetteer*.

Europa and *Statesman's Yearbook* are the two best yearbooks providing concise information on countries throughout the world. They have much in common; yet each has its own approach and each provides some unique information not found in the other. For example, "Diplomatic Representation" in *Europa* and "Diplomatic Representatives" in *Statesman's Yearbook* contain different information. *Europa* has more descriptive and directory information than the *Statesman's Yearbook*, and the former's inclusion of a summary or the full text of each country's constitution is a good feature.

The Worldmark Encyclopedia deals with the United Nations and related agencies in Volume 1 and with countries by continent as Africa, Americas, Asia and Oceania, and Europe in the other four volumes. The first volume is appended with supplements, such as Polar Region, World Tables, Conversion Tables, Abbreviations and Acronyms, glossary of religious holidays, glossary of special terms, and general bibliography. There is a detailed index. Information on each country is presented under 50 headings, including location, size, and extent; topography; climate; flora and fauna; environment; population; migration; ethnic groups; languages; religions; transportation; history; government; political parties; and many others. Each volume has an index to countries.

World Quality of Life Indicators provides data taken from ABC-Clio's *Kaleidoscope: Current World Data* (no longer published) for 171 countries and territories. Data are arranged in uniform format for each country and territory under twelve topics: location, area, population, vital statistics, health care, ethnic composition, religion, language, education, economic data, travel notes, and government. Most of the information contained herein can be found in other reference sources, such as *Encyclopaedia Britannica*'s "World Data" and *Worldmark Encyclopedia*, both noted earlier. However, the availability of other reference sources does not detract from the value of this book. It is concise for quick reference, and its line-by-line listing of data is convenient for use.

Subfield

The Peoplepedia: The Ultimate Reference on the American People. Les Krantz and Jim McCormick. New York: Henry Holt, 1996. 474 p. ISBN 0805037276. (D68)

Peoplepedia consists of three parts covering three categories of American people: the American Mindset, the American Collective, and American Individuals. The first part, "The American Mindset," deals with how Americans feel about issues. Some 70 issues are presented in alphabetical order from advice, allies, anxieties, baby boomers and retirement, baseball, black children, busing, and celebrities to gift preferences, marijuana, and narcissism in the family to women and work. There are photos and statistical information. These issues may be grouped into seven categories, as the authors state: "(a) assessment of societal changes, (b) confidence in various institutions, (c) familial relationships, (d) perceptions of public figures, (e) personal preference issues, (f) satisfaction levels, and (g) trust." Data are drawn from a number of polls, including the *Peoplepedia* Opinion Poll.

The second part, "The American Collective," consists of eleven chapters dealing with education, facts of life, families, the generations, health and body, pastimes, populations, possessions, religion, sexuality and gender, and the workplace. Each chapter provides an overview and topics relating to the chapter theme with rich statistical data and some photos. Data are drawn from many government sources.

Over half of the book is devoted to the third part, "The American Individuals: Notable Americans," a who's who of the *Peoplepedia*. Some 1,350 individual profiles are included. Each profile is given an address, and if complete, year of birth, achievements, and education, and a biographical sketch. Some of the biographees have photos. This part is appended with "Notable Americans by Profession." All biographees are classified into some 21 professions. Each profession lists names of the biographees with criteria for inclusion—a good feature.

The book answers many interesting questions about American people.

The publisher lists a number of questions that are certainly of interest to many people. They are, for example, "Who are the most respected professionals in their field, and how can you contact them?"; "How many people live in mobile homes, nursing homes, and jails?"; and "What is the demographic makeup of our newest immigrants?"

AREA STUDIES

General

> *African Studies WWW Virtual Library.* New York: Vibe. http://www.vibe.com/history/africanstudies/africanwww.html (D69)
> *Asian Studies WWW Virtual Library.* Canberra, Australia: Australian National University, Coombs Computing Unit. http://coombs.anu.edu.au/wwwvl-asianstudies.html (D70)
> *Latin American Studies WWW Virtual Library.* Austin, TX: University of Texas. http://www.lanic.utexas.edu/las.html (D71)
> *Middle East Network Information Center.* Austin, TX: University of Texas. http://menic.utexas.edu/mes.html (D72)

The preceding are four Web sites for area studies. African Studies contains a number of categories: Resources Located on the Continent of Africa, Links to Historically Black Colleges and Universities, Links to African Related Organizations, Other Related Sites, Major List of Other Resources, and the Schomburg Center of the New York Public Library. Its Web site (http://www.nypl.org/research/sc/sc.htm) (D73) provides collections, digital sources such as *African American Women Writers of the 19th Century*, online exhibitions, selected Internet sources, and the Schomburg program. Its Kaiser Index is noted in Chapter 17.

Asian Studies WWW Virtual Library (AS WWW VL) contains three categories of sources: Asia-Pacific Global Resources; Regional Resources, and Individual Countries/Territories Resources. Resources in the Global Resources are further grouped into nine areas, such as Asian Studies WWW Monitor, Annotated Guide to WWW Search Engines, Chinese and Japanese Art History, Study Abroad Asia, and so on. Regional Resources are of eight kinds: Middle East, Caucasus, Central Asia, South Asia, South East Asia, Pacific Ocean, East Asia, and Asian Continent as a whole. There are 63 countries and territories included in Individual Countries/Territories Resources. For each country, there is a link to sources. For instance, the button for China links to the China WWW Virtual Library: Internet Guide for China Studies at the Institute of Chinese Studies, Heidelberg University, whereas Japan is linked to the Stanford Guide to Japan Information Resources.

The other two Web sites are maintained at the University of Texas at

Austin. *Latin American Studies* groups resources by country and subject. Twenty-eight countries and the Caribbean are included. By subject, the site lists more than 40 topics for choosing, from African Diaspora, Agriculture, Anthropology, Business, to Statistics, Trade, and Women. For each country, it lists sources grouped into Academic Research Resources, Discussion Groups, Economy and Finance, General, Government, Internet and Connectivity, Magazines, Newspapers, Science and Technology, and Travel and Tourism. Links are provided. For Middle Eastern Studies, the site *Middle East Network Information Center* contains Subject Categories, including Ancient History/Archaeology, Business/Finance/Economics, Government/Country Profiles, Maps/Travel and Regional Information, News Media/Newsgroups, Religion, and Oil Energy, and Natural Resources. In the category of Additional Research Resources, it lists sources grouped into Conferences, Internet/Networking, K-12 Educational Resources, Libraries/Electronic Publishing, Middle East Academic Programs, Centers and Institutes, Organizations/Associations, Reference, and Search the Internet. Twenty-three countries in the Middle East are included, with links provided for many resources.

Encyclopedias

> *The Cambridge Encyclopedia of Africa.* Roland Oliver and Michael Crowder, eds. Cambridge: Cambridge University Press, 1981. 492 p. ISBN 0821230969. (D74)
>
> *The Cambridge Encyclopedia of Latin America and the Caribbean.* Simon Collier, Harold Blakemore, and Thomas E. Skidmore, eds. Cambridge: Cambridge University Press, 1985. 456 p. ISBN 0521262631. (D75)
>
> *The Cambridge Encyclopedia of the Middle East and North Africa.* Trevor Mostyn, ed. Cambridge: Cambridge University Press, 1988. 504 p. (D76)
>
> *Encyclopedia of the Modern Middle East.* Reeva S. Simon, Philip Mattar, and Richard W. Bulliet, eds. New York: Macmillan Reference, 1996. 4 vols. ISBN 0028960114. (D77)

The three Cambridge encyclopedias have a similar format and arrangement by broad subject. Maps and illustrations are substantial. The encyclopedia on Africa contains more than 180 articles contributed by nearly 100 authors grouped into the African Continent, the African Past, Contemporary Africa, and Africa and the World. The encyclopedia of Middle East and North Africa contains some 110 articles contributed by over 80 authors grouped into six parts: Lands and Peoples, History, Societies and Economics, Cultural, The Countries, and Inter-State Relations. The third encyclopedia on Latin America and the Caribbean contains 82 articles by 68 authors arranged by topic, such as the physical environment, the economy, the peoples, history, and culture. Although people are noted elsewhere in the encyclopedias, there is no listing of biographies.

Encyclopedia of the Modern Middle East is a compendium of knowledge about the Middle East since 1800. It "encompasses the interaction of political, historical, social, economic, and cultural movements as well as relevant persons (both living and dead), places, and events" (Preface). Nearly 4,000 entries of terms, concepts, parties, organizations, agencies, and persons cover fields in politics, economics, religion, history, literature, the arts and others. A substantial number of entries are biographies, including profiles of many Americans, including Dean Acheson, John Foster Dulles, John Jernegan, and Franklin Delano Roosevelt. Maps and photos are many, and most entries provide a bibliography. It is appended with Genealogies and Lines of Succession, Biographical Entries by Category, and Index.

Dictionaries

Scarecrow Press has published a number of dictionaries series on area studies, which include the following:

> *African Historical Dictionary Series*, no. 1– . Lanham, MD: Scarecrow Press, 1974– . Irregular. (D78)
>
> *Asian Historical Dictionaries Series*, no. 1– . Lanham, MD: Scarecrow Press, 1972– . Irregular. (D79)
>
> *Latin American Historical Dictionaries*, no. 1– . Lanham, MD: Scarecrow Press, 1967– . Irregular. (D80)
>
> Oceania Historical Dictionaries Series, no. 1– . Lanham, MD: Scarecrow Press, 1992–   . Irregular. (D81)

This area of dictionaries series covers prominent personalities, occurrences, places, and organizations of a particular country or region. All dictionaries series have a similar format and arrangement. In general each dictionary consists of two parts: dictionary and bibliography. The *African Historical Dictionary Series* has published more than 60 titles, including *Historical Dictionary of Gabon* (2nd ed., David E. Gardinier, 1994, 466 p., ISBN 0810827689, series no. 58) (D82). One recent title in the *Asian Historical Dictionaries Series* is *Historical Dictionary of Taiwan* (John F. Copper, 1993, 178 p., ISBN 0810826089, series no. 12) (D83). Over 20 dictionaries have appeared in the *Latin American Historical Dictionaries Series*. One of its recent publications is *Historical Dictionary of Honduras* (2nd ed. Harvey K. Meyer and Jessie H. Meyer, 1994, 708 p., ISBN 0810828456, series no. 25) (D84). *Oceania Historical Dictionaries Series* is the newest series. One of its titles is *Historical Dictionary of Papua New Guinea* (Ann Turner, 1994, 334 p., ISBN 081082874X, series no. 4) (D85).

Handbooks, Yearbooks, and the Like

General

> *Area Handbook Series,* 1961– . U.S. Library of Congress, Federal Research
>   Division. Washington, DC: GPO. Print & digital. (D86)
> *Background Notes on the Countries of the World.* Washington, DC: U.S.
>   Dept. of State, Bureau of Public Affairs, Office of Public Communi-
>   cation. Irregular. ISSN 05019966. Print & digital. (D87)
> *Government on the WWW.* http://www.gksoft.com/govt (D88)
> *World Factbook.* U.S. Central Intelligence Agency. Springfield, VA: National
>   Technical Information Service. Annual. ISSN 02771527. Print & dig-
>   ital. (D89)

The *Area Handbook Series,* formerly the work of Foreign Area Studies
at American University, is now prepared by the Library of Congress under
the Country Studies/Area Handbook Program sponsored by the Department of the Army. Each handbook, with exceptions, is devoted to a particular country, "describing and analyzing its political, economic, social,
and national security systems and institutions, and examining the interre-
lationships of those systems and the ways they are shaped by cultural factors" (Foreword).

Each country studies/area handbook in the series begins with a country
profile, a summary of the geography, population, languages, religion, economy, government, and other aspects, followed by detailed coverage in a
number of chapters. The number of chapters in the handbooks varies. In
general, all handbooks include chapters on historical setting, the society,
the economy, government and politics, and national security. The appendix
consists of a bibliography of books and periodical articles corresponding
to each chapter, and a glossary. In most handbooks, statistical tables are
also provided. Country Studies/Area Handbook Series is also available
on the Library of Congress Web site (http://lcweb2.loc.gov/frd/cs/
cshome.html). The online version consists of 85 countries.

Background Notes and *World Factbook* are also government
publications. *Background Notes* is a series of pamphlets on selected countries and on international organizations. *Background Notes* is also available
on the Internet (http://www.state.gov/www/background_notes). It is organized by Geographic Regions and International Organizations. Geographical
Regions contain Africa, Middle East and North Africa, East Asia and the
Pacific, South Asia, Europe and Canada, and Latin America and the Caribbean. Countries are arranged in alphabetical order in each area. For each
country, information contains geography, history, government, political
conditions, economy, foreign relations, U.S. relations with the country,
principal U.S. officials, and, in addition, general travel and busi-

ness information. The category of International Organizations lists the Association of Southeast Asian Nations, the European Community, the Organization of American States, and the United Nations.

World Factbook, formerly *National Basic Intelligence Factbook,* is compiled from information supplied by a number of agencies, including the American Geophysical Union, Bureau of the Census, Central Intelligence Agency, Defense Intelligence Agency, Defense Mapping Agency, Department of State, National Science Foundation, and many others. It contains maps and more detailed information as compared with *Background Notes.* *World Factbook* is available online via Lexis-Nexis and on CD-ROM and the Internet (http://www.odci.gov/cia/publications/factbook).

Simple listings of parliaments, ministries, offices, law courts, embassies, city councils, public broadcasting corporations, central banks, multinational organizations, and political parties are included in *Governments on the WWW.* The database is organized by areas and categories. There are six areas: worldwide governments, European governments, African governments, American governments, Asian governments, and Oceania governments. By categories, there are multinational organizations, heads of state, parliaments, law courts, representation in foreign countries, political parties, broadcasting, currency, elections, intellectual property, and statistics. The Table of Contents lists name of country or territory, number of entries, file size, and date of last change. The database contains over 9,000 entries from 205 countries and territories. It also provides links to many countries and territories.

Subfield

> *Africa Contemporary Record,* 1968/69– . Colin Legum, ed. New York: Holmes and Meier. Annual. ISSN 00653845. (D90)
> *Africa South of the Sahara,* 1971– . London: Europa. Annual. ISSN 00653896. (D91)
> *The Far East and Australasia,* 1969– . London: Europa. Annual. ISSN 00713791. (D92)
> *Latin American and Caribbean Contemporary Record,* v. 1– , 1981/82– . New York: Holmes and Meier. Annual. ISSN 07361700. (D93)
> *South America, Central America, and the Caribbean,* 1988– . London: Europa, 1987– . Biennial. ISSN 02680661. (D94)
> *The Middle East and North Africa,* 1948– . London: Europa. Annual. ISSN 00768502. (D95)

Listed here are two contemporary records and four surveys. *Africa Contemporary Record* consists of three parts: (1) current issues, (2) country-by-country review, and (3) documents. The third part is further divided into international relations, constitutional developments, political affairs, regional affairs, social issues, economic issues, and table of statistics.

Latin American and Caribbean Contemporary Record records events, issues, documents, and data. The 1986/87 edition (1989, pagination varies, ISBN 0841911703), with 26 contributing authors, consists of four parts: (1) current issues and essays; (2) country-by-country review, containing 30 articles on countries and areas grouped into South America, Central America, and Mexico, and the Caribbean; (3) documents (about 23); and (4) economic, social, and political data, with over 120 tables. There is a name index and a subfield index.

The four surveys provide invaluable reference sources for geography, history, economy, statistical data, and other information about the areas. All are compiled in a similar format and arrangement. Each of the yearbooks consists of three parts. Part 1 is the general survey, a background introduction. Part 2 deals with regional organizations. Part 3, the country surveys, provides detailed information about individual countries that in general includes physical and social geography, recent history, economy, statistical survey, directory, and bibliography. The directory lists government agencies and key personnel. In fact, all yearbooks are the expanded versions of *Europa* noted earlier. The statistical survey and directory in *Europa* are retained with expansion of the introductory survey and the addition of a bibliography.

NOTES

1. "Foreword," *International Encyclopedia of the Social Sciences*, vol. 1 (New York: Macmillan and Free Press, 1968–   ), p. xvi.

2. "Introduction," *International Encyclopedia of the Social Sciences*, vol. 1 (New York: Macmillan and Free Press, 1968–   ), p. xiii.

3. David L. Sills, "Editing a Scientific Encyclopedia," *Science* 163 (1969): 1173.

4. Barratt Wilkins, "Sub-field Dictionaries," *RQ* 9, no. 3 (1970): 234–36.

Chapter 5

Statistical Sources

Most statistical sources are produced by government agencies. The U.S. government is, in fact, the most important principal source for statistical information on practically all aspects of life. The statistical system of the U.S. government is decentralized, with the Office of Information and Regulatory Affairs, Office of Management and Budget (OMB), as a coordinating agency.

THE STATISTICAL SYSTEM

The U.S. statistical system may be divided into four categories: (1) a central coordinating agency, (2) general-purpose statistical collection agencies, (3) analytical and research agencies, and (4) administrative and regulatory agencies.

The central coordinating agency is the Office of Information and Regulatory Affairs, Office of Management and Budget (OMB) (http://www.whitehouse.gov/WH/EOP.OMB/html/OMBhome.html) (E1), charged with the responsibility to prevent duplication, achieve balance, and develop procedures for an integrated system of governmental statistics. Its general operations are fourfold: (1) statistical planning and cooperation, (2) review of agency questionnaires and forms, (3) statistical standards and definitions, and (4) international statistical programs.

General-purpose statistical collection agencies have as their primary functions collection, compilation, analysis, and publication of statistics in specified fields for general use. They constitute a large proportion of the federal government's statistical activities and are the most important producers of statistical information. But the production of general-purpose statistical information is not limited to these agencies. Agencies in other categories also publish statistical information for general use. There are five major agencies in this category, of which the Bureau of the Census and the Bureau of Labor Statistics are the most productive publishers.

The Bureau of the Census (http://www.census.gov) (E2), Department of Commerce, is the largest general-purpose statistical collection agency. It conducts the censuses and sample surveys and collects and publishes statistics on industry, trade, construction, commodity, manufacturers, and so on; and it provides statistical services to other agencies. For publications of the Bureau of the Census, refer to *Census Catalog and Guide*, 1946– (U.S. Bureau of the Census, Washington DC: GPO. Annual. ISSN 0007618X) (E3). The *Guide*, formerly *Census Catalog*, introduces the Bureau's services—an overview of its products, guides, methodologies, and statistical anthologies—and lists all the bureau's publications with an indication of their forms, such as printed reports, microfiche, computer tapes, online access, diskettes, and maps. The *Guide* is supplemented by *Monthly Product Announcement*, 1981– (U.S. Bureau of the Census, Washington, DC: GPO) (E4). It is also available on the Web. The Bureau's online database, CENDATA, marketed through Dialog (File 578, 579, 580) and DataStar (File CENDATA), is no longer published. Instead, it has been expanded into *CenStats*, accessible on the Web, noted later.

The Bureau's Web site displays eleven function buttons: (1) News, (2) Access Tools, (3) Subjects A to Z, (4) Search, (5) Censtats—Censtore, noted later, (6) Just for Fun, (7) About the Census Bureau, (8) User Manual, (9) New on the Site, (10) Population Clock, and (11) Economic Clock. The Search button provides word search, place search, map search, staff search, and other search engines. Search for Subjects A to Z uses words or phrases, separated by commas. Some documents are in Portable Document Format (PDF). Access Tools provides Datamap, 1990 Census Lookup, Tiger Map Server, Census CD-ROMs at the University of California, and the Data Extraction System. For a listing of publications, select the About the Census Bureau button. It displays, for instance, customer service information, contacts, employment opportunities, executive staff roster, fellowship opportunities, publications, statistical activities, and surveys. Publications are organized by subject, from Agriculture, Business, Foreign Trade, Government, International to Population and Transportation.

The Bureau of Labor Statistics (http://www.bls.gov) (E5), Department of Labor, is the principal general-purpose statistical collection agency in labor economics and industrial relations. It provides statistical sources on a variety of subjects, including the labor force, employment and unemployment, industrial and occupational employment, hours and earnings in nonagricultural industries, wages and industrial relations, occupational safety and health, and productivity.

The home page displays ten categories for choosing: Data; Economy at a Glance; Keyword Search of BLS Web Pages; Surveys & Programs; Publications & Research Papers; Regional Information; Mission, Management and Jobs; Other Statistical Sites; What's New; and Contact Information. The user may use the Data button to obtain time series data, series report, FTP, and most news releases. Economy at a Glance is a table of current data on the various economic indicators. Surveys and Programs is organized by statistical categories into Employment and Unemployment, Prices and Living Conditions, Compensation and Working Conditions, Productivity and Technology, Employment Projections, International Programs, and Other Surveys. Publications and Research Papers includes *Monthly Labor Review Online* (hard copy since 1915, ISSN 0027044X) (E6), *Compensation and Working Conditions Online* (hard copy, monthly, ISSN 00981818) (E7), and *Occupational Outlook Handbook*, noted in Chapter 10. A listing of statistical sites on the World Wide Web is provided in Other Statistical Sites. The list is divided into Principal U.S. Federal Statistical Agencies and International Statistical Agencies. The former contains 11 Web sites, including Bureau of Economic Analysis, Bureau of Transportation Statistics, Census Bureau, Economic Research Service, National Center for Education Statistics, and Statistics of Income. The latter includes nearly 60 Web sites of foreign countries and territories and eight Web sites of international agencies.

The National Agricultural Statistics Service (NASS) (http://www2 .hqnet.usda.gov/nass) (E8), Department of Agriculture, is charged with statistical programs of general interest and coordination of all statistical work in the department. It provides statistical sources of information on such subjects as crop acreage, crop and livestock production, inventories and forecasts, price farmers pay and receive, parity index, farm employment, and wage rates.

The NASS home page is organized into two categories: Statistical Information and Agency Information. Statistical Information includes Publications, Graphics, Historic Data, Search State Information, Statistical Research, and Census of Agriculture. Agency information includes Agency Information, Customer Service, Coming Events, Other Links, and NASS Kids. Graphics provides graphics on crops, economics, livestock, and research. In Historic Data, items include Crops Data, Livestock Data, Rankings, Agricultural Statistics on CD-ROM, Statistical Highlights of U.S. Agriculture, and Statistical Bulletin. The census of agriculture taken every five years provides comprehensive agriculture data for every county in the nation.

The National Center for Health Statistics (NCHS) (http://www.cdc.gov/nchswww/default.htm) (E9), Department of Health and Human Resources, is a principal source of national statistics on births, deaths, marriages, divorces, life tables, health status, and needs of the population. From its Web home page, the user may select *FASTATS*, Products, Data Warehouse, News Releases and Fact Sheets, and NCHS Web Search. NCHS activities include thirteen categories, such as aging, AIDS, data on America's children, healthy people 2000, minority health, national death index, and public health conferences on records and statistics. *FASTATS* is an index to subjects (including individual state) from A to Z and provides statistical data. For each subject are given various data, comprehensive data, and some related links. The Center's Web site also links to *FEDSTATS*, noted later, and other sites.

The National Center for Education Statistics (NCES) (http://nces.ed.gov) (E10), Department of Education, collects, reports, and provides statistics on elementary, secondary, higher, and adult education, relating to enrollments, graduates and degrees granted, personnel, school facilities and finance, and on libraries. Its home page displays buttons for choosing, such as News, Publications, Data, and Surveys. The Publications button displays reports released in the last 90 days; data products released in the last six months; publications by subject; the *Digest, The Condition*, and other compendia; publications by survey and program area; issue briefs, data products, and technical reports. *The Condition* and the *Digest* will be noted in Chapter 11.

Publications of these five agencies are either completely or substantially covered by the *American Statistics Index*, noted later.

Analytical and research agencies use statistics collected by other agencies for interpretative purposes, including preparation of composite measures. The principal analytical and research agencies are the Council of Economic Advisors, the Bureau of Economic Analysis of the Department of Commerce, the Economic Research Service of the Department of Agriculture, the Board of Governors of the Federal Reserve System, the Board of Mines of the Department of the Interior, the Mining Enforcement and Safety Administration of the Department of the Interior, the Domestic and International Business Administration of the Department of Commerce, the Consumers and Food Economics Institute of the Department of Agriculture, and the Manpower Administration of the Department of Labor.

Administrative and regulatory agencies collect statistics primarily as a by-product of their administrative and cooperating responsibilities. The Social Security Administration and the Social and Rehabilitation Service belong to the administrative agencies. The regulatory agencies include the Interstate Commerce Commission, the Federal Power Commission, the Federal Communications Commission, the Civil Aeronautics Board, and the Federal Reserve Board.

ACCESS TO SOURCES

Bibliographies

United States

Federal statistical sources may be found in such bibliographies as *Monthly Catalog*, the catalogs of the Bureau of the Census and the Bureau of Labor Statistics noted earlier, Appendix I of the *Statistical Abstracts of the United States*, noted later, and the Congressional Information Service's indexes, noted next.

International

For international and foreign statistical sources, readers are advised to consult works mentioned in indexes and abstracts and the sources of information in this chapter. A useful bibliography of foreign statistical sources is:

> *Sourcebook of Global Statistics*. George Thomas Kurian. New York: Facts on File, 1985. 413 p. ISBN 087196063X. (E11)

This is a listing of 207 books and serials issued by official and private international and national organizations. Each entry has four sections: (1) basic bibliographic data—title, year of publication, language, number of pages, edition, indexes, base period, updating, scope, sources of data, and organization; (2) contents; (3) new features, graphs, tables, and charts; (4) evaluation, publisher, most recent price, availability on tape, and availability on database.

Indexes and Abstracts

> *American Statistics Index*, 1973– . Washington, DC: Congressional Information Service. Base edition, monthly, and annual supplement. ISSN 00911658. Print & digital. (E12)
>
> *Statistical Reference Index: A Selected Guide to American Statistical Publications from Sources Other Than the U.S. Government*, 1980– . Washington, DC: Congressional Information Service. Monthly with quarterly and annual cumulations. ISSN 0278604X. Print & digital. (E13)
>
> *Index to International Statistics: A Guide to Statistical Publications of International Intergovernmental Organizations*, 1983– . Washington, DC: Congressional Information Service. Monthly, with quarterly and annual cumulations. Print & digital. (E14)

Statistical Universe. Washington, DC: Congressional Information Service. http://www.lexis-nexis/universe. (E15)

Statistics Sources, 1960– . Jacqueline Wasserman O'Brien and Steven R. Wasserman, eds. Detroit: Gale Research. Annual. ISSN 0585198X. (E16)

American Statistics Index (ASI) is a comprehensive guide to all federally produced statistical data, whether published in serial or monograph form. It consists of a base edition and the monthly and annual supplements. The *ASI* 1974 base edition covers the entire range of federal statistical publications, including business, economics, and natural resources. But scientific and experimental observations, technical studies, and data stemming from specific scientific and technical research and development projects are generally excluded. Also excluded are classified or confidential data. Every year, it indexes and abstracts more than 7,500 titles, including over 800 periodicals.

ASI is published in two volumes: index and abstracts. The index volume has (1) an index by subject and names, being an index to subject, to corporate authors, and to individual authors; (2) an index by three categories: geographic, economic, and demographic, and further divided by state, industry, age, or some other standard category; (3) an index by titles; (4) an index by agency report numbers; (5) an index of SuDoc numbers; and (6) a guide to selected standard industrial classifications. The abstracts volume provides summaries of entries and full bibliographical information of entries, arranged by accession numbers and agencies. The first *ASI* cumulative index, for 1980–1984, was published in 1985. Since *ASI* does not cover congressional publications containing data of limited statistical interest, the publisher's other work, *CIS/Index to Publications of the U.S. Congress,* noted in Chapter 7, should be consulted. The *ASI* database is also available online as part of *Statistics Universe,* noted later.

Statistical Reference Index (SRI) is a selective listing of abstracts of statistical information issued by associations and institutes, corporations and commercial organizations, university and independent research centers, and state government agencies, with stress on production, costs, earnings in key industries and commercial and business sectors, business and finance, and economics. Arrangement is patterned after *ASI. SRI* is available on the Web as part of *Statistics Universe,* noted later.

Index to International Statistics (IIS) and *Statistics Sources (SS)* provide extensive international coverage of statistical sources. It may be noted that although not as extensive as these three bibliographies, *PAIS,* noted in Chapter 4, is also a good source for current foreign publications. *IIS* is a welcome addition to the index family of the Congressional Information Service, indexing approximately 1,500 publications issued by some 90 organizations, including the United Nations, specialized agencies, the Organization for Economic Corporation and Development, the European Community, the Organization of American States, and other intergovernmental regional and special purpose organizations. Coverage is limited to publications in English. Other language publications are included if no English version exists. Arrangement is similar to that of *ASI*. *IIS* is also available on the Web as part of *Statistics Universe*, noted later.

The CIS also maintains microfiche and CD-ROM library collections on sources indexed in its indexes as *Statistical Masterfile: ASI, SRI & IIS* (E17). The *Masterfile* enables the user to search three CIS indexes at once.

In 1998, Congressional Information Service developed the Universe Library, a Web-based database consisting of *Statistical Universe, Congressional Universe, State Universe, History Universe*, and Lexis-Nexis Academic Universe. *Congressional Universe* will be noted in Chapter 7. *Statistical Universe* contains the three indexes mentioned earlier—*ASI, SRI*, and *IIS*—and provides full-text documents. According to the publisher, over 60 percent of documents covered by *Statistical Universe* are currently available on government Web sites.

As compared with its print counterparts, *Statistical Universe* has four features: (1) It is updated monthly, rather than quarterly; (2) it provides the user an option of advanced searches, if search is conducted in Lexis-Nexis; (3) the search result has a more precise answer set than *Statistical Master File*; and (4) it provides a link back to the main abstract and links to many government Web sites. For links to government Web sites, there is "List of Links" on the home page. Data can be searched by subject, title, agency, comparative data, SuDoc number, Monthly Catalog number, and Library of Congress number; and search can be confined to *The Statistical Abstract of the United States*, noted later.

Statistics Sources is "a subject guide to data on industrial, business, social, educational, financial, and other topics for the United States and internationally" (subtitle). The 22nd, 1999 edition (Jacqueline Wassermand O'Brien and Steven R. Wasserman, eds., 1998, 2 vols., ISBN 0787624594) contains more than 2,000 sources over 20,000 specific subjects with nearly 100,000 citations. Sources are arranged alphabetically by subject; for each subject are indicated the publication or publications in which statistics on that subject can be found. The book is preceded by three sources from which data are incorporated into the main body: "Selected Bibliography of Key Statistical Sources," "Federal Statistical Telephone Contacts," and "Federal Statistical Data Bases." It features the listing of some organizations, government agencies, or trade and professional groups considered to be important sources even if they do not ordinarily publish statistics. There are two appendixes: A, Source Publications and B, Sources of Nonpublished Statistical Data.

SOURCES OF INFORMATION

Encyclopedias

International Encyclopedia of Statistics. William H. Kruskal and Judith M.
Tanur, eds. New York: Free Press. 1978. 2 vols. ISBN 0029179602.
(E18)

The encyclopedia is an assemblage of statistics articles in the *International Encyclopedia of the Social Sciences* with addition of new articles. As its introduction states, "the present work reproduces and amends the IESS statistics articles, the statistical biographies, and many of the social science articles with statistical import [and] to these have been added five new articles and 12 new biographies." There is a detailed name, title, and subject index.

Dictionaries

A Dictionary of Statistical Terms. 4th ed. Maurice G. Kendall and William
R. Buckland. London: Longman, 1982. 213 p. ISBN 0582470080.
(E19)
Statistical Tables for the Social, Biological and Physical Sciences. F. C. Powell,
comp. London: Cambridge University Press, 1982. ISBN
0521241413. (E20)

These two works provide concise definitions of statistical terms. The *Dictionary* contains nearly 3,000 terms, including statistical models. In Powell's work, an explanation of statistical terms and procedure precedes tables. Tables are based on journals and books. It concludes with a guide to texts.

Directories

The Web sites of government agencies such as the Bureau of the Census and the Bureau of Labor Statistics and a number of statistical databases including *Fedstats*, noted later, are good sources for locating statistics databases and other directory information.

STATISTICAL SOURCES

Statistical sources may be found in many familiar reference works, such as *Statesman's Yearbook, Europa World Year Book*, and *World Almanac and Book of Facts*, 1868– (New York: World Almanac, annual, ISSN 00841382) (E21). Titles contained in this chapter are limited to those that are devoted primarily to statistics. *Statistical Universe*, just noted, is also a source for finding statistical sources.

General

> Geospatial and Statistical (GeoStat) Data Center. Charlottesville, VA: University of Virginia, Fisher Library. http://www.lib.virginia.edu/socsci (E22)

Geospatial and Statistical (Geostat) Data Center was created in 1998 as a result of merging the Social Sciences Data Center and the Geographic Information Center. The Social Sciences Data Center contains Data Collections, Hypertext Documents, Social Sciences Links, and so on. Hypertext Documents is a collection of reference materials for the quantitative social sciences researcher. The Social Sciences Links category links databases throughout cyberspace. It links to Government Information Resources, the Center for Survey Research, and Resources at Other Colleges and Universities, including Princeton University Data Library, University of Michigan's Population Studies Center, and University of California at San Diego's Social Sciences Data Collection.

United States

General

> *Statistical Abstract of the United States*, 1878– . U.S. Bureau of the Census. Washington, DC: GPO, 1879– . Annual. Print & digital. (E23)
>
> *Historical Statistics of the United States, Colonial Times to 1970*. U.S. Bureau of the Census. Bicentennial ed. Washington, DC: GPO, 1975. 2 vols. Print & digital. (E24)
>
> *County and City Data Book*, 1949– . U.S. Bureau of the Census. Washington, DC: GPO, 1952– . Irregular. (E25)
>
> *County and City Extra: Annual Metro, City and County Data Book*. Deirdre A. Gaquin and Mark S. Littman, eds. Lanham, MD: Bernan Press, 1998. 1,033 p.+. ISBN 0890590931. (E26)
>
> *State and Metropolitan Area Data Book*, v. 1– , 1979– . U.S. Bureau of the Census. Washington, DC: GPO, 1980– . Irregular. (E27)
>
> *Places, Towns and Townships*. 2nd ed. Deirdre A. Gaquin and Richard W. Dodge, eds. Lanham, MD: Bernan Press, 1998. 924 p. ISBN 0890590729. (E28)
>
> *CenStats*. http://www.census.gov (E29)
>
> *Fedstats*. http://www.fedstats.gov (E30)
>
> *STAT-USA*. http://www.stat-usa.gov (E31)
>
> White House Briefing Room. http://www.whitehouse.gov/WH/html/briefroom.html (E32)

The *Statistical Abstract* is the most useful summary of statistics on social, political, and economic organizations of the United States. Data are selected from both government and private publications and some unpublished materials. Its coverage is international, though emphasis is placed on national data of the United States. The 1997 edition begins with a map showing U.S. census divisions and regions, weights and measures, a guide to tabular presentation, selected state rankings, and telephone contacts. The main statistics tables and graphic charts are grouped into 31 sections by subject, such as population; vital statistics; health and nutrition; education; law enforcement, courts, and prisons; geography and environment; parks, recreation, and travel; elections; state and local government finances and employment; federal government finance and employment; and national defense and veterans affairs. It contains over 1,400 tables from 250 federal, private, and international sources. The volume also features *USA Statistics in Brief* (1997, 12 p., ISBN 0160427347), the pocket-size booklet insert in front of the book, 1986 population estimates for metropolitan areas, and new data on national and state population projections, the elderly, employment projections by industry and occupation, election results by congressional districts, participation in sports activities, and income data for the 50 largest cities.

Statistical Abstract also serves as a guide to other statistical publications and sources through the use of its introductory text to each section and the source notes appearing below each table and graphic chart. There are five appendixes: (1) Guide to Sources of Statistics, Guide to State Statistical Abstracts, and Guide to Foreign Statistical Abstracts—useful bibliographies of primary and secondary sources arranged by subject, states, and countries respectively. The guide to foreign statistical abstracts is limited to only 26 countries. (2) Metropolitan Area Concepts and Components and Population of Metropolitan Statistical Areas. (3) Statistical Methodology and Reliability, describing methods of collecting data, a measure of their validity, and reference to further readings. (4) Index to Tables Having *Historical Statistics, Colonial Times to 1970* Series. (5) Index to Tables Having *State and Metropolitan Area Data Book* Series.

Statistical Abstract is also available on CD-ROM and the Internet. Its online version can be accessed via a number of Web sites, such as the Web sites of the Census Bureau, *Statistical Universe*, all noted earlier, *Fedstats*, noted later, and the Web directly (http://www.census.gov/stat_abstract/).

Statistical Abstract is supplemented by *Historical Statistics, State and Metropolitan Area Data Book*, and *City and County Data Book*. *Historical Statistics* is the third in the Historical Statistics Series. It supersedes the previous two editions: *Historical Statistics of the United States, 1789–1945*, published in 1949, and *Historical Statistics of the United States, Colonial Times to 1957*, issued in 1960. *Historical Statistics* is an indispensable, convenient statistical reference to sources dating back to 1610, arranged in

24 chapters of major subjects with a detailed alphabetical subject index. More than 12,500 statistical time series constitute the present edition. The specific source notes, description of statistical tables, and definitions of terms contained therein serve also as a guide to original published sources. *Historical Statistics* on CD-ROM is marketed through Cambridge University Press.

The two data books present information by areas and are considered small-area supplements to *Statistical Abstract. State and Metropolitan Area Data Book* (1997–98, 5th ed., 1998, pagination varies) is a collection of data from statistical publications and electronic sources, both government and private. It provides the most current data on the nation's metropolitan (metro) areas and states. There are three categories of tables: (1) Tables for 50 States and the District of Columbia: 56 tables of 869 data items. (2) Ten tables of 159 data items for all metro areas and three tables of 43 data items for metro counties. (3) One table for central cities. The 56 tables for the states cover area and population; vital statistics; health and hospitals; education; crime; housing; labor, employment, and earnings; income; energy; motor vehicles and highway statistics; foreign commerce; services; social welfare; and so on. There are five appendixes such as Notes and Explanations, Geographic Concepts and Codes, and Alphabetic Listing of PMSAs with CMSAs, and a subject index.

The *County and City Data Book* (12th ed., 1994, 928 p.+, ISBN 0160450403) contains data arranged in four tables: A, 220 items of data for the United States as a whole; B, same 220 items of data for counties and county-equivalents; C, 104 items of data for cities (incorporated places with 25,000 or more inhabitants in 1990); and D, 1990 population and 1990 census income data for places of 2,500 or more inhabitants. It covers 23 categories of data, such as agriculture, banking, climate, crime, education, elections, federal funds and grants, government finances and employment, health, household, journey to work, and vital statistics. It also provides at the beginning three tables of area rankings. There are four appendixes: Source Notes and Explanations, Geographic Information, City Maps by State, and Table Outlines. Both data books are also available on diskettes and CD-ROM.

The two commercial publications by Bernan Press complement the government data books. *County and City Extra* contains maps and rankings of counties, cities, metropolitan areas, and congressional districts on a number of key demographic and economic characteristics. It features 1996 population estimates by age and race for counties, median household income and poverty estimates for 1993, and state data tables including 1996 population estimates by race and Hispanic origin, age of householder, house ownership rates, and immigrants to the United States in 1996 by state of intended residence. Five basic tables are offered: Table A, data for states; Table B, data for states and counties; Table C, data for metropolitan areas;

Table D, data for cities of 1990 population of 25,000 or more; and Table E, data for congressional districts. Appendixes are: (A) Geographical Concepts and Codes; (B) Metropolitan Statistical Areas and Components; (C) Metropolitan Statistical Areas and Components by State; (D) Maps of States and Congressional Districts; (E) Cities by County; and (F) Sources Notes and Explanations.

For cities of population of below 25,000, refer to the companion volume, *Places, Towns and Townships*. The book contains three tables: Table A, Incorporated Places and Minor Civil Divisions of 10,000 or More Population; Table B, Incorporated Places of 2,500 or More Population; and Table C, All Places. There are two appendixes: Geographic Concepts and Sources Notes and Explanation.

The preceding list includes four Web sites for statistical sources. *Censtats*, a fee-based electronic subscription service from the Bureau of Census, provides nine searchable databases: County Business Patterns, USA Counties, Annual Survey of Manufacturers, ZIP Business Patterns, Census Tract/Street Index, Building Permits, International Trade Data, Occupation by Sex, Race and Hispanic Origins, and Consolidated Federal Funds Report. For instance, the County Business Patterns database lists SIC code, SIC description, number of employees for week, 1st quarter payroll, annual payroll. The ZIP Code Business Patterns provides number of establishments, number of employees, annual payroll in 1,000, first quarter payroll in $1,000, and total establishments. Also, it gives a table that lists SIC Code, SIC description, total establishments, and number of establishments by employment-size class. There are breakdowns for some SIC descriptions. Census Bureau databases can be searched by word, place (Gazetteer), and map (formerly DataMap). It also provides access to *Statistical Abstract of the United States*.

Fedstats is maintained by the Federal Interagency Council on Statistical Policy. According to the Council, over 70 U.S. government agencies produce statistics. *Fedstats* provides access to fourteen of them: Bureau of the Census, Bureau of Economic Analysis, Bureau of Justice Statistics, Bureau of Labor Statistics, Bureau of Transportation Statistics, Economics Research Service, Energy Information Administration, Environmental Protection Agency, Internal Revenue Service: Statistics of Income Division, National Agricultural Statistics Service, National Center for Education Statistics, National Center for Health Statistics, National Science Foundation: Science Resource Studies, and Social Security Administration.

Fedstats provides links to key statistics of 70 agencies arranged in alphabetical order. It links to, for instance, one of the most widely used sources of statistics, *The Statistical Abstract of the United States*.

STAT-USA, a fee-based database produced by the Department of Commerce, provides statistics on U.S. business, economics, and trade available from the federal government. Its sources are broadly grouped into State of the Nation for U.S. Economy, and Globus and NTDB (National Trade Data Bank) for international market research, trade opportunities, country analysis, and NTDB.

For current and brief federal government statistics, a good source is the White House Briefing Room. The Briefing Room contains Economic Statistics Briefing Room (ESBR) and Social Statistics Briefing Room (SSBR). All statistics are maintained and updated by federal agencies. In ESBR, statistics are grouped into Production, Sales, Orders and Inventories; Output; Income, Expenditures, and Wealth; Employment, Unemployment, and Earnings; Prices; Money, Credit, and Interest Rates; Transportation; and International Statistics. Subjects in SSBR are organized into Crime Statistics, Demographic Statistics, Education Statistics, and Health Statistics. Crime Statistics, for example, includes Violent Crime Measures, Homicide Rates by Age, Violent Crime Rates by Sex of Victim, Property Crime Rates, and Arrests for Drug Abuse Violations, produced by the Bureau of Justice Statistics and the Federal Bureau of Investigation. Education Statistics, provided by the National Center for Education Statistics, includes International Comparisons of Mathematics and Science Proficiency, Trends in Academic Progress, Dropout Rate, and so on. The Briefing Room also links to *Fedstats*, noted earlier.

Subfield

Statistics on the subdisciplines of the social sciences will be discussed in Part 2 of this book. Some statistics sources of general interest follow:

> *The Comparative Guide to American Suburbs*. Milpitas, CA: Toucan Valley Publications, 1997, 800 p. ISBN 1884925618. (E33)
> *Profiles of America: An Informational, Statistical and Relocation Encyclopedia of All U.S. Cities, Towns, and Counties*. Milpitas, CA: Toucan Valley Publications, 1995. 16 vols. ISBN 1884925030. (E34)
> *State Rankings: A Statistical View of the 50 United States*. 1990– . Kathleen O'Leary Morgan, Scott Morgan, and Mark A. Uhlig, eds. Laurence, KS: Morgan Quitno Press. Annual. ISSN 10573623. (E35)

The Comparative Guide covers suburban communities in the 50 largest metro areas, with rankings (title page). Any suburban community incorporated with a 1994 population estimate of 10,000 or greater is included. Each suburban community contains name or name origin, county, land area, elevation, government type, chamber of commerce, local newspaper(s), economy, safety, housing, and education.

Profiles of America is organized by region, then by state and county. It covers 3,140 counties and county-equivalents, 19,325 incorporated municipalities, 3,640 census designated places, and 8,451 minor civil divisions (called towns and townships). There are 33 elements of data for communities, including type, population, population by race, population by Hispanic origin, land area, population density, education, surbordinate note, change note, history, unemployment rate, total labor force, per capita income, high school graduation rate, college graduation rate, school districts, four-year colleges, two-year colleges, building permits issued for new housing units, median house value, median rent, and so on.

The ninth edition of *State Rankings* (1998, 575 p., ISBN 1566923298) provides 569 tables of state comparisons, classified by subject into fifteen categories, including agriculture, crime and law enforcement, defense, economy, education, employment and labor, energy and environment, geography, government finance: federal, government finance: state and local, health, housing, population, social welfare, and transportation. For instance, in number of crimes, California leads at 12 percent of the total crimes in 1996. On the other hand, California is at the top in national total of assets of savings institutions in 1997. The state of Montana ranks at the top in 31.6 percent of recent change in new business incorporations from 1995 to 1996. At the end are "Sources," a listing of agencies, and an index.

International

General

Publications of international and foreign statistical sources are many. For international statistical sources, *UNDOC*, noted in Chapter 7, and catalogs of publications issued by the United Nations and its specialized agencies should be used. All statistical activities of the United Nations are carried on under the guidance of the Statistical Commission of the Economic and Social Council. The central unit for collection, analysis, and publication of statistics is the United Nations Statistical Office. The works noted below are indispensable references:

> *Statistical Yearbook; Annuaire Statistique*, 1948– . United Nations, Statistical Office. New York, 1949– . Annual. ISSN 00828459. (E36)
> *Monthly Bulletin of Statistics—United Nations*, v. 1–27, 1919–1946, 1947– . United Nations, Statistical Office. New York. ISSN 00417432. Print & digital. (E37)
> *World Statistics in Brief*, 1976– . United Nations, Statistical Office. New York. Annual. ISSN 02801820. (E38)

Statistical Yearbook is one of the annuals on statistics published by the United Nations. Others in the social sciences include *Demographic Yearbook*, noted in Chapter 17, and *International Trade Statistics Yearbook* and *National Accounts Statistics*, noted in Chapter 10.

Statistical Yearbook is a compendium of important comparable data among nations. The 1993 edition (40th issue, 1995, 841 p.), a collection of data up to 31 December 1994 from over 40 different international and national sources, contains 20 chapters in four parts. Part I, World and Region Summary, highlights the principal trends in the development of the world and region economy. Part II is Social Statistics, an extension of the first part, providing statistical information on individual countries divided by subject, such as population and human settlement, education and literacy, health and child-bearing and nutrition, and culture and communications. Part III, Economic Activity, deals with national accounts and industrial production; financial statistics; labor force; wages and prices; agriculture, hunting, forestry and fishing; manufacturing; transport; energy; and intellectual property, science and technology. Part IV is International Economic Relations, including tables on international merchandise trade, international tourism, balance of payments, international finance; and development assistance. It ends with "Statistical Sources and References" and an index (English only). There are three annexes: I, Country and Area Nomenclature, Regional and Other Groupings; II, Conversion Coefficients and Factors; and III, Tables Added and Omitted. *Statistical Yearbook* is also available on machine-readable data file.

Statistical Yearbook serves as an abstract of international statistics. For details, other publications issued by the United Nations and its specialized agencies must be consulted. The *Yearbook* is supplemented by *Monthly Bulletin of Statistics*, which contains more current data. The monthly provides economic and social statistics from more than 200 countries and territories and quarterly statistics on industrial production. It is also online as *MBS On-line* (http://www.un.org) (E39).

A handy compendium of statistical data in a nutshell is *World Statistics in Brief*. This pocket-size work provides statistical data on 159 countries in various fields such as demography, labor force, national accounts, agriculture and industry, trade, finance, transport, and education.

Subfield

> *The Illustrated Book of World Rankings*. George Thomas Kurian, ed. Armonk, NY: Sharpe Reference, 1997. 403 p. ISBN 1563248921. (E40)
> *The New Book of World Rankings*. 3rd ed. George Thomas Kurian; updated by James Marti. New York: Facts on File, 1991. 324 p. ISBN 0816019312. (E41)

The two Kurian books complement each other as scoreboards that compare and rank over 190 nations on their performance over 50,000 variables. *The New Book* is arranged in 230 sections of topics grouped into 23 chapters. Each section provides an explanation of the topic, with highlights in a box that contains number of countries, mid-part, period covered, type of ranking, regions, most and least, and a table. For instance, in government expenditures in percentage of GDP, Israel leads (63.81%), followed by Ireland (60.4%) and Hungary (59.7%). India is ranked top in milk production (24.2 billion metric tons), followed by Pakistan (8.59 billion) and China (2.408 billion).

The Illustrated Book contains 25 sections by topic, such as vital statistics, population, race and religion, military power, economy, finance and banking, trade, labor, transportation, consumption, and education and 300 subsections of topics. Each subsection provides an explanation of the topic and statistical data of ranking, with source and many with graphics. In age of nations, China is on the top (1523 B.C.), followed by Ethiopia (1000 B.C.) and Japan (660 B.C.). China leads in steel production (8.343 billion tons) and next are Japan (8.246 billion) and the United States (7.85 billion). On top in the military expenditures is Russia ($311 million), followed by the United States ($304.1 million) and France ($35.26 million). There are two appendixes (Sources of Global Statistics and Classification of Countries) and an index. The book includes a CD-ROM.

Chapter 6

Periodicals

Several types of aids to using periodical publications are available. Indexes and abstracts, current awareness service, and selective dissemination of information are discussed in Chapter 3. This chapter will deal with the other two types of aids, bibliographies or directories and union lists. Reference sources in periodicals will also be noted. Readers will notice that items listed here use the term "serials" or "periodicals" for their titles. According to the *Anglo-American Cataloging Rules*, a serial is defined as "a publication in any medium issued in successive parts bearing numerical or chronological designations and intended to be continued indefinitely. Serials include periodicals, newspapers, annuals (reports, yearbooks, etc.); the journals, memoirs, proceedings, transactions, etc., of societies; and numbered monographic series."[1] But periodicals are not defined in the current *Rules*.

A periodical has the same characteristics as a serial, which are periodicity, seriality, and continuity. A periodical is published more frequently than annually and contains separate articles, stories, or other writings. As such, newspapers, proceedings, indexes, abstracts, bibliographies, and directories, even though they are published continuously and indefinitely, are not periodicals.[2] Such a distinction is, however, generally ignored.

In library practice, the difference between a serial and a periodical is not a semantic one. The difference lies in the frequency of publication. Any publication issued more than twice a year is generally considered to be a periodical. In this book, the two terms, serial and periodical, are used interchangeably.

BIBLIOGRAPHIES

General

Books and Periodicals Online, 1987– . Washington, DC: Library Technology Alliance. Annual. ISSN 08840911. Print & digital. (F1)

Gale Directory of Publications and Broadcast Media, ed. 1— , 1880– . Detroit: Gale Research. Annual. ISSN 08921636. Print & digital. (F2)

The Serials Directory: An International Reference Book, ed. 1– , 1986– . Birmingham, AL: EBSCO. Annual. Quarterly updates. ISSN 08864179. Print & digital. (F3)

Standard Periodical Directory, 1964/65– . New York: Oxbridge Communications, 1964– . Annual. ISSN 00856630. Print & digital. (F4)

Ulrich's International Periodicals Directory, ed. 1– . New York: Bowker, 1987– . Annual. Quarterly updates. ISSN 00000175. Print & digital. (F5)

For periodicals available online, database directories mentioned in Chapter 3 are excellent sources. *Books and Periodicals Online*, formerly *Directory of Periodicals Online: Indexed, Abstracted and Full-Text*, in three major fields: law and business, medicine and social science; and science and technology, is a comprehensive worldwide directory of books and periodicals, both online and on CD-ROM. It contains 85,000 sources from over 200 countries. Each entry contains source title, country, ISSN number, ISBN number, database name, coverage code, coverage dates, and vendor contact information. It is also accessible on the Internet (http://www.periodicals.net). Boolean operators, fields, and date ranges can be used for searching.

Gale Directory of Publications, well known by its former title, *Ayer Directory of Publications*, is an annual guide to publications and broadcasting stations including newspapers, magazines, journals, radio stations, television stations, and cable systems (subtitle). The 132nd edition (Kristin B. Mallegg, ed., 1998, 4 vols., ISBN 0787615161) lists sources by states and after states Canada in volumes 1 and 2. Newsletters and directories are excluded. Volume 3, "Indexes and Tables," consists of Abbreviations, Symbols, and Codes; Industry Activity; Industrial Statistics; Broadcast and Cable Networks; News and Feature Syndicates; Publishers Index; Subject Index; Newspaper Feature Editors; and Master Name and Keyword Index. Volume 4 contains regional market index and maps. The Subject Index includes a number of categories of publications, such as Agricultural Publications; Ethnic Publications including Black, Foreign Language, Hispanic, and Jewish publications; Fraternal Publications including College, Religious, and Women's publications; Newspapers; Radio Station Formats; and Traded, Technical, and Professional Publications.

The Gale Directory presents over 37,000 items of more than 10,000 publishers. The contents of entries vary. For magazines and newspapers, there are nearly 30 items in each entry, such as title, subtitle, address, e-mail, frequency, print method, column width, column depth, subscription, advertisement rates, circulation, online, and feature editors. There is *An Interedition Service Providing New Listings and Updates to Listings in the Main Volume*. The directory is available on CD-ROM, an online database marketed through Dialog (File 469) as *Gale Database of Publications and Broadcast Media*, noted in Chapter 4, and on the Galenet, noted in Chapter 1.

The database, updated semiannually, has much broader coverage than its print counterpart. It contains more than 65,000 sources from Gale's four print products: *Gale Directory of Publications and Broadcast Media, Directories in Print, City and State Directories in Print*, and *Newsletters in Print*.

The *Serials Directory* and *Ulrich's* are two comprehensive listings of periodicals. The former, compiled primarily on the basis of CONSER and MARC-S files and EBSCO's own internal database, is a competitor to *Ulrich's*. In its eleventh edition (1997, 5 vols., ISBN 1888151118), volumes 1–4 are a serials listing of approximately 160,000 titles classified in alphabetical order by some 140 subject headings, with over 380 subheadings, with over 11,000 cross-references. Each entry has up to 50 elements of information, including main entry, date of publication, volume information, ISSN, type of serials, country of publication, frequency, price, publisher, up to four classifications (the Library of Congress, Dewey Decimal, Universal Decimal, and the National Library of Medicine), CODEN, index availability, book reviews, advertising, circulation, descriptive listing, wire services, and so on. Volume 1 also has four tables: Wire Services, Country of Publication by Code, Country of Publication by Country, Unit of Currency, and Index of Abstracts.

Volume 4 contains newspapers and alphabetical title index. Volume 5, an index volume, consists of ISSN, New Title Index, Serials Online Index, Serials on CD-ROM Index, Controlled Circulation Index, Book Review Index, Copyright Center Index, Advertising Accepted Index, and Ceased/Suspended, Title Change. It is updated by *Update* (F7), a quarterly interedition. The *Directory* and its updates are also available on CD-ROM and on the Web (http://www.epnet.com).

The best-known bibliography of serials is *Ulrich's*, produced from the Bowker International Serials Database.[3] Its 35th edition (1997, 5 vols., ISSN 08352380) lists under more than 550 subject classes over 165,000 periodicals, newspapers, irregulars and other elusive materials from 70,000 publishers in 200 countries, and ceased serials in the last three years. For each serial, information includes DDC and LC classification, country code, ISSN, title and language, year first published, frequency, current subscription information, toll-free number, e-mail address, URL, subscription and distributor addresses, key personnel: editor(s) and publisher, rights and permissions contact and telephone, e-mail address and Web sites, advertising contact and full-page rates, special features, circulation, abstracting and indexing coverage, document type, availability in electronic media: CD-ROM or online, document delivery services, copyright clearance center, bibliographic history including ISSN for former titles, description of contents and intended readership, and refereed serials identification.

The first three volumes are periodicals arranged in alphabetical order under 554 subject classes. Volume 4 is a listing of refereed serials, controlled circulation serials, serials available on CD-ROM, serials available online, vendor listing/serials online, cessation, index to publications of international organizations (international organizations, international congress proceedings, European Community, and United Nations), ISSN index, title change index, and title index. Volume 5 is newspapers.

Ulrich's is updated quarterly by *Ulrich's Update* (F8), formerly *Ulrich's Quarterly*, 1977–1987. *Ulrich's* online, *Ulrich's International Periodicals Directory*, updated monthly (F9), is marketed through Dialog (File 480), Ovid (File ULRI), Lexis-Nexis (File ULRICH), and SilverPlatter. The CD-ROM version, *Ulrich's on Disc* (F10), operates for both Windows and DOS systems. It provides a number of access points. On each search screen are displayed 22 search fields, such as title, ISSN, keyword, keyword in title, personal name, country, price, circulation, indexing and abstracting, electronic vendor, publication code, year first published, and Coden number. As compared with the online database, it has fewer fields and is not as powerful as the online version for precise searching results.

The *Standard Periodical Directory*, formerly irregular, became an annual, lists in its 21st edition (1998, 2,272 p., ISBN 0917460898) 90,000 periodicals in the United States and Canada arranged alphabetically by title under some 250 subject headings. The term "periodical" is broadly used to include "any publication having a frequency of issue of at least once every two years" (Preface), such as consumer magazines, trade journals, newsletters, government publications, house organs, directories, transactions and proceedings of scientific societies, yearbooks, and guides. Its bibliographical data are adequate. Compared with the two directories just mentioned, it has far less coverage and is limited to periodicals published in the United States and Canada. The *Directory*, however, includes many house organs. Each entry provides, if available, name of publisher, address, phone, e-mail, personnel, brief description, subscription, circulation, advertisement (trim size, number of pages, and so on). There are two indexes: online and title/ISSN. It is also on CD-ROM and the Internet (http://www.mediafinder.com).

Selective

Other bibliographies and directories for specific purpose or particular form are many. Below are some representative titles:

Magazines for Libraries. 9th ed. Bill Katz and Linda Sternberg Katz. New York: Bowker, 1997. 1,402 p. ISBN 0835222179. (F11)

Oxbridge Directory of Newsletters, 1979– . New York: Oxbridge Communications. Annual. ISSN 01637010. Print and digital. (F12)

Katz is a classified annotated selection tool for the general reader, and school, junior college, college, university, and public libraries (subtitle), primarily limited to American magazines. Its ninth edition lists over 7,304 titles classified under more than 150 topics. Newsletters are generally not included. Each entry includes title, ISSN, date founded, frequency, price, editor, publisher and address, Internet-WWW, illustrations, index, advertising, circulation, sample, date volume ends, refereed, CD-ROM, microform, online, reprint, indexed, book reviews, audience, and annotation. In almost all topics, basic periodicals and basic abstracts and indexes are presented. In general, each topic has an introduction describing the periodicals listed under the topic and the periodical publishing situation in the field. There are two indexes: title and subject.

The 1998 edition of *Oxbridge Directory of Newsletters* lists over 28,000 newsletters published in the United States and Canada classified into more than 180 categories. Newsletters in the social sciences include those in accounting, business and industry, civil rights, consumer interests, credit card holders, economics, education, geography, government, history, insurance, international affairs, investment, labor, law, psychology and psychiatry, taxes, and youth. Each entry consists of title, publisher, personnel, editorial description, general information (year established, frequency, trim size, number of pages, method of printing, availability of online, and so on), subscription, and acquisitions. There are five indexes: multipublisher, publishers by state, online, title/ISSN, and title change. The directory is also available on CD-ROM and the Internet (http://www.mediafinder.com).

Subfield

For bibliographies of periodicals in the social sciences and related fields, the following title may be useful:

World List of Social Science Periodicals. 8th ed. Prepared by UNESCO Social Science Documentation Centre with the cooperation of the International Committee for Social Science Information and Documentation. Paris: UNESCO, 1991. 446 p. ISBN 9230027340. (F13)

The fourth edition of the *World List* represents the first extension of the social sciences of a subsystem of UNISIST (The World Science Information Programme)—the International Serials Data Series—and the first of the world Social Sciences Information Services Series, an output of UNESCO's

Social Science Documentation Centre and DARE Data Bank. It "includes only scientific periodicals devoted to the social science disciplines, that is, those that regularly publish original research, field studies or articles signed by scholars or specialists in the fields covered" (Introduction). Publications of news and information about social issues, or of statistics and economic conditions, translations or reprints, and doctrinal works are excluded.

The current, eighth edition lists 4,459 periodicals. It is organized into four sections: (1) an alphabetical index of titles, (2) full entry for each periodical arranged by country of publication and alphabetically by title within each country, (3) a subject index, and (4) an index of bibliographic and abstracting periodicals by discipline. An annex gives a list of abstracting and indexing services known to cover the periodicals on a regular basis.

UNION LISTS

> *Union List of Serials in Libraries of the United States and Canada.* 3rd ed. Edna Brown Titus, ed. New York: Wilson, 1965. 5 vols. (F14)
>
> *New Serial Titles: A Union List of Serials Commencing Publication after Dec. 31, 1949.* Washington, DC: Library of Congress, 1953– . Monthly with annual cumulation. ISSN 00286680. (F15)

The third edition of *Union List of Serials (ULS)* includes the second edition, two supplements, and additional new titles of 11,892 serials that began publication prior to 1950. It lists in one alphabet 156,449 titles held by 956 libraries with information on changes of titles, holding information, and suspension of publications prior to 1950. The *Union List of Serials* does not, however, have a subject approach.

The *New Serial Titles*, a serial publication itself, continues *ULS*, providing information as a union list on serials that began publication after December 31, 1949. It is now produced from OCLC tapes as part of the CONSER (Cooperative Online Serials) Program, which began in 1975. Its earlier feature, "Classed Subject Arrangement," has been discontinued.

REFERENCE SOURCES IN PERIODICALS

Periodicals provide a wealth of reference sources in addition to articles. *Fortune's 500, U.S. News & World Report*'s "Best Colleges," "The Devil's Dictionary of Insurance" in *Best Reviews*, and *Smith College Studies in Social Work*'s abstracts of doctoral dissertations are a few examples of widely scattered reference sources contained in periodicals.

A review of 3,000 periodicals in all fields yields some 1,300 periodicals that carry reference sources.[4] Seventeen types of reference sources each of which appears in more than 50 periodicals are chosen: abstracts and indexes; article reviews; AV reviews; awards, prizes, and the like; bibliographies; biographies; book reviews; calendars, events, and the like; career opportunities; contents reproduction; directories; dissertations, theses listing; guides; meetings; necrology; news; and rankings and ratings. Other types published by fewer than 50 periodicals are also included provided they are of high reference value, such as glossaries and research in progress.

Some highlights of the study may be noted as follows.[5] All numbers of periodicals are from the study, and the number of periodicals of a particular subdiscipline is provided in parentheses.

Reviews are the most popular reference sources in periodicals. They include reviews of print materials (article reviews, book reviews, literature reviews, magazine reviews, technical reviews, and telegraphic reviews), reviews of nonprint materials (art reviews, audiovisual reviews, CD-ROM reviews, database reviews), and software reviews), products reviews (hardware reviews, instrument reviews, teaching aid reviews, and test reviews), and other reviews (exhibition reviews, performance reviews, and seminar reviews). Book reviews dominate in reference sources. Of the 1,275 periodicals that carry book reviews, 683 in the social sciences accounted for 54 percent of the total. Law (116) has the largest number of periodicals with book reviews, followed by history (88), psychology (55), education (50), and political science (43).

Social science periodicals also dominate bibliographies, indexes, and abstracts with 133 periodicals, or 60% of 222 periodicals identified as carrying the sources. History (31) leads other subdisciplines, followed by law (19), education (9), and business (8). Many abstracts are summaries of proceedings and conference papers, as in psychology. Periodicals in all subject fields that carry contents reproduction number nineteen, of which thirteen are in the social sciences.

Biographies and news about people include awardees, conversations, dedications, honorees, members, officers, retirements, and tributes. Also included are many "bests," such as the richest and the best paid. Periodicals that publish biographical sources are accounted for 239 with 116 periodicals in the social sciences. Law (25) has the most periodicals, followed by business (18), education (8), and political science (7). For obituaries and necrology, 94 periodicals in the social sciences are identified, with periodicals in law (19) on the top, followed by history (14), psychology (11), political science (7), economics (5), and geography (5).

Information on awards, grants, prizes, fellowships, and scholarships can be found in many periodicals. In the social sciences, 81 periodicals carry information on awards, grants, prizes, fellowships, and the like. History has 10 periodicals, education 9, sociology 6, and law and political science 5 each. Many awards and prizes are presented by societies and associations and are therefore published in their organs.

Rankings and ratings are published in 52 periodicals in the social sciences, predominately in business (27).

A total of 54 periodicals are identified to carry listings of doctoral dissertations and master's theses, of which 36 are in the social sciences. By sub-discipline, business, economics, and history have five or more periodicals each with these listings.

A directory includes a general directory for locating names and addresses; professional directory for members, officers of a profession; institutional directory listing organizations, institutions, societies, and the like; and trade directory, listing companies, manufacturers, industries, and other business organizations. These directories may be found in 68 periodicals in the social sciences. By number of periodicals, education (11) leads, followed by business (10), law (10), and history (5). Many periodicals provide directories of membership, committees, officers, courses, programs, and so on.

A guide is a tool that offers basic information or instructions. In the social sciences, 55 periodicals provide guides. By the number of periodicals, business has 16, followed by education (8), and law (8). Some guides also serve as bibliographies or directories. In this respect, guides, bibliographies, and directories are used interchangeably. One popular item is the buyer's guide, which appears in many periodicals.

Quite a few organizations, societies, and institutions provide placement in their official organs. Career opportunities are also listed in the periodical advertisements. In the social sciences, 39 periodicals are identified as providing information on career opportunities. Business (8) leads in the number of periodicals.

The term *calendar* refers to chronology, courses, meetings, events, and performance. The social sciences have 84 periodicals that carry such information.

Quite a number of periodicals carry news. News may include meetings. Over 180 periodicals in the social sciences carry such information. Law (32) leads other subdisciplines in the number of periodicals. Others, in rank order, are business (20), history (20), education (15), political science (11), psychology (5), and sociology (5).

Most meetings are found in periodicals published by societies, associations, and institutions. Information on meetings is also found in calendars and news columns. The social science periodicals that carry meeting news, reports, and minutes number 164. History (24) has the largest number of periodicals, followed by education (17), psychology (16), law (14), business (6), economics (6), geography (6), and political science (6).

Not many periodicals in the social sciences carry glossaries; only 4 do.

Periodicals are the best source for research in progress. In the social sciences, a dozen or so periodicals carry such information.

Listed hereafter are types of reference sources and a listing of periodicals that carry reference sources as their regular features. Both types and periodicals are selective.

Access to Sources

Bibliographies, Abstracts and Indexes

Abstracts that are summaries of proceedings and conference papers are excluded.

Business

American Printer, v. 4– , 1982– . Chicago: MacLean Hunter Publishing. Monthly. ISSN 07446610 (F16). "Literature."

International Labor and Working-Class History, 1972– . Champaign, IL: University of Illinois Press. 2/year. ISSN 01475479 (F17). "Current Research."

International Labor Review, 1921– . Switzerland: ILO Publications. Bimonthly. 00207780 (F18). "Bibliography: ILO [International Labor Office] Publications." An annotated bibliography.

Journal of Banking and Finance, 1977– . Amsterdam: North-Holland. 6/year. ISSN 03784266 (F19). "Latest Publications." An annotated bibliography.

Journal of Future Markets, The, 1981– . New York: John Wiley & Sons. Bimonthly. ISSN 02707314 (F20). "Futures Bibliography." A classified unannotated bibliography.

Journal of Marketing, 1934– . Chicago: American Marketing Association. Quarterly. ISSN 00222429 (F21). "Marketing Literature Review." A selective listing based on article abstracts from the business literature database.

Journal of Risk and Insurance, The, 1933– . Orlando, FL: American Risk and Insurance Association. Quarterly. ISSN 00224367 (F22). "From the Library Shelf: Abstracts."

Journal of Small Business Management, 1963– . Morgantown: West Virginia University, Bureau of Business Research. Quarterly. ISSN 00472778 (F23). "Resources." An annotated bibliography of books and periodical articles.

Journal of Systems Management, 1950– . Cleveland, OH: Association for Systems Management. Monthly. ISSN 00224839 (F24). "Recommended Reading." An annotated bibliography of books and periodical articles.

Economics

Journal of Economic Literature, v. 7– , 1969– . Nashville, TN: American Economic Association. Quarterly. ISSN 00220515 (F25). "Annotated Listing of New Books," a classified bibliography; "Current Periodicals" consisting of "Contents of Current Periodicals," "Subject Index of Articles in Current Periodicals with Selected Abstracts," and "Index of Authors of Articles in the Subject Index."

Journal of Vocational Behavior, 1971– . San Diego, CA: Academic Press. Bimonthly. ISSN 00018791 (F26). Annual review of the vocational behavior literature.

International Journal of Physical Distribution and Logistics Management, 1970– . Bradford, England: MCB University Press. ISSN 00207527 (F27). "Logistics Abstracts."

Education

Comparative Education Review, 1956– . Chicago: University of Chicago Press. Quarterly. ISSN 00104086 (F28). Annual listing of comparative and international education periodical articles, classified by subject.

Research in the Teaching of English, 1967– . Urbana, IL: National Council of Teachers of English. Quarterly. ISSN 00345271 (F29). An annotated bibliography of research in the teaching of English.

Review of Education, The, 1975– . New York: Gordon and Breach Science Publishers. Quarterly. ISSN 00985597 (F30). An annotated bibliography of selected titles.

Geography

Cartography and Geographic Information Systems, v. 17, no. 1– . 1990– . Bethesda, MD: American Congress on Survey and Mapping. Quarterly. ISSN 10509844 (F31). "Recent Literature."

Geographical Magazine: The Monthly Journal of the Royal Geographical Society, 1935– . Putney, England: World Publications. Monthly. ISSN 0016741X (F32). "Geographic Sources. . . ."

Research and Exploration, 1985– . Washington, DC: National Geographic Society. Quarterly. ISSN 8755724X (F33). "New Titles." A listing of books.

History

American Historical Review, The, 1895– . Washington, DC: American Historical Association. 5/year. ISSN 00028762 (F34). "Documents and Bibliographies." A classified listing of works by subject, country, and region.

Canadian Historical Review, The, 1920– . Downsview, Canada: University of Toronto Press. Quarterly. ISSN 00083755 (F35). "Recent Publications Relating to Canada." A classified listing of books, periodical articles, and theses.

Catholic Historical Review, The, 1915– . Washington, DC: Catholic University of America Press. Quarterly. ISSN 00088080 (F36). "Periodical Literature."

English Historical Review, The, 1888–   . Essex, England: Addison Wesley Longman. Quarterly. ISSN 00138266 (F37). "Notices of Periodical and Occasional Publications . . ." A classified listing.

History and Theory: Studies in the Philosophy of History, 1960–   . Middletown, OH: Ohio Wesleyan University. Quarterly. ISSN 00182656 (F38). "Beiheft." A yearly issue that contains bibliographies.

Journal of American History, The, 1914–   . Bloomington, IN: Organization of American Historians. Quarterly. ISSN 00218723 (F39). "Recent Scholarship." Beginning with volume 70(1), it combines with the Book Notes section, arranged by subject, and within subject, alphabetically by author, first articles, then dissertations, and finally books.

Journal of Southern History, The, 1935–   . Houston, TX: Southern Historical Association. Quarterly. ISSN 00224642 (F40). Since 1964, an annual selected bibliography on Southern history in periodicals, classified but not annotated.

Journal of the Early Republic, 1981–   . Indianapolis, IN: Society for Historians of the Early American Republic. Quarterly. ISSN 02751275 (F41). "Recent Articles."

Recusant History, 1957–   . Durham, England: Catholic Record Society. 2/year. ISSN 00341932 (F42). "Newsletter" including theses and theses in progress.

Seventeenth Century News, 1942–   . College Station: Texas A & M University, Department of English. Quarterly. ISSN 00373028. "Abstracts of Recent Articles." (F43)

Western Historical Quarterly, The, 1970–   . Logan, UT: Western History Association. Quarterly. ISSN 00433810 (F44). "Recent Articles." An unannotated listing of periodical articles.

Law

Common Market Law Review, 1963–   . Dordrecht, The Netherlands: Kluwer Academic Publishers. Quarterly. ISSN 01650750 (F45). "Survey of Literature."

Comparative Labor Law Journal, 1976–   . Philadelphia: The Law School and the Wharton School of the University of Pennsylvania and the U.S. National Branch of the International Society for Labor Law and Social Security. Quarterly. ISSN 01479202 (F46). "Selected Current Bibliography."

Criminal Law Bulletin, 1964–   . New York: Warren, Gorham and Lamont. 6/year. ISSN 00111317 (F47). "From the Legal Literature" and annual case digest index.

Federal Communications Law Journal, 1977–   . Los Angeles: University of California. 3/year. ISSN 01637606 (F48). "Article Digest."

Hastings Communications and Entertainment Law Journal, 1988–   . San Francisco: University of California, Hastings College of Law. Quarterly. ISSN 10616578 (F49). "Abstracts." Classified abstracts of periodical articles, monographs, and pamphlets, with an "Index to Abstracts." Bibliographies on various topics.

Issues in Law and Medicine, 1985– . Terre Haute, IN: National Legal Center for the Medically Dependent and Disabled. Quarterly. ISSN 87568160 (F50). "Abstracts." Abstracts of periodical articles.

Journal of Air Law and Commerce, The, 1930– . Dallas, TX: Southern Methodist University. Quarterly. ISSN 00218642 (F51). "Bibliography." A classified listing of monographs and periodical articles.

Journal of Criminal Justice: An International Journal, 1973– . Elmsford, NY: Pergamon Press. Bimonthly. ISSN 00472352 (F52). "Current Publications Abstracts."

Michigan Law Review, 1902– . Ann Arbor, MI: Michigan Law Review Association. 8/year. ISSN 00262234 (F53). "Periodical Index: Subject Index of Articles, Comments, Notes and Recent Developments Appearing in Leading Law Reviews." A classified listing.

Natural Resources and Environment, 1985– . Chicago: Section of Natural Resources Law of the American Bar Association. Quarterly. ISSN 08823812 (F54). "Nuggets." An annotated bibliography.

Real Estate Law Journal, 1972– . New York: Warren, Gorban and Lamont. Quarterly. ISSN 00486868 (F55). "Survey of Articles" and "Digest of Selected Articles."

Political Science

Foreign Affairs, 1922– . New York: Council on Foreign Relations. 5/year. ISSN 00157120 (F56). "Source Material." Divided into two categories: documents and other publications.

Human Rights Internet Reporter, 1976– . Cambridge, MA: Human Rights Internet. Quarterly. ISSN 0275049X (F57). "Bibliography." A classified annotated bibliography with geographic, subject, and organizational indexes. Organizational addresses are referred to the "Master Lists" in its Supplement, updated annually, containing "the names and addresses of organizations whose material is reviewed in the Reporter, and information on how to obtain serial publications cited in the Reporter" (Introduction).

International Review of Administrative Sciences, 1957– . London: Sage Publications. Quarterly. ISSN 00208523 (F58). "Bibliography—A Selection." A classified annotated bibliography.

Journal of Agricultural Taxation and Law, v. 5, no. 1– , 1983– . Boston: Warren, Gorham and Lamont. Quarterly. ISSN 07459181 (F59). "Article Digests."

Journal of Taxation, The, 1954– . New York: Warren, Gorham and Lamont for Tax Research Group. Monthly. ISSN 00224863 (F60). "Tax Literature." An annotated bibliography.

Psychology

Aggressive Behavior: A Multidisciplinary Journal Devoted to the Experimental and Observational Analysis of Conflict in Humans and Animals,

1975– . New York: Wiley-Liss. 6/year. ISSN 0096140X (F61). "A Guide to the Literature on Aggressive Behavior."

Reading Psychology: An International Quarterly, 1979– . Bristol, PA: Taylor and Francis. ISSN 02702711 (F62). "ERIC Research Reviews." An annotated bibliography.

Sociology

Ageing and Society, 1981– . Cambridge, England: Cambridge University Press. Quarterly. ISSN 0144686X (F63). "Abstracts."

British Journal of Social Work, The, 1971– . Oxford, England: Oxford University Press. 6/year. ISSN 00453102 (F64). "Abstracts." Abstracts of periodical articles with comments on various subjects, such as psychiatry and psychology, sociology, social policy, law, criminology, and philosophy.

Journal of the American Planning Association, 1979– . Washington, DC: American Planning Association. Quarterly. ISSN 01944363 (F65). "Literature in Planning." A classified bibliography of articles [contents reproduction], documents, and reports.

International Migration Review: A Quarterly Studying Sociological, Demographic, Economic, Historical, and Legislative Aspects of Human Migration Movements and Ethnic Group Relations, 1964– . Staten Island, NY: Center for Migration Studies. Quarterly. ISSN 01979183 (F66). "Review of Reviews," a unique classified listing of reviews.

International Review of Social History, 1937– . Cambridge, England: Cambridge University Press. 3/year. ISSN 00208590 (F67). "Bibliography," a classified annotated listing.

Studies in Family Planning, 1963– . New York: Population Council. 6/year. ISSN 00393665 (F68). "Current Publications." Abstracts of articles, books, and reports.

Contents Reproduction

Business

Accounting Review, The, 1926– . Sarasota, FL: American Accounting Association. Quarterly. ISSN 00014826 (F69). "Contents of Accounting Research Journals."

Journal of Accounting & Economics, 1979– . Amsterdam: North-Holland. Quarterly. ISSN 01654101 (F70). Contents reproduction at the end of each issue.

Journal of Business Finance & Accounting, 1974– . Oxford, England: Basil Blackwell. 6/year. ISSN 0306686X (F71). Contents reproduction at the end of some issues.

Economics

Journal of Economic Literature (listed earlier, see F25). "Contents of Current Periodicals."

Education

> *Journal of Research in Music Education*, 1953–   . Reston, VA: Music Educators National Conference. Quarterly. ISSN 00224294 (F72). "Research Resources."

History

> *American Historical Review, The* (listed earlier, see F34). "Collected Essays."

Law

> *American Journal of International Law*, 1907–   . Washington, DC: American Society of International Law. Quarterly. ISSN 00029300 (F73). "International Legal Materials."
> *Student Lawyer*, 1972–   . Chicago: American Bar Association Law Student Division. Monthly. ISSN 0039274X (F74). "Resources." Contents, organizations, publications, and so on.

Political Science

> *Public Finance*, 1946–   . Koenigstein, Germany: Foundation Journal Public Finance. Quarterly. ISSN 00333476 (F75). "New Publications," tables of contents of books; "Contents of Journal."

Psychology

> *American Journal of Psychiatry, The*, 1844–   . Washington, DC: American Psychiatric Association. Monthly. ISSN 0002953X (F76).

Sociology

> *Journal of Regional Science*, 1958–   . Cambridge, MA: Blackwell Publishers. Quarterly. ISSN 00224146 (F77). "Selected Titles from Current Journals."
> *Journal of the American Planning Association*, 1979–   . Washington, DC: American Planning Association. Quarterly. ISSN 01944363 (F78). "Periodical Literature."
> *Towns Planning Review*, 1910–   . Liverpool, England: Liverpool University Press. Quarterly. ISSN 00410020 (F79). "Selected Titles from Current Journals."

Theses and Dissertations

Anthropology

> *Journal of Contemporary Ethnography: A Journal of Ethnographic Research*, 1972–   . Newbury Park, CA: Sage Publications. Quarterly. ISSN 08912416. (F80). "Dissertation Abstracts."

Business

Journal of Business, The, 1928–   . Chicago: University of Chicago Press. Quarterly. ISSN 00219398 (F81). Annual listing of dissertations since 1954.

Journal of International Business Studies, 1970–   . Columbia, SC: University of South Carolina. 3/year. ISSN 00472506 (F82). "Dissertation Abstracts," published since 1974.

Journal of Risk and Insurance (listed earlier, see F22). "Doctoral Dissertations and Closely Related Fields."

MIS Quarterly: Management Information Systems, 1977–   . Minneapolis, MN: Society for Management Information Systems. Quarterly. ISSN 02767783 (F83). "MIS Doctoral Dissertations." An annual listing since 1983.

Omega: International Journal of Management Science, 1973–   . Kidlington, Oxford, England: Elsevier Science. Bimonthly. ISSN 03050483 (F84). "International Register of Theses and Dissertations."

Economics

Canadian Journal of Agricultural Economics, 1952–   . Ottawa, Canada: Canadian Agricultural Economics and Farm Management Society. 3/year. ISSN 00083976 (F85). "M.Sc. and Ph.D. Theses Submitted at Canadian Universities."

Economic Journal, The, 1891–   . Oxford, England: Basil Blackwell. 6/year. ISSN 00130133 (F86). An annual listing of thesis titles for degrees in the United Kingdom since 1973.

Journal of Economic History, The, 1941–   . Cambridge, England: Cambridge University Press. Quarterly. ISSN 00220507 (F87). "Summaries of Doctoral Dissertations." An annual listing in June issue.

Journal of Economic Literature (listed earlier, see F25): "Doctoral Dissertations in Economics." An annual listing.

Education

Journal of Curriculum and Supervision, 1985–   . Alexandria, VA: Association for Supervision and Curriculum Development. Quarterly. ISSN 08821232 (F88). "Abstracts of Selected Doctoral Dissertations in Supervision;" "Dissertations in Supervision . . ."

Roeper Review: A Journal on Gifted Education, 1978–   . Bloomfield Hills, MI: Roeper School. Quarterly. ISSN 02783193 (F89). "Recent Doctoral Dissertation Research on Gifted Education."

Geography

Professional Geographer, 1949–   . Washington, DC: Association of American Geographers. Quarterly. ISSN 00330124 (F90). Listings of dissertations and master's theses, and dissertations in progress, from 1950 to 1979 and, since 1984, listing of doctoral dissertations.

History

Canadian Historical Review, The (listed earlier, see F35). "Recent Publications Relating to Canada." A listing of books, periodical articles, and theses classified by subject and province.

Journal of American History, The (listed earlier, see F39). "Recent Scholarship." Beginning with volume 70(1), it combines with the Book Notes section, arranged by subject, and within subject, alphabetically by author, first the articles, then the dissertations, and finally the books.

Journal of the Early Republic (listed earlier, see F41). "Recent Dissertations."

New Zealand Journal of History, The, 1967– . Auckland, New Zealand: University of Auckland. 2/year. ISSN 00288322 (F91). "Research." Theses completed, research essays completed, and theses in progress.

Recusant History (listed earlier, see F42). "Newsletter" including theses and theses in progress.

Western Historical Quarterly (listed earlier, see F44). "Sources and Literature." "A List of Dissertations." An annual listing since 1970.

Political Science

Diplomatic History, 1977– . Wilmington, DE: Scholarly Resources. Quarterly. ISSN 01452096 (F92). "Doctoral Dissertations in U.S. Foreign Affairs." An annual listing.

PS: Political Science and Politics, 1968– . Washington, DC: American Political Science Association. Quarterly. ISSN 00323497 (F93). "Doctoral Dissertations in Political Science." An annual listing, formerly published in American Political Science Review.

Psychology

Journal of Creative Behavior, 1967– . Buffalo, NY: Creative Education Foundation. Quarterly. ISSN 00220175 (F94). "Bibliography of Recent Doctoral Dissertations on Creativity and Problem-Solving."

Sociology

American Annals of the Deaf, 1847– . Washington, DC: Convention of American Instructors of the Deaf. 5/year. ISSN 0002726X (F95). "Research on Deafness: Doctoral Dissertations."

Research on Social Work Practice, 1990– . Newbury Park, CA: Sage Periodicals Press. Quarterly. ISSN 10497315 (F96). "Doctoral Dissertations in Practice Research."

Smith College Studies in Social Work, 1930– . Northampton, MA: Smith

College School for Social Work. 3/year. ISSN 00377317 (F97). "Abstracts of Doctoral Dissertations" and "Abstracts of Master's Theses."

Research in Progress

Cultural Anthropology

American Antiquity: Journal of the Society for American Archaeology, 1935– . Washington, DC: The Society. Quarterly. ISSN 00027316 (F98). Current research.

Business

Accounting Review, The, 1926– . Sarasota, FL: American Accounting Association. Quarterly. ISSN 00014826 (F99). "Research in Accounting."
Business Horizons, 1957– . Bloomington, IN: Indiana University. Bimonthly. ISSN 00076813 (F100). "Research Clearinghouse."

Economics

Atlantic Economic Journal, 1973– . Edwardsville, IL: Southern Illinois University. Quarterly. ISSN 01974254 (F101). "Anthologies." Summaries of research and research in progress, comments on a printed article and comments on errors in one's own previously printed work (editor's note).
Industrial and Labor Relations Review, 1947– . Ithaca, NY: Cornell University. Quarterly. ISSN 00197939 (F102). "Research in Progress."
International Labor and Working-Class History (listed earlier, see F17). "Current Research."

Geography

Research and Exploration, 1985– . Washington, DC: National Geographic Society. Quarterly. ISSN 8755724X (F103). "Reports Received." Reports regarding progress and completion of projects supported by the National Geographic Society grants, published in each summer issue.

History

New Zealand Journal of History, The (listed earlier, see F91). "Research." Theses completed, research essays completed, and theses in progress.
Quaker History, 1906– . Haverford, PA: Friends Historical Association, Membership Office, Haverford College Library. 2/year. ISSN 00335053 (F104). "Research in Progress."
Recusant History (listed earlier, see F42). "Newsletter." A bibliography including theses in progress.
Speculum: A Journal of Medieval Studies, 1926– . Cambridge, MA: Medi-

eval Academy of America. Quarterly. ISSN 00387134 (F105). "Varia—Bibliography of Editions and Translations in Progress."

Political Science

> PS: *Political Science and Politics* (listed earlier, see F93). A section on dissertations in preparation.
> *Public Opinion Quarterly*, 1937– . Chicago: University of Chicago Press. ISSN 0033362X (F106). Brief reports of research in progress.

Sources of Information

Biographical Sources

Biographies and news about people include awardees, conversations, dedications, honorees, members, officers, retirements, and tributes. They include many "bests," such as the richest and the best paid. This information is also found in periodicals under Rankings and Ratings, noted later. A number of periodicals carry necrology or obituaries. They are generally excluded.

Business

> *American Printer* (listed earlier, see F16). "News Makers" and "Names and Faces."
> *Institutional Investor: The Magazine for Finance and Investment*, 1967– . New York: Institutional Investor. Monthly. ISSN 00203580 (F107). "CEO Interview."
> *Management Accounting*, 1919– . Montvale, NJ. National Association of Accountants. Monthly. ISSN 00251690 (F108). "Trends"; "Promotions & New Positions."
> *Personnel Management*, 1969– . London: Personnel Publications. Monthly. ISSN 00315761 (F109). "Profile."

Education

> *Childhood Education: A Journal for Teachers, Teachers-in-Training, Teacher Educators, Parents, Day Care Workers, Librarians, Pediatricians and Other Child Caregivers*, 1924– . Wheaton, MD: Association for Childhood Education International. 5/year. ISSN 00094056 (F110). "Later Leaders in Education."

Directories and Guides

Some guides also serve as bibliographies or directories. In this respect, guides, bibliographies, and directories are used interchangeably. Rankings and ratings, noted later, can also serve as a guide. One popular item is the buyer's guide. Directories of membership, committees, officers, courses, programs, and the like are omitted.

Anthropology

> *Current Anthropology: A World Journal of Sciences of Man*, 1960–   . Chicago: University of Chicago. Quarterly. ISSN 00113204 (F111). "Institutions."

Business

> *American Machinist*, 1877–   . New York: McGraw-Hill. Monthly. ISSN 00029858 (F112). "Outstanding Services Directory;" guides to products/services/manufacturers; "Casebook" for problem-solving techniques used by other companies.
>
> *Buildings: The Facilities Construction and Management Journal*, 1906–   . Cedar Rapids, IA: Stamats Communications. ISSN 07332408 (F113). "Directory of Real Estate Related Organizations."
>
> *Business Week*, 1929–   . New York: McGraw-Hill. Weekly. ISSN 00077135 (F114). Investing.
>
> *Chain Store Age: The Magazine for Retail Executives*, v. 51–   , 1975–   . New York: Lebhar-Friedman. Monthly. ISSN 10870601 (F115). Directories on various topics, such as annual store planning, equipment and construction services seminars; retailers; fixture manufacturers; and lighting supplies.
>
> *Drug and Cosmetic Industry*, 1914–   . Duluth, MN: Harcourt Brace Jovanovich. Monthly. ISSN 00126527 (F116). Directories on various topics, such as skin care materials suppliers; consulting and special services; packages and packaging materials; machinery and equipment; raw materials; associations; trade name; and supplier's address.
>
> *Euromoney: The Monthly Journal of International Money and Capital Markets*, 1969–   . London: Euromoney Publications. Monthly. ISSN 00142433 (F117). Guides to investment, European domestic bond market, currencies, borrowers of foreign markets, Euromoney, etc.
>
> *Forbes*, 1917–   . New York: Forbes. Weekly. ISSN 00156914 (F118). Annual money guide.
>
> *Foreign Service Journal*, 1924–   . Washington, DC: American Foreign Service Association. 11/year. ISSN 00157279 (F119). Annual AFSA's [American Foreign Service Association] foreign service tax guide.
>
> *Fortune*, 1930–   . Chicago: Time. Biweekly. ISSN 00158259 (F120). Investor's guide.
>
> *Fuel Oil and Oil Heat with Air*, 1922–   . Fairfield, NJ: Industry Publications. Monthly. ISSN 10609725 (F121). Oil heat buyer's guide.
>
> *In Business*, 1979–   . Emmaus, PA: J. G. Press. Bimonthly. ISSN 01902458 (F122). "Directory of Environmental Entrepreneurs" and "Directory of Green Retailers."
>
> *Inc.: The Magazine for Growing Companies*, 1979–   . Boulder, CO: Tech-

nology Publishing. Monthly. ISSN 01628968 (F123). "Buyer's Guide to Office Equipment and Technology."

Institutional Investor (listed earlier, see F107). Directories on various topics, such as pensions, foreign exchange, public finance, and defined contributions.

International Management, 1947– . Surrey, England: Reed Business Publishing. Monthly. ISSN 00207888 (F124). "The Top 500 Industrial Companies."

Mergers and Acquisitions, 1965– . Philadelphia: MLR Enterprises. Bimonthly. ISSN 00260010 (F125). "M&A [Mergers & Acquisitions] Rosters;" "Middle Market Profile."

Office, The, 1935– . Stamford, CT: Office Publications. Monthly. ISSN 00300128 (F126). Buyers' guides to copying equipment, PC and business computers, facsimile systems, telephone systems, electronic typewriters, shredders, copier control systems, dictation equipment, and so on.

Personnel Journal, 1922– . Costa Mesa, CA: ACC Communication. Monthly. ISSN 00315745 (F127). Guides to software, recruitment markets, and so on.

Personnel Management (listed earlier, see F109). Guides to parks and recreation, computers, and so on.

Progressive Grocer: The Magazine of Super Marketing, 1922– . Stamford, CT: Edgar B. Walzer. Monthly. ISSN 00330787 (F128). Manuals on supermarket sales and nonfoods sales.

Purchasing, 1915– . Boston: Cahners Publishing. Semimonthly. ISSN 00334448 (F129). Services available for freight hauling; and buyer's guide on writing instruments, facsimile, and so on.

Security: The Magazine for Security Decision Makers, 1964– . Denver, CO: Cahners Publishing. Monthly. ISSN 08908826 (F130). Product, service, supplies guide.

U.S. News & World Report, 1933– . New York: United States News & World Report. Weekly. ISSN 00415537 (F131). Annual money guide; career, and so on.

Education

American School and University, 1928/29– . New York: Buttenheim. Monthly. ISSN 00030945 (F132). "Resources for Educational Administrators." A listing of companies for product and service literature and information.

Educational Researcher, 1972– . Washington, DC: American Educational Research Association. 9/year. ISSN 0013189X (F133). "Directory of State and Regional Research Associations" and "Special Interest Group Annual Directory."

Intervention School and Clinic: An Interdisciplinary Journal Directed to an International Audience of Teachers and Specialists Working with Capable but Underachieving Children and Youth, 1965– . (Formerly:

Academic Therapy). 5/year. ISSN 0001396X (F134). "Tips for Teachers" on practical teaching suggestions.

Media and Methods, 1964– . Philadelphia: Society of Educators. 5/year. ISSN 00256897 (F135). "Who's Who in Educational Media"; "The Media and Methods Buyer's Guide"; and buyer's guides to computers, networking, and so on.

NCA *Quarterly: A Publication of the North Central Association of Colleges and Schools*, 1988– . Boulder, CO: The Association. Quarterly. ISSN 10433511 (F136). "Directory of Accredited Schools and Candidates for Accreditation."

Law

ABA Journal: The Lawyer's Magazine. 1915– . Chicago: American Bar Association. Monthly. ISSN 07470088 (F137). Annual legal software directory.

Compleat Lawyer, The, 1984– . Chicago: American Bar Association. Quarterly. ISSN 07419066 (F138). Tips for general practice on a variety of subjects, including legal publications, databases, research techniques, and landlord-tenant matters.

Legal Assistant Today, 1983– . Costa Mesa, CA: James Publishing Group. Bimonthly. ISSN 07417772 (F139). "Legal Services Directory."

Mental and Physical Disability Law Reporter, 1976– . Washington, DC: American Bar Association. Bimonthly. ISSN 08837902 (F140). "Directory of Cases and Legislation."

Practical Lawyer, The, 1955– . Philadelphia: American Law Institute– American Bar Association, Committee on Continuing Professional Education. 8/year. ISSN 00326429 (F141). "Practice Checklists."

Student Lawyer (listed earlier see F74). Directory of schools arranged by country for studies in the summer; state listings of bar exam dates, requirements, and bar review courses.

Volta Review, The: Journal of the Alexander Graham Bell Association for the Deaf, 1899– . Washington, DC: Alexander Graham Bell Association for the Deaf. 7/year. ISSN 00428639 (F142). "Directory of Services."

Women Lawyers Journal, 1911– . Chicago: National Association of Women Lawyers. Quarterly. ISSN 00437468 (F143). "Roster of Private Practitioners."

Political Science

National Voter, The, 1951– . Washington, DC: League of Women Voters of the United States. 6/year. ISSN 00280372 (F144). "Listing of State Leagues."

PS: Political Science and Politics (listed earlier, see F93). "Listing of Regional and State Political Science Associations;" "Listing of Area Studies Organizations"; "Organizations Related to the Study of Political Science."

Rankings and Ratings

Business

Across the Board: Reporting to Management on Business Affairs, 1939– . New York: Conference Board. 10/year. ISSN 01471554 (F145). The top 100 corporations.

Advertising Age, 1930– . Chicago: Crain Communication. Semiweekly. ISSN 00018899 (F146). Rankings on national and international advertising agencies by gross income; top leading national advertisers, top events, top newsmakers, top products, and so on.

American Druggist, 1871– . New York: Stanley Siegelman. Monthly. ISSN 0002824X (F147). Top hospital OTC [Over the Counter] drugs; top prescription drugs dispensed in U.S.; most recommended by OTC pharmacists.

American Machinist, 1877– . New York: McGraw-Hill. Monthly. ISSN 00029858 (F148). Top machine tool companies.

American Printer (listed earlier, see F16). The AP [American Printer] top.

Best's Review (Life/Health Insurance Edition), v. 69, no. 9– , 1969– . Oldwick, NJ: A. M. Best. Monthly. ISSN 00059706 (F149). "Best's Rating Monitor," leading life companies.

Best's Review (Property/Casualty Insurance, v. 77, no. 1– , 1976– . Oldwick, NJ: A. M. Best. Quarterly. ISSN 01617745 (F150). "Best's Rating Monitor," leading property/casualty companies and groups, insurance premium distribution, auto insurance, property insurance, Workers' Compensation and general compensation insurance, and leading writers of medical malpractice insurance.

Black Enterprise, 1970– . New York: Earl G. Graves Publishing. Monthly. ISSN 00064165 (F151). The top B. E. [*Black Enterprise*] Industrial/ Service, the largest black-owned enterprises, the largest black-owned auto dealerships, the largest black banks and S&Ls, the largest black insurance companies, and the most black-owned franchise units.

Buildings: The Facilities Construction and Management Journal (listed earlier, see F113). Top product picks.

Business Week (listed earlier, see F114). Best of the year—winners and losers; best of the year in product design, advertising, entrepreneurs, innovation, and public service; best mutual funds; corporate scoreboard; executive pay; best small corporations; best product designs; the corporate elite; and best-performing information technology companies.

Chain Store Age: The Magazine for Retail Executives (listed earlier, see F115). The top executives, the nation's top retailers, and the top discount stores.

Drug and Cosmetic Industry (listed earlier, see F116). "Package of the Month."

Euromoney: The Monthly Journal of International Money and Capital Mar-

kets (listed earlier, see F117). "The European Five Hundred," "The World's Top Money Managers," "The Asian One Hundred."

Forbes (listed earlier, see F118). Rankings of American industry, performance ratings of mutual funds, Forbes 500 executive compensation, Forbes international 500 survey, 100 largest foreign investments in the U.S., 100 largest U.S. multinationals, 100 top U.S.-traded foreign stocks, best small companies in America, 400 largest privately owned companies in U.S., America's 400 richest people.

Fortune (listed earlier, see F120). The top airlines, best cities for business, "America's Fastest Risers," "The Global 500," "The Fortune 500."

Inc.: The Magazine for Growing Companies (listed earlier, see F123). Executive compensation survey, the fastest-growing cities in America, "The Inc. 500: America's Fastest Growing Private Companies."

Institutional Investor: The Magazine for Finance and Investment (listed earlier, see F107). "Investor Relations: The Best Annual Reports," "Ranking the World's Largest Bank," rankings of America's top money managers.

Mergers and Acquisitions (listed earlier, see F125). Top mergers and acquisitions, largest transactions.

Progressive Grocer: The Magazine of Super Marketing (listed earlier, see F128). "Store of the Month," "Outstanding Independents."

Purchasing (listed earlier, see F129). "Masters Ranking Guide."

Stores, 1912–   . New York: NRMA Enterprises. Monthly. ISSN 00391867 (F152). Top specialty stores, top department stores, and "Best Stores of the Year."

U.S. News & World Report (listed earlier, see F131). Rankings of the top small stocks and the best mutual funds.

Education

Business Week (listed earlier, see F114). The Best B-Schools, a biannual.

U. S. News and World Report (listed earlier, see F131). Best colleges, best graduate schools, best tuition values, and career guide.

Political Science

Human Rights Internet Reporter (listed earlier, see F57). UNDP [United Nations Development Program] World Freedom Index.

NOTES

1. Michael Gorman and Paul W. Winkler, eds., *Anglo-American Cataloging Rules*, 2nd ed., prepared by the American Library Association and others (Chicago: American Library Association, 1978), p. 570.

2. *Anglo-American Cataloging Rules*, prepared by the American Library Association and others (North American edition) (Chicago: American Library Association, 1967), p. 345.

3. For a history of *Ulrich's*, refer to Charles D. Patterson, "Origins of Systematic Serials Control: Remembering Carolyn Ulrich," *Reference Service Review* 16 (1988): 79–92.

4. Tze-chung Li, "Reference Sources in Periodicals: A Demographic Study," *Journal of Information, Communication, and Library Science* 3, no. 4 (1997): 25.

5. Ibid.

Chapter 7

Government Publications

This chapter deals with primarily U.S. government publications, with some reference to foreign and international government publication sources. A government publication, or government document, may be defined as "informational matter which is published as an individual document at government expense or as required by law."[1] By this definition, any work published at government expense by either private or public printer is a government publication.

THE GOVERNMENT PRINTING OFFICE

Most of the publications of federal agencies are produced by the Government Printing Office (GPO). The Government Printing Office, created as a part of the Legislative Branch by Congressional Joint Resolution 25 of June 23, 1860, is charged with executing orders for printing and binding placed by Congress and the departments, independent establishments, and agencies of the federal government, distributing government publications as required by law, and printing, for sale to the public, documents that are not of a confidential nature. Its activities are detailed in the Printing Act of January 12, 1895, as amended. Government publications cover practically all fields of human knowledge, in various forms and different media, and for all walks of life. The issuance of some documents is expressly stipulated by the Constitution, laws, and regulations. The Printing Act requires the Superintendent of Documents to publish such documents as the *Monthly Catalog* and the *Congressional Record*, both noted later.

In 1994, the Government Printing Office developed its Web site, listed here, under the Government Printing Office Electronic Information Access Enhancement Act of 1993.[2]

> GPO Access. Washington, DC: Government Printing Office. http://www.access.gpo.gov/su_docs/ (G1)

The Web site consists of Access to Government Information Products, Services Available to Federal Agencies, Business and Contacting Opportunities, Employment Opportunities, and Establishing Links to Documents in GPO WAIS Databases. GPO Access provides free electronic access to information products of the federal government.

Services of GPO Access may be divided into the following categories: (1) government information databases, (2) individual federal agency files for download, and (3) tools for finding government information. Government information databases are referred to for popular regulatory materials, critical congressional materials, important business materials, and useful reference tools. They include the Constitution of the United States of America, *United States Code, Federal Register, Code of Federal Regulations, Congressional Record*, Congressional Bills, Congressional Calendars, Congressional Directory, Congressional Documents, *Congressional Record Index*, Congressional Reports, the Budget of the United States, Campaign Reform Hearings, *Commerce Business Daily, Economic Indicators, Economic Report of the President, Government Manual, House Rules Manual, Senate Manual*, Supreme Court Decisions, and many others. They are mostly current.

Federal Web sites hosted by GPO Access include the Equal Employment Opportunity Commission, Federal Labor Relations Authority, Merit Systems Protection Board, Office of Compliance, Office of Government Ethics, Office of Special Counsel, Office of Thrift Supervision, and many others. Over twenty databases are available online via GPO Access. GPO Access also provides links to federal agency Internet sites and Pathway Indexer, an indexed search of more than 1,350 official U.S. federal agency and military Internet sites. One of the links is to some 500 certified electronic federal depository libraries by state and area code.

The Federal Bulletin Board (FBB) lists over 4,500 individual federal agency files for free download. Tools for finding government information include *Monthly Catalog of U.S. Government Publications (MOCAT)*, noted later, for locating titles available through the Federal Depository Library Program; the Sales Product Catalog (SPC) for finding and purchasing currently available products, finding titles for individual federal agency files available for download; the Government Information Locator Service (GILS), for identifying and searching federal information resources; and Locate Federal Depository Libraries for locating federal depository libraries by state or area.

GPO Access Government CD-ROM Publications lists GPO's CD-ROM products. Products related to the social sciences include Congressional Record, Education Statistics, National Criminal Justice Database, Survey of Current Business, U.S. Code, and U.S. Foreign Affairs, some of which are noted in the following chapters.

Free text and phrase (in quotation marks) can be searched. The Boolean logical operators, the proximity operator ADJ, and word truncation are available for searching. The number of records retrieved defaults to 40, with a maximum number of 200.

DEPOSITORY LIBRARIES

Many libraries are designated by law as depositories. They receive government publications free but are obligated to make them available for the free use of the general public and not to dispose of them without authorization. The law provides that a depository may dispose of government publications after retention for five years, if it is served by a regional depository library, and that a depository that is not served by a regional depository library or that itself is a regional library shall retain government publications permanently except superseded publications or those issued later in bound form; these may be discarded as authorized by the Superintendent of Documents.

There are two less known categories of depository libraries: Patent and Trademark Depository Libraries and the Bureau of the Census Depository Libraries. Since numerous government publications are in digital format readily accessible on the Internet, users may not use a depository library for access to them.

In each state, there are libraries designated as depositories for state government publications. The United Nations also designates libraries worldwide as depositories to receive its publications. In the United States, over 40 libraries in 27 states, the District of Columbia, and Puerto Rico are United Nations depositories, where United Nations documents are available for use.

GUIDES

Of all the guides to U.S. government publications, this work is considered a reference classic:

> *Government Publications and Their Use*, 2nd rev. ed. Lawrence F. Schmeckebier and Roy B. Eastin. Washington, DC: The Brookings Institution, 1969. 502 p. (G2)

It is intended "to describe the basic guides to government publications, to indicate the uses and limitations of available indexes, catalogs, and bibliographies, to explain the systems of numbering and methods of titling, to call attention to certain outstanding compilations or series of publications, and to indicate how the publications may be obtained" (Foreword). An important feature of the work is its thorough description of contents, series and subseries, history of editions and changes, problems of arrangement and citations, defects and usefulness of a particular item, and the way to find materials under seemingly confused headings.

Guides for current interest include:

> *Government Information on the Internet*. Greg R. Notess. Lanham, MD: Bernan Press, 1997. 778 p. ISBN 0890590818. (G3)
>
> *Guide to Popular U.S. Government Publications*. 4th ed. Frank W. Hoffman and Richard J. Wood. Englewood, CO: Libraries Unlimited, 1997. 285 p. ISBN 1563084627. (G4)
>
> *Introduction to United States Government Information Sources*. 5th ed. Joe Morehead. Englewood, CO: Libraries Unlimited, 1996. 333 p. ISBN 1563084856. (G5)
>
> *Locating United States Government Information: A Guide to Sources*. 2nd ed. Edward Herman. Buffalo, NY: Hein, 1999. 580 p. ISBN 1575882035. (G6)

In contrast to the thorough analysis of *Government Publications and Their Use*, Morehead's *Introduction* is characterized by its clarity and conciseness as a good introductory guide to the use and administration of government documents. The book, formerly *Introduction to United States Public Documents*, in eleven chapters, provides an account of the general and specialized sources, in print and nonprint formats, that comprise the bibliographic textual structure of federal government information (Preface). It begins with a new chapter on public access in the electronic age, followed by two chapters (2–4) on Government Printing Office programs and services, depository libraries, and general bibliographic services. Chapters 5–8 discuss publications of three branches of the U.S. government. Statistical sources, technical reports, and geographical sources are presented in chapters 9–11. Over 60 figures complement the text. There are three indexes: personal name, title/series, and subject.

Locating United States Government Information contains nineteen chapters: chapters 1–3, general indexes; chapters 4–8, congressional publications, including three major electronic resources (Library of Congress, *GPO Access*, and *Thomas*) on the Internet; chapters 9–10 dealing with index, guides to legislation, and regulations; chapters 11–15, statistics sources including census information; chapter 16, technical reports; chapters 17–18, Freedom of Information Act, Privacy Act, and acquisitions of government publications; and chapter 19, directories to government offices. The number of sample pages as illustrations is substantial. Most chapters include exercises and answers.

More than 1,300 entries are contained in *Guide to Popular U.S. Government Publications*. It is an annotated, classified bibliography, with no mention of the availability of digital format information. There are a title index and a subject index.

Government Information on the Internet contains 1,282 entries of Internet resources, including both U.S. governmental and nongovernmental sites, with stress on the federal government. Major sites for state government, international and intergovernmental organization, and foreign countries are also briefly listed. Entries are arranged by subject and agencies into 18 chapters in an alphabetical order, including agriculture, business and economics, census and other statistics, Congress, education, environment, health sciences, international, legal information, libraries, popular government reference sources, social services, state governments, the White House, and so on.

For each entry, if complete, are given entry number, title, sponsoring agency, primary access, alternative access method, resource summary subject headings, and SuDoc numbers. The resource summary provides information on organization, principal features, menu items, and significant links.

The primary access lists URLs that include e-mail, Gopher, FTP, Telnet, and Web. The alternative access simply lists other Internet sites of the primary access. In some cases, it gives the Internet sites of other agencies or organizations, such as the *GPO Access* (noted earlier) gateway; there are thirteen sites in the alternative access, including eleven institutions of higher learning.

BIBLIOGRAPHIES OF BIBLIOGRAPHIES

Bibliographies of bibliographies of government publications may be found in general bibliographies, indexes, guides, catalogs and the like mentioned elsewhere in this chapter. Bibliographies listed in the *Monthly Catalog*, noted later, for instance, can be located through the use of its subject index under "bibliography."

BIBLIOGRAPHIES

United States

General

Bibliographic Guide to Government Publications—U.S., 1974– . Thorndike, ME: G. K. Hall. Annual. ISSN 03602796. (G7)

The former title of the *Bibliography* is *Government Publications Guide*, which includes both U.S. and foreign publications. Since 1975, it has been published separately as *Bibliographical Guide to Government Publications-U.S.* and *Bibliographical Guide to Government Publications—Foreign*, listed later. These two guides are arranged in a single alphabetical order by main entries, added entries, titles, series titles, and subject headings. These guides are parts of G. K. Hall's *Bibliographic Guides Series* mentioned in Chapter 3. The *Guide—U.S.* covers federal, regional, and state government documents.

Federal

The bibliographical coverage of U.S. government publications is an unbroken chain from 1774 to the present, as shown in the following titles:

> *A Descriptive Catalogue of the Government Publications of the United States, September 5, 1774–March 4, 1881.* Benjamin Perley Poore. Washington, DC: GPO, 1885. 1,392 p. (48th Cong., 2nd sess. Senate Misc. doc. no. 67) Reprint ed., Ann Arbor, MI: Edwards, 1983; New York: Johnson Reprint, 1962. (G8)
>
> *Comprehensive Index of the Publications of the United States Government, 1881–1893.* John G. Ames, Chief of the Document Division, Department of the Interior. Washington, DC: GPO, 1935. 1,590 p. (58th Cong., 2nd sess. House Misc. doc. no. 754). Reprint ed., Ann Arbor, MI: Edwards, 1953; New York: Johnson Reprint, 1970. (G9)
>
> *Checklist of United States Public Documents, 1789–1909.* 3rd ed. Washington, DC: GPO, 1911. v. 1. 1707 p. Reprint ed., Ann Arbor, MI: Edwards, 1953; New York: Kraus, 1962. (G10)
>
> *Catalog of the Public Documents of Congress and Other Departments of the Government of the United States for the Period March 4, 1893–December 31, 1940.* Washington, DC: GPO, 1896–1945. vols. 1–25. (G11)
>
> *Monthly Catalog of United States Government Publications,* 1895– . Washington, DC: GPO, 1895– . Monthly. Print & digital. (G12)

Poore's *Catalogue* presents a chronological list of documents, most of which are congressional publications issued from the first Continental Congress to the date of adjournment of the 46th Congress. Poore is continued by the Ames *Comprehensive Index*, which lists publications covering the period from the 47th to the 52nd Congress in three-column format. Like Poore, Ames stresses congressional documents. For publications of other branches of government, Poore and Ames are supplemented by the *Checklist of United States Public Documents*, a shelf list arranged by issuing offices.

Catalog of the Public Documents of Congress and Other Departments of the Government of the United States, generally referred to as *Document*

Catalog, distinguished by its detailed treatment and dictionary arrangement, is one of the best bibliographies of government publications, listing both congressional and departmental publications. It supersedes the *Monthly Catalog* for the period covered. Since the demise of the *Document Catalog* in 1940, the *Monthly Catalog (MOCAT)* has been the basic, indispensable bibliography of government publications.

In 1976, the *Monthly Catalog* began to use *Anglo-American Cataloguing Rules* and Library of Congress main entries. Subjects are derived from the *Library of Congress Subject Headings*. The *Monthly Catalog* is now produced in four formats: hard copy, CD-ROM, online database (*GPO Monthly Catalog*), and tape (*GPO Cataloging Tapes*). In 1996, with the introduction of the CD-ROM version, its hard-copy version provides only short entries and "Title Keyword Index." Only CD-ROM, online, and tape versions carry traditional features of long entries.

The online version of the *Monthly Catalog* is GPO *Monthly Catalog*, 1976– , (G13) marketed via Dialog (File 66), Ovid, and FirstSearch. As an extended version of the hard-copy counterpart, it provides longer entries. A sample entry includes title, source, conference title, conference year, conference location, series, publisher, report number, call number (LC, Dewey, Local), language, document type, geographic location, note, and descriptor. Its Web site, as part of *GPO Access*, noted earlier, provides two types of cataloging information: TEXT and HTML. TEXT is for full cataloging record and HTML for full cataloging record with hyperlink to an electronic document.

The *Monthly Catalog* is complemented by *GPO Sales Publications Reference File (PRF)* (G14) and *U.S. Government Books: Publications for Sale by the Government Printing Office* (quarterly, ISSN 07342764) (G15). *PRF*, published in two versions, microfiche and magnetic tape, serves as a catalog of publications in print. Its online version is *GPO Publications Reference File*, marketed through Dialog (File 166) (G16). It indexes public documents currently for sale, and forthcoming and recently out-of-print publications. Data include availability, prices, and stock numbers. *U.S. Government Books* lists books for sale in all fields.

For government reference sources, there is:

Government Reference Books, 1968/69– . Englewood, CO: Libraries Unlimited. Biennial. ISSN 00725188. (G17)

The thirteenth edition of *Government Reference Books*, compiled by LeRoy C. Schwarzkopf (1994, 370 p., ISBN 5630818141) annotates 1,120 titles that have been distributed to depository libraries. Entries are grouped into four parts: general references, social sciences, science and technology, and arts and humanities. The book contains over 650 titles in the field of the social sciences. There is an author/title/subject index. The work used to include serials. Now most serials are included in a companion volume, *Government Reference Serials*, also compiled by LeRoy C. Schwarzkopf (Englewood, CO: Libraries Unlimited, 1988, 344 p., ISBN 0872874516) (G18) that lists 583 titles that have been distributed to depository libraries.

States

For a long time, the *Monthly Checklist of State Publications*, v. 1– , 1910–1994 (U.S. Library of Congress, Exchange and Gift Division, Washington, DC: GPO, monthly) (G19) served as the only extensive bibliography of state government publications. It records state documents received by the Library of Congress, being a holding list of the Library. Monographs, including those in series and annual publications, are arranged by state and issuing agency. Periodicals are listed semiannually in the June and December issues, with the December list cumulative for the year. An annual index to the monographs is published early the following year. It is no longer published. The user may use state Web sites via *GPO Access*, noted earlier, to locate some of the state publications.

Serials

> *Guide to U.S. Government Publications*. Donna Andriot, ed. Manassas, VA: Documents Index, 1996. 1,629 p. (G20)
> *Monthly Catalog Periodical Supplement, 1977–* . Washington, DC: GPO. Annual. Print & digital. (G21)
> *U.S. Government Periodicals Index*, 1970– . Bethesda, MD: Congressional Information Service. Quarterly with annual cumulation. ISSN 10763163. (G22)

Andriot's *Guide* is a listing of serials, periodicals and reference tools published by U.S. government agencies. More than 35,000 entries are arranged by agencies, some with concise annotations. It features "the Agency Class Chronology which gives the complete history of current Class number assignments and traces them back historically to previous number assignments" (Preface). There are three indexes: agency, title, and keyword in title.

For a listing of periodicals published by U. S. government agencies, refer to *Monthly Catalog Periodicals Supplement*, a part of the *Monthly Catalog*. The *1998 Supplement* (36, 340 p.) includes serials issued three or more times a year. It also provides information on classification changes, ceased publications, periodicals made available online, publications no longer listed for other reasons, and so on. There are six indexes: author, title, subject, series/report, stock number, and title keyword.

Formerly *Index to U.S. Government Periodicals*, the *U.S. Government Periodicals Index* covers approximately 11,000 articles from more than 180 periodicals. Normally indexed materials include technical, research, and policy analysis; papers and reports; general interest feature articles; historical analysis; military doctrine, military operations, profiles of activities of U.S. citizens abroad; safety procedures and illustrative accident accounts; interviews; speeches; congressional testimony; scientific correspondence; conference reports; book reviews; photo essays; poems; and periodical cumulative indexes. There are two indexes: subjects and names. It is also available on CD-ROM and magnetic tape.

International

> *Bibliographic Guide to Government Publications—Foreign,* 1974– . Thorndike, ME: G. K. Hall. Annual. ISSN 0360280X. (G23)
>
> *Guide to Country Information in International Governmental Organization Publications.* Marian Shaaban, ed. Chicago: American Library Association, Government Documents Round Table, 1996. 343 p. (G24)
>
> *International Information: Documents, Publications, and Electronic Information of International Governmental Organizations.* 3rd ed. Peter I. Hajnal, ed. Englewood, CO: Libraries Unlimited, 1997. 528 p. ISBN 1563081474. (G25)
>
> *UNDOC: Current Index,* 1950– . New York: United Nations. Quarterly with annual cumulation on microfiche. ISSN 02505584. (G26)

The *Guide—Foreign* is a companion of the *Guide—U.S.* noted earlier. The 1997 edition (1998, 2 vols., ISBN 0783881657) includes "public documents of all national governments so far as they are published or attainable, official gazettes, parliamentary debates and papers, censuses, statistical annuals and reports, and journals and monographs relating to major activities of governmental departments and agencies" (Introduction). The bibliography is based on materials cataloged at the Library of Congress and the New York Public Library.

Guide to Country Information is a bibliography of publications since 1988, arranged by seven geographical areas and formatted into eight sections: 1, Worldwide/Multiregional; 2, Africa; 3, Asia/Pacific; 4, Europe; 5, Latin America/Caribbean; 6, Middle East; 7, North America; and 8, Guides, Catalogs, and Indexes. Within each of the seven geographical sections, publications are arranged by subject and within subject by issuing agency. It is complemented by the *Guide to Official Publications of Foreign Countries* (Gloria Westfall, ed., Chicago: American Library Association, Government Documents Round Table, 1990, 359 p.) (G27).

International Information is both a directory and a bibliography, consisting of fourteen chapters in three parts. Part 1, "Institutions," has seven chapters on the international setting, the United Nations, the European Union, Organization for Economic Co-operation and Development, the

League of Nations, International Development Research, and the G7. Part 2, "Resources," in five chapters deals with electronic and print resources, the United Nations Scholars Work Station at Yale University, and resources of non-IGO organizations. Part 3 comprises two chapters, which are devoted to bibliographical processes. The fourteen chapters are contributed by nineteen authors, including the editor. It concludes with a bibliography, not annotated, and an index.

UNDOC is a successor to *Checklist of United Nations Documents, 1946–1949, United Nations Documents Index,* 1950–1973, and *UNDEX.* It lists all documents and publications except those of a confidential nature. *UNDOC* consists of two parts: Part 1 contains Documents and Publications; Personal/Corporate Name Index, and Title Index; and Part 2 is the Subject Index. It covers documents and publications received by the Dag Hammarskjöld Library, including reports and studies, resolutions and decisions, draft resolutions, meeting records, and miscellaneous records. Press releases and most conference room papers are excluded.

DIRECTORIES

> *Directory of Government Document Collections and Librarians.* 6th ed. Judy Horn, ed. Bethesda, MD: Congressional Information Service, 1991. 650 p. ISBN 0912380152. (G28)

The directory consists of ten sections: (1) Guide to libraries, collections, and staff. This section lists libraries in geo-alphabetical order by state, city, and institution, and by library within an institution. Each entry description includes directory and collection information and staff. (2) Library index—an alphabetical listing. (3) Documents collections index—in four subsections: state, local, international, and foreign. (4) Special collections index alphabetically arranged by subject. (5) Library school instructors, government documents. (6) State document authorities, an alphabetical listing, by state, of agencies and individuals responsible for administering their respective state collections programs. (7) State data centers, an alphabetical listing by state of the Bureau of the Census State Data Centers and individuals responsible for providing access to census data. (8) Personal name index. (9) Other names to know—retired documents librarians and other librarians involved in government document activities. (10) Association and government offices. The appendix includes subject terms, agency names, and acronyms, and a data collection questionnaire.

PUBLICATIONS OF THE BRANCHES OF GOVERNMENT

The remainder of this chapter will discuss briefly government publications of the three branches of government. An important reference to government agencies, their creation, authority, organization, activities and chief officials is:

United States Government Manual, 1935–   . U.S. Office of the Federal Register, National Archives and Records Administration. Washington, DC: GPO, Annual. Print & digital. (G29)

The *Manual* has in the main three parts: Legislative Branch, Judicial Branch, and the Executive Branch, preceded by the American Constitution. It also contains selected multilateral organizations, selected bilateral organizations, and four appendixes: standard federal regions, commonly used abbreviations and acronyms, terminated and transferred agencies, and agencies appearing in the *Code of Federal Regulations*. The online version of the *Manual*, the *United States Government Manual Online* (1995–   ) can also be accessed through the *GPO Access* Web site noted earlier.

Publications of the Legislative Branch

The Congress consists of the Senate and the House of Representatives. Article 1 of the Constitution provides that "all legislative powers herein granted shall be vested in a Congress of the United States." But the function of Congress is not limited to making law. The Congress is also charged with non-lawmaking functions, such as constituent, judicial, electoral, inquisitorial, and other administrative functions. In lawmaking, the Congress shares with the President the legislative power, which is deliberately divided. Every law and every joint resolution require the President's signature.

Congress does its main work through committees. Committee reports are an indispensable tool for gaining insight into congressional activities. There are four kinds of committees. The Standing Committees are the most important in legislation. Joint Committees consist of members of both bouses. Conference Committees are temporary committees formed for the purpose of ironing out differences between the two houses. Special or Select Committees are also temporary committees to conduct special investigation of matters not directly related to legislation.

The definition of congressional publications is confusing. Some identify congressional publications with the congressional set. Others consider congressional publications as those published under the authority of Congress as a whole, of either house, or of any committee of either house. Since the publication of hearings is not authorized by Congress, they are technically not congressional publications. For the purpose of this book, congressional publications are defined broadly to include any publication authorized by or originated in Congress. Space limitations do not allow listing all congressional publications. Manuals, proceedings and debates, bills, journals of both houses, the congressional set, hearings, prints, and some other publications will be briefly mentioned.

General

> *Congressional Universe.* Bethesda, MD: Congressional Information Service. http://web.lexis-nexis.com/congcomp (G30)
>
> *Thomas: Legislative Information of the Internet.* Washington, DC: Library of Congress. http://thomas.loc.gov (G31)

Congressional Universe, formerly *Congressional Compass,* provides information published by or about Congress. Sources are grouped into several areas, such as Congressional Publications; Bills, Laws and Regulations; Members and Committees, Inside Washington, Hot Topics in Congress, and List of Links. Reports, documents, committee prints, testimony, and bills are in full text. Members and Committees includes biographical sketches and committee assignments. List of Links lists annotated links to other Web sites about the American political process. Web sites are arranged in categories, including Congressional Sites, Political Parties, News and Other Organizations Sites, and University Sites.

Most sources are from recent years. They can be found on other Web sites, such as *GPO Access,* noted earlier, or *Thomas,* noted next. But, CIS/ Indexing and abstracts, CIS legislative histories, Congressional committee prints, Congressional testimony, Congressional committee schedules, and voting records are unique.

Thomas, constructed in 1995, provides access to congressional information grouped into six categories: Congress Now, Bills, *Congressional Record* (including Résumés of Congressional Activity) and *Annals of Congress,* Committee Information, The Legislative Process, and Historical Documents. The category Bills includes Bill Summary and Status, Bill Text, Votes, Public Laws by Law Number, and Major Legislation. Committee Information consists of Committee Reports, Committee Home Pages, and House Committees. *Thomas* also links to other *Thomas* home pages. *Thomas* will also be mentioned in Chapter 14.

Indexes

The following are three commercially published indexes to congressional publications:

> *CIS/Index,* 1970– . Washington, DC: Congressional Information Service. Monthly with quarterly and final cumulations. ISSN 00078514. Print & digital. (G32)
>
> *CIS U.S. Serial Set Index, 1789–1969.* Washington, DC: Congressional In-

formation Service, 1975–1977. 12 parts; 36 vols. ISBN 0912380268.
Print & digital. (G33)
Congressional Index, 75th Congress, 1937/38– . Chicago: Commerce Clearing House, 1957– . Weekly throughout session. Looseleaf. (G34)

According to the Congressional Information Service, there are 910,000 pages in 4,400 titles of congressional publications a year. *CIS/Index* or the *Index to Publications of the United States Congress* is intended to include practically every document issued by Congress. It consists of two sections. Section 1 is abstracts of documents issued by Congress during the previous month. Section 2 contains the Index of Subjects and Names, Index of Titles, Index of Bill Numbers, List of Reports Received by Number, List of Documents Received by Number; and List of Senate Hearings by Number, List of Senate Prints by Number. There are two appendixes: 1, Index of Committee and Subcommittee Chairmen, and 2, List of Bibliographic Date Additions and Revisions.

Its *Annual*, the *CIS/Annual*, contains materials that the monthly and quarterly *CIS/Index* does not list. The 1997 *CIS/Annual* (3 vols., ISBN 0886924308) consists of abstracts, index, and legislative histories volumes. The Index volume contains Index of Subjects and Names, Supplementary Indexes (indexes of titles, bill numbers, report numbers, document numbers, Senate hearings numbers and Senate print numbers), Index of Superintendent of Documents Numbers, and Index of Committee and Subcommittee Chairmen. The Legislative volume contains Table of Public Laws and Legislative Histories. CIS also publishes four-year cumulations. Full text of documents are available on microfiche. *CIS/Index* and *CIS/Annual* are available online via Lexis-Nexis.

Beginning in 1989, CIS is marketing *Congressional Masterfile 2* (G35), the *CIS/Index* on CD-ROM, from 1970 to the present with quarterly updates. The CD-ROM for pre-1970 congressional indexes is noted next.

A retrospective index to more than 325,000 individual titles and more than 11 million pages in 14,000 separate serial set volumes is the *CIS U.S. Serial Set Index*. Each of the twelve parts contains an index of subjects and keywords and finding lists. The finding lists include (1) Private Relief and Related Actions—Index of Names of Individuals and Organizations, (2) Numerical List of Reports and Documents, and (3) Schedule of Serial Volumes. Its companion work is the full-text collection of the serial set on microfiche, *CIS U.S. Serial Set on Microfiche, 1789–1969*.

Beginning in 1989, the *CIS U.S. Serial Set Index* is available on CD-ROM as *Congressional Masterfile 1* (G36). *Congressional Masterfile 1* includes four CIS retrospective indexes: *CIS U.S. Serial Set Index, CIS U.S. Congressional Committee Hearings* (G37), *CIS Index to Unpublished*

U.S. Senate Committee Hearings (G38), and *CIS U.S. Congressional Committee Prints Index* (G39).

Congressional Index in two volumes reports twice a week during weeks when Congress meets. The first volume includes biographies of members of the Senate and deals primarily with Senate actions including hearings, bills, resolutions, status of bills, and voting records. The section "Status of Senate Bills" reports all legislative actions on bills, from hearings to enactment. Also included are reorganization plans, treaties, nominations, and enactments-vetoes. The second volume deals with the House, including biographies of members of the House and House hearings, bills, resolutions, status of bills, and voting records. At the end is the "Last Report Letter," which contains summaries of legislation highlights of the preceding week. Following these summaries is a list showing which measures were acted upon during the week. Each section has an introduction with explanations of terms. There are a subject index (including headline legislation) and an author index. One of its most useful features is the summaries of public bills and resolutions.

Congressional Index is an index primarily to legislation, providing quick reference to the status of all legislation pending in Congress, with brief reports on the progress of public bills and resolutions from introduction to final disposition. It thus differs from *CIS/Index* both in purpose and stress. Subscribers to the *Congressional Index* receive the Friday newsletter, *The Week in Congress* (G40), prepared each week during which Congress is in session.

Manuals

Constitutions, Jefferson's Manual, and Rules of the House of Representatives. U.S. Congress, House. Washington, DC: GPO, 1824–   . Print & digital. (G41)

Senate Manual, Containing the Standing Rules, Orders, Laws, and Resolutions Affecting the Business of the United States Senate; Jefferson's Manual; Declaration of Independence; Articles of Confederation; Constitution of the United States, etc. U.S. Congress, Senate. Washington, DC: GPO, 1820–   . Print & digital. (G42)

These manuals are two official handbooks of the organization, procedures, and operation of the Congress. The *House Manual*, a biennial, "contains the fundamental source material for parliamentary procedure in the House of Representatives; the Constitution of the United States; applicable provisions of *Jefferson's Manual; Rules of the House*; provisions of law having the force of a rule of the House; and pertinent decisions of the Speakers and other presiding officers of the House and of the committees of the whole which have interpreted the Rules and other procedural authority used in the House of Representatives." A summary work is *House Practice: A Guide to the Rules, Precedents and Procedures of the House* (William Holmes Brown, Washington, DC: GPO, 1996, 536 p., ISBN 016053786X) (G43).

The title of the *Senate Manual*, issued for each new Congress, is self-explanatory. It also contains historical documents and statistical data. Both House and Senate manuals can be accessed through the *GPO Access* Web site.

Procedures and Debates

> *Congressional Record*, March 4, 1873–   . U.S. Congress. Washington, DC:
> GPO. Print & digital. (G44)

For records before 1873, reference should be made to *Debates and Proceedings* (also known by its binder's title, *Annals of Congress*, 1st Congress–18th Congress, 1789–1834, 42 vols. (Publ. 1834–1856) (G45), *Register of Debates*, 18th Congress, 2nd sess.–25th Congress, 1st sess., 1824–1837, 14 vols. in 29 (Publ. 1825–1837) (G46), *Congressional Globe*, 23rd Congress–42nd Congress, 1833–1873, 46 vols. in 108 (Publ. 1834–1873) (G47).

The *Record*, published daily when Congress is in session, records congressional proceedings and debates divided into four sections: Proceedings of the House, Proceedings of the Senate, Extensions of Remarks, and Daily Digest. Each section is in consecutive number designated by H, S, E, and D respectively. The section, "Extension of Remarks," formerly the appendix until the 90th Congress, is for members of Congress to extend their remarks. The *Daily Digest* section serves as a summary of congressional activities, presenting chamber actions, committee meetings, bills signed by the President, and other information. The semimonthly and annual indexes consist of two parts: an index to proceedings and the extensions of remarks and an index to the history of bills and resolutions. The annual volume cumulates the daily *Congressional Record* in one numerical order, arranged chronologically. The Daily Digest section is cumulated in a separate volume.

The *Record* purports to be a verbatim record, though in fact it is by no means a true one.[3] Speeches never delivered appear as if they had. Speeches actually delivered may have been substantially rewritten or deleted. Materials printed in the daily *Record* disappear in the bound volume. There are justifications for such a practice.[4] (1) It helps to conserve precious House time. Thus the *House Manual*, Section 929, clearly stipulates that "leave to print in the *Congressional Record* shall be exercised without unreasonable freedom." (2) It permits members to correct any grammatical errors and to modify impolitic statements made in the stress of debate. (3) It provides one more means by which constituents can gain insight into the thinking of their representatives. *Congressional Record*, 1994 (103rd Congress, Second Session) forward, *Congressional Record Index*, 1983 forward, and *History of Bills* 1983 forward, can be accessed via *GPO Access*. *Congressional Record*, *Congressional Record Index*, and *Annals of Congress* can also be found in *Thomas* and *Congressional Universe*, both noted earlier.

Bills and Resolutions

In each house, legislative actions involve four types of proposals, numbered in series when introduced and having a distinctive designation for each house. A bill is a general statutory proposal designated as "H.R." or "S." according to the house in which the legislation is formally introduced. A resolution known as a simple resolution, designated as "H. Res." or "S. Res.," deals with matters that affect only the business, procedures, or organization of one house, such as the establishment of a committee, authorization to print a report, and the like. A joint resolution, designated as "H. J. Res." or "S. J. Res.," has the legal effect of law. With the exception of those proposing an amendment to the Constitution, a joint resolution requires the approval of both houses and the President. The distinction between a bill and a joint resolution is difficult. In general, a joint resolution deals with matters of incidental, unusual, or inferior purposes of legislating. A concurrent resolution, designated as "H. Con. Res." or "S. Con. Res.," is used for matters wholly within the authority of the Congress and in which both houses are interested. Concurrent resolutions are issued for such matters as joint sessions and the appointment of joint committees.[5] Its most significant use is provided for in various statutes that permit the Congress to disapprove presidential reorganization plans and to terminate certain powers granted to the President by statute.[6]

Current bills and resolutions are found in the *Congressional Record*, House and Senate *Journals, Calendars, Thomas*, and in:

> *Digest of Public General Bills and Selected Resolutions with Index*. 74th Cong., 2nd sess.– . U.S. Library of Congress, Legislative Reference Service. Washington, DC: GPO, 1936– . (G48)

The *Digest* is normally published during each session of a congress in two cumulative issues, with monthly supplements and a final edition at the conclusion of the session. According to its foreword, "the principle purpose of the *Digest* is to furnish in the form of a brief summary, the essential features of public bills and resolutions and changes made therein during the legislative process. It also indicates committee action, floor action and enactments and includes a subject, author, specific title and identical bill index."

Calendars

The calendar is an agenda and a list of the business of the Congress. According to Rule VIII of the *House Manual*, there are five legislative calendars: (1) the Union Calendar, which refers to "bills raising revenue, general appropriations bills, and bills of a public character directly or indirectly appropriating money or property"; (2) the House Calendar, including "all bills of a public character not raising revenue and not directly or indirectly appropriating money or property"; (3) the Private Calendar, listing "all bills of a private character"; (4) the Consent Calendar for noncontroversial bills; and (5) the Discharge Calendar, a listing of motions to discharge committees.

The Calendars of the United States House of Representatives and History of Legislation (G49), issued daily when the House is in session, contains calendars, public laws, private laws, reported bills sequentially referred, "Bills in Conference," and "Bills through Conference." The two sections on bills in conference and bills through conference are arranged by date with bill number, brief of title, conferees, report filed, and report agreed to. When tracing legislative history, of particular reference value are "History of Bills and Resolutions." For subjects of bills, consult the subject index printed in the Monday issue of the *Calendars*. It indexes all legislation of both houses that has been reported by the committees and acted upon by either or both houses and special House reports. Senate resolutions not of interest to the House are not included. The final edition of the *Calendars* categorizes the status of bills and resolutions of the session.

The Senate *Calendar of Business* (G50), also issued daily when the Senate is in session, carries under Rule VIII of the *Senate Manual* "General Orders," which lists in table order number, number and author of bills, the title and by whom reported. Also included are "Resolutions of Motions Over, Under the Rule," "Motions for Reconsideration," "Bills in Conference" arranged as in the *House Calendars*, and "Status of Appropriation Bills." Its inclusion in every issue of a list of Senate membership and of members of various committees is a handy source of reference. In tracing legislative history, however, the *Senate Calendar* is less helpful, for it does not have the numerical section of the *House Calendar*. Neither does it have a subject index and the final edition of the *House Calendar*. In the Senate, there is an additional calendar, the *Executive Calender* (G51), listing treaties and nominations from the president.

Both House and Senate *Calendars* are available on *GPO Access*. They are *Congressional Calendars—House* (G52), 104th Congress (1995–1996) forward, and *Congressional Calendars—Senate* (G53), 104th Congress (1995–1996) forward.

Journals

The *House Journal* (G54) and the *Senate Journal* (G55) are the only publications required by the Constitution. Article I, Section 5, of the Constitution provides that "each house shall keep a journal of its proceedings, and from time to time publish the same excepting such parts as may in their judgement require secrecy." The journals are day-to-day records of proceedings, including roll call, all motions, all actions taken, the votes, and messages from the President. They do not, however, contain debates, speeches, or explanatory remarks. For these materials, as well as the verbatim record of the proceedings, the *Congressional Record* should be consulted.

The House and Senate journals have indexes to names, subjects, titles, actions on bills and resolutions, and both list "History of Bills and Resolutions," which may also be found in the *Congressional Record*. In addition, the *House Journal* has proceedings of the House subsequent to *sine die* adjournment, rules of the House of Representatives, and questions of order decided in the House.

Proceedings of executive sessions are printed in the *Senate Executive Journal* (G56). The *Senate Executive Journal* is a separate series and is not a part of the congressional set, noted below. *Journals* of both houses and the *Senate Executive Journal* are available on *GPO Access*, noted earlier.

Congressional Set

The congressional set or serial set consists of House and Senate journals (not included in the set since the 83rd Congress, 1953), House and Senate reports, and House and Senate documents. Each bound volume is given a "serial number." Volumes are numbered consecutively beginning with the 15th Congress (1817). House and Senate documents and reports of the first fourteen Congresses (1789–1817) were reprinted in *American State Papers, Documents, Legislative and Executive, of the Congress of the United States* (Washington, DC: Gales and Seaton, 1832–1961) (G57).

The serial numbers of the congressional set are listed in the *Checklist* and *Document Catalog*, both noted earlier, and in *Numerical Lists and Schedule of Volumes of the Reports and Documents of Congress* (1933/34– . Washington, DC: GPO, 1934–) (G58). Since the demise of the *Document Catalog*, the *Numerical Lists* has been an indispensable tool for obtaining serial numbers of congressional reports and documents.

The formats of congressional reports and documents vary. Some are issued in bound volumes; others in unbound, or pamphlet form, later combined into the bound serial set. There is no clear-cut demarcation of materials to be printed as reports or documents. Materials may be printed in both reports and documents, such as *Impeachment of Richard M. Nixon*

(H. Doc. 93–339; H. Rep. 93–1305). A document series may include reprints of committee prints.

Reports

The *House Reports* (G59) and the *Senate Reports* (G60) in general include only reports of committees. Reports on investigations, including testimony taken, are sometimes included. They are the most useful sources of legislation, and the minority reports are particularly valuable in illuminating the main issues of controversy. The reports may be published as both House and Senate reports, such as *Examination of President Richard M. Nixon's Tax Returns for 1969 Through 1972* (H. Rep. 93–966; S. Rep. 93–758). House and Senate reports are available on *GPO Access* as *Congressional Reports* (G61), 104th Congress (1995–1996) forward.

Documents

The *House Documents* (G62) and the *Senate Documents* (G63) in general contain three categories of materials: (1) a large variety of reports originating in executive departments and independent bodies; (2) reports originating in Congress including committee activities, committee-sponsored studies, and background information and miscellaneous materials such as tributes, prayers, portrait unveilings, and memorial addresses; and (3) materials originating outside the government, such as the annual report of the Girl Scouts of the U.S.A. The House and Senate documents contain many materials considered basic in a reference collection, such as *The Constitution of the United States of America* (S. Doc. 99–16), noted in Chapter 14. House and Senate reports are also available on *GPO Access* as *Congressional Documents* (G64), 1994 (103rd Congress, Second Session) forward.

Executive Reports and Documents

The *Senate Executive Reports* (G65) and the *Senate Executive Documents* (G66) are separate published series and do not form a part of the congressional edition. The *Senate Executive Report*, a numbered series, contains Senate committee reports on treaties and nomination of high officials in the executive branch and the judiciary. The Senate *Executive Documents*, a lettered series, deals exclusively with presidential messages seeking the advice and consent of the Senate on treaties.

Hearings

The *House Hearings* (G67) and the *Senate Hearings* (G68) contain the transcripts of testimony before the committees on a variety of subjects. Hearings serve many purposes: (1) They provide an opportunity to interested parties to present their views on an issue; (2) they represent one of the means by which members can obtain detailed knowledge and understanding of a proposal; (3) they inform the public and interested groups that a particular measure is under consideration, thus providing the voters with an opportunity to make their wishes known in advance of congressional action; (4) in this regard, they provide a political climate to change, thus facilitating acceptance of the program under discussion; (5) they may prove beneficial in pointing out implications of the language of a bill which had not been foreseen; and (6) they may also serve as a source of ideas regarding legislative proposals not directly associated with the subject under consideration.[7]

Committee Prints

Special reports and studies prepared for the use of a committee are published as *Committee Prints* (G69). The prints describe, analyze, or evaluate legislation, programs, and public policy. They are prepared by committee staff or others on a variety of topics.

Publications of the Executive Branch

The executive branch consists of the executive office of the President, executive departments, and a number of independent agencies. All current presidential proclamations and executive orders and regulations of government agencies having general applicability and legal effect are published by its Office of the Federal Register in the *Federal Register*, noted in Chapter 14. Presidential materials are also found in the congressional publications previously mentioned. The *Congressional Record*, the journals of both houses, and the Congressional edition, for instance, are good sources for locating presidential addresses, remarks, and messages to Congress. Publications of the executive branch, including departments and agencies, are numerous. Two titles deserve attention:

> *Weekly Compilation of Presidential Documents*, August 2, 1965– . Washington, DC: U.S. Office of the Federal Register. Print & digital. (G70)
> *Public Papers of the Presidents of the United States, Containing the Public Messages, Speeches, and Statements of the President*. U.S. Office of the Federal Register. Washington, DC, 1958– . Annual. (G71)

The *Weekly Compilation*, issued every Monday, contains the President's addresses and remarks, announcements, appointments, and nominations (not including promotions of members of the uniformed services, nominations to the service academies, or nominations of foreign service officers), communications to Congress, meetings with foreign leaders, proclamations, and other presidential materials released by the White House during the preceding week. It has a four-quarter "Cumulative Index to Prior Issues" and separately published semiannual and annual indexes.

The *Weekly Compilation* is cumulated to form the annual *Public Papers of the Presidents*. Not all materials are included, however. Therefore, the *Public Papers of the Presidents* is not a substitute for the former reference.

There was no uniform publication of presidential papers comparable to the *Congressional Record*, noted earlier, and the *United States Reports*, noted in Chapter 15, until 1958, when the series of the *Public Papers of the Presidents* was begun. The basic text of each volume consists of "oral statements by the President or of writings subscribed by him, and selected from (1) Communications to the Congress; (2) Public addresses; (3) Transcripts of news conferences; (4) Public letters; (5) Messages to heads of States; (6) Statements on miscellaneous subjects; and (7) Formal executive documents promulgated in accordance with Law."[8] Published volumes cover Presidents Hoover, Truman, Eisenhower, Kennedy, Johnson, Nixon, Ford, Carter, Reagan, Bush, and Clinton.

For earlier presidential public papers, there is *A Compilation of the Messages and Papers of the Presidents 1789–1897* . . . , compiled by James D. Richardson (New York: Bureau of National Literature, 1917, 20 vols.) (G72). According to Schmeckebier and Eaton, "the compilation does not contain all the early messages, nor does it include the accompanying papers, in many cases, more important than the messages, which are often mere letters of transmittal."[9]

Publications of the Judicial Branch

There are two types of federal courts: constitutional and legislative. Constitutional courts are those established by Article III of the Constitution, which provides that "the judicial power of the United States shall be vested in one Supreme Court, and in such inferior courts as the Congress may from time to time ordain and establish." They consist of the Supreme Court, courts of appeals, and district courts. Legislative courts are created as necessary and proper means to carry into execution powers granted to the federal government on the basis of other authority than Article III of the Constitution. They include the Court of Claims, the Court of Customs and Patent Appeals, the Customs Court, territorial courts, and the Court of Military Appeals.

For court decisions, see titles discussed in Chapter 14. One item significant to reference work is:

The Third Branch: Bulletin of the Federal Courts, 1968–   . Washington, DC: The Federal Judicial Center. Monthly. (G73)

It is a joint publication of the administrative office of the United States Courts and the Federal Judicial Center. *The Third Branch* publishes brief information about the judiciary and presents legislative outlook, state-federal judicial councils, personnel, calendar, and the like.

NOTES

1. 44 U.S.C. 1901.

2. Nina Platt, "GPO Access: Government at Its Best?" *Database* 21, no. 2 (1998): 41–43.

3. *Congressional Quarterly's Guide to Congress* (2nd ed., 1976), p. 497.

4. Charles L. Clapp, *The Congressman: His Work as He Sees It* (Washington, DC: The Brookings Institution, 1963), p. 135.

5. Laurence F. Schmeckebier and Roy R. Eastin, *Government Publications and Their Use* (Washington, DC: The Brookings Institution, 1969), p. 176.

6. Emmette S. Redford and others, *Politics and Government in the United States* (New York: Harcourt, Brace and World, 1965), p. 412.

7. Clapp, *Congressman*, pp. 265–266.

8. 1 C.F.R. 10.3.

9. Schmeckebier and Eastin, *Government Publications*, p. 331.

Part II

Subdisciplines of the Social Sciences

Chapter 8

Cultural Anthropology

Anthropology is the science devoted to the study of people, the study of differences and similarities of all aspects of people's ways of life without limitation in time and space.[1] One branch of anthropology is physical anthropology, which studies the genetics and the physical traits of human groups; it is a part of human biology. The remainder, a large and more diverse part, is cultural anthropology. Cultural anthropology examines the variations of behavior among human groups and describes the character of the various cultures and the process of stability, change, and development that are characteristic of them.[2]

In theory, anthropology also includes archaeology, the study of remains of the past, and linguistics, the science of language, for both artifacts and language are part of culture. But, in practice, they are separate from other parts of cultural anthropology.[3] In traditional American practice, anthropology is often divided into physical anthropology, cultural anthropology, archaeology, and linguistics.[4] Cultural anthropology may be divided into ethnology, which depicts and analyzes the cultural characteristics of peoples; ethnography, which describes data collected in the field; and social anthropology, which aims at understanding and explaining the diversity of human behavior by a comparative study of social relationships. To some, cultural anthropology and social anthropology are synonymous.[5] A subfield of social anthropology is applied anthropology, which applies anthropological knowledge to practice use. It does not simply study the variations of human life, but aims at achieving a goal, analogous to the work of an engineer or medical doctor.[6]

The first undergraduate anthropology courses offered in the United States were taught in 1879 at the University of Rochester and in 1882 at the

University of Lewisburg (now Bucknell University).[7] The University of Vermont followed in 1885.[8]

ACCESS TO SOURCES

Guides

The following are two guides:

> *Cultural Anthropology: A Guide to Reference and Information Sources.* Josephine Z. Kibbee. Englewood, CO: Libraries Unlimited, 1991. 205 p. ISBN 0872877396. (H1)
>
> *Introduction to Library Research Anthropology.* 2nd ed. John M. Weeks. Boulder, CO: Westview Press, 1998. 401 p. ISBN 0813390036. (H2)

The Kibbee guide has a broad coverage, not limited to cultural anthropology. It includes physical anthropology, applied anthropology, medical anthropology, cognitive anthropology, economic anthropology, political anthropology, urban anthropology, anthropology of education, anthropology of women, and related subjects. Some 700 annotated entries are grouped into nine chapters. The first four chapters deal with anthropology and subfields of anthropology. Chapters 5 and 6 cover humanities and additional topics, such as visual anthropology, history of anthropology, ethnohistory, and museums. The last three chapters contain area studies, periodicals, and supplemental resources. The chapter on supplemental resources contains anthropological organizations and institutes, libraries and archives, and publishers. Of the 700 entries, nearly 130 entries are in area studies and over 130 entries are supplemental resources. The book is one of the guides in *Reference Sources in the Social Sciences Series.* Some guides in the *Series* will be mentioned in other chapters.

The Weeks *Introduction* is "intended for the undergraduate student about to begin a research project . . . simply an introduction to the mechanics and resources of library use" (Preface). The main part of the book is "Library Resources in Anthropology," preceded by four chapters on anthropology as an academic discipline, basic services available for research, library research, and library catalog. The main part is organized into nineteen chapters according to format, such as catalogs, guides, bibliographies, dictionaries and encyclopedias, handbooks, book reviews and yearbooks, indexes and abstracts, journal literature, biographies, directories, government documents, atlases and maps, theses and dissertations, digital sources, audiovisual materials, and Human Relations Area Files. Most of these sources are annotated. There are four appendices: (A) Library of Congress Classification Scheme for Anthropology and Related Subjects; (B) Major Anthropology Collections in United States and Canadian Libraries; (C) Arrangement of the *Outline of Culture Materials*, and (D) Arrangement of the *Outline of World Cultures*. Author, ethnic or cultural group, and geographic place indexes are provided.

Bibliographies of Bibliographies

Compared with other disciplines, the number of published bibliographies in cultural anthropology is small. The bulk of the bibliographies of anthropology in Webb, noted in Chapter 3, would have contracted immensely if bibliographies on area studies had been eliminated. A bibliography of bibliographies is:

> *Anthropological Bibliographies: A Selected Guide.* Margo L. Smith and Yvonne M. Damien, eds. Library-Anthropology Resource Group, comp. South Salem, NY: Redgrave, 1981. 307 p. ISBN 0913178632. (H3)

This guide lists more than 3,200 bibliographies, filmographies, and discographies, either separately published or concealed, in multiple languages, classified into eight sections that are further divided by country, area, or topic. The eight sections are Africa, Americas, Asia, Europe, Oceania, U.S.S.R., topical, and addendum. Some of the entries are briefly annotated. According to its preface, the bibliography is also intended to update Gordon D. Gibson's two bibliographies: "A Bibliography of Anthropological Bibliographies: Africa" and A Bibliography of Anthropological Bibliographies: The Americas" published in *Current Anthropology* (1960– . Chicago: University of Chicago Press, 5/year, quarterly, ISSN 00113204) (H4) in 1969 and 1959 respectively, and J. D. Pearson's *A World Bibliography of Oriental Bibliographies* (Totowa, NJ: Rowman and Littlefield, 1975, 727 p., ISBN 0874717507) (H5). It may be noted that *Current Anthropology*, an international and interdisciplinary journal, publishes articles in anthropology and related fields, discussion and criticism, reports, and others. It features the "CA treatment," that is, articles accepted for publication are sent to commentators selected internationally for their comments. Their comments are published together with the article or in a later issue in "Discussion and Criticism."

Bibliographies

General

The following are major bibliographies in anthropology:

> *Catalogue of the Peabody Museum of Archaeology and Ethnology Library: Authors.* Boston: G. K. Hall, 1963. 26 vols. (H6)

Catalogue of the Tozzer Library of the Peabody Museum of Archaeology and Ethnology: Authors. Supplement, 1–4. Boston: G. K. Hall, 1970–1979. (H7)

Catalogue of the Peabody Museum of Archaeology and Ethnology: Subjects. Boston: G. K. Hall, 1963. 27 vols. (H8)

Catalogue of the Tozzer Library of the Peabody Museum of Archaeology and Ethnology: Subjects. Supplement, 1–4. Boston. G. K. Hall, 1970–1979. (H9)

The Tozzer Library Index to Anthropological Subject Headings. 2nd rev. ed. Boston: G. K. Hall, 1981. 177 p. ISBN 0816104050. (H10)

Bibliographic Guide to Anthropology and Archaeology, 1987– . Thorndike, ME: G. K. Hall, 1988– . Annual. ISSN 08968101. (H11)

International Bibliography of Social and Cultural Anthropology: Bibliographie Internationale d'Anthropologie Sociale et Culturelle, 1958– . London: Routledge, 1958– . Annual. Print & digital. (H12)

The *Catalogue of the Peabody Museum* is published in two sections: authors and subjects. The authors section includes personal authors, editors, translators, museums, societies, and other institutions, main entries for journals, and contents of monograph series. The subjects section covers general and physical anthropology, ethnology, and prehistoric archaeology, arranged primarily by geographical areas with topical subdivisions. The *Catalogue* is the most comprehensive bibliography of anthropology with its main strength in American archaeology and ethnology. It includes materials in English, French, German, Spanish, and Slavic languages. Anthropological materials in oriental and Arabic languages are, however, not duplicated here. For these materials, the catalogs of other libraries of Harvard University may be used. Items included in the Catalogue are books, articles, review articles (not published in *Reviews in Anthropology*), articles on anthropologists and anthropologists' informants, article-length obituaries, major discussions of articles, newsletters two or more pages in length, and all articles written by Harvard anthropology and Peabody Museum staff regardless of topic. One outstanding feature is the inclusion of journal articles.

The fourth *Supplement* (1979, 7 vols., ISBN 0816102538) adds some 100,000 entries since the third supplement, the personal library of Lloyd Cabot Briggs of primarily North African materials, and 247 new periodicals. The library catalog has been updated on microfiche covering collections through June 1986 as the *Author and Subjects Catalogues of the Tozzer Library,* 2nd ed. (Boston: G. K. Hall, 1988, ISBN 0816117314) and is continued by *Bibliographic Guide to Anthropology and Archaeology.* The supplement is no longer published. The Guide is also available on CD-ROM as *Anthropology Bibliography on Disc.* (H13)

The Tozzer Library Index to Anthropological Subject Headings is a useful guide to materials classified by subject. It lists the headings and cross-references appearing in the subjects section of the *Catalogue*.

The *International Bibliography*, one of the four parts of *International Bibliography of the Social Sciences* mentioned in Chapter 3, lists in its 1995 volume (1996, 333 p., ISBN 0415152143) over 3,800 entries of books and periodicals. In spite of its extensive coverage, the bibliography has not received much attention from anthropologists. Of the four parts of the *International Bibliography*, it is the least in demand.[9] According to Appel and Gurr, 89 percent of social scientists surveyed were not aware of the existence of the *International Bibliography of the Social Sciences*.[10] *International Bibliography* is also available on CD-ROM and on the *BIDS-IBSS* Web, noted in Chapter 3.

Subfield

> *A Bibliography of North American Folklore and Folksong*. 2nd rev. ed. Charles Haywood. New York: Dover, 1961. 2 vols. (H14)
>
> *Bibliography of Native North Americans*. New Haven, CT: Human Relations Area Files. Digital. (H15)
>
> *Ethnographic Bibliography of South America*. Timothy J. O'Leary. New Haven, CT: Human Relations Area Files, 1978. 414 p. (H16)
>
> *Guide to Research on North American Indians*. Arlene B. Hirschfelder, Mary Gloyne Byler, and Michael A. Dorris. Chicago: American Library Association, 1983. 330 p. ISBN 0838903535. (H17)
>
> *Indians of North America Methods and Sources for Library Research*. Marilyn L. Haas. Hamden, CT: Library Professional Publications, 1983. 163 p. ISBN 0208019804. (H18)
>
> *Indians of North and South America*. Carolyn E. Wolf and Karen R. Folk, comp. Metuchen, NJ: Scarecrow, 1977. 576 p. ISBN 0810810263. (H19)
>
> *Indians of North and South America Supplement*. Carolyn E. Wolf and Nancy S. Chiang, comp. Metuchen, NJ: Scarecrow, 1988. 654 p. ISBN 0810821273. (H20)
>
> *Indians of North and South America Second Supplement*. Carolyn Wolf, comp. Lanham, MD: Scarecrow, 1997. 452 p. ISBN 0810833018. (H21)
>
> *The Indians of South America: A Bibliography*. Thomas L. Welch, comp. Washington, DC: Organization of American States, Columbus Memorial Library, 1987. 594 p. ISBN 0827025998. (H22)

The Haywood bibliography is one of the first comprehensive bibliographies of its kind, listing over 40,000 books, articles, recordings, and musical arrangements with occasional brief annotations. The work, a compendium of vast traditional heritage in lore and song, is divided into two books. Book 1 deals with the American people north of Mexico. Book 2 is concerned with the American Indians north of Mexico. It has a detailed, 130-page index. Though considered to be weak in local history sources and inconsistent in form of entry,[11] it is, on balance, an indispensable reference work. [12]

Bibliography of Native North Americans (BNNA) is one of the three current electronic products of the Human Relations Area Files, noted later. It replaces *Ethnographic Bibliography of North America* (4th ed., George P. Murdock and Timothy J. O'Leary, New Haven, CT: Human Relations Area Files, 1975, 5 vols.) (H23) and *Ethnographic Bibliography of North America: 4th edition supplement 1973–1987* (M. Marlene Martin and Timothy J. O'Leary, New Haven, CT: Human Relations Area Files, 1990, 3 vols., ISBN 0875362540) (H24). *BNNA* contains the *Ethnographic Bibliography of North America*'s 50,000 citations plus 15,000 new entries. In general, full bibliographic information is given for each citation, including author's full name, the full title and subtitle, the place of publication, the publisher, and the date of publication. It is now available on CD-ROM and on the HRAF Web site, noted later.

Ethnographic Bibliography of South America lists over 20,000 entries limited to South America. The bibliography is also organized by geographical area and within area by tribal groups. The 1978 publication is a reprint of the work published in 1963, with corrections.

The *Guide to Research on North American Indians* annotates 1,100 items divided into 27 chapters, with a wide coverage including archaeology, prehistory, urban life, religion, and philosophy. The Haas book serves as an introduction to the use of libraries and to bibliographies. It contains three parts: Part 1, library methodology and reference works, includes a brief introduction to subject headings, classification systems, and call numbers, followed by reference works by form. An annotated topical bibliography and an unannotated bibliography by tribe constitute Part 2 and Part 3 respectively.

Also listed here are four comprehensive bibliographies. *Indians of North and South America* and its two supplements compiled on the basis of the collection at the Willard E. Yager Library-Museum, Hartwick College, Oneonta, NY (subtitle) cover books, theses, microform and essays. These bibliographies provide 4,387, 3,542, and 3,495 entries respectively.

More than 9,000 items are included in *The Indians of South America*. It is an unannotated bibliography in many languages, based on the collection of the Columbus Memorial Library, Organization of American States. The bibliography is classified into five divisions: general works, topical works, specific peoples, specific regions, and specific languages and dialects. Mexico, Panama, and Central America are not covered.

Subject bibliographies are also provided in the handbooks listed in the section on handbooks. They are excellent sources for publications on American Indians.

Theses and Dissertations

From 1870 to 1954, doctoral dissertations were published in the *Yearbook of Anthropology*, noted later, and the listing was continued by *Current Anthropology*, noted earlier, until 1968. Current listings of doctoral dissertations in anthropology may be found in *The AAA Guide*, noted later. For master's theses, an extensive bibliography is *Masters' Theses in Anthropology: A Bibliography of Theses from United States Colleges and Universities*, by David R. McDonald (New Haven, CT: HRAF, 1977, 453 p., ISBN 0875362176) (H25). The bibliography lists over 3,700 theses grouped into five categories: social/cultural anthropology, archaeology, physical anthropology, linguistics, and subject undetermined. Theses listing can also be found in journals, noted in Chapter 6.

Reviews

Book reviews are published in many periodicals in anthropology. Two publications devoted to reviews in anthropology are:

> *Annual Review of Anthropology*, 1972– . Palo Alto, CA: Annual Review. Annual. ISSN 00846570. (H26)
> *Reviews in Anthropology*, v. 1– , 1974– . Amsterdam: Gordon and Breach Science. Quarterly. ISSN 00938157. (H27)

The *Annual Review* continues the *Biennial Review of Anthropology* (1959–1971). Each volume includes several chapters of greater or lesser scope. Each chapter is an extensive review in a particular topic of the most significant output of anthropologists appended with a list of literature cited. Volume 26 of the *Annual Review* (1997, 686 p., ISBN 0824319265) consists of six major topics: overview, archaeology, biological anthropology, linguistics and communicative practices, theme I: governmentality, and theme II: religion. There are four indexes: author, subject, cumulative contributing authors, and cumulative titles. The *Review* is one of the four reviews in the social sciences published by Annual Reviews. The other three cover political science, psychology, and sociology, noted separately in the chapters that follow. The Table of Contents can be viewed through the publisher's web site (http://www.annualreviews.org).

Another major reviewing organ is *Reviews in Anthropology*. It publishes review essays in anthropology and related fields of the social and behavioral sciences. About fifteen review essays are published in each issue.

Indexes

In the early 1950s, George P. Murdock pointed out the almost complete lack of abstracts and periodical summaries and expressed his disappointment at the discontinuation of notices of periodical articles in *American Anthropologist*.[13] Since then, there has been an impressive improvement in indexing and abstracting services in anthropology. The commencement of *Biennial Review of Anthropology*, the publication of Harvard's Peabody Museum *Catalogues* and the index of the Royal Anthropological Institute, the issuance of two periodicals, *Current Anthropology* and *Review in Anthropology*, and the launching of *Abstracts in Anthropology* and *Anthropological Literature* exemplify the advances made.

International Bibliography of Social and Cultural Anthropology, Harvard's Peabody Museum *Catalogues*, and G. K. Hall's *Guide* are bibliographies and indexes to periodical articles as well. The current indexes in anthropology include:

> *The Anthropological Index to Current Periodicals in the Museum of Mankind Library*, v. 1–32, 1963–1994. London: Royal Anthropological Institute. Quarterly. ISSN 00035467. Print & digital. (H28)
>
> *Anthropological Literature: An Index to Articles and Essays*, v. 1– , 1979– . Cambridge, MA.: Tozzer Library, Harvard University. Quarterly. ISSN 01903373. Print & digital. (H29)

The Anthropological Index is a classified listing of periodical articles in archaeology, ethnomusicology, physical anthropology, cultural anthropology, and human biology, with an author index for each volume. The 1994 volume lists over 9,500 entries organized in five parts: (1) general; (2) Africa; (3) Americas; (4) Asia; and (5) Australasia, Pacific. It ceased publication with volume 32, 1994. It is now accessible via the Web, as *The Anthropological Index Online* (http://lucy.ukc.ac.uk/AIO.html) (H30) and *Social Science Ready Reference*, noted in Chapter 3.

Anthropological Literature indexes some 1,000 serials and edited works. Books (not edited), film, video reviews, interviews, and conference reports are not included. Its format varies. The print format was replaced by microfiche in 1984. Since 1989, *Anthropological Literature* has resumed its print format. Beginning with number 3 of volume 14 (1992), it added a Review Supplement. Reviews are divided into eight categories: (1) books and journals; (2) films and videos; (3) sound recordings; (4) databases, including CD-ROMs; (5) microform publications; (6) computer software; (7) exhibits; and (8) other (e.g., conferences, slide sets, etc.) *Anthropological Literature* covers anthropology and related fields, such as sociology, history, ethnohistory, demography, geography, international development, and human genetics.

Each issue contains five sections: bibliographic citations, subject index, list of authors indexed, list of journals indexed, and list of edited works and series indexed. The fourth issue of each volume cumulates the indexes. The 1997 volume lists 9,000 items. *Anthropological Literature* is on CD-

ROM as *Anthropological Literature on Disc* (H31). A ten-year compilation, updated annually and produced by G. K. Hall, it provides some 98,000 entries. It is also available via the RLG Web site, noted in Chapter 2.

The two indexes, the *International Bibliography* and Harvard's *Catalogues*, duplicate one another to a certain extent. Rexford S. Beckham in reviewing *Anthropological Index*, the *International Bibliography*, and the *Catalogue* considered the duplication of efforts a great waste and suggested that if the scope of the *Index* and the *International Bibliography* were changed to coincide with that of Harvard's *Catalogues*, the mechanism of any one activity could provide bibliographic data for the other two.[14]

Abstracts

Abstracts in Anthropology, v. 1– , 1970– . Amityville, NY: Baywood. 8/year. ISSN 00013455. (H32)

Abstracts in Anthropology is arranged topically under four areas: linguistics, cultural anthropology, archaeology, and physical anthropology, published on rotation, one issue on linguistics and cultural anthropology and the next issue on archaeology and physical anthropology. The area of cultural anthropology includes applied anthropology, social policy; arts; cultural ecology; economics; ethnohistory; kinship; medical anthropology; minorities; political structure and process, law; psychological anthropology; social organization; sociocultural change; symbol systems; theoretical, methodological, and general; and urban studies. Each issue abstracts books, periodical articles, and papers, with an author and a subject index. The 1998 volume contains some 3,000 entries.

Contents Reproduction

For contents reproduction, refer to *Current Contents* and *ABS Pol Sci*. Both have partial coverage of anthropological periodicals. The following is a content reproduction in anthropology:

International Current Awareness Service: Anthropology and Related Disciplines, 1990– . London: Routledge. ISSN 09601511. (H33)

International Current Awareness Service: Anthropology and Related Disciplines is one of four parts of *ICAS* noted in Chapter 3.

SOURCES OF INFORMATION

General

> *Human Relations Area Files.* New Haven, CT: Human Relations Area Files. Print & digital. (H34)
> *WWW Virtual Library: Anthropology.* Flagstaff, AZ: Anthro Tech. http:// anthrotech.com/resources/ (H35)

The Human Relations Area Files (HRAF), founded in 1949, is a non-profit research corporation controlled by major universities and research institutions aiming at contributing to an understanding of people and cultures. It contains some one million pages of descriptive data from a variety of sources (books, articles, and manuscripts) in the field of cultural anthropology throughout the world. Data are arranged by culture and subject classification system developed by HRAF, entitled *Outline of Cultural Materials (OCM)* by George Peter Murdock and others (5th rev. ed., New Haven, CT: HRAF, 1987, 247 p., ISBN 0875366546) (H36). The area of cultural classification around which each file is organized follows the *Outline of World Cultures*, also by Murdock (6th rev. ed., New Haven, CT: HRAF, 1983, 259 p., ISBN 0875366643) (H37). These works provide access to the contents of the files. HRAF was released in annual installments on sheets as *Paper Files*, including duplicate or original pages of published or unpublished sources on particular cultures or societies. From the 1950s to 1993, annual installments up to installment 42 were published on microfiche as the *HRAF Microfiles* (H38). *The HRAF Collection* (H39) is another file program, which consists of selected files on 3 × 5 microfiche. A subject index to over 4,000 sources in HRAF was published in 1972, entitled *Index to the Human Relations Area Files* (8 vols. with supplements, 1979–) (H40). HRAF is now only available on CD-ROM and on the Web (http://www.yale.edu/hraf/home.htm).

HRAF has three electronic collections available on CD-ROM and on the Web: Ethnography, Archaeology, and *Bibliography of Native North Americans (BNNA)*, noted earlier. *Collection of Ethnology* consists of three annual installments: 43–45. Each installment provides access to 40,000 pages of subject text, with 40 percent of new documents on Asia, Africa, North and South America, the Middle East, and Oceania. *Collection of Archaeology* includes archaeological materials released by installments. These installments contain twelve to fifteen major traditions worldwide. Each tradition typically contains an overview and descriptive materials on five to seven sites.

WWW Virtual Library: Anthropology is an extensive resource guide to all branches of anthropology, including applied anthropology, archaeology, biophysical anthropology, cultural anthropology, education, and linguistic anthropology. Its links to bibliographies, organizations and institutes, specialized fields, and directories of anthropologists are a valuable reference tool. Directories of Anthropologists contains over 100 profiles of anthropologists compiled at the Minnesota State University, Mankato, and Anthropologist's Addresses, some sixteen links to different directories, such as Anthropology and Archaeology Academics List, Email Address in Forensics, and World Wide Email Directory of Anthropologists.

In the Cultural Anthropology field, it presents a brief note on cultural anthropology and eighteen sections of topics, such as Agricultural Anthropology, Bibliographies, Cyber Anthropology, Ethnographies, Gerontology, Indices and General, Journals, Organizations, Regional Studies, and Psychological Anthropology.

Encyclopedias

General

> *The Encyclopedia of Cultural Anthropology.* David Levinson and Melvin Ember, eds. New York: Henry Holt, 1996. 4 vols. ISBN 0805028773. (H41)
> *Encyclopedia of Social and Cultural Anthropology.* Alan Barnard and Jonathan Spencer, eds. London: Routledge, 1996. 658 p. ISBN 041509996X. (H42)
> *The Encyclopedia of World Cultures.* David Levinson, ed. Boston: G. K. Hall, 1994. 10 vols. ISBN 0816118086. (H43)

For a long time, there was no significant encyclopedia of anthropology. By coincidence, two encyclopedias with good coverage of social and cultural anthropology appeared in 1996.

The Encyclopedia of Cultural Anthropology contains 340 articles contributed by 310 scholars on approaches, methods, concepts, and topics in cultural anthropology and selected information on linguistics, biological anthropology, and archaeology. It covers nine subject areas: (1) major subfields of anthropology; (2) framework and major organizing concepts such as humanism, psychoanalysis, and cultural materialism; (3) methods of data collection and analysis; (4) specific topics in anthropological study such as dance, marriage, and slavery; (5) specific theories of human culture and behavior; (6) cultural regions and subregions; (7) major recent controversies in cultural anthropology; (8) aspects of the profession of cultural anthropology; and (9) topics from linguistics, biological anthropology, and archaeology of special relevance to cultural anthropology.

Articles are arranged in alphabetical order, from Adaptation, Adolescence, Adornment to World Religions and Writing Systems. Each article is signed, concluding with a bibliography, and many articles have *see* and *see also* references. The coverage is broad, including such topics as birth, computers, crime, decision-making, games, gangs, cities, market, marriage, martial arts, Marxism, money, nationalism, taxation, and transnationalism. Many subfields of anthropology are discussed including advocacy, applied, biological, business, clinical, critical, economic, educational, humanistic, legal, linguistic, medical, policy, political, practicing, psychological, scientific, and urban anthropology. But the *Encyclopedia* lacks an article on cultural anthropology per se. A listing of anthropological periodicals is given as an appendix. There is an article, subject, and name index.

The one-volume encyclopedia contains three parts: (1) main text of 231 entries arranged alphabetically, from Aboriginal Australia, Adoption and Fostering, Africa: East to Witchcraft and Sorcery and Work; (2) some 200 biographical sketches; (3) Glossary. There are three indexes: name, people and place, and subject.

A monumental work on cultures is the *Encyclopedia of World Cultures*. Culture is referred to as "the way of life of the people—both past and present—and the factors that have caused the culture to change over time and place" (Preface). It is arranged by region into the following volumes: (I) North America (Canada, Greenland, and the United States of America); (II) Oceania (Australia, New Zealand, Melanesia, Micronesia, and Polynesia); (III) South Asia (Afghanistan, Bangladesh, Burma [now Myanmar], India, Pakistan, Sri Lanka, and the Himalayan states); (IV) Europe (Central, Western, and Southeastern Europe); (V) East and Southeast Asia (Japan, Korea, mainland and insular Southeast Asia, and Taiwan); (VI) Russia and Eurasia/China (including Mongolia); (VII) South America; (VIII) Middle America and the Caribbean (Central America, Mexico, and the Caribbean); and (IX) Africa and the Middle East. The book contains "about fifteen hundred summaries along with maps, glossaries, and indexes of alternate names for the cultural groups" (Preface). Each volume consists of a Preface (same in every volume), Introduction, Maps and Cultures, Glossary, Filmography, and Ethnonym Index. Some volumes provide appendixes, which vary in scope. Articles (descriptive summaries) range from a few lines to six pages, with cross references. Each article usually contains culture name, ethnonyms, orientation (identification, location, demography, and linguistic affiliation), history and cultural relations, settlements, economy, kinship, marriage and family, sociopolitical organization, religion and expressive culture, bibliography, and author's name.

Each of the first nine volumes concludes with Glossary, Filmography, and Ethnonym Index. Appendixes vary. For instance, volume 1 covers "Extinct Native American Cultures," and volume 9 contains "Additional African Culture" and "Ethnonym Index to Appendix." Volume X, Indexes, contains "The Task of Ethnography," an article by Paul Hockings, List of Cultures by Country, an Ethnonyms Index, and a Subject Index.

Subfield

American Folklore: An Encyclopedia. Jan Harold Brunvand, ed. New York: Garland, 1996. 794 p. ISBN 0815307519. (H44)

Encyclopedia of Human Evolution and Prehistory. Ian Tattersall, Eric Delson, and John Van Covering, eds. New York: Garland, 1988. 603 p. ISBN 0824093755. (H45)

Encyclopedia of Native American Tribes. Carl Waldman. Illustrated by Molly Braun. New York: Facts on File, 1988. 293 p. ISBN 0816014213. (H46)

The Cambridge Encyclopedia of Archaeology. Andrew S. Sherratt. New York: Crown, 1980. 495 p. ISBN 0517534975. (H47)

American Folklore contains North American folklore, including Canadian but excluding in general the folklore of Native Americans. Its coverage ranges "from traditional areas like folklore, scholarship, film and folklore, history and folklore, mass media and folklore parody in folklore, and public folklore to such leading-edge topics as body lore, coding in American folk culture, cultural studies, computer folklore, empowerment, organizational folklore, and postmodernism" (Preface). It includes many biographies and illustrations are plenty. Articles are signed with references, and in many cases, cross-references.

Encyclopedia of Human Evolution and Prehistory contains over 1,200 articles (including 50 biographies) contributed by forty authors. Articles are heavily cross-referenced and appended with further readings. Illustrations are many. A good article preceding the main body of the work is "A Brief Introduction to Human Evolution and Prehistory." Also good is the subject list by topic, a summary of major topics that provides a quick reference to the entire subject coverage of the encyclopedia.

A representative sampling of Indian tribes, as well as some general cultural categories of Native Americans, is presented in *Encyclopedia of Native American Tribes.* There are over 250 color illustrations. The *Encyclopedia* concludes with a glossary and a further reading list.

The *Cambridge Encyclopedia* is an outstanding reference work. Fifty-four scholars contributed 64 articles. Articles are organized into three parts under ten headings. It ends with a bibliography, a further reading list, and an index.

Dictionaries

General

Anthropological Glossary. Roger Pearson, ed. Malabar, FL: Robert E. Krieger, 1985. 282 p. ISBN 0898745101. (H48)

Dictionary of Anthropology. Thomas Barfield, ed. Malden, MA: Blackwell, 1997. 626 p. ISBN 11577180577. (H49)

Dictionary of Anthropology. Charlotte Seymour-Smith. Boston: G. K. Hall, 1986. 305 p. ISBN 0816188773. (H50)

Anthropological Glossary, expanded from part of the author's work, *Introduction to Anthropology* (1974), contains terms in all fields of anthropology, such as cultural anthropology, physical anthropology, archaeology, linguistics, and regions of planets. Definitions are brief.

The dictionary by Barfield "focuses primarily on topics in cultural and social anthropology, but also includes related topics in archaeology, biological anthropology, and linguistics" (Preface). Over 500 terms and biographies are included in alphabetical order, with cross-references and further reading. Its integrated bibliography contains almost 3,000 separate citations. There is a long bibliography (pp. 502–626).

A good dictionary is the Seymour-Smith work, also published under the title *Macmillan Dictionary of Anthropology* (New York: Macmillan, 1986, 305 p., ISBN 0333365909) (H51), which also stresses theoretical and conceptual issues. The dictionary includes biographies of persons deceased or born before 1920. Length of articles varies from one short paragraph to a two-page entry on "economic anthropology." Articles are cross-referenced, and bibliographical references are given with the name of the author/editor throughout the text. For bibliographical citation of references cited, refer to a selective bibliography and further readings at the end of the book (pp. 293–305). The bibliography covers both books and periodical articles.

Subfield

A Concise Dictionary of Indian Tribes of North America. Barbara A. Leitch. Algonac, MI: Reference Publications, 1979. 646 p. ISBN 0917256093. (H52)

Funk and Wagnalls Standard Dictionary of Folklore, Mythology and Legend. Maria Leach, ed. New York: Funk and Wagnalls, 1972. 1,236 p. (H53)

Historical Dictionary of North American Archaeology. Edward B. Jelks and Juliet C. Jelks, eds. Westport, CT: Greenwood Press, 1988. 760 p. ISBN 0313243077. (H54)

Larousse Dictionary of World Folklore. Alison Jones. New York: LKC, 1996. 512 p. ISBN 0752300431. (H55)

The Macmillan Dictionary of Archaeology. Ruth D. Whitehouse, ed. London: Macmillan, 1983. 597 p. ISBN 0333271904. (H56)

A Concise Dictionary provides profiles of Indian tribes in alphabetical order. Each entry gives a brief history, tribe life, language, religion, and tradition. Most entries are appended with a bibliography. There are maps and a glossary.

The Leach dictionary contains an international sampling of gods, folk heroes, culture heroes, tricksters, festivals and rituals, food customs, games, and tongue twisters. Entries range from one or two short, unsigned paragraphs to some articles longer than ten pages. Occasionally, bibliographies and references are provided. It is more than a dictionary. Its article on "Museum" includes an international directory of museums. There is a key to 2,305 countries, regions, cultures, culture areas, peoples, tribes, and ethnic groups. The dictionary was compiled on the descriptive principle. It belongs to no "school of folklore," adheres to no "method," advocates no "theory," according to the author. More than one definition, if available, is given to represent varying and controversial points of view.

Another book of international coverage of folklore is the *Larousse Dictionary*. Entries are presented in A-Z order. Some are supplied with illustrations. It also includes Further Reading, Biographical Notes on Prominent Folklore, and a Calendar of festivals and folkloric events throughout the world.

The Macmillan Dictionary defines terms in archaeology with substantial cross-references. Lower-case letters ad, be, or bp (before present) indicate uncalibrated radiocarbon dates, whereas the capital letters AD, BC, or BP are used for dates to represent a "real" or calendar year. It also uses in general *pinyin* instead of the Wade-Giles system of transliteration for Chinese names.

Directories

Anthropology Resources on the Internet. Allen H. Lutins. http://www.nitehawn.com/alleycat (H57)

The AAA Guide: A Guide to Departments of Anthropology, 1962– . Washington, DC: American Anthropological Association. Print & digital. (H58)

Anthropology Resources on the Internet, last updated in August 1998, is a listing of Internet resources. Web sites are grouped into General, Archaeology, Archaeological Sites/Digs, Field School/Job Opportunities, Linguists, Cultural Anthropology, Physical Anthropology, Museums, Academic Institutions, Other Institutions, Commercial Sites, Journals, and Other Anthropology Resource Collections. It provides links to all web sites listed. For instance, it provides links to *The Anthropological Index of the Royal Anthropological Institute*, noted earlier, *Anthropology Review Database*, and *Anthropology on the Internet: A Review and Evaluation of Networked Resources*, by Brian Schwimmer (H59).

Schwimmer's work, published in *Current Anthropology* (from June 1996) includes "Reference List of URL's," a listing of Web sites. Web sites in the list are grouped into E-mail Discussion Lists, Newsgroups, Research Consortia and Collections, Scholarly Journals and Societies, Anthropology Departments, Research Centers and Institutes, Area Studies, Museums, U.S. Government Information, and International Agencies.

The directories just mentioned can be accessed through the Web site of the American Anthropological Association (http://www.ameranthassn.org) (H60). On its home page, select "Anthropology Resources on the Internet" to link to these Web sites.

The 36th edition, 1997/1998, of the *Guide* lists 551 academic departments, museums, research firms, and government organizations and, in addition, membership, statistical data, and Ph.D. dissertations in anthropology. It covers the United States and Canada. A typical listing for a department includes program, degrees offered, faculty, staff, chair, anthropologists in other departments, students, degrees granted, academic year system, academic requirements, special programs, special resources and research facilities, publications, address, and cross-references. Also listed are sources of degrees held by individuals, breakdowns of number of individuals and positions, locations of academic departments by state, enrollment, total degrees granted, Ph.D. degrees granted, and recent Ph.D. dissertations in anthropology. Its statistical information contains locations of academic departments, highest degree offered, student enrollment, number of degrees granted by category, and Ph.D. degrees granted. There are indexes of individuals in programs and of academic departments by state.

Biographies

> *Biographical Directory of Anthropologists Born Before 1920*. Library-Anthropology Resource Group, comp. Thomas L. Mann, ed. New York: Garland, 1988. 245 p. ISBN 082405833X. (H61)
>
> *Fifth International Directory of Anthropologists*. Chicago: University of Chicago Press, 1975. 496 p. ISBN: 0266790770. (H62)
>
> *Women Anthropologists: A Biographical Dictionary*. Ute Gacs and others, eds. Westport, CT: Greenwood Press, 1988. 428 p. ISBN 0313244146. (H63)

The *Biographical Directory* lists 3,485 biographical sketches. Each entry contains "dates of birth and death, birthplace, profession, major contributions, and published sources of biographical information" (Preface). It also provides statistical data indicating the number of biographies by country and by career and graphs for birth and death dates. There is an index of topic and geographic region.

A listing of anthropologists is also provided in *The AAA Guide*, just noted. But the *Guide* does not provide biographical sketches; neither does it include anthropologists outside the United States and Canada. The *Fifth International Directory* profiles over 4,300 anthropologists all over the world. It provides a number of indexes for the convenience of use, including a geographical index, a chronological index, four sections of subject/methodological indexes (cultural anthropology, archaeology, physical anthropology, and linguistics), and an institutional location/residence index.

Women Anthropologists consists of articles on 58 women anthropologists. The work may be considered as a biobibliography, for each article is appended with references and works about and by the biographee. There are two appendixes: Field Work Areas and Chronology of Birth Dates.

Handbooks, Yearbooks, and the Like

There are significant handbooks, especially on American Indians.

> *Handbook of Method in Cultural Anthropology*. Raoul Naroll and Ronald Cohen, eds. Garden City, NY: Natural History Press for the American Museum of Natural History, 1970. 1,017 p. (H64)
>
> *Handbook of American Indians North of Mexico*. Frederick Webb Hodge. Washington, DC: GPO, 1907–1910. Reissued in 1972. 2 vols. (U.S. Bureau of American Ethnology Bulletin 30). Reprint ed., New York: Rowman and Littlefield, 1965. (H65)
>
> *Handbook of Middle American Indians*. Robert Wauchope, gen. ed. Austin: University of Texas Press, 1964–1976. 16 vols. (H66)
>
> *Handbook of North American Indians*. William C. Sturtevant, gen. ed. Washington, DC: Smithsonian Institution, 1978– . 20 vols. (H67)
>
> *Handbook of South American Indians*. Julian Haynes Steward. Washington, D.C.: GPO, 1946–1959. U.S. Bureau of American Ethnology Bulletin 143. Reprint: New York: Cooper Square, 1963. 7 vols. (H68)

A Handbook of Method in Cultural Anthropology contains 49 articles in seven parts: general introduction, general problems, the fieldwork process, models of ethnographic analysis, comparative approaches, problems of categorization, and special problems of comparative method. It focuses on how to plan and to do research with some discussion on research techniques. Practically all articles are appended with a bibliography. There is an article by Timothy J. O'Leary on ethnographic and related bibliographies.

The four handbooks on Indians are outstanding works. Hodge is an encyclopedic dictionary, an outgrowth of a compilation of tribal names. It deals with "all the tribes north of Mexico, including the Eskimo, and those tribes south of the boundary more or less affiliated with those in the United States." Entries contained therein, in alphabetical order, cover "relations between the aboriginals and the government; their archaeology; manners, customs, arts, and industries; brief biographies of Indians of note; and words of aboriginal origin that have found their way into the English language." There are "Synonyms" as cross-references and a "Bibliography" at the end of the book.

Steward is intended "to provide a concise summary of existing data that will serve as a standard reference work for the scholar, a text book for the student, and a guide to the general reader," says its introduction. It centers attention on the culture of each tribe at the time of its first contact with Europeans. The seven volumes are (1) The Marginal Tribes, (2) The Andean Civilizations, (3) The Tropical Forest Tribes, (4) The Circum-Caribbean Tribes, (5) The Comparative Ethnology of Southern American Indians, (6) Physical Anthropology, Linguistics, and Cultural Geography of South American Indians, and (7) Index. Its treatment of culture is most extensive in such topics as subsistence activities, villages and houses, dress and ornaments, transportation, manufactures, political and social life, religion, mythology, and lore and learning. Also included of reference value are terminology, mostly archaeological terms (volume 2, pp. 74–79 and pp. 975–978); a glossary used in the fields of basketry, weaving, ceramics, and metallurgy (volume 5, pp. 773–782); and bibliographies elsewhere in the work.

Both Hodge and Steward belong to the series of *Bulletin of the Bureau of American Ethnology*, 1896–1965, of the Smithsonian Institution (H69). The *Bulletin* consists of two subseries: *Anthropological Papers*, nos. 1–80, 1938–1965 (H70), and *River Basin Survey Papers*, nos. 1–29, 1963–1965 (H71). It terminated with number 200 as the Bureau itself was replaced, along with the Department of Anthropology of the National Museum, by the Smithsonian Office of Anthropology. The office not only has broader activities than its predecessors but also continues work on the native peoples of the Americas and is expanding its research programs in Africa, Asia, and the Pacific. A new series of worldwide scope is *Smithsonian Contributions to Anthropology, 1965–* (Washington, DC: Smithsonian Institution Press, irregular, ISSN 00810223) (H72).

Handbook of Middle American Indians is intended to fill the gap between Hodge and Steward. The first eleven volumes consist of nearly 200 articles by specialists arranged in eight parts: (1) natural environment and early cultures (Volume 1), (2) archaeology of southern Mesoamerica (volumes 2–3), (3) archaeological frontiers and external connections (volume 4), (4) linguistics (volume 5), (5) social anthropology (volume 6), (6) ethnology (volumes 7–8), (7) physical anthropology (volume 9), and (8) archaeology of northern Mesoamerica (volumes 10–11). Each article provides the references cited in it, and there are full citations at the end of each volume. Volumes 12 through 15 constitute the *Guide to Ethnohistorical Sources*, edited by Howard F. Cline. Volume 16 is *Sources Cited and Artifacts Illustrated*, edited by Margaret A. L. Harrison and Majorie S. Zengel.

A handbook still in progress is *Handbook of North American Indians*. Planned to be a 20-volume set, it is intended to be "an encyclopedic summary of what is known about the prehistory, history, and cultures of the aboriginal peoples of North America who lived north of the urban civilizations of central Mexico" (Preface). The 20 volumes, published and planned, are (published volumes are indicated by year of publication in parentheses): (1) Introduction, (2) Indians in Contemporary Society, (3) Environment, Origins, and Population, (4) History of Indian-White Relations, (5) Arctic (1984), (6) Subarctic (1981), (7) Northwest Coast, (8) California (1978), (9) Southwest (1979), (10) Southwest (1983), (11) Great Basin (1986), (12) Plateau, (13) Plains, (14) Southeast, (15) Northeast (1978), (16) Technology and Visual Arts, (17) Languages, (18) Biographical Dictionary, (19) Biographical Dictionary, and (20) Index.

NOTES

1. A. L. Kroeber, ed., *Anthropology Today* (Chicago: University of Chicago Press, 1953), p. xiii.

2. David G. Mandelbaum, "Cultural Anthropology," in *International Encyclopedia of the Social Sciences*, vol. 1 (New York: Macmillan and Free Press, 1968–), p. 313.

3. Joseph H. Greenberg, "Anthropology," in *International Encyclopedia of the Social Sciences*, vol. 1 (New York: Macmillan and Free Press, 1968–), p. 303.

4. Ibid., p. 306.

5. Gail M. Kelly, "Anthropology," in Bert F. Hoselitz, ed., *A Reader's Guide to the Social Sciences*, rev. ed. (New York: Free Press, 1960), p. 45.

6. Lucy Mair, "Applied Anthropology," in *International Encyclopedia of the Social Sciences*, vol. 1 (New York: Macmillan and Free Press, 1968–), p. 325.

7. Elizabeth Tooker, "A Note on Undergraduate Courses in Anthropology in the Latter Part of the Nineteenth Century." *Man in the Northeast* 39 (1990): 39–51.

8. Ibid.

9. Maurice B. Line, "The Information Uses and Needs of Social Scientists: An Overview of INFROSS," *Aslib Proceedings* 23 (1971): 419.

10. John S. Appel and Ted Gurr, "Bibliographic Needs of Social and Behavioral Scientists," *American Behavioral Scientist* 7 (1964): 53.

11. Reviewed by Gerald D. McDonald, *Library Journal* 76 (1951): 862. See also review in *United States Quarterly Book Review* 7 (1951): 326: "Omissions are few, and rarely notable, but errors of spelling, bibliographic inexactitude, and the usual slips inherent in reference volumes of this kind are too numerous for comfort."

12. Favorably reviewed by Stith Thompson, *American Anthropologist* 53 (1951): 553–554.

13. George P. Murdock, "The Processing of Anthropological Materials," in *Anthropology Today* (Chicago: University of Chicago Press, 1953), p. 481.

14. Rexford S. Beckham, "Anthropology," *Library Trends* 15, no. 4 (1967): 696.

Chapter 9

Business

Business, considered applied economics, deals with activities for the purpose of making profit and improvement. The core of business as a discipline is threefold[1]: (1) to study the technical aspects of business administration, such as accounting and advertising; (2) to study management, which deals with planning, organizing, staffing, directing, and controlling[2]; and (3) to study leadership in business.

The number of reference sources in business in digital format is abundant and overwhelming. Business is part of economics. Reference sources in economics cover many aspects of business. On the other hand, many business sources are of reference importance to economics. It must be noted that the listing of a number of sources here in this chapter and in economics is subjective. Business reference sources stress currency, as evidenced by many available online databases.

ACCESS TO SOURCES

Guides

> *Business Information: How to Find It, How to Use It*. 2nd ed. Michael R. Lavin. Phoenix, AZ: Oryx Press, 1992. 499 p. ISBN 0897745566. (J1)
> *Business Information Sources*. 3rd ed. Lorna M. Daniells. Berkeley, CA: University of California Press, 1993. 725 p. ISBN 0520081803. (J2)
> *Handbook of Business Information: A Guide for Librarians, Students, and Researchers*. 2nd ed. Diane Wheeler Strauss. Englewood, CO: Libraries Unlimited, 1988. 537 p. ISBN 0872876071. (J3)
> *International Business Information: How to Find It, How to Use It*. Ruth A.

Pagell and Michael Halperin. Phoenix, AZ: Oryx, 1998. 445 p. ISBN 1573560502. (J4)

Lavin's book consists of five parts with title and subject indexes. The five parts are (I) Introduction, sources and forms of business information; (II) Getting Started, consisting of five chapters on reference tools for locating experts, finding reference materials, finding books, documents, and statistical reports, and searching journals, newspapers, and news services; (III) Information about Companies in seven chapters dealing with national and specialized businesses, private and public corporate finances, basic and special investment advice and analysis; (IV) Statistical Information, consisting of four chapters on statistical reasoning, population and housing, general economic and industry statistics; and (V) Special Topics, also in four chapters on states and local areas, marketing information, business law sources, and taxation and accounting. It contains business sources of information, sample pages, explanation of terms, and how to read and interpret financial data. The book serves well as a guide, particularly to those who are unfamiliar with the terms used in business and finance.

Its companion, *International Business Information*, patterned after Lavin, consists of sixteen chapters in five parts: (I) Introduction, (II) Company Information, (III) Marketing, (IV) Industrial and Economic Statistics, and (V) International Transactions. Part II has seven chapters on accounting standards and practices, company information issues, directory sources, financial sources, electronic sources, corporate affiliations and change, and special topics. Part III, in four chapters, deals with international marketing issues, sources, research, marketing operations, and exporting and importing. Part IV contains two chapters on economic statistics and industry information. The final part, also in two chapters, covers international trade and payments and financial markets. Some chapters are attached with appendixes. There are eight appendixes in Part II, such as sample U.K. and French Balance Sheets, Company Definitions—Glossary, Company WWW Sources—A Checklist, and Selecting an International Database—A Checklist. It features more than 140 exhibits and over 130 tables for illustration.

A well-known guide, Daniells contains 21 chapters that may be grouped into two parts. Part 1 (chapters 1 through 8) describes the basic business reference sources and data on current business and economic trends. Chapters 9 through 20 constitute part 2, with stress on management, listing works in specific subfields of business, including handbooks, textbooks, reference sources, and periodicals. Stress is placed primarily on print sources, although business-related databases and CD-ROMs are included. Chapter 21 is a bookshelf of important reference works basic to almost any small office library. Daniells is a guide to both reference sources and the significant literature in business.

The *Handbook of Business Information* has features of both Lavin and Daniells in reference sources. It contains explanations of business terms and the use of key sources with illustrations. It is divided into two parts. The first part, consisting of eight chapters, deals with business sources of information in general arranged according to form. The other ten chapters in part 2 provide sources of information on specific fields of business, such as marketing, accounting, taxation, banking, stocks, bonds, mutual funds, futures, options, insurance, and real estate. It is one of the best sources in the field.

Bibliographies

A good number of bibliographies in business have been published.

> *Bibliographic Guide to Business and Economics*, 1975–   . Thorndike, ME: G. K. Hall. Annual. ISSN 03602782. (J5)
> *Directory of Business and Financial Services*. 8th ed. Mary McNierney Grant and Riva Berleant-Schiller, eds. Washington, DC: Special Libraries Association, 1984. 189 p. [reprint, 1995. ISBN 0783786859]. (J6)
> *Encyclopedia of Business Information Sources*, ed. 1–   . Detroit: Gale Research, 1970–   . Irregular. ISSN 00710210. (J7)
> *Harvard Business School Core Collection: An Author, Title, and Subject Guide*. Boston: Baker Library Reference Services, Harvard Business School, 1997. 413 p. ISBN 007103823X. (J8)
> *The Quality Management Sourcebook: An International Guide to Materials and Resources*. Christine Avery and Diana Zabel. London: Routledge, 1996. 327 p. ISBN 0415108314. (J9)

G. K. Hall's *Bibliography* is one of its bibliographic guides series, as noted earlier. It lists books, reports, and other materials on all aspects of business and economics. The *Bibliography* is basically a holding list of the Library of Congress and the New York Public Library.

The Grant and Berleant-Schiller directory "deals exclusively with information services that provide continuous coverage of some facet of business activity [and] provide the information that should help users determine the applicability of each service to their needs" (Introduction). It describes nearly 1,200 publications, databases, and services. The term "services" is defined as "information distributed by individuals or companies which make a business of compiling and publishing for general distribution, data and statistics on a given subject, kept up to date by revised and supplemental data issued either regularly or irregularly" (Introduction).

The *Encyclopedia*, first published in 1965 under the title *Executive's Guide to Information Sources*, is a simple listing of publications and sources. Its thirteenth edition (James Woy, ed., 1998, 1,114 p., ISBN 0787624411) provides "more than 32,000 citations covering over 1,100 subjects of interest to business personnel" (title page). It includes abstracts and indexes, almanac and yearbooks, bibliographies, biographical sources, CD-ROM databases, directories, encyclopedias and dictionaries, financial ratios, handbooks and manuals, Internet databases, online databases, price sources, research centers and institutes, and many others (title page). Arrangement is alphabetical by topic from "Abbreviations" to "Zoning."

Harvard's core collection was established in 1969. The 1997 edition of the *Harvard Business School Core Collection* contains approximately 3,500 titles with a cutoff date of July 1996. Titles are arranged by subject in alphabetical order from accounting, accounting firms, action research to Xerox corporation, young adults, and Zero Coupon Securities. Some titles are annotated. New to this edition are titles that are designated as Core Classics, have won awards, or have been selected for "best books" lists. Its "Notable Books: Awards and Best Books Lists" includes American Libraries Outstanding Reference Sources, the Bancroft Prizes Listing by Subject, and the Wildman Medals. It has an appendix, Publishers' Names and Addresses, and four indexes (Author, Title, and Core Classics, and Notable Books: Awards and Best Books Index).

The *Quality Management Sourcebook* is an annotated bibliography of books, periodical articles, and nonprint materials and a listing of associations, consultants, and so on. It contains five chapters: (1) Introduction to general sources; (2) Application of TQM (Total Quality Management) arranged by SIC (Standard Industrial Classification Code); (3) Focus on Specific Aspects of Quality Management; (4) Quality in the Future: What Role Does ISO 9000 Play?; and (5) Resource Materials, including training materials, executive development programs, quality management consultants survey, TQM associations, and so on. There are a glossary and three indexes: name, title, and subject.

Theses and Dissertations

National Business Education Yearbook, 1963–   . (Reston, VA: National Business Education Association, annual, ISSN 10490256) (J10) publishes "Research Studies in Business Education Completed and Underway." Listings of dissertations are also carried in a few periodicals, as noted in Chapter 6.

Research in Progress

National Business Education Yearbook, noted above, also publishes research in progress in its "Research Studies in Business Education Completed and Underway." Research in progress may also be found in periodicals, as noted in Chapter 6.

Indexes

General

For locating periodical articles in business, some general indexes and indexes other than business should not be overlooked. *Reader's Guide to Periodical Literature*, a general index, and subject indexes such as *PAIS International, Social Sciences Index, Applied Science and Technology Index*, and *Engineering Index* all have coverage of business material. The following indexes are of particular importance:

> *Business Index*, v. 1– , 1979– . Foster City, CA: Information Access Company. Monthly updating. ISSN 02733684. Microfilm and digital. (J11)
>
> *Business Periodicals Index*, 1958– . Bronx, NY: H. W. Wilson. 11 monthly issues, with quarterly and annual cumulations. ISSN 00076961. Print & digital. (J12)
>
> *IAC F & S Index United States*, 1960– . Foster City, CA: Information Access Company. Monthly (optional weekly) with quarterly and annual cumulations. ISSN 07473206. Print & digital. (J13)
>
> *IAC F & S Index Europe*, 1978– . Foster City, CA: Information Access Company. Monthly with quarterly and annual cumulations. ISSN 02774536. Print & digital. (J14)
>
> *IAC F & S Index International*, 1967– . Foster City, CA: Information Access Company. Monthly with quarterly and annual cumulations. ISSN 02774528. Print & digital. (J15)

Both *Business Index (BI)* and *Business Periodicals Index* are cumulative, subject indexes, but in different format. *BI* is a three-year cumulative index in a reel film to over 800 journals and some newspapers. It has more extensive coverage than *Business Periodicals Index*, noted next. Periodicals indexed in *BI* with a few exceptions are all included in *Trade & Industry Database*, noted later.

Business Periodicals Index indexes over 300 periodicals in the English language in accounting, acquisitions and mergers, advertising, banking, building and construction, chemical industry, communications, computers, drugs and cosmetics, economics, electronics, engineering, finance and investments, food industry, government regulations, industrial relations, insurance, international business, marketing, occupational health and safety, and others, with a separate index to book reviews. The index is also available online and on CD-ROM.

The F & S indexes, expanded by Predicasts from the former *Funk & Scott Index of Corporations and Industries* (1960–1967), now published by the Information Access Company, cover business activities worldwide. All three indexes are organized by Standard Industrial Classification (SIC) number, by company name, and by country. Each issue consists of two sections: Section 1, Industries and Products (yellow pages) and Section 2,

Companies (white pages). For each entry are provided one or two lines of summary, in addition to a citation. They serve as a quick reference without referring to the source. About 2,500 newspapers, trade journals, government documents, newsletters, and special reports are indexed. They are marketed online as *IAC F & S Index* (J16) through Dialog (File 18) from 1980 forward and DataStar (File PTIN) from 1978 to date.

It may be noted that for SIC codes, an indispensable reference is the *Standard Industrial Classification Manual* (U.S. Office of Management and Budget, Washington, DC: NTIS, 1987, 705 p.) (J17). It lists titles and description of industries in 99 major groups. The SIC (Standard Industrial Classification) code is the federal economic standards classification by industry, developed as a means for the comparability of establishment data on the U.S. economy. An establishment is "a unit, generally at a single physical location, where business is conducted or where services or industrial operations are performed."[3] The SIC system begins with nine major categories: agriculture, forestry and fishing; mining; construction; manufacturing; transportation, communications, and public utilities; wholesale trade; retail trade; finance, insurance, and real estate; and services. They are further broken down to 2-digit, 3-digit, and finally 4-digit codes.

The new codes, NAICS (North American Industrial Classification System), contain six digits, as opposed to four digits in SIC. They are published as the *North American Industry Classification System* (Executive Office of the President, Office of Management and Budget, Washington, DC: GPO, 1997, 1,247 p., ISBN 0934213577) (J18). The publication consists of four parts: Part I, Titles and Descriptions of Industries; Part II, Numerical List of Short Titles; Part III, Appendices; and Part IV, Alphabetical Index. Beginning January 1, 1997, federal statistical data are collected and based on NAICS. Its appendixes consist of (A) 1997 NAICS United States Structure, Including Relationship to 1987 United States SIC, and (B) 1987 United States SIC Matched to 1997 United States NAICS. The appendixes provide a comparable list of SIC/NAICS. The comparable list can also be accessed on the Bureau of the Census Web site (http://www.census.gov).

The *IAC F & S Index United States* lists products, industries, and company activities in the United States. It indexes 750 publications including business-oriented newspapers, trade magazines, and special reports. The *IAC F & S Index Europe* covers the Common Market, Scandinavia, other regions of Western Europe, and Eastern Europe. Business activities in Canada, Latin America, Africa, the Middle East, Asia, and Oceania are provided in the *IAC F & S Index International*.

Subfield

Accounting and Tax Index, 1921/23– . Ann Arbor, MI: UMI. Quarterly with annual cumulation. ISSN 10630287. Print & digital. (J19)

Banking Information Index, 1982/83– . Louisville, KY: UMI. Monthly with annual cumulation. ISSN 1075282X. Print & digital. (J20)

Insurance Periodicals Index, 1963– . Chatsworth, CA: NILS Publishing and Special Libraries Association, Insurance and Employee Benefits Division. Annual. ISSN 0074073X. Print & digital. (J21)

Accounting and Tax Index, formerly *Accountants' Index*, indexes English-language periodicals, books, pamphlets, and government documents by author, title, and subject. More than 1,000 publications are scanned for inclusion. It covers accounting, taxation, and related subjects, such as financial management, compensation, consulting, and the financial services industry. The index is also available online as *Accounting and Tax Database* (J22) marketed through ProQuest and Dialog (File 485). The database, updated weekly, runs from 1971 forward and contains full text of articles in a number of serials.

Over 220 periodicals on banking trends, topics, issues, and corporations with focus on practical banking management are indexed in *Banking Information Index*, formerly *Banking Literature Index*. It is a classified index of over 650 subject headings. *Banking Information Index* is part of the *Banking Information Source* database (J23), updated weekly, marketed through ProQuest, Lexis-Nexis, and Dialog (File 268). *Banking Information Source* consists of the index and *FINIS* (*Financial Industry Information Service*) (J24). The database contains selected full-text materials from 1994 forward.

The *Insurance Periodicals Index* indexes 35 journals. Its coverage is broad, including accounting, AIDS, alcohol abuse, asbestos, HMOs (health maintenance organizations), PPOs (preferred provider organizations), stocks taxation, workers' compensation, and so on. Its database, updated weekly, is marketed through Dialog (File 169) from 1984 to date.

Abstracts

General

ABI/INFORM, 1971– . Louisville, KY: UMI. Weekly. Digital. (J25)

Business Dateline, 1985– . Louisville, KY: UMI. Weekly. Digital. (J26)

IAC Business A.R.T.S., 1976– . Foster City, CA: Information Access Company. Weekly. Digital. (J27)

IAC Management Contents, 1974–   . Foster City, CA: Information Access Company. Digital. (J28)

IAC Newsearch. Foster City, CA: Information Access Company. Daily. Digital. (J29)

IAC PROMT (Predicasts Overview of Markets and Technology), 1972– . Foster City, CA: Information Access Company. Daily. Digital. (J30)

Wilson Business Abstracts, 1990–   . Bronx, NY: H. W. Wilson. 9/year or quarterly. Print & digital. (J31)

ABI/INFORM indexes and abstracts 1,000 journals in English on management and administration, with selected full-text. *ABI/INFORM* provides the major source information in business. The database is marketed through Dialog (File 15), DataStar (File INFO), Ovid (File INFO), Questel-Orbit (File INFO), and FirstSearch.

Business Dateline is a full-text database of over 350 business publications. It contains the full text of articles of more than a hundred regional publications in the United States and Canada. The database is marketed directly from the provider and through Dialog (File 635), Ovid (File INFO), and FirstSearch.

The coverage of *IAC Business A.R.T.S* (*Applied Research, Theory, and Scholarship*) is much broader than its title indicates. It covers art, anthropology, economics, education, ethnic studies, government, history, literature, political science, and so on. Over 1,550 periodicals commonly held in selected academic libraries are abstracted with full-text articles from 500 periodicals. The database is marketed through Dialog (File 88) and DataStar (File ACAD).

IAC Management Contents (publishers, title, and form vary) began as a contents reproduction service to U.S. and foreign journals. Publication of the printed version has ceased. It is now available on CD-ROM and online. The database indexes and abstracts 150 journals covering accounting, decision science, finance, industrial relations, managerial economics, marketing, operations research, organization behavior, and public administration. The database is updated daily in *Newsearch*, noted later, and monthly with approximately 1,000 records per update. It is marketed through Dialog (File 75), DataStar (File MGMT), Ovid (File MGMT), and FirstSearch.

IAC Newsearch, a daily (current 45 days only), provides abstracts and full-text of over 1,700 sources of news stories, articles, and book reviews on many subjects, such as arts and entertainment; business and economics; company and industry; consumer preference; finance; management; new product announcements; stocks, bonds and commodities; and news. It is the front runner of IAC, updating IAC's nine databases, including *IAC Business A.R.T.S.*, *IAC Legal Resource Index*, *IAC's Magazine Database*, *IAC Management Contents*, *IAC Trade & Industry Database*, and IAC's news and magazine databases, noted elsewhere in this and other chapters. The database is marketed through Dialog (File 211).

IAC PROMT lists abstracts and full-text records from more than 1,000 sources on new products and technologies, research, market trends, plant production and capacities, sales and shipment data, and general management and industry news. It is the broadest and the most current database and should be the first one of IAC's products turned to for business information. The database is marketed through Dialog (File 16), DataStar (Files PTSP, PT91, PT86, and TRPT), Questel-ORBIT (file PROMT), and Lexis-Nexis.

Other Information Access Company databases relating to business may be noted: (1) *Industry Express* (J32), a full-text database updated daily (current 30 days), covers general business news, economic and trade sources, and government policy issues. It is marketed through Dialog (File 12). (2) *Trade & Industry Database*, 1981– (J33), a weekly bibliographic and full-text database, provides over 1,000 sources from trade and business publications and news releases, including *The Value Line Investment Survey, Standard & Poor's Industry Surveys*, and *OECD Economic Surveys*. It complements *IAC PROMT*, noted earlier. The database is marketed through Dialog (File 148), DataStar (File INDY and ID91), and Lexis-Nexis. (3) *IAC National Newspaper Index*, 1979– (J34), covers a number of newspapers and indexes front-to-back five newspapers—*Christian Science Monitor, Los Angeles Times, The New York Times, The Wall Street Journal*, and *The Washington Post*. The database is marketed through Dialog (File 111, updated weekly) and DataStar (NNIN, updated monthly). One feature of IAC's news database is its AT (article type) field search for limiting retrieval of articles by type (nearly 30 of them), such as bibliography, biography, calendar, editorial, illustration, interview, obituary, review, and transcript.

Wilson Business Abstracts indexes and abstracts articles of over 300 English language business periodicals. Abstracts are 50–150 words in length and included for biographical sketches, corporate profiles, interviews, product reviews, and obituaries. It uses the same subject headings as *Business Periodical Index*, noted earlier. The other version of *Wilson Business Abstracts* is *Wilson Business Abstracts—Full-Text*. *Wilson Business Abstracts* is available on CD-ROM, as Wilsondisc and marketed through Silver-Platter. Its online database is included in Wilsonline and marketed through FirstSearch and Ovid (File WBUS).

Subfield

Management and Marketing Abstracts, 1976– . Leatherhead, Surrey, England: Pira International. Monthly. ISSN 03082172. Print & digital. (J35)

Operations Research Management Science: An International Literature Digest. Davenport, IA: Executive Sciences Institute. Monthly. ISSN 00303658. (J36)

Personnel Management Abstracts, 1955– . Chelsea, MI: Personnel Management Abstracts. Quarterly. ISSN 0031577X. (J37)

Management and Marketing Abstracts (formerly *Marketing Abstracts*) contains over 70,000 references and abstracts of articles of over 200 management journals. It covers management, marketing, business developments, personnel issues, management techniques, environmental issues, employment legislation, and company strategy and planning. Stress is on European sources. It is also available on CD-ROM as Dialog's OnDisc, updated quarterly, and online marketed through DataStar (File MMKA).

In *Operations Research Management Science*, a classified abstracting service, all entries are published in a same format on one sheet of one or two pages in length. Each entry contains title, authors, journal, purpose, summary, and results.

Another classified abstracting service in management is *Personnel Management Abstracts*, a guide to the literature of management, human resources and personnel (subtitle). It abstracts books and articles of some 100 periodicals. Each issue consists of two indexes: index to periodical literature, indexed by authors' names; and index to companies and other organizations referred to in the abstracts.

SOURCES OF INFORMATION

General

Business is one of the fields with a large number of databases available. Over 110 databases are currently marketed by Dialog. These are grouped into General Company and Industry News; Company Directories and Financials; Mergers and Acquisitions; Country and Market Research; Trade, Business Opportunities, and Events; and Management, Economics, and Banking.

All major business source providers make available databases, including Disclosure Information Group, Dun and Bradstreet, Moody's, Information Access Company, National Register, and Standard & Poor's. Below are some databases providing information on business in general.

> *Business & Industry*, 1974– . Beachwood, OH: Responsive Database Services. Digital. (J38)
>
> *Dow Jones Interactive*. New York: Dow Jones. http://www.djinteractive.com (J39)
>
> *Hoover's Online*. Austin, TX: Reference Press. http://www.hoovers.com (J40)
>
> *IAC InSite*. Foster City, CA: Information Access Company. http://www.iac-insite.com (J41)
>
> *Lexis-Nexis Academic Universe*. Bethesda, MD: Congressional Information Service. http://web.lexis-nexis.com/universe/ (J42)
>
> *Profound*. Mountain View, CA: Dialog Corp. http://www.profound.com (J43)

Business & Industry, updated daily, contains events, facts, figures, and products of public and private companies worldwide. It indexes and abstracts, some with full-text, 1,400 sources such as general business press, trade magazines, newspapers, newsletters, and dailies. There are nearly 90 industry names for the convenience of searching, including aerospace and defense, agriculture, airline, automotive, banking, beer, business services, fast foods, financial services, insurance, mail order, metals, oil and gas, online services, portable computers, securities, software, and utilities. Also, there are listings of concept terms and marketing terms for searching. The database provides information on market size, market share, forecasts, demographics, mergers and acquisitions, foreign investment, capacity, product development, and markets. It is available on CD-ROM via Dialog and SilverPlatter and online marketed through Dialog (File 9), DataStar (File BIDB), and FirstSearch, and on the Web (http://www.rdsinc.com).

Business & Industry is one of the three business databases of *RDS Business Reference Suite* on the Web. The other two are *TableBase*, 1997– , weekly (J44), and *Business & Management Practices*, 1995– , weekly (J45). These two databases are also marketed via Dialog (File 93 and File 13). The *Suite*'s home page displays the databases for choosing. Boolean logical and positional operators and field limitation can be used for searching. The search results indicate full-text or abstracts.

The home page of *Dow Jones Interactive* displays four major categories for searching: Business Newsstand, Publications Library, Company & Industry Center, and Historical Market Data Center. Business Newsstand covers major news and business publications, 50 top U.S. newspapers, and press release wires. Top newspapers and magazines include *The Wall Street Journal, The New York Times, The Washington Post, Los Angeles Times, Financial Times, The Wall Street Journal Europe, The Asian Wall Street Journal, Barron's, Forbes, Fortune, Far Eastern Economic Review*, and *Smart Money*.

In Publications Library, search may be conducted by words, company, industry, and person. There are also choices for result, such as full article, headline only, lead paragraph only, and headline and lead paragraph. Company & Industry Center provides four categories of reports: company, industry, country, and market research. Company Reports contains Financial Snapshot, Financial Profile, Company Screening Reports, Company/Industry Comparison Reports, Investext Analyst Reports, Multex Analyst Reports, Dun & Bradstreet Reports, and SEC Full-Text Filings. Country Reports derive from EIU [Economist Intelligence Unit] Country Information. Historical Market Data Center consists of Historical Pricing including Exchange Rates, Dividend, and Capital Change Reports. A user may find information here on stocks, options, mutual funds, and market indices. The database also links to *Dow Jones Business Directory*, noted later.

Hoover's Online contains information of public and private companies in the United States and around the world, including 9,000 U.S. public companies, 2,800 U.S. private companies, and 1,400 foreign companies and U.S. subsidiaries of foreign companies. It provides Company Profiles and Company Capsules. Company can be searched by company name, ticker symbol, or keyword. Company Capsules is also available on CD-ROM. In addition, the producer publishes a number of hard-copy business sources of information, including handbooks such as *Hoover's Handbook of American Business* (1998, 2 vols., ISBN 157311037X) (J46) and guides such as *Hoover's Guide to Media Companies* (1996, 300 p., ISBN 18789753967) (J47) and *Hoover's Guide to the Top Chicago Companies* (1996, 40 p., ISBN 1878753681) (J48).

IAC InSite consists of Business InSite, Market InSite, Newsletter InSite, Computer InSite, Health & Wellness InSite, Consumer InSite, and Company InSite. All InSites derive from IAC's databases repectively, such as *IAC Trade and Industry Database, IAC Newsletter Database*, and *IAC Promt*. Business InSite contains over 1,000 trade and industry publications. Market InSite offers resources of monitoring the activities of companies worldwide, the products and technologies they produce, and the markets in which they compete. Newsletter InSite contains leading industry and company newsletters worldwide, with full-text of over 500 publications. Some 100 journals, newsletters, and popular publications that cover the computer, electronics, and telecommunications industries are included in Computer InSite. Health & Wellness InSite contains 170 professional and general-interest health publications and health-related articles from over 3,000 business and popular magazines, with more than 70 percent of the articles in full text. More than 350 general publications are included in Consumer InSite. Business InSite, Computer InSite, and Health & Wellness InSite also refer to Company InSite, which provides information on 140,000 companies (111,000 U.S. and 30,000 foreign), of which 95 percent are privately held.

Lexis-Nexis Academic Universe is a database of news, business, and legal research drawn from nearly 6,000 English-language resources, including newsletters, journals, wires, and broadcast transcripts. It provides access to news, business directories, SEC documents, corporate profiles, statutes, federal and state case law, law reviews, and state legal material. It interfaces with Lexis-Nexis, reaching many of its vast legal sources. Some sources are available on both *Academic Universe* and *Congressional Universe*, noted in Chapter 7.

Its home page displays eighteen research topics: Top News; General News Topics; Company News; Industry & Market News; Government & Political News; Legal News; Company Financial Information; Country Profiles; State Profiles; Biographical Information; Reference & Directories; General Medical & Health Topics; Medical Abstracts; Accounting, Auditing, & Tax; Law Reviews; Federal Case Law; U.S. Code, Constitution, &

Court Rules; and State Legal Research. Each topic has a scope note, such as Industry & Market News, which is described as "Learn about industry forecasts, trends, and the forces driving an industry." Company News, according to the scope note, is to "find out the latest information about a specific company such as Microsoft, Time Warner, or General Motors." In each research topic, there is a listing of source material for selection. To a certain extent, *Academic Universe* duplicates *Congressional Universe*, such as *U.S. Code, Code of Federal Regulations*, congressional testimony, congressional committee schedules, *National Journal*, and *Congress Daily*.

Academic Universe uses two levels of menu search: the first level is the main menu, and the second level is the source. The user must select the first level and then specific source in the second level for searching. In free-text searching, Boolean logical and positional operators, proximity, and date range can be used.

Profound can be accessed via dialup or the Internet. *Profound* consists of mainly six databases: Researchline, Brokerline, Countryline, Wireline, Newsline, and Companyline. Researchline contains over 45,000 full-text market research reports. Brokerline has over 250,000 analysts' reports from brokerage houses. News is provided in Wireline and Newsline. Companyline contains financial reports on companies worldwide. *Profound* also offers quotes in its Exchange, listing reports recently added and additional sources.

Encyclopedias

The Encyclopedia of Management. 3rd ed. Carl Heyel. New York: Van Nostrand Reinhold, 1982. 1,371 p. ISBN 0442251651. (J49)

Glenn G. Munn's Encyclopedia of Banks and Finance. 8th ed. Rev. and exp. F. L. Garcia. Boston: Bankers, 1983. 1,024 p. ISBN 0872670422. (J50)

International Encyclopedia of Business and Management. Malcolm Warner, ed. London: Routledge, 1996. 6 vols. (J51)

Articles in Heyel, contributed by 203 specialists, range from a concise half-page statement to more detailed discussion of 20 pages or more. Heyel also includes biographies of management pioneers. References cited or information references at the end of most articles are a useful feature. Another feature is its guide to "core subject" readings, a planned, topical sequence reading program. Its appendixes include AACSB accredited universities and colleges offering programs in business administration; sources of information on associations, societies, special services, and publishers; and periodicals mentioned in the text. It complements Garcia, noted next.

Garcia contains 4,000 entries on banking, business, and financial terms. Its "in-depth entries provide historical background, analysis of recent trends, illustrative examples, statistical data, and citation of applicable laws and regulations" (Publisher's Foreword). There is a quick index. Garcia is an outstanding reference work for banks and trust companies, financiers, brokers, investors, speculators, lawyers, and students in courses in applied economics.

A new encyclopedia is the *International Encyclopedia of Business and Management*. It covers accounting; business economics; business history; finance; human resources management and industrial/labor relations; international business; management education and comparative management; management information systems; manufacturing management; marketing; operations management; operations research; and organization behavior and strategy. It also covers biographies and topics by continent, region, and nation. Biographical coverage is broad, including philosophers, psychologists, and military strategists, such as Machiavelli, Freud, and Sun Tzu. Each article has cross-references and further reading. Volume 6 is an index to key terms, concepts, countries, and names.

Dictionaries

The Blackwell Encyclopedia of Management. Cary L. Cooper and Chris Argyris, eds. Cambridge, MA: Blackwell, 1997. 12 vols. (J52)

Dictionary of Business and Economics. Rev. and exp. ed. Christine Ammer and Dean S. Ammer. New York: Free Press/Collier Macmillan, 1986. 507 p. ISBN 0029014808. (J53)

Oxford Dictionary for the Business World. Oxford: Oxford University Press, 1993. 966 p. ISBN 0198631251. (J54)

The *Blackwell Encyclopedia* consists of eleven dictionaries in eleven volumes:

Volume 1: *The Blackwell Encyclopedic Dictionary of Accounting*. Rashad Abdel-Khalik, ed. 308 p. ISBN 1557869431.

Volume 2: *The Blackwell Encyclopedic Dictionary of Strategic Management*. Derek F. Channon, ed. 350 p. ISBN 1557869669.

Volume 3: *The Blackwell Encyclopedic Dictionary of Management Information Systems*. Gordon B. Davis, ed. 263 p. ISBN1557869480.

Volume 4: *The Blackwell Encyclopedic Dictionary of Marketing*. Barbara R. Lewis and Dale Littler, eds. 274 p. ISBN 1557869391.

Volume 5: *The Blackwell Encyclopedic Dictionary of Managerial Economics*. Robert McAuliffe, ed. 233 p. ISBN 1558669650.

Volume 6: *The Blackwell Encyclopedic Dictionary of Organizational Behavior*. Nigel Nicholson, ed. 628 p. ISBN 0631187812.

Volume 7: *The Blackwell Encyclopedic Dictionary of International Management.* John O'Connell, ed. 317 p. ISBN 1557869243.

Volume 8: *The Blackwell Encyclopedic Dictionary of Finance* Dean Paxson and Douglas Wood, eds. 225 p. ISBN 155786912X.

Volume 9: *The Blackwell Encyclopedic Dictionary of Human Resource Management.* Lawrence H. Peters, Charles R. Creek, and Stuart A. Youngblood, eds. 438 p. ISBN 155786943X.

Volume 10: *The Blackwell Encyclopedic Dictionary of Operations Management.* Nigel Slack, ed. 256 p. ISBN 1557869057.

Volume 11: *The Blackwell Encyclopedic Dictionary of Business Ethics.* Patricia H. Werhane and R. Edward Freeman, eds. 701 p. ISBN 1557869421.

All volumes have a similar format. Entries are arranged in alphabetical order with cross-references and bibliography. Volume 12 is a cumulative index.

The work by Ammer and Ammer is a dictionary of terms, concepts, organizations, and biographies. Definitions are relatively long on topics ranging from economic theory to business applications, such as accounting, business law, insurance, real estate, and public finance. It concludes with a selected bibliography. The appendix includes sources for economic and financial data.

The *Oxford Dictionary* contains terms in business and accounting, commodity, computer, financial, and stockbroking markets. It also covers place names and biographies of leading figures in the business world. Pronunciation is provided. There are eight appendixes: checklist for a business plan, compiling graphs and charts, world times, some points of English usage, punctuation marks, Royal mail services, paper sizes and types, and checklist for a business speech.

Directories

Business is one field that has been overwhelmed with directories. Company information can be found in a number of directories. The following are some representative directories broadly divided into United States, international, and subject.

United States

American Business Directory. Omaha, NE: American Business Information. Monthly. Digital. (J55)

America's Corporate Families and International Affiliates, 1983–   . Parsippany, NJ: Dun & Bradstreet Information Services. Annual. ISSN 07404018. (J56)

Brands and Their Companies. 15th ed. Susan E. Edgar, ed. Detroit: Gale
Research. 1996. 2 vols. ISBN 0810302101. (J57)

D&B—Dun's Electronic Business Directory. Parsippany, NJ: Dun & Bradstreet Information Services. Quarterly. Digital. (J58)

D&B—Dun's Market Identifiers. Parsippany, NJ: Dun & Bradstreet Information Services. Digital. (J59)

D&B—Million Dollar Directory, 1959– . Parsippany, NJ: Dun's Marketing
Services. Annual. ISSN 10513442. Print & digital. (J60)

Dow Jones Business Directory. New York: Dow Jones. http://bus-
dir.dowjones.com (J61)

Standard & Poor's Corporations. New York: Standard & Poor's. CD-ROM.
Monthly. Digital. (J62)

Standard & Poor's Register of Corporations, Directors, and Executives,
1928– . New York: Standard & Poor's. Annual. ISSN 01981061.
Print & digital. (J63)

Ward's Business Directory of U.S. Private and Public Companies, 1961– .
Detroit: Gale Research. Annual. ISSN 10488707. Print & digital. (J64)

Both *American Business Directory (ABD)* and *D&B—Dun's Electronic
Business Directory* provide comparative description of records. Over 10
million U.S. businesses are listed in *American Business Directory*, marketed
through Dialog (File 531). It covers public companies, private companies,
small businesses, government agencies, professionals, and schools. A typical
record contains business name, address, telephone, county, MSA, type of
industry, primary SIC and yellow page product line(s), employees, location
sales, and top executives. It is basically an electronic yellow pages, enhanced with other information.

Also, over 10 million businesses in the United States are listed in *Dun's
Electronic Business Directory*, marketed through Dialog (File 515). It
covers agriculture, business services, communications, construction, finance, insurance, manufacturing, mining, professional services, public administration, public utilities, real estate, retail, transportation, and
wholesale. For each record are listed company name, address, telephone
number, region, industry group, Standard Industrial Classification, type of
company, D-U-N-S number, number of employees, and country population. It may be noted that D-U-N-S (Data Universal Numbering System)
number is a distinctive nine-digit company identifier. It links to the D-U-
N-S numbers of parents, subsidiaries, headquarters, and branches of millions of corporate members worldwide. As compared with *American
Business Directory*, its links to D-U-N-S numbers is unique and its listing
of mailing address and secondary SICs are not found in *American Business
Directory*, but the latter lists executives. For more detailed information,
such as sales, assets, and affiliations, other sources should be used. All
records in *Dun's Electronic Business Directory* are also available in *D&B—
Dun's Market Identifiers (DMI)* (Dialog File 516), noted next.

Dun's Market Identifiers (DMI), marketed through Dialog (File 516) and Lexis-Nexis, provides information on companies as does *Dun's Electronic Business Directory*, but *DMI* is more current and contains more information, such as sales, sales growth, employment growth, number of accounts, accounting firm, bank, and corporate executives. In addition, it provides three types of reports: Business Information Report (BIR), Payment Analysis Report (PAR), and Supplier Evaluation Report (SER). D&B's two databases and *American Business Directory* complement each other. In a comparative study of *ABD* and *DMI*, Michael R. Lavin concluded that each contains information not found in the other and both offer important advantages for business directory users.[4]

America's Corporate Families consists of two volumes. Volume 1 provides full descriptions of 9,000 U.S. parent companies and their 45,000 subsidiaries and divisions. Volume 2 lists 1,700 U.S. parents with their 13,000 foreign subsidiaries and 2,500 foreign parents with their 6,000 U.S. subsidiaries. It complements *Million Dollar Directory*, noted later.

For trade and company name identification, refer to *Brands and Their Companies* (formerly *Trade Name Directory*). It provides "consumer products and their manufacturers with addresses and phone numbers" (subtitle), including 68,000 manufacturers and distributors, 326,000 consumer brands, and 20,000 brands new to this edition. Materials are arranged in two sections of listings: brands and company. The brands section is an alphabetical listing of all brands. The company section contains company names, addresses, and phone numbers, with fax and toll-free numbers if available.

Million Dollar Directory consists of two sets: *Series* (ISSN 07342861) and *Top 50,000 Companies* (ISSN 07429649). The 1998 *Series* (5 vols., ISBN 1562036416) provides profiles of 160,000 leading American public and private companies (subtitle), of which 136,000 are privately owned businesses. Volumes 1 to 3 (white pages) list businesses alphabetically by company name. Criteria for inclusion are (1) 180 or more employees in a headquarter or single location, and 900 or more at that location, if the company is a branch, or (2) $9,000,000 or more in sales volume. For each company are given address and telephone number, type of business, sales volume, employment size, up to six SIC codes, D-U-N-S number, officers and directors, members of the board of directors, and founded/ownership date. Volumes 4 and 5 provide cross-reference businesses by Standard Industrial Classification (blue pages) and geography (yellow pages).

The *Top 50,000 Companies* selects from the *Series* some 50,000 that have an intangible net worth of over $1,850,000. Companies listed in both sets are indexed in the *Million Dollar Directory Master Index*. *Million Dollar Directory* and *Reference Book of Corporate Management*, noted later, are also available on CD-ROM, *D-U-N-S Million Dollar Disc (DDS)* (J65), updated quarterly. *DDS* lists over 180,000 businesses with net worth of $500,000 or more and nearly 500,000 biographies.

Million Dollar Directory can also be accessed through the Internet as *D&B Million Dollar Database* (http://www.dnbmdd.com) (J66). The database provides "information on over 1,250,000 U.S. leading public and private businesses . . . [that] includes industry information with up to 24 individual 8-digit SICs, size criteria (employees and annual sales) type of ownership, principal executives and biographies" (home page).

A listing of Web sites and briefs are provided by *Dow Jones Business Directory*. The directory has a broad coverage, including government and law. The home page displays the following groups for choosing: Career, Companies in the Dow, Economy, Financial Markets, Government & Politics, Industries, Law, Personal Finance, Reference, and Small Business. Each group is further divided. Companies in the Dow, for instance, lists Dow Jones Industries, Dow Jones Transportation, Dow Jones Utilities, and Industries, for reviews of other companies organized by industry. Reference is categorized by Career Resources, Company Information, Consumer Tips, Demographics & Research, Encyclopedias & Reference Works, Management Resources, Small Business Reference, Tax Reference, and Travel. A record contains key reasons to use a site, cost, summary, and key site pages.

One of its features is the Web site linkage. The category of Company Information, for example, lists a number of Web sites for searching information on companies, such as *Business Wire, CompaniesOnline, Hoover's Online*, noted earlier, *Standard & Poor's Equity Investor Services*, and *Web100: Big Business on the Web*. All these Web sites can be linked by clicking their URLs. It may be noted that *CompaniesOnline* (http://www.companiesonline.com) (J67), developed by Dun & Bradstreet in partnership with Lycos, a search engine company noted in Chapter 1, is to "discover the U.S. companies behind the Websites." Its home page displays search by criteria, featured companies of the week, and browse by industry. Each record provides D-U-N-S number, phone number, location type, immediate parent, ultimate parent, contact name, annual sales, trade name(s), Web address, ownership structure, and ownership.

Standard & Poor's Corporations, on CD as Dialog's Ondisc, consists of three databases: (1) *Standard & Poor's Corporate Descriptions Plus News* (Dialog File 133), noted later in the Investment Services section; (2) *Standard & Poor's Register—Biographical* (Dialog File 526) (J68); and (3) *Standard & Poor's Register—Corporate* (Dialog file 527) (J69). The last two databases will be noted next as parts of *Standard & Poor's Register*. *Standard & Poor's Corporation* provides information on more than 12,000 publicly traded companies, including over 1,000 major international companies traded on U.S. exchanges, more than 45,000 leading private corporations, and 70,000 key business executives from both public and private companies.

Standard & Poor's Register is one of the most widely used reference tools. As the publisher advertised, there are 89 ways to profit from using the directory, such as information on potential acquisition candidates, pro-spective client lists, targeted mailing lists, and fund-raising campaigns. Volume 1 is a corporate listing of over 56,000 entries in alphabetical order by business name, including address, officers, SIC code(s), and when available, assets, number of employees, sales, products, and the like. Volume 2 is an individual listing of directors and executives, over 71,000 entries, including their titles/positions, business addresses, residence addresses, and when obtainable, year and place of birth, education, and fraternal memberships. Volume 3 is an index consisting of (1) Standard Industrial Classification Index, (2) Standard Industrial Classification Codes, (3) Geographical Index, (4) Corporate Family Indices, (5) Obituary Section, (6) New Individual Additions, and (7) New Company Additions. Also included in volume 3 is a brief introduction to the "S&P 500." *Standard & Poor's Register* is updated by *Standard & Poor's Register of Corporations, Directors, and Executives Cumulative Supplement* (J70) between editions. Its database constitutes a part of Dialog's CD-ROM, *Standard & Poor's Corporations*, noted earlier, and is marketed through Lexis-Nexis and Dialog in two files: *Standard & Poor's Register—Biographical*, semiannual updates (Dialog File 526) (J71) and *Standard & Poor's Register—Corporate*, quarterly updates (Dialog File 527) (J72).

The 1999 edition of *Ward's* (8 vols., 1998, ISBN 0787625027) contains 90,000 companies. Volumes 1 to 3 list companies in alphabetical order. A typical entry provides company name, address, phone, fax, toll-free number, URLs, e-mail, financial figures, sales, total assets, operating revenues, or gross billings, number of employees, up to 4-digit SIC codes with descriptions, 6-digit NAICS codes with descriptions, company type, immediate parent, ticker symbol and stock exchange, fiscal year end, year founded, import/export status, up to five officers' names and their titles, and description of products or services. Volume 4 is a geographical listing. Volume 5 lists rankings of sales within 4-digit SIC codes. State rankings by sales within 4-digit SIC listing, ranked by sales within 6-digit NAICS listing are provided in volumes 6 to 8. Although subsidiaries are indicated, they are not grouped under their parent companies. Its special features provide many interesting data, such as 100 largest publicly held U.S. companies for each state, 100 largest privately held U.S. companies for each state, both ranked by sales volume, and 100 largest employers for each state. *Ward's* also contributes to *IAC Company Intelligence* (J73), marketed through Dialog (File 479), DataStar (File INCO), and Lexis-Nexis. The database is characterized by company news.

International

> *D&B—Global Corporate Linkages*. Parsippany, NJ: Dun & Bradstreet Information Services. Bimonthly. (J74)

Directory of American Firms Operating in Foreign Countries. 15th ed. New York: Uniworld Business Publications, 1999. 3 vols. ISBN 0836000412. (J75)

Directory of Corporate Affiliations, 1968– . New Providence, NJ: National Register. Annual. ISSN 07369778. Print & digital. (J76)

International Directory of Company Histories. Editors vary. Detroit: St. James, 1990– . Irregular. (J77)

Worldscope Company Database, 1988/89– . Bridgeport, CT: Worldscope-Disclosure Partners. Print & digital. (J78)

A relatively new database is *Global Corporate Linkages* (Dialog File 522), providing information on company structure and family hierarchy worldwide. A very useful tool for looking for parent company, branches, and subsidiaries, it lists name of holding company, primary and secondary SICs, parent D-U-N-S number, domestic D-U-N-S number, corporate family hierarchy, and company name, location, and D-U-N-S number. For more detailed information, such as sales, assets, and/or key personnel, other sources should be used.

Directory of American Firms lists, in volume 1, part 1, American firms operating in foreign countries in alphabetical order. Each entry contains U.S. company name, address, phone/fax, subsidiaries or affiliates, some key personnel, Web site address, annual revenue, and number of employees. Volume 1, part 2, and volumes 2 and 3 are listings of countries from A to Z of the American firms' foreign operations.

A comprehensive coverage of corporation subsidiaries is the *Directory of Corporate Affiliations,* a standard "Who Owns Whom" directory. The five-volume set consists of a master index (vols. 1 and 2) with cross-references to over 40,000 businesses, subsidiaries, and affiliates of U.S. corporations; U.S. public companies (vol. 3); U.S. private companies (vol. 4); and international public and private companies (vol. 5). It provides information on parent companies of over 40,000 businesses, providing for each entry address and telephone number, state of incorporation, ticker symbols, stock exchange, transfer agents, number of affiliates, type of business, number of employees, sales, total assets, total liabilities, net worth, and top corporate officers and their divisions, subsidiaries, and affiliates. The directory is available on CD-ROM as *Corporate Affiliations Plus* (J79) and online as *Corporate Affiliations* (J80) marketed through Dialog (File 153) and Lexis-Nexis.

The first five volumes of the *International Directory* published in 1990 cover 1,200 companies, arranged by 36 industries. Companies in each industry are presented in alphabetical order. Beginning with volume 7, 1993, entries of all companies are arranged in a simple alphabetical order, no longer grouped by industry. Criteria for inclusion vary. In the first five volumes, companies to be included "have achieved a minimum of two billion U.S. dollars in annual sales, or they are leading influences in their respective industries or geographical locations." In later volumes, criteria have been revised to include most companies whose annual sales have achieved a minimum US$500 million, and in recent volumes a minimum of $100 million.

The current volume is volume 24, published in 1998. It provides directory information in a box, such as legal name, address, telephone, toll-free, fax, and Web site and a statement of public, private, state, or parent ownership. Entries in general have a Company Perspectives box, a short summary of the company's mission, goals, and ideals. The main body of entry provides historical development of the company followed by principal subsidiaries, principal divisions, principal operating units, and further reading. There are two indexes, both cumulative: Index to Companies and Index to Industries.

Worldscope consists of five volumes: (1) Users' Guide; (2) Asia, Africa, Australia; (3) Europe; (4) and (5), North America. Over 3,000 industrial companies from 18 industries and 24 countries are listed. Each entry in a one-page format gives the company's information including financial statement data, financial ratios and growth rates, per share data and investment ratios, five-year annual growth rates, financial ratios, five-year average, and accounting practices. Volume 1 also provides country averages, industry averages, company rankings worldwide, company rankings within the country, company rankings within the country by industry, company rankings within the industry, and company indexes. Each of the other four volumes is preceded by three indexes: worldwide, country, and industry. This is a useful, handy reference for principal companies in the world. Its database is marketed through Dow Jones, Lexis-Nexis, and FirstSearch.

Subfield

Included here are directories for different types of business.

Accounting

> *Who Audits America*, 1976– . Menlo Park, CA: Data Financial Press. Semiannual. ISSN 01490281. (J81)

As the subtitle states, it is "a directory of publicly held corporations and the accounting firms who audit them," organized in three sections: (1) Companies, a two-line listing of companies, new companies added, and companies removed from the previous edition; (2) Auditors, a summary of auditor clients, big accounting firms, and other accounting firms with state lists, changes of auditors by clients, officers of national accounting firms, and auditor codes; and (3) Appendices, listing industry codes, and state codes. The work is also available on magnetic tape.

Advertising

> *Standard Directory of Advertising Agencies*, 1917–   . New Providence, NJ: National Register. 2/year. ISSN 00856614. Print & digital. (J82)
> *Standard Directory of Advertisers*, 1964–   . New Providence, NJ: National Register. Annual. Print & digital. (J83)
> *Standard Directory of International Advertisers and Agencies*, 1984–   . New Providence, NJ: National Register. Annual. Print & digital. (J84)

The *Standard Directory of Advertising Agencies* and *Standard Directory of Advertisers* are known as the agency red books, also available on CD-ROM. The January 1999 issue of *Standard Directory of Advertising Agencies* (1998, 1,558 p.+, ISBN 0871217297X) lists advertising agencies in six sections: Advertising Agencies, House Agencies, Media Buying Services, Sales Promotion Agencies, Public Relations Firms, and CyberAgencies. It also provides U.S. Agency Brands Ranked by Gross Income, Top 10 Agencies by U.S. Media Billings, and World Top 50 Advertising Agencies.

For information on company advertisers, a well-known publication is the *Standard Directory of Advertisers*. The 1999 edition (1998, 2 vols., ISBN 0872172880) lists in volume 1, Business Classifications, some 25,000 advertiser companies in the United States and Canada that spend at least $200,000 on national or regional campaigns a year. Businesses are classified into 52 categories, including appliances, cleaning agents, cultural and recreational entertainment, financial services, food retailers, government and state agencies, schools and colleges, shoes, wines and liquors, and so on. Each entry contains name, address, telecommunication data, electronic addresses, company data, business descriptions, advertising expenditures, and advertising media. It has a ranking listing of 200 largest advertisers on the basis of the amount of appropriations. Volume 2 is Indexes consisting of Product Categories by State, Brandname, Standard Industrial Classification, and Personnel. The *Directory* is available online through Lexis-Nexis. The international directory, known as the international red book, lists more than 3,000 international advertisers and advertising agencies in over 90 countries. It is available on CD-ROM.

Banking and Finance

> *Thomson/Polk Bank Directory*, 1872–   . Skokie, IL: Thomson Financial Publishing. Annual. ISSN 10578986. (J85)

Thomson/Polk Bank Directory (formerly *Rand McNally Bankers Directory*, *Rand McNally International Bankers Directory*, and *Thomson Bank Directory*), called by the publisher the "Bankers' Blue Book," lists over 130,000 banks worldwide. The 1998 edition (1998, 5 vols., ISBN

1563102668) lists in volumes 1 and 2, United States and Dependencies, banks by state and location, and in volumes 3 and 4, World, banks by country and location. Each entry contains seventeen items of information, such as bank legal title, institution charter type, general information, funds processing, memberships, holding company, asset rank, financial figures, bank profit, balance sheet, officers, and branches. Volume 5 is a Reference Section, which consists of Principal Correspondents Directory, Correspondents Performance: Interbank Liability Guidelines for the 2,000 Largest U.S. Banks, World Time Zone Map, Explanation of Listings, Title and City Abbreviations Guide, and Currency Abbreviations.

Employment

A fair number of publications appear on career opportunities, ranging from entry-level careers to choosing a company. A comprehensive guide to career opportunities is:

> *The Career Guide*, 1983/84– . Parsippany, NJ: Dun & Bradstreet. ISSN 08910596. (J86)

Formerly *Dun's Employment Opportunities Directory*, *The Career Guide* (1997, 6,032 p., ISBN 1562036378) consists of seven sections: Section 1, Employers Alphabetically, limited to American companies with at least 1,000 employees (white pages); Section 2, Employers Geographically (white pages); Section 3, Employers by Industry Classification (blue pages); Section 4, Employer Branch Offices Geographically (green pages); Section 5, Disciplines Hired Geographically (pink pages); Section 6, Employers Offering Work Study or Internship Programs (blue pages); and Section 7, Personnel Consultants Geographically (white pages). For each company are listed educational/experience specialties generally hired by the company, career opportunities, training and career development, benefits, and employment inquiries address.

Franchising

> *Franchise Handbook: Online*. Milwaukee, WI: Enterprise Magazines. http://www.franchise1.com (J87)

The Web site provides three main areas for information. A user may search franchise companies by alphabetical listing, category, and featured franchise companies. For each company are given company's name, address, contact person, phone and e-mail, description of the operation, number of franchised units, number of company-owned units, in business since, franchise fee, training and support provided, and more information. Its arrangement and information are similar to *Franchise Opportunities Handbook*, 1965– (Washington, DC: U.S. Department of Commerce, Minority Business Development Agency, biennial) (J88). The print version (1994, 302 p.) includes Government Assistance Programs, Non-Government Assistance Programs and Index, and the main body—Sources of Franchising Information—listing companies by categories in alphabetical order from art supplies to water conditioning. There are three indexes: franchising participants, alphabetical, and by categories. The Web site also provides latest news, a directory of business opportunities, and links to franchise information.

Insurance

Two Best's reports are indispensable:

> *Best's Insurance Reports: Life-Health*, 1906– . Oldwick, NJ: A. M. Best. Annual. ISSN 10758690. (J89)
>
> *Best's Insurance Reports: Property-Casualty*, 1900– . Oldwick, NJ: A. M. Best. Annual. ISSN 01483218. (J90)

The two reports were originally published in one and have similar formats. The separate report on each institution listed includes a review of the institution, history, management and operations, investments, operating statistics, and its statistical exhibits. It also gives Best's policyholders ratings and Best's financial size category. The objective of Best's rating system is "to provide an overall opinion of an insurance company's ability to meet its obligations to policyholders" (Overview of Best's Rating System and Procedures, Section IV). Ratings consist of nine codes grouped into two levels: Secure Best's Ratings and Vulnerable Best's Ratings. A++ and A+ (superior), A and A− (Excellent), B++ and B+ (very good) belong to Secure Best's Ratings level. B and B− (fair), C++ and C+ (marginal), C and C− (weak), D (poor), E (under regulatory supervision), F (in liquidation), and S (rating suspended) are in the Vulnerable Best's Ratings level. Also, there is financial performance ratings (FPR) grouped into two levels: Secure FPR Ratings and Vulnerable FPR Ratings. FPR 9 (very strong), FPR 8 and 7 (strong), and FPR 6 and 5 (good) belong to the Secure level, whereas from FPR 4 (fair), FPR 3 (marginal), FPR 2 (weak) to FPR 1 (poor) are rated vulnerable.

In *Life-Health Report*, according to the 1998 edition, only 47 companies are rated A++ or 4.3 percent and 160 companies rated A+ or 14.7 percent. In *Property-Casualty Report*, the 1998 edition indicates that 33 companies are rated A++ and 102 companies A+, constituting 2.8 percent and 8.6 percent respectively.

Management

> *D&B Consultants Directory*. Parsippany, NJ: Dun & Bradstreet, 1998. 3,605 p. ISBN 156203653X. (J91)

It consists of three sections: Consultants Alphabetically (white pages), including 30,000 consulting firms in the United States, Consultants Geographically (yellow pages), and Consultants by Activity (blue pages). For each firm are given firm name, trade style, phone, D-U-N-S number, SIC codes, most recent annual sales volume, number of employees, geographic territory served, principal officers, complete other "location" listings, and, if available, state of incorporation, indication of public ownership, and indication of public family ownership.

Manufacturing

> *Thomas Register of American Manufacturers and Thomas Register Catalog File*, 1906– . New York: Thomas Publishing. Annual. ISSN 03627721. Print & digital. (J92)
> *Thomas Food Industry Register*, 1898– . New York: Thomas Publishing. Annual. ISSN 1061284X. Print & digital. (J93)

For information on manufacturers other than food industry, there is *Thomas Register of American Manufacturers and Thomas Register Catalog File* (formerly *Thomas Register of American Manufacturers*), now in 34 volumes (88th ed., 1998). Volumes 1 to 23, Products and Services, list 57,000 products and services in alphabetical order. There are two indexes in volume 23: Product Index and Trademarks and Brand Names Index. Volumes 24 to 26, Company Profiles, contain 152,000 U.S. companies in alphabetical order. Each entry includes company name, address, zip code, phone and fax numbers, e-mail and URL addresses, branch offices, asset ratings, and company offices. Catalogs from 2,500 companies are provided in volumes 27 to 34, arranged alphabetically by company name and cross-referenced in the first 26 volumes. Appended in volume 34 is Inbound Logistics Guide that contains Transportation Services, Locator Indexes, and Company Profiles.

One *Thomas Register* feature is the assets ratings, which indicate approximate minimum total tangible assets in nine categories ranging from 250M+ (over $250,000,000), to 100M+ (over 100,000,000), to NR (not rated). The ratings are not, however, a credit, financial liability, or net worth rating.

It is available on CD-ROM, online database, *Thomas Register Online*, marketed through Dialog (File 535) (J94), and the Web, *Thomas Register*, http://www.thomasregister.com. The online version consists of both *Tho-*

mas Register and its companion, *Thomas Food Industry*, noted next. It enables the user to search a huge database of 180,000 companies, over 60,000 product and service classification headings, and 124,000 brand names. Searching on the Web is not as volatile as in Dialog. However, it provides three search options: company name, product/service, and brand name.

A companion work for the food industry is *Thomas Food Industry Register* (formerly *Thomas Grocery Register*) in three volumes (1998–1999 edition, 1998, ISBN 188794429X). It contains 30,000 companies and more than 120,000 listings under 6,000 products. Volume 1, Equipment, Supplies & Services, and Distribution, consists of equipment, supplies and services; wholesalers/distributors: combined list; wholesalers/distributors listed by specialty; brokers/manufacturers' agents: combined list; brokers/manufacturers' agents listed by specialty; importers; exporters; warehouses; transportation; and index to volume 1. Volume 2, Food Products, lists food products, ethnic food, health food, food service, vendors, private label manufacturers, industrial ingredients, and index to volume 2. Products are arranged in alphabetical order, from abalone to zucchini. Volume 3, Company Profiles, includes brandnames and trademarks, trade associations, industry convention calendar, government resource guide, and international trade boards. It is also available on CD-ROM, online database, and the Web, noted earlier.

Marketing

> *Directory of Manufacturers' Sales Agencies, 1998–1999*. Laguna, CA: Manufacturers' Agents National Association, 1998. 1,104 p. Print & digital. (J95)
>
> *Market Share Reporter: An Annual Compilation of Reported Market Share Data on Companies, Products, and Services*. Detroit: Gale Research, 1980– . Annual. ISSN 10529578. (J96)

The *Directory* is intended to locate an agent/rep to market products or services. Some 25,000 agents are listed. It is organized into three sections. Section 1 lists members of MANA (Manufacturers' Agents National Association), providing information such as agency name, address, phone number, key contact, services offered, customers, products sold, number of field sales people, territory covered, and other data. Section 2 is a listing geographically by state that each agency member covers and products the agency sells. Section 3 is an alphabetical listing of manufacturers/principals and others who are directly involved in marketing. The *Directory* is also available on disk and CD-ROM.

The ninth edition of *Market Share Report* (Robert S. Lazich, ed., 1998, 577 p., ISBN 0787624489) contains 2,000 entries arranged under 440 SIC

codes. It is "a unique resource for competitive analyses, diversification planning, marketing research, and other forms of economic and policy analyses" (Introduction). Market shares are referred to mainly four categories:
corporate market share, institutional market shares, brand market shares,
and product, commodity, services, and facility shares. The market share is
given either by sales or percentage or both, documented by sources. For
instance, under SIC 2033 (Juices), market shares for Canada's orange juice
are given as Tropicana at 60 percent, Lassonde 18 percent, and other 22
percent. There is a table of over 540 topics in alphabetical order from
abrasives and accounting services, to yogurt bars and yttrium. Its companions are *European Market Share Reporter* (1993– , biennial) (J97) and
World Market Share Reporter (1996– , biennial, ISSN 10786703) (J98).

Real Estate

> *National Referral Roster*, 1962– . Cedar Rapids, IA: Stamats Communi-
> cations. Annual. ISSN 10751084. Print & digital. (J99)

This is a simple listing of residential real estate firms, their addresses,
persons in charge, and telephone and fax numbers arranged in alphabetical
order by state, city, and company. In addition, it provides descriptions of
real estate organizations, such as the National Association of Realtors, National Marketing Institute of Real Estate Management, Society of Real Estate Counselors, FIABC-USA (American Chapter, International Real Estate
Federation), American Institute of Real Estate Appraisers, and Women's
Council of Realtors. It is also available on the Web (http://www.
roster.com).

Biographies

Many directories mentioned above consist of biographical information.
The *Standard & Poor's Register*, for instance, provides extensive biographical sources in business. The following biographies and biography index
may also be mentioned:

> *Reference Book of Corporate Management*, 1967– . Parsippany, NJ: Dun
> & Bradstreet. Annual. ISBN 07356498. Print & digital. (J100)
> *Who's Who in Finance and Industry*, ed. 1– . New Providence, NJ: Marquis
> Who's Who, 1936– . Biennial. ISSN 00839523. Print & digital.
> (J101)

Reference Book of Corporate Management, formerly *Dun & Bradstreet
Reference Book of Corporate Management*, contains listings of more than
30,000 men and women who are officers and directors of the 2,400 com-

panies of greatest investor interest. "Companies of greatest investor interest" refers to those with annual sales of $20 million or more and/or 1,000 or more employees. These companies, according to Dun & Bradstreet, have a combined revenue equal to 80 percent of the gross national product and employ 20 million people. For individuals who are both directors and officers, biographical data include age, education, and business positions presently and previously held, and for directors who are officers, present principal business connections are shown. *Reference Book of Corporate Management* is also available on CD-ROM as *D-U-N-S Million Dollar Disc*, noted earlier.

Who's Who in Finance and Industry, a member of the Marquis Who's Who family, lists North American business executives and international professionals in the fields of "accounting, advertising, banking and finance, communications, construction and engineering, industrial and commercial firms, insurance, investment companies, retail trade, transportation, utilities, as well as other sectors of the business community" (Preface). Each biographical sketch provides such information as name, position, vital statistics, education, family status, career and career-related activities, civic and political activities, nonprofessional directorships, military record, decorations and awards, lodges and clubs, writings, and address. The biography is available on CD-ROM, as part of Marquis Who's Who, a database noted in Chapter 4.

Statistical Sources

> *Business Statistics of the United States.* 1997 edition. Courtenay M. Slater, ed. Lanham, MD: Bernan Press, 1998. 398 p. ISBN 0890590834. (J102)

It contains some 2,000 economic time series, predominantly from federal government sources from 1968 through 1996, with background notes. It is organized into four parts: (I) The U.S. economy, including gross domestic product; consumer income and spending; industrial production and capacity utilization; business sales, inventories, and investment; prices, employment costs, productivity, and profits; and employment, hours, and earnings, money and financial markets, U.S. foreign trade and finance, international comparisons. (II) Industry profiles, including data by industries and government. (III) Historical Data. (IV) State and Regional Data. The four parts are preceded by the editor's notes on U.S. Economic Patterns: the 1960s to 1990s, Developments in Economic Statistics: the Consumer Price Index, Development in Economic Statistics: North American Industry Classification System. At the end are Notes, which provide information on data sources, definitions, methodology, and revisions.

Handbooks, Yearbooks, and the Like

AMA Management Handbook. 3rd ed. John J. Hampton, ed. New York: AMACOM, 1994. Pagination varies. ISBN 0814401058. (J103)

Barron's Finance and Investment Handbook. 4th ed. John Downes and Jordan Elliot Goodman, eds. Hauppauge, NY: Barron's, 1995. 1,392 p. ISBN 0812057295. (J104)

CRB Commodity Yearbook, 1939– . New York: John Wiley. Annual. ISSN 10468226. Print & digital. (J105)

AMA Management Handbook is a collection of essays grouped into 16 sections with an editor for each section. Topics covered include management, marketing, sales and distribution, human resources, accounting, finance, research and technology, manufacturing, information system and technology, purchasing, corporate relations, risk management and insurance, entrepreurship and small business, international business, service industry and public sector and nonprofit management.

Investment is extensively covered in *Barron's Finance and Investment Handbook.* The *Handbook* consists of five parts. Part 1 addresses 30 basic investment alternatives, a useful guide to investors. Parts 2 and 3 deal with how to read an annual report and the financial pages respectively. Part 4 is a dictionary of 2,500 terms. Part 5, Financial and Investment Ready Reference, contains sources of information, major financial institutions, mutual funds, futures and options contracts, historical data, and public trade companies. There are three appendixes: Selected Further Reading, Currencies of the World, and Abbreviations and Acronyms.

CRB Commodity Yearbook (formerly *Commodity Yearbook*) reports changing trends in supply, demand, and prices of some 100 basic commodities arranged in alphabetical order from aluminum, antimony, apples to wool and zinc. The 1998 *Yearbook* (Bridge Commodity Research Bureau, 79, 316 p., ISBN 0471270577) provides over 900 tables, price charts, and graphs for more than 100 commodities and future markets, with seasonal patterns and historical data since 1986. They are updated by *Commodity Year Book Statistical Abstract Service* (Chicago: Bridge Publishing, 3/year, ISSN 00103241) (J106). The *Yearbook* is also complemented by the following publications and services: *CRB Commodity Index Report* (Chicago: Bridge Information Systems, weekly) (J107), providing CRB price index data in over 550 markets; *CRB Futures Market Service,* 1934– (Chicago: Bridge Publishing, weekly, ISSN 10574883) (J108), in blue sheet, providing information on the fundamentals that are influencing the markets, and *CRB Futures Perspectives* (formerly *Commodity Chart Service*), 1956– (Chicago: Bridge Publishing, weekly, ISSN 07307217) (J109). Future Perspectives is released in three editions: full (Financial and Agricultural), Financial, and Agricultural, providing bar charts of more than 80 international futures and cash markets. All publications listed are available in digital format.

Bridge's digital service consists of the Bridge DataCenter, the CRB InfoTech, and the CRB/Market Center. The Bridge DataCenter is a daily trade analysis dial-in service, providing quotes, news, analysis, trend analysis, and recommendations. The CD-ROM product is the CRB InfoTech. It is particularly useful for decades of historical price data. CRB/Market Center is on the Internet (http://crbindex.com).

INVESTMENT SERVICES

For a listing of investment services, refer to the guides by Daniells and Lavin, noted earlier. Listed here are the best-known services:

Moody's

> Moody's Manuals, 1929– . New York: Moody's Investors Services. Annual. Print & digital.
>
> Moody's Corporate News—US, 1983– . New York: Moody's Investors Service. Weekly. Digital. (J110)
>
> Moody's Corporate News—International, 1983– . New York: Moody's Investors Service. Weekly. Digital. (J111)
>
> Moody's Corporate Profiles. New York: Moody's Investors Service. Weekly. Digital. (J112)
>
> Moody's FIS Online. New York: Moody's Investors Service. http://www.fisonline.com (J113)

Moody's Manuals and their news reports are published in eight areas:

Moody's Bank and Finance Manual (ISSN 05450152) (J114) covers banks, insurance companies, investment companies, unit investment trusts and miscellaneous financial enterprises, real estate companies, and real estate investment trusts.

Moody's Industrial Manual (ISSN 05450217) (J115) covers all corporations on the New York, American, and regional stock exchanges and international companies.

Moody's Municipal and Government Manual (ISSN 05450233) (J116) covers United States and dependencies, states and municipalities, and other units.

Moody's OTC Industrial Manual (ISSN 01927167) (J117) covers over-the-counter industrial firms.

Moody's Public Utility Manual (ISSN 05450241) (J118) covers electric and gas utilities, gas transmission companies, and telephone and water companies.

Moody's Transportation Manual (ISSN 0545025X) (J119) covers railroads, airlines, steamship companies, bus and truck lines, oil pipelines, bridge companies, automobile and truck leasing and rental companies, and railroad systems.

Moody's International Manual (ISSN 02783509) (J120) covers corporations and national and supranatinoal institutions in one hundred countries.

Moody's OTC Unlisted Manual (ISSN 08905282) (J121), a relatively new publication since 1986, covers over-the-counter security firms in the United States unlisted on national or regional stock exchanges.

Each of the manuals is updated in its *News Reports* (J122), published either weekly or biweekly. News Reports, except for Moody's *Municipal and Government Manual*, can also be accessed online, noted later.

Coverage of the manuals is of two categories: visibility coverage at a fee and standard coverage. The former consists of types of coverage with different scales of fee, namely visibility-ultra, visibility-plus, visibility-select, and visibility-basic. The visibility coverage is fuller and has special features not found in the standard coverage. For instance, the visibility-plus coverage includes, in addition to the standard coverage, (1) financial information, such as seven-year presentation of income accounts, balance sheets, and financial and operating ratios coverage; (2) detailed description of the company's business; and (3) capital structure. For a visibility ultra-coverage, the company may place a page of advertising matter.

In each manual, there is a special feature section with a variety of data, including Moody's yield average, Dow Jones stock average, statistical data, and other reference sources of information. For instance, the special section in *Moody's Bank and Financial Manual* presents such interesting information as largest banks in the free world and in the United States, largest domestic bank holding companies, and largest life insurance companies. The *Manual* itself also provides additional information in addition to finance. In the *International Manual*, each country has in general the following information: profile, including people, geography, political establishment and economy; finance, currency, and banking; production, resources, and services; international transactions; and external loans, if any. Most countries are provided with a map. This serves as a concise political handbook.

One of the features of Moody's manuals is ratings, which provide investors with a simple system of gradation by which the relative investment qualities of bonds and stocks may be rated. In fact, Moody's Investors Service and Standard & Poor's are two of the biggest rating services. They are competitors in publications and services as well. In Moody's, there are nine symbols for bond ratings, from Aaa (best quality), Aa (high quality), A (upper medium grade obligations) to Ca (speculative in a high degree) and C (the lowest-rated class). A similar scale applies to Moody's preferred stock ratings. There are other ratings in some *Manuals*. The rating symbols indicate least investment risk or highest investment quality to greatest investment risk or lowest investment quality. All *Moody's Manuals* are indexed in *Moody's Complete Corporate Index*, an index to over 40,000 corporations and institutions listed in the manuals. *Moody's Manuals* are also available on microfiche and, on a selective basis, online as *Moody's Corporate Profile*, noted next.

Listed here are three databases. *Moody's Corporate News—US*, marketed through Dialog (File 556), is the equivalent of Moody's six news reports: *Bank & Finance News Reports, Industrial News Reports, OTC News Reports, Public Utilities News Reports, Transportation News Reports*, and *OTC Unlisted News Reports*. *Moody's Corporate News—International*, also marketed through Dialog (File 557), is the equivalent of *Moody's International News Reports*. Both databases provide textual and tabular records on a variety of topics, such as annual reports, interim reports, acquisitions, mergers, purchase offers, debt offerings, contracts, new products, name change, and expansions.

Moody's Corporate Profiles, marketed through Dialog (File 555), contains profiles of all companies on the New York and American stock exchanges and most active companies traded over the counter. A profile consists of address and telephone number, D-U-N-S number, stock exchange, ticker, primary and secondary SIC, business description, business line analysis, interim dividends, interim earnings with quarterly development and Moody's comment, annual earnings and dividends, financials for five years (earnings and balance sheet), statistical record for five years (book value and price/earnings ratio), and capitalization. *Moody's Corporate Profile* may be considered as a capsule of *Moody's Manuals* and *Moody's News Reports*.

A newcomer is *FIS Online* on the Web. Currently, it offers *Company Data Direct* (J123) providing information on more than 10,000 public companies in the United States drawn from Moody's manuals. It is also available on CD-ROM as *Moody's Company Data*, monthly (J124). A companion to Moody's Company Data is *Moody's International Company Data*, monthly (J125).

In addition, Moody's has published a variety of reference sources in finance, including *Moody's Bond Survey* (weekly, ISSN 00270822) (J126); *Moody's Bond Record* (monthly with annual cumulative issue, ISSN 01481878), listing 56,000 fixed-income issues with bond ratings and other ratings, such as short-term debt ratings, mutual fund ratings, insurance financial strength ratings, and bank financial strength ratings (J127); *Moody's Dividend Record* (twice a week with annual cumulative issue, ISSN 01927019) (J128), providing dividend data of 17,000 securities; and *Moody's Handbook of Common Stocks* (quarterly, ISSN 00270830) (J129), providing "access to basic financial and business information of more than 950 stocks with high investor interest" (Introduction) and special features in each issue, such as industry review—automobiles and trucks in the Fall 1998 issue. For information on Moody's, its Web site (http:// www.moodys.com) gives a listing of buttons for selection, such as ratings, research, data, economic, directory, managed funds, and insurance.

Standard & Poor's

> *Standard & Poor's Corporation Records*, 1940– . New York: Standard & Poor's. Looseleaf. Semimonthly and daily revisions. ISSN 0277500X. Print & digital. (J130)
>
> *Standard & Poor's Corporate Description Plus News*. New York: Standard & Poor's. Semimonthly. Digital. (J131)
>
> *Standard & Poor's Stock Reports*, 1933– . New York: Standard and Poor's. Looseleaf with quarterly bound issue. Print & digital.

The *Standard & Poor's Corporation Records* in six volumes arranged in alphabetical order contains descriptions of some 12,000 publicly held corporations with extensive statistics. Similar to *Moody's Manuals*, the *Records* consists of two types of description. Full or standard coverage is accorded to corporations that pay a fee to be included. Other corporations will receive much briefer coverage. Each volume consists of, in general, three sections: (1) index section for the volume, (2) list of subsidiary companies and cross references, and (3) descriptions. A statistical section in the last volume gives a mutual fund summary and foreign bonds statistics. The *Standard & Poor's Corporation Records Daily News* (5/week, ISSN 01964674) (J132) updates the *Records* and provides news on companies. The *Records* also provide ratings, but their bond rating was discontinued. Current bond ratings are to be found in *Standard & Poor's Bond Guide*, 1938– (New York, monthly, ISSN 02773988) (J133). The *Bond Guide* represents comparative financial and statistical information on bonds with Standard & Poor's Bond Quality Ratings, ranging from "AAA" to "D" to most of them. A companion to the *Bond Guide* is *Standard & Poor's Stock Guide*, 1942– (monthly, ISSN 07374135) (J134), compiled in a similar format.

The *Records* are available in microfiche and online marketed through Dialog as *Standard & Poor's Corporate Descriptions Plus News* (File 133). The database provides financial information and news on some 12,000 publicly held companies. Its sources include stockholder reports, press releases, 10-K, 10-Q, 8-K reports, filing with other regulatory agencies, newspapers, wire service reports, and releases from stock exchanges. A typical record contains company profile, including address, phone, type of company, stock ticker, employees, shareholders, incorporation year, primary and secondary SIC; recent news; company description; corporate background; bond descriptions; annual report data; and management discussion. The database is updated by *Standard & Poor's Daily News* (Dialog

File 132) (J135). As compared with Dialog File 133, it has the same coverage but fewer access points.

Standard & Poor's Stock Reports covers a total of about 4,600 traded and distributed security issues reported in three separate areas, as follows. With the exception of foreign companies, investment companies, and certain finance-oriented companies, all include, if available, S & P common stock ranking, a measurement of past earnings and dividend growth, and beta point assigned. *Stock Reports* consists of three reports as follows:

Standard & Poor's Stock Reports: New York Stock Exchange (ISSN 01604899) (J136) covers stocks listed on the New York Stock Exchange.

Standard & Poor's Stock Reports: American Stock Exchange (ISSN 01911112) (J137) covers stocks listed on the American Stock Exchange.

Standard & Poor's Stock Reports: NASDAQ and Regional Exchanges (ISSN 01631993) (J138) covers over-the-counter stocks traded in the National Association of Securities Dealers Automated Quotations (NASDAQ) system or on regional exchanges. The system is a network of dealers who sell and buy stocks.

All Stock Reports are published in the same format of a two-page company report. In general, all report stock, summary, common share earnings, dividend data, balance sheet statistics, fundamental position/company position, finance, capitalization, revenues/sales, and recent developments. These reports are also available on the Web, *Standard & Poor's Investor Center* (http://www.stockinfo.standardpoor.com/mks.htm) (J139). The Web site is an expanded version of Stock Reports. It contains Stock Report, updated quarterly; Standard & Poor's News Headlines, updated daily; Standard & Poor's Wall Street Consensus, updated weekly; Historical Price Chart, updated daily; and Business Wire Press Release, updated daily. A useful reference to investors, *Standard & Poor's Wall Street Consensus* provides information gathered from analysts at over 150 firms and Standard & Poor's own analysis, with recommendations to buy, hold, and sell.

Value Line

The Value Line Investment Survey, 1933– . New York: Value Line. Weekly. Looseleaf. ISSN 00422401. Print & digital. (J140)

The Value Line Investment Survey is published in three sections: (1) Selection and Opinion, including the Value Line view, advisable investment strategy, performance stock highlights, Value Line averages, and best- and worst-performing industries. (2) Summary and Index, including rating 1,700 stocks for future relative price performance and price safety. (3) Ratings and Reports, on subjects in alternate issues, one page of information for each company on stock price, capital structure, current position, annual rates, quarterly sales, earnings per share, quarterly dividend paid, Value Line's opinion and ratings on the company's financial strength, stock's price stability, price growth persistence, earnings predictability, Beta (the stock's sensibility to market fluctuation), statistical milestones, and summary of company's business. *Investment Survey* is also available on CD-ROM. Value Line's Web site (http://www.valueline.com) provides information on stocks, mutual funds, financial planning, and quarterly review, lists a number of its products and services, and offers a useful "Glossary of Investment Terms."

Disclosure

> *Disclosure Database.* Bethesda, MD: Disclosure. Weekly. Digital. (J141)
> *EdgarPlus—SEC Basic Filings.* Bethesda, MD: Disclosure. Daily. Digital. (J142)

In the earlier days, Disclosure compiled company reports to the U.S. Securities and Exchange Commission (SEC) and published only paper and microfiche. These were later joined and eventually replaced by digital format. Disclosure is now available on CD-ROM as *Compact Disclosure* and online as *Disclosure Database*, marketed through Dialog (File 100).

Disclosure Database covers 10-K, 20-F, 10-Q, 8-K, 10-C, proxy statement, registration statement, and annual report to shareholders. It provides long records with detailed data such as company name, address, telephone, status, location, exchange, ticker symbol, Fortune number, Forbes number, D-U-N-S number, SIC, description of business, segment data, five-year summary, cash flow statement, income statement, balance sheet assets, quarterly assets, quarterly liabilities, quarterly income statement, weekly data price information, earnings information, dividend information, filings, officers, ownership, exhibits, other corporate events, president's letter, and management discussion. Its related products include *Access Disclosure Index*, 1968– , daily (Dialog File 534) (J143), an index to the SEC and other regulatory agencies publications, and *Disclosure/Spectrum Ownership*, 8/ year (Dialog File 540) (J144), providing public company ownership derived from *Disclosure Database*.

EdgarPlus (Edgar stands for Electronic Data Gathering, Analysis and Retrieval), a file extracted from company reports filed with the SEC, is more current and divided by filing and document types. It consists of five separate databases marketed through Dialog: *EdgarPlus—6-K, 8-K, and 10-C Filings* (File 776), *EdgarPlus—Annual Reports* (File 777), *EdgarPlus—20-K and 20-F Filings* (File 778), *EdgarPlus—10-Q Filings* (File 779), and *EdgarPlus—Proxy Statements* (File 780). Also in the Edgar family are *Ac-*

cess Disclosure Index, just noted, *EdgarPlus—Williams Act Filings* updated daily (File 773), *EdgarPlus—Prospectuses* updated daily (File 774), *EdgarPlus—Registration Statements* updated daily (File 775). *EdgarPlus* is also available on the Web (http://www.disclosure-investor.com). For a listing of filings, refer to "SEC Filings Guide" (http://www.disclosure-investor.com/retail/help/see-guide).

Some reports to the SEC can also be retrieved online from *SEC Online* (Hauppauge, NY: SEC Online, semiweekly) (J145) marketed through Dialog. *SEC Online* consists of four databases: Dialog File 541 for annual reports to shareholders; Dialog File 542 for 10-K and 20-F; Dialog File 543 for 10-Q; and Dialog File 544 for proxy statements.

Bloomberg

Bloomberg Online. New York: Bloomberg, L. P. http://www.Bloomberg.com) (J146)

Bloomberg is popularly used among brokerages. The database features current, quick, and easy-to-read data on markets. Its home page displays areas for choosing as follows: Markets, News, Energy, Sports, Analysis, Products, Lifestyles, and so on. Markets is further divided into World Markets and U.S. Markets, with a number of subtopics under each. World Markets provides equity indices, international yield curves, key cross-currency rate, currency calculator, currency for region, and Bloomberg EMU update. For U.S. Markets topics, there are Treasury curve, municipal bond yields, active futures, most active options, U.S. composite, NYSE movers, NASDAQ movers, AMEX movers, S&P index, industry group movers, Dow 30, top mutual funds, regional indices, and interest rates. Its News on Business includes top news, company news, mutual funds, securities firms, U.S. equity preview, U.S. equity movers, Bloomberg columns, and small business news.

Bloomberg also provides tools for investors. In its Analysis, there are calculators for calculating mortgage, educational cost, exchange rates, and savings. In addition, Analysis includes resources such as bond information, company connection, corporations, Hoover's Search, stocks and stock exchanges, and U.S. tax forms.

NEWS SERVICES

A number of sources covering news have been noted such as *Bloomberg Online*, *Moody's News Reports*, and *Standard & Poor's Corporate Descriptions Plus News*. Following are some news services:

Barron's: The Dow Jones Business and Financial Weekly, 1921– . New York: Dow Jones. ISSN 10778039. Print & digital. (J147)

Time Warner's Pathfinder. New York: Time. http://www.pathfinder.com (J148)

The Wall Street Journal, 1889– . Eastern edition. New York: Dow Jones. 5/week. ISSN 00999660. Print & digital. (J149)

The Wall Street Transcript, 1963– . New York: Wall Street Transcript Corp. Weekly. ISSN 00430102. Print & digital. (J150)

World Reporter. Mountain View, CA: Dialog Corp. Digital. (J151)

Barron's is a newspaper devoted to business, with a conservative tone. Each issue has articles on various aspects of business, and its sections on "Up and Down Wall Street" and "Investment News & Views" are current and informative. "The Trader," a valuable department for the stock market, occupies half of its contents. In addition, its advertisements and current corporate reports highlight the financial situations of some corporations. It can be accessed through Dow Jones News Retrieval, and it is on the Web (http://www.barrons.com).

Pathfinder is a network of news and entertainment. Its home page displays highlights of news, a table of contents, and links to other sites, such as CNN, Time, Fortune, Money, Mutual Funds, Life, and Asianweek. "Pathfinder Network Guide" gives a listing of sources grouped by subject, such as News; Money and Business; Entertainment; Health, Family, and Living; Personalities; Sports; Net Culture; Travel; and Community. In Money and Business, it provides quotes, business coverage and personal finance and investment tools and links to CNN, *Fortune*, Hoover's Business Resources, Money Daily, Quick Quotes, and many others.

The Wall Street Journal, published in four editions (Eastern, Midwest, Southwest, and Western) covers general news, with stress on business information. Each issue consists of three parts: (1) national and international news; (2) company products, technology, business, regulations and law; and (3) money and investment including financial tables, charts, and so on. It has a separately published index, *The Wall Street Journal Index*, 1958– (Ann Arbor, MI: UMI, monthly with annual cumulation, ISSN 00837075, print & digital) (J152). The index consists of two sections: corporate news and general news. *The Wall Street Journal* is available online, accessible through Dow Jones News Retrieval and on the Web (http://www.wsj.com).

Each issue of *The Wall Street Transcript (TWST)* consists of the following columns: *TWST* Roundtable, CEO Awards, and Executive's Corner. Of particular value to business and finance are its Roundtable, where invited participants discuss a particular industry, and the Executive's Corner. The Executive's Corner includes CEO interviews and speeches. The former contains interviews with the CEO of one or two corporations; the latter presents short notes on the financial situation of some 100 corporations. A related publication is *CEO Interviews*, 1986– (weekly, ISSN 08879168) (J153), which presents an "inside look by chief executives at future prospects of their company and industry" (Publisher). Each issue contains an average of 20 interviews.

International business news is provided in *World Reporter*, a database (Dialog File 20) produced by Dialog, Dow Jones, and Financial Times Information. It includes newspapers, business periodicals, newswires on a variety of subjects, such as accounting, advertising, aerospace and defense, agriculture, automotive, banking and finance, electronics, engineering, economic news, European community, investments, marketing, politics, retailing, and many others. Its geographical coverage includes Europe, Asia, Pacific, Middle East, Africa, North America, and Latin America. Many sources are full-text.

NOTES

1. Bert F. Hoselitz, "Economics," in Bert F. Hoselitz, ed., *A Reader's Guide to the Social Sciences*, 2nd ed. (New York: Free Press, 1970), p. 280.

2. Harold Koontz and Cyril O'Donnell, *Essentials of Management* (New York: McGraw-Hill, 1974).

3. *Standard Industrial Classification Manual* (Washington, DC: U.S. Office of Management and Budget, NTIS, 1987), p. 12.

4. Michael R. Lavin, "A Clash of Titans: Comparing America's Most Comprehensive Business Directories," *Database* 21, no. 3 (1998): 44–48.

Chapter 10

Economics

Economics, as defined by Paul A. Samuelson, is "the study of how people and society end up choosing, with or without the use of money, to employ scarce productive resources that could have alternative uses, to produce various commodities and distribute them for consumption, now or in the future, among various persons and groups in society."[1] Economics deals with allocating resources to produce goods and services and achieving the full use of resources to meet human needs and desires.

Economics is broadly divided into two branches: microeconomics and macroeconomics.[2] Microeconomics studies the parts of the economic system, focusing on the problem of resource allocation. Macroeconomics studies the whole or aggregates of the economic system. It deals with money, the price level, and the level of employment. Macroeconomics is concerned with the broad effects of economic problems affecting the whole economy of a country or of the world, such as the devaluation of the dollar.

Because economics is the study of human behavior in the business part of human life, it shares with other subdisciplines of the social sciences the problem of methodology, the normative and positive approaches. In the positive approach, economists appeal to the facts and will not accept any statement without adequate verification. The normative approach is based on some kind of value judgment, dealing with what ought to be. Economics is now accepted as essentially a positive science.[3] The study of economics demands, therefore, some knowledge of quantitative methods. The intensive use of mathematics and statistics in the study of economic problems has led to the development of the discipline of econometrics. There are, however, economic phenomena that cannot be subjected to precise quantitative measurement. As Ronald H. Wolf pointed out, "in achieving economic justice through economic policy, judgements must be made which require a weighing of conflicting interests and goals and of advantage against disadvantage, all of which are immeasurable."[4]

The subfields of economics vary. Albert Rees mentioned eight of them: (1) mathematical economics theory; (2) history of economic thought, a study of works of economists and their contributions; (3) economic history and its related field, economic development; (4) industrial organization, the study of the problems in the structure of firms, industries, and markets; (5) agricultural economics, the study of the use of resources, production, and distribution in agriculture; (6) public finance, the study of the activities of the state and their impact on the economy, including the level of income and employment, the tax system, and government expenditure; (7) labor economics, dealing with wages, employment, and labor forces; and (8) international economics, dealing with the world economy, such as balance of payments and international trade.[5] Business, a part of economics, is treated separately in the preceding chapter. Readers should be aware that many reference sources in business are not exclusive and can very well be listed in economics. On the other hand, many titles in this chapter can also be classified as business reference sources.

ACCESS TO SOURCES

Guides

Information Sources in Economics. 2nd ed. J. Fletcher, ed. London: Butterworths, 1984. 139 p. ISBN 0408114711. (K1)

The Fletcher book, formerly *The Use of Economic Literature* (1971), is a collection of articles that fall into three parts: libraries, materials, and subjects. The first three chapters, dealing with British and American libraries strong in economic material, literature search, and organization of libraries, make up the first part. The second part consists of eight chapters referring to the different kinds of materials most used by economists, including bibliographies, periodicals, unpublished materials, databases and data banks, government documents, and statistical sources. The third part comprises thirteen chapters on various subject areas. Emphasis is placed on British publications.

Bibliographies

General

The earliest comprehensive bibliography in economics must be credited to John Ramsay McCullock for his work entitled *The Literature of Political Economy: A Classified Catalogue of Selected Publications in the Different*

Departments of That Science, with Historical, Critical and Biographical Notices (1840; reprint ed., New York: Kelley, 1964, 407 p.) (K2).[6] One of the earlier bibliographies completed in the twentieth century is Harold E. Batson's *A Selected Bibliography of Modern Economic Theory, 1870–1929* (New York: Dutton, 1930; reprint ed., New York: Kelley, 1968, 224 p.) (K3). Batson covers in two parts the main fields of modern theoretical economics, with the exception of money and banking. The first part is a select annotated bibliography of books and articles arranged by subject, while the second part is an author bibliography including English and American, German and Austrian, and French authors.

For current bibliographies, refer to:

> *International Bibliography of Economics. Bibliographie Internationale de Science Economique*, 1962– . London: Routledge, 1955– . Annual. ISSN 0085204X. Print & digital. (K4)
> *Resources for Economists on the Internet (RFE)*. Bill Goffe. http://econ-wpa.wustl.edu/EconFAQ/EconFAQ.html (K5)

International Bibliography serves as both a bibliography and an index. It is one of the four parts of *International Bibliography of the Social Sciences*, noted in Chapter 3. The annual provides an extensive, but not annotated, listing of books, periodical articles, and government publications in various languages.

A popular digital bibliography is *Resources for Economists on the Internet* (RFE). It lists resources on the Internet divided into some 30 subjects, such as U.S. Macro and Regional data; World and Non-U.S. data; Finance and Financial Markets; Working Papers; Bibliographical Databases and Information; Indices to Journals; On-line Journals; Societies and Associations; Academic Research Organizations and Institutes; Directories to Universities, Organizations, and Economists; Mailing Lists, and Internet Resources. It can be accessed through a number of Web sites, such as *Agricultural Virtual Library, ERS, FinWeb, NetEc,* and *EconData,* all noted next.

It may be noted that *Journal of Economic Literature*, listed in the section on indexes next, has a section on new books. The *Journal* provides an extensive annotated bibliography.

Subfield

> *Labor in America: A Historical Bibliography*. Santa Barbara, CA: ABC-Clio, 1985. 307 p. Clio Bibliography Series, no. 18. ISBN 0874363977. (K6)
> *Money Management Information Source Book*. Alan M. Rees and Judith Janes. New York: Bowker, 1983. 299 p. ISBN 0835217388. (K7)

Public Finance: An Information Sourcebook. Marion B. Marshall. Phoenix, AZ: Oryx Press, 1987. 287 p. ISBN 0897742761. (K8)

The bibliography of labor in America provides 2,865 annotated entries of periodical literature grouped into five periods: (1) labor in America: multiperiod; (2) early American labor to 1865; (3) labor in post-bellum America to 1900; (4) labor in the new century, 1900 to 1945; and (5) modern labor from 1945 to 1982. It features the SPindex (Subject Profile Index), that is, a string of descriptors including both generic and specific terms arranged in a single alphabetical sequence to present a profile of a given article.

Money Management Information Source Book consists of eleven chapters. Chapter 1 is an introduction to the information need on money management. Chapter 2 deals with bibliographies and selection tools. Chapters 3–7 are the heart of the book listing more than 600 titles on the subject. The remaining four chapters cover periodicals, newsletters, pamphlets, and investment and securities reference sources. There are a subject index, an author index, and a title index.

Public Finance is an annotated bibliography of over 1,200 titles classified in twelve chapters. Eleven chapters deal with such topics as public finance theory and practice, management, federal government finances, tax policy, revenues, fiscal relations, and expenditures. One chapter lists core library collections. There are three indexes: author, title, and subject.

Theses and Dissertations

A few journals publish dissertations as their regular features, as listed in Chapter 6. An annual list of doctoral dissertations in economics in American universities and colleges was published in *American Economic Review* (1911– . Nashville, TN: American Economic Association, ISSN 00028282) (K9) from 1911 to 1986. *American Economic Review* is considered the most prestigious journal in economics.[7]

Research in Progress

A number of journals carry research in progress. They are listed in Chapter 6.

Reviews

Quite a few journals in economics carry review essays and book reviews, such as *Economica* (1934– . London: London School of Economics, quarterly, ISSN 00130427) (K10), *Economic History Review* (1927– . Oxford: Blackwell Publishers, quarterly, ISSN 00130117) (K11), *Journal of*

Economic History (1841– . Cambridge, England: Cambridge University Press, ISSN 00220507) (K12), and *Journal of Monetary Economics* (1975– . Amsterdam: North-Holland, 6/year, ISSN 03043932) (K13). A substantial number of book reviews were published in *American Economic Review*, just noted, until 1969, and since then they have been carried in *Journal of Economic Literature*, noted later.

Indexes

For locating periodical articles in economics, some general indexes and other subject indexes should not be overlooked. General indexes, including *Reader's Guide to Periodical Literature*, and subject indexes such as *Applied Science and Technology Index, Business Periodicals Index, Engineering Index, Social Sciences Index*, and *PAIS International* cover economic material. There are excellent indexing and abstracting services in economics, particularly in the field of business noted earlier. The *International Bibliography of Economics*, already mentioned, is also an extensive index to periodical articles in economics with worldwide coverage. Of particular importance are the following titles:

> *Index of Economic Articles in Journals and Collective Volumes*, 1886/
>   1924– . Nashville, TN: American Economic Association, 1961– .
>   Annual. ISSN 0536647X. Print & digital. (K14)
> *Journal of Economic Literature*, v. 1– , 1963– . Nashville, TN: American
>   Economic Association. Quarterly. ISSN 00220515. Print & digital.
>   (K15)

The *Index of Economic Articles in Journals and Collective Volumes* supersedes *Index of Economic Journals* (v. 1–7). The first five volumes were published in 1961–1962, covering the period from 1886 to 1959. Volume 7 was the first to cover a two-year period. Volume 7A, entitled *Index of Economic Articles in Collective Volumes*, a companion to Volume 7, was published in 1969, covering the period from 1964 to 1965. Later in 1972, volume 6A, *Index of Economic Articles in Collective Volumes*, 1960–1963, was published. Beginning with volume 8, the present title was adopted to reflect the index's coverage of articles in both economic journals and collective volumes for a one-year period. One of its problems is its time lag. It is available on CD-DOM and online noted next.

Journal of Economic Literature (*JEL*), covering articles published in various languages, continues the *Journal of Economic Abstracts* (v. 1–6, 1963–1968, Cambridge, MA: Harvard University, quarterly). The present title was adopted due to expansion of three areas: (1) original articles and reviews of the recent literature; (2) book reviews and bibliographical listings, including dissertations formerly in *American Economic Review*, noted earlier; and (3) articles in journals, including contents reproduction, index to periodical articles, and selected abstracts. As compared with the *International Bibliography of Economics, JEL* duplicates about 80 percent of the periodicals indexed in the *International Bibliography*. But *JEL* is more current than the annual and complements the latter in economic history and American publications. Since *JEL* also compiles the *Index*, just mentioned, the relationship between *JEL* and the *Index* is obviously close. Journals included in the *Index* are those indexed in *JEL*, collective volumes are selected from the annotated books, and the classification system is a more detailed version of *JEL*.

The bibliographical sections of *JEL*'s digital version, EconLit (K16), are available on CD-ROM marketed through Silver Platter and online marketed through Dialog (File 139) and FirstSearch. The database is updated monthly and is therefore more current than its print counterpart. The digital version, being an expanded *JEL*, adds citations to articles in collective volumes in the annual *Index of Economic Articles*, journal citations and abstracts not printed in *JEL*, and *Abstracts of Working Papers in Economics*, noted next.

Abstracts

> *Abstracts of Working Papers in Economics*, 1986– . New York: Cambridge University Press. 5/year. ISSN 09510079. Print & digital. (K17)
> *AgEcon Search: Research in Agricultural and Applied Economics*. St. Paul, MN: University of Minnesota. Monthly. http://agecon.lib.umn.edu (K18)

Each issue of *Abstracts of Working Papers in Economics* provides approximately 375 to 400 abstracts of papers. According to the editor, working papers in economics are produced by scholars at over 60 of the world's preeminent research organizations. These research centers produce more than 1,500 working papers per year. *Abstracts* is particularly valuable for unpublished materials. Its database, *AWPE* (K19), is marketed through Ovid and constitutes a part of *JEL* marketed through Dialog (File 139), noted earlier.

AgEcon Search, developed at the University of Minnesota with the support and cooperation of the American Agricultural Economics Association, the Economic Research Service of the U.S. Department of Agriculture, and the Farm Foundation, is an index of reports and access to full-text reports in agricultural and applied economics. A user may search the entire database or limit search to a particular institution. Abstracts are provided for each paper, and most papers are in full-text that can be downloaded. Papers included in *AgCon Search* are also listed in *WopEc*, noted later.

There are a few abstracts in digital format, such as *SRRN, Abstracts in Economic History*, and *Economic Working Papers Abstracts*. They will be noted in General Sources under Sources of Information next.

Contents Reproduction

> *International Current Awareness Service: Economics and Related Disciplines*, 1990– . London: Routledge. Monthly. ISSN 0960152X. Print & digital. (K20)

This is one of the four parts of *International Current Awareness Service*. It covers economics and related disciplines of statistics and mathematics, noted in Chapter 3.

One of the regular features of the *Journal of Economic Literature* is its section on contents reproduction. The publication of contents of periodicals in economics is also found in *Current Contents: Social and Behavioral Sciences*, noted in Chapter 3, and *ABS Pol Sci*, noted in the chapter on political science.

SOURCES OF INFORMATION

General

The following are Web sites that provide general sources in economics. Included in these sources are bibliographies, data, abstracts, indexes, directories, and full-text materials.

> *Agricultural Economics Virtual Library*. Lubbock, TX: Texas Tech University. http://www.aeco.ttu.edu/aecovl/ (K21)
> *Economic History Services*. The Cliometric Society, the Economic History Association, and the History of Economics Society. http://www.eh.net (K22)
> *Economic Research Service*. Washington, DC: U.S. Department of Agriculture. http://www.econ.ag.gov (K23)
> *FinWeb*. http://www.finweb.com (K24)
> *NetEc*. St. Louis: Washington University. http://nete.cwustl.edu (K25)
> *SSRN*. Social Science Electronic Publishing. http://www.ssrn.com (K26)

Agricultural Economics Virtual Library provides the following menus for searching: Mega Resources; Academic Departments; Usenet News; Mailing Lists; Journals and Research; Markets; Policy; Trade; Associations; Software; Other "Index" Pages; Extension; Data on the Web; and Add New Resource. Both Academic Departments and Associations are directories of Web sites. Academic Departments consists of the listing of the University of Victoria, *Economics Departments, Institutes and Research Centers*

Worldwide (EDIRC) (K27), and *Agricultural Economics Institutes in Germany*. *EDIRC* provides information on 3,519 institutions in 157 countries and territories. Associations lists directories giving Web sites of each department and association. Journals and Research: Listing of Journals and Research Resources Closely Related to Agricultural Economics provides resource/journal title and description/organization. Other "Index" Pages divides the sources into Independent, Agriculture Virtual Library, and Other Virtual Library. The category of Independent lists, for instance, *Resources for Economists on the Internet*, noted earlier.

Economic History Services is "designed to assist economic historians in sharing information abut their work" (home page). It provides *Abstracts in Economic History (AEH)* (K28), *Book Reviews (BRBEH)* (K29), Calendar, Course Syllabi, Databases, *EH.Net* Discussion Lists, and Other Websites. *AEH, Eh.Net's* main service, provides abstracts of all types of work in economic history and related fields including journal articles, working papers, conference presentations, dissertations, and contributions to anthologies. *BRBEH* groups book reviews in full-text into two categories: Business History and Economic History.

Database consists of Data Series Online and Databases Survey. Data Series contains U.S. Population Series, Labor Series, and Greenback Series. Databases Survey contains a number of surveys. *EH.Net* Discussion Lists provides direct link to Archives of *EH.Net* Lists, including economic history of informal discussion, economic history of Eastern Europe, history of economics ideas, and Economic History Society of Australia and New Zealand.

Its Other Websites contains *Internet Resources for Economic Historians* (K30), a WWW sites directory. Web sites are grouped into Professional Organizations; Academic Journals; WWW Pages for Colleges and Academic Departments; Individual Pages; Museums, Institutes, and Archives; Companies with Historical Information; Handy Sites; Stock Exchanges; Ongoing Seminars in Economic History; U.S. Government Sites; Library Catalogs; Major Listings of Historical Information; Economics Working Paper Archives; and Data Sets. Some 26 organizations are given in Professional Organizations. Academic Journals lists nearly 20 journals, their policies, subscription rates, and editorial boards, and many with tables of contents or abstracts of articles. Companies with Historical Information lists Chrysler, Ford, Wells Fargo, and J. P. Morgan. Also listed are representative library catalogs, such as Harvard Online Catalog (HOLLIS), and COPAC, noted in Chapter 2. Its Handy Sites group is of general reference value. It lists SIC Finder, Zip Code Finder, Area Code (U.S. and International) Finder, Scout Report (weekly publication of new and newly discovered Internet resources of interest to researchers and educators), World Clock, and CNN/Koblas Currency Converter.

FinWeb lists Internet resources in financial economics. It consists of several databases, including journals, working papers, databases, other sites, and miscellaneous. Journals lists nearly 20 electronic journals and provides links to Uncover, noted in Chapter 2, and *Resources for Economists on the Internet*, just noted. The working papers database links to other sites, such as *EconWPA* and *NetEc*, both noted next. A number of databases are included in Databases, including International Directory of Finance and Economics Professionals, FreeEdgar, EconData noted later, Holt's Stock Market Reports, J. P. Morgan's Home Page, Merrill Lynch, QuoteCom, and the Chicago Mercantile Exchange's Home Page. Other Sites continue the listing of Web sites such as the Rand Corporation and On-line Services for Business Schools. The category of Miscellaneous Databases contains such sites as Federal, State, City and Foreign Government Sites; U.S. and Foreign Business Schools; and Nobel Laureates in Economics.

Primarily for working papers is *NetEc*. It consists of six databases: *Printed Working Papers (BibEc)* (K31), *Electronic Working Papers (WopEc)* (K32), *Code for Economics and Econometrics (CodEc)* (K33), *World Wide Web Resources in Economics (WebEc)* (K34), home page papers in economics (HoPec), and jokes for economists and economics (JokEc). It offers paper abstracts and papers in full text.

WebEc is a directory of resources grouped into 30 categories, such as Economics and Teaching, Methodology and History of Economic Thought, Economic Data, International Economics, Labor and Demographics, Law and Economics, Business Economics, Economics of Networks, Guides, Institutions, Libraries, Publishing, Internet, and Reference Shelf. Most categories are further divided. The category of International Economics, for example, consists of international affairs, international trade, international organizations, and international treaties. The Reference Shelf category lists economists, meetings, jobs, fun, and miscellaneous. Of particular reference value are *Directory of Quantitative Macroeconomists* (K35), *Directory of International Economists* (K36), and *EDIRC* (*Economics Departments, Institutes and Research Centers in the World*), noted earlier. *Directory of Quantitative Macroeconomists*, prepared by Université du Québec à Montréal, provides, in a typical record, name, personal information, teaching materials, recent academic working papers, and links. *Directory of International Economists* is simply a listing of URL or e-mail addresses of individuals and organizations.

NetEc also collaborates with other databases including *Economic Working Paper Archives (EconWPA)* (http://econwpa.wustl.edu) (K37), and *Resources for Economists on the Internet* (RFE) noted earlier. *EconWPA* provides full-text working papers in economics classified into 22 subject areas according to *Journal of Economic Literature* classification.

SSRN (Social Science Research Network) comprises the Accounting Research Network (ARN), Economics Research Network (ERN), Financial Economics Network (FEN), Legal Scholarship Network (LSN), and Litigation Support Network (LIT). These networks are for distributing over 8,000 abstracts of papers, accessing to archives and other materials, and downloading over 1,800 electronic documents. ARN provides abstracts of five journals, such as Auditing Litigation and Tax, Financial Accounting, and Managerial Accounting. ERN produces abstracts of some 20 journals, including Development Economics, Econometrics, Economic and Business History, Environmental Economics, International Trade, Labor, Monetary Economics, and Public Economics. LAN publishes abstracts of Latin American Business and Latin American Economics. Abstracts of seven journals are included in FEN, as, for instance, Banking and Financial Institutions, Capital Markets, Corporate Finance and Organizations, Derivatives, and Real Estate. Search can be conducted for All Paper Series, Accepted Paper Series, and Working Paper Series.

Encyclopedias

> *Encyclopedia of American Economic History: Studies of the Principal Movements and Ideas.* Glenn Porter, ed. New York: Scribner's, 1980. 3 vols. ISBN 0684162717. (K38)
>
> *The McGraw-Hill Encyclopedia of Economics.* 2nd ed. Douglas Greenwald, ed. New York: McGraw-Hill, 1994. 1,093 p. ISBN 0070244103. (K39)
>
> *Survey of Social Science: Economics Series.* Frank Magill, ed. Pasadena, CA: Salem Press, 1991. 4 vols. ISBN 0893567256. (K40)

Encyclopedia of American Economic History is one of the three encyclopedias compiled on the same principle and format. The other two, on political science, are noted in Chapter 17. The *Encyclopedia of American Economic History* is a collection of 72 essays classified into five parts: (1) the historiography of American economic history, (2) the chronology of American economic history, (3) the framework of American economic growth, (4) the institutional framework, and (5) the social framework. It covers some aspects of social history such as articles on family, women, and urbanization.

Articles on some 310 subjects by 178 authors are included in the *Encyclopedia of Economics*. Subjects are selected from 1,400 terms included in *The McGraw-Hill Dictionary of Modern Economics*, noted next. The *Encyclopedia* "is thoroughly cross-referenced and indexed, with extensive bibliographical references to guide the reader who wants to know more about the subject and how it relates to other subjects" (Preface). Arrangement is in alphabetical sequence from "Acceleration Principle," "Balance of International Payments" to "Yield Curve" and "Zero Population Growth." Article length varies from less than two pages to over 20 pages. There are two appendixes: (1) classification of articles by economic fields, a listing of ten broad fields, and (2) a timetable of economic events, technological development, financial development, and economic thought.

The *Survey* is one of the four Survey Series (Economics, Government & Politics, Psychology, and Sociology). The other surveys will be noted in chapters 14, 15, and 16 respectively. All surveys have similar arrangement, consisting of three parts for each article: overview, applications, and context. The present *Survey* contains 393 articles, averaging six pages in length, arranged in alphabetical order.

Dictionaries

The McGraw-Hill Dictionary of Modern Economics: A Handbook of Terms and Organizations. 2nd ed. New York: McGraw-Hill, 1983. 656 p. ISBN 007024376X. (K41)

The MIT Dictionary of Modern Economics. 4th ed. David W. Pearce, ed. Cambridge, MA: MI Press, 1992. 474 p. ISBN 026216132X. (K42)

The New Palgrave: A Dictionary of Economics. John Eatwell, Murray Milgate and Peter Newman, eds. London: Macmillan, 1987. 4 vols. ISBN 0935859101. (K43)

The New Palgrave Dictionary of Economics and the Law. Peter Newman, ed. London: Macmillan Reference, 1998. 3 vols. ISBN 033367667X. (K44)

The New Palgrave Dictionary of Money and Finance. Peter Newman and others, ed. Groves Dictionaries, 1992. 3 vols. ISBN 156159041X. (K45)

The *McGraw-Hill Dictionary* consists of two parts: (1) Terms, about 1,425 modern economic terms; and (2) Organizations, describing briefly some 235 private, public, and nonprofit agencies, associations, and research organizations concerned with economics and marketing. Definitions are longer than one sentence, with economic data, charts, tables, and diagrams frequently cited and, in some cases, presentation of both sides of an issue. One valuable addition is that most definitions are current and sources for further information on the terms are indicated.

One-sixth of the content has been changed in the new edition of *The MIT Dictionary*. It contains 2,800 entries. Definitions are brief, with cross-references. For a fuller state-of-the-art account of any of the theoretical entries, the editor suggests use of *The New Palgrave*, noted next.

The three *New Palgrave* dictionaries are companions. All feature historical perspectives in most entries and present quite often two or more essays of different points of view on similar subjects. *The New Palgrave: A Dictionary of Economics* is a successor to the *Dictionary of Political Economy*, edited by R. H. Inglis Palgrave and published in 1894, and to *Palgrave's Dictionary of Political Economy*, edited by Henry Higgs and published in 1925. The editors intend "to provide a thorough account of contemporary economic thought but also, like Palgrave himself, to have it set in historical perspective" (Editors' Preface). It contains 2,000 entries, of which over 700 are biographical. The criterion for inclusion of living economists is that they were born before January 1, 1916. Some 50 entries in *Palgrave's Dictionary* are reproduced to ensure the continuity between the old Palgrave and the new. Articles are signed and most are appended with bibliographies and are extensively cross-referenced. There are four appendixes: (1) a list of entries by author, (2) a list of biographies included in the 1925 edition of *Palgrave's Dictionary* but omitted from the new one, (3) a list of entries in *Palgrave's Dictionary* by author, and (4) an analysis of all the subject entries by 53 fields of study and a classification of all the biographies by country of the subject. There is an analytical index. The old *Palgrave's Dictionary* is still useful for biographical sketches of deceased economists, classical economic theory, and historical matters.

The New Palgrave Dictionary of Economics and the Law contains 399 essays of over 6,800 distinct items, with an average of about 5,000 words for each essay. Entries are listed alphabetically, preceded by Subject Classification, which classifies the 399 essays under seven headings and 75 subheadings. The seven headings are: society, economy, polity, law in general, common law systems, regulation, and biographies. Each essay provides cross-references, subject classification, and bibliography. It is concluded with "Statutes, Treaties and Directories" and "Cases." There is no index.

The New Palgrave Dictionary of Money and Finance contains 1,008 articles on public accounting, investment consumption spending, banking and finance, balanced budget, and the money systems of major countries. Each article is appended with a bibliography and a glossary.

Directories

The *McGraw-Hill Dictionary*, just noted, also serves as a directory. Other directories in economics include:

Directory of U.S. Labor Organizations, 1982/83– . Washington, DC: BNA Books. Annual. ISSN 07346786. (K46)

Directory of Foreign Labor Organizations. Washington, DC: U.S. Department of Labor, Bureau of International Labor Affairs. 4 vols. Looseleaf. (K47)

Economic Departments with Ph.D. Programs in American and Canadian Universities. Albany, New York: University of Albany. http://www.albany.edu/eco_phds.html (K48)

International Economic Institutions. 5th rev. ed. M. A. G. Van Meerhaeghe. Dordrecht, The Netherlands: Kluwer Academic, 1987. 368 p. ISBN 9024735130. (K49)

World Index of Economic Forecasts, Including Industrial Tendency Surveys and Development Plans. 4th ed. Robert Fildes, ed. Brookfield, VT: Gower, 1995. 663 p. ISBN 0566074885. (K50)

Directory of U.S. Labor Organizations is the successor to the discontinued government publication, *Directory of National Unions and Employee Associations.* About 300 American labor organizations are grouped into three parts: Part 1, outlines of structure of AFL-CIO Executive Council; Part 2, AFL-CIO headquarters and central body offices; and Part 3, major AFL-CIO and independent unions in the United States. Labor organizations are arranged in alphabetical order. Each entry gives address, officers, publication, convention, membership, and locals. There are three indexes: Labor Organizations by Abbreviations; Labor Organizations by Common Name; and Labor Organization Officers.

Directory of Foreign Labor Organizations lists labor organizations by regions and by state within regions. The four volumes cover, respectively, Africa; American Republics; Europe; and East Asia/Pacific, Near East, and South Asia. Each organization lists, if complete, name, address, telephone, chief officers, other top officers, department or service heads; membership; jurisdiction; political affiliation; publications; and international affiliations.

Drawn from *Peterson's Guide to Graduate Programs in the Humanities, Arts, & Social Sciences,* noted in the next chapter, *Economic Departments with Ph.D. Programs* lists departments and programs, including agricultural economics. It provides links to the departments and programs. The Web site also links to other sites. They are Economics Departments in the U.S.; Economics Departments Outside the U.S.; Economics Departments, Institutes, and Research Centers in the World; and American Colleges and Universities, Canadian Colleges and Universities, and Colleges and Universities All over the World.

International Economic Institutions describes ten international economic institutions: the International Monetary Fund, the World Bank for Reconstruction and Development, the International Development Association, the General Agreement on Tariffs and Trade, the United Nations Conference on Trade and Development, Benelux, the Organization for Economic Cooperation and Development, the Council for Mutual Economic Assistance, the European Community, and the European Free Trade Association. Each entry covers in detail origins, objectives, organization, functions and operation, appraisal, and bibliography.

Profiles of 217 forecasting organizations are provided in the *World Index.* The *Index* consists of four sections: (1), a review of macroeconomic forecasts and surveys; (2), who's who in economic forecasting, profiles of the forecasting organizations; (3), the forecasters; and (4), trade cycle and tendency surveys. The who's who section contains profiles of the forecasting organizations. Detailed information is given in the macroeconomic forecasters. In this section, for each organization are given address and contact information, but the main feature is a checklist of the coverage of the forecasts and surveys (Introduction). It has four indexes: organization index, country index, exchange rate index, and commodities and other specialist subject index, followed by a section of "Who's Who in Economic Forecasting."

The Web sites noted also include directories in economics. They are, for instance, *Resources for Economists on the Internet* in *Net.Ec* and *Internet Resources for Economic Histories* in *Economic History Services*.

Biographies

Biographies of economists may be found in encyclopedias and dictionaries in economics and in the social sciences in general. The following are some representative biographies:

> *Great Economists before Keynes: An Introduction to the Lives and Works of One Hundred Great Economists of the Past.* Mark Blaug. Brighton, UK: Wheatsheaf, 1986. 286 p. ISBN 0745001602. (K51)
> *Great Economists since Keynes: An Introduction to the Lives and Works of One Hundred Modern Economists.* Mark Blaug. Brighton, UK: Wheatsheaf, 1985. 267 p. Dist. by Harvester Press. ISBN 0710807554. (K52)
> *Men and Ideas in Economics: A Dictionary of World Economists Past and Present.* Ludwig H. Mai. Totowa, NJ: Littlefield and Adams, 1975. 270 p. ISBN 0822602849. (K53)
> *Who's Who in Economics: A Biographical Dictionary of Major Economists, 1700–1986.* 2nd ed. Mark Blaug, ed. Cambridge, MA: MIT Press, 1986. 936 p. ISBN 0262022567. (K54)

Blaug's two companion books profile two hundred economists with photos for most of them. Each profile contains career, contributions, and important work, ending with secondary literature for further information. Length of entries varies from two to four pages. The two books are complemented by *Who's Who in Economics* that contains some 1,000 living and 400 deceased economists. Each entry includes name, date and birthplace, current post, past posts, degrees, offices and honors, editorial duties, principal fields of interest, chief publications, and principal contributions. The criterion for inclusion is that a biographee publishes more or less regularly in one of the hundreds of learned journals of economics. Appendixes include (1) index of principal fields of interest, (2) index of country of residence if not United States, (3) index of country of birth if not United States, and (4) names without an entry.

Men and Ideas in Economics provides biographical profiles of major economics thinkers in the past and a few from the present day. Arrangement is alphabetical by name. Appendixes include (1) the present-day generation of economists, (2) an outline of periods and schools in economic thought, and (3) bibliography.

It may be noted that readers may find useful a biographical listing in a special issue of *American Economic Review*, noted earlier. Volume 75, Number 6, 1985, is a special issue commemorating the centennial of the American Economic Association. The issue includes five articles concerning the history of economics, "Biographical Listing of Members" (pp. 71–549), classification of members by category, supplementary information and statistical data about members, and chairs of departments of economics in the United States.

Statistical Sources

As mentioned in Chapter 7, government agencies are the most productive publishers of statistics. Many titles listed next are government products.

United States

> *Consumer Price Index Detailed Report*, 1919– . Washington, DC: U.S. Bureau of Labor Statistics. Monthly. ISSN 0095926X. Print & digital. (K55)
>
> *EconBase: Time Series and Forecasts*. Eddystone, PA: WEFA Company. Monthly. Digital. (K56)
>
> *EconData*. University of Maryland. http://www.inform.umd.edu/ EdRes.Tpopic/Economics/EconData/Econdata.html (K57)
>
> *Economic and Energy Indicators*, 1949– . Springfield, VA: NTIS. Semi-monthly. ISSN 00130125. Print & digital. (K58)
>
> *Economic Report of the President*, 1947– . Washington, DC: Council of Economic Advisers. Annual. ISSN 01931180. Print & digital. (K59)
>
> *Handbook of U. S. Labor Statistics: Employment, Earnings, Prices, Productivity*. 1st ed. Eva E. Jacobs, ed. Lanham, MD: Bernan Press, 1997. 316 p. ISBN 0890590621. (K60)
>
> *Moody's Industry Review*, 1984– . New York: Moody's Investors Service. Semiannual. ISSN 10473114. (K61)
>
> *Standard & Poor's Industry Surveys*, 1973– . New York: Standard & Poor's. Semiannual with monthly supplements. ISSN 01964666. (K62)
>
> *Survey of Current Business*, 1921– . Washington, DC: Bureau of Economic Analysis. Monthly. ISSN 00396222. Print & digital. (K63)
>
> *U.S. Industrial & Trade Outlook*. New York: DRI/McGraw-Hill with Standard & Poor's and U.S. Dept. of Commerce/International Trade Administration, 1998. Pagination varies. ISBN 0070329311. (K64)

Consumer Price Index Detailed Report (CPI), formerly *Consumer Price Index*, covers consumer expenditures on food and beverages, housing, apparel, transportation, medical care, recreation, education and communications, and other goods and services. *CPI* is also on the Web (http://www.stats.bls.gov/cpihome.htm). *CPI*'s home page displays summary and tables and provides an overview of *CPI* stating data available, coverage, source of data, reference period, forms of publication, uses of the data, and major research in progress.

EconBase and *EconData* are two databases that provide immense statistical sources. *EconBase* collects data mostly from government agencies, such as the Bureau of Economic Analysis, Bureau of Labor Statistics, Bureau of the Census, and Federal Research Board. Over 11,000 time series are given on more than 20 subjects including agriculture, balance of payments, capital expenditures, construction and housing, exchange rates, finance, foreign trade, government finance, interest rates, labor force, population, price indexes, retail sales, and transportation. A typical record gives series code, corporate source, SIC code, start date, frequency, and data. The database is marketed through Dialog (File 565).

EconData consists of times series data collected from a number of U.S. agencies, divided into U.S. National, further divided into Accounts, Labor Price, and BusInd; State and Local; and International. Time series are in the form of banks for the G regression and model building program. Data regularly dated are grouped into annual data, quarterly data, and monthly data. For instance, under annual data of U.S. National are listed Annual National Income and Product Accounts, Annual Jobs, Hours, and Output, Gross Output by Detailed Industry, and International Sales and Purchases of Private Services. *EconData* also provides links to other economics resources, such as *Resources for Economists on the Internet, Economic Working Paper Archives*, and *WebEd*, all noted earlier.

EconData is one of the services of Inforum at the University of Maryland. Inforum provides Academic Resources by Topic. A number of topics are useful to social sciences research, including Business and Law Resources, Disability Resources, Economics Resources, Education Resources, History Resources, Social Issues Resources, Statistics Resources, United States and World Politics, Culture and History, and Women's Studies Resources.

Economic and Energy Indicators, formerly *Economic Indicators*, presents in each issue economics data on the following seven categories: total output, income, and spending; employment, unemployment, and wages; production and business activity; prices; money, credit, and security markets; federal finance; and international statistics. Data are for the current year with breakdown by month and for the previous years. For an annual summary, refer to the President's annual economic report, noted next. *Economic and Energy Indicators* can be accessed on the White House Web and *GPO Access*, noted in Chapters 15 and 7 respectively.

The annual economic report of the President, transmitted to Congress each year, is the best source for an overview of the U.S. economy and the administration's achievements. The 1998 report (407 p., ISBN 0160494192) by President Clinton consists of two parts: the President's report and the Annual Report of the Council of Economic Advisers (CEA). The CEA report consists of seven chapters on high-employment economy, macroeconomic policy and performance, economy well-being of children, economic inequality, economy efficiency, antitrust enforcement, and opening market. There are two appendixes: Report to the President on the Activities of the Council of Economic Advisers during 1997 and Statistical Tables Relative to Income, Employment, and Production. The annual report is also available on the Web site of *GPO Access.*

Since the *Handbook of Labor Statistics* (1924/26–1989, Washington, DC: Bureau of Labor Statistics, irregular, ISSN 00829055) (K65), is no longer published in print format, *Handbook of U.S. Labor Statistics* is a welcome publication. It is grouped in nine parts: (I), Population, Labor Force, and Employment Studies; (II), Employment, Hours, and Earnings, Nonagricultural Payrolls; (III), Projections of Employment by Occupation and Industry; (IV), Productivity and Related Costs; (V), Compensation of Employees; (VI), Prices and Living Conditions; (VII), Occupational Injuries and Illness; (VIII), Work Stoppages; and (IX), Foreign Labor and Price Statistics. Each part is preceded by Notes, a concise description of the data. The government publication, *Handbook of Labor Statistics*, is available on CD-ROM and on the Internet (http://www.bls.gov).

Moody's Industry Review and *Standard & Poor's Industry Survey* are fine analyses of major domestic industries. *Standard & Poor's Industry Survey* consists of basic and current analysis of more than 1,000 companies in 120 industries. The basic analysis provides prospects for a particular industry, an analysis of trends and problems, composite individual data, and comparative company analysis. The current analysis provides latest developments and available industry, market, and company statistics, and S & P investment outlook. The work also includes an earnings supplement that lists revenues and earnings of more than 1,200 companies.

Moody's Industry Review is much more concise, basically a statistical reference containing financial information, operating data, and rankings on 4,000 companies in 139 industry groups. The information is arranged alphabetically by industry in 144 industry groups such as advertising, cable and pay TV systems, computers, electronic power, gaming, insurance, measuring and control instruments, railroad, savings and loan associations, unclassified/unranked, and so on. Each industry consists of three parts: comparative statistics, financial data—latest annual rankings, and composite stock price movements.

Survey of Current Business provides information on business, industry, and economic outlook. It is also available on the Web site of Bureau of Economic Analysis (BEA) (http://www.bea.doc.gov/bea.pubs.htm). BEA "is the nation's economic accountant, preparing estimates that illuminate key national, international, and regional aspects of the U.S. economy" (home page). Data are provided in three areas: National Accounts, International Accounts, and Regional Accounts. In National Accounts, there are GDP and related data, articles, and industry and wealth data. Data, articles, and survey forms are included in International Accounts. Regional Accounts also includes three topics: data, articles, and other products. Data in all areas are classified into description, estimate and time period, scope, and format. Data may be in either HTML, PDF, WKS, spreadsheet, or ASCII format. Additional national and regional data are available on *STAT-USA*, noted in Chapter 5.

U.S. Industry & Trade Outlook continues the *U.S. Industrial Outlook*, a government document no longer published. As its title page indicates, the book is an industry-by-industry overview of the U.S. economy—from manufacturing to high tech to service industries, containing 600 tables and charts, 100 industry reviews, analyses, and forecasts, and geographical snapshots of industry and trade trends. The Outlook consists of 50 chapters on different subjects, such as coal mining, electricity production and sales, construction, textiles, chemical and allied products, metals, electrical equipment, information services, computer equipment, entertainment, wholesaling, professional business services, and education and training. Data are collected from public and private sectors.

International

International Financial Statistics Yearbook; Statistiques Financieres Internationales Annuaire, 1976– . Washington, DC: International Monetary Fund. ISSN 02507463. (K66)

International Trade Statistics Yearbook; Annuaire Statistique du Commerce Internationale, 1950– . New York: United Nations. ISSN 1010447X. (K67)

National Accounts Statistics: Main Aggregates and Detailed Tables, 1958– . New York: United Nations. Annual. ISSN 02593025. (K68)

Yearbook of Labour Statistics. 50th issue. Geneva: International Labour Office, 1997. 1,269 p. ISBN 9220073544. (K69)

World Economic Outlook, 1980– . Washington, DC: International Monetary Fund. Semiannual. ISSN 02566877. Print & digital. (K70)

International and domestic financial data on exchange rates, international liquidity, money and banking, international transactions prices, production, government finance, and interest rates are provided in monthly *International Financial Statistics*, 1948– (Washington, DC: International Monetary Fund, ISSN 00206725) (K71). Data in the monthly publication form the basis for the annual *International Financial Statistics Yearbook*.

International Trade Statistics Yearbook "provides the basic information for individual countries' external trade performance in terms of the overall trends in current value as well as in volume and price, the importance of trading partners and the significance of individual commodities imported and exported" (Introduction). It consists of two volumes: Volume 1, Trade by Country, providing tables for 153 individual countries and thirteen summary tables indicating world trade by region, countries, commodities, and trade and so on; and Volume 2, Trade by Commodity.

National Accounts Statistics partially superseded *Yearbook of National Accounts Statistics*. Its 38th issue presents national accounts estimates for 175 countries and areas in four parts: (1) Summary Information; (2) Final Expenditures on Gross Domestic Product: Detailed Breakdowns and Supporting Tables; (3) Institutional Sector Accounts: Detailed Flow Accounts; and (4) Production by Kind of Activity: Detailed Breakdowns and Supporting Tables.

Yearbook of Labour Statistics provides principal labor statistics over 190 countries and areas or territories. It is organized into nine chapters as economically active population, employment, unemployment, house of work, wages, labour cost, consumer prices, occupational injuries, and strikes and lockouts. Appendixes include International Standard Industrial Classification of All Economic Activities (ISIC) (revisions 2 and 3), International Classification by Status in Employment (ICSE 1993), International Standard Classification of Occupations (1968 and 1988), International Standard Classification of Education (SCED), References, and Order of Arrangement of Countries, Areas and Territories. There is an index (countries, areas, and territories included in each table). For more recent statistical data, refer to *Bulletin of Labor Statistics*, 1965– (4/year plus supplements, ISSN 00074950) (K72).

An outstanding reference for global economic outlook is the *World Economic Outlook* by the International Monetary Fund, originally published as an annual. *World Economic Outlook* provides projection and analysis for individual country. Each entry consists of three sections: (1) an overview, recent developments and short-term prospects, and analysis of industrial and developing countries; (2) supplementary notes; and (3) statistical appendix, presenting tables in eight categories: output and employment, inflation, financial policies, foreign trade, current account transactions, current account financing, external debt and debt service, and medium-term reference scenario. It is available on the Web (http://www.imf.org). *World Economic Outlook*, released in May 1998, contains five chapters: (1) Global Economic Prospects and Policy Consideration; (2) Global Repercussions of the Asian Crisis and Other Issues in the Current Conjuncture; (3) The Business Cycle, International Linkages, and Exchange Rates; (4) Financial Crises: Characteristics and Indicators of Vulnerability; and (5) Progress with Fiscal Reform in Countries in Transition, ended with

Annexes and Statistics. Each chapter contains surveys, box(es), table(s), and figures.

Handbooks, Yearbooks, and the Like

Handbooks

> *The Handbook of Economic and Financial Measures.* Frank J. Fabozzi and Harry I. Greenfield, eds. Homewood, IL: Dow Jones-Irwin, 1984. 517 p. ISBN 0870944665. (K73)
>
> *Handbook of United States Economic and Financial Indicators.* Frederick M. O'Hara, Jr. and Robert Sicignaro. Westport, CT: Greenwood Press, 1985. 224 p. ISBN 0313239541. (K74)
>
> *Occupational Outlook Handbook,* 1949– . U.S. Bureau of Labor Statistics. Washington, DC: GPO. Biennial. ISSN 00829072. Print & digital. (K75)

The *Handbook of Economic and Financial Measures* contains 21 chapters by 23 contributors, grouped into six parts: (1) measures of aggregate economic activity, (2) government deficit and trade balance, (3) money supply and capital market conditions, (4) inflation, (5) firms and consumers, and (6) forecasting. Some chapters are appended with references or sources of data.

In *Handbook of United States Economic and Financial Indicators,* an indicator is defined as any standard measure of economic activities. Entries of indicators are arranged in alphabetical order. Each entry contains up to nine elements such as brief description, derivation, use, compiler, publisher, announced in, announced frequency, cumulation, and more information.

A superb career guide is the *Occupational Outlook Handbook.* The 1998–1999 edition (1998, 528 p., ISBN 016049348X) provides guidance to approximately 250 occupations. For each occupation, it describes what workers do on the job, the training or education requirements, and employment outlook. It contains an index to the *Dictionary of Occupational Titles* (4th ed., rev., U.S. Department of Labor, Employment and Training Administration; Hawthorne, NJ: Career Press, 1991, 2 vols., ISBN 1564140105) (K76). It does not list, however, 1980 Standard Occupational Classification (SOC) codes. The earlier edition of the *Handbook* should be retained pending publication of the new codes. Although the *Handbook* and the *Dictionary* are compiled by different agencies, they are companions. The *Handbook* is updated by *Occupational Outlook Quarterly,* 1957– (Washington, DC: U.S. Bureau of Labor Statistics, ISSN 01994786) (K77) that provides a continuous flow of current information between editions. It is also available in reprint form and on CD-ROM and on the Internet (http://www.bls.gov).

Yearbooks and the Like

> Consumers Index to Product Evaluations and Information Sources, 1974– . Ann Arbor, MI: Pierian Press, 1973– . Quarterly with annual cumulation. ISSN 00940534. Print & digital. (K78)
> Consumer Sourcebook, 1974– . Detroit: Gale Research. Irregular. ISSN 07380518. (K79)

Consumer Index, organized into sixteen main subject headings, gives summaries to articles and codes (e, r, or d) to specific products. The codes e, r, or d stand for evaluation or test, recall, and description respectively.

Compiled for the purpose of assisting consumers in handling complaints, Consumer Sourcebook provides more detailed information. The seventh edition, 1991, lists approximately 6,200 federal, state, and local government agencies and offices.

NOTES

1. Paul A. Samuelson, *Economics*, 10th ed. (New York: McGraw-Hill, 1976), p. 3.

2. Albert Rees, "Economics," in *International Encyclopedia of the Social Sciences*, vol. 4 (New York: Macmillan and Free Press, 1968–), pp. 472–480.

3. Alan Day, "Economics," in Norman MacKenzie, ed., *A Guide to the Social Sciences* (New York: New American Library, 1966), p. 108.

4. Ronald H. Wolf, "Economics," in John U. Michaelis and A. Montgomery Johnston, eds., *The Social Sciences: Foundations of the Social Studies* (Boston: Allyn and Bacon, 1965), p. 156.

5. Rees, "Economics," pp. 482–484.

6. Emma Lila Fundabunk, *The History of Economic Thought and Analysis: A Selective International Bibliography* (Metuchen, NJ: Scarecrow Press, 1973), pp. xiii–xix.

7. John Fletcher, ed., *Information Sources in Economics* (London: Butterworths, 1984), pp. 58–62; Allan M. Cartter, *An Assessment of Quality in Graduate Education* (Washington, DC: American Council on Education, 1966), p. 8.

Chapter 11

Education

Education is a body of information and skills and a process through which to transmit them to the new generation.[1] The main purpose of education, as John Dewey has written, "is to prepare the young for future responsibilities and for success in life, by means of acquisition of the organized bodies of information and prepared forms of skill which comprehend the material of instruction."[2] But Dewey also recognizes the value of progressive development.[3] Education may, therefore, be viewed as a body of knowledge and a process to transmit knowledge and to improve upon and preserve it as well.[4]

There are three areas of primary concern in education.[5] The first is training in practical livelihood skills. It is represented by the form of apprenticeship, from unskilled labor to the sophisticated profession, such as a physician's internship in a hospital. The second area of concern is training in mores, customs, and cultural heritage. It takes the form of instruction or exhortation with the purpose of shaping the mind and spirit of man. The third area is training in subject disciplines basic to intellectual life.

Formal education is generally given in an institution organized specifically for such a purpose. It has become a universal pattern that formal education is carried on by distinctive institutions, primarily schools. Present-day schooling retains the three-level system developed in Western Europe, namely primary schools, secondary schools, and universities.[6] Levels of schooling are designed to equip the population with different degrees of knowledge, from basic to advanced. The educational structure resembles a pyramid with the largest number of individuals enrolled at the base or primary level; the number decreases at each successive level.

Education is generally regarded as a professional field. Knowledge is

sought in the professional field to prepare an individual for a specific occupation; it differs from the academic field in which the imparting of a
body of information is the primary aim without explicit concern as to its
practical application.[7] There has been an increased interest since the 1960s
in developing education as an academic field. An obvious movement toward this is the establishment in 1968 of the American Education Studies
Association, which aims at promoting "the academic study of the educative
process and the school as a fundamental societal institution."[8]

The subfields of education as a discipline include the philosophical foundations of education, policies for education, historical foundations of education, comparative and international education, social and economic
foundations of education, control and administration of education, curriculum studies, the teaching process, educational psychology, and educational research methods.[9] Education depends heavily upon and draws from
other disciplines for its basic content, but it is distinguished by its unique
characteristics, that is, its learning processes, and problems. Education may
also be studied by level of processes which divides it into preschool, elementary, secondary, higher, adult, teacher, and special education.

ACCESS TO SOURCES

Guides

Guides listed here should be studied for a good grasp of reference sources
in education. An old standby is *Documentation in Education* by Arvid J.
Burke and Mary A. Burke (New York: Teachers College Press, 1967, 413
p.) (L1). The Burke guide, formerly *How to Locate Educational Information and Data* by Carter Alexander and Arvid J. Burke, is one of the best
guides in the social sciences, although dated in many respects. Designed as
both a guide to individual research in the use of the literature and a text
for class instruction, it covers most of the general reference works usually
included in the library school's basic course in reference and bibliography.

> *A Bibliographic Guide to Educational Research*. 2nd ed. Dorothea M. Berry.
>   Metuchen, NJ: Scarecrow Press, 1980. 215 p. ISBN 0810813513. (L2)
> *Education: A Guide to Reference and Information Sources*. Lois J. Buttlar.
>   Englewood, CO: Libraries Unlimited, 1989. 258 p. ISBN
>   0872876195. (L3)
> *A Guide to Sources of Educational Information*. 2nd ed. Marda Woodbury.
>   Washington, DC: Information Resources Press, 1982. 430 p. ISBN
>   0878150412. (L4)

Berry's work is an annotated list of over 700 items in education and
related fields by form, including books, periodicals, research studies, government publications, and special types of materials such as children's lit-

erature, textbooks, and tests and measurements. The second edition has given more attention to international and comparative education, bilingual and multicultural education, education of minorities, special education, and vocational education, as the preface states.

The book by Buttlar contains over 900 titles in 676 entries of print sources and entries of databases, research centers, and periodical literature. It is divided into 20 chapters that may be grouped into two categories: general reference sources in four chapters and reference sources in education in sixteen chapters. It is a valuable addition to the guides in education.

A more extensive work is the Woodbury book. It is both a guide to sources and a directory dealing with four types of information: (1) printed materials, (2) education libraries or quasi-libraries (information centers), (3) organizations and government agencies, and (4) special search or bibliographical services. Both Berry and Woodbury complement Burke in some subject areas, particularly Woodbury, which features lists of organizations, institutions, and government agencies.

Bibliographies of Bibliographies

> *An Annotated Bibliography of ERIC Bibliographies 1966–1980.* Joseph Gerald Drazan. Westport, CT: Greenwood Press, 1982. 520 p. ISBN 0313226881. (L5)

The Drazan work is an annotated listing of over 3,200 bibliographies in *Resources in Education*, noted later, arranged in about 600 subjects. All entries give full title, an imprint, pagination, and ED accession number. This is a good source to the vast quantity of bibliographies in English on education and related topics.

Bibliographies

A good number of bibliographies have been published in education. Well-known earlier bibliographies include *Hints toward a Select and Descriptive Bibliography of Education* by G. Stanley Hall and John M. Mansfield (Boston: Heath, 1893, 309 p.) (L6) and *Bibliography of Education* by Will S. Monroe (New York: Appleton, 1897, 202 p.) (L7).

Of current interest, the bibliographies are:

> *Bibliographic Guide to Education*, 1975–   . Thorndike, ME: G. K. Hall. Annual. ISSN 01476505. (L8)
>
> *El-Hi Textbooks and Serials in Print*, 1970––   . New York: Bowker. Annual. ISSN 00000825. (L9)
>
> *The Educational Software Selector*, 1984–   . Hampton Bays, NY: Educational Products Information Exchange (EPIE) Institute. Digital. (L10)

G. K. Hall's *Bibliographic Guide* is primarily a holding list of the Teacher's College Library of Columbia University, with additional entries from the New York Public Library. It updates the *Dictionary Catalog of the Teachers' College Library* (Boston: G. K. Hall, 1970, 36 vols.) (L11) and its three Supplements (1971, 5 vols., ISBN 0816109583; 1973, 2 vols., ISBN 0816109583; and 1977, 10 vols., ISBN 0816100179) (L12).

Since the demise of *Education Book List* (Washington, DC: Pi Lambda Theta, 1968–1975) (L13), *El-Hi Textbooks and Serials in Print* (formerly *American Education Catalog, Textbooks in Print* and *El-Hi Textbooks in Print*) has become the only current, extensive general-education bibliography in the United States. It consists of six indexes. The subject index is the main section. The 1998 edition (126th ed., 1998, 2 vols., ISBN 0835240622) lists, in 22 broad subject categories, "90,120 elementary, junior, and senior high school textbooks and pedagogical books, appearing in 107,834 bibliographic records" (Foreword). It includes related teaching materials, K-12 (subtitle). The other five indexes are the title index, author index, series index, serials subject index, and serials title index.

The Educational Software Selector (*TESS*) consists of sections on software descriptions, contents of program packages, summary listings by hardware, and software suppliers. The heart of the book is software descriptions that provide information to products for all grade levels organized by subject. Each entry lists name, types, uses, scope, grouping, description, components, configurations, availability, and reviews. Appendixes include a glossary, EPIE courseware evaluations, and forms for selection and use of software. *TESS* is a valuable software selection reference. It is now available only on CD-ROM.

Theses and Dissertations

A number of bibliographies of theses and dissertations have been published. Retrospective bibliographies of theses on education include *Research Studies in Education: A Subject and Author Index of Doctoral Dissertations, Reports and Field Studies, and a Research Methods Bibliography, 1941/51–1970* (Bloomington, IN: Phi Delta Kappa, 1953–1972) (L14); and *American Dissertations on Foreign Education: A Bibliography with Abstracts* (Franklin Parker, Troy, NY: Whitston, 1971–1990) (L15). *Research Studies in Education* consists of four sections: (1) doctoral dissertations completed, (2) author, (3) research method bibliography, and (4) an ERIC document index related to research methods. Confined foreign education is *American Dissertations on Foreign Education*, now defunct. Each volume is devoted to a particular area or country.

Doctoral dissertations on a particular subject field are listed in journals. Refer to Chapter 6 for journal listings.

Reviews

Many education journals have book reviews as a regular feature. A journal devoted to reviews of books and films is *Educational Studies: A Journal in the Foundations of Education*, 1970– (Statesboro, GA:, American Educational Studies Association, Georgia Southern University, quarterly, ISSN 00131946) (L16), formerly *Educational Studies: A Journal of Book Reviews in the Foundations of Education* (1970–1975). The *Journal* publishes a substantial number of timely reviews of new publications in the foundations of education field. Beginning in 1987, it publishes a special section that groups together several reviews on a theme. In the subfield, *Higher Education: Handbook of Theory and Research*, noted later, serves as an annual review of literature in higher education.

Indexes

General

> *Current Index to Journals in Education*, 1969– . Phoenix, AZ: Oryx Press. Monthly with semiannual cumulations. ISSN 00113565. Print & digital. (L17)
> *Education Index*, 1929– . New York: Wilson, Monthly with semiannual cumulations. ISSN 00131385. Print & digital. (L18)
> *State Education Journal Index*, 1963– . Westminster, CO: State Education Journal Index. Annual. ISBN 00390046. (L19)

Current Index to Journals in Education (CIJE) is a computer-compiled monthly, a project of the Educational Resources Information Center (ERIC), formerly the Educational Research Information Center. ERIC, created in 1964, is part of the U.S. Department of Education's National Library of Education and consists of sixteen clearinghouses, eleven adjunct clearinghouses, and support components.[10] The clearinghouses collect, abstract, and index education materials for the ERIC database. The database of nearly one million records of journal articles, research reports, and curriculum and teaching guides is the heart of ERIC.[11] The ERIC Document Reproduction Service (EDRS) produces and sells microfiche and paper copies of documents. Documents can be delivered electronically through the EDRS Web site (http://www.edrs.com).

CIJE currently covers approximately 830 educational and education-related journals, arranged by subjects that conform to topics presented in the *Thesaurus of ERIC Descriptors* (13th ed., James E. Houston, ed., Phoenix, AZ: Oryx Press, 1995, 744 p., ISBN 0897747887) (L20). *CIJE* annotates articles and in this respect may be considered an abstracting service. All articles listed in *CIJE* are indexed with descriptive notes by one of the sixteen ERIC Clearinghouses. Each issue consists of Main Entry, arranged by accession number; the Subject Index, an ERIC controlled vocabulary; an Author Index; a Journal Contents Index; and a Source Journal Index. Complete information about each entry includes accession number, clearinghouse number, article title, author, journal title, volume number, issue number, pages, publication, reprint availability, descriptors, identifiers, annotation, and annotator's initials. The Source Journal Index lists all periodicals indexed and their ordering information. *CIJE*, a companion to *Resources in Education (RIE)*, an abstract journal noted later, lists "current findings, project and technical reports, speeches, unpublished manuscripts, and books" (Introduction). *CIJE* and *RIE* are available on CD-ROM and online and the Internet, noted later.

Education Index covers 70 years of significant educational output and stood as the sole important index in education until 1969 when *CIJE* began its publication. It is a cumulative author and subject index to 350 educational journals and yearbooks. *Education Index* has been enhanced with abstracts and full-text, noted later. The index is available online as Wilsonline and on CD-ROM as Wilsondisc.

Education Index and *CIJE* are complemented by *State Education Journals Index*, started with the purpose of covering periodicals not indexed in *Education Index*. It is a classified index arranged by topic in alphabetical order, from absenteeism and academic freedom to year-round school and youth. Currently, it indexes some 115 periodicals published by state educational associations.

Subfield

> *The Business Education Index*, 1940– . Little Rock, AR: Delta Pi Epsilon Society. Annual. ISSN 00684414. (L21)
>
> *Physical Education Index*, 1978– . Cape Girardeau, MO: Benoak. Quarterly. ISSN 01919202. (L22)
>
> *A-V Online*, 1964– . Albuquerque, NM: Access Innovations. Quarterly. Digital. (L23)

The Business Education Index is a publication of the National Honorary Professional Graduate Society of Business Education. It is a subject index classified by over 110 subject headings.

Physical Education Index is "a subject index to domestic and foreign periodicals which are published in English or contain summaries in English." Stress is placed on dance, health, physical education, physical therapy, recreation, sports, and sports medicine. Over 180 periodicals are indexed.

For indexes to educational media, one should consult the publications of the National Information Center for Educational Media (NICEM), now a division of Access Innovations, and its database, *A-V Online*. *A-V Online* contains over 440,000 records with a broad coverage on athletics, education in general, foreign languages, health and safety education, history, management, psychology, science, and vocational and technical education, and education-related fields, such as history, management, psychology, and science. All media types are indexed, including CD-ROM, video, film, filmstrips, tapes, slide, software, model, overheads, and transparency. *A-V Online* is available on CD-ROM from SilverPlatter and NICEM as *International Directory of Educational Audiovisual (IDEA)* (L24) and online marketed through EBSCOhost, SilverPlatter, The Library Cooperation, NICEM Net (http://www.nicem.com), and BiblioFile as *NICEM A-V MARC* (L25). *IDEA*, drawn from the NICEM masterfile with quarterly update, contains more than 322,000 bibliographic records of education media items since 1984 and over 24,000 records of producers and distributors. Boolean logical operators, truncation, and date range can be used for searching.

Most of NICEM's print versions are no longer published, except the following titles:

> *Film and Video Finder*, 1987– . Medford, NJ: Plexus. Biennial (5th ed., 1997. 3 vols.). ISSN 08981581. Print & digital. (L26)
>
> *Index to AV Producers and Distributors*, 1971– . Medford, NJ: Plexus. Biennial. (10th ed., 1997. 626 p.). ISSN 10443967. (L27)
>
> *NICEM Thesaurus*. Albuquerque, NM: NICEM, 1998. 300 p. ISBN 0893202002. (L28)

The *Finder* contains 123,000 records of in-print films and video materials. It is also a part of *AV Online*. The *Index*, formerly *Index to Producers and Distributors*, is a directory listing 23,600 producers and distributors in alphabetical order by name. Some 4,300 subject terms used *in A-V Online* are recorded in *NICEM Thesaurus*. The *Thesaurus* contains a hierarchical term list constructed into 26 major categories and up to nine levels of terms within the hierarchy.

Abstracts

General

> *Resources in Education*, 1966– . Washington, DC: GPO. Monthly with semiannual cumulative indexes. ISSN 01979973. Print & digital. CD-ROM. (L29)
>
> *ERIC*, 1966– . Washington, DC: U.S. Department of Education, Office of Educational Research and Improvement, Educational Resources Information Center. Monthly. Digital. (L30)

Wilson Education Abstracts, 1994–   . Bronx, NY: H. W. Wilson. Monthly. Print & digital. (L31)

Resources in Education (RIE), formerly *Research in Education* (1966–1974), adopted the present title in 1975 to reflect its coverage as not limited to reporting research projects and results. *RIE* adds 12,000 items a year of recent report literature related to education. It consists of two sections: Document Section and Index Section. The latter provides subject index, author index, institution index, publication type index, and clearinghouse number/ED number cross-reference index. There are semiannual index cumulations. As mentioned earlier, both *RIE* and *CIJE* constitute the *ERIC* database, noted next.

ERIC contains two print counterparts: *CIJE* and *RIE.* It is available online marketed through Dialog (File 1), Ovid (File ERIC), Questel-ORBIT (File ERIC), DataStar (File ERIC), FirstSearch, and EBSCOhost and on CD-ROM from Dialog, OCLC, SilverPlatter, and EBSCOhost. Over 30,000 records are added each year. Abstracts of selected documents in *ERIC* are also provided by *Educational Technology Research and Development,* 1953–   (Washington, DC: Association for Educational Communications and Technology, quarterly, ISSN 10421629) (L32).

ERIC is also available on Web sites. The user may use *ERIC* Systemwide site at http://www.aspensys.com/eric (L33) or *AskERIC* at http://www.askeric.org (L34), or the new Web address http://www.accesseric.org. For search on specific clearinghouse resources, there are a number of Web sites, such as http://eric-web.tc.columbia.edu for urban education, http://www.indiana.edu/~eric_rec for Reading, English, and Communication, and http://ericir.syr.edu/ithome for information and technology.

As noted earlier, *Education Index* has been enhanced with abstracts as *Wilson Education Abstracts* and in 1997, the *Abstracts* was added with full-text as *Wilson Education Abstracts—Full-Text* (monthly, digital) (L35). *Wilson Education Abstracts* cites articles in over 400 periodicals and yearbooks in English languages published worldwide. The online version including *Wilson Education Abstracts—Full-Text* is available on CD-ROM marketed as Wilsondisc and through SilverPlatter and online and on the Web. The online database, *Education Abstracts* (L36), is marketed through Dialog (File 437), Ovid, and FirstSearch.

Subfield

Educational Administration Abstracts, 1966–   . Thousand Oaks, CA: Sage. Quarterly. ISSN 00131601. (L37)

Exceptional Child Education Resources, 1969–   . Reston, VA: Council for Exceptional Children. ISSN 01604309. Print & digital. (L38)

Higher Education Abstracts, 1965– . Claremont, CA: Claremont Graduate
University. Quarterly. ISSN 07484364. (L39)

Research into Higher Education Abstracts, 1966– . Abingdon, Oxon, England: Carfax for the Society for Research into Higher Education. 3/
year. ISSN 00345326. (L40)

Sociology of Education Abstracts, 1965– . Abington, Oxon, England: Carfax. Quarterly with annual cumulative indexes. ISSN 00380415. (L41)

Educational Administration Abstracts abstracts over 100 journals that
are of interest to practicing administrators. Abstracts are classified under
fifteen headings with an author index and a subject index. Each issue provides 150 abstracts.

Exceptional Child Education Resources, formerly *Exceptional Child Education Abstracts*, provides more than 85,000 abstracts of over 200 periodicals, books, conference papers and proceedings, dissertations, and
government publications in education and special education fields. Each
issue contains some 800 entries with separate author, title, and subject
indexes. It is available on CD-ROM marketed through SilverPlatter.

Formerly *College Student Personnel Abstracts* (1965–1983), *Higher Education Abstracts* is "a compilation of abstracts from journals, conference
proceedings, and research reports pertaining to college students, faculty,
administration, and related topics" (title page). Some 120 periodicals are
regularly reviewed for abstracts. Abstracts are classified into nearly 50
headings grouped into four parts: (1) students, (2) faculty, (3) administration, and (4) higher education, with an author and a subject index.

Over 280 journals are regularly reviewed for abstracts in *Research into
Higher Education Abstracts*. The serial abstracts journal articles, books,
chapters in a book, and theses and dissertations describing research on
higher education. Reference works, reviews, and important articles of general interest are also included.

Sociology of Education Abstracts, an international abstracting service,
covers books and journal articles. It regularly reviews 600 periodicals for
inclusion. Each issue consists of journal abstracts, book abstracts, an author index, and a subject index. The 1988 volume provides 584 abstracts
of publications on the sociological study of education with annual cumulative author and subject indexes.

Contents Reproduction

Abstracts of educational journals are included in *Current Content: Social
and Behavioral Sciences*, noted in Chapter 3. The following is a content
reproduction service in education:

Contents Pages in Education, 1986– . Abingdon, Oxon, England: Carfax.
Monthly. ISSN 02659220. (L42)

It produces content pages from over 600 periodicals of education worldwide. Tables of contents of about 2,400 periodical issues appear in a year. Contents reproduction may also be found in periodicals, noted in Chapter 6.

SOURCES OF INFORMATION

General

> *The Gateway to Educational Materials (GEM)*. Washington, DC: National Library of Education. http://www.thegateway.org (L43)
>
> *U.S. Network for Educational Information (USNEI)*. Washington, DC: National Library of Education. http://ed.gov/NLE/usnei.html (L44)

The two Web sites were created by the National Library of Education. *The Gateway to Educational Materials* (*GEM*) provides "one-stop, any stop access to high quality Internet lesson plans, curriculum units and other education resources" (home page). It contains some 2,800 resources from over 40 collections, including *AskERIC*, Federal Resources for Educational Excellence, Library of Congress, Microsoft *Encarta*, Newton's Apple Lesson Plans, Smithsonian Education, Treasure Island Web Unit, Virtual Reference Desk, and U.S. Department of Education. Its home page displays *GEM* access points, full-text, subject, keyword, or title search. For keyword search, it provides a listing of topics in alphabetical order. The character C provides, for instance, such topics as CD-ROM databases, calculator, California Gold Rush, calligraphy, caloric values (nutrition), cameras, and cancer. For each topic are given title, reading levels, and keyword subjects. A typical record for a title contains title, link to resource, *GEM* subject, keywords, grade/grade range, description, form, resource type, date, language of resource, publisher, creator, cataloging agency, and rights management.

U.S. Network for Educational Information (USNEI) is "a national information service in the area of international education, especially for educators, students, and parents interested in coming to the United States or going abroad to study or teach" (home page). Sources of information are grouped into Education Around the World and Education in the United States. Education Around the World is organized into six categories: Non-U.S. Education Systems, Going Abroad, U.S. Study Abroad Programs, Studying in Another System, Teaching Overseas, and Additional Resources. There is a brief description of each category and there are a number of topics in a category, such as the Non-U.S. Education Systems category, further divided into General Information, International Information Sources, Regional Information Sources, National Information Sources, and

Institutional Directories. International Information Sources is basically a listing of governments on the Web.

Education in the United States is also organized by category into General Introduction, Organization of U.S. Education, Structure of U.S. Education, U.S. Institutions and Programs, Visiting the United States, Studying in the United States, Teaching in the United States, and Additional Resources. It serves as an excellent nutshell of American education and a directory source.

Encyclopedias

The earliest comprehensive encyclopedia is *A Cyclopedia of Education*, edited by Paul Monroe (New York: Macmillan, 1911–1913, 5 vols.) (L45). Though in existence for over 70 years, it is still useful for retrospective information. There is a wealth of information on universities, school systems, subjects taught in school, and biographies. Of current interest are the following encyclopedias:

General

> *Encyclopedia of American Education*. Harlow G. Unger, ed. New York: Facts on File, 1996. 3 vols. ISBN 08160299946. (L46)
> *Encyclopedia of Education*. Lee C. Deighton, ed.-in-chief. New York: Macmillan, 1971. 10 vols. ISBN 0028953002. (L47)
> *Encyclopedia of Educational Research*. 5th ed. Harold E. Mitzel, ed.-in-chief. Sponsored by the American Educational Research Association. New York: Free Press, 1982. 4 vols. ISBN 0029004500. (L48)
> *The International Encyclopedia of Education*. 2nd ed. Torsten Husén and T. Neville Postlethwaite, eds.-in-chief. London: Pergamon Press, 1994. 12 vols. ISBN 0080410464. (L49)
> *World Education Encyclopedia*. George Thomas Kurian, ed. New York: Facts on File, 1988. 3 vols. ISBN 0871967480. (L50)

Encyclopedia of American Education contains nearly 2,500 entries on various topics of American education, including administration, pedagogy, history, reform, child labor, church-state conflicts, civil rights, minority education, and women's education (Preface). It describes terms, concepts, court decisions, laws, and organizations and provides biographical sketches. Entries are arranged alphabetically with cross-references and bibliographical reference. Its usefulness would have been enhanced if citations were provided for court decisions and laws. There are four appendixes and an index. The four appendixes are Chronology; Significant Federal Education Legislation, 1787–1993; Significant U.S. Supreme Court Decisions in Education; and Graduate School Offerings in Education, Undergraduate Education Majors, and Undergraduate Majors at American Colleges.

The *Encyclopedia of Education* consists of more than 1,000 articles on the history, theory, research, philosophy, and structure of education and on a variety of related disciplines such as art, economics, English, history, industrial arts, mathematics, sociology, and psychology. A few biographies are included. Articles are signed, and most of them are appended by bibliographies for further study. The *Encyclopedia* primarily deals with American education though articles on the educational systems of over 100 countries and territories are presented. The index volume (10) includes an enlarged "Guide to Articles" with cross-references, a detailed subject index, and a directory of contributors, with brief biographical sketches.

Encyclopedia of Educational Research consists of 256 signed articles by 217 contributors providing concise summaries of research on most of the important aspects of education, with many references for further study. Articles are arranged alphabetically by topic, ranging from Academic Freedom and Tenure to Women's Education and Writing, Composition, and Rhetoric. The current edition increased by 56 percent over the previous edition and added such new concepts and topics as Computer-Based Education, Drug Abuse Education, and Equity Issues in Education.[12] An Organizing Scheme preceding the articles serves well the content outlines that classify all articles into eighteen broad headings.

International education is well covered by the encyclopedias listed here, encyclopedias in the subfields, and handbooks. *The International Encyclopedia of Education* updated its first edition and two supplements. It contains 1,266 articles with an average of 4,000 words each in 22 "mega" fields, such as adult education, anthropology of education, comparative and international education, curriculum, economics of education, educational administration, educational evaluation, education of children with special needs, educational policy and planning, national systems, special education, preschool education, teaching, and technical and vocational education and training. Articles are arranged in alphabetical order from abilities and aptitudes, ability grouping and tracking to Zimbabwe: system of education. Over 140 national systems of education are presented. Each article concludes with references and further reading. Volume 12 consists of a classified list of entries, name index, subject index, and list of major education journals.

There are a few by-products of the encyclopedia, including *The International Encyclopedia of Teaching and Teacher Education*, noted next. These works primarily draw articles from the parent encyclopedia (first and second editions).

World Education Encyclopedia consists of five sections: (1) global education, (2) 93 major countries, (3) 33 middle countries, (4) 55 minor countries, and (5) appendixes and index. The division of countries into major, middle, and minor is based on the availability of information. "All major countries follow the information schedules closely, middle countries follow the outline rather loosely, and minor countries generally present the information in no particular order," as noted by the author. The information schedule consists of, in general, the following topics: basic data; history and background; constitutional and legal foundations; education system—overview; preprimary and primary education; secondary education; higher education; administration, finance, and educational research; nonformal education; teaching profession; summary; glossary; and bibliography.

Subfield

Encyclopedia of Careers & Vocational Guidance. 9th ed. William E. Hopke, ed. Chicago: J. G. Ferguson, 1993. 4 vols. ISBN 0894341499. (L51)

The Encyclopedia of Comparative Education and National Systems of Education. T. Neville Postlethwaite, ed. Oxford: Pergamon Press, 1988. 777 p. ISBN 0080308538. (L52)

Encyclopedia of Special Education. Cecil R. Reynolds and Lester Mann, eds. New York: John Wiley, 1987. 3 vols. ISBN 0471828580. (L53)

Concise Encyclopedia of Special Education. Cecil R. Reynolds and Elaine Fletcher-Janzen, eds. New York: John Wiley, 1990. 1,215 p. ISBN 0471515272. (L54)

International Encyclopedia of Higher Education. Asa S. Knowles, ed.-in-chief. San Francisco: Jossey-Bass, 1977. 10 vols. ISBN 0875893236. (L55)

The International Encyclopedia of Teaching and Teacher Education. 2nd ed. Lorin W. Anderson, ed. New York: Pergamon Press, 1996. 684 p. ISBN 0080423043. (L56)

Encyclopedia of Careers & Vocational Guidance covers, according to the Introduction, two aspects of career information. Volume 1, Industry Profiles, covers structures and career paths of all industries. Volumes 2–3 cover information on each job. The volume on Industry Profiles lists over 70 industries in alphabetical order, from accounting and advertising to wildlife management and wood. In the other three volumes, careers are also arranged in alphabetical order. Each career gives definition, history, nature of the work, requirements, special requirements, opportunities for experience and exploration, methods of entering, advancement, employment outlook, earnings, and conditions of work and is appended with sources of additional information and related articles. It complements Occupational Outlook, noted in Chapter 10. It has three appendixes and an index. The three appendixes are: Resources and Associations for Individuals with Disabilities; Internships, Apprenticeships, and Training Programs; and DOT [Dictionary of Occupational Titles] Index.

As just mentioned, The Encyclopedia of Comparative Education and The International Encyclopedia of Teaching and Teacher Education are two of the by-products of the parent encyclopedia, The International Encyclopedia *of Education. The Encyclopedia of Comparative Education* contains 159 articles describing the educational systems of 159 countries drawn primarily from the parent encyclopedia, with or without revisions. Articles are arranged in two parts: Part 1, comparative education consisting of articles dealing with history, concepts, and methods and articles on major aspects of comparative education; and Part 2, national systems of education.

The International Encyclopedia of Teaching and Teacher Education is one of Pergamon's single-volume encyclopedia series drawing upon articles in the *International Encyclopedia of Education*, with revisions and additions. Other single volumes in the series include encyclopedias on national systems, adult and continuing education, economics of education, and education technology. The encyclopedia listed here contains 140 articles including eleven section introductions, all signed, grouped into two parts, teaching and teacher education. At the end, there are a list of contributors, a name index, and a subject index.

The encyclopedia consists of two parts. Part A, Teaching, has eight sections. It deals with (1) The Nature and Characteristics of Teachers (seventeen articles in three groups: metaphors of teachers, a psychological view of teachers, and sociopolitical view of teachers); (2) Theories and Models of Teaching (nine articles); (3) Instructional Programs and Strategies (nine articles); (4) Teaching Skills and Techniques (28 articles in four groups: planning the classroom, classroom management, teaching in the classroom, and assessing and evaluating); (5) School and Classroom Factors (sixteen articles in three groups: frame factors, classroom environments, and paraprofessionals, substitute teachers, parents, and families; (6) Students and the Teaching-Learning Process (thirteen articles in two groups: student entry characteristics: cognitive and affective, and classroom processes); (7) Teaching for Specific Objectives (ten articles); and (8) The Study of Teaching (six articles).

Part B, Teacher Education, contains three sections: (1) Concepts and Issues in Teacher Education (ten articles in three groups: students and teachers, organization and curriculum, and accreditation and certification); (2) Generic Initial Teacher Education (six articles); and (3) Continuing Teacher Education (five articles). In both Part A and Part B, there is an introduction for each section dealing with the subject and highlighting articles in the section.

As compared with the first edition, according to the editor, the present one provides new conceptual frameworks.[13] First, the framework is developed for teachers, schools, classroom, students, teaching, and learning. Second is the framework on the relationship of various areas of teacher education. Articles are arranged in six sections: (1) concepts and models; (2) methods and paradigms for research; (3) teaching methods and techniques; (4) classroom processes; (5) contextual factors; and (6) teacher education.[14]

Encyclopedia of Special Education covers education of the handicapped and other exceptional children and adults and the disciplines of psychology, medicine, and politics as well. Terms, organizations, and biographies are organized in alpabetical order from "AAMD Adaptive Behavior Scales" to "Zygosity." Articles are signed and most of them appended with references for further information. Entries in the encyclopedia can be grouped into seven categories: (1) biographies, (2) educational and psychological tests, (3) interventions and service delivery, (4) handicapping conditions, (5) related services, (6) legal, and (7) miscellaneous entries. Its condensed version is the *Concise Encyclopedia of Special Education.*

The *Concise Encyclopedia* retains 80 percent of the coverage of the original encyclopedia and adds new articles. About 90 percent of the original articles were condensed, but articles on living biographees have been deleted. There is a subject index.

International Encyclopedia of Higher Education contains approximately 1,800 entries in alphabetical order grouped into nine categories: (1) national systems of higher education (198 countries and territories), (2) essays on contemporary topics (282 articles), (3) fields of study (142 fields), (4) educational associations (314 national, international and regional educational associations, organizations, societies, committees, and commissions), (5) research centers and institutes (911 centers and institutes), (6) reports on higher education (71 reports), (7) documentation centers (201 centers listed in the international directory at the end of volume 9), (8) a listing of acronyms, and (9) glossary of terminology in volume 1. Volume 10 is a detailed subject index. It stresses directory information and contemporary topics on higher education. There is, however, no biography.

Dictionaries

General

Dictionary of Education. 3rd ed. Carter V. Good. Prepared under the auspices of Phi Delta Kappa. New York: McGraw-Hill, 1973. 681 p. (L57)
A Dictionary of Education. Derek Rowntree. Totowa, NJ: Barnes & Noble, 1982. 354 p. ISBN 0389202630. (L58)
Dictionary of Education. Denis Lawton and Peter Gordon. London: Hodder & Stoughton, 1993. 200 p. ISBN 0349531797. (L59)
The Facts on File Dictionary of Education. Jay M. Shafritz, Richard P. Koeppe, and Elizabeth W. Soper. New York: Facts on File, 1988. 503 p. ISBN 0816016364. [reprint 1996, ISBN 0608028096] (L60)

Good is an outstanding dictionary "concerned with technical and professional terms and concepts in the entire area of education" (Preface). It contains 33,000 entries and cross-references. Pronunciation is given for difficult words. Educational terms used in Canada, England, and Wales are grouped at the end of the book. As a general policy, names of persons, institutions, school systems, organizations, places, and titles of publications and journals are excluded. The dictionary has a close relationship with the earlier edition of the *Encyclopedia of Education Research*. The fields and authors represented in the encyclopedia originally published in 1941 served the purpose of inviting experts in education to assume responsibility for selecting terms and formulating definitions. The professional vocabulary in education was identified for the dictionary on the basis of the encyclopedia.

There are many complements to Good in foreign terminology, biographies, and organizations, including a few noted later. The Rowntree work contains terms used in the United States and the United Kingdom, concepts, educational theorists and practitioners, and a limited number of associations, committees, societies, and agencies. It is particularly useful for terms with different meanings in the two countries.

The dictionary by Lawton and Gordon also provides brief definitions. It consists of three sections: (1) Discussion of Core Key Concepts, (2) Dictionary: An Alphabetical List of Definitions, and (3) Acronyms and Abbreviations. Its Discussion section provides analysis of the relationships between keywords, a useful feature.

The *Facts on File Dictionary of Education* provides concise definitions of terms. It also includes entries of significant persons, court decisions, and organizations.

Subfield

> *Dictionary of Gifted, Talented, and Creative Education Terms*. Mary M. Frasier, Jo Ann Carland, and E. P. Torrance, eds. New York: Trillium Press, 1984. 135 p. ISBN 0898240212. (L61)
>
> *A Dictionary of Reading and Related Terms*. Theodore L. Harris and Richard E. Hodges. Newark, DE: International Reading Association, 1981. 400 p. ISBN 0685026396. (L62)

Dictionary of Gifted, Talented, and Creative Education Terms is a compilation of definitions in the words of experts with sources indicated. As such, it may be considered a dictionary of quotations. Appendixes include a bibliography, listing sources for the definitions; associations; journals and publications; tests; and test publishers.

A Dictionary of Reading and Related Terms includes 4,780 entries and some 620 subentries with illustrative contexts. It provides more than one definition in many entries with pronunciation in a number of words. There are two appendixes: (1) word-meaning equivalents for selected dictionary entries in French, Spanish, German, Danish, and Swedish and (2) bibliography, a classified listing of books followed by journals and specialized dictionaries and handbooks.

Directories

United States

There are many directories of American institutions. The field is over-whelmed by the number of publications, their similar arrangement and format, and the duplication of information. No directory can claim to be up to date. Even the bulletin or catalog of an academic institution becomes dated soon after its publication. Fortunately, many institutions have created Web sites from which current information about the institution can be found. Web sites noted earlier, such as *GEM* and *USNEI*, all provide links to college and university Web sites. Below are representative directories:

General

Below are Web sites providing information on undergraduate studies, graduate studies, and others:

> *CollegeSource Online.* San Diego, CA: Career Guidance Foundation. http://www.cgf.org (L63)
>
> *Educational Resource Organizations Directory.* Washington, DC: U.S. De-partment of Education. http://www.ed.gov/BASISDB/EROD.direct/SF (L64)
>
> *Petersons.Com: The Education & Career Center.* Princeton, NJ: Peterson's. http://www.peterson.com (L65)
>
> *US News.edu.* New York: U.S. News & World Report Inc. http://usnews.com (L66)
>
> *U.S. Universities and Community Colleges.* Austin: TX: University of Texas. http://www.utexas.edu/world.univ/ (L67)

More than 8,000 college catalogs are available on *CollegeSource Online*. The database contains cover-to-cover catalogs from 2-year, 4-year, gradu-ate, and professional schools. The user may search schools by keyword, criteria, and alphabetical order. Criteria refer to tuition, enrollment degree, affiliation (public, for profit, and so on), state, and major. Each school catalog provides school profile data and the year of coverage of the current catalog. Some school's catalogs appear not to be up to date.

Educational Resource Organizations Directory lists organizations that provide information and assistance on education. It contains State/Territory Report, States Map, and States/Territories List. Educational Resources in States/Territories List are arranged by individual state and District of Co-lumbia in alphabetical order and by Outlying Areas. Outlying Areas include American Samoa, Commonwealth of the Northern Mariana Islands, Federated States of Micronesia, Guam, Puerto Rico, Republic of Palau, Republic of the Marshall Islands, and Virgin Islands. More than 2,200 organizational records are listed. Take the state of Illinois, for example. Educational Resources for Illinois contains thirteen agencies classified into two categories: State Services and Resources and U.S. Department of Education Sponsored State & Regional Services and Resources, including State Education Agency, Regional Office, Comprehensive Regional Assistance Center, Eisenhower Regional Math/Science Consortium, Regional Technology in Education Consortium, State Literacy Resource Center, State Director for Vocational-Technical Education, Desegregation Assistance Center, and ERIC Resource Collections in Illinois. A typical record for each agency gives brief description of the agency, address, person in charge, person to contact, telephone number, fax number, and URL. It provides links to all Web sites listed in the directory.

The directory is one of many sources provided by the U.S. Department of Education Web site (http://www.ed.gov) (L68). The Web site groups sources into Funding Opportunities, Student Financial Assistance, Research & Statistics, News & Events, Programs & Services, Publications & Products, and Other Sites. Student Financial Assistance provides information on aids and opportunities available. Research & Statistics contains Statistics, Assessment, Research—Offices & Organizations, and Research—Publications & Products. Two statistical publications in Research & Statistics, *Digest of Education Statistics* and *The Condition of Education*, produced by the National Center for Education Statistics (NCES), will be noted next. Many of the Department of Education's publications in the category of Publications & Products are available on the Web. The category of Other Sites is a listing of over 20 Web sites classified into ED-Funded Internet Resources, Other Government Internet Resources for Education and Libraries, State Agencies and Resources, Educational Institutions and Education Support Institutions, Libraries, Educational Associations and Organizations, Curricular Resources and Networking Projects, and General Catalogs and Subject Trees on Education.

Peterson's home page displays sixteen categories of information on institutions, programs, and related topics. The categories are Private Schools, Colleges & Universities, Graduate Study, Studying Abroad, Careers & Jobs, Summer Programs, Special Schools, Test Preparation, Distance Learning, Financing & Education, Executive Education, Learning Adventures, Enrollment Message Center, CollegeQuest, MBA Programs, and LifeLong Learning. Each category is organized by topics. In the College & University category, topics include College Searches, Professional Degree Programs, Undergraduate College Features, International Student Information, Competitive Colleges Consortium, Regional Colleges Consortium, Search for Graduate Schools and Program, Search for Distance Learning Program, and Search for a Study Abroad Program. Some topics are further organized by subtopics. Not every institution is described. Full information about a particular institution is referred to Peterson's other publications.

US News.edu is the College & Careers Center site that provides information on education and careers in four areas: College, Financial Aid, Graduate School, and Careers. College contains College Ratings, Find a College, Find a Community College, and Comparison Work Sheet. In Financial Aid are given Find a Scholarship, Best Values Rankings, and Compare Aid Awards. For Graduate School, there are more topics, including Grad Ratings, Find a Business School, Find a Law School, Find a Medical School, Find an Engineering School, and Find an Education School. Careers include Search the Bureau of Labor Statistics and Career Survey. In College Rankings, national liberal arts colleges are ranked Top 25, 26th-40th, second tier, third tier, and so on. The print counterpart of its school directory is the annual *America's Best Colleges* (issue for 1999 published in 1998, 286 p.) (L69).

U.S. Universities & Community Colleges contains two sections: Universities and Community Colleges. Institutions are arranged alphabetically and by state, including District of Columbia and territories. It provides a listing of Web sites of universities and colleges, including *American Universities* (http://www.clas.ufl.edu/clas/american-universities.html) (L70) and *College and University Home Pages* (http://www.mit.edu:8001/people/cdemello/univ.html) (L71). *American Universities* is a listing of Web sites of universities and colleges that grant bachelor's or advanced degrees, arranged in alphabetical order. *College and University Home Pages* presents over 2,500 home pages of American and international institutions. It is not quite as well updated as it should be.

Colleges and Universities

> *American Universities and Colleges*, 1928– . New York: Walter de Gruyter. Quadrennial. ISSN 00660922. (L72)
> *American Community Colleges*, 1940– . Phoenix, AX: Oryx Press. Quadrennial. ISSN 10797599. (L73)
> *College Blue Book*, 1923– . New York: Macmillan. Biennial. ISSN 00695572. Print & digital. (L74)
> *The College Handbook*, 1941– . New York: The College Board. Annual. ISSN 00695653. (L75)
> *Peterson's Guide to Four-Year Colleges*. Barbara Lawrence, ed. Princeton, NJ: Peterson's. ISSN 08949336. Print & digital. (L76)
> *Peterson's Guide to Two-Year Colleges*, 1970– . Barbara Lawrence, ed. Princeton, NJ: Peterson's. Annual. ISSN 08949328. Print & digital. (L77)

American Universities and Colleges (15th ed., 1997, 1,841 p. ISBN 3110146894) consists of survey articles on higher education and on professional education in the United States, institutional exhibits, appendixes, and indexes. Profiles of over 1,900 institutions are arranged by state and within state in alphabetical order by institution. For each institution, if information is available, are given characteristics, accreditation, history, structure, calendar, characteristics of freshmen, admission, degree requirements, distinctive educational programs, degrees conferred, fees and other expenses, departments and teaching staff, enrollment, characteristics of student body, foreign students, student life, publications, library collections, finances, buildings and grounds, and chief executive officer. Appendixes are (1) an academic costume code and an academic ceremony guide; (2) tables of earned doctorates and master's degrees; (3) ROTC units; (4) summary data by state for institutions; and (5) American Council on Education. There are an institutional index and a general index.

Its companion volume, *American Community Colleges* (formerly *American Junior Colleges* and *American Community, Technical, and Junior Colleges*), lists in its tenth edition (Robert H. Atwill and David Pierce, eds., 1995, 909 p., ISBN 0897748743) over 1,180 two-year colleges arranged by state, followed by territories. Information for each entry is grouped into (1) general background, (2) academic, and (3) financial. It provides similar types of information as *American Colleges and Universities* does except for a few items generally insignificant for two-year colleges, such as foreign students, degrees conferred, and publications. It also provides two indexes: subject and institution. There are no appendixes. These two companion directories cover all institutions that are regionally accredited or are recognized candidates for accreditation.

The 1999, 36th edition (1998, 1,754 p., ISBN 0874475902) of *The College Handbook* contains profiles of more than 3,200 four-year and two-year institutions. The Handbook features guidance information and advice for choosing a college. Each entry begins with a few items of general information, followed by sections on degrees awarded, majors, academic programs, academic regulations, freshman admissions, student life, student activities, athletics, student services, annual expenses, financial aid, and address/telephone. It is also available on CD-ROM as *College Explorer* (L78). The CD-ROM version enables the user to link to college Web sites.

It may be noted that the publisher, The College Board, founded in 1900, is a national membership association of schools and colleges with the purpose of facilitating student access to colleges. Other useful publications of the College Board include *College Costs Financial Aid Handbook* (1998, 700 p., ISBN 0874475910) (L79) and *The Scholarship Handbook* (1998, 620 p., ISBN 0874475945, also on CD-ROM) (L80), and *Index of Majors and Graduate Degrees* (1998, 695 p., ISBN 0874475929) (L81). *College Costs* profiles institutions on tuition and fees, undergraduate aid, freshman aid, policies to reduce costs, payment plans, application procedures, and contact. Information on scholarships, internships, loans for undergraduate and graduate students are provided in *The Scholarship Handbook*. Its CD-ROM version, *Fund Finder* (L82), links to the Internet for other college funding options. *Index of Majors* indexes approximately 3,200 colleges by 600 major fields of study. Colleges are listed under each field with degree(s) indicated.

The College Board also developed College Board Online (http://www.collegeboard.org) (L83), providing guides to both teachers and students. For instance, it assists the student to search for colleges, scholarships, and career opportunities; to register for the SAT and send scores; to prepare for the SAT II Writing Tests and AP Exams; to access the Online Essay Evaluation Service; and to apply online for admissions.

The *College Blue Book* (1997, 26th ed., 1998, ISBN 0028647580) consists of five volumes: Volume 1, narrative descriptions of more than 3,000 institutions in the United States and Canada; Volume 2, tabular data, alphabetically arranged by state or province, giving for each institution data on type, costs, accreditation, enrollment figures, faculty, and name of the chief administrative officers or registrar; Volume 3, degrees offered by college and subject; Volume 4, occupational education, and Volume 5, scholarships, fellowships, grants, and loans.

Peterson's two annual guides to undergraduate study, the four-year directory (1999, 29th ed., 1998, 3,258 p., ISBN 1560799870) and two-year colleges directory (1999, 29th ed., 1998, 807 p., ISBN 1560799935), present profiles and special announcements of colleges in the United States (also four-year colleges in Canada) organized in alphabetical order. Descriptions listed therein are of two kinds: concise and in-depth two-page information. The former contains, for each institution, general information, undergraduate profile, freshman data, enrollment patterns, admissions, graduate requirements, expenses, financial aid, special programs, housing, campus life/student services, athletics, majors, and contact. The latter provides, in addition to concise information, more space describing the institution and includes location, faculty, academic facilities, and a photograph. The four-year directory provides Quick Reference College Search Indexes, including state-by-state-summary, entrance difficulty index, cost ranges index, and major index. Quick Reference College Search Indexes also are provided in a two-year directory that includes state-by-state summary and what majors are offered where.

The annual guides are also available online as *Peterson's College Database* (L84) in Dialog (File 214), Dow Jones News Retrieval, and Ovid (File PETE). One good feature of the database is its structure, which enables search by fields. Dialog File 214, for instance, has over 70 fields. The user may qualify the search by field, such as percent Asian American undergraduates, percent freshmen scoring 21 or over on ACT composite, room and board, career services, total enrollment, expenses, financial aid, full-time faculty, major, part-time faculty, special programs, percentage men undergraduates, and percentage women undergraduates. Peterson's publications can also be found on its Web site, noted earlier.

Peterson's also provides The Universal Application, (L85), a handy application tool for applying to colleges. A user may have access to it through the Internet: http://www.ApplyToCollege.com or http://CollegeQuest.com.

Graduate Studies

> *Directory of Graduate Programs*, 1972/73– . Princeton, NJ: Educational Testing Service. Biennial. ISSN 07430506. (L86)
>
> *Peterson's Graduate and Professional Programs: An Overview*, 1966– . Barbara Lawrence, ed. Princeton, NJ: Peterson's. Annual. Print & digital. (L87)
>
> *Peterson's Graduate and Professional Programs: Business, Education, Health, Information Studies, Law, and Social Work*, 1966– . Barbara Lawrence, ed. Princeton, NJ: Peterson's. Annual. Print & digital. (L88)
>
> *Peterson's Graduate and Professional Programs: The Humanities, Arts, and Social Sciences*, 1966– . Barbara Lawrence, ed. Princeton, NJ: Peterson's. Annual. Print & digital. (L89)

Directory of Graduate Programs, published under the sponsorship of the Graduate Record Examinations Board and the Council of Graduate Schools, provides two types of information: (1) tabular format, presenting data on highest degree and number of degrees awarded, number of faculty and students, tuition and fees, admission prerequirements, and financial aid, and (2) narrative account, describing briefly such topics as application deadlines, degree requirements, library holdings, and research and computer facilities. It lists accredited graduate institutions in the United States grouped into four volumes: (1) Natural Sciences; (2) Engineering; (3) Social Sciences; and (4) Arts, Humanities, and Other Fields.

Peterson's Graduate and Professional Programs (33rd ed., 1998, ISBN 1560799811) consists of six books. Listed here are three books. Its title varies, formerly known as *Peterson's Annual Guides to Graduate Study*. Book 1 presents an overview of programs in more than 1,700 accredited institutions of higher learning in the United States and Canada. Book 2, The Humanities, Arts, and Social Sciences, contains over 10,900 programs in 124 disciplines. It is organized in 28 sections in two parts. Part A, Directory of Institutions with Programs in the Humanities, Arts, and Social Sciences, consists of academic and professional programs in these fields. Part B consists of Research and Training Opportunities in these fields.

Book 6, Business, Education, Health, Information Studies, Law, and Social Work, provides information on graduate programs in the United States and Canada in 44 sections, also in two parts. Part A, Directory of Institutions with Programs in Business, Education, Health, Information Studies, Law, and Social Work, consists of academic and professional programs in these fields. Part B consists of Research and Training Opportunities in these fields. The other three books deal with biological sciences; physical sciences, mathematics, and agricultural sciences; and engineering and applied sciences respectively. Each book contains a graphical summary of graduate and professional work and descriptions of American and Canadian institutions in one or more fields. Descriptions are of two kinds: one paragraph and two pages. *Peterson's* digital version, *Peterson's Gradline* (L90), is available on CD-ROM marketed through SilverPlatter and online through Dialog (File 273). Information can also be found on Peterson's Web, noted earlier.

Schools

> *Patterson's American Education*, 1904–   . Mount Prospect, IL: Educational Directories. Annual. ISSN 00790230. (L91)
> *Patterson's Elementary Education*, 1989–   . Mount Prospect, IL: Educational Directories. Annual. ISSN 10441417. (L92)

The two Patterson directories are compiled on the same pattern, and both are simple listings of schools. *Patterson's American Education* (1999, 95th ed., Wayne Moody, ed., 1998, 901 p., ISBN 0910536740) lists 11,300 public school districts, 32,000 public secondary schools, 5,000 private and Catholic secondary schools, and more than 6,000 postsecondary schools, a total of over 48,000 schools. It is organized in two parts: Part 1, secondary schools, arranged by state, and Part 2, Patterson's schools classified by academic fields. It is a convenient reference for quick information on schools and their addresses, officers, and districts.

The 1999, 11th edition of *Patterson's Elementary Education* (Wayne Moody, ed., 1998, 987 p., ISBN 0910536759) lists more than 13,000 public school districts, more than 66,000 public, private, and Catholic elementary schools, and more than 14,000 middle schools, a total of 93,987 schools. Also included are Superintendents and Catholic, Lutheran, and Seventh-Day Adventist schools.

Special

> *Vocational Careers Sourcebook: Where to Find Help Planning Careers in Skilled Trade and Non-technical Vocations.* 3rd ed. Kathleen E. Maki and Kathleen M. Savage, eds. Detroit: Gale Research, 1997. 701 p. ISBN 0810364700. (L93)

The *Vocational Careers Sourcebook* "profiles 134 vocational occupations, ranging from aircraft mechanic and animal caretaker to welder and woodmaker" (Highlights). Each profile consists of eleven categories of information, such as job descriptions, career guides, associations, standard/

certification examinations, educational directories and programs, basic reference guides and handbooks, periodicals, and meetings and conventions. It contains over 6,500 entries. There are three appendixes: (I) Electronic Career Resources; (II) State Occupational and Professional Licensing Agencies; and (III) Employment Growth Rankings and Statistics.

International

> *World of Learning*, ed. 1– , 1947– . London: Europa. Annual. ISSN 00842117. (L94)
>
> *Commonwealth Universities Yearbook*, 1914– . London: Association of Commonwealth Universities. Annual. ISSN 00697745. (L95)
>
> *International Handbook of Universities and Other Institutions of Higher Education*, 1959– . Paris: International Association of Universities. Biennial. ISSN 00746215. (L96)

World of Learning is the most extensive listing of institutions of higher learning worldwide. It lists international organizations, libraries, archives, museums, art galleries, societies, and institutions in over 170 countries and areas. The United States is given more extensive coverage that occupies 14 percent of the main text. One of its features is a listing of officers and, in many cases, faculty members of institutions of higher learning. Its 49th edition (2,080 p., 1998, ISBN 1857430492) covers some 200 countries and territories. There are six indexes: institutions, learned societies, research institutes, libraries and archives, museums and art galleries, and universities. For more detailed information on foreign institutions, the other two directories noted next should be consulted.

Commonwealth Universities Yearbook (1997–1998, 73rd ed., 1997, 2 vols., ISBN 0851431607) describes over 600 Commonwealth universities of good standing arranged by countries and region in alphabetical order. Thirty-five countries and regions are covered. Each country section includes a list of universities and a national introduction for each of the fourteen countries at the beginning of those countries. A full entry contains title, address, executive head and other principal officers, academic staff, dean/heads of faculties, contact officers, campus, and college heads. Appendixes include ACU [Association of Commonwealth Universities] members of former Commonwealth Countries: People's Republic of China/Hong Kong; Commonwealth of Learning; and Commonwealth Scholarship and Fellowship Plan. There are two indexes: Index to Institutions and Index to Personal Names.

For institutions of higher education in all parts of the world not covered by the *Commonwealth Universities Yearbook* and *American Universities and Colleges*, consult the *International Handbook*. Each entry, if complete, contains officers, brief descriptions of the history and structure, academic year, admission requirements, fees, language of instruction, library, academic staff, and student enrollment. Information is concise. Since it covers the United States and United Kingdom, the *Handbook* complements the *Commonwealth Universities Yearbook* and *American Universities and Colleges*. The *Handbook* is limited to degree-granting institutions of university level. For other institutions, refer to *World List of Universities*. The 30th edition (1993, 1,304 p., ISSN 1561591009) (L97) contains over 4,000 institutions in 169 countries.

Financial Aid

Most print or database directories provide information on financial aid. For instance, *College Blue Book* has one volume devoted to financial aid. The Web sites of the Department of Education, *Peterson.com*, and *USNews.edu* all provide information on financial aid.

Rating

One who is interested in the rating of academic programs may consult *An Assessment of Quality in Graduate Education* by Allan M. Cartter (Washington, DC: American Council on Education, 1966, 131 p.) (L98); *A Rating of Graduate Programs* by Kenneth D. Roose and Charles J. Anderson (Washington, DC: American Council on Education, 1970, 115 p.) (L99), a follow-up study; and *An Assessment of Research-Doctorate Programs in the United States* by the Committee on an Assessment of Quality Related Characteristics of Research-Doctorate Programs in the United States (Washington, DC: National Academy Press, 1982, 5 vols.) (L100).

An annual rating of colleges has been provided since 1987 in *U.S. News & World Report*, noted in Chapter 6, and in *USNews.edu*, noted earlier.

Frequently mentioned yet controversial are two Gourman reports: *The Gourman Report: Rating of Undergraduate Programs in American and International Universities*, 1967– (Los Angeles: National Education Standards, biennial, ISSN 10497188) (L101) and *The Gourman Report: A Rating of Graduate and Professional Programs in American and International Universities*, 1967– (Los Angeles: National Education Standards, biennial, ISSN 1049717X) (L102). Both works are based on data submitted by the selected institutions in the form of a questionnaire, but no further details are given regarding their rating method and the weight of scores. Another popular rating is *Rugg's Recommendations on the Colleges*, 1980– (Frederick E. Rugg, ed., Atascadero, CA: Rugg's Recommendations, annual) (L103). It classifies selected colleges into three groups: most selective, very selective, and selective.

The following is an extensive rating in education:

Educational Rankings Annual. Detroit: Gale Research. Annual. ISSN
00774472. (L104)

Its 1999 Annual (Lynn C. Hattendorf Westney, ed., 1998, 730 p., ISBN
0787611875) contains "3700 rankings and lists on education, compiled
from educational and general interest published sources" (subtitle). It is
arranged in alphabetical order by subject—some 400 subjects plus many
see references. In each item are given the ranking title, ranking basis/back-
ground, number lists, ranking, and source. Some items provide remarks for
"additional details relating to the list from the source materials" (Sample
Entry). It has a detailed dictionary index providing a listing of rankings
under each subject and institutions.

The book has international coverage, including Australia, Canada,
China, England, Taiwan, and other countries. The term "educational" in
the title is broadly construed to include books, publishing, journals, dictionaries, encyclopedias, hospitals, libraries, museums, employment, and
many others.

Biographies

American Men and Women of Science and *Directory of American Scholars*, mentioned in Chapter 4, are familiar biographies for educators. Biographies in education include:

> *Biographical Dictionary of American Educators.* John F. Ohles, ed. Westport,
> CT: Greenwood Press, 1978. 3 vols. ISBN 0837198933. (L105)
> *Biographical Dictionary of North American and European Educationists.* Pe-
> ter Gordon and Richard Adrich. London: Worurn Press, 1997. 528
> p. ISBN 0713002050. (L106)
> *Leaders in Education: A Biographical Directory.* 5th ed. Jacques Cattell
> Press, ed. New York: Bowker, 1974. 1,309 p. ISBN 0835206998.
> (L107)
> *Who's Who in American Education,* 1988–   . New Providence, NJ: Marquis
> Who's Who. Biennial. ISSN 104567203. Print & digital. (L108)

Biographical Dictionary of American Educators contains 1,665 educators "who have been major figures in the development of American education." As stated in the introduction, "the content of each biographical
sketch is basically a short description of the subject's education, employment, contributions to education, and participation in professional activities." Each entry is appended with references for further information. It
consists of five appendixes: (1) place of birth, (2) state of major service, (3)
field of work, (4) chronology of birth years, and (5) important dates in
American education.

Some 500 biographies are included in *Biographical Dictionary of North*

American and European Educationists, a companion to the authors' *Dictionary of British Educationists*. The criteria for inclusion are: "entries were almost entirely restricted to those whose main careers were from 1800 onwards" and "none of the subjects is still alive" (Introduction). Each biography is about one page long and concludes in most cases with a select bibliography.

The book contains educationists in some 20 countries. However, more than half of biographees are Americans, followed by educationists in Germany, Canada, France, Switzerland, Russia, Belgium, and other countries. By quick check, countries represented by fewer than two biographies each are Bulgaria, Czech, Finland, and Greece. Coverage appears not to be balanced.

Most of the biographies can be found in other reference sources, such as the *Encyclopaedia Britannica* and the *Columbia Encyclopedia*. The book is well written and features in one place collection of prominent education lists in North America and Europe.

Leaders in Education has the same criteria for inclusion as those stated in *American Men and Women of Science* and *Directory of American Scholars*. About 17,000 biographical sketches of decision makers and outstanding contributors to the work of the educational community in the United States and Canada are presented. One feature is its inclusion of an index to biographies by area of specialization.

Who's Who in American Education is one of the Marquis Who's Who publications. It lists biographical sketches of some 27,000 educators. All Marquis Who's Who publications including the present one are available on CD-ROM marketed through Bowker and online marketed through Dialog, noted in Chapter 4.

Statistical Sources

The Chronicle of Higher Education Almanac, 1988– . Washington, DC: Chronicle of Higher Education. Annual. ISSN 10437967. (L109)

The Condition of Education: A Statistical Report on the Condition of American Education, 1975– . Washington, DC: U.S. Department of Education, National Center for Education Statistics. Annual. ISSN 00984752. Print & digital. (L110)

Digest of Educational Statistics, 1962– . Washington, DC: U.S. Office of Educational Research and Development. Annual. Print & digital. (L111)

UNESCO Statistical Yearbook. Annuaire Statistique, 1962– . Paris: UNESCO. Annual. ISSN 00827541. (L112)

The Chronicle of Higher Education Almanac presents "facts about higher education in the U.S., each of the 50 states, and D.C." (contents page). It covers basically demographics, political leadership, colleges and universities, faculty members, students, and money. The 1998/1999 issue provides three parts of information: The Nation, The States, and Resources and Notes. The Nation divides data into five categories, namely, general, students, faculty and staff, resources, and institutions. The students category, for instance, contains average SAT scores, average ACT scores, proportion of undergraduates receiving financial aid, educational attainment, colleges with the most freshman Merit Scholars, student financial aid, computers with the largest enrollments, enrollment, attitudes and characteristics of freshmen, characteristics of recipients of doctorates, foreign students, earned degrees, and many others. The second part, The States, covers demographics, political leadership, colleges and universities, faculty members, students, money, and miscellany for each state and the District of Columbia. Miscellany is an anecdote. Resources and Notes is a bibliography.

The Chronicle of Higher Education Almanac is a supplement to *The Chronicle of Higher Education*, 1966– (Weekly, ISSN 00095982, print & digital, http://chronicle.com) (L113). The journal reports news, trends, and events in the entire spectrum of higher education, national and international. It contains articles, news on campus, bulletin board (job available), calendar of coming events, grants, deaths, and a limited number of book reviews. Of particular interest are the many statistical data on various topics. Its history section contains selected stories of the past and is available for free access on the Internet (http://chronicle.com/free/history).

The two publications by the National Center for American Statistics (NCAS) are important statistical sources of American education. *The Condition of American Education*, an annual report to Congress, contains 60 indicators on the most significant national measures of the condition and progress of education. The 1997 report (1997, 411 p., ISBN 0160490731) is organized by six sections of indicators: (A) Access, Participation, and Progress; (B) Achievement, Attainment, and Curriculum; (C) Economic and Other Outcomes of Education; (D) Organization and Management of Educational Institutions; (E) Climate and Diversity of Educational Institutions; and (F) Financial and Human Resources of Educational Institutions. Each section offers a summary followed by indicators. For instance, Section B contains fourteen current indicators, including Trends in the reading proficiency of 9-, 13-, and 17-year-olds, trends in writing proficiency in grades 4, 8, and 11; trends in the mathematics proficiency of 9-, 13-, and 17-year-olds, educational attainment, international comparisons of educational attainment by age, and so on. The second volume (1997, 470 p.) is *The Condition of Education Supplemental and Standard Error Tables*.

Digest of Educational Statistics is a compilation of statistical information from government and private sources covering American education from kindergarten through graduate school. The 1997 *Digest* (33rd ed., 1997,

529 p., ISBN 0160493439) consists of seven chapters: (1) all levels of education, (2) elementary and secondary education, (3) postsecondary education, (4) federal programs for education and related activities, (5) outcomes of education, (6) international comparison of education, and (7) learning resources and technology. Over 400 tables are included. Also included are a guide to sources and definitions. This is a most useful, significant statistical data book in education. The two publications can be accessed on the NCES Web (http://nces.ed.gov), noted in Chapter 5.

At the international level, an indispensable tool is *UNESCO Statistical Yearbook*, providing statistics relating to the educational, scientific, and cultural life and activities of some 200 countries and territories. Data are gathered mainly from official replies to UNESCO questionnaires and special surveys. Statistical sources are grouped in ten parts: Reference Tables, Education, Education by Country, Public Expenditure on Education, Research and Experimental Development, Summary Tables for Culture and Communication Subjects by Groups of Countries, Printed Matter, Films and Cinema, Broadcasting, and Cultural Heritage. Each part is further divided, such as in Education by Country, into Education Structure and Enrollment Ratios, Education at the Pre-Primary Level, Education at the First Level, Education at the Second Level, and Education at the Third Level. The Printed Matter part is further divided into Libraries, Book Production, Newspapers and Periodicals, International Trade in Printed Matter, and Cultural Paper. There are seven appendixes: (A) Member States and Associate Members of UNESCO; (B) School and financial years; (C) Exchange rates; (D) List of selected UNESCO statistical publications; (E) Tables that have appeared in past editions of the Yearbook; (F) Introductory texts in Russian; and (G) Introductory texts in Arabic.

Handbooks, Yearbooks, and the Like
Handbooks

Educational Research, Methodology, and Measurement: An International Handbook. 2nd ed. John P. Keeves, ed. Oxford, England: Pergamon Press, 1997. 964 p. ISBN 0080427103. Resources in Education Series, vol. 7. (L114)

Handbook of Research on Teaching. 3rd ed. Merlin C. Wittrock. New York: Macmillan, 1986. 1,037 p. ISBN 0029003105. (L115)

Handbook on Continuing Higher Education. Quentin H. Gessner, ed. Washington, DC: American Council on Education. New York: Macmillan, 1987. 304 p. ISBN 0029116201. (L116)

Higher Education: Handbook of Theory and Research, 1985– . John C. Smart, ed. Edison, NJ: Agathon Press. Annual. ISSN 08824126. (L117)

International Handbook of Education Systems. J. Cameron and others, eds. Chichester, England: John Wiley, 1983–1984. 3 vols. (L118)

International Handbook of Bilingualism and Bilingual Education. Christina Bratt Paulston, ed. Westport, CT: Greenwood Press, 1988. 803 p. ISBN 0313244847. (L119)

Educational Research, one of the by-products of the parent encyclopedia, *The International Encyclopedia of Education,* noted earlier, contains 115 articles that were drawn from the parent encyclopedia with addition of articles specially prepared for the handbook. It consists of four sections: (1) the methods of educational inquiry, (2) the creation, diffusion, and utilization of knowledge, (3) measurement for educational research, and (4) research techniques and statistical analyses.

Handbook of Research on Teaching, a project of the American Educational Research Association, was produced with four objectives: (1) summarizing or reviewing research theories and methods of research on teaching, (2) presenting known research on teaching, (3) offering theoretical explanations of the research findings, and (4) providing organized coverage of the subject matter. It contains 35 articles by 58 authors grouped into five parts: (1) theory and method of research on teaching, (2) research on teaching and teachers, (3) the social and institutional context of teaching, (4) adapting teaching to differences among learners, and (5) research on the teaching of subjects and grade levels.

Two handbooks listed above deal with higher education. The purpose of the *Handbook on Continuing Higher Education* is "to provide a practical, comprehensive overview of continuing education within postsecondary institutions . . . a sourcebook for professional continuing educators who develop, administer, deliver, and evaluate continuing education programs offered by colleges and universities as part of their outreach effort" (Preface). It contains thirteen articles on such topics as historical perspective, components of continuing higher education, financial structure, needs assessment, and marketing strategies. At the end, there are "Suggested Readings" and an index.

Higher Education: Handbook of Theory and Research serves as an annual review of literature on diverse topics on higher education theory and research. Each article is intended "to provide an integrative review of extant research on the selected topic; to critique that research in terms of its conceptual and methodological rigor; and to set forth an agenda for future research," as noted in the preface.

International Handbook of Education Systems adopted the framework of entries from the National Profiles of Educational Systems, compiled by the British Council. The framework consists of a number of topics, such as geography, population, society and culture, history and politics, the economy, the education system, educational administration, educational finance, development and planning of the education system, the system in operation, trends, and problems and possibilities. The handbook arranges countries by region in three volumes: Volume 1, Europe and Canada; Volume 2, Africa and the Middle East; and Volume 3, Asia, Australasia, and Latin America.

Twenty-seven articles are contained in *International Handbook of Bilingualism and Bilingual Education*. The first two articles serve as an introduction to bilingualism and bilingual education and languages of the world. The other 25 articles deal with case studies in different countries including Arabic nations, Bolivia, Canada, China, England, Mexico, Singapore, Spain, Sweden, and the United States. It concludes with a glossary and a bibliographic essay.

Yearbooks and the Like

> *Educational Media and Technology Yearbook*, 1975– . Donald P. Ely and Barbara B. Minor, eds. Englewood, CO: Libraries Unlimited. ISSN 87552094. (L120)
>
> *Requirements for Certification of Teachers, Counselors, Librarians, Administrators for Elementary Schools, Secondary Schools, Junior Colleges*, 1935– . John Tryneski, ed. Chicago: University of Chicago Press. ISSN 00801429. (L121)

Published in cooperation with the Association for Educational Communications and Technology, *Educational Media and Technology Yearbook* (formerly *Educational Media Yearbook*) is a combination of handbook, directory, biography, and bibliography. It consists of five parts: (1) educational media and technology: trends and issues, (2) leadership profiles in educational media and technology, (3) organizations and associations in North America, (4) graduate programs, and (5) mediagraphy—a bibliography of print and nonprint sources.

Requirements for Certification (62nd ed., John Tryneski, ed., 1997, 243 p., ISBN 0226813185) provides concise certification requirements for elementary schools, secondary schools, junior colleges, and colleges arranged by state and within state by type of certification. This is a useful, handy reference to certification requirements for teachers, librarians, and administrators.

NOTES

1. John Dewey, *Experience and Education* (New York: Collier Books, 1938), p. 17.

2. Ibid., p. 18.

3. Ibid., p. 73ff.

4. Stella Van Pettern Henderson, *Introduction to Philosophy of Education* (Chicago: University of Chicago Press, 1947), pp. 38, 25ff.

5. Arthur Bestor, "Education and the American Scene," in Brand Blanshard, ed., *Education in the Age of Science* (New York: Basic Books, 1960), pp. 57–59.

6. C. Arnold Anderson, "Education and Society," in *International Encyclopedia of the Social Sciences* (New York: Macmillan and Free Press, 1968–   ), vol. 4, p. 522; A. H. Halsey, "Educational Organization," in *International Encyclopedia of the Social Sciences*, vol. 4, pp. 528–529.

7. John A. Laska, "Current Progress in the Foundations of Education," in Margaret Gillett and John A. Laska, *Foundation Studies in Education: Justification and New Directions* (Metuchen, NJ: Scarecrow Press, 1973), pp. 123–124.

8. Ibid., pp. 122, 129–130; John Walton, "Education as an Academic Discipline," in Gillett and Laska, *Foundation Studies*, pp. 119–121.

9. Based on the *Classification of Educational Studies*, a periodical.

10. *All about ERIC* (Washington, DC: U.S. Department of Education, 1998), p. 1.

11. Ibid., p. 3.

12. "Preface," in Harold E. Mitzel, ed. *Encyclopedia of Education Research*, 5th ed. (New York: Free Press, 1982), p. ix.

13. "Preface," in Lorin W. Anderson, ed., *International Encyclopedia of Teaching and Teacher Education*, 2nd ed. (New York: Pergamon Press, 1996), pp. xv–xviii.

14. Ibid.

Chapter 12

Geography

Geography may be simply defined as the science that describes the earth's surface, but the study of geography is complex because such study cannot be separated from the space above, the land below, and its relationship to the people who live on it.[1] Geography finds a place in the natural sciences and the social sciences. As pointed out by Richard Hartshorne, modern geography studies the earth as the space in which people live and their environment as well.[2] The human-earth relationship is the distinctive subject matter of geography, which results naturally in two branches of geography: physical geography and human geography.[3] Physical geography studies the earth, the outer space above, and the land below. It may be further divided into geomorphology, hydrology, oceanography, climatology and meteorology, pedology, and biogeography, to study rivers, seas, oceans, climate, soil, and the distribution of plants and animals respectively.[4] Human geography overlaps to a great extent with other subfields of the social sciences. It has been divided into political geography, economic geography, cultural geography, social geography, and statistical geography, to study political, economic, cultural, and social phenomena in their areal context.[5] Statistical geography is devoted to quantitative methods in the study of human-earth relationship.

ACCESS TO SOURCES

Guides

A Guide to Information Sources in the Geographical Sciences. Stephen Goddard, ed. London: Croom Helm, 1983. 273 p. ISBN 038920403X. (M1)

The Literature of Geography: A Guide to Its Organization and Use. 2nd ed. J. Gordon Brewer. Hamden, CT: Linnet Books, 1978. 264 p. ISBN 020801683X. (M2)

A Guide to Information Sources serves as an introduction to bibliographical resources in thirteen chapters arranged in three main categories: (1) the systematic approach dealing with geomorphology, historical geography, agricultural geography, and industrial geography; (2) sources of regional information consisting of Africa, South Asia, the United States and the former U.S.S.R.; and (3) tools for the geographer including maps, atlases, gazetteers, aerial photographs, satellite information, statistical sources, and archival materials.

The Brewer book "is planned as an introductory guide, identifying the most useful, the most significant, and the most authoritative sources within each branch of the subject" (Introduction). It consists of thirteen chapters. The first two chapters deal with the scope, structure, use, and organization of the literature. Six chapters discuss the literature by form, such as bibliographies, cartobibliography, monographs, periodicals, statistics, and government publications. Two chapters cover the history and geographical thought and techniques and methodology. The remaining three chapters are for the literature classified by topic into physical geography, human geography, and regional geography. The second edition adds a chapter on cartobibliography and expands the earlier edition with 400 more reference sources.

Bibliographies

General

> *Bibliographie Géographique Internationale*, 1891– . Paris: Centre National de la Recherche Scientifique. Annual. ISSN 12749249. (M3)
> *Current Geographical Publications*, 1938– . Milwaukee: University of Wisconsin at Milwaukee Library, American Geographical Publications. Monthly. ISSN 00113514. (M4)
> *Geographical Bibliographies for American Libraries.* Chauncy D. Harris, ed.-in-chief. Washington, DC: Association of American Geographers, 1985. 437 p. ISBN 089291193X. (M5)
> *Geography and Cartography: A Reference Handbook.* C. B. Muriel Lock. London: Bingley, 1976. 762 p. ISBN 0208015221. (M6)

Although a French-language publication, *Bibliographie Géographique Internationale* includes an English-language introduction and English-language titles and subject headings. It lists books and periodical articles arranged by broad subject with three indexes: authors, subjects, and places.
Current Geographical Publications, a library holding list, publishes ad-

ditions to the American Geographical Society Collection and the University of Wisconsin–Milwaukee. It is an unannotated bibliography of books and periodical articles classified into four sections: topical, regional, maps, and selected books and monographs.

Geographical Bibliography is a joint project of the Association of American Geographers and the National Geographic Society. It was originally published as *A Basic Geographical Library: A Selected and Annotated Book List for American Colleges*, compiled and edited by Martha Church, Robert E. Huke, and Wilbur Zelinsky (Washington, DC: Association of American Geographers, 1966, 152 p.) (M7), which was superseded by *A Geographical Bibliography for American College Libraries*, compiled and edited by Gordon R. Lewthwaite, Edward T. Price, Jr., and Harold A. Winters (Washington, DC: Association of American Geographers, Commission on College Geography, 1970, 214 p.) (M8). The present book is an annotated bibliography of 2,903 titles grouped into seven parts: (1) general aids and sources; (2) history, philosophy, and methodology; (3) systematic fields of physical geography; (4) systematic fields of human geography; (5) applied geography; (6) regional geography; and (7) publications suitable for school libraries. There is a name, title, and subject index. Since the listing focuses primarily on publications for the period 1970–1984, the earlier edition should be consulted for publications before 1970.

The Lock book combined the author's two previous titles, *Geography: A Reference Handbook* (New York: Bingley, 1968, 179 p.) (M9) and *Modern Maps and Atlases: An Outline Guide to Twentieth Century Publications* (London: Bingley, 1969, 619 p. ISBN 0851570720) (M10). It is a combination of directory, bibliography, and biography, listing 1,393 entries of books, organizations, periodicals, symposia, maps, globes, atlases, and deceased geographers. Many entries are cross-referenced. It is a good reference book of international coverage, though with a British bias.

Subfield

Bibliographic Guide to Maps and Atlases, 1979–   . Thorndike, ME: G. K. Hall. Annual. ISSN 01975889. (M11)

Guide to Atlases: World, Regional, National, Thematic: An International Listing of Atlases Published since 1950. Gerard L. Alexander. Metuchen, NJ: Scarecrow Press, 1971. 671 p. ISBN 081080414X. (M12)

Guide to Atlases Supplement: World, Regional, National, Thematic: An International Listing of Atlases Published 1971 through 1975 with Comprehensive Indexes. Gerard L. Alexander. Metuchen, NJ: Scarecrow Press, 1977, 362 p. ISBN 0810810115. (M13)

Bibliographic Guide to Maps and Atlases includes maps, atlases, globes, books, journal articles, and analytics. It is basically a catalog of the Research Libraries of the New York Public Library and the Library of Congress. The guide serves as a supplement to the *Dictionary Catalog of the Map Division, the Research Libraries, the New York Public Library* (Boston: G. K. Hall, 1971, 10 vols., ISBN 0816107831) (M14).

The two Alexander books list atlases in four groups: (1) world atlases, arranged chronologically by publisher; (2) regional atlases, arranged in alphabetical order by region and within region by publisher; (3) national atlases, arranged by continent and within continent by publisher; and (4) thematic atlases, arranged by subject and within subject by publisher in alphabetical sequence. Each atlas gives the name of the publisher, title, edition, author, place of publication, date of publication, number of pages, colored maps, and size of atlas.

It may be noted that *Bulletin of the Geography and Map Division, Special Libraries Association*, 1947–   (3/yr, ISSN 00361607) (M15), provides as its regular feature bibliographical services. It publishes book reviews and listings of new maps, new atlases, new books, new government publications of interest, and recent publications of interest.

Theses and Dissertations

For doctoral and master's theses in geography, there are *A Bibliography of Dissertations in Geography, 1901–1969: American and Canadian Universities* (Chapel Hill, NC: University of North Carolina Department of Geography, 1978, 96 p.) (M16); *A Bibliography of Dissertations in Geography: Supplement, 1962–1982* (Chapel Hill, NC: University of North Carolina Department of Geography, 1983, 145 p.) (M17), both compiled by Clyde E. Browning; and *A Bibliography of Master's Theses in Geography: American and Canadian Universities*, by Merrill M. Stuart (Tualatin, OR: Geographic and Area Study Publications, 1973, 274 p.) (M18). The two Browning works contain 3,852 titles, and Stuart gives 5,054 master's theses. Dissertations are also listed from 1979 to the present in *Guide to Programs in Geography in the United States and Canada* and in *Geobase*, both noted later. For journal listings of theses, refer to Chapter 6.

Research in Progress

The journal listing of research in progress is noted in Chapter 6.

Reviews

Two journals devoted to reviews are:

Progress in Human Geography: An International Review of Geographical Work in the Social Sciences and Humanities, 1977– . London: Edward Arnold. Quarterly. ISSN 03091325. (M19)

Progress in Physical Geography: An International Review of Geographical Work in the Natural and Environmental Sciences, 1977– . London: Edward Arnold. Quarterly. ISSN 03091333. (M20)

They are companions. Each consists of four sections: (1) substantial review articles covering a wide range of materials in the subject fields as indicated by the title, (2) classics revisited, (3) progress reports in a host of subdivisions, and (4) book reviews. *Progress in Human Geography* "publishes reviews of current research and theoretical developments on any aspect of social, economic, political and cultural geography and their interconnections with related disciplines" (Journal policy). Its 1997 volume published fifteen articles, four classics in human geography revisited, fourteen progress reports, and 86 book reviews.

Indexes

Bibliographie Géographique Internationale, mentioned earlier, is also an index to periodical articles. The following is an extensive abstracting service in geography.

Abstracts

Geobase, 1980– . Norwich, England: Elsevier Science. Monthly. Digital. (M21)

Geographical Abstracts: Human Geography, 1966– . Norwich, England: Elsevier Science. Monthly. ISSN 09539611. Print & digital. (M22)

Geobase consists of the print counterpart of *Geographical Abstracts: Human Geography, Geographical Abstracts: Physical Geography, Geological Abstracts, Ecological Abstracts,* and others. The database covers fully or partially 5,000 journals and, in addition, books, monographs, proceedings, reports, and theses and dissertations. The database is marketed through Dialog (File 292) and Questel-Orbit (File GEOB). One of its print counterparts is *Geographical Abstracts: Human Geography.*

Human Geography, combining the former *Geographical Abstracts: Economic Geography, Geographical Abstracts: Social and Historical Geography,* and *Geographical Abstracts: Regional and Community Planning,* covers articles, books, theses and dissertations, and other materials worldwide. It is a classified bibliography of abstracts with an author index. Its companion, *Geographical Abstracts: Physical Geography,* 1960– (monthly, ISSN 09540504) (M23), provides abstracts formerly covered by *Geographical Abstracts: Landforms and the Quaternary Sedimentology, Geographical Abstracts: Climatology and Hydrology*, and *Geographical Abstracts: Remote Sensing Photogrammetry and Cartography*.

SOURCES OF INFORMATION

General

> *GeoWorld History*. New York: GeoHistory. http://www.geohistory.com (M24)
>
> *The World-Wide Virtual Library: Geography*. Paris: International Council on Monuments and Sites. http://www.icomos.org/WWW_VL_Geography.html (M25)

GeoWorld History is available on the Internet and CD-ROM, providing over 5,000 original, linked history articles, photos and maps on various aspects of history from 3000 B.C. to the present. *GeoWorld History* includes biographies and business information, although its emphasis is on geographical sources. Its CD-ROM version has two products: *GeoHistory Maps: Europe to Eurasia* (M26) and *GeoHistory Maps: The Americas* (M27). Its home page displays four choices for login: GeoWorld, Americas, GeoInvest, and GeoNews. It also displays buttons of Map of the Week, Photo of the Week, This Week in History, and Weekly World News Update for search.

GeoWorld contains maps, Timelines, Slides, Current Events, Links, and so on. Maps are organized by category, such as Contemporary Political, Ancient World, Early A.D. Period, Middle Ages, and Modern Era. Many maps can be enlarged. In each category, there are images with slide shows. Timeline is for current events and 3,000 years of history. The user may search by period, divided into Ancient World–1913, 1914–1989, and each year from 1990 to 1998. Current Events contains places for current events, leaders from 2500 B.C. to the present, and nations, with concise descriptions. Links provides "Recommended Internet Links," organized into seventeen categories, including Europe and Great Britain, Americas, Africa, Asia, World, Map Resources, School Sites, China, Middle East and Persian Gulf, Japan, Latin America, Russia and Eastern Asia, and so on.

Americas provides Maps and Articles, Photos, and Recommended Links. Maps and Articles can be searched by category, such as America Expands, A Period of Slavery, The Civil War, and Presidential Election. Topics for Photographs include Civil War, Native Americans, World War I, Labor, and People. Internet Links is also organized by category such as Indians and Explorers, American Revolution, American Expansion, Slavery Dispute, The U.S. Civil War, The Cold War, and Presidential Elections.

The Virtual Library is organized into three categories: General Information, Information about Countries, and Information about Educational Institutions. The General Information category lists a number of sources, including SUNY/Buffalo list of resources, American Geophysical Union Home Page, Institute of Arctic and Alpine Research, CIA World Factbook, Geography Branch of the German Virtual Library, and Cybergeo. Information about countries includes regions, such as Asian studies, and individual countries, such as Brazil, China, Germany, India, and Thailand. Some twelve departments of geography are listed in Information about Educational Institutions.

Encyclopedias

> *Companion Encyclopedia of Geography: The Environment and Humankind.* Ian Douglas, Richard Huggett, and Mike Robinson, eds. London: Routledge, 1996. 1,021 p. ISBN 0415074177. (M28)
>
> *Encyclopedia of World Geography.* Peter Haggett and others, eds. Marshall Cavendish, 1993. 24 vols. ISBN 1854356313. (M29)

Companion Encyclopedia emphasizes a people-and-environment theme. It contains 45 chapters grouped into six parts: (I) A Differentiated World, "focusing on the evolution of the earth through geological, and up to historical, time" (Preface); (II) A World Transformed by the Growth of a Global Economy; (III) The Global Scale of Habitat; (IV) A World of Questions; (V) Changing Worlds, Changing Geographies; and (VI) Geographical Futures. Coverage is broad, including such topics as human evolution, religion, and the quality of life: human welfare and social justice. Each chapter is signed and appended with References and Further Reading. It has a subject and name index.

Encyclopedia of World Geography is organized by geographic area. The regional description includes physical geography, habitats, animal and plant life, agriculture, industry, cultures, cities, government, and environments. The description of country focuses on environment, society, economy, and history. Volume 24 is an index volume that contains a general index, thirteen thematic indexes, and a glossary. It may be noted that for current information about countries and areas, encyclopedias noted in Chapter 4 and a number of handbooks, yearbooks, and the like noted in Chapter 15 are good sources.

Dictionaries

> *Dictionary of Concepts in Human Geography.* Robert P. Larkin and Gary L. Peters. Westport, CT: Greenwood Press, 1983. 286 p. ISBN 0313227292. (M30)

The Dictionary of Human Geography. 3rd ed. R. J. Johnston, Derek Gregory and David M. Smith, eds. Cambridge, MA: Blackwell, 1994. 724 p. (M31)

Longman Dictionary of Geography: Human and Physical. Audrey N. Clark. Longman, 1985. 724 p. ISBN 0582352614. (M32)

Dictionary of Concepts in Human Geography is historical, providing for each of the more than 100 concepts definitions from earliest to most recent and tracing the evolution of the concept as it is understood by geographers, as stated in the preface. The dictionary is one of the concept dictionaries series. All dictionaries in the series have a uniform format, that is, each entry consists of four parts: (1) definitions; (2) historical growth of the term; (3) a bibliography of material including books and periodical articles; and (4) additional sources of information. Its usefulness would be enhanced if a listing of terms contained in the text were provided. Other dictionaries that have been published in the series include *Dictionary of Concepts in History*, noted in Chapter 13, and *Dictionary of Concepts in Physical Geography*, by Thomas P. Huber, Robert P. Larkin, and Gary L. Peters (New York: Greenwood Press, 1988, 291 p., ISBN 0313253692) (M33). The addition of an outline of concepts in *Dictionary of Concepts in Physical Geography* is a welcome feature.

Dictionary of Human Geography contains 700 entries contributed by 45 authors. It defines concepts, terms, and institutions but excludes biographies. Geographers' contributions are noted in the relevant articles. Articles are signed, and many of them are cross-referenced and appended with references and/or suggested reading. Length of articles varies from one paragraph to over two pages.

The *Longman Dictionary* defines terms in geography, plant products, and other commodities. Terms in cartography, geology, and geomorphology are, in general, excluded. Many geographical terms are cited from *A Glossary of Geographical Terms*, edited by Dudley Stamp and Audrey N. Clark (3rd ed., New York: Longman, 1979, 571 p., ISBN 0582352584) (M34). Entries are alphabetically arranged and most of them cross-referenced. Appendixes include Greek and Latin roots and conversion tables.

Also complementing the *Longman Dictionary* are two of Stamp's earlier works: *A Glossary of Geographical Terms* (New York: John Wiley, 1961, 539 p.) (M35) and *Dictionary of Geography* (New York: John Wiley, 1966, 492 p.) (M36). The *Glossary* features citations from other sources, but no gazetteer or biographical information, whereas the *Dictionary* consists of terms, place names, and biographies.

Directories

GISLinx. Wylie, TX: GISLinx. http://www.gislinx.com (M37)

Great GIS Net Sites. Cambridge, MA: Harvard Design and Mapping Company. http://www.hdm.com (M38)

Internet Resources for GIS. Worcester, MA: College of the Holy Cross. http://perseus.holycross.edu/PAP/General/Res.Starting.html (M39)

Guide to Programs in Geography in the United States and Canada—AAG Handbook and Directory of Geographers. Washington, DC: Association of American Geographers. Annual. ISSN 08821542. (M40)

Guide to U.S. Map Resources. David A. Cobb, comp. Chicago: American Library Association, 1986. 196 p. ISBN 0838904394. (M41)

World Directory of Map Collections. 3rd ed. IFLA Section of Geography and Map Libraries, comp.; Lorraine Dubreuil, ed. Munich: Saur, 1993. 310 p. IFLA Publication 63. ISBN 3598217919. (M42)

Listed here are three Web sites. *GISLinx* is intended to provide a listing of sources organized into 22 categories and over 800 links. A user can look for categories of data, services, publications, government sites, GIS in Canada, GIS Resources, GIS indices, GIS events, and other GIS sites. The Government Sites category, for instance, gives four subcategories: Local/Municipal Government Agencies, Other Government Agencies (non-U.S.), U.S. Federal Government Agencies, and State/Provincial Government Agencies. Each subcategory consists of a number of sites. For instance, the subcategory of U.S. Federal Government Agencies contains some 70 Web sites, such as CIA—World Map database, National Imagery and Mapping Agency, The Federal Web Locator, U.S. Census Bureau, USGS—Digital Maps, and USGS GIS—General, just to name a few.

The home page of *Great GIS Net Sites* displays some twenty categories of sources for choosing, including GIS Books, GIS Conferences, Classic GIS Sites, Online GIS, GIS WWW Resources, Worldwide Government Agencies, U.S. Federal Government Agencies, State/Provincial Government Agencies, GIS Mapping Companies, and Colleges, Universities and Research Institutes. The GIS WWW Resources category lists a number of resources, including CIA World Databank, CIA World Fact Book, Geographic Data Locators, Geographic Gopher, and many others. Colleges, Universities, and Research Institutes is a directory of over 80 institutions worldwide created by the University of Maine, Orono.

Internet Resources for GIS lists sources organized into nine categories, such as University-based resources, Information gateways, Professional organizations, Research, Cartography, Other GIS-related sites, and so on. "University-based resources" consists of the Kingston Center for GIS, SciNet, and University of Edinburgh GIS World Wide Web Server. The server links GIS worldwide. "Information gateways" includes CTI (Computers in Teaching Initiative) Geo-Information Gateway, and Guide to GIS Resources on the Internet. The CTI Geo-Information Gateway provides links to a number of topics, such as human geography, physical geography, cartography, general references and information sources, GIS, and place information. In "Professional organizations" are listed the Association for Geographic Information, which has a list of online resources for GIS, and the American Society for Photogrammetry and Remote Sensing. "Cartography" lists digital charts of the world, ordnance surveys, and UK borders. "Other GIS-related sites" links to a number of databases on the Internet, including *U.S. Geological Survey.*

U.S. Geological Survey (http://www.usgs.gov) (M43) is one of the best sources for GIS on the Internet. Its "Internet Resources" lists directory services, scientific research resources, and World Wide Web search services.

The *Guide to Programs,* formerly *Guide to Graduate Departments of Geography* and *Guide to Programs in Geography in the United States and Canada—AGA Membership Directory,* provides current information on programs, research facilities, admissions, financial aid, and faculty arranged alphabetically by name of the institution under United States and Canada, with additional listings of private industry and government agencies. As noted earlier, recently completed dissertations and theses under each graduate department of geography are also included in each edition of the *Guide.* For other publications and information of the Association of American Geographers, refer to its Web site (http://www.aag.org) (M44). The Web site also provides links to seventeen related organizations, including American Geographical Society, Consortium of Social Science Associations, GeoBusiness Association, Geographers on Film, National Geographic Society, and Royal Geographical Society.

The two directories of map collections complement each other with different coverage, as their titles indicate. *Guide to U.S. Map Resources* lists 919 collections that represent over 12 million maps. In general, collections with fewer than 500 maps are not included. Arrangement is alphabetical by state and within states, by city. Each entry consists of name of the institution, address, telephone number, responsible person, special strengths, holdings (maps, aerial photographs, satellite imagery, atlases, globes, wall maps, raised relief maps, books, gazetteers, and serial titles), and information on cataloging, classification, access, circulation, equipment, and map depositories. Its introduction is particularly informative, for it provides statistical data on map collections. At the end are sources for cartographic information, including: (1) U.S. Geological Survey Depositories, (2) Defense Mapping Agency Depositories, (3) National Cartographic Information Centers and Affiliates, (4) State Information Resources, (5) State Mapping Advisory Committees, and (6) Map Societies. It has a specialized collections index.

World Directory of Map Collections is a listing of over 500 collections in 67 countries and territories. Information for each collection, if complete, consists of institutional name and address, the person in charge, telephone number, cable address and telex number, the date of establishment, the number and categories of staff, area, size of collection, scale of basic collection, seating capacity, originals and other forms, copying restrictions, reproduction services, storage equipment, conservation procedure, and bibliographical references.

Biographies

> *Geographers: Biobliographical Studies*, 1977– . T. W. Freeman, ed. London: Mansell. Annual. ISSN 03086992. (M45)
> *Biographical Dictionary of Geography*. Robert P. Larkin and Gary L. Peters. Westport, CT: Greenwood Press, 1993. 361 p. ISBN 0313276226. (M46)

Geographers is edited on behalf of the Working Group on the History of Geographical Thought of the International Geographical Union and the International Union of the History and Philosophy of Science, with a purpose of "showing the evolution of geography as a science and of geographical thought throughout the world," according to its introduction. It contains some 20 articles of individuals. Each article consists of three parts: (1) biography that includes education, life, and work; scientific ideas and geographical thought; and influence and spread of ideas; (2) bibliography and sources; and (3) chronology of the biographee. There are a personal names index, organizations and related references, a subject index, and a cumulative list of biobibliographies in earlier volumes.

Some 77 geographers are listed in *Biographical Dictionary of Geography*. Each entry consists of four sections: (1) an essay highlighting the life of the person and his or her contributions, (2) a selective bibliography of major works, (3) a chronology of the person's life, and (4) biographical reference sources for further reading.

Gazetteers

A gazetteer is a dictionary of place names for identification.

United States

> *American Places Dictionary: A Guide to 45,000 Populated Places, Natural Features, and Other Places in the United States*. Frank R. Abate, ed. Detroit: Omnigraphics, 1994. 4 vols. ISBN 1558887474. (M47)
> *Omni Gazetteer of the United States of America: A Guide to 1,500,000 Place*

Names in the United States and Territories. Frank R. Abate, ed. Om-
nigraphics, 1992. 11 vols. ISBN 1558883363. (M48)
TIGER Mapping Service. Alexandria, VA: U.S. Census Bureau. http://ti-
ger.census.gov (M49)
The United States Dictionary of Places. 1st ed. New York: Somerset, 1998.
644 p. ISBN 0403098998. (M50)

Listed here are two dictionaries of American place names. *American
Places Dictionary* covers political entities (states, counties and county
equivalents, legally incorporated places, unincorporated places), American
Indian reservations, major U.S. military installations, and major U.S. geographical features (mountains and ranges, rivers, natural landmarks, and
so on). Its four volumes cover North East, South, Midwest, and West respectively. The entry contents vary. For states are given the state seal, a
map, introductory information, population, area, coastline, elevation, state
capital, largest city, second largest city, largest county, housing, distribution
of population by race and Hispanic origin, admission date, location, name
origin, state symbol or emblem, state motto and nickname, telephone area
code(s), time zone(s), abbreviations, part of (region). An "Editor's Miscellany: American Places and American Names—Curiosities and Peculiarities"
provides interesting facts, such as early U.S. capitals, geopolitical peculiarities, unusual official state symbols, historical development and changes
in counties, some out-of-the-ordinary place names, and first name, last
name places. Volume 4 also includes appendixes and a general index. Appendixes are: (A) Indian Reservations; (B) Major U.S. Military Installations;
and (C) Major U.S. Geographic Features.

The other dictionary, *The United States Dictionary of Places*, consists of
two sections: main entries and Map section. The main entries section contains place names organized by city within state in alphabetical order. Each
entry lists name, population, census designated place, elevation in feet, latitude and longitude, and location note including name origin. The map
section contains some 50 pages of maps (pp. 556–606). There is a place
index.

In *Omni Gazetteer*, place names are broadly defined to include hospitals,
institutions of higher learning, parks, and so on. The complete set consists
of nine volumes; each covers a region as follows: (1) New England; (2)
Northeastern States, including District of Columbia; (3) Southeast, including Puerto Rico, Virgin Islands; (4) South Central States; (5) Southwestern
States; (6) Great Lakes States; (7) Plains States; (8) Mountain States; and
(9) Pacific, including Pacific Territories. Each region contains a number of
states and territories if applicable. For instance, the Great Lakes States region contains Illinois, Indiana, Michigan, Minnesota, Ohio, and Wisconsin.

Information is entered in line entry. There are six columns for each line
entry: (1) Main entry names and variants (Zip); (2) Type of features or

population; (3) City (or city equivalent); (4) USGS map name—USGS topographic map (1:24,000 scale); (5) Latitude and longitude coordinates; and (6) Source(s) and other data.

The other two volumes are the National Index and Appendixes. Appendixes contain Index of United States Geological Survey (USCS) Topographic Map Names; Index of Feature Types and Generic Names Used with U.S. Place Names; National Register of Historic Places—National List; List of State and City Federal Information Processing Standards (FIPS) Place Codes; Bureau of Indian Affairs List of American Indian Reservations; Federal Aviation Administration (FAA) National List of 16,000 Airports, Heliports, and Seaplane Bases; and FAA National List of 60,000 Elevated Landmarks and Structures—Obstructions to Air Navigation.

TIGER Mapping Service (TMS) is "The Coast to Coast Digital Map Database" (subtitle), providing national scale, street-level maps on the Web. The *TMS* home page provides two major sources: U.S. Gazetteer and GIS Gateway. GIS (Geographic Information System) is a computer system for storing, retrieving, integrating, and analyzing data related to geographical locations. U.S. Gazetteer identifies places and obtains census data from the 1990 Census Lookup server. A user may search a place by entering name of the place, state (optional) or a 5-digit zip code. At present, no street names are provided in maps. *U.S. Gazetteer Place and Zipcode Files* used in *TMS* is available for downloading. The user may also use for identifying geographic entities the *USGS Geographic Names Information System* (http://www-nmd.usgs.gov/www/gnisofrm.html) (M51).

TMS also provides GIS Gateway. The Gateway is organized into five categories: Other GIS Gateways on the WWW, University Sites, Resource collections and documents containing detailed information, metadata sources, and information servers. Titles in Other GIS Gateways such as GISLinx are listed earlier.

International

The Columbia Gazetteer of the World. Saul B. Cohen, ed. New York: Columbia University Press, 1998. 3 vols. ISBN 0231110405. (M52)
The Hutchinson Guide to the World. 3rd ed. Phoenix, AZ: Oryx, 1998. 666 p. ISBN 1573562203. (M53)
Merriam-Webster's Geographical Dictionary. 3rd ed. Springfield, MA: Merriam-Webster, 1997. 1,361 p. (M54)

In terms of the number of place names and coverage, *The Columbia Gazetteer*, formerly *Columbia Lippincott*, is the largest and most extensive among the gazetteers. The new edition contains 165,000 entries with 25,000 new entries. It provides name changes, variant spellings, pronunciation, coordinates, population data, and physical, political, economic, historical, and cultural descriptions. It is more than a gazetteer; some entries receive long descriptions, such as China, which is described in eight columns.

There are two parts in the *Hutchinson Guide*: Countries of the World and World Gazetteer. The first part covers 192 sovereign countries. Each country has 50 categories of information, such as government, economy, resources, population, transportation, history, and practical information. Part 2 contains 65,000 entries of cities, towns, regions, provinces, and geographical features. There are three appendixes: Administrative Divisions, World Geography, and Countries and Population. The Appendix of World Geography provides ranks, including deepest depressions, largest deserts, longest rivers, highest mountains, and largest islands.

Merriam-Webster's, formerly *Webster's New Geographical Dictionary*, provides "in text and maps, essential information on spelling, pronunciation, type of feature, location, and depending on the nature of the entry, population, size (as area, height, depth, or length), economy, history, and other matter of importance" (Preface). It contains more than 8,000 entries and 252 maps. Incorporated places with a population of 2,500 or more in the United States and 4,500 or more in Canada are included. Each entry includes the place name, pronunciation, alternate forms, identification, location, area and population, geographical and physical features, economic data, history, and items of general interest, such as names of colleges and universities. Also included are a glossary and explanatory front matter.

Atlases and Maps

An atlas is a collection of maps. A map is "a drawing or representation, usually on a flat surface, of part or all of the surface of the earth or of some other heavenly body, of the heavens, etc., indicating a specific group of features, as land masses, countries, planets, etc., in terms of their relative size and position."[6] In general, maps are classified into general purpose maps and thematic maps. The general purpose maps refer to physical, political, economic, and cultural maps. Maps on a particular aspect or aspects in an area, such as population, soil, minerals, atmosphere, climates, food, plants, energy, topology, and the like are thematic.

Virtually all maps give information on location, scale, and symbols. Scale is the measurement of reduction of earth surface. It refers to the ratio between the distance on the map and the distance on the earth's surface. At a scale of 1:10,000, 1 unit of distance on the map (1 centimeter or millimeter or foot) represents 10,000 units (10,000 centimeters or millimeters or feet) of distance on the surface of the earth. The smaller the ratio, the larger the map scale, and vice versa. The larger the map scale, the more detailed—and the more changes and additions are required in updating. To keep the *Rand McNally Road Atlas* up to date requires 20,000 additions and changes each year, in contrast to updating a world map with far less detail that might require a few hundred changes.[7] If every town and place name is included, a map requires a scale of one inch for five miles; at that scale, an Illinois map would be more than six feet long, and a national road atlas would weigh more than your spare tire.[8] Grid lines measured by latitude and longitude are used to pinpoint location. Symbols are represented by point, line, and area. For instance, cities are represented by dots or circles and boundaries by a solid line.

General

> Perry-Castañed Library Map Collection. Austin, TX: University of Texas Library. http://www.lib.utexas.edu/Libs/PCL/Map_collection/Map_collection.html (M55)

This map collection Web site groups maps into two categories: Online Maps of Special Interest and Online Maps of General Interest. The second category is divided by regions, countries, and states, such as Maps of the World, Maps of Africa, Maps of The Americas, Maps of Asia, Maps of the United States, and Maps of Texas. Maps of The World includes World Map, Muslim Distribution, Standard Time Zones, Vulnerable Single-Commodity-Dependent Economies, World City Maps, World Gross Domestic Product Per Capita, and World Market Size by Gross Domestic Product. Countries are arranged in alphabetic order by name under each region. Most maps were produced by the U.S. Central Intelligence Agency.

More than 700 maps of the United States are arranged into U.S. Electronic Map Collections by Type, U.S. Territories Electronic Map Collections, and Maps of the United States. Maps by type, for instance, contains Historical Maps; Maps of National Parks, Monuments, and Historic Sites; Maps of Major Metropolitan Areas (from the U.S. National Atlas); Maps of the United States; and State Maps with County Boundaries. State Maps also contains city maps and historical city maps.

United States

> Map Collections. Washington, DC: Library of Congress, National Digital Library. http://lcweb.loc.gov (M56)
> Mapquest. Mountville, PA: GeoSystems Global. http://www.mapquest.com (M57)
> The National Atlas of the United States of America. Reston, VA: U.S. Geological Survey, 1998. http://www.atlas.usgs.gov (M58)
> Rand McNally Commercial Atlas and Marketing Guide. Chicago: Rand McNally. Annual. Print & digital. (M59)

Map Collections is one of the five types of collections in *American Memory* available on the Web, noted in the next chapter. *American Memory* is a part of the National Digital Library of the Library of Congress. The Library of Congress holds more than 4.5 million items. Only a small fraction of its maps collection is converted into digital format available in *American Memory* on the Web. Maps collections in *American Memory* cover the period from 1597 to 1988, organized by categories into Cities and Towns, Conservation and Environment, Discovery and Exploration, General Maps, Immigration and Settlements, General Maps, Military Battles and Campaigns, and Transportation and Communication. Maps are also found in other collections of *American Memory*. Since it is menu-driven, the user may find maps very easily. For instance, "the Cities and Towns category includes maps that depict individual buildings to panoramic views of large urban areas. . . . Record the evolution of cities illustrating the development and nature of economic activities, educational and religious facilities, parks, street patterns and widths, and transportation systems" (Web description). Click the button of Cities and Towns, and a listing of maps is displayed for selecting. The image may be enlarged by selecting desired zoom level and window.

For acquisitions of maps, driving directions, and planning a trip (hotels, dining, city information, weather, etc.), *Mapquest* is an excellent source. Of particular usefulness are its door-to-door driving instructions, which depict the route from start to destination, a marked road map, and road directions with distance.

The *National Atlas* includes both electronic and paper map products. The former print version of *The National Atlas of the United States of America* (1970) is no longer published. The current electronic version "shows the distribution of the principal aquifers that supply ground water to the United States, Puerto Rico and the U.S. Virgin islands. . . . Each principal aquifer is classified as one of the six types of permeable geologic material: unconsolidated deposits of sand and gravel, semiconsolidated sand, sandstone, carbonate rocks, interbedded sandstone and carbonate rocks, and basalt and other types of volcanic rock. The general distribution of glacial deposits that contain numerous productive aquifers in the north-central and northeastern parts of the conterminous United States is also shown" (home page).

Maps printed from *The National Atlas of the United States of America* of 1970 are of two kinds: Thematic Maps and Reference Maps. Some maps are out of print, many maps are available, and a few have been revised. General reference maps contain most of the 40,000 place names recorded in the index. General reference maps vary in scale, for instance, maps for the 50 states at scale of 1:2,000,000 (approximately 1 inch to 31.5 miles); outlying areas from 1:250,000 to 1:1,000,000, and 27 largest cities at 1: 500,000. Some maps are out of print; others have been revised and are available for sale. Thematic maps convey concepts of human-environment relationships and interactions. Thematic maps are limited to three scales: 1: 7,500,000, 1:17,000,000, and 1:34,000,000. There are 765 maps on pages of 19" × 14" size, with explanatory textual material. These maps represent "physical features, historical evolution, economic activities, socio-cultural conditions, administrative subdivision, and place in world affairs" (Introduction, 1970).

The *Rand McNally Commercial Atlas* (1999, 130th ed., 1998, 572 p.) is organized in six sections: (1) U.S. State/County/City Maps; (2) Metropolitan Area Maps; (3) Transportation/Communications; (4) Economy; (5) Population; and (6) State Maps and Index of Places with Statistics. Each section "is preceded by an introduction which summarizes the content of that section, provides the definitions of the terms and concepts used, and describes some ways to effectively use the data" (Preface). The book features rich statistical data. Basic business data are provided for each state.

International

Goode's *World Atlas*, 1922– . Edward B. Espenshade, Jr., ed. Chicago: Rand McNally. Quadrennial. (M60)

National Geographic Atlas of the World. 2nd rev. ed. Washington, DC: National Geographic Society, 1995. Pagination varies. ISBN 0792230361. (M61)

New International Atlas. 25th anniversary ed. Chicago: Rand McNally, 1994. Pagination varies. ISBN 0528836935. (M62)

The Times Atlas of the World. 9th comprehensive ed. London: Times Books, 1992. Pagination varies. ISBN 0812920775. (M63)

World Reference Atlas. London: Dorling Kindersley, 1996. 751 p. ISBN 0789410850. (M64)

Formerly Goode's *School Atlas*, Goode's (19th ed., 1995, 371 p.) is organized in four sections: (1) Introduction, which briefly describes geography and maps, map scale, map projections, and earth-sun relations and world time zones; (2) World Thematic Maps, which contains 60 maps on political, physical, landforms, climatic regions, soils, ecoregions, birth rate, agricultural products, exports, and many others; (3) Regional Maps; and (4) Major Cities Maps. Also included are Geographical Tables and Indexes. The Pronouncing Index indexes approximately 34,000 names of features.

The *National Geographic Atlas of the World* provides maps from the solar system to the earth. The new edition features more space for China and Southeast Asia and the addition of world resources maps indicating the location of minerals, energy sources, and food-growing regions. Texts accompany maps. At the end, there are geographic comparisons, temperature and rainfall, population of major cities, a glossary, and an index of place names.

The *New International Atlas* is organized in the following sequence: world, continent, and ocean maps, regional maps, and metropolitan maps. Areas are mapped in five series in metric system of measurement: (1) The continents at 1:24,000,000, the oceans at 1:48,000,000, and the world at 1:75,000,000. (2) Major world regions at 1:12,000,000. (3) Inhabitated areas at either 1:6,000,000 or 1:3,000,000. (4) Key Regions at 1:1,000,000. (5) Major metropolitan areas at 1:300,000. Local geographic names are used. It is appended with glossary and abbreviations of geographical terms, world information table of population, population density, capital, and political status for every country in the world, metropolitan areas table, population of cities and towns, and an index to 160,000 place names.

The Times Atlas of the World in one volume is based on the prominent *The Times Atlas of the World* (Mid-Century ed., John Bartholomew, ed., Boston: Houghton Mifflin, 1955–1959. 5 vols.) (M65). The five-volume set contains 120 plates. The new one-volume edition has 123 plates, with an obvious addition, for instance, of a plate on Antarctica. All "Key to Adjacent Areas" plates in the five-volume set are deleted to reduce the size of the new *Times Atlas*.

The *Times Atlas* consists of eight thematic maps and 115 general purpose maps. Thematic maps at scales of 1:58,000,000 to 1:200,000,000 include plates of the world and of minerals, climatology, climate and food potential, vegetation, mankind, food, energy, and politics. The general purpose maps are grouped by region, country, and cities at scales of 1:50,000 to 1:55,000,000. Indexes include Glossary and Abbreviations; Abbreviations Used in the Index, Chinese Place-Names, and Index-Gazetteer of the Maps. The new edition adopts the *pinyin* system instead of the Wade-Giles system for Chinese place names. There is a comparative table of differences between *pinyin* and Wade-Giles. Its Index-Gazetteer provides more than 200,000 place names.

A family edition of *The Times Atlas of the World* (2nd ed., London: Times Books, 1985, 64,143 p., ISBN 0812929497) (M66) consists of two parts. Part 1 is the Guide to States and Territories. Each country or territory contains name, status, area, population, currency, organizations, and national flag. Part 2 is Maps, arranged by region, such as Oceania, Asia, Europe, Africa, North America, and South America, followed by Antarctica, Indian Ocean, Pacific Ocean, and Atlantic Ocean.

The *World Reference Atlas* contains four main sections: (1) The World Today, (2) The Nations of the World, (3) Global Issues, and (4) Index-Gazetteer. There are four elements in each section: maps, charts, icons, and text. "The central section of the book is the Nations of the World which includes detailed mapping and encyclopedic information for every one of the world's 192 countries as defined by UN" ("How the Atlas Works").

For each country, it provides official name, national flag, brief country profile and eighteen consistent headings, such as climate, transportation, tourism, people, politics, world affairs, aid, defense, economics, resources, environment, media, crime, chronology, education, and world ranking. Ranking covers eight areas: life expectancy, infant mortality, GNP per capita, daily calorie intake, literacy, schooling, education, and human development.

Subfields

United States

Atlas of American History. 3rd ed. Martin Gilbert. New York: Routledge, 1995. 138 p. (M67)

The Atlas of American History. Rev. ed. Robert H. Ferrell and Richard Natkiel. New York: Facts on File, 1995. 192 p. ISBN 086034419. (M68)

We the People: An Atlas of America's Ethnic Diversity. James Paul Allen and Eugene James Turner. New York: Macmillan, 1988. 315 p. ISBN 0029014204. (M69)

The Women's Atlas of the United States. Anne Gibson and Timothy Fast. New York: Facts on File, 1988. 248 p. ISBN 0816011702. (M70)

In historical atlases, the Historical Geography of the United States by Charles Oscar Paullin and edited by John K. Wright (1932, 162 p., 166 plates) (M71) has been mentioned as the first adequate atlas. For recently published historical atlases, refer to The Atlas of American History, a supplement to the Dictionary of American History, noted in the next chapter. It contains 147 black-and-white maps arranged chronologically, with an alphabetical index to places mentioned on the maps. The maps are arranged in such a way as to indicate the growth and expansion of the United States.

The Facts on File atlas covers the colonial era to the two world wars and America in a divided world in the 1980s. It also contains three map essays: territorial expansion of the United States of America, population of the United States of America, and presidential elections.

We the People serves as a guide to the ethnic heritage of America. It provides geographical and demographic data on 67 ethnic groups classified by region such as North American, Western European, Eastern European, Southern European, Middle Eastern, African, Middle and South American, and Asian and Pacific Islanders. There are 115 patterns of ethnic origins. Each group is provided with a historical account of settlement and immigration and statistical data on its population, countries with largest population, and countries with highest percentage.

The Women's Atlas contains seven chapters on demography, education, employment, family, health, crime, and politics. There are a bibliography for maps corresponding to the seven chapters and additional references and suggestions for further reading.

International

> *National Geographic Atlas of World History.* Noel Grove. Washington, DC: National Geographic Society, 1997. 400 p. ISBN 0792270487. (M72)
>
> *The Times Atlas of World History.* 4th ed. Geoffrey Parker, ed. Maplewood, NJ: Hammond, 1994. 360 p. ISBN 0723005346. (M73)
>
> *Archaeological Atlas of the World.* David Whitehouse and Ruth Whitehouse. London: Thames & Hudson, 1975. 272 p. (M74)
>
> *Atlas of Classical Archaeology.* M. I. Finley, ed. New York: McGraw-Hill, 1977. 256 p. ISBN 007021025X. (M75)
>
> *The World Atlas of Archaeology.* Boston: G. K. Hall, 1985. 423 p. ISBN 0816187479. (M76)

The *National Geographic Atlas of World History* consists of six sections: (1) Early Man to 500 B.C., The Ancient World; (2) 500 B.C. to A.D. 500, The Classical Age; (3) 500 to 1400, Isolated Realms; (4) 1400 to 1700, New Links and Contacts; (5) 1700 to 1900, Quickening Change; and (6) Twentieth Century, Vanishing Empires. Each section is arranged chronologically and "opens with a world map that shows developments of various points of the compass, along with an essay about what was happening and why" (book jacket). It is substantially supplemented by illustrations and maps. Appendix contains Highlights of Chinese History; Roman Rulers; Historical Periods of Japan; Major Wars; Rulers of England and Great Britain, France, and Russia; Prime Ministers of Great Britain and Canada; and Presidents of the United States.

The Times Atlas of World History focuses on social history and cultural achievements of different civilizations from 9,000 B.C. to the 1990s. It begins with a world chronology, which serves as a "key to the individual places and maps" (p. 15), followed by seven sections: (1) Human origins and early cultures, (2) the first civilizations, (3) the classical civilizations of Eurasia, (4) the world of divided regions, (5) the world of the emerging West, (6) the age of European dominance, and (7) the age of global civilizations. There are a glossary and a geographical index.

The preceding list contains three atlases of archaeology. *Archaeological Atlas of the World* presents 103 maps that cover the whole world and pinpoint 5,000 pre- and proto-historic sites. Each map is provided with explanatory notes. The book is arranged in seven parts: Old World; Africa, Western Asia; the Mediterranean; Europe with Russia; South and East Asia; Australasia and the Pacific; and the Americas.

Atlas of Classical Archaeology contains fifteen chapters on Britain Roman, East of Palmyra, Roman Rhine-Danube Frontier, North Africa, Sicily, Italy, Greece, Cyprus, Black Sea, Asia Minor, and so on, with emphasis on

Europe. Also included are a chronological table, Roman Emperors, a glossary, and an index.

The World Atlas of Archaeology, the English edition translated from *Le Grand Atlas de l'Archéologie*, is claimed by the publisher as a dossier of the earliest discoveries in a scope wider than any general survey of archaeology. It contains 25 papers on historical Europe, the early Middle Ages, the Byzantine world, Islam, the Near East, China, Vietnam, Africa, the modern period, and so on. Each article presents the archaeological background. The book is rich in color illustrations and plates. It concludes with a bibliography, a glossary, and an index.

Handbooks, Yearbooks, and the Like

Handbooks

> *Cities of the World*. 5th ed. Detroit: Gale Research, 1998. 4 vols. ISBN 0810376911. (M77)

This is a compilation of current information on cultural, geographical, and political conditions in the countries and cities of six continents, based on the Department of State's "Post Reports," with articles on 33 countries for which no "Post Reports" exist. Some 2,000 cities in 193 countries are presented alphabetically by country in four volumes: (1) Africa; (2) the Western Hemisphere (exclusive of the United States); (3) Europe and the Mediterranean Middle East; and (4) Asia, the Pacific, and the Asiatic Middle East. Each country consists of major cities, other cities (with less description), and country profile. Major cities consist of geographical location, brief history, schools, recreation, and entertainment. A country profile consists of geography and climate; population; government; arts, science, and education; commerce and industry; transportation; communications; health; clothing and services; local holidays; recommended reading; and notes for travelers. Each volume has a cumulative index. For current information, refer to the *Consular Affairs Home Page* (Bureau of Consular Affairs, Department of State, http://travel.state.gov) (M78). It provides Travel Warnings/Consular Info Sheet, Services/Information for Americans Abroad, Travel Publications, Passport Information, Visa Services, Judicial Assistance, U.S. Embassy and Consulate Websites Worldwide, and so on.

Geographical Names

> *The American Counties*. 4th ed. Joseph N. Kane. Scarecrow, 1983. 546 p. ISBN 0810815583. (M79)
> *Bibliography of Place-Name Literature: United States & Canada*. 3rd ed.

Richard B. Sealock, Margaret M. Sealock, and Margaret S. Powell. Chicago: American Library Association, 1982. 442 p. ISBN 0838903606. (M80)

Placenames of the World. Adrian Room. Jefferson, NC: McFarland, 1996. 441 p. (M81)

Place-Name Changes, 1900–1991. Adrian Room, comp. Metuchen, NJ: Scarecrow, 1993. 296 p. ISBN 0810826003. (M82)

The American Counties is a book of "Origins of County Names, Dates of Creation & Organization, Area, Population Including 1980 Census Figures, Historical Data & Published Sources" (subtitle). It begins with an introduction, being a brief description of the origins of county names and data, followed by five chapters on counties. These chapters include counties by county, counties by state, counties by date, counties whose names have changed, county seats, and persons for whom counties have been named. It also provides a listing of independent cities by state and Alaska boroughs. Population data are based on the 1980 census.

Bibliography of Place Name Literature is a listing of 3,599 items from place name literature, books, periodicals, and some unpublished material as well. It is limited to place names in the United States and Canada.

Placenames of the World presents origins and meanings of names for over 5,000 natural features, countries, capitals, territories, cities and historic sites (subtitle). It begins with an introduction to the type and pattern of naming places. Each place name comprises three elements: name, main entry with the origin of the name, background and history, and identification of the named place. Cross-references and earlier names are provided for some entries. A glossary consists of Language Cited and Non-English Language Placename Components. There are seven appendixes: (1) Indigenous Country Names; (2) Roman Names of Towns and Cities; (3) Bilingual Placenames; (4) Coastal Touristic Names; (5) Inhabitants of Towns and Cities; (6) Civic Coats-of-Arms; and (7) Words from Names. The book concludes with a select bibliography.

Many place names have been changed, particularly in China, the former Soviet Union, and a number of countries in Africa, as stated in *Place-Name Changes*. Each entry lists present name, identification, location, former name(s), and year or years of renaming. It is appended with Official Names of Countries and a bibliography.

NOTES

1. "Geography," in *New Encyclopaedia Britannica*, vol. 19 (Chicago: Encyclopedia Britannica, 1974), p. 917.

2. Richard Hartshorne, "Geography," in *International Encyclopedia of the Social Sciences*, vol. 6 (New York: Macmillan and Free Press, 1968–   ), p. 115.

3. Ibid.

4. John Small and Michael Witherick, *A Modern Dictionary of Geography* (London: Edward Arnold, 1986), p. 161.

5. Harold H. Sprout, "Political Geography," in *International Encyclopedia of the Social Sciences*, vol. 6, p. 116.

6. *The Random House Dictionary of the English Language*, p. 874.

7. James Pearre, "These Folks Help Us along Life's Highway," *Chicago Tribune*, November 29, 1974.

8. Ibid.

Chapter 13

History

What is history? The Durants define it simply as the events or record of the past.[1] But history as a discipline is more than a body of information about past human events; it has a distinct purpose. History is concerned with "why" and "with what results," and particularly with the nature of historical evidence and reliability. As Henry Steele Commager explains, history consists of three processes: the collection of facts, the organization of these facts, and the interpretation of the facts.[2] Interpretation is what makes history different from erudition, which merely collects and records facts of the past. The discipline of history is to reconstruct the past of the human race with the purpose of investigating causes and effects to contribute to an explanation of present problems.[3]

The relationship of history to the social sciences is obvious. The social sciences are considered fundamentally historical in character.[4] But history differs from the social sciences in function. Historians reconstruct the past and interpret the evidence to explain existing problems, the solution of which falls within the purview of the social scientists.

One of the primary functions of historians is to interpret evidence. But historical evidence originates beyond the historian's own experience. The historian depends on others for the material over which he has no control. Commager states:

Clearly history is not a science in the sense that chemistry or biology are sciences. It cannot submit its data to scientific experiments; it cannot repeat its own experiments; it cannot control its materials. . . . Yet it is equally clear that history uses or aspires to use the scientific method. This is, it tests all things which can be tested, and holds fast to what it finds to be true, in so far as it is able to make any findings at all.[5]

How are things tested? In Arthur M. Schlesinger's view, the procedures of historical studies resemble those employed by a court of law.[6] In testing the evidence, the historian "combines the functions of detective, prosecuting attorney, lawyer for the defendant, judge, or jury" to seek the truth. [7]

History may be studied by period, by area, and by subject matter. By period, history is generally divided into ancient, medieval, and modern. In the area approach, the historian specializes in a a particular geographical unit, such as a continent, a nation, or groups of nations. The approach by subject matter is generally considered within the proper sphere of a particular discipline.

One of the developments in historical studies is oral history, developed by Allen Nevins at Columbia University in 1948. Oral history consists of obtaining a record, first by interviewing, later by tape recording, from the lips of living persons on all phases of life.[8] The end product of oral history is not the tape but a transcript.

ACCESS TO SOURCES

Guides

General

There are quite a few guides in history. Readers may find the following guides helpful:

> Reference Sources in History: An Introductory Guide. Ronald H. Fritze, Brian E. Coutts, and Louis A. Vyhnanek. Santa Barbara, CA: ABC-Clio, 1990. 319 p. ISBN 0874361648. (N1)
> Teaching Bibliographic Skills in History: A Sourcebook for Historians and Libraries. Charles A. D'Aniello, ed. Westport, CT: Greenwood Press, 1993. 385 p. ISBN 0313252661. (N2)

Reference Sources in History "is designed to provide an introduction to the major reference works for all periods of history and for all geographical areas" (Preface). It contains 685 reference works divided by form into fourteen chapters, such as guides, handbooks, and manuals for history; bibliographies; book review indexes; periodical guides and core journals; periodical indexes and abstracts; guides to newspapers, newspaper collections, and newspaper indexes; dissertations and theses; government publications and legal sources; dictionaries and encyclopedias; biographical sources; and geographical sources and atlases. The book complements The Historian's Handbook: A Descriptive Guide to Reference Works (Helen J. Poulton, Norman: University of Oklahoma Press, 1972, 304 p., ISBN 0806109858) (N3) in new titles and works in digital format.

Intended as a source of ideas for teaching history students how to use the library and do bibliographic research, D'Aniello "is neither a guide to history reference sources nor a fully developed instructional program" (Preface). However, it contains many reference sources. The book consists of ten chapters divided into four parts. Part I, The Study of History, deals in two chapters with historical methodologies and research and history and interdisciplinary history. Part II, Bibliographic Instruction in History, has two chapters on finding and using historical materials and bibliographic instruction in history. Five chapters are in part III, Special Topics. They include using catalogs and indexes, using reference sources, sources for interdisciplinary research, using electronic information sources, and using the finding aids to archive and manuscript collections. Part IV, or Chapter 10, is a selected annotated bibliography of books and articles on teaching the bibliography of history. A chapter on sources for interdisciplinary research in part III is a concise guide to reference sources in the social sciences and the humanities.

For research and in-depth study, significant guides include:

> The American Historical Association's Guide to Historical Literature. 3rd ed. Mary Beth Norton, ed. New York: Oxford University Press, 1995. 2 vols. ISBN 0195057279. (N4)
>
> Introduction to Ancient History. Hermann Bengtson. Translated by R. I. Frank and Frank D. Gilliard. Berkeley: University of California Press, 1970. 213 p. ISBN 0520017234. (N5)
>
> Guide to the Study of Medieval History. Rev. ed. Louis John Paetow. Prepared under the auspices of the Medieval Academy of America. New York: Crofts, 1931; Reprint ed., New York: Kraus, 1980. 645 p. ISBN 0927681011. (N6)
>
> Literature of Medieval History, 1930–1975. Gray Cowan Boyce, comp. and ed. Millwood, NY: Kraus, 1981. 5 vols. ISBN 0527104620. (N7)

The *Guide to Historical Literature*, first published in 1931, has long been regarded as a standard work that furnishes directions for the best means of gaining a broader knowledge of history. The book, contributed by some 370 authors, "contains 26,926 bibliographic citations that are divided into forty-eight sections. Each section comprises an introductory essay, a guide to contents, and an annotated bibliography" (Introduction). Some sections deal with specific country, such as China, Japan, Korea, Britain, France, Italy, Germany, Russia/Soviet Union, Canada, Australia, and the United States. Most cited works were published after the 1961 edition. Each annotation is followed by the initials of the contributors. The annotated bibliography contains, in general, reference works, following by topic, country, and/or period. The type of reference works varies in each section. A type in general includes bibliographies, biographies, chronologies, encyclopedias, dictionaries, geographies, atlases, research guides, and general histories and textbooks.

Bengtson, Paetow, and Boyce deal with history by period. Bengtson, a standard text for German university students, consists of nine chapters dealing with the scope of ancient history, the history of the study of antiquity, the fundamentals of the study of ancient history, the sources, the monuments, and various disciplines. Each chapter is appended with bibliographies. A chapter on the sources gives a detailed discussion on the study and criticism of the original sources. There are two chapters devoted to reference sources: "Reference Works and Journals" and "Select Bibliography." The bibliography (pp. 176–198) has two parts. Part 1 covers general works, and Part 2 is studies organized in correspondence to the arrangement of *Cambridge Ancient History*, noted later.

Paetow consists of three parts. Part 1 lists the most important general books in the study of medieval history. Parts 2 and 3 are topical, including philosophy, theology, language, Roman and canon law, medieval books and libraries, and medieval art. Each section in parts 2 and 3 is further divided into (1) outline, presenting the subject matter of the section in an orderly fashion; (2) special recommendations for reading; and (3) bibliography, a classified list of the most important special books and articles. Its coverage of English history is, however, sparse. Paetow is supplemented by Boyce. Boyce's *Literature of Medieval History* follows closely the pattern of the Paetow *Guide*. Its volume 5 is an index to personal name authors and personal name subjects.

United States

> *Harvard Guide to American History*. Rev. ed. Frank Friedel, ed. Cambridge, MA: Belknap Press of Harvard University Press, 1974. 2 vols. ISBN 0674375602. (N8)
>
> *Research Guide to American Historical Biography*. Washington, DC: Beacham Publishing, 1988–1991. 5 vols. (N9)

The *Harvard Guide to American History*, a successor to the *Guide to the Study and Teaching of American History* by Edward Channing, Albert Bushnell Hart, and Frederick Jackson Turner (Boston: Ginn, 1922, 650 p.) is an outstanding reference to books, articles, and other bibliographical materials. It is now expanded into two volumes with stress on economic, social, cultural, political, and diplomatic history. The two volumes differ in their arrangement. Volume 1 is topical, under 29 broad subject headings; whereas volume 2 is chronological. Some features in the earlier edition, such as sections on the nature of history and its relationship with other fields of knowledge and on prehistoric times and a summaries section that outlines the topic treated within the section, no longer appear. The new *Guide* reflects, however, newer approaches and media and adds materials on the history of special subjects and on domestic issues and foreign relations since 1945. The *Guide* is a standard work used to evaluate library strength in American history.[9]

The *Research Guide* (editors vary) was first published in a three-volume set (1988, ISBN 0933833091) that contains 278 profiles. Volume 4 (1990, ISBN 0933833210) and volume 5 (1991, ISBN 0933833245) contain a total of 174 profiles. Volumes 4–5 add women, native Americans, and minorities. Each entry contains chronology; activities of historical significance; overview of biographical sources; evaluation of principal biographical sources; overview and evaluation of primary sources; museums, historical landmarks, and societies; and other sources. Its latest volume consists of two appendixes: Historical Figures Grouped by Era and Selected Museums and Historical Landmarks. There is a Cumulative Index for volumes 1–5 of Figures and Sources Reviewed.

Bibliographies

General

The guides just mentioned are also extensive bibliographies. For general bibliographies on history by period, a comprehensive work is the Cambridge history series: *The Cambridge Ancient History* (Cambridge: Cambridge University Press, 1928–1939, 12 vols.; 2nd ed., 1982–1996, vols. 3–10; 1997, vol. 13; 3rd ed., 1970–1975, vols. 1–2; Plates, 1927–1959, 5 vols.; Plates, new ed. to vols. 1–7, 1977–1984; Plates to vols. 1–7, 1994–1997) (N10), covering the period from Egypt and Babylonia to the fourth century (A.D. 324); *The Cambridge Medieval History* (Cambridge: Cambridge University Press, 1911–1956, 8 vols.; 2nd ed., 1966–1967, vol. 4; new ed., 1998, vols. 5–7) (N11), covering the period from the Christian Roman Empire and the foundation of the Teutonic Kingdom to the era of the Renaissance; and *The Cambridge Modern History* (Cambridge: Cambridge University Press, 1902–1926, 14 vols.) (N12), covering the period from the Renaissance to the early twentieth century. The Cambridge history series has full bibliographies at the end of each volume.

A new edition of *The Cambridge Modern History* is *The New Cambridge Modern History* (Cambridge: Cambridge University Press, vols. 1–12, 1957–1960, vols. 1–12; 1979, vol. 13, companion volume; Atlas, 1970, vol. 14; 2nd ed., 1968, vols. 1–12, 14; 2nd ed., 1968, vol. 12) (N13). But the new *Cambridge* does not contain the feature of extensive bibliographies. To supply this omission, John Peter Charles Roach compiled *A Bibliography of Modern History* (Cambridge: Cambridge University Press, 1968, 388 p.) (N14). Roach contains books and periodical articles arranged in three sections that correspond to the three volumes of the new Cambridge. It is less detailed than the bibliographies in the old Cambridge series, since it does not include manuscript sources and its reference sources to journals are quite limited.

For current bibliographies, one may refer to *American Historical Review*, noted in Chapter 6. The following are significant bibliographies:

Annual Bulletin of Historical Literature: Publications of the Year, 1911– .
   Oxford, England: Blackwell Association, 1912– . ISSN 00663832.
   (N15)
International Bibliography of Historical Sciences, 1926– . Munich: Saur,
   1930– . Annual. ISSN 00742015. (N16)
International Medieval Bibliography, 1967– . Leeds, England: University of
   Leeds, 1968– . Semiannual. ISSN 00207950. (N17)

The *Annual Bulletin* is a classified guide to each year's output of books and articles with an author index. The *International Bibliography* lists both books and periodical articles arranged by period and area according to the scheme developed by the International Committee of Historical Sciences, with an author-proper name index and a geography index.

For the medieval topics, *International Medieval Bibliography* provides a listing of articles, notes, and similar literature, but not reviews. Entries are classified into 57 topics, which are further divided by areas. Beginning with volume 21, part 1, 1988, it includes articles on Western medieval topics published in Israel and Japan. The part lists over 4,100 items with an author index and a general index.

Subfield

Oral History

Oral History: A Reference Guide and Annotated Bibliography. Patricia Pate
   Havlive. Jefferson, NC: McFarland, 1985. 148 p. ISBN 0899501389.
   (N18)
Oral History Collection of Columbia University. 4th ed. Elizabeth B. Mason
   and Louis N. Starr. New York: Oral History Research Office, 1979,
   306 p. ISBN 0960249206. (N19)

The Havlive book is primarily an annotated bibliography of 773 items grouped in two parts: bibliographies of oral history and books and articles on oral history. A six-page introduction that precedes the bibliography briefly mentions reference sources, journals, colloquia, and subject headings. There is an author, title, and subject index. Since the items are arranged in alphabetical order by main entry, author, or title, the use of an index is necessary for locating a particular item by subject.

The oral history collection at Columbia University is the oldest and perhaps the largest in the world. The Mason and Starr bibliography represents the transcripts of 3,638 persons interviewed on all phases of American history from the 1880s to the present. The growth rate of Columbia's collection is between 15,000 and 25,000 pages a year. The work is arranged under 2,697 names with short biographical sketches and some subjects in alphabetical order. For a nationwide bibliography of oral history, one may consult the *National Union Catalog of Manuscript Collections*, noted in Chapter 3.

United States

A bibliography of bibliographies is *Bibliographies in American History: Guide to Materials for Research* by Henry Putney Beers (2nd ed., New York: Wilson, 1942, 487 p.) (N20), a classified listing of more than 11,000 items including concealed bibliographies, compilations in progress, and manuscript bibliographies. It is continued by *Bibliographies in American History, 1942–1978: Guide to Materials for Research*, also by Beers (Woodbridge, CT: Researcher, 1982, 2 vols., ISBN 0892350385) (N21). Some 11,700 items are included in the continuation. The work covers the period from World War II through the late 1970s.

Some good retrospective bibliographies may be found in *American Nations: A History from Original Sources by Associated Scholars*, edited by Albert Bushnell Hart (New York: Harper and Row, 1904–1918, 28 vols.) (N22) and *History of American Life* (New York: Macmillan, 1929–1948, 13 vols.) (N23). In each volume there is a "Critical Essay on Authorities," a select bibliography of monographs and special treatises upon the general subject of the volume.

The following are major retrospective bibliographies on American history:

> *Writings on American History, 1902–1961.* Publishers and, title vary. Annual. (N24)
> *Writings on American History, 1962–1973: A Subject Bibliography of Articles.* Millwood, NY: KTO Press, 1976. 4 vols. (N25)
> *Writings on American History: A Subject Bibliography of Articles, 1973/74–1990.* White Plains, NY: Kraus, 1974–1994. Annual. (N26)

Writings on American History has gone through many changes. Its title, publisher, frequency, and coverage vary. *Writings, 1902–1961* covered materials on the United States, Canada, and Latin America in the first two decades. With volume 13, it was published as a supplement to or as volume 2 of the *Annual Report* of the American Historical Association. Beginning with the 1936 volume, the scope was changed to include only writings on the history of the United States and its outlying possessions. *Writings* includes books and periodical articles with annotations.

One drawback of *Writings* was its time lag. *Writings 1960* was not published until 1972. After the appearance of the 1961 issue, *Writings* was replaced by the new *Writings*, which began publication in 1974. The new

Writings dropped annotations and its coverage was limited to periodical articles. Its listing was derived solely from the "Recently Published Articles" (RPA), 1976–1987, that appeared in the *American Historical Review*.[10]

Writings, 1962–1973 intended to fill the gap between the demise of the old *Writings* and the emergence of the new. *Writings* is an index to articles, containing more than 33,000 citations in 86,099 entries because of multiple listings from 510 journals. It consists of three parts: chronological, geographical, and subject, with an author index. Both *Writings*, old and new, and "Recently Published Articles" are no longer published.

Current bibliographies include:

Bibliographic Guide to North American History, 1977–   . Boston: G. K. Hall. Annual. ISSN 01476491. (N27)

United States History. Ron Blazek and Anna Perrault. Englewood, CO: Libraries Unlimited, 1994. 411 p. ISBN 0872879844. (N28)

The G. K. Hall guide is one of the company's bibliographic guide series. It is basically a library catalog of the Library of Congress and the New York Public Library.

Over 940 annotated titles are presented in *United States History*. The work is organized by chapters in two parts. Part 1, U.S. History General Sources, covers bibliographies, dictionaries, encyclopedias, chronologies, source books, statistics, demographic sources, and atlases and geographical sources. Part 2, U.S. History—Topics and Issues, consists of six chapters on politics and government, diplomatic history and foreign affairs, military history, social, cultural, and intellectual history, regional history, and economic history. Titles available in digital format are indicated. There are two indexes: author/title and subject.

Genealogy

Guide to Genealogical Research in the National Archives. Washington, DC: U.S. National Archives and Record Service, 1983. 304 p. ISBN 0911333002. (N29)

The Librarian's Guide to Genealogical Research. James Swan. Highsmith Press, 1998. 120 p. ISBN 1579500110. (N30)

There are a number of guides to genealogical records. *Fundamentals of Genealogical Research* by Laureen R. Jaussi and Gloria D. Cheston (3rd ed., Salt Lake City, UT: Deseret Books, 1977, 414 p., ISBN 0877470936) (N31) provides information on genealogical records and services with an international coverage. *How to Find Your Family Roots* by Timothy Field Beard with Denise Demong (New York: McGraw-Hill, 1977, 1,007 p.,

ISBN 0070042101) (N32) is a good source book. It lists sources by states and the District of Columbia.

Guide to Genealogical Research represents the largest collection of records for genealogical research. As noted in Chapter 3, the National Archives and Record Service houses millions of records on population and immigration, military, particular population groups, and other records such as land records, claims records, court records, and so on. It provides huge and valuable sources for genealogical research.

Theses and Dissertations

Extensive bibliographies of doctoral dissertations in history have been compiled by Warren F. Kuehl: *Dissertations in History: An Index to Dissertations Completed in History Departments of United States and Canadian Universities, 1873–1960* (Lexington: University of Kentucky Press, 1965, 249 p., ISBN 0813112648) (N33); *Dissertations in History*, volume 2, 1961–1970 (Lexington: University of Kentucky Press, 1972, 237 p., ISBN 0813112649) (N34); and *Dissertations in History, 1970–1980* (Santa Barbara, CA: ABC-Clio, 1985, 466 p., ISBN 087436356X) (N35). These bibliographies contain over 23,600 dissertations completed during the 1873–1980 period. The American Historical Association also published *Doctoral Dissertations in History*, 1976–1994 (semiannual, ISSN 01459929) (N36), which lists both dissertations in progress and dissertations completed. The semiannual is now incorporated in *Directory of History Departments and Organizations*, noted later. Both *America: History and Life* and *Historical Abstracts*, noted later, carry abstracts of dissertations. In addition, quite a number of history journals carry listings of doctoral dissertations, as noted in Chapter 6.

Research in Progress

The semiannual *Doctoral Dissertations in History* and *Directory of History Departments and Organizations*, both noted above, carry research in progress. Research in progress may also be found in periodicals noted in Chapter 6.

Reviews

A number of periodicals give ample space to book reviews. The best-noted periodicals for book review are *The American Historical Reviews*, 1895– (Washington, DC: American Historical Association, 5/year, ISSN 00028762) (N37), *English Historical Review*, 1886– (Essex, England: Addison Wesley Longman, quarterly, ISSN 00138266) (N38), *History: The Journal of the Historical Association*, 1912– (Oxford, England: Blackwell, quarterly, ISSN 00182848) (N39), and *Speculum: A Journal of Medieval Studies*, 1926– (Cambridge, MA: Medieval Academy of America, quarterly, ISSN 00387134) (N40). *The American Quarterly*, 1949– (Baltimore: American Studies Association and Johns Hopkins University Press, quarterly, ISSN 00030678) (N41) is noted for its annual bibliographical review on special topics. Below are two periodicals devoted to book reviews:

> *History: Reviews of New Books*, 1972– . Washington, DC: Heldref. Quarterly. ISSN 03612759. (N42)
>
> *Reviews in American History*, 1973– . Baltimore: Johns Hopkins University Press. Quarterly. ISSN 00224642. (N43)

History reviews an average of over 80 books per issue. Reviews are arranged by area, country, and subject. *Reviews in American History* carries long, critical reviews. Over 20 reviews are published each issue.

America: History and Life, noted next, features an index to book reviews. An extensive index to book reviews is *Index to Book Reviews in Historical Periodicals, 1972–1976*, compiled by John W. Brewster and Deborah Gentry (Metuchen, NJ: Scarecrow Press, 1976–1979, 6 vols.) (N44). Some 3,000 periodicals are indexed.

Indexes

Some indexes and abstracts noted in Chapter 3 have strong coverage of history, such as *Humanities Index*. Until the 1950s, *Writings* and the "Recently Published Articles," both noted earlier, were the major indexing services. Some bibliographies mentioned earlier also serve as indexing services, such as *International Bibliography of Historical Sciences* and *International Medieval Bibliography*. The following is a significant index in history:

> *Combined Retrospective Index to Journals in History, 1838–1974*. Arlington, VA: Carrollton Press, 1977. 9 vols. ISBN 0840801750. (N45)

The Combined Retrospective Index is one of the three sets in a series, *Combined Retrospective Index Sets* or *CRIS*, claimed by the publisher to be "the great leap backward in retrospective indexing of the social science literature." *CRIS* provides access to over 400,000 articles of 531 journals in three areas: history, political science, and sociology. *CRIS/History* indexes 243 English-language periodicals covering all periods and areas in history, arranged by 342 subject categories, each with its own chronological and keyword index. It is divided into two parts: vols. 1–14, world history, and vols. 5–9, United States history.

Abstracts

America: History and Life, 1955–   . Santa Barbara, CA: ABC-Clio. 5/year.
  ISSN 00027065. Print & digital. (N46)
Historical Abstracts, 1955–   . Santa Barbara, CA: ABC-Clio. Quarterly.
  ISSN 03632725. Print & digital. (N47)

America: History and Life (AHL) covers the United States and Canadian history, area studies, current affairs, and history-related fields. It is arranged by subjects listing "article abstracts and citations of reviews and dissertations" (subtitle) selected from 2,100 journals in 40 languages. *AHL* was published earlier in a format of a four-part series: (1) Articles, Abstracts, and Citations, (2) Index to Book Reviews, (3) American History Bibliography, and (4) Annual Index. Beginning with volume 26, 1989, it no longer carries separate parts. Now *AHL* consists of five issues in each volume. The first three issues have issue indexes. There is no issue index in issue 4. The fifth issue is a cumulative subject and author index that supersedes all issue indexes. It also includes a book, microforms, and film/video index; a list of abstractors; and a list of periodicals.

AHL is organized in six parts: (I) North America; (II) Canada; (III) United States of America: National History to 1945; (IV) United States of America: 1945 to Present; (V) United States of America: National, State, and Local History; and (IV) History, the Humanities, and Social Sciences. The length of abstracts varies. Articles from journals central to the historian's interest are covered with abstracts of 75–100 words. Others provide in general one- to two-sentence annotations.

Historical Abstracts: Bibliography of the World's Historical Literature (HA) was inspired by the example of the defunct *Social Science Abstracts*, noted in Chapter 3. The original aim was to provide full bibliographical descriptions with abstracts of the world's periodical literature pertaining to the period 1775–1945. Starting with volume 10, it limited its entries on Canada and the United States to topics dealing with foreign relations only to avoid duplication with *America: History and Life (AHL)*. Abstracts covering international relations are the only ones duplicated in *AHL*. In 1972, *HA* expanded its coverage from 1775 to the present. It further expanded its coverage from 1430 to the present in 1973 and since then has not carried writings on North America.

HA abstracts articles from approximately 21,000 journals in more than 50 languages covering political, diplomatic, economic, social, cultural, and intellectual history and related subjects in the social sciences and humanities in all countries of the world, except the United States and Canada. Sources are predominately French, German, Russian, Spanish, and Italian. *HA* covers (1) all branches of world history from 1450 to the present: history of the social sciences, the humanities, technology, and medicine; (2) related social sciences and humanities: area and interdisciplinary studies, the social sciences, the humanities with historical perspective; and (3) the historical profession: bibliography and methodology of history, archival and library collections, professional institutions, the teaching of history, and historical societies and meetings. It is organized into two parts with four issues in each part: Part A, Modern History Abstracts, 1450–1914, and Part B, Twentieth Century Abstracts, 1914 to the present. Entries in each part are grouped into three sections: (1) General, (2) Topics, and (3) Area or Country. Issues 1 and 2 are appended with an index. Issue 4 is a cumulated annual index.

Both *AHL* and *HA* use the Subject Profile Index (SPIndex). The SPIndex system produces a subject-geographic-biographic index arranged in a single alphabetical sequence with all relevant forms grouped together to provide a brief profile on the cited work. All terms in a string can be searched.

A backward step to supplement *AHL* is *America: History and Life: A Guide to Periodical Literature, Volume 0* (Santa Barbara, CA: ABC-Clio, 1972, 537 p.) (N48), which includes periodical literature from 1954 to 1983. It lists 6,154 abstracts that appeared in *HA*, volumes 1–16, 1955–1959, relating to American and Canadian history and studies. Both *AHL* and *HA* are available on CD-ROM and online marketed through Dialog (File 38 and File 39 respectively).

SOURCES OF INFORMATION

General

> *American Memory*. Washington, DC: Library of Congress. http://lcweb2. loc.gov (N49)
>
> *The Annals of America*. Chicago: Encyclopaedia Britannica, 1968–1974. 21 vols. ISBN 0878271996. (N50)
>
> *Historic Documents*, 1972–   . Washington, DC: Congressional Quarterly. Annual. ISSN 0892080X. (N51)
>
> *Makers of America*. Chicago: Encylopaedia Britannica, 1971. 10 vols. ISBN 0878270000. (N52)
>
> *WWW-VL-History*. Lawrence, KS: University of Kansas. http://history. cc.ukans.edu/history/WWW_history_main.html (N53)

American Memory's "Today in History" began on April 1, 1997. It is designed to present daily historical facts highlighted by materials from the American Memory collections consisting of "primary source and archival materials relating to American culture and history" (home page). These historical collections are part of the National Digital Library. Its home page gives three choices: Search, Browse, and Learn, and in addition,

Showcase, which displays new collections and sample collections. As of October 1998, there were 40 collections including African American Perspective, A Century of Lawmaking, Continental Congress, Detroit Publishing Company, Map Collections, Pioneering the Upper Midwest, Votes for Women, and George Washington Papers.

Collections are in five formats, that is Photos & Prints, Documents, Motion Pictures, Maps, and Sound Recordings, all arranged by title keywords in alphabetical order. Photos & Prints provide invaluable visual sources for research, including 2,100 baseball cards, 1,100 Civil War photographs, over 4,600 photographs from the Great Depression to World War II, over 14,000 photographs of Washington as It Was, 888 views of Around the World in the 1890s: Photographs from the World's Transportation Commission, and portraits of presidents and first ladies.

Documents are textual collections. There are 20 collections including the titles just noted. Some ten collections of motion pictures include Early Motion Pictures, 1897–1920; The Last Days of a President: Films of McKinley and the Pan-American Exposition, 1901; and the Spanish-American War, 1898–1901. Maps are noted in the previous chapter. Sound Recordings contains five collections, such as Northern California Folk Music from the Thirties and American Leaders Speak, 1918–1920.

The two Encylopaedia Britannica sets, *The Annals* and *Makers of America*, are documentary works in a similar format but with different emphasis. Each volume of the main set, *Annals*, covers a certain period, beginning with Christopher Columbus's letter written in 1493 to Scott Suchanan's message published in 1968. Each also contains a short introduction as an overview of the events of the period and a general description of the selections in the volume, followed by a chronology of the events of the period and maps.

The eighteen text volumes contain 2,202 selections of American writings with nearly 5,000 illustrations. The writings include laws, court decisions, messages of the presidents, formal declarations of other members of the government, speeches and writings of government figures, private papers, newspaper editorials and reports, magazine articles, diaries, and fiction. Each selection has a headnote to explain the background of the work. At the end of each volume is an alphabetical index of authors contained in the volume.

The *Annals Conspectus* in two volumes is a list of 25 major themes or great issues that form its chapters. Each chapter begins with an essay on the issue, followed by "Outlines of Topics" representing various subthemes under the major theme, "Reference," referring to the text volumes "Cross-References" and "Recommended Readings." The *Conspectus* serves as a typical index to the *Annals*.

Volume 21 of the *Annals*, published in 1971, is a detailed index, providing access to the *Annals* not provided by the *Conspectus*. It consists of three parts: (1) an overall table of contents of both the *Annals* and the *Conspectus*; (2) a Proper Name Index to both sets; and (3) an Authors and Sources Index to the eighteen text volumes. Its appendixes contain "Bibliography of Recommended Readings," with full bibliographical details to the lists of recommended readings that appear at the end of each chapter; "Bibliography of Additional Source Materials" of about 2,000 works; and "Index of Subjects."

The *Annals* has been continuously published since 1974: Volume 19, 1969–1973 (1974, 439 p., ISBN 087827197X); Volume 20, 1974–1976 (1977, 388 p., ISBN 085229316X); and Volume 21, 1977–1986 (1987, 679 p., ISBN 0852294751). Each volume has an index.

With stress on the history of American pluralism is *The Makers of America*, which contains over 730 documents. Each volume covers a period from the first comers, 1736–1800, to emergent minorities, 1955–1970. Bibliographies of recommended readings are given. There are five indexes: ethnic, proper name, topical, author, and source.

Historic Documents provides access to the raw materials of contemporary history. It "contains official statements, Supreme Court decisions, reports, special studies, communiques, treaties, and speeches related to events of national and international significance" (Preface). Materials are arranged by month. There is a cumulative index for 1983–1987.

A rich collection of historical documents is offered in *WWW-VL-History*. The home page provides two indexes at the beginning: The History Index ordered alphabetically and The History Index ordered chronologically and geographically. All sources are grouped into Major Heritage Group Web sites and Some Useful Sites. Under the former, there are AmDocs Documents for the Study of American History, American Academy of Research Historians of Medieval Spain, First World War Documents Archives, and a number of collections on the State of Kansas. The AmDocs contains the full text of documents from a letter of Christopher Columbus to the King and Queen of Spain in 1494 to the present Clinton State of the Union Speech of 1993.

Encyclopedias

General

General encyclopedias, such as *Encyclopaedia Britannica* and *Encyclopedia Americana*, are the most frequently used reference for historical topics. Below are encyclopedias in history in general and by period.

The Encyclopedia of Ancient Civilizations. Arthur Cotterell, ed. New York: Mayflower, 1980. 367 p. ISBN 083172790X. (N54)

The Encyclopedia of the Renaissance. Thomas G. Bergin and Jennifer Speake, eds. New York: Facts on File, 1987. 454 p. ISBN 0816013152. (N55)

An Encyclopedia of World History: Ancient, Medieval and Modern, Chronologically Arranged. 5th ed. William Leonard Langer. Boston: Houghton Mifflin, 1972. 1,569 p. ISBN 0395135923. (N56)

Great Events from History. Frank N. Magill, ed. Englewood Cliffs, NJ: Salem Press, 1972–1975. 9 vols. (N57)

Great Events from History II. Frank N. Magill, ed. Englewood Cliffs, NJ: Salem Press, 1991–1995. (N58)

Great Events: The Twentieth Century. Pasadena, CA: Salem Press, 1992. 10 vols. ISBN 0893567965. (N59)

The Encyclopedia of Ancient Civilizations is a survey of civilizations, with emphasis on "their emergence, development, interaction, decline" (Preface). Articles contributed by 38 scholars cover Egypt, West Asia, India, Europe, China, and America. It features rich illustrations, some 300 of them, and 28 maps.

In *The Encyclopedia of the Renaissance*, articles are arranged in alphabetical order with black-and-white photographs and color plates. It is strong in biographies. At the end are a bibliography and a chronological table. One weakness is its lack of an index.

An Encyclopedia of World History, a successor to Ploetz's *A Manual of Universal History* (trans. and enl. by William H. Tillinghast; rev. under the editorship of Harry Elmer Barnes, Boston: Houghton Mifflin, 1925, 766 p.), gives concise outlines of historical developments throughout the world through the year 1970. It has a detailed index of nearly 200 pages. Langer, with the addition of illustrations to supplement the text, was also published under the title *The New Illustrated Encyclopedia of World History: Ancient, Medieval, and Modern History Chronologically Arranged and Illustrated with More Than 2,000 Photographs, Maps, Charts and Drawings* (New York: Harry N. Abrams, 1975, 2 vols.) (N60). The text of Langer remains unchanged.

Great Events from History contains three sets: Ancient and Medieval Series (1972, 3 vols.), Modern European Series (1973, 3 vols.), and American Series (1975, 3 vols.). About 1,000 historical events in summary form are presented in chronological order. The articles are signed. Each article has four sections: (1) quick reference materials at the beginning showing type of events, time, locale, and principal personages involved, if applicable; (2) summary of the event, describing the basic facts and some of the causes and effects; (3) pertinent literature, which presents two reviews of books and articles written about the event; and (4) additional recommended reading. In each set, there are an alphabetical list of events, a keyword index for events, a category index for type of events, principal personages, pertinent literature reviews, and literature for additional recommended reading.

Great Events from History II consists of the following sets: *Science & Technology* (1991, 5 vols., 2,610 p., ISBN 0893566373); *Human Rights* (1992, 5 vols., 2,880 p., ISBN 0893566438); *Arts & Culture* (1993, 5 vols., 1,678 p., ISBN 0893568074); *Business & Commerce* (1994, 5 vols., 2,678 p., ISBN 0893568139); and *Ecology & the Environment* (1995, 2,296 p., ISBN 0893567515).

Subfield

The American Heritage Encyclopedia of American History. John M. Faragher, ed. New York: Holt, 1998. 1,106 p. ISBN 0805044388. (N61)

The Cambridge Historical Encyclopedia of Great Britain and Ireland. Christopher Haigh, ed. New York: Cambridge University Press, 1985. 392 p. (N62)

Civilization of the Ancient Mediterranean Greece and Rome. Michael Grant and Rachel Kitzinger, eds. New York: Scribner's, 1988. 3 vols. ISBN 0684175940. (N63)

Encyclopedia of American History. 7th ed. Richard B. Morris and Jeffrey Morris, eds. New York: Harper and Row, 1996. 1,278 p. ISBN 0062700553. (N64)

Encyclopedia of Asian History. Ainslie T. Embree, ed. New York: Scribner's, 1988. 4 vols. ISBN 0684186195. (N65)

Encyclopedia of Jewish History: Events and Eras of the Jewish People. Ilana Shamir and Shlomo Shavit, eds. New York: Facts on File, 1986. 288 p. ISBN 0816012202. (N66)

Two encyclopedias listed here deal with American history. The *Encyclopedia of American History* provides "the essential historical facts about American life and institutions" from the era of discovery and exploration to 31 December 1993. It consists of four parts. Part 1, Basic Chronology, presents the major political and military events arranged in time sequence. Part 2, Topical Chronology, deals with constitutional developments, American expansion, and demographic, economic, scientific, technological, and cultural trends with many statistical data. Part 3 presents biographical sketches of 450 notable Americans. Part 4, Structure of the Federal Government, contains tables on the three branches of government. There are maps and charts.

The American Heritage Encyclopedia of American History contains nearly 3,000 entries, including more than 1,000 biographies. It covers government, law, science, education, economics, immigration, labor movement, the frontier, exploration, warfare, art, regions, literature, culture, and Supreme Court decisions. Entries are cross-referenced, many with bibliography and illustration. Appendixes include Declaration of Independence, Constitution of the United States, Presidents of the United States, Vice Presidents of the United States, Chief Justices of the United States, Associate

Justices of the Supreme Court, States of the United States, and Timetables of American History (pp. 1068–1077).

The *Civilization of the Ancient Mediterranean* contains 97 articles by 88 scholars on the people, customs, government, religion, and arts from 2000 B.C. to the fall of Rome in A.D. 476. Articles are arranged under thirteen broad topics: history, land and sea, population, agriculture and food, technology, government and society, economics, religion, private and social life, women and family life, literary and performing arts, philosophy, and the visual arts. There are 175 photographs and line drawings. Each article concludes with a bibliography consisting of sources and studies.

The *Cambridge Historical Encyclopedia* contains 61 articles contributed by 60 experts arranged under seven topics: (1) Britons and Romans, c. 100 B.C.–A.D. 409; (2) Saxons, Danes and Normans, 409–1154; (3) Medieval Empire: England and Her Neighbours, 1154–1450; (4) Reformation and Inflation, 1450–1625; (5) Disorder to Stability: Britain and Ireland, 1625–1783; (6) Political Reform and Economic Revolution, 1783–1901; and (7) From Imperial Power to European Partner, 1901–1972. Also included is a Who's Who, short biographical sketches of most individuals mentioned in the text.

Encyclopedia of Asian History provides entries "on history in its sense of a chronological record of past events along with an interpretation of their meaning and significance" (Preface), and thus attention has not been given to art, religion, and literature. The term "Asia" refers to, according to its preface, "Iran and Central Asia; the Indian subcontinent or South Asia; Southeast Asia, which comprises the great sweep of islands of the Indonesian archipelago and the Philippines as well as to mainland countries of Burma, Thailand, Laos, Kampuchea, Vietnam, and Malaysia; and East Asia which includes China, Korea, and Japan." More than 400 experts contributed over 3,000 articles arranged in alphabetical order from "Abangan" to "Zunbil." The length of articles varies from one paragraph to over twelve pages, all signed. Some articles include maps. The encyclopedia concludes with a synoptic outline and a general index. The synoptic outline, a guide to the organization and classification of the encyclopedia, consists of "Topical Outline" and "Outline of Contents."

The *Encyclopedia of Jewish History* "offers concise information about events, eras, and key figures in the annals of the Jewish people from the dawn of history until modern times," as stated in the preface. Its preface also states: "It contains 100 historical entries and a dozen appendices on culture and ethnography. Each entry comprises a central article of around 800 words and some ten additional integrated feature items, including illustrations, photographs, maps, and diagrams." The encyclopedia concludes with a chronological chart of Jewish and world history, a glossary, and a general index.

Dictionaries

General

History is replete with dictionaries. The one-volume encyclopedias just mentioned may also be regarded as dictionaries. Listed here are dictionaries in history in general and by period.

> *Dictionary of Concepts in History*. Harry Ritter. Westport, CT: Greenwood Press, 1986. 490 p. ISBN 0313227004. (N67)
>
> *Dictionary of Historical Terms*. 3rd ed. Chris Cook. London: Macmillan, 1998. 384 p. ISBN 0333673476. (N68)
>
> *A Dictionary of Eighteenth-Century World History*. Jeremy Black and Roy Porter, eds. Oxford: Blackwell, 1994. 840 p. ISBN 0631180680. (N69)
>
> *A Dictionary of Nineteenth-Century World History*. John Belchem and Richard Price, eds. Oxford: Blackwell, 1994. 746 p. ISBN 0631183523. (N70)
>
> *A Dictionary of Twentieth-Century World History*. Jan Palmowski. Oxford: Oxford University Press, 1997. 683 p. ISBN 0192800167. (N71)
>
> *Dictionary of Twentieth-Century History: 1914–1990*. Peter Teed. Oxford: Oxford University Press, 1992. 520 p. ISBN 0192116762. (N72)
>
> *Dictionary of the Middle Ages*. Joseph R. Strayer, ed. New York: Scribner's, 1982–1989. 13 vols. (N73)

Dictionary of Concepts in History belongs to the concept dictionaries series noted in the previous chapter. Like the other series dictionaries, each entry consists of four parts: (1) the definition of the idea, (2) the history of the idea, (3) an annotated list of references, and (4) suggested readings. There is no listing of terms contained therein for quick reference.

The Cook dictionary, formerly *Macmillan Dictionary of History Terms*, contains terms on a worldwide basis. It includes foreign words that have become part of the historical vocabulary. Entries are arranged in alphabetical order from AAA, Abbasid, ABC countries to Zoroastrianism and Zouave.

The three world history dictionaries cover the periods 1700–1799, 1800–1899, and 1900–1996 respectively. Entries are concise with cross-references, maps, and chronologies. The eighteenth-century dictionary also provides a dynastic chart. Another twentieth-century dictionary of international coverage is Peter Teed. The dictionary provides concise definitions in alphabetical order, from Abboud, Sudanese general, abd al-Aziz ibn Saud, King of Saudi Arabia, to Zog, King of Albania, and Zulu. Political and military terms dominate.

The *Dictionary of the Middle Ages* covers the period roughly from A.D.

500 to 1500 and the geographical scope of the Latin West, the Slavic world, Asia Minor, the lands of the caliphate in the East, and the Muslim-Christian areas of North Africa. It contains some 5,000 signed articles including biographies. Each article is appended with a bibliography. Volume 13 is an index volume.

Subfield

Concise Dictionary of American History. David William Voorhees, ed. New York: Scribner's, 1983. 1,140 p. ISBN 0684173212. (N74)

Dictionary of American History. Rev. ed. James Truslow Adams, ed.-in-chief. New York: Scribner's, 1976. 8 vols. ISBN 0684138565. (N75)

Dictionary of American History: Supplement. Robert H. Ferrell and Joan Hoff, eds. New York: Scribner's, 1996. 2 vols. ISBN 0684819579. (N76)

Dictionary of American History. Rev. and enl. ed. Michael Martin and Leonard Gelber. Totowa, NJ: Littlefield, 1981. 742 p. ISBN 0822601249. (N77)

Dictionary of Asian American History. Hyung-chan Kim. New York: Greenwood Press, 1988. 627 p. ISBN 0313237603. (N78)

Dictionary of Mexican-American History. Matt S. Meier and Feliciano Rivera. Westport, CT: Greenwood Press, 1981. 498 p. ISBN 0313212031. (N79)

The concise dictionary is a condensed one-volume edition of *Dictionary of American History* (*DAH*) noted next, handy for quick reference. It reduced *DAH* by shortening some long articles, omitting less important ones, and rearranging certain materials. As it is based on *DAH*, noted next, biographies are not included.

The *Dictionary of American History* contains about 6,200 entries on events, trends, Supreme Court decisions, ideas, organizations, and places, arranged in alphabetical order with many cross-references. The revised edition has increased its coverage on science, technology, the arts, native American Indians, and Afro-Americans. Some 1,200 are newly written articles, with 500 subjects not covered in the earlier edition. Articles contributed by approximately 800 authors are signed and have references to most of them. Volume 8, published in 1978 (ISBN 0684150786), is an index.

The two-volume Supplement contains 757 new and revised entries. New articles cover such topics as Cable News Network, Computer Viruses, Cybernetics, Desktop Publishing, Helsinki Accords, Iran-Contra Affairs, North American Free Trade Agreement, Thomas Confirmation Hearings, and Vegetarians.

DAH is a companion volume in a series that includes the following: (1) *Dictionary of American Biography* (New York: Scribner's, 1928–1937, 20 vols. and Index; rept., 1943 and 1945) (N80); and *Supplements* 1–10 (New

York: Scribner's, 1944–1995) (N81), which record the lives of outstanding people in the history of America. Beginning with the third supplement, each has a cumulative index to all preceding supplements. Its concise version, *Concise Dictionary of American Biography* (5th ed., New York: Scribner, 1997, 2 vols., ISBN 0684805499) (N82), lists over 19,000 Americans who died before 1981. (2) *Album of American History* (James Translow Adams, ed.-in-chief. New York: Scribner's, 1969, 6 vols.) (N83); and *Supplement, 1968 to 1982* (New York: Scribner's, 1985) (N84), which record some 6,300 illustrations with brief explanatory narratives "to tell the history of America through pictures made at the time the history was being made" (Foreword). (3) *Atlas of American History* (2nd rev. ed. New York: Scribner's, 1984, 306 p., ISBN 0684184117) (N85), which contains 147 places from the fifteenth century to 1912 recording where the events happened.

The earlier editions of *DAH*, *DAB*, *Album*, and *Atlas* are adapted to form the work *Record of America: A Reference History of the United States* (Joseph F. X. McCarthy, New York: Scribner's, 1974, 10 vols., ISBN 068413862X) (N86). Volumes 1–8 of the *Record* contain the text arranged alphabetically by topic on the colonial and national history of the United States, with pictorial and graphic illustrations. Volumes 9–10 deal with resources listing official documents, writings, speeches, diaries, memoirs classified by eight periods from 1492 to 1974; books for further reading; general bibliography; and chronological tables. It is a very useful reference geared to use by the general public and students, although it is in some aspects dated.

It may be noted that *DAB* after its Tenth Supplement will no longer be published. Instead, a new publication entitled *The Scribner Encyclopedia of American Lives* (N87), covering people who died between 1981 and 1990, will be published. Oxford University Press announced it will publish *American National Biography* (N88), prepared under the auspices of the American Council of Learned Societies. It will be in 24 volumes containing 17,500 entries contributed by more than 6,000 authors.

In the preceding list are two outstanding dictionaries of the history of American minorities. The *Dictionary of Asian American History* consists of two sections. Section 1 is a collection of fifteen essays on historical development of Asian Americans and their places in the American social order. Section 2 is the dictionary that defines some 800 entries of "major events, persons, places, and concepts that have left indelible marks on the collective experience of Asian and Pacific Americans" (Preface). Also included are an extensive bibliography about Asian and Pacific Asians and a historical chronology of Asians in America, the 1980 census data, and a general subject index.

The *Dictionary of Mexican American History* "covers the period from the Texas revolt against Mexico in 1835, which marked the birth of the 'Mexican American' to the beginning of the decade of the Hispanic in

1980" (Preface). It contains terms, events, institutions, developments, organizations, and personalities. There are eight appendixes: (1) bibliography of general works, (2) chronology of Mexican American history, (3) the complete text of the Treaty of Guadalupe Hidalgo and the Protocol of Querétaro, (4) glossary of Chicano terms, (5) Mexican American journals, (6) tables of census, education, employment, and immigration statistics, (7) figures, and (8) maps.

Directories

> *Directory of Historical Agencies in North America.* 13th ed. Betty Pease Smith. Nashville, TN: American Association for State and Local History, 1986. 686 p. ISBN 0910050775. (N89)
> *Directory of History Departments and Organizations,* 1975/76– . Washington, DC: American Historical Association. Annual. ISSN 10778500. Print & digital. (N90)

The best source for locating historical agencies is the *Directory of Historical Agencies in North America.* Its first edition under the title *Historical Societies in the United States: A Handbook* gave 583 listings. The number of listings has increased to 9,375 in the current edition. The directory consists of two parts: (1) historical agencies in America, arranged by state, followed by territories, and within states by city; and (2) historical agencies in Canada arranged by province and within provinces by city. Each entry provides name, address, telephone, founding date, person in charge, staff, publication, programs, and period of collections. There are a general index and a special interest index; the latter is a classified index under twelve categories.

The AHA's *Directory,* formerly *Guide to Departments of History,* is a guide to "colleges, universities, and research institutions in the United States and Canada" (subtitle). The 1998–1999 edition contains more than 800 departments and research institutions with e-mail and Web addresses for many of them and individual e-mail addresses for more than 6,000 historians. According to AHA's Web description, the *Directory* includes affiliations, degree information, rank, and specializations; all Ph.D. programs; research facilities and programs; contact addresses and information; department specializations; enrollment statistics, tuition figures, and application deadlines; recent doctoral recipients and their dissertation titles; current history dissertations in progress; and indexes of entries by name and by state arranged in alphabetical order. The *Directory* is under three parts: (1) United States, (2) Canada, and (3) research institutions.

A limited version of the *Directory* is available on the Web (http://chnm.gmu.edu/aha/pubs/directories.htm). A user may search U.S. schools,

Canadian Schools, and Historical Organizations. Links are provided to individual Web site if available.

Biographies

Biographical sources about historians are many. *Biography of American Scholars*, noted in Chapter 4, including biographies of historians, is a most useful one. Biographies of deceased historians may be found in "Obituaries" in the *Hispanic American Historical Reviews* and "Recent Deaths" in the *American Historical Review*. The following are biographies of historians:

> *American Historians, 1607–1865.* Clyde N. Wilson, ed. Detroit: Gale Research, 1984. 382 p. Dictionary of Literary Biography Series, no. 30. (N91)
>
> *American Historians, 1866–1912.* Clyde N. Wilson, ed. Detroit: Gale Research, 1986. 467 p. Dictionary of Literary Biography Series, no. 47. (N92)
>
> *Twentieth Century American Historians.* Clyde N. Wilson, ed. Detroit: Gale Research, 1983. 519 p. Dictionary of Literary Biography Series, no. 27. (N93)
>
> *The Superhistorians: Makers of Our Past.* John Barker. New York: Scribner's, 1982. 365 p. ISBN 068416664X. (N94)

The first three reference works are part of *Dictionary of Literary Biography (DLB)* (Detroit: Gale Research, 1978–   ) (N95). *DLB* covers different groups of writers organized by genre, topic, and period. The three volumes deal with American historians. The Barker book is more than a biography. It presents achievements of thirteen great historians and analyzes their thinking and contributions. The thirteen historians are Herodotus, Thucydides, Augustine, Petrarch, Machiavelli, Voltaire, Scott, Ranke, Marx, Nietzche, Du Bois, Toynbee, and Wells. According to the author, their lives and achievements "constitute a history of history in the West."

Handbooks, Yearbooks, and the Like

General

> *Chronicle of the World.* New York: DK Publishing, 1996. 1,175 p. ISBN 078940334X. (N96)
>
> Chronology of the Modern World, 1763–1992. 2nd ed. Neville Williams and Philip Waller. Oxford: Helicon, 1994. 1,136 p. ISBN 0091782740. (N97)
>
> *Chronology of World History.* H. E. Mellersh and Neville Williams. Santa Barbara, CA: ABC-Clio, 1999. 4 vols. ISBN: 1576071553. (N98)

The People's Chronology: A Year-by-Year Record of Human Events from Prehistory to the Present. James Trager. New York: Holt, 1995. 1,312 p. ISBN 0805017860. (N99)

Random House Timetables of History. 2nd rev. ed. R. Castello. New York: Random House, 1996. 320 p. ISBN 0679769609. (N100)

Timelines of the 20th Century. David Brownstone and Irene Franck. Boston: Little, Brown, 1996. 506 p. ISBN 0316114065. (N101)

The Timetables of History: A Horizontal Linkage of People and Events. 3rd rev. ed. Bernard Grun. New York: Simon and Schuster Trade, 1991. 688 p. ISBN 0671749196. (N102)

The greatest duplication occurs among chronologies. Encyclopedias and dictionaries in history noted earlier all contain chronologies. All titles just listed list events by date. *Chronicle of the World* begins with World Timeline. Events are arranged in chronological order under two headings of politics and society and technology and culture. It covers from 3.5 million B.C. to 1995. Its companion volume, *Chronicle of America*, will be noted next.

Chronology of the Modern World presents chronology on two-page spreads. The left side of the page records chronological events by month. The right side of the page lists significant achievements in politics; economics; law and education; science, technology, discovery, etc.; scholarship; fine arts and architecture; music; literature; the press; drama and entertainment; sports; statistics; birth and deaths.

Both the *Chronology of World History* and the *Timetables of History* list events by date for the period as indicated by their titles. The *Chronology of World History* contains 70,000 events in four volumes: (1) The Ancient and medieval world, prehistory–A.D. 1491; (2) The expanding world, 1492–1775; (3) The changing world, 1776–1900; (4) The modern world, 1901–1998. A main index and a title index are provided in each volume. In general, events are grouped for each year in four categories: (1) politics, government, and economics; (2) science, technology, and medicine; (3) arts and ideas; and (4) society. Categories are further divided, such as the category of "Society" consists of subcategories of education, everyday life, media and communication, religion, and sports. The *Chronology* features also mini-chronologies for at-a-glance information, and births and deaths of noteworthy people at the end of each year.

The People's Chronology includes not only major happenings but also historical developments of such topics as "canned food, the steam engine, small-pox vaccine, the railroad, the sewing machine, electric lighting, x-rays, the motorcar" (Preface). It also features 30 graphic symbols (art, food and drink, music, population, and so on) for quick reference.

Timelines is "a chronology of 7,500 key events, discoveries, and people" (subtitle) from 1900 to 1994. Information is organized in four vertical subject columns (politics and war; science, technology, and medicine; arts and literature; and social, economic, and everyday life) from left to right across each two-page spread. There is a detailed index.

United States

> *Almanac of American History.* Arthur S. Schlesinger, Jr., gen. ed. New York: G. P. Putnam's, 1983. 623 p. ISBN 0399128530. (N103)
> *Chronicle of America.* Rev. ed. New York: DK Publishing, 1995. 1,016 p. ISBN 0789420910. (N104)
> *Encyclopedia of American Facts and Dates.* 10th ed. Gorton Carruth. 1997. 1,096 p. ISBN 0062701924. (N105)
> *The Longman Handbook of Modern American History, 1763–1996.* Chris Cook and David Waller. London: Longman, 1998. 451 p. ISBN 0582084881. (N106)
> *The Timetables of American History.* Laurence Urdang, ed. New York: Simon and Schuster, 1981. 470 p. ISBN 0671252453. (N107)

Almanac of American History covers the period from 986 through 1982, organized into five groups: (1) founding a nation, 986–1787; (2) testing a union, 1788–1865; (3) forging a nation, 1866–1900; (4) expanding resources, 1901–1945; and (5), emerging as a world power, 1945 forward.

A companion to *Chronicle of the World*, noted above, *Chronicle of America* is organized in eight periods: (1) A New World B.C.–1606; (2) Conceived in Liberty, 1607–1763; (3) Harvest of Freedom, 1764–1788; (4) A Perfect Union? 1789–1849; (5) A House Divided, 1850–1877; (6) Yearning to Breathe Free, 1878–1916; (7) Saving the Dream, 1917–1945; and (8) The Eagle Ascendant, 1946–1993. The revised edition extended the period from 1994 to 1996.

Longman's recently updated companions include *The Longman Handbook of Modern European History, 1763–1997* (3rd ed., Chris Cook and John Stevenson, comp., Longman, 1998, 550 p., ISBN 0582304161) (N108) and *The Longman Handbook of Modern British History, 1714–1995* (3rd ed., Chris Cook and John Stevenson, comp., Longman, 1996, 543 p., ISBN 0582293049) (N109).

One widely used chronology is Carruth. It covers a vast number of interesting events in the American past from 986 through 1996, arranged in chronological order and divided into four fields in vertical columns. The four columns are (1) exploration and settlement, wars, government, civil rights, statistics; (2) publishing, arts and music, popular entertainment, architecture, theater; (3) industry, science, education, philosophy and religion; and (4) sports, social issues and crime, folklore, fashion, and holidays. There is a detailed index.

The Timetables of American History is chronologically arranged from 1000 to 1980 in four vertical columns: (1) history and politics, (2) the arts,

(3) science and technology, and (4) miscellaneous. Each column is further divided into events in America and events elsewhere in the world. This approach is convenient for concurrent events that ocurred elsewhere in the world.

NOTES

1. Will Durant and Ariel Durant, *The Lessons of History* (New York: Simon and Schuster, 1968), p. 14.

2. Henry Steele Commager, *The Study of History* (Columbus, OH: Charles E. Merrill, 1965), p. 5.

3. Gaetano Salvemini, "The Social Sciences and History," in Arthur W. Thompson, ed., *Gateway to the Social Sciences*, rev. ed. (New York: Holt, Rinehart and Winston, 1965), pp. 3–5.

4. John Herman Randall, Jr., "History and the Social Sciences," in Thompson, *Gateway to the Social Sciences*, p. 379.

5. Commager, *Study of History*, p. 12.

6. Arthur M. Schlesinger, "History: Mistress and Handmaid," in The Brookings Institution, *Essays on Research in the Social Sciences* (1951; reprint ed., Port Washington, NY: Kennikat Press, 1968), pp. 139–157.

7. Ibid., pp. 150–151.

8. Elizabeth Rumics, "Oral History: Refining the Term," *Wilson Library Bulletin* 40 (1966): 602–605.

9. For instance, Crick has used the *Guide* to evaluate library collections in England. See B. R. Crick, "A Survey of Library Resources in the United Kingdom for Teaching History and Literature in the Universities," *Journal of Documentation* 14 (1958): 109–118.

10. *American Historical Review* 80, no. 4 (1975): 1099.

Chapter 14

Law

Laws are rules governing human behavior that can be enforced by the authority of a state. The main sources of American laws are the Constitution, legislation, and common law. Article 6, paragraph 2, of the Constitution provides: "This Constitution and the laws of the United States which shall be made in pursuance thereof; and all treaties made, or which shall be made, under the authority of the United States, shall be the supreme law of the land." Other constitutional provisions relating to legislation are found in Article 1, sections 7 and 8. American statutory laws include three categories of legislation, namely the act, the joint resolution, and the treaty.

The other source of American laws is common law. If Congress has not legislated to apply to a case, the judge must apply common law. Common law is judge-made law and develops according to the doctrine of *stare decisis*, which requires that, once a rule has been established by a court, it shall be followed in all similar cases.[1] In deciding a case, when there are competing principles or there is no principle that precisely fits the case, the judge must select the principle or make new principles. Thus, the American judiciary not only interprets and applies law, but also makes laws, as if it acted like Congress. But common law can be repudiated, replaced, or revised by legislation.

One unique feature of American judiciary is its power over other branches of government commonly referred to "judicial review" or "judicial supremacy," by which the court may invalidate an act of Congress or an executive order of the executive branch.[2] In the United States, actions of the court have deeply affected the style and substance of government and politics. The collection of judicial publications becomes a must for most libraries.

Information sources about law are rich and extensive. A less known, yet useful, source is the informational pamphlets and brochures published by state bar associations. It is estimated that over 460 pamphlets on various topics are available from state bar associations.[3] In bibliographical control, there is a parallel pattern in laws, regulations, treaties, and court decisions.

ACCESS TO SOURCES

Guides

There is no shortage of guides in law. The following two titles are excellent tools for sources in law.

> *Fundamentals of Legal Research*. 7th ed. J. Myron Jacobstein, Roy M. Mersky, and Donald J. Dunn. New York: Foundation Press, 1998. 810 p. ISBN 1566626137. (P1)
>
> *How to Find the Law*. 9th ed. Morris L. Cohen, Robert C. Berring, and Kent C. Olson. St. Paul, MN: West Publishing, 1989. 718 p. ISBN 0314533184. (P2)

These works cover practically the same major sources and both feature clarity and richness in illustrations. Jacobstein, Mersky, and Dunn is a successor to the *Pollock's Fundamentals of Legal Research* (4th ed., edited by Jacobstein and Mersky) (P3). It features definitions and summaries in most of the chapters and the helpful appendixes, which include citation forms and selective legal materials and their abbreviations, as well as a table of legal abbreviations. The book is also available in an abridged version, *Legal Research Illustrated: Abridgement of Fundamentals of Legal Research* (1998, 569 p., ISBN 1566627125) (P4).

The book by Cohen, Berring, and Olson consists of articles contributed by others. Its coverage is admirably balanced and well coordinated. Additional readings are given in many chapters for further studies. Its appendixes include state legal research guides and bibliographies, state primary legal sources, coverage of West regional reporters, sources of federal regulatory agency rules, regulations, and adjudications, and subject guide to selected looseleaf services. The guides to legal research used to pay little attention to trade bibliography, selection tools, bibliographical details of sources cited, and reference sources. The chapter on nonlegal research sources, including reference sources in the social sciences, adds more flavor to the book. An abridged version is *Finding the Law* (10th ed., Robert C. Berring, 1995, 331 p.) (P5). It does not include the chapters in *How to Find the Law* on general and social science sources and on foreign, international, and comparative law materials. Morris L. Cohen's other guide, a good brief introduction to basic sources in law, is *Legal Research in a Nutshell* (6th ed., Morris L. Cohen and Kent C. Olson, St. Paul, MN: West

Publishing, 1996, 397 p., ISBN 0314095896) (P6). It is much more condensed than *Finding the Law*, yet it includes sources on English, foreign, and international law.

Bibliographies

Legal bibliography has a wide spectrum of coverage, including laws, statutes, regulations, court decisions, treaties, digests, and other documents, and is characterized by its currency, coordination, and comprehensiveness. Indexing and abstracting are prompt and extensive. The field of law originated the citation index. There is an imposing array of bibliographies, substantially annotated, of statutes, regulations, and court decisions. Not a single piece of legislation or common law escapes the attention of legal bibliography.

The bibliography of books and periodical articles began flourishing in the 1960s. Two of Harvard Law School's excellent, selective bibliographies, however, were discontinued: *Current Legal Bibliography* (CLB), 1960–1983 (9/year) (P7), listing works primarily in English, and *Annual Legal Bibliography (ALB)*, 1961–1983 (P8), including *Current Legal Bibliography*, being an international bibliography of some 10,000 monographs and 2,500 serials. It may be regarded as the counterpart of the *International Bibliography of the Social Sciences*, noted in Chapter 4.

The following bibliographies are important:

> *Bowker's Law Books and Serials in Print: A Multimedia Sourcebook*, 1982– . New York: Bowker. Annual & Supplement. ISSN 00000752. (P9)
>
> *Law Books, 1876–1981: Books and Serials in Law and Its Related Subjects.* New York: Bowker, 1981. 4 vols. ISBN 0835213978. Monthly supplements and annual cumulations. (P10)
>
> *Law Books in Print: Law Books in English Published Throughout the World*, 1957– . Dobbs Ferry, NY: Glanville. Triennial. ISSN 00758221. (P11)
>
> *Law Books Published*, 1969– . Dobbs Ferry, NY: Glanville. 2/year. ISSN 00239240. (P12)
>
> *International Legal Books in Print*, 1991– . W. Sussex, England: Bowker-Saur. Irregular. (P13)

Bowker's Law Books and Serials in Print contains some 51,900 monograph titles and serials titles extracted from Bowker's American Book Publishing Record and Serials Bibliography databases. The 1998 edition (3 vols., ISBN 0835239861) consists of volume 1, books—subject index; volume 2, books—title index, books—author index, and books publishers and distributors/symbols and abbreviations; and volume 3, serials—subject index, vendor listing/serials online, serials—title index, audio cassettes—subject index, video cassettes—title index and subject index, software—subject index, and multimedia publishers' and distributors' symbols and abbreviations. Its subject indexes follow the Library of Congress subject headings. The book is updated by Bowker's *Law Books and Serials in Print Supplement* between editions (*Supplement*, 1998, 737 p., ISSN 000011031) (P14).

Bowker's is a continuation of *Law Books* that contains approximately 130,000 monograph titles and 4,000 serials titles. Volumes 1–3 are subjects classified under 39,000 Library of Congress subject headings. Volume 4 includes author and title indexes, serials subject, law and law-related publications and publishers and distributors, and law and law-related online database producers and vendors.

The seventh edition of *Law Books in Print* (Nicholas Triffin and Alice Pidgeon, comp., 1994, 6 vols., ISBN 087802039X) includes "virtually all major types of law materials: monographs, looseleafs, treaties, multivolume sets, and reprints (including government publications, if commercially reprinted) . . . many law-related and inter-disciplinary titles with law related contents . . . especially in such fields as political science, business and economics, environmental affairs, and international relations" (Preface). It covers "Law Books in English Published throughout the World and in Print through 1993" (subtitle). But legal materials in very short pamphlets on marginal subjects, juvenile materials, and general government documents not commercially reprinted are excluded. Volumes 1–2 are author/title listings. Volumes 3–5 are subject listings and part of a publishers' directory. Volume 6 consists of publisher listing, series listing, and publishers' directory. *Law Books in Print* is supplemented by the semiannual *Law Books Published*.

Each issue of *Law Books Published* contains Author Index, Subject Index, Publisher Index, Series Index, and Publisher Directory. Volume 30, number 1 (298 p.), was published in 1998.

The second edition of *International Legal Books in Print* (1992, 2 vols., ISBN 1857390016), a companion to *Bowker's Law Books and Serials in Print*, contains some 29,000 author/title entries. Each entry, if complete, includes author, title, state of responsibility, edition, number of volumes, imprint, place of publication, size, series title, annotation, ISBN and ISSN, binding, price, and frequency. For international publications in law, it complements *Law Books in Print* and *Law Books Published*.

Theses and Dissertations

A Listing of Law School Theses and Dissertations. Sanford R. Silverburg. Buffalo, NY: Hein, 1995. Looseleaf. ISBN 0899419038. (P15)

It is a simple listing of more than 4,500 graduate theses and dissertations produced at American law schools, arranged by author in alphabetical order. There are a subject index and a listing of degree-granting institutions.

Reviews

The number of book reviews published in law periodicals is small. In general, law periodicals do not publish many book reviews; an exception is the *Michigan Law Review*.[4] David F. Cavers regarded law school journals as less hospitable to book reviews. In his findings, eleven law school journals carried one to eleven book reviews in a year.[5] The *Michigan Law Review*, 1902– (Ann Arbor: Michigan Law Association, 8/year, ISSN 00262234) (P16), carries an annual survey of books relating to law.

Indexes

There exists a proliferation of indexes in law, such as indexes to laws and statutes, administrative regulations, court decisions, and treaties and other international agreements, mentioned elsewhere in the chapter. The indexes to legal periodicals and Harvard's two ceased law bibliographies, *CLB* and *ALB*, all noted earlier, are good sources. Readers may also notice that an index in a field other than law yet noted for its coverage of legal periodicals is *PAIS*, noted in Chapter 3. The titles listed next are indexes geared to providing access to legal sources.

General

> *Index to Legal Periodicals and Books*, 1908– . New York: H. W. Wilson. Monthly except September with annual cumulation. ISSN 00194077. Print and digital. (P17)
>
> *Current Law Index: Access to Legal Periodicals*, 1980– . Sponsored by the American Association of Law Libraries. Foster City, CA: Information Access Company. Monthly with quarterly and annual cumulations. ISSN 01961780. Print & digital. (P18)
>
> *Index to Foreign Legal Periodicals*, 1960– . Published for the American Association of Law Libraries. Berkeley: University of California Press. Quarterly. ISSN 0019400X. Print & digital. (P19)
>
> *Index to Periodical Articles Related to Law*, 1958– . Roy M. Mersky and Donald J. Dunn, eds. and comps. Dobbs Ferry, NY: Glanville. Quarterly. ISSN 00194093. (P20)

Index to Legal Periodicals and Books, formerly *Index to Legal Periodicals*, the oldest of the four, indexes articles, books, decisions, case notes, bibliographies, biographies, and book reviews from over 700 periodicals and 1,400 monographs published in the United States, Canada, Great Britain, Ireland, Australia, and New Zealand. The *Index* is one of the H. W. Wilson indexing services, yet it differs from most other Wilson indexes in both its coverage and its arrangement. It has international coverage of common law–system countries. Its arrangement features four parts: Subject and Author Index, Table of Cases, Table of Statutes, and Book Reviews. The *Index* used to be sponsored by the American Association of Law Libraries (AALL). As a result of disagreement over the editorial policy, AALL sponsored instead publication of the *Current Law Index*, noted later. The index is available online as Wilsonline and marketed through Lexis-Nexis and Ovid (File WILP), on the Web as WilsonWeb, and on CD-ROM as Wilsondisc and marketed through SilverPlatter.

The *Current Law Index* indexes over 1,000 periodicals in law and allied disciplines published in the United States, Canada, the United Kingdom, Ireland, Australia, and New Zealand. It contains four parts: Subject Index, Author/Title Index, Table of Cases, and Table of Statutes. By random check, periodicals indexed in the *Index to Legal Periodicals (ILP)*, with a few exceptions, are all covered in the *Current Law Index*. The improvement of *ILP* in providing bibliographic citations of titles under both subject and author and including more periodical titles makes the two indexes strong competitors.

The *Current Law Index* is also available in other media. The CD-ROM, *LegalTrac* (P21), covers over eight years of *Current Law Index* and information from other IAC databases. It is also available online as *IAC Legal Resource Index* (P22) on Dialog (File 150), DataStar (File LAWS), and the two law databases, Lexis-Nexis and Westlaw.

Index to Foreign Legal Periodicals: A Subject Index to Selected International and Comparative Law Periodicals and Collections of Essays, as the title indicates, indexes periodicals primarily outside the common law system. More than 500 periodicals and several collections of essays published in some 60 countries and territories are regularly indexed. It is arranged by subject with an author index and translations of subject headings. It is also available on CD-ROM from SilverPlatter.

The purpose of *Index to Periodical Articles Related to Law* is twofold: it indexes articles from journals that do not appear in the *Index to Legal Periodicals and Books, Current Law Index, Legaltrac, Legal Resources Index,* and *Index to Foreign Legal Periodicals,* and it emphasizes the application of the social and behavioral sciences to law. As such, the *Index* selects articles from such nonlaw journals as *AAUP Bulletin, Penthouse,* and *Playboy.* Each issue is arranged into two parts: an index to articles arranged by subject and an author index. The last issue of each volume cumulates the first three issues and contains a list of the journals indexed. There are also ten-year and five-year cumulations. Cumulations are arranged into four parts: a subject index, an index to articles, a list of journals indexed, and an author index.

Subfield

> *Criminal Justice Periodical Index*, 1975– . Ann Arbor, MI: UMI. 3/year.
> ISSN 01455818. Print & digital. (P23)

Criminal Justice Periodical Index (formerly *Crime and Delinquency Literature*) consists of author and subject indexes, indexing some 150 periodicals published in the United States, England, and Canada. It covers abortion, arrest, child abuse, crime, statistics, drug abuse, forensic science, gun control, legal aid, police, prisons, terrorism, and violence. Its online database, updated monthly, is marketed through Dialog (File 171). The publisher also provides copy article and microform services.

Abstracts

Listed here are three abstracting services in criminal justice and criminology:

> *Criminal Justice Abstracts*, 1968– . Monsey, NY: Willow Tree Press. Quarterly. ISSN 01469177. Print & digital. (P24)
> *Criminology, Penology and Police Science Abstracts*, 1961– . Amsterdam: Kugler. Bimonthly. ISSN 09288759. (P25)
> *NCJRS*, 1972– . Rockville, MD: U.S. National Institute of Justice, National Criminal Justice Reference Service. Irregular. Digital. (P26)

The first two abstracting services are a result of a merge of publications. *Abstracts on Crime and Juvenile Delinquency* (formerly *Crime and Delinquency Literature*) and *Information Review on Crime and Delinquency* were merged into the present *Criminal Justice Abstracts*. *Criminal Justice Abstracts* provides abstracts of books, journal articles, dissertations, and reports published worldwide. It is arranged broadly by topics, such as crime, the offender, and the victim; juvenile justice and delinquency; police; courts and the legal process; adult corrections; and crime prevention and control strategies. The 1998 volume abstracts over 800 entries. It has a subject and a geographic index. The abstracting service is also available on CD-ROM marketed through SilverPlatter and online through SilverPlatter and Westlaw.

Criminology, Penology and Police Science Abstracts, a merger of *Excerpta Criminologica* and *Abstracts in Criminology and Penology*, publishes in its volume 37 (1997) about 3,700 abstracts classified in nine categories: (1) criminology and other disciplines; (2) offenses, deviant behavior; (3) victim; (4) juvenile justice and delinquency; (5) criminal law; (6) crime policy; (7) police; (8) courts; (9) corrections. In each issue there are subject index, author index, and journals abstracted. Cumulative indexes appear in the last issue of each volume.

NCJRS (*National Criminal Justice Reference Service*), sponsored by the National Institute of Justice under the Omnibus Crime Control and Safe Streets Act of 1968, as amended, indexes and abstracts over 200 periodicals. It has an international coverage on many topics, including AIDS, corrections, courts, crime, criminology, drugs, law enforcement, juvenile justice, policy, probation, parole, statistics, and victim services. There are over 140,000 records in the database with monthly updates including books, reports, journal articles, and unpublished materials. The database is marketed through Dialog (File 21). *NCJRS* is also available on the Web as *NCJRS Abstracts Database* (http://www.ncjrs.org) (P27). The database on the Web can be searched by author, subject, and title, and both Boolean logical operator and limited search by date are available. For the convenience of subject search, *NCJRS* has published an annual *National Criminal Justice Thesaurus* (ISSN 01986546) (P28).

Contents Reproduction

Currently, there is no publication devoted to contents reproduction in law. *Legal Contents*, 1972–1989 (Philadelphia: Institute for Scientific Information, semimonthly, ISSN 02795787) (P29), formerly *Contents of Current Legal Periodicals*, reproduced tables of contents of over 300 legal periodicals. It is no longer published. For active contents reproduction, refer to *Contents Pages from Law Reviews and Other Scholarly Journals* (Austin: University of Texas School of Law, http://tarlton.law.utexas.edu/tallons/content_search.html) (P30) and *The Table of Contents of Law Journals* on *Hieros Gamos*, a Web site, noted later.

Citations

Shepard's Citations is the earliest and the most comprehensive citations service in the social sciences. It consists of a series of over 70 citations intended to give legal researchers the judicial history and interpretation of every reported decision, the legislative history and all cases citing a statute, and other legal documents and materials. Three citations of Shepard's citations may be mentioned:

Shepard's Code of Federal Regulations Citations. Colorado Springs, CO: Shepard's Citations, 1986– . 5/year with supplements and annual cumulation. ISSN 0730465X. Print & digital. (P31)
Shepard's Federal Statute Citations. Colorado Springs, CO: Shepard's Citations, 1927– . Semimonthly. ISSN 1089411X. Print & digital. (P32)
Shepard's United States Citations: Supreme Court Reporter. Colorado

Springs, CO: Shepard's Citations, 1887– . Semimonthly. ISSN 10890718. Print & digital. (P33)

All three are compilations of citations. One is a compilation of citations to the *Code of Federal Regulations*, presidential proclamations, executive orders, and reorganization plans. The other, formerly *Shepard's United States Citations: Statutes and Court Rules*, contains citations to the United States Constitution, *United States Code, United States Statutes at Large*, federal court rules, and federal sentencing guidelines. The third compiles citations to decisions of the U.S. Supreme Court. All citations also appear in a number of titles. Citations are supplemented by soft-covered periodical issues. Shepard's Citations are available online marketed through Lexis-Nexis, noted later.

Uniform Citations

One unique feature in law is the standardized citation style. The following is well known on the subject in the legal profession.

A *Uniform System of Citation*. 16th ed. Cambridge, MA: Harvard Law Review Editors, 1996. 365 p. (P34)

Known as the "*Bluebook*," it is arranged in seven parts: General Rules of Citation and Style; Cases; Constitution, Statutes, and Legislative, Administrative, and Executive Materials; Books, Periodical Materials, and Other Secondary Sources; Services; Foreign Materials; and International Materials. It concludes with Tables of Abbreviations and an index. It is an authoritative text on the subject. The earlier-mentioned *Index to Legal Periodicals* complies with the *Bluebook* in its citations.

SOURCES OF INFORMATION

General

Lexis-Nexis. Dayton, OH: Lexis-Nexis. Digital. (P35)
Westlaw. St. Paul, MN: West Group. Digital. (P36)
FedLaw. Washington, DC: U.S. General Services Administration. http://www.legal.gsa.gov (P37)
Hieros Gamos. Houston, TX: Lex Mundi. http://www.hg.org (P38)
Jurist: The Law Professors' Network. Pittsburgh: University of Pittsburgh School of Law. http://jurist.law.pitt.edu (P39)
Legal Information Institute. Ithaca, NY: Cornell Law School. http://www.law.cornell.edu (P40)
Thomas: Legislative Information on the Internet. Washington, DC: Library of Congress. http://www. thomas.loc.gov, noted in Chapter 7.

Lexis-Nexis and *Westlaw* are the two large databases devoted to law. *Lexis-Nexis*, formerly *Lexis* of Mead Data Central, also noted in Chapter 1, is the first database with full-text commercially available. The system uses the Lexis terminal with a special keyboard, or a compatible terminal, by telephone to search legal materials. Materials in the Lexis-Nexis system are divided into over 180 libraries arranged alphabetically by the name of the library. Each library consists of a number of files. The 180 libraries include 50 individual state, news, laws, regulations, trade, business and finance, law reviews, marketing, quotes, and foreign countries. The States Library (STATES), for example, has 53 libraries, one each for the 50 states plus the District of Columbia, Puerto Rico, and the Virgin Islands. There are duplications of files in the States Library and individual state libraries, such as the state of Alabama (ALA). Its Citations Library (CITES) includes autocite and Shepard's Citation Services, noted earlier. In the Law Reviews Library (LAWREV), some 200 law reviews are grouped into areas, such as Group Files, Annotations and Indexes, Law Reviews by Jurisdiction, Law Reviews by Topics, Individual Law Reviews and Law Journals, and Individual State Bar Journals. A well-known directory, *Martindale-Hubbell Law Directory*, noted later, is available as one of its libraries.

Lexis-Nexis combines menu and free-text searching. One may bypass the menu display and the use of some key functions by entering dot commands, such as .cl for library change and .cf for file change, for fast and more efficient searching and for using a terminal other than that of *Lexis-Nexis*. For the convenience of searching, *Lexis-Nexis* developed Freestyle, a concept searching program. It is also available on the Web (http://www.lexis-nexis.com) For a listing of libraries and files and for quick reference, refer to *Directory of Online Services*, 1994– (Dayton, OH: Lexis-Nexis, annual, ISSN 10812024) (P41).

Westlaw is also a full-text database for computer-assisted legal research (CALR). Its databases are grouped according to topics, such as General Materials: State and Federal, Texts and Periodicals, Specialized Materials, Antitrust, Bankruptcy, Communication, Criminal Justice, Energy and Utilities, Environmental Law, Financial Services, Government Contracts, Immigration, Intellectual Property, International Law, Labor, Legal Services, Military Law, Securities, and Taxation. In 1997, it developed KeyCite in competition with *Shepard's Citations*. Two recent surveys find that KeyCite provides more citations than Shepard's.[6] It also includes databases supplied by other producers, such as the Bureau of National Affairs (BNA) and Commerce Clearing House (CCH).

Westlaw combines menu and free-text searching. The logical and positional operators and the familiar West's topic and key number system are available for ease of use. It developed the first concept search, called WIN (Westlaw Is Natural). It is also available on the Web (http://www.westlaw.com). For the convenience of using *Westlaw* and for database descriptions, there is *Westlaw Reference Manual* (4th ed., St. Paul, MN: West Publishing, 1990, 580 p., ISBN 0314683143) (P42).

Materials in *FedLaw* are grouped into eight main categories: Topical and Title Index, Federal Laws and Regulations by Subject Category, Federal Judiciary, Legislative Branch, State and Territorial Laws, Arbitration and Mediation, General Research and Reference, and Professional Associations and Organizations. The Topical and Title Index is an alphabetical listing of topics and titles. Federal Laws and Regulations contains 61 subjects and many subcategories arranged in alphabetical order from acquisition, agriculture, appropriations, banking, business, to tax, trade, and transportation, and provides links to the federal agencies. All federal courts are listed in the category of Federal Judiciary. For Supreme Court Decisions, it refers to other Web sites, such as Cornell's *Legal Information Institute (LII)*, noted later. Legislative Branch includes Congress, Legislation, Congressional Budget Office, General Accounting Office, Government Printing Office, Library of Congress, Office of Compliance, Office of Technology Assessment through September 1995 (GPO), and Superintendent of Documents, GPO. General Research and Reference offers sources on various topics and titles, such as *Dow Jones, Farmer's Almanac*, finding people, places, and things, locating federal government agencies, publications, and news (Fox News, the *New York Times, USA Today*, the *Wall Street Journal*, and so on), and currency. Over 1,060 entities are given in Professional Associations and Organizations.

Comprehensive legal sources worldwide are provided by *Hieros Gamos*. The Web site contains HG I, HG II, and HG III. HG I has 12 directories on bar, governments, associations, law schools, law firms, publishers, services, vendors, law sites, legal education, mediators, and online services. Its Global bar lists bar associations in 150 countries. Other directories provide information on all governments of the world, legal associations worldwide, every law school, and law firms and laws worldwide (telneting Lexis and Westlaw for laws).

HG II contains 200 practice areas, 400 discussion groups, and 50 guides to doing business. HG III is resources consisting of law study, employment, Internet law library, law news, seminars, legal guides, and law and law-related journals. The table of contents of 750 journals can be searched.

Jurist provides "An online forum where law professors can find information important to their daily work as teachers and scholars, and where they can share knowledge and exchange ideas with a global community of colleagues, law students, lawyers and interested citizens." It has three affiliates: *Jurist Australia, Jurist Canada*, and *Jurist UK*. First on the Web site is news, including U.S. Legal News, U.S. Supreme Court News, U.S. Law School News, Foreign Legal News, U.S. Legal Press, and New in Jurist. Other areas of service include JuristChat, conferences, course page, resources page, online articles, worldwide dean's list, faculty lounge, student lounge, and so on. It also provides links to sources and services, such as *Lexis, Westlaw*, U.S. Supreme Court Cases and Oral Argument, Federal Cases and Legislation, Law Reviews Online, Legal Dictionary, Lawyer Locator (Mardindale-Hubbell), Law Library Catalogs, and Legal Internet.

Primarily for legislation information, *Thomas* consists of six categories: Congress Now, Bills, Congressional Record, Committee Information, Legislative Process, and Historical Documents. It also provides current Congress House and Senate directories, Congressional Internet Services, and Library of Congress Web Links. The Library of Congress Web Links contains four main Web sites: Legislative Branch, Executive Branch, Judicial Branch, and State/Local.

The Legislative Branch contains Congressional Mega Sites, Members of Congress, Committees of Congress, Congressional Organizations and Commissions, Calendars and Schedules, Floor Proceedings, Legislation, *United States Code*, House and Senate Rules, Roll Call Votes, Executive Business of the Senate, Legislative Process, Congressional Internet Services, and Legislative Branch Support Agencies. The Executive Branch is the official federal government Web Site, which groups the Web sites into Executive Branch; Independent Agencies; Boards, Commissions, and Committees; and Quasi-Official Agencies. Laws, regulations, and court opinions are provided in the Judicial Branch. The Judicial Branch contains *The Constitution of the United States of America* and its 1996 Supplement, Statutes (*U.S. Code* and Statutes), Regulations (*Federal Register* and *Code of Federal Regulations*), Judicial Opinions (Federal Court, Circuit Courts of Appeal, and State Courts), Court rules, Executive Branch Materials, Law Journals, and Law-Related Internet Sites.

Supreme Court Opinions and Federal Rules are accessed through Cornell's *LII*, noted later, and Circuit Courts of Appeals are accessible through different Web sites. It may be noted that laws and regulations can be accessed through a number of Web sites. *GPO Access*, noted in Chapter 7, is one of them.

The *Legal Information Institute (LII)* provides access to laws, regulations, rules, and court decisions. Its home page displays the following topics: law about constitutions and codes, court opinions, law by source of jurisdiction, American Legal Ethics Library, Cornell Law School, directories, current awareness, and the *LII* and its publications. Each topic is further divided by subtopics. The constitutions and codes topic consists of *U.S. Code* (Acts of Congress), U.S. Constitution, *Code of Federal Regulations*, and federal rules. The topic law by source or jurisdiction includes federal law, state law, and law from around the world. "Law from around the world" is organized into two categories: (1) national law material, which is divided by region, such as North America, South America, Australia and New Zealand, Asia, Europe, Middle East, and Africa; and (2) by resources of international law, which includes international trade law materials, UN materials, treaties dealing with the environment, and so on. *LII* provides links to other Web sites; for instance, for treaties it links to *The Multilateral Project* of the Fletcher School of Law and Diplomacy.

Subfield

Constitution

The Constitution of the United States appears in the *United States Code, United States Code Annotated (USCA)*, and *United States Code Services (USCS)*, all noted later, though it does not constitute a part of the Code. The Constitution is heavily annotated with numerous court cases in both *USCA* and *USCS*. *United States Code Annotated, Constitution of the United States Annotated* (Bicentennial ed., St. Paul, MN: West Group, 1987, 9 vols. with pocket, cumulative supplements) (P43), contains thousands of judicial decisions of both federal and state courts interpreting and applying the Constitution. Of similar approach but less extensive is *United States Code Service, Constitution* (Rochester, NY: Lawyers Cooperative/Bancroft-Whitney, 1977, 2 vols., with pocket supplements) (P44), which is part of the Total Client-Service Library and encompasses a research guide to law review articles and *American Jurisprudence*, noted later, and interpretative notes and decisions. The Total Client-Service Library (TCSL) refers to all publications by the Lawyers' Co-operative on annotations, forms, proofs, and trial techniques.

The best separate work on the United States Constitution annotated is:

> *The Constitution of the United States of America: Analysis and Interpretation. Annotations of Cases Decided by the Supreme Court of the United States to June 29, 1992.* Prepared by the Congressional Research Service, Library of Congress. Johnny H. Killian and George A. Costello, eds. Washington, DC: GPO, 1996. 2,444 p. Supplemented by pocket-part. Print & digital. (P45)

Previously edited by Edward S. Corwin, the work is an indispensable research tool to the interpretation of the Constitution through Supreme Court decisions. It begins with an introduction, a brief survey of the Court's treatment of the doctrine of constitutional law. Analysis and interpretation are organized by Articles and Amendment, heavily documented. At the end are acts of Congress held constitutional in whole or in part by the Supreme Court, state constitutional and statutory provisions and municipal ordinances held unconstitutional on their face or as administered, Supreme Court decisions overruled by subsequent decisions, and a table of cases. *Constitution of the United States* is revised every ten years; supplements are published in odd years between editions. The 1996 Supplement (published in 1997) is the latest. The book and its supplement can be accessed through the Web sites, noted earlier and *GPO Access*, noted in Chapter 7.

A compilation of both federal and state constitutions is *Constitutions of the United States, National and State*, ed. 1–   (Dobbs Ferry, NY: Oceana for Legislative Drafting Research Fund of Columbia University, 1962–   , looseleaf) (P46). It consists of six binders and an index binder, updated by continuous replacements. Each constitution is preceded by notes that briefly explain the history and source of the constitution.

Statutes

There are three legislative forms of statutory laws: slip laws (P47), session laws, and subject compilations. The slip law is the first official text of a statute and is issued shortly after enactment in a pamphlet or single sheet. Each law is given an identifying number, the chronological order of enactment, and the number of the Congress that enacted it. Slip laws are cumulated, corrected, and issued in bound volumes in chronological order at the end of each session of Congress. The official session laws are the *United States Statutes at Large*, noted next. It supersedes the slip laws. Also noted next, the *United States Code* is a subject compilation of current text of all general and permanent federal laws in force.

> *United States Statutes at Large* . . . , 1789–   . Boston: Little, 1845–1873; Washington, DC: GPO, 1873–   . Print & digital. (P48)
> *United States Code*. 1994 ed. Washington, DC: GPO, 1995. 34 vols. with supplements. Print & digital. (P49)

Contents of the *Statutes at Large* vary. Beginning with Volume 65, 1951, each volume contains, as required by law, laws (public, private, and joint resolutions), reorganization plans, concurrent resolutions, proclamations by the President, and any proposed amendments to the Constitution.[7] Documents are arranged under each category in chronological order by date of passage of the act. In the *Statutes at Large*, public laws are those that apply to the people generally of the nation or state, whereas private laws are enacted to affect only an individual or a small number of persons.[8]

Under the terms of a reorganization act, the President is granted power to reorganize the executive branch of government, but the plan for reorganization must be submitted to Congress for approval, and either house may veto it within 60 days. When approved by Congress, a reorganization plan has the force of law. A concurrent resolution deals with matters in which both houses are interested; it does not have the legal effect of law.[9] Proclamations, like executive orders, are expressions of the President's action. There is not much difference between the two. It is generally considered that proclamations are used for matters of widespread interest.[10] Proclamations are also published in the *Federal Register*, noted next, and the publications of the President. The *United States Code Congressional and Administrative News* (St. Paul, MN: West Group, 1942–   , monthly with annual cumulation) (P50) carries advance session laws.

West's *News* includes all public laws currently enacted, legislative history (Congressional Committee Reports explaining the background, history, and purpose of legislation), executive orders and proclamations, reorganization plans, administrative rules, and regulations of general interest. One of its features is the general review of issues before Congress, new laws, and President's messages. It has a cumulative index and tables, including one on *USC* and *USCA*, and sections amended, repealed, and new. There is a permanent bound volume for each session of Congress.

The *United States Code (USC)*, the compilation of federal laws by subject into 50 titles, "contains the general and permanent laws of the United States, in force on January 4, 1995" (title page). It was first published in 1926 and is revised every six years, with bound cumulative supplements until the next edition. Two supplements have been published: *Supplement I* (1995) and *Supplement II* (1996). *USC* publishes public, general, permanent laws. Private laws are excluded. The *Code* and its supplements establish *prima facie* the laws of the United States, except for 22 titles that have been enacted into positive laws. For laws classified in other titles, *Statutes at Large* is the authoritative text.

Volumes 1 to 26 of the *United States Code* contain 50 titles. Volume 26 includes Popular Names. Volumes 27 to 28 are Tables, including revised titles; *Statutes at Large*, 1789–1994; Executive Orders; Proclamations; Reorganization Plans; and so on. Since *USC* is largely drawn from the *Statutes at Large*, references from *USC* to the *Statutes at Large* are necessary. One of the tables in the Tables volumes is "Statutes at Large," showing where the acts of Congress will be found in *USC*. A General Index is provided in volumes 29 to 35.

There are two commercial publications of the Code: *United States Code Annotated* (St. Paul, MN: West Group, 1927–   ) (P51) and *United States Code Service Lawyers' Edition* (Rochester, NY: Lawyers' Co-operative/Bancroft-Whitney, 1972–   ) (P52). *USCA* aims to add to the framework of the law the constructions that the courts have placed upon it and to include in the text historical data with comments on the sources. It consists of the text of the statute, citations to the original acts in the *Statutes at Large*, citations to the *United States Code*, historical notes, cross-references, library references, *Code of Federal Regulations*, and notes of decisions. The "Notes of Decisions" includes library references and most significantly one-paragraph summaries of every court decision that has interpreted the law. The library references give references to the West Key Number Digests and to *Corpus Juris Secundum*.

The West Key Number is a fixed number given to specific points of case law. Every point of case law has its own Key Number. The Key Number

Digests are arranged by main topics, headings, and numerous subheadings. The Key Number will enable a researcher to find a point under the same identical Key Number in all West Digests and West Reporters.

A researcher may use one of three methods to seek information in *USCA*: the General Index volumes, to find descriptive words or fact words that give reference to the appropriate Title and, in some instances, section number in *USCA*; directly to the Title; or the Popular Name Table in the last volume of the General Index for acts of Congress. *USCA* is supplemented by annual pocket-part services and interim pamphlets, and the session law service, *United States Code Congressional and Administrative News*, noted earlier.

USCS, renamed after the *Federal Code Annotated*, is annotated to decisions of federal and state courts and contains history of each code section with amendment notes and references to the *Code of Federal Regulations*. It also features separate additional volumes on uncodified law and treaties, court rules, administrative rules of procedure, rules of bankruptcy and official form, United States Code Guide to relevant materials, and tables.

USCS is updated by pocket and cumulative supplements, *Advance Service* (P53) and *Later Case Service* (P54). The *Advance Service*, a monthly pamphlet, contains newly enacted public laws, presidential proclamations, executive orders, amendments to court rules, and selective administrative regulations. The *Later Case Service*, published in September and January, contains the notes of new cases decided. The January issue cumulates the September issue, which is then itself cumulated in the annual pocket supplement published in April.

Both *USCA* and *USCS* are substantially annotated to the court decisions, with numerous references to related topics and neatly interwoven with publishers' other publications. *USCA* is more extensive than *USCS*. It follows the text of the government publication, *United States Code*, whereas *USCS* adheres to the text of the *Statutes at Large*.

Both the *Statutes at Large* and the *United States Code* are accessible through the *GPO Access* Web site, noted in Chapter 7, and the Web sites noted earlier. They are also on the commercial Web sites, *Lexis-Nexis* and *Westlaw*.

Regulations

The Federal Register Act of 1935 requires that all executive orders and administrative regulations be published in the *Federal Register*. The subject compilation of the *Federal Register* becomes the task of the *Code of Federal Regulations* (CFR).

Federal Register, March 14, 1936– . Washington, DC: GPO. Daily except Saturday, Sunday, and official holidays. Print & digital. (P55)

Code of Federal Regulations, 1938– . Washington, DC: GPO, 1949– . Print & digital. (P56)

The *Federal Register* publishes the following documents as required by law:[11]

1. Presidential proclamations and Executive orders, except those not having general applicability and legal effect or effective only against federal agencies or persons in their capacity as officers, agents, or employees thereof;
2. Documents or classes of documents that the President may determine from time to time have general applicability and legal effect; and
3. Documents or classes of documents that may be required so to be published by Act of Congress.

In addition, when the Director of the Federal Register considers that publication of the document is in the public interest, he may allow that document to be published.[12]

The document refers to "a Presidential proclamation or Executive order, and an order, regulation, rule, certificate, code of fair competition, license, notice, or similar instrument, issued, prescribed, or promulgated by a Federal agency."[13] "Documents having general applicability and legal effect" means "any document issued under proper authority prescribing a penalty or course of conduct, conferring a right, privilege, authority, or immunity, or imposing an obligation, and relevant or applicable to the general public, numbers of a class, or persons in a locality, as distinguished from named individuals or organizations."[14]

The *Federal Register* publishes regulations and notices of federal agencies in four basic categories:[15] (1) presidential documents. Other public presidential documents not required to be published in the *Federal Register* can be found in the *Weekly Compilation of Presidential Documents*, noted in Chapter 7; (2) rules and regulations, that is, regulatory documents having general applicability and legal effect, most of which are keyed to and codified in the *Code of Federal Regulations*; (3) proposed rules; and (4) notices, such as notices of hearings and investigations, committee meetings, agency decisions and rulings, delegation of authority, filing of petitions and applications, agency statements of organization and functions, and Sunshine Act meetings. Each issue also lists both current and cumulative *CFR* parts affected.

An index to the *Federal Register* is issued monthly in cumulative form, with an annual volume for the calendar year. The index is broadly arranged by subject. A detailed index to the *Federal Register* is commercially available, entitled *CIS Federal Register Index*, 1984– (Bethesda, MD: Congressional Information Service, looseleaf, weekly, with interim and permanent semiannual cumulations, ISSN 07412878) (P57). It indexes the contents of every issue of the *Federal Register*, except agency notices of meetings held under the government in the Sunshine Act or the Federal Advisory Committee Acts. *CIS Federal Register Index* consists of three indexes and a calendar: Subjects and Names, CFR Section Numbers, Federal Agency Docket Numbers, and "Calendar of Effective Dates and Comment Deadlines."

CFR was first published in 1938 and, since its second edition, published in 1949, has been continuously revised. It is revised at least once a year and issued on a quarterly basis, each quarter for a number of titles. It contains the text of new and amended rules in force arranged by 50 titles to conform to titles of *USC*. *CFR* does not reflect the complete history of the regulation with the text of all changes and revisions and does not contain all materials appearing in the *Federal Register*. It is a *prima facie* evidence of the text of the original documents.

The *CFR Index and Finding Aids*, revised annually, contains five parts. (1) subject/agency index for rules currently codified in *CFR*; (2) a list of agency-prepared indexes; (3) a table of laws and presidential documents cited as authority for regulations currently codified in the *CFR*; (4) a list of *CFR* titles, chapters, subchapters, and parts; and (5) an alphabetical list of agencies appearing in the *CFR*. A more detailed index is *Index to the Code of Federal Regulations* (Bethesda, MD: Congressional Information Service, 1978– , ISSN 01989014, annual with quarterly supplements) (P58). It is basically a subject index. The 1997 edition (4 vols., ISBN 0886924251) consists of Subject Index, Geographic Index, Index by New and Revised *CFR* Section Numbers, List of Descriptive Headings, Administrative History of the *CFR*. Each supplement contains Subject Index to New, Revised, and Deleted Rules and *CFR* Section number. The index lists changes with the Federal Register citation and date.

For changes, additions, and removals in *CFR*, consult *LSA (List of CFR Section Affected)* (P59), a monthly. It has four annual issues published on rotation (December for Titles 1–6, March for Titles 7–27, June for Titles 28–41, and September for Titles 42–50).

Both *Federal Register* and *Code of Federal Regulations* are available online from *Lexis-Nexis* and *Westlaw*. *Federal Register* is also marketed through Dialog (File 180) from 1988 forward. The online database features field searching. For instance, in Dialog, the user may limit the search to *CFR* Section affected, agency, and document types, which includes presidential documents, rules and regulations, proposed rules, notices, and Sunshine meetings.

Treaties and Other International Agreements

United States

Treaties, by Article 2, section 2, paragraph 2, of the Constitution, are international agreements concluded with the advice and consent of the Senate. Other international agreements, generally referred to as "executive agreements," are those concluded within the power of the President without the advice and consent of the Senate.[16] For complete texts of treaties and other international agreements to which the United States is a party, the following official publications are indispensable:

> *Treaties and Other International Agreements of the United States of America, 1776–1949.* Comp. under the direction of Charles I. Bevans. Washington, DC: GPO, 1968–1976. 13 vols. (P60)
> *Treaties and Other International Acts Series,* no. 1501– . Washington, DC: GPO, 1945– . (P61)
> *United States Treaties and Other International Agreements,* 1950– . Washington, DC: GPO. Annual. ISSN 00833487. Print & digital. (P62)
> *Treaties in Force: A List of Treaties and Other International Agreements of the United States in Force,* 1929– . Washington, DC: GPO. Annual since 1958. ISSN 00830194. (P63)
> *Current Treaty Index: A Cumulative Index to the United States Slip Treaties and Agreements,* 1982– . Igor I. Kavass and Adolf Sprudzs, comps. Buffalo, NY: Hein. Annual. ISSN 07318189. (P64)
> *A Guide to the United States Treaties in Force.* Igor I. Kavass, ed. Buffalo, NY: Hein, 1998. 3 vols. ISBN 1575883880. (P65)

The earliest significant official compilation of texts of United States treaties and agreements is *Treaties and Other International Acts of the United States of America* edited by Hunter Miller (Washington, DC: GPO, 1931–1948, 8 vols.) (P66) for the period from 1776 to 1949. The Bevans work "is designed to present in a convenient form the English texts or, in cases where non-English text was signed, the official United States Government translations of treaties and other international agreements entered into by the United States from 1776 to 1950" (Preface). It is essentially a collection of texts. Multilateral treaties were published in the first four volumes. Volumes 5 to 12 deal with bilateral treaties arranged by country. Each volume has a brief index. Volume 13 is a general index. A few categories of bilateral agreements are not included, many of which may be found in Miller's work, just mentioned.

Treaties and Other International Acts Series (TIAS), issued singly in pamphlets, continues two separate publications: "Treaty Series" (1908–1946) and "Executive Agreement Series" (1929–1945). Because the combined numbers in these two series has reached 1,500, the two series begin with 1,501. These are slip forms of treaties and other international agreements, similar to slip laws. Items of *TIAS* are cumulated and bound into *United States Treaties and Other International Agreements (UST).*

UST is the official publication of legal evidence of treaties and international agreements to which the United States is a party. Prior to this, treaties and other international agreements were published in the *Statutes at Large.* *UST* is arranged in numerical order as originally published in the slip form.

Other official publications that carry treaties and other international agreements include Senate *Executive Documents*, noted in Chapter 7, and the *U.S. Department of State Dispatch* (formerly *U.S. Department of State Bulletin*), 1939– (Washington, DC: GPO, weekly, ISSN 10517693) (P67), which provides up-to-date information on treaties and other international agreements.

Treaties in Force serves as an index to treaties and other international agreements in force. It refers to *UST, TIAS*, and other documents for the texts. For a detailed index to *TIAS*, refer to *Current Treaty Index*. Each issue consists of a numerical list of documents and three indexes: chronological, country, and subject index.

A Guide to the United States Treaties in Force is intended to complement *Treaties in Force*, providing correlation between the bilateral categories and the multilateral subject headings, numerical and subject lists of bilateral and multilateral agreements in force, and chronological lists of dates in multilateral agreements. There are three parts. Part 1 contains a numerical list of bilateral and multilateral treaties and agreements of the United States in force on January 1, 1997; a numerical list of agreements listed in *Treaties in Force* January 1, 1996, but not listed in *Treaties in Force* January 1, 1997; a numerical list of agreements newly listed in *Treaties in Force* January 1, 1997; a numerical list of agreements entered into force after January 1, 1997; and a numerical list of nonbinding and other unrecorded international agreements.

In Part II are given a country list of bilateral and multilateral treaties and agreements of the United States in force January 1, 1997; a country list of bilateral and multilateral treaties and agreements listed in *Treaties in Force* January 1, 1996, but not listed in *Treaties in Force* January 1, 1997; a country list of bilateral and multilateral treaties and agreements listed in *Treaties in Force* January 1, 1997; a subject list of bilateral and multilateral treaties and agreements of the United States in force January 1, 1997; a subject list of bilateral and multilateral treaties and agreements listed in *Treaties in Force* January 1, 1997; and a subject list of bilateral and multilateral treaties and agreements newly listed in *Treaties in Force* January 1, 1997. Part III consists of a chronological index to United States multilateral agreements in force on January 1, 1997, a directory of multilateral treaties by countries and international organizations, and United States multilateral treaties and agreements in force on January 1, 1997.

International

Compilations of international treaties concluded from A.D. 1648 to the present are:

> *The Consolidated Treaty Series*. Clive Parry, ed. and comp. Dobbs Ferry, NY: Oceana, 1969–1981. 231 vols. ISBN 0379130004. (P68)

League of Nations Treaties Series: Publications of Treaties and International Engagements Registered with the Secretariat of the League, v. 1, 1920–v. 105, 1946. Geneva: League of Nations. Print & digital. (P69)

The Multilateral Project. Medford, MA: Fletcher School of Law and Diplomacy, Tufts University. http://www.tufts.edu/fletcher/multilaterals.html (P70)

United Nations Treaties Series: Treaties and International Agreements Registered or Filed and Recorded with the Secretariat of the United Nations. New York: United Nations, 1946– . Print & digital. (P71)

The Consolidated Treaty Series reproduces treaties concluded between 1648 and 1919. Volumes 227 to 231 are appendixes listing Dutch colonial agreements from 1648 to 1799 as supplements to the main series. The series is indexed in three parts by *Index-Guide to Treaties: Based on the Consolidated Treaty Series* . . . Dobbs Ferry, NY: Oceana, 1979–1986, ISBN 0379130017) (P72): (1) *Index-Guide to Treaties: General Chronological List,* Paul Irwin, comp. (vol. 1) and Brian H. W. Hill, comp. (vols. 2–5), 1979–1985 (5 vols.); (2) *Index-Guide to Treaties: Special Chronological List, 1648–1920,* Michael A. Meyer, comp., 1984, 2 vols., an index to (a) colonial and like treaties and (b) postal, telegraphic, and similar agreements; and (3) *Index-Guide: Party Index* (Brian H. W. Hill, comp., 1986, 5 vols.), arranged by country from Afghanistan to Zanzibar.

The *League of Nations Treaties Series,* published as a supplement to the *Official Journal of the League of Nations,* lists over 4,800 documents. There are nine cumulative volumes of indexes. It is continued by the *United Nations Treaty Series.* Over 1,200 volumes of the *United Nations Treaty Series* have been published. Each volume consists of two parts: (1) treaties and international agreements registered with the Secretariat, and (2) treaties and international agreements filed and recorded by the Secretariat. The time lag of publication is about six years.

There is a *Cumulative Index,* no. 1– , 1956– (P73) published irregularly. The 1988 *Treaties Series Cumulative Index* (no. 22) covers treaties and international agreements contained in volumes 1,252 to 1,300 of the *United Nations Treaties Series* (UNTS). There are two sections: section 1, Chronological Index in the order of the dates on which they were adopted, signed or opened for signature or accession, and so on. Section 2 is an Alphabetical Index by party and by subject. *United Nations Treaty Series* can be accessed on the Internet as *The United Nations Treaty Collection* (http://www.un.org/Depts/Treaty) (P74).

All multilateral treaties can be accessed through *The Multilateral Project* at the Fletcher School of Law and Diplomacy. The Multilateral Project, begun in 1992, is a full-text database of international multilateral conventions and other instruments. The file is organized by eleven subject areas: atmosphere and space, flora and fauna—biodiversity, cultural protection, diplomatic relations, general, human rights, marine and coastal, other environmental, trade and commercial relations, rules of warfare, arms control, and gulf area borders.

Court Decisions

The United States Reports, v. 1– , 1754– . Washington, DC: GPO. (P75)

There are three forms of Supreme Court decisions. The first official text, issued as a pamphlet with separate pagination shortly after the decision date, is the slip decision or slip opinion (P76). The slip decisions are cumulated together as the Preliminary Print, or Advance Sheet, in cumulative page number. At the end of each term, the Preliminary Prints are published in a bound volume as The United States Report.

Two commercial Supreme Court reports with substantial annotations may be mentioned: The Supreme Court Reporter, v. 1– , 1882– (St. Paul, MN: West Group) (P77), which incorporates West's Key Number Digest System and is one of the units of the National Reporter System. United States Supreme Court Reports Lawyers' Edition, 1790–1955, 2nd Ser., 1956– (Rochester, NY: Lawyers Co-operative/Bancroft-Whitney) (P78) with complete headnotes, summaries of decisions, statements of cases, points and authorities of counsel, annotations, tables, and parallel references. The latter features briefs of counsel in a separate section in the bound volume. It is supplemented by Advance Reports (P79), published twice monthly while the Supreme Court is in session. Full texts of opinions of the Supreme Court the day after they are announced are published in The United States Law Week, 1935– (Washington, DC: Bureau of National Affairs, looseleaf, ISSN 01488139, print & digital) (P80).

The United States Law Week consists of two parts: General Law Sections and Supreme Court Sections. The first part contains two regular sections and a Statute Section, which is issued only when laws of general interest or importance are passed by Congress. The two regular sections are: (1) Summary and analysis of current legal development and (2) new court decisions, federal agency rulings, and special articles on nondecisional matters of interest to the legal profession. The second part also contains two sections, 3 and 4: (3) Journal of proceedings of the Supreme Court, summary of orders of the court, cases docketed and summary of cases recently filed, calendar or hearings scheduled and special articles on the Supreme Court's work, and (4) Opinions of the Supreme Court. Section 4 presents Supreme Court decisions in full text with digest-headnotes.

Its popular Supreme Court proceedings is updated daily electronically as U.S. Law Week's Supreme Court Today (P81). The Law Week's companion is United States Law Week Summary and Analysis, 1933– (weekly, ISSN 01905252) (P82) providing a summary of recent legal development.

U.S. Law Week is available online through *Lexis-Nexis* and *Westlaw* and on the Web (http://subscript.nba.com).

The Supreme Court Bulletin publishes court decisions, appended by index to opinions, index to docket case table, dockets, and statutes tables. But the two online systems, LEXIS and Westlaw, provide the most current, up-to-date court decisions.

It may be noted that the *Legal Information Institute (LII)*, mentioned earlier, has an extensive coverage of court decisions. Its court opinions topic consists of decisions of the U.S. Supreme Court, other federal courts, the New York Court of Appeals, and other state courts. The Supreme Court decisions are offered under the auspices of Project Hermes. Decisions are listed from 1990 to the present, but *LII*'s collection of historical, most important decisions of the U.S. Supreme Court covers the whole period of the Court existence. Court decisions can be searched by party name, topic, or opinion author. The collection is also available on CD-ROM. In addition, *LII* offers current awareness service, sending synopses of the Court's decisions via e-mail. Court decisions of the International Court of Justice since 1996 in full text can be accessed. *LII*'s International Court of Justice file includes all decisions, the Statutes of the International Court of Justice, the Charter of the United Nations, information about the ICJ (Court, Judges, Annual Report, Gallery of Images, and UN News), and research resources (German ICJ Research Guide and International Law Web Sites).

Lower federal court decisions and state court decisions are reported in the National Reporter System of the West Group. The System includes seven regional units and federal and state units listed later. These units are published either weekly or semiweekly, with annual bound volumes.

Atlantic Reporter, 1886–1938; 2nd series, 1938– . Weekly. ISSN 87502637. Print & digital. (P83)

North Western Reporter, 1879–1942; 2nd series, 1942– . Weekly. ISSN 87502704. Print & digital. (P84)

North Eastern Reporter, 1885–1936; 2nd series, 1936– . Weekly. Print & digital. ISSN 0275262X. (P85)

Pacific Reporter, 1883–1931; 2nd series, 1931– . Weekly. ISSN 87502666. Print & digital. (P86)

South Eastern Reporter, 1887–1939; 2nd series, 1939– . Weekly. ISSN 05844215. Print & digital. (P87)

South Western Reporter, 1886–1928; 2nd series, 1928– . Weekly. ISSN 67502682. Print & digital. (P88)

Southern Reporter, 1887–1941; 2nd series, 1941– . Weekly. ISSN 87502690. Print & digital. (P89)

Supreme Court Reporter, 1882– . Semiweekly and interim edition. ISSN 07333978. Print & digital. (P90)

Federal Reporter, 1880–1924; 2nd series, 1924– . Weekly. Print & digital. (P91)

Federal Supplement, 1932– . Weekly. Print & digital. (P92)
Federal Rules Decisions, 1941– . Weekly. Print & digital. (P93)
Military Justice Reporter, 1975/76– . Weekly. ISSN 01477315. Print & digital. (P94)
California Reporter, 1960– . Weekly. ISSN 87502623. Print & digital. (P95)
New York Supplement, 1932/33– . Weekly. Print & digital. ISSN 8750264X. (P96)

Each unit of regional reporter consists of several states and includes in full all state appellate court decisions. The *Federal Reporter, Federal Supplement*, and *Federal Rules Decisions* cover lower federal court decisions. Court decisions of California and New York are too numerous for inclusion in the regional reporters; only the highest court decisions are printed therein. Other court decisions are included in the *California Reporter* and *New York Supplement*.

The National Reporter System can be accessed online through Westlaw. Another reporting service consists of the *American Law* (1st series, 2nd series, 3rd series, and 4th series–) *Reports, ALR 3d, Cases and Annotations*, 1945– (P97), and *American Law Reports, ALR Federal, Cases and Annotations*, 1969– (P98), both published by Lawyers Co-operative/Bancraft-Whitney. They annotate lower federal court decisions and state court decisions.

Digests

A court decision digest is a summary of facts and points of law decided by the court. West Group has published digests in two kinds: (1) The *American Digest* (P99) includes all reported cases of the nation from both the federal and state levels in the following units: *Century Digest*, 1658–1896 (P100); *Decennial Digest* (P101) (1st–8th, 1897–1976, and 9th in two parts: part 1, 1976–1981, and Part 2, 1981–1986, 10th, 1986–1991); and *General Digest*, 1986– (8th series, 1991–1996, 9th series, 1996–) (P102); (2) Digests for certain courts. They are published in five units: *United States Supreme Court Digest*, 1754– (P103); *Federal Digest*, 1754– (P104); *Modern Federal Practice Digest*, 1960–1975 (P105); *West's Federal Practice Digest*, 2nd, 1976– (P106); and *United States Court of Claims Digest*, 1855– (P107). The *Federal Digest, Modern Federal Practice Digest*, and *Federal Practice Digest* cover the decisions of all federal courts including the United States Supreme Court. The other digest system is the Lawyers Co-operative's *American Law Reports* and *ALR Federal*, both noted earlier, and *Digest of United States Supreme Court Reports*, 1948– (22 vols. in many parts, with cumulative pocket supplements) (P108). Volume 15 in four parts is a Table of Cases. Volumes 16 in five parts contains the Constitution and Court Rules.

Encyclopedias

General

The titles listed here are two dinosaurs in the encyclopedia world:

American Jurisprudence: A Modern Comprehensive Text Statement of American Law, State and Federal. 2nd ed. Rochester, NY: Lawyers Co-operative, 1962–1976. 82 vols in 88. Updated by pocket parts and replacement volumes. Print & digital. (P109)

Corpus Juris Secundum: A Contemporary Statement of American Law as Derived from Reported Cases and Legislation. St. Paul, MN: West Group, 1936–1974. 101 vols. in 136. Updated by pocket parts and replacement volumes. Print & digital. (P110)

West's Encyclopedia of American Law. Minneapolis, MN: West Group, 1996– . ISBN 0314201548. (P111)

In contrast to other encyclopedias in the social sciences, the two legal encyclopedias are statements of the law. *American Jurisprudence (AJ) 2nd* emphasizes statutory law, whereas *Corpus Juris Secundum (CJS)* is primarily based on reported cases. Both are arranged by broad topics, but definitions of words and phrases are interfiled alphabetically with topics and both are updated continuously. *AJ 2nd* is a comprehensive text statement of American federal and state laws. It has six volumes of General Index (1998) and one volume of Table of Statutes, Rules, and Regulations Cited (1999 edition, 1998) that includes a Popular Names Table.

CJS is included in the West Key Number system, which makes *CJS* compatible with all other key number publications and features a summary at the head of each section stating the prevailing rules, full history of each case, and footnotes giving both reporter and state report citations. It has three volumes of General Index (1998) and one volume of 1999 Table of Statutes, Rules, and Regulations Cited showing where various statutes, rules, and regulations are cited throughout *Corpus Juris Secundum.*

The *West's Encyclopedia* replaces the earlier set, *Guide to American Law: Everyone's Legal Encyclopedia* (St. Paul, MN: West, 1983–1985, 12 vols. ISBN 0314732241; latest Supplement, 1995) (P112). It contains over 4,000 entries of terms, concepts, events, movements, cases, and persons significant to U.S. law. Each entry of legal term provides a definition, followed by explanatory text if necessary. Entries are documented with cross-references and some with illustrations. Eleven volumes have been published. Each volumes has abbreviations and a bibliography at the end, and some volumes have a special section, Milestones in the Law. The section provides opinions of the lower courts, the briefs presented by the parties to the U.S. Supreme Court, and the decisions of the Supreme Court. At the end of each volume, Abbreviations, and Bibliography Volume 11, Appendix, published in 1988 includes documents, laws, and manuscripts, such as the Magna Charta of the English law, Stamp Act, Treaty of Paris, women's rights, Presidential speeches, legal scholarships, and so on.

Subfield

> *Encyclopedia of the American Constitution.* Leonard W. Levy, ed. New York: Macmillan, 1986. 4 vols. ISBN 0029186102. Print & digital. (P113)
>
> *Encyclopedia of the American Constitution. Supplement I.* Leonard W. Levy, Kenneth L. Karst, John G. West, Jr., eds. New York: Macmillan, 1992. 668 p. ISBN 0029186781. Print & digital. (P114)
>
> *Encyclopedia of Crime and Justice.* Sanford H. Kadish, ed. New York: Free Press/Macmillan, 1983. 4 vols. ISBN 0029181100. (P115)

Encyclopedia of the American Constitution contains 2,100 articles arranged in an alphabetical order. The articles, contributed by 262 authors, are signed, and most are appended with a short bibliography. "The subjects fall into five general categories: doctrinal concepts of constitutional law (about fifty-five percent of the total words); people (about fifteen percent); political decisions, mostly of the Supreme Court of the United States (about fifteen percent); public acts, such as statutes, treaties, and executive orders (about five percent); and historical periods (about ten percent) . . . the articles vary in treatments of major subjects of constitutional doctrine, which may be as long as 6,000 words, and articles on periods of constitutional history, which may be even longer" (Preface). The seven appendixes include the birth of the Constitution and important events in the development of American constitutional law. Also included are a glossary and three indexes: case, name, and subject. The Supplement updates the main encyclopedia, including over 300 articles. The main work and its supplement are available on CD-ROM, produced in 1996.

English law is extensively treated with some reference to European and other legal systems in *Encyclopedia of Crime and Justice.* The length of articles varies from 1,000 to 10,000 words, arranged in alphabetical order by topics from "abortion" to "youth gangs and groups." Articles are signed and appended with a bibliography. It has a glossary and two indexes: legal and general.

Dictionaries

Dictionaries range from less than 200 pages to the mammoth, *Words and Phrases*, listed later.

General

Black's Law Dictionary. Rev. 6th ed. St. Paul, MN: West Publishing, 1990.
    1,657 p. ISBN 031476271X. (P116)
Law Dictionary. 4th ed. Steven H. Gijis. Hauppauge, NY: Barron's, 1996.
    643 p. ISBN 0812030966. (P117)

Black's Law Dictionary is perhaps the most widely used law dictionary,
containing "definitions of the terms and phrases of American and English
jurisprudence, ancient and modern" (title page), by the late Henry Campbell Black (1860–1927). The new and revised words and terms were prepared by Joseph R. Nolan and Jacqueline M. Nolan-Haley. It features
citations appended to definitions and some entries with pronunciation.

Law Dictionary contains more than 3,000 legal terms documented with
citations. Pronunciation for some terms and phrases are supplied. There
are five appendixes: The Constitution of the United States, ABA Model
Rules of Professional Conduct (1983), Federal Judicial Circuits, Federal
Judicial System, and U.S. Supreme Court Justices, 1789–1996.

Subfield

United States

The Constitutional Law Dictionary. Ralph C. Chandler, Richard A. Ensten,
    and Peter G. Renstrom. Denver, CO: ABC-Clio, 1985– . (P118)
Words and Phrases. Permanent edition. St. Paul, MN: West Group,
    1940– . Updated by pocket parts and replacement volumes. (P119)

A part of ABC-Clio's Dictionaries in Political Science Series, The Constitutional Law Dictionary focuses on concepts of constitutionalism and
terms common to American constitutional law and Supreme Court decisions. It features long definitions and a paragraph of "significance" on each
term's historical and current relevance. Volume 1 consists of eight chapters
dealing with constitutionalism, First to Eighth Amendments, equal protection and privacy, and words and phrases. Some 120 terms are defined. The
Constitutional Law Dictionary Supplement covers the 1983–1984, 1984–
1985, and 1985–1986 terms of the Supreme Court. Volume 2 deals with
constitutionalism, judicial power, executive power, legislative power, federalism, the commerce power, the federal taxing and spending power, state
economic regulations and due process, the cabinet clause, leading Supreme
Court justices, and legal words and phrases. Over 140 terms are defined.
The chapter on constitutionalism appears to be reproduced from volume
1. Some 40 terms of the chapter are listed in both volumes.

Words and Phrases is a unique dictionary. Definitions of words and phrases contained therein are based on judicial constructions. They are the exact languages of the federal and state courts from the earliest times.

International

> *Parry and Grant Encyclopedic Dictionary of International Law.* John P. Grant, Anthony Parry, and Arthur D. Watts. New York: Oceana, 1986. 564 p. ISBN 0379208288. (P120)
> *Dictionary of International Law and Comparative Law.* James R. Fox. Dobbs Ferry, New York: Oceana, 1992. 495 p. ISBN 0379204304. (P121)

Parry and Grant is a dictionary of concepts, doctrines, principles, cases, and jurists, arranged in alphabetical order. Its emphasis is on contemporary coverage. Entries are cross-referenced and provided with sources. Appendixes include seven documents, such as the Charter of the United Nations, Vienna Convention of the Law of Treaties, and Universal Declaration on Human Rights.

Dictionary of International Law and Comparative Law is an outgrowth of answers to questions about international law at the Dickinson School of Law. In addition to words and phrases, it features defining agencies, organizations, events, cases, and documents. Most of the definitions are documented, but its coverage of comparative law is quite limited.

Directories

> *Legal dot Net.* Newport Beach, CA: Internet Exchange International. http://www.legal.net (P122)
> *Law and Legal Information Directory*, 1980– . Jacqueline Wasserman O'Brien and Steven R. Wasserman. Detroit: Gale Research. Biennial. ISSN 0740090X. (P123)
> *Martindale-Hubbell Law Directory*, 1931– . New Providence, NJ: Martindale-Hubbell. Annual. ISSN 01910221. Print & digital. (P124)

For a listing of attorneys, reference may be made to *Legal dot Net*. Its Directory of Legal Services is for advertisements, paid to be listed. Its Attorney Registry is free, arranged by area of practice and by state. There are over 40 practices in alphabetical order, from appellate, aviation law to workers' compensation and wrongful termination. By state, place names are also arranged in alphabetic order. Place names include the 50 states of the United States, the District of Columbia, U. S. territories, and foreign countries and places. For each entry of attorney under place names are given name, address, e-mail, phone, fax, year admitted, state admitted, area of practice, and note. But the listing is far from complete. *Legal dot Net* also provides links grouped into Attorneys and Law Related Businesses, Computer Tech and Related Businesses, General News Sites, Government Information Sites, International Law Sites, Law Schools, Legal Reference Sites, Libraries, and Other Sites of Interest.

Law and Legal Information Directory may be considered as a directory of directories. Its eighth edition (Steven Wasserman, Jacqueline Wasserman o'Brien, and Bonnie Shaw Pfaff, eds., 1995, 2 vols., ISBN 081038809X) contains "more than 33,000 National and International Organizations, Bar Associations, Bar Examination and Admission to Legal Practice Requirements, the Federal Court System, Highest State Courts, Federal Regulatory Agencies, Law Schools, Continuing Legal Education, Paralegal Education, Scholarships and Grants, Awards and Prizes, Special Libraries, Information Systems and Services, Research Centers, Legal Periodicals, Book and Media Publishers, State Lawyer Disciplinary Agencies, Lawyer Referral Services, Legal Aid Offices, Public Defender Officers, Legislative Manuals and Registers, Small Claims Courts, Corporation Departments of States and Provinces, Law Enforcement Agencies, Bill Status of State Legislation, and State Agencies" (subtitle). Materials are organized into 40 chapters. Each entry contains name of organization, phone number, fax number, address, chief official and title, and description of the organization's activities.

A most comprehensive directory in the legal profession is *Martindale-Hubbell Law Directory*, formerly *Martindale's American Law Directory* and *Hubbell's Legal Directory*. Its 129th edition (1997, 19 vols., ISBN 1561602221) comprises Practice Profiles Bar Roster; Patent and Trademark Practice Profiles Section; Professional Biographies Section; and Services, Supplies, Consultants Section. Some 900,000 lawyers and law firms worldwide are included. The additional two index volumes contain (1) alphabetical index and Services, Supplies, Consultants National Alphabetical Index and (2) Areas of Practice Index, Administrative Law–Zoning Law. One of its features is ratings, such as general recommendation rating and the firm rating, based upon confidential recommendations from lawyers and judges.

Published as parts of the *Directory* are *Martindale-Hubbell Law Digest* (2 vols., ISBN 1561602507) (P125), concise digests of laws of 50 states and the District of Columbia; *Martindale-Hubbell International Law Digest* (1 vol., ISBN 1561602507) (P126), concise digests of laws of 70 countries; and *Martindale-Hubbell International Law Directory* (3 vols., ISBN 156160223X) (P127). The *International Law Directory* consists of a Directory of Law Firms, Alliances, Networks, Clubs, Associations and Other Affiliations; a Professional Biographies Section; and a detailed index. Some 100,000 lawyers and 8,000 law firms in 150 countries are included.

The *Martindale-Hubbell Law Directory* is now published in four formats: print, CD-ROM, online via *Lexis-Nexis,* noted earlier, and on the Internet (http://www.martindale.com). The *Digest* can be accessed through *Lexis-Nexis.*

Biographies

The *Martindale-Hubbell Law Directory* serves as both a directory and a biography. Other biographies include:

> *The American Bar—The Canadian Bar—The Mexican Bar—The International Bar: The Professional Directory of Lawyers of the World,* 1919– . Sacramento, CA: Forster-Long. Annual. (P128)
> *The American Bench: Judges of the Nation,* 1977– . Sacramento, CA: Forster. Biennial. ISSN 01602578. (P129)
> *Almanac of the Federal Judiciary,* 1984– . New York: Aspen Law and Business. Looseleaf. Semiannual supplements. (P130)
> *The First One Hundred Justices: Statistical Studies on the Supreme Court.* Albert P. Blaustein and Roy M. Mersky. Hamden, CT: Archon Books, 1978. 210 p. ISBN 0208012907. (P131)
> *Who's Who in American Law,* lst ed.– , 1977– . New Providence, NJ: Marquis Who's Who. Biennial. ISSN 01627880. Print & digital. (P132)

The eightieth edition of *The American Bar* (titles vary) 1998, 2 vols., ISBN 093139838X) is an international directory of lawyers. "Volume 1 contains the Individual Attorney Index and the Firm Name and Location Index as well as the law firm listings for Alabama-Massachusetts. Volume 2 contains law firm listings for Michigan-Wyoming, Canada, Mexico and international, and Patent and Trademark Agents Outside the United States and Canada" (Explanatory Foreword). A condensed version is *The American Bar Reference Handbook, Including the Canadian Bar, the Mexican Bar, the International Bar* (1998, 1,205 p.) (P133). The two-volume set does not contain organizational and biographical data.

The American Bench lists biographical sketches of judges of the nation. Its ninth edition (1997/98, 1998, 2,575 p., ISBN 0931398371) provides profiles of "over 18,000 judges from all levels of federal and state courts with jurisdictional, structural and geographical information on the courts they serve. . . . All information received as of May 15, 1997 has been incorporated" (Foreword). It contains 52 sections, one section for the United States Court and one for each of the 50 states and the district of Columbia. Each section is divided into three parts: Court Outline, Maps, and Biographies. One useful feature is its descriptive information on each court in the state including court location, jurisdiction, and method of selecting judges. At the end is a glossary.

Almanac of the Federal Judiciary has similar coverage. It consists of two volumes: Volume 1, profiles and evaluations of all judges of the U.S. District courts, and Volume 2, profiles and evaluations of all judges of the U.S. Circuit Courts and the U.S. Supreme Court. Each profile, if complete, includes noteworthy rulings, lawyers' evaluation, and the judges' special guidelines.

The First One Hundred Justices is an interesting study of justices from John Jay to William Hubbs Rehnquist. It consists of five chapters: (1) a biography of the Supreme Court: the first 100; (2) rating the justices: the best and the worst; (3) selection of capable justices: factors to consider; (4) nominated but did not serve; and (5) counting the opinion: the first 34,000 decisions. The appendix has eleven tables giving in tabular form statistical data on the members of the Supreme Court, occupants of Supreme Court seats, judges of the judges, prior judicial experience, the multiple nominees, opinions by justices, and average number of opinions per justice per term. The "Selected Bibliography" (pp. 155–203) lists over 700 items of bibliographies, biographies, articles, and monographs on the Supreme Court, and other publications dealing with analysis of Supreme Court decisions or pending cases.

Compared with *The American Bar, The American Bench,* and *Almanac of the Federal Judiciary, Who's Who in American Law* has much less coverage, but it includes educators and law librarians. Biographical sketches are arranged in alphabetical order in the familiar style of *Who's Who in America.* The 1996–1997 *Who's Who in American Law* (9th ed., 1997, 977 p., ISBN 0837935113) provides 22,000 biographical entries. Its index to fields of practice and interest is a useful reference. It is available on CD-ROM and online as part of *Marquis Who's Who,* marketed through Dialog (File 234), noted in Chapter 4.

Handbooks, Yearbooks, and the Like

> *Federal Judiciary Almanac.* 3rd ed. W. Stuart Dornette and Robert R. Cross. New York: John Wiley, 1987. 1,116 p. ISBN 0471615485. (P134)
>
> *The Lawyer's Almanac.* 18th ed. New York: Aspen Law and Business, 1998. Pagination varies. ISSN 02779544. (P135)
>
> *The Supreme Court Compendium: Data, Decisions, and Developments.* Lee Epstein and others. Washington, DC: Congressional Quarterly, 1994. 741 p. ISBN 0871877716. (P136)

Federal Judiciary Almanac contains four parts: Part 1, Supreme Court of the United States; Part 2, Federal Circuit Courts of Appeal; Part 3, Federal District Courts; and Part 4, Special Courts. There are over 70 chapters; each chapter deals with a particular court. For each chapter are given in general four sections: (1) directory information, (2) statistical data, (3) biographies of all judges, and (4) a listing of other court officials.

The Lawyer's Almanac contains five main sections: (1) The Legal Profession, including 700 largest firms with information on partnership tracks, salaries, billing rates and the compensation of corporate counsel, over 100 top Internet legal research sites, members of the Association of American Law Schools and officers of the American Bar Association, its sections and divisions, and information for state bar associations; (2) The Judiciary, including federal and state benches; (3) Government Departments and Agencies; (4) Statutory Summaries and Checklists; and (5) Commonly Used Abbreviations. The new edition also includes complete text of the mandatory continuing legal education (MCLE) requirements for the 38 state jurisdictions.

The Supreme Court Compendium provides data on the Supreme Court, justices, the environments in which the Court operates, and case decisions and impacts. There are ten chapters. Except for the last chapter, which deals with other courts in the judicial system, the nine chapters on the Supreme Court may be grouped into three areas: the Supreme Court as an institution, the individual justices, and the Supreme Court and its impact on the political process. Each chapter has an introduction that explains data choices, the scope of data, and details on the tables. With a few exceptions, all data are presented in tabular format. Hundreds of topics are covered in the 166 tables and five figures.

For the Supreme Court as an institution, readers may locate in the *Compendium* a chronology of important events, key Congressional legislation, reporting systems, budget, salaries, employees, administrative officers, caseload, number of petitions granted review, landmark decisions, and more. On individual justices, biographical information is provided on birth and childhood, family background, education, marriage, experience, confirmation, rating and rank, and voting behavior. Data on the political process and impact of the Supreme Court include such information as success rate of the Solicitor General as an amicus curiae, success rates of federal agencies as a party to a case and public opinions on the Supreme Court decisions. The book ends with the U.S. Constitution, selected readings, and an index.

NOTES

1. Robert K. Carr, *The Supreme Court and Judicial Review* (Westport, CT: Greenwood Press, 1942), pp. 17–19.

2. Ibid., 23.

3. Kay L. Audrus, "Citizen Access to Legal Information," *Library Journal* 112, no. 11 (1987): 39.

4. Fred R. Shapiro, comp., *The Most-Cited Law Review Articles* (Buffalo, NY: Hein, 1987), pp. 12–14.

5. David F. Cavers, "Book Reviews in Law Reviews: An Endangered Species," *Michigan Law Review* 77 (1979): 328–329.

6. Fred R. Shapiro, "KeyCite and Shepard's—Coverage and Currency of Citations to Recent Cases: A Comparative Study." *Legal Information Alert* 17, no. 4 (1998): 1–3; Elizabeth M. McKenzie, "New Kid on the Block: KeyCite Compared to Shepard's," *AALL Spectrum* (October 1998): 8–9, 29.

7. 1 *U.S.C.* 112.

8. *Black's Law Dictionary*. See also brief discussion of public and private laws, Laurence F. Schmeckebier and Roy B. Eastin, *Government Publications and Their Use*, 2nd rev. ed. (Washington, DC: The Brookings Institution, 1969), pp. 206–208.

9. For different kinds of resolutions, see Chapter 8.

10. For discussion of proclamations and executive orders, see Schmeckebier and Eastin, *Government Publications*, pp. 340–345.

11. 44 *U.S.C.* 1505.

12. 1 *C.F.R.* 5.1 and 5.3.

13. 44 *U.S.C.* 1501; 1 *C.F.R.* 1.1.

14. Ibid.

15. 1 *C.F.R.* 5.9.

16. For categories of other international agreements that can be made by the President, see *Digest of International Law* 14 (1970): 227.

Chapter 15

Political Science

Political science emerged as an independent academic discipline in the nineteenth century. There is no consensus on the use of the words "political" and "science" in this connection. Some feel that the term "science" should not be used at all.[1] However, it is generally considered that "science" is not used here rigidly, to mean knowledge acquired and verified by observation, measurement, and logical deduction, but rather denotes in a broader sense the systematic search for knowledge relative to a determined subject, with or without adequate verification.[2]

Political science, the study of politics, is concerned with the organization of human beings into the state. The study of politics may focus on power, institutions, policy process, functions, ideologies and movements, international relations, or political behavior.[3] At an international conference of political scientists held at UNESCO House in September 1948, it was generally considered that political science is concerned with four major areas, which are political theory; government; political parties, groups, and public opinion; and international relations.[4] In the United States, the subjects of public law and public administration are added to the discipline of political science.

According to Charles Merriam, important subdivisions of political science in the United States are (1) political theory, which deals with the broad problems of systematic politics, including the ends, types, and trends of government; (2) political institutions, which study the government by branch, by area, or by function; (3) public law, which deals with legal powers and duties of public agencies; (4) public administration, which studies the processes and practices of administration; (5) political parties and public opinion, which deal with political processes and behavior; and (6) international relations, which study technical problems of international law, diplomacy, and world government.[5]

ACCESS TO SOURCES

Guides

Political science surpasses most other disciplines of the social sciences in the quantity of its guides, perhaps because political science has a wide appeal. By coincidence, two guides of enduring value appeared in the 1930s:

> *Student's Guide to Materials in Political Science.* Laverne Burchfield. New York: Holt, 1935. 426 p. (Q1)
>
> *Guide to the Diplomatic History of the United States, 1775–1921.* Samuel Flagg Bemise and Grace Gardner Griffin. Washington, DC: GPO, 1935. 979 p. Reprint ed., Gloucester, MA: Peter Smith, 1959. (Q2)

The two guides are modern classics. Burchfield, prepared under the direction of the Sub-Committee on Research of the Committee of Policy of the American Political Science Association, is a partially annotated guide to significant works in political science and its allied fields arranged in topics with an outline and a general statement for each topic and to sources of information, which includes bibliographies, newspapers, serials, dissertations, and directories.

The Bemise and Griffin guide, like Burchfield, covers both literature and sources of information. It consists of two parts: (1) bibliographical chapters, topically and chronologically arranged, and (2) remarks on the sources, containing an analysis of printed state papers and manuscript and archival sources. The closing date for the bibliographical chapters is 1921 because "that year, the U.S. concluded a peace treaty with Germany and Austria-Hungary, and in which assembled the Washington Conference, marks the end of a period in American as well as Enriopean diplomatic history, and in 1933 appeared . . . *Foreign Affairs Bibliography* covering the period 1919–1932" (Preface). Although it does not have a subject index, there are a detailed scheme of classification and many cross-references.

For over 30 years, Burchfield and Bemise and Griffin remained the only comprehensive guides in political science, until other guides began to appear in the 1960s. The following are guides worth noting:

> *Guide to American Foreign Relations since 1700.* Richard Dean Burns, ed. Santa Barbara, CA: ABC-Clio, 1983. 1,311 p. ISBN 0874363233. (Q3)
>
> *Information Sources in Politics and Political Science: A Survey Worldwide.*

Dermot Englefield and Garvin Drewry, eds. London: Butterworths, 1984. 509 p. ISBN 0408114703. (Q4)

The Information Sources of Political Science. 4th ed. Frederich Holler. Santa Barbara, CA: ABC-Clio, 1986. 417 p. ISBN 0874363756. (Q5)

Political Science: A Guide to Reference and Information Sources. Henry E. York. Englewood, CO: Libraries Unlimited, 1990. 249 p. ISBN 0872877949. (Q6)

The *Guide to American Foreign Relations since 1700* is intended to expand the Bemise and Griffin book. It annotates monographs, essays, periodical articles, and documents classified in 40 categories, with author and subject indexes. Appendixes include (1) makers of American foreign policy and (2) bibliographical sketches of secretaries of state, 1781–1982. The guide has a much broader coverage than the Bemise and Griffin book, which focuses on legal and political relations between and among sovereign nations.

A good review of literature is the Englefield and Drewry book, a collection of 24 essays grouped into four parts: (1) resources dealing with bibliographical aids to the study of politics; (2) approaches to the study of politics and government, dealing with theory, concept, and methodology; (3) politics and government: United Kingdom in six chapters on textbooks, party politics, parliament and ministers, public administration, judiciary, and local government; and (4) politics and government overseas, comprising chapters on the United States; Central and Southern America; Australia, Canada, New Zealand, and South Africa; Western Europe; the European Community; Eastern Europe; East Asia; South Asia; Sub-Saharan Africa; the Middle East and North Africa; and international organizations. Although emphasis is placed on British publications, it is a fine piece of work for significant literature and for reference sources in the field. There is a subject index. A title/name index would enhance its usefulness.

The Information Sources of Political Science consists of three parts. Part 1, The Political Reference Theory, "advances an alternative, unique conception of political inquiry" (Preface). Part 2, the heart of the book, consists of seven chapters: (1) general reference sources; (2) social sciences; (3) American government, politics, and public law; (4) international relations and organizations; (5) comparative and area studies of politics and government; (6) political theory; and (7) public administration. This part lists 2,423 entries of reference sources, an increase of 38 percent over its previous edition. Part 3, The Indexes, provides four access points—author, title, subject, and topology.

York contains over 800 annotated titles with an author/title index and a subject index. Titles are organized into six chapters: General Social Science Reference Sources, Social Science Disciplines, Political Science—General Reference Sources (Economics, Education, History, Psychology, and

Sociology and Related Fields), Political Science—Geographic Fields (International, Africa, Americas, Asia and the Middle East, Britain, Europe, and United States), Political Science-Topical Fields, and Public Policy. The section on the United States is further divided into General, Presidency, Congress, and State and Local Government, but no judiciary. Some titles on judiciary are listed under the sub-section General. It has good coverage of area studies.

Bibliographies

General

> *International Bibliography of Political Science. Bibliographie Internationale des Sciences Sociales*, 1962– . London: Routledge, 1954– . Annual. ISSN 00852058. Print & digital. (Q7)

International Bibliography of Political Science is one of the four parts of *International Bibliography of the Social Sciences*, mentioned in Chapter 3.

Subfield

> *American Presidency: A Bibliography*. Fenton S. Martin and Robert U. Goehlert. Washington, DC: Congressional Quarterly, 1987. 506 p. ISBN 0871874156. (Q8)
>
> *American Presidents: A Bibliography*. Fenton S. Martin and Robert U. Goehlert. Washington, DC: Congressional Quarterly, 1987. 756 p. ISBN 0871874164. (Q9)
>
> *The United States Congress: A Bibliography*. Robert U. Goehlert and John R. Sayre. New York: Free Press, 1982. 376 p. ISBN 0029119006. (Q10)
>
> *The Supreme Court and the American Republic: An Annotated Bibliography*. D. Grier Stephenson, Jr. New York: Garland, 1981. 281 p. ISBN 0824093569. (Q11)
>
> *Current World Affairs: A Quarterly Bibliography*, 1975– . Alexandria, VA: George A. Daoust. ISSN 10504850. (Q12)
>
> *Foreign Affairs Bibliography: A Selected and Annotated List of Books on International Affairs*. New York: Bowker for the Council on Foreign Relations, 1933– . Publisher varies. (Q13)

The first four bibliographies deal with the three branches of the U.S. government. *American Presidency* and *American Presidents*, compiled with the same format, cover the presidency as an institution and presidents respectively. The former contains over 8,500 entries classified into thirteen chapters on such topics as perspectives on the presidency, the presidency and the law, the organization of the presidency, the selection of presidents, and extrapresidential topics (first ladies, families, cartoons, health, and so on). The latter contains over 13,000 entries from Washington to Reagan. Both bibliographies have author and subject indexes.

The United States Congress focuses on the history, development, and legislative process of Congress. It is an unannotated listing of more than 5,600 entries of books, articles, dissertations, theses, research notes, and some government documents, classified into fourteen topics, such as history and development, congressional processes, reform of Congress, powers of Congress, congressional investigations, foreign affairs, committees, legislative analysis, legislative case studies, leadership in Congress, pressures on Congress, Congress and the electorate, congressmen, and support and housing of Congress. There are an author index and a subject index.

Some 1,300 entries of books, journal articles, and court decisions are contained in *The Supreme Court and the American Republic*. It consists of six sections: research aids, general works, origins, institutional development, constitutional interpretation, and biographical and autobiographical materials. An author index and a cases index are provided.

The bibliographical coverage of foreign affairs from 1775 to the present is extensive. Bemise, mentioned earlier, covers the period from 1775 to 1921 and is continued by *Foreign Affairs*, 1922–   (New York: Council on Foreign Relations, bimonthly, ISSN 00157120, print & digital) (Q14) and the *Foreign Affairs Bibliography*, noted next. One of the regular features of *Foreign Affairs* is the classified annotated bibliography, "Recent Books on International Relations," arranged in eight broad categories: general, American politics, the Western Hemisphere, western Europe, the Soviet Union and East Europe, the Middle East, Asia and the Pacific, and Africa. The books are the fundamental sources for the compilation of the *Foreign Affairs Bibliography*. The journal also publishes "Source Materials," an unannotated listing of materials divided into two parts: (1) documents, further classified by region and subject, and (2) other publications.

The *Foreign Affairs Bibliography* is limited to books, the majority of which are in English and the Western European languages. Government documents are generally excluded. The work is arranged under three major headings: general international relations, the world since 1914, and the world by region. Its subject matter includes history, politics, diplomacy, economics, international law, world organization, social problems, and racial problems. Author and title indexes are given in each volume.

Theses and Dissertations

Journals that carry dissertations, including *The American Political Science Review*, now continued by *PS: Political Science and Politics*, are noted in Chapter 6.

Research in Progress

Research in progress can be found in periodicals noted in Chapter 6.

Reviews

For review of the literature, the well-known extensive work is the book section of the leading journal, *American Political Science Review*, 1906– (Washington, DC: American Political Science Association, quarterly, ISSN 00030554) (Q15). An annual review of books in political science is *The Political Science Reviewer: An Annual Review of Books*, 1971– (Wilmington, DE: Intercollegiate Studies Institute, annual, ISSN 00913715) (Q16). The work grew out of the dissatisfaction with the book review section of leading journals, considered to be little more than a listing of current publications, and is intended to evaluate the central points, themes, or factual content of the books under review. Each issue contains about ten reviews at length, with citations to related works, of current studies and textbooks, reprints, and the great classics as well. For library selection, librarians would prefer a shorter and more concise book review.

Two review publications are worth noting:

> *Annual Review of Political Science*, 1986–1990, 1997– . Palo Alto, CA: Annual Reviews. ISSN 10942939. (Q17)
> *Perspectives on Political Science*, 1972– . Washington, DC: Heldref. Quarterly. ISSN 10457097. Print & digital. (Q18)

The *Annual Review* is one of the four reviews in the social sciences. All reviews are in the same format, as mentioned in Chapter 8. Its Table of Contents can be viewed through the publisher's Web site (http://www.annualreviews.org).

Perspectives, formerly *Perspective: Monthly Reviews of New Books on Government/Politics/International Affairs* incorporated with *Teaching Political Science*, publishes reviews classified in eight categories: the United States; Central and South America; Europe/USSR; Africa and the Middle East; Asia and the Pacific; International Relations, Laws, and Organization; Comparative Politics; and Theory and Methodology. New books are reviewed from one to eight months after publication. It is also available on CD-ROM.

Indexes

Political science is one of the subdisciplines of the social sciences that have been serviced by extensive indexes and abstracts. *International Bib-*

liography of Political Science, already mentioned, is an index to periodicals in political science worldwide. A retrospective index is *Combined Retrospective Index to Journals in Political Science 1886–1974* (Washington, DC: Carrollton Press, 1977–1978, 6 vols.) (Q19), one of the CRIS series previously noted.

Abstracts

> *American Foreign Policy and Treaty Index*, 1993– . Bethesda, MD: Congressional Information Service. Quarterly with annual cumulation. ISSN 10886141. (Q20)
>
> *International Political Science Abstracts. Documentation Politique Internationale*, 1951– . Paris: International Political Science Association. Bimonthly. Publisher and frequency vary. ISSN 00208345. Print & digital. (Q21)
>
> *Universal Reference System: Political Science, Government and Public Policy Series*. Princeton, NJ: Princeton Research, 1965–1969. 10 vols. (Q22)
>
> *Universal Reference System: Political Science, Government and Public Policy Series*. Supplement. Princeton, NJ: Princeton Research, 1969–1979. Annual. (Q23)
>
> *Political Science Abstracts*, 1980– . New York: IFI/Plenium Press. Annual. ISSN 07318022. (Q24)

American Foreign Policy and Treaty Index, formerly *American Foreign Policy Index*, is a guide to foreign policy and foreign relations publications of the U.S. government (subtitle). It covers journals, conference proceedings, special reports, and selected monographs. It is also available on CD-ROM.

International Political Science Abstracts, the oldest of the abstracting services, is a listing of abstracts of journal articles from over 900 periodicals, but not all periodicals are fully abstracted. Entries are arranged in six broad categories: (1) methods and theory; (2) political thinkers and ideas; (3) government and administrative institutions; (4) political processes; (5) international relations; and (6) national and area studies. It has cumulated annual subject and author indexes. It is also produced on CD-ROM. The service of printing articles abstracted therein for a fee is available.

The *Universal Reference System (URS)* is a computer-produced annotated bibliography of books, articles, papers, and documents, based on a classification scheme developed by Alfred de Grazia, known as the Grazian Index Scheme. It is published in three forms: the ten-volume basic library, cumulative quarterly supplements, and bound annual supplements. The ten-volume basic library, referred to as Codexes, covers the following political and behavioral science subfields:

1. International Affairs
2. Legislative Process, Representation, and Decision Making
3. Bibliography of Bibliographies in Political Science, Government and Public Policy
4. Administrative Management: Public and Private Bureaucracy
5. Current Events and Problems of Modern Society
6. Public Opinion, Mass Behavior, and Political Psychology
7. Law, Jurisprudence, and Judicial Process
8. Economic Regulation, Business, and Government
9. Public Policy and the Management of Science
10. Comparative Government and Cultures

Each Codex contains from 2,000 to 4,000 items, with full citations and concise summaries. In illustrating the first volume of the *Universal Reference System Political Science, Government and Public Policy Series*, Alfred de Grazia explains the unique characteristics of his index scheme:

Its value derives in part from the depth of its indexing. Whereas most keyword indexes in bibliographies rely solely on titles (perhaps augmented with additional keyword(s), the URS input is not only annotated but is also tagged with an average of twenty "Standard" and "Unique" descriptors per item. Moreover, from two to four of these descriptors are identified as "Critical" descriptors and are given special treatment in indexing.[6]

The *Supplement* is continued by the *Political Science Abstracts*, a classified bibliography with abstracts dealing with government and especially public administration, state and local government, the legislative and executive branches, and the judiciary. Since the abstracts are arranged by item number, it is necessary to use the index to locate the abstracts on a particular subject.

Contents Reproduction

The *ABC Pol Sci. Advance Bibliography of Contents: Political Science and Government*, 1969–   . Santa Barbara, CA: ABC-Clio. 6/year with annual index. ISSN 00010456. Print & digital. (Q25)

International Current Awareness Service: Political Science and Related Disciplines, 1990–   . London: Routledge. Monthly. ISSN 09601538. (Q26)

These two works reproduce edited tables of contents. The *ABC Pol Sci*, a bibliography of contents: political science and government (subtitle), also available on CD-ROM, covers some 300 journals, both foreign and domestic, on political science, government, and related disciplines such as law, sociology, and cultural anthropology. Each issue is arranged in alphabetical order by title with subject and author indexes and in addition, a list of periodicals. The publisher also provides an article copying service for a number of periodicals for a fee. *ICAS* is noted in Chapter 3.

SOURCES OF INFORMATION
General

> *Political Science Virtual Library*. Storrs, CT: University of Connecticut. http://www.lib.uconn.edu/PoliSci (Q27)

Resources are grouped into eight categories: Department of Political Science and Government, Libraries, Journals and Collections of Papers, Professional Associations and Research Institutions, Some FTP Servers, News Groups and ListServes, Other Lists and Searching Tools, and WWW Virtual Library: Related Fields. More than 200 departments and eight libraries worldwide are listed. It provides a listing of over 20 journals and some 16 organizations plus additional lists for searching. Of particular reference interest are two lists: Other Lists and Searching Tools and World Wide Web Virtual Library: Related Fields. The former includes political science personal homepages, Galaxy: Political Science, The National Political Index, International Political Economy Network, Political Science Resources, and Political Scientists' Personal Home Pages. The latter provides eight virtual library Web sites, including German Resources in Political Science, History, International Affairs, Politics and Economics, Social Sciences, and United Nations and other international organizations.

Subfield

United States

> The White House. Washington, DC. http://www.whitehouse.gov (Q28)
> The House of Representatives. Washington, DC. http://www.house.gov (Q29)
> The Senate. Washington, DC. http://www.senate.gov (Q30)
> The Federal Judiciary. Washington, DC. http://www.uscourts.gov (Q31)
> The Democratic National Committee. Washington, DC. http://www.democrats.org (Q32)
> The Republican National Committee. Washington, DC. http://www.rnc.org (Q33)

Also listed here are Web sites for the three branches of American government and two major political parties. The White House Web site provides the following categories of information: The President and Vice-President: their accomplishments, their families, and how to send them electronic mail; Interactive Citizens' Handbook: a guide to information about the federal government; White House History and Tours; The Virtual Library: contents of the White House Web site and the archive of White House documents; What's New; Site News; The Briefing Room (noted in Chapters 5 and 10); and White House for Kids.

The House of Representatives home page displays the following categories for choosing: What's New; House Operation; House Directory; House Office Web Sites including Member Offices, Committee Offices, Leadership Offices, Other House Organizations, Commissions, and Task Forces; Media Galleries; This Week on the House Floor; Currently on the House Floor; Annual Congressional Schedule; The Legislative Process; Roll Call Votes; House Committee Hearing Schedules and Oversight Plans; *Thomas* (noted in Chapter 7); and Internet Law Library.

Some categories are worth noting. House Directory lists members and committees, consisting of current Congressional profile, House documents, house links, and mailing labels of members and committees. House Web Sites provide links to members in alphabetical order, some 21 committees, members who hold House leadership positions, House organizations, House commissions, House task forces, and House media galleries (radio, television, daily press, and periodical press). The House Web site also provides links to *Thomas* and *GPO Access* (noted in Chapter 7).

The Senate Web site provides a number of choices: Legislative Activities, Committees, Senators, Learning about the Senate, Other Resources, and What's New. The category of Legislative Activities consists of Legislation, Schedules and Rules, and Detailed Activities. The former includes Committee Meetings and Hearings, Pending Business, Recess Calendar, Full Text of Standing Rules of the Senate. Others, such as *Daily Digest, Senate Calendar of Business,* Congressional bills, and *Congressional Record* are accessible via *GPO Access.* The latter, Detailed Activities, includes roll call votes, legislative calendar, executive calendar, committee actions, nominations, and treaties. The Senators category provides a directory of Senators by name, directory of Senators by state, contacting Senators on the Internet, Senate leadership, and class membership.

Learning about the Senate contains The Senate Historical Office, Senate Art and Historical Collections, Brief History of the Senate, Publications about the United States Senate, Full Text Standing Rules of the Senate, Planning Your Visit to the Senate, a Virtual Reality Tour of the U.S. Capitol, the Legislative Process, and a Glossary of Senate terms. Other Resources include Other Sources of Government Info on the Internet, Senate Internet Usage Policies, Frequently Asked Questions, and Lobby Registration. Ten Web sites are listed in Other Sources of Government Information on the Internet, including Web sites of the House of Representatives, Library of Congress, the Government Printing Office, *Thomas*, and the White House.

The Federal Judiciary Web site contains "information from and about the Judicial Branch of the U.S. Courts" (home page). It has the following categories: What's New, Frequently Asked Questions, For Public Review, Links, Search, Employment Opportunities, About the U.S. Courts, Publications and Directories, Newsroom, and Federal Judiciary Channel. Links provide access to eleven sites, the District of Columbia, and Federal Circuits, International Trade, and others, such as the American Judicature Society, Federal Court Clerks Association, Federal Judicial Center, *Thomas*, the United States Sentencing Commission, and Citizens for Independent Courts. Its Publications and Directories provides Directory of Electronic Public Access Services. The services now include the U.S. Supreme Court Electronic Bulletin Board System, U.S. Supreme Court Clerk's Automated Response Systems (CARS), and ABBS (Appellate Bulletin Board System).

The two major political parties maintain their Web sites dealing with issues, position, party publicity, and participation in party politics.These two Web sites provide mirrors of each party's activities and accomplishments. The Democratic National Committee's Web site offers Democratic Platform, Democratic Record of Accomplishments, Democratic Position Papers, and State by State Accomplishments. On the other hand, the Republican National Committee's Web site presents major issues and accomplishments, such as national security, improving America's schools, reducing taxes and simplifying the tax code, Republican agenda for America's students, reforming welfare, and preserving the American family.

International

United Nations. New York: United Nations Department of Public Information. http://www.un.org (Q34)
Columbia International Affairs Online (CIAO). Monthly update. New York: Columbia University Press. http://www.ciaonet.org (Q35)

The United Nations home page displays a number of choices, including About the UN; Conference and Events; General Information; UN Reform; Audio, Visual, Webcast; Publications and Sales; Databases; UN News; UN Document; UN Around the World; UN Member States; and main subjects, such as Peace and Security, International Law, Economic and Social Development, Human Rights, and Humanitarian Affairs. The UN Publications and Sales category lists publications, stamps, and online publications, including *UN Chronicle*, 1964– (formerly *UN Monthly Chronicle*, New York: United Nations Publications, 11/year, ISSN

02517329). There are some ten electronic products, such as *Statistical Year-book on CD-ROM* and *Witstat CD-ROM* (Women's Indicators and Statistics Database). Access to online databases is provided in the Databases category.

Selected official UN documents are listed in the UN Documents category. They are United Nations Documentation Research Guide, Daily List of Documents Issued at Headquarters, Document Alert, UN Conference Documents, UN Documents in German, UN Secretary-General, Security Council, General Assembly, Economic and Social Council, and UN-I-QUE (UN Info Quest). Current documents, such as resolutions, can be searched from the listings. Among the main subjects, International Law lists the International Court of Justice, International Criminal Court, International Law Commissions, International Trade Law, Law of the Sea, Treaties, and other international tribunals. Peace and Security provides general information, United Nations Peacekeeping, General Assembly, Disarmament, United Nations Special Commission (UNSCOM), Special Representatives or Envoys of the Secretary-General, Preventive Action and Peacemaking, Security Council, and others.

Columbia International Affairs Online (CIAO) is a database of full text of working papers from 66 contributing institutions such as Academy of Political Science, The Brookings Institution, Carnegie Endowment for International Peace, Cato Institute, Copenhagen Peace Research Institute, Council on Foreign Relations, London School of Economics, Stockholm Institute for Peace Research, and The Woodrow Wilson International Center for Scholars. *CIAO* contains some 25,000 pages of conference proceedings, papers and books, and abstracts from selected journals of international affairs. It can be searched through author, institution, subject, keyword, date, and title.

Encyclopedias

General

> *The Encyclopedia of Democracy*. Seymour Martin Lipset, ed. Washington, DC: Congressional Quarterly, 1995. 4 vols. ISBN 0871876752. (Q36)
> *Survey of Social Science: Government and Politics Series*. Frank N. Magill, ed. Pasadena, CA: Salem Press, 1995. 5 vols. ISBN 0893567450. (Q37)

The *Encyclopedia* contains "417 original articles on countries, geographical regions, historical eras, important individuals, philosophical concepts, and many other issues important to an understanding of democracy" (Preface). There are 124 biographies. The length of articles ranges from 300 to 8,500 words. Articles are arranged in alphabetical order. Each volume has an index. An appendix provides the texts of 20 primary source documents, including Pericles' Funeral Oration (431 B.C.), Magna Carta (1215), American Declaration of Independence (1776), constitutions of the United States (1787), Norway (1814), Argentina (1853), Japan (1949), the Federal Republic of Germany (1949), and the Czech Republic (1993), and Summit of the Americas Declaration of Principles (1994).

The *Survey* series is one of the four sets noted in Chapter 3, containing 342 articles on 12 political subject areas. It also includes a 500-term glossary, cross-references, and an annotated bibliography in each article.

Subfield

American Government

> *Encyclopedia of the American Legislative System: Studies of the Principal Structures, Processes, and Policies of Congress and the State Legislature Since the Colonial Era.* Joel H. Silbey, ed. New York: Charles Scribners' Sons, 1994. 3 vols. ISBN 0684192438. (Q38)
>
> *Congress A to Z: A Ready Reference Encyclopedia.* 2nd ed. Michael Nelson, ed. Washington, DC: Congressional Quarterly, 1993. 547 p. ISBN 0871878267. (Q39)
>
> *The Presidency A to Z: A Ready Reference Encyclopedia.* 2nd ed. Michael Nelson, ed. Washington, DC: Congressional Quarterly, 1998. 603 p. ISBN 1568023596. (Q40)
>
> *The Supreme Court A to Z: A Ready Reference Encyclopedia.* 2nd ed. Kenneth Jost, ed. Washington, DC: Congressional Quarterly, 1998. 584 p. ISBN 156802357X. (Q41)
>
> *Encyclopedia of the American Presidency.* Leonard W. Levy and Louis Fisher, eds. New York: Simon and Schuster, 1994. 4 vols. ISBN 0132759837. (Q42)
>
> *Encyclopedia of the United States Congress.* Donald C. Bacon, Roger H. Davidson, and Morton Keller, eds. New York: Simon and Schuster, 1995. 4 vols. ISBN 0132763613. (Q43)

The American Congress and legislative systems are covered in two encyclopedias. *Encyclopedia of the American Legislative System* contains 91 essays grouped into six parts: The American Legislative System in Historical Context; Legislative Recruitment, Personnel, and Elections; Legislative Structure and Processes; Legislative Behavior; Legislatures and Public Policy; and Legislature within the Political System. Most essays are cross-referenced, and each essay includes a bibliography.

Encyclopedia of the United States Congress contains 1,056 articles with illustrations, tables, and charts, arranged in alphabetical order. It covers laws, events, biographies, institutions, treatises, states, cases, government agencies, and publications. The back of volume 4 contains The Constitution of the United States, Glossary, Synoptic Outline of Contents, and an index.

The three A-to-Z encyclopedias complement Congressional Quarterly's three guides, noted later. The three-encyclopedia set "provides the most concise and accessible ready-reference information about the history, powers, and operations of the three branches of government" (Preface). All encyclopedias are concluded with Reference Material that includes Appendixes, Constitution of the United States, Bibliography, and Index. The number of appendixes varies. There are 26 appendixes in *Congress A to Z*, such as House Floor Leaders, 1899–1993; Senate Floor Leaders, 1911–1993; Congressional Committee Chairs since 1947; Women Members of Congress, 1917–1993; Black Members of Congress, 1870–1993; Hispanic Members of Congress, 1877–1993; Cases of Expulsion in the House; Cases of Expulsion in the Senate; Censure Proceedings in the House; Censure Proceedings in the Senate; Salaries; U.S. House of Representatives Organizational Chart; U.S. Senate Organizational Chart; Capital Attractions; and U.S. Government Organizational Chart. In *The Supreme Court A to Z*, there are seven appendices: Reference Material; Supreme Court Nominations, 1789–1994; Seat Chart of the Justices; Constitution of the United States; U.S. Government Organization Chart; Online Sources of Decisions; and How to Read a Court Citation.

Encyclopedia of the American Presidency deals with the powers and prerogatives of the executive office, the multiple roles of the President, and relationship with Congress. It contains 1,011 articles by 335 contributors arranged in alphabetical order from ABM (Antiballistic Missile System), Act of State Doctrine, Administrative Procedure Act, and also-rans to Yalta Conference and *Youngstown Sheet and Tube Co. v. Sawyer*. It covers a variety of topics, including statutes, public policy, party politics, media, public opinion, issue networks, contemporary events, treaties, and court decisions. Articles are signed with cross-references and appended with a bibliography. Volume 4 has Tables on presidents: personnel information, cabinets, other officials, and elections, and Synoptic Outline of Contents, a classified listing of entry titles grouped into (1) The Presidency, (2) Policies and Issues, (3) Laws and Legal Cases, (4) Historical Events and Politics, and (5) Photographs.

Foreign Relations

Encyclopedia of American Foreign Policy: Studies of the Principal Movements and Ideas. Alexander DeConde, ed. New York: Scribner's, 1978. 3 vols. ISBN 0684155036. (Q44)

Encyclopedia of U. S. Foreign Relations. Bruce W. Jentleson and Thomas G. Paterson, eds. New York: Oxford University Press, 1997. 4 vols. ISBN 0195110552. (Q45)

Encyclopedia of American Foreign Policy and *Encyclopedia of Political History*, noted later, are compiled on the same principle, dealing with principal movements and ideas. Each is a collection of essays organized by topic in alphabetical order. Articles are appended with bibliographies and cross-references. *Encyclopedia of American Foreign Policy* contains 95 signed articles on topics ranging "from broad concepts such as isolationism and national self-determination to specific topics, such as the Monroe Doctrine and the Marshall Plan" (Preface). It also includes "Biographies" in volume 3 (pp. 995–1138).

More than 1,000 signed articles contributed by 373 authors are contained in *Encyclopedia of U. S. Foreign Relations*. They cover the period from 1776 to the 1990s. Length of articles ranges from a column to several pages. Most entries have cross-references and further reading. It provides three appendixes: (1) Chronology of U.S. Foreign Relations; (2) Table of National Data; and (3) Classified Bibliography of Reference Works.

Human Rights

> *Encyclopedia of Human Rights*. 2nd ed. Edward H. Lawson, ed. Philadelphia: Taylor and Francis, 1996. 1,715 p. ISBN 1560323620. (Q46)

The *Encyclopedia* is "a compendium that brings together materials about international, regional, and national activities undertaken between the years 1945 and 1996 to promote and protect the enjoyment of human rights and fundamental freedoms by everyone without distinction" (User's Guide). It provides information on international instruments, international organizations, promotion, monitoring, supervision of implementation of human rights, state of human rights in 186 countries and territories, and biographical profiles of Nobel Peace Prize winners. One of the features is the inclusion of many full-text documents. It is an excellent source of activities by international organizations on human rights. Each entry is cross-referenced and ends with a bibliography. The country entry provides background information on government structure, geography, population, languages, and so on. The length of entries varies. Over 20 pages are for the United States and 10 pages for China. There are two appendixes: (A) A Chronological List of International Instruments Concerned with Human Rights and (B) Status of International Human Rights Convention.

Political History

> *Encyclopedia of American Political History: Studies of the Principal Movements and Ideas*. Jack P. Greene, ed. New York: Scribner's, 1984. 3 vols. ISBN 0684170035. (Q47)

Compiled on the same principle as *Encyclopedia of American Foreign Policy*, just noted, *Encyclopedia of American Political History* contains 90 signed articles on political events, documents, issues, themes, institutions, process, and developments. Topical articles are preceded by "Historiography of American Political History." Topics range from ideas such as liberalism and Republicanism to specific topics such as cabinet and suffrage.

International

> *Encyclopedia of Government and Politics.* Mary Hawkesworth and Maurell Kogan, eds. London: Routledge, 1992. 2 vols. ISBN 0415030937. (Q48)
>
> *Encyclopedia of the United Nations and International Agreements.* 2nd ed. Edmund Jan Osmanczyk. Philadelphia: Taylor and Francis, 1990. 1,220 p. ISBN 0850668336. (Q49)
>
> *World Encyclopedia of Political Systems and Parties.* 2nd ed. George E. Delury, ed. New York: Facts on File, 1987. 2 vols. ISBN 0816015392. (Q50)

Eighty-four articles are grouped into ten parts in *Encyclopedia of Government and Politics*: (I) Introduction; (II) Political Theory: Central Concepts; (III) Contemporary Ideologies; (IV) Contemporary Political Systems; (V) Political Institutions; (VI) Political Forces and Political Processes; (VII) Centripetal and Centrifugal Forces in the Nation-State; (VIII) Policy Making and Policies; (IX) International Relations; and (X) Major Issues in Contemporary World Politics. Governments are not separately presented except for international government, which includes the United Nations, the International Court of Justice, the World Bank, and the International Monetary Fund. All articles are signed, and each is concluded with references and further reading. The encyclopedia can be used as a textbook for the course in comparative and international government. There is a name and subject index.

The *Encyclopedia of the United Nations and International Agreements* defines terms, international conferences, agreements, conventions, treaties, and declarations with cross-references. Most entries are given sources. The length of entry varies from one sentence to five or more pages, such as the one on cases of the International Court of Justice. Some international organizations are included, but most are not. There is no mention of the standard for inclusion or exclusion of international organizations. It has three indexes: a selective index; an index of agreements, conventions, and treaties; and an index of names. Its appendixes include World Population Statistics, 1985–2025, Words Frequently Found in UN Documents, Acronyms, and Official Abbreviations.

The standard entry in the *World Encyclopedia of Political Systems and Parties* consists of the system of government, an introduction to the institutions of government, and the electoral system including suffrage, registrations, and balloting procedures. Arrangement is by country, followed by smaller countries and territories.

Dictionaries

Dictionaries in political science may be grouped into six categories according to their purposes and scope: (1) terms of political science in general; (2) terms of historical significance, long past or contemporary; (3) terms of contemporary persons and events; (4) terms of political ideologies and methodologies; (5) terms of American government; and (6) terms of other subjects in political science. Listed here are some representative titles in the first three categories. All other titles are listed in the subfields section.

General

> *Cassell Dictionary of Modern Politics*. CIRCA Research and Reference Information. London: Cassell, 1994. 340 p. ISBN 030434432X. (Q51)
>
> *A Dictionary of Modern Politics*. 2nd ed. David Robertson. London: Europa, 1993. 495 p. ISBN 0946653755. (Q52)
>
> *Safire's New Political Dictionary: The Guide to the New Language of Politics*. William Safire. New York: Random House, 1993. 930 p. ISBN 0679420681. (Q53)

Cassell's Dictionary contains terms, concepts, countries, and international organizations, arranged in alphabetical order. There are no biographies. However, names are mentioned in entries and are indexed. Definitions are brief.

About 50 percent longer than the first edition of *A Dictionary of Modern Politics*, it contains terms, biographies, political parties, conferences, international organizations, and so on. One feature is that in an entry, a word or concept that has an entry of its own is in boldface.

Safire's defines some 1,800 terms in over 1,100 entries. It supplements *American Political Terms: An Historical Dictionary* by Hans Sperber and Travis Trittschuh (Detroit: Wayne State University Press, 1962, 516 p.) (Q54). The latter, patterned after the *Oxford English Dictionary*, the *Dictionary of Americanisms*, and the *Dictionary of American English*, defines terms and identifies the origin and history of American political terms and their usage with references to sources. *Safire's* emphasizes contemporary usage, while *American Political Terms* is historical and philological. Included in *Safire's* are such words and phrases as foot-in-mouth disease, political correctness, floo-floo bird, eleventh commandment, read my lips, and hooverize.

Subfield

American Government

> The American Dictionary of Campaigns and Elections. Michael L. Young. Lanham, MD: Hamilton Press, 1987. 246 p. ISBN 0819154466. (Q55)
>
> The American Political Dictionary. 10th ed. Jack C. Plano and Milton Greenberg. Fort Worth, TX: Harcourt Brace, 1996. 702 p. ISBN 0030173175. (Q56)
>
> The Dorsey Dictionary of American Government and Politics. Jay M. Shafritz. Chicago: Dorsey Press, 1988. 661 p. ISBN 0256056390. (Q57)

The three dictionaries listed here deal with American government. With focus on party politics, *The American Dictionary of Campaigns and Elections* defines "the major notions, concepts, tools and terms associated with the contemporary American political campaign," according to the Preface. Over 700 entries are provided. There are a bibliography and a topical index.

Plano and Greenberg's *The American Political Dictionary* consists of court decisions and statutes divided into fourteen chapters on political ideas; the United States Constitution and the federal union; parties, politics, pressure groups, and elections; the legislative branch; the executive branch; public administration; the judicial process; civil liberty; finance and taxation; and so on. Each chapter has four sections: (1) terms, (2) important agencies, (3) important cases, and (4) important statutes. Each entry is first defined or described, then followed by a statement of its historical or contemporary significance to American government and politics. An index contains a complete listing of all major entries as well as significant terms discussed within major entries. The book also serves as a guide.

Of a different arrangement is *The Dorsey Dictionary*, which contains over 4,000 entries in alphabetical order on American national, state, or local government and politics, Supreme Court decisions, biographies, laws, political slang, scholarly and professional journals, and associations and organizations. Most entries conclude with citations of bibliographic sources. The dictionary also features boxes, photographs, and illustrations. Its appendixes provide useful references, such as guides to American government documents, statistical information, and online databases.

Foreign Relations

> Dictionary of American Diplomatic History. 2nd ed. John E. Findling. Westport, CT: Greenwood Press, 1989. 674 p. ISBN 0313260249. (Q58)
>
> Dictionary of American Foreign Affairs. Stephen A. Flunders and Carl N.

Flunders. New York: Macmillan, 1993. 833 p. ISBN 0028971469. (Q59)

International Relations: A Practical Dictionary. 5th ed. Lawrence Ziring, Jack C. Plano, and Roy Olton. Santa Barbara, CA: ABC-Clio, 1995. 458 p. ISBN 0874368979. (Q60)

The preceding are three good international relations dictionaries. *Dictionary of American Foreign Affairs* contains approximately 1,400 entries in alphabetical order, covering the period from 1776 to the present. "Subject entries include applicable dates and participants, key background information, a description or summary of the item, and, as appropriate, an assessment of its outcome or significance [and] biographical entries provide birth, death, and relevant active dates and focus on the person's role in foreign affairs" (Introduction). There are eight appendixes: (A) Timeline of U.S. Foreign Affairs, (B) The Executive Branch, (C) Diplomatic Corps, (D) Congressional Committees, (E) Conference and Summits, (F) Glossary, (G) Guide to Further Sources, and (H) Maps.

The Findling *Dictionary* identifies nearly 600 persons associated with U.S. foreign policy from the Revolution through 1978. Some 800 nonbiographical entries are provided, with basic background information and commentaries as to their significance for diplomatic events, terms, treaties and international agreements, and organizations. Maps and organization charts are given in front of the main body of entries. Each entry gives bibliographical sources. Appendixes include (A) Chronology of American Diplomatic History, from 1776 to 1988; (B) Key Diplomatic Personnel Listed by Presidential Administration; (C) Initiation, Suspension, and Termination of Diplomatic Relations; (D) Place of Birth; and (E) Locations of Manuscript Collections and Oral Histories (arranged by biographees).

International Relations contains 714 entries of terms, concepts, court decisions, agencies, international agreements, and treaties classified in twelve chapters within the chapter in alphabetical order. The twelve chapters are Nature and Role of Foreign Policy; Ethnicity, Nationalism, and Interpretation; Geography, Environment, and Population; International Economics and Development; War and Military Policy; Arms Control and Arms Reduction; Diplomacy, Peacekeeping, and Peacemaking; International Law; International Organizations; U.S. Foreign Policy; and Patterns of Political Organization. Each entry consists of two parts: (1) definition with cross-references and (2) significance, presenting the entry's impact on international relations. For convenient use, the book provides a guide to major concepts, a listing of terms contained in the text arranged in alphabetical order. The dictionary is one of the *Clio Dictionaries in Political Science* series. The series consists of dictionaries on various subjects, including dictionaries on area studies.

Philosophy and Theory

> A *Dictionary of Political Thought*. Roger Scruton. New York: Hill and Wang, 1985. 512 p. ISBN 0809015242 paper. (Q61)

A *Dictionary of Political Thought* defines the terms of principal political ideas. According to its preface, the dictionary's emphasis is on "conceptual rather than factual, exploring the formulation of doctrines rather than their specific application," and as such, "political events are mentioned only when they cast light on intellectual conceptions." It also includes biographies of political thinkers.

Public Administration

> *The Facts on File Dictionary of Public Administration*. Jay M. Shafritz. New York: Facts on File, 1985. 610 p. ISBN 0816012660. (Q62)

The dictionary has an interdisciplinary coverage, including theory, concepts, practices, institutions, literature and people in public administration, and in economics, law, psychology, statistics, history, and medicine as well. Many articles are provided with cross-references and references for further reading.

Directories

The best inexpensive manual that serves also as a directory of the federal government is the *United States Government Manual*, noted later. The following are representative directories:

United States

General

> Carroll's Government Personnel Charts and Directories. Washington, DC: Carroll Publishing. http://www.carrollpub.com (Q63)
> *The Federal Web Locator*. Villanova, PA: Villanova University, School of Law, Center for Information Law and Policy. http://www.law.vill.edu/Fed-Agency/fedwebloc.html (Q64)
> *The FedWorld Information Network*. Springfield, VA: National Technical Information Service. http://www.fedworld.gov (Q65)
> *Washington Information Directory*, 1975–1976– . Washington, DC: Congressional Quarterly. Annual. ISSN 08878064. (Q66)

The Carroll's directory online consists of its print counterparts as follows:

Carroll's Federal Directory: Executive, Legislative, and Judicial (formerly *Federal Executive Directory*), bimonthly, ISSN 10804919 (Q67), and *Carroll's Federal Directory Annual* (formerly *Federal Executive Directory Annual*), ISSN 10932089 (Q68), listing over 35,000 key personnel in the federal government.

Carroll's Federal Regional Executive Directory (formerly *Federal Regional Executive Directory*), semiannual, ISSN 10823182 (Q69), listing over 20,000 key personnel in regional federal agencies.

Carroll's State Directory (formerly *State Executive Directory*), 3/year, ISSN 10821929 (Q70), and *Carroll's State Directory Annual* (formerly *State Executive Directory Annual*), ISSN 10932070 (Q71), listing over 37,000 key personnel in state governments.

Carroll's County Directory (formerly *County Executive Directory*), semiannual, ISSN 10861114 (Q72), listing over 28,000 key personnel in some 3,100 counties, boroughs, and parishes.

Carroll's Municipal Directory (formerly *Municipal Executive Directory*), semiannual, ISSN 1083933X (Q73), listing over 38,000 key personnel in municipal governments.

The preceding two directories combined into an annual as:

Carroll's Municipal–County Directory Annual (formerly *Municipal–County Directory Annual*), ISSN 10932054 (Q74).

Carroll's Military Facilities Directory (formerly *Military Facilities Directory*), semiannual, ISSN 10932062 (Q75), listing decision-makers at 550 military installations and centers with a brief description of each installation and center.

All the preceding directories are in digital format, on CD-ROM as *Carroll's Government Suite*, and on the Web. One feature of the digital format is information updating. Information is updated more often on CD-ROM and continuously on the Web.

Its home page provides a number of choices for searching, such as Federal Military, Federal Civilian, State Government, and County (including Municipal) Government. For Federal Civilian, three choices are displayed: Executive Branch, Legislative Branch, and Judicial Branch. Executive Branch is further divided into White House, Executive Agencies, and Other Executive Links. Its links provide access, for example, under State Government, to staff pages for the Governor, Senators, House Members, and the state's official home page, and to various other pages concerned with the state. Likewise it provides links to county and municipal pages across the country.

Also listed here are two Internet directories. *The Federal Web Locator* is intended to provide "one shopping point for federal government information on the World Wide Web" (home page). All federal government Web servers are organized by government functions into Federal Legislative Branch, Federal Judicial Branch, Federal Executive Branch, Federal Independent Establishments and Government Corporations, Federal Government Consortium and Quasi-Official Agencies, Federal Board, Commissions, and Committees, and Selected Multilateral Organizations and International sites. Over 90 Web sites are listed. In addition, it lists 25 nongovernmental federally related Web sites and over 15 search engines.

FedWorld is for government Web sites and documents search. Hundreds of U.S. government Web sites can be searched through the database of Search U.S. Government Information Servers. Over 450,000 government reports in 375 subject areas from more than 200 U.S. government agencies can be searched and ordered online. Its home page displays the following choices: Search U.S. Government Web Sites, Other Important Government Information, Subject-Based U.S. Government Web Sites (Gateways), Executive Branch Agency Web Sites, and U.S. Federal Agencies and Commissions. A user may click one of the choices and do further searching. For instance, Other Important Government Information offers six items for searching: *Code of Federal Regulations, Commerce Business Daily, Federal Register*, Library of Congress Thomas System, *U.S. Code*, and White House Home Page.

Washington Information Directory belongs to the first category, a useful government "yellow pages." It begins with listings of executive office, executive departments, and federal agencies, followed by subject listings organized by categories such as communications and the media; economics and business; education and culture; employment and labor; energy; advocacy; health; housing and urban affairs; law and justice, and so on. For each subject, it provides three categories of information: (1) departments and agencies of the federal government, (2) Congress, and (3) nongovernmental organizations in Washington, D.C. Agencies and organizations are briefly described. It ends with "Handy Reference Lists" that include foreign embassies, governors, and mayors of major cities. There are name and subject indexes.

Subfield

> *Congressional Directory for the Use of the United States Congress*, 1809– .
> Washington, DC: Congressional Quarterly. Annual. ISSN 01609890.
> Print & digital. (Q76)
> *Congressional Staff Directory*, 1959– . Alexandria, VA: Congressional
> Quarterly Staff Directory. 3/year. ISSN 00698938. (Q77)
> *Federal Staff Directory*, 1982– . Alexandria, VA: Congressional Quarterly
> Staff Directory. Annual. ISSN 07353324. (Q78)
> *Judicial Staff Directory*, 1986– . Alexandria, VA: Congressional Quarterly
> Staff Directory. Annual. (Q79)

The four directories deal with the three branches of government. *Congressional Directory* is a combination of biography and directory. It includes a biographical section on members of Congress, an alphabetical list of members of Congress, committees, committee assignments, the Executive Branch, the judiciary, administrative or legislative assistants and secretaries, the District of Columbia, international organizations, diplomatic representatives and consular offices, press representatives and services, statistical information, maps of congressional districts, a subject index, and an index of individual names. The biographical section supplements *Biographical Directory of the American Congress*, noted in the biographies section next. *Congressional Directory* is available on the Web on *GPO Access*, noted in Chapter 7.

The staff directories are three of the six directories published by Congressional Quarterly Staff Directories. The other three are *Federal Regional Staff Directory* (2/year, ISSN 10924000) (Q80), *State Staff Directory* (3/year, ISSN 10907203) (Q81), and *Municipal Staff Directory* (annual, ISSN 10924019) (Q82). *Congressional Staff Directory* (1998 Summer edition, 1,312 p., ISBN 0872891437) focuses on the staff of the members of Congress and features over 3,000 staff biographies. Biographies are short—only a few lines. It consists of the following major sections: State Delegations; Senate; Joint Committees, Agencies, Offices, and Organizations; House of Representatives; and 14,000 Counties and Cities and Their Districts. The *Directory* also includes information on members of Congress, their assignments and committees, and key personnel of the Executive Branch, and in this respect it duplicates the *Congressional Directory*. There are also a keyword subject index and an index of individuals.

The *Federal Staff Directory* is published in two editions (volumes) each year. It consists of five sections: (1) the agencies of the Executive Office of the President and presidential advisory organizations; (2) the executive departments; (3) independent agencies; (4) quasi-official, international, and nongovernment organizations; and (5) key executive biographies. There are two indexes: (1) keyword in context subject index and (2) individuals. Volume 2 is an update.

The 1989 *Judicial Staff Directory* (3rd ed., 888 p., ISBN 0872890759) consists of seven sections: (1) the federal courts, (2) the U.S. district courts, (3) the bankruptcy court, (4) maps of court jurisdictions, (5) index of judges, (6) biographies of judges and staff containing 1,400 of them, and (7) index of individuals, some 16,000 persons in the volume.

International

> Directory of International Organizations. Hans-Albrecht Schraepler. Washington, DC: Georgetown University Press, 1996. 424 p. ISBN 0878406077. (Q83)
>
> Yearbook of International Organizations, 1910– . Munich: Saur. Annual. ISSN 00843814. Print & digital. (Q84)

These two directories are for international organizations. The *Directory of International Organizations* is organized in six parts: (I) United Nations System; (II) North Atlantic Treaty Organization (NATO); (III) Regional Organizations of Worldwide Importance; (IV) Economic Organizations of Worldwide Relevance; (V) The Commonwealth and the Commonwealth of Independent States; and (VI), Other Organizations of Worldwide Relevance. Each organization lists, in general, name, address, purpose, members, structure, resources, activities, achievements, and institutions. Also included in the book are Abbreviations, Events in the History of International Cooperation, and Membership of International Groupings.

Yearbook of International Organizations, a comprehensive directory, provides information on organizations, administrators, embassies, and government agencies worldwide. The 34th edition 1997/98 (Union of International Associations, ed., 1997, ISBN 3598233574) consists of four volumes. Volume 1, Organization Descriptions and Cross-References, lists more than 13,000 organizations. Each entry provides when available nineteen elements of information, such as name, address, telephone number, e-mail address, founding date, structure, staff, finance, languages, IGO relations, NGO relations, activities, information services, publications, and members.

Volume 2 is a Country Directory of Secretariats and Membership, consisting of international organizations classified by countries or secretariat and international organizations classified by countries of membership. Volume 3 is a subject guide and index. Volume 4, Bibliography, has four main sections: (A) publications of international organizations, (B) publications on concerns of international organizations, (C) bibliography on transnational organizations, and (D) general index. Some appendixes are provided in all volumes. Volume 1 has the most appendixes, including Types of Organization; Legal Status of International Non-governmental Organizations; Statistics; Related Reference Works; Union of International Associations; Profile, and so on. The yearbook is also available on CD-ROM, entitled *Yearbook Plus of International Organizations and Biographies on CD-ROM* (4th ed., 1998/1999, ISBN 3598403917) (Q85).

Biographies

Biographical information can be found in many places. The American Political Science Association published irregularly a biographical directory of its membership, *Biographical Directory of the American Political Science Association*, 1945– (Washington, DC: The Association) (Q86). There are numerous general biographies containing biographies of politicians, statesmen, and political scientists. Dictionaries such as *Dictionary of American Diplomatic History* and *Dictionary of American Foreign Affairs*, already mentioned, and many yearbooks, handbooks, and almanacs, some of which will be noted later, also devote a considerable portion of their pages to biographies.

United States

> The Almanac of American Politics: The Senators, The Representatives, and the Governors: Their Records and Election Results, Their States and Districts. Michael Barone and Grant Ujifusa. Washington, DC: National Journal, 1997, 1,632 p. ISBN 0892340800. (Q87)
>
> The Almanac of the Executive Branch, 1997–98. Peggie Rayhawk and Gary P. Osifchin. Washington, DC: Almanac Publishing, 1997. 815 p. ISBN 1886222061. (Q88)
>
> Biographical Directory of the American Congress 1774–1996. Alexandria, VA: CQ Staff Directories, 1997, 2,108 p. ISBN 0872891240. (Q89)
>
> Biographical Directory of the United States Executive Branch, 1774–1989. Robert Sobel, ed. Westport, CT: Greenwood Press, 1990. 567 p. ISBN 0313265933. (Q90)
>
> Political Profiles. New York: Facts on File, 1976– . (Q91)
>
> Politics in America, 1984– . Phil Duncan, ed. Washington, DC: Congressional Quarterly. Biennial. ISSN 10646809. (Q92)
>
> Who's Who in American Politics: A Biographical Directory of United States Political Leaders, 1967/68– . New York: Bowker. Biennial. ISSN 00000205. Print & digital. (Q93)

These sources deal primarily with members of the legislative and executive branches. For biographies in the judiciary, refer to sources listed in Chapter 14.

The Barone and Ujifusa *Almanac* begins with a guide to usage, abbreviations, and a brief introduction to the nation, the regions, the presidency, the House, and the Senate. It lists for each political unit governor, senators, mayors, and congressional district followed by statistical data on the people, share of federal tax burden, share of federal expenditures, political lineup, and presidential vote. For each governor are listed party affiliation, career, office, and election result. For each senator or representative are indicated party affiliation, career, offices, committee membership, group ratings, *National Journal* ratings, key votes, and election.

The Almanac of the Executive Branch profiles over 830 key officials and presents a brief history of each cabinet level department, its jurisdiction, and a current organization chart for the department. It is arranged by agencies: Office of the President, Office of the Vice President, Executive Agencies, Office of the First Lady, Office of Mrs. Gore, followed by departments, independent agencies and government corporations, and selected multilateral organizations. Appendixes are (A) Agency Acronyms and Abbreviations, (B) Government Internet Sites, and (C) Agencies Appearing in the *Code of Federal Regulations*. It also provides a name index and an agency/

subject index. Both the almanac and the work noted next are basically dossiers.

Politics in America presents profiles of senators and representatives, arranged by state, followed by nonvoting representatives in the House. Each biographical sketch concludes with committees, electors, campaign finance, voting studies, key votes, and interest group ratings.

Two directories listed here provide biographical information on two branches of government. The *Biographical Directory*, an outstanding reference work, no longer published by the government, consists of two categories of information. The first is a directory of executive officers, the Continental Congress, representatives under each apportionment, and Congress from 1789 to 1989. The second is a listing of biographies of more than 11,000 individuals divided into two sections: (1) biographies of Presidents who were not members of Congress, and (2) biographies of those who have served in Congress. A few entries are appended with bibliographies. For biographies of current members of Congress, refer to *Congressional Directory*, noted later.

Of equally good standing is the *Biographical Directory of the United States Executive Branch*, patterned after the earlier edition of the *Biographical Directory of the American Congress*. The work "contains career biographies of all cabinet heads, as well as of presidents, vice-presidents, and presidents of the Continental Congress" (Preface). Arranged in an alphabetical order, each biography contains a short biographical reference to important primary and secondary works to be consulted for additional information. It has superb indexes, eight altogether. They are: presidential administrations; heads of state and cabinet officials; other federal government services; state, county, and municipal government services; military services by branch; education; place of birth; and marital information.

One of the best of its kind, *Political Profiles* is a contemporary of *Dictionary of American Biography* in politics, though not limited to deceased persons. When completed, it will consist of six volumes of more than 2,500 biographies of people who have dominated American politics since the end of World War II. The Preface states that the work is intended to provide "a richness of personal detail, political context and historical perspective unavailable in any other biographical reference work." The guiding principles for inclusion are that (1) the individual had an important, measurable impact on American politics or (2) the individual, though not of lasting political importance, had achieved such fame or notoriety that, for a moment, the person captured the political attention of the nation. All senators and some representatives are included, as well as persons with less achievement in politics, such as Francis Gary Powers, the U-2 pilot, and Lee Harvey Oswald, the alleged assassin of John F. Kennedy.

Each volume, except *The Nixon/Ford Years*, covers the period of a single presidential administration and is preceded by a review of political activities and events during the years of that administration. The biographical account emphasizes the activity or occupation for which the subject was most noted during the years of the presidential administration covered by the volume. Thus, some persons may appear in more than one volume. Sources for further information are frequently supplied. Five volumes have been published so far: *The Truman Years* (Eleanora W. Schoenebaum, ed., 1978, 714 p., ISBN 0871964538), *The Eisenhower Years* (Eleanora W. Schoenebaum, ed., 1977, 757 p., ISBN 0871964523), *The Kennedy Years* (Nelson Lichtenstein, ed., 1976, 621 p., ISBN 0871964503), *The Johnson Years* (Nelson Lichtenstein, ed., 1976, 741 p., ISBN 0871064511), and *The Nixon/Ford Years* (Eleanora W. Schoenebaum, ed., 1979, 787 p., ISBN 0871064546).

Who's Who in American Politics contains biographical sketches of over 27,000 men and women who make the American form of government work at the national, state, and local levels. Categories selected include President, Vice-President, cabinet officers, members of Congress, subcabinet officials, governors and staff officials, officials of political parties, and other political leaders. As entries are based primarily on replies to questionnaires, biographical sketches vary in length. For persons whose positions warrant inclusion, but for whom no information is available, names, addresses, and positions are listed. In addition to biographies, the book includes a roster of the President and members of his cabinet, state delegates to the Congress, governors of the states, state chairmen, and a geographical index. The book is arranged by residence. *Who's Who in American Politics* is part of *Bowker Biographical Directory* marketed through Dialog (File 236), noted in Chapter 4.

Handy biographical works may be noted:

> *Facts About the Presidents: A Compilation of Biographical and Historical Information.* 6th ed. Joseph Nathan Kane. New York: H. W. Wilson, 1993. 432 p. ISBN 0824208455. (Q94)
>
> *Facts About the Congress.* Stephen G. Christianson. New York: H. W. Wilson, 1996. 635 p. ISBN 0824208838. (Q95)
>
> *Facts About the Supreme Court of the United States.* Lisa Paddock. New York: H. W. Wilson, 1996. 569 p. ISBN 082420896X. (Q96)

The three *Facts About* books are companions. *Facts About the Presidents* consists of two parts: part 1 is a biographical compilation of data about presidents, arranged in chronological order, from Washington to Clinton. Part 2 provides comparative data and statistics on the presidents as individuals and on the office of the presidency.

Facts About the Congress covers over 200 years of Congress from 1789 to 1995, organized by chapters from the 1st Congress (1789–1791) to the 104th Congress, 1st session (1995–1996). Each chapter contains dates on which the sessions of Congress met, gains and losses by the major parties, a background summary of contemporary events, a detailed roster of the party leadership, important changes in Congress's organization and administration, a chronology of important dates for the Congress, major legislation passed, a summary of important proposed legislation that failed to pass, statistics on presidential nominations, appointments, and confirmations for the judicial and executive branches, votes, important scandals, chronology, relations with the president, and further reading.

Facts About the Supreme Court is arranged chronologically from the Jay Court (1789–1795) to the Rehnquist Court (1986–   ). Each court provides background, members of the court, judicial biography, significant cases, and political composition. There are three appendixes, a glossary, sources for further study, an index of cases, and a general index. Appendixes include United States Code Annotated, 1995, Title 28, Judiciary and Judicial Procedure 1995, Section Concerning the Supreme Court of the United States, and Rules of the Supreme Court of the United States.

At the state and local levels, there are:

Biographical Directory of American Colonial and Revolutionary Governors, 1607–1789. John W. Raimo. Westport, CT: Greenwood Press, 1980. 521 p. ISBN 0930466071. (Q97)

Biographical Directory of the Governors of the United States, 1789–1978. Robert Sobel and John Raimo, eds. New York: Meckler, 1978. 4 vols. ISBN 0930466004. (Q98)

Biographical Directory of the Governors of the United States, 1978–1983. John W. Raimo, ed. Westport, CT: Greenwood Press, 1985. 352 p. ISBN 0930466624. (Q99)

Biographical Directory of the Governors of the United States, 1983–1988. Marie M. Mullaney. New York: Mecklermedia, 1989. 307 p. ISBN 0685254372. (Q100)

Biographical Directory of the Governors of the United States, 1988–1993. Marie M. Mullaney. Westport, CT: Greenwood Press, 1994. 440 p. ISBN 0313283125. (Q101)

Biographical Dictionary of American Mayors, 1820–1980. Melvin G. Holli and Peter d'A. Jones, eds. Westport, CT: Greenwood Press, 1981. 451 p. ISBN 09313211345. (Q102)

Facts About the States. 2nd ed. Joseph Nathan Kane, Janet Podell, and Steven Anzovin. New York: H. W. Wilson, 1993. 624 p. ISBN 0824208498. (Q103)

The five biographical directories of governors are prepared on a similar pattern. Biographical entries are arranged by state and within state in chronological order. Each biography, if complete, presents basic information such as dates of birth and death, ancestry and family, religion and political affiliation, electoral results, and political and private careers. Also appended to each article are sources and in many cases, the location where the governor's papers are housed. The 1978 directory contains approximately 2,000 and its supplement 87 biographies. The supplement has added photographs. Colonial and revolutionary governors are broadly defined to include those who held effective executive powers in the colonies that later became the first thirteen states. Over 380 entries are included in the *Biographical Directory of American Colonial and Revolutionary Governors*.

Biographical Dictionary of American Mayors is a collective biography contributed by one hundred experts of 679 mayors of the fifteen leading American cities (Baltimore, Boston, Buffalo, Chicago, Cincinnati, Cleveland, Detroit, Los Angeles, Milwaukee, New Orleans, New York, Philadelphia, Pittsburgh, San Francisco, and St. Louis). Entries are arranged alphabetically by name, and each entry is appended with sources. The twelve appendixes are a useful reference, including a chronological list of mayors by city; classified listings of mayors by political party affiliation, ethnic background, religious affiliation, place of birth; and demographic data on the fifteen cities.

A concise dossier of every state, Washington, DC, and Puerto Rico is presented in *Facts About the States*. The book provides for each political entity full name, postal abbreviations, inhabitants, admitted to the union, capital city, state name and nicknames, motto, song, symbols, flag, geography and climate, national sites, history, demography, government and politics, finance, economy, environment, culture and education, unusual state facts, literature, guides to resources, and selected nonfiction sources. It concludes with comparative tables on area, population, order of settlement and statehood, geography, demography, presidential elections, finance, transportation, department of defense, and education.

International

> *Chiefs of State and Cabinet Members of Foreign Governments*. U.S. Intelligence Agency, Directorate of Intelligence. Washington, DC: NTIS. Bimonthly. ISSN 01622951. (Q104)
>
> *Current World Leaders*, 1957– . Santa Barbara, CA: International Academy. Bimonthly. ISSN 01926802. (Q105)
>
> *International Yearbook and Statesmen's Who's Who*, 1953– . London: European Association of Directory Publishers. Annual. 00749621. (Q106)
>
> *Who's Who in the United Nations and Related Agencies*. 2nd ed. Stanley R. Greenfield, ed. Detroit, MI: Omnigraphics, 1992. 800 p. ISBN 1558887628. (Q107)

Chiefs of State and Cabinet Members of Foreign Governments is a simple listing of officials and their titles arranged by countries with an alphabetical name index. *Current World Leaders* (title and publisher vary; formerly

Current World Leaders—Biography and News), merged with *Almanac of Current World Leaders*, provides up-to-date information on world leaders, including news, biographies, feature articles, reports from government, public and private agencies, and official and opposition speeches. It also contains other information formerly carried on in the *Almanac*, such as major cities, population, area, membership in international organizations, state, government, political party leaders (key government officials), and alliances.

The *International Yearbook* consists of two parts. Part 1 lists United Nations, intergovernmental organizations, and other international and national organizations. Part 2 provides information primarily on states of the world and dependent states and territories with a biographical section. About half of the contents is devoted to biographical sketches of individuals of international standing in government, commerce, industry, and education.

Who's Who in the United Nations and Related Agencies provides biographical sketches of members and principal officials of international governments and United Nations Secretariat staff members holding the rank of P-5 (Section Chief) and above, or corresponding grades. In addition, the book also includes for quick reference such information as organizational roster, member states of the United Nations from 1946 to 1974, United Nations depository libraries, and World Federation of United Nations Associations.

Statistical Sources

> *America at the Polls: A Handbook of American Presidential Election Statistics.* Alice V. McGillivray and Richard M. Scammon. Washington, DC: Congressional Quarterly, 1994. 2 vols. ISBN 1568020511. (Q108)
>
> *American Votes: Handbook of Contemporary American Election Statistics,* 1956– . Washington, DC: Congressional Quarterly. Biennial. ISSN 0065678X. (Q109)
>
> *Gallup Poll,* 1971– . Wilmington, DE. Annual. ISSN 0195962X. (Q110)
>
> *Public Opinion Online (POLL).* Storrs, CT: Roper Center for Public Opinion Research. Digital. (Q111)
>
> *Vital Statistics on American Politics, 1997–1998.* 6th ed. Harold W. Stanley and Richard G. Niemi, eds. Washington, DC: Congressional Quarterly, 1997. ISBN 1568023758. (Q112)
>
> *Vital Statistics on Congress, 1995–96.* Norman J. Ornstein, ed. Washington, DC: Congressional Quarterly. 291 p. ISBN 0871878453. (Q113)

America at the Polls covers nineteen presidential elections, from Harding to Clinton. Data are arranged chronologically by presidential election in reverse order. Each volume consists of three sections. The first section presents national summary tables of the state-by-state electoral votes, total votes, and percentages for each presidential election year. The second section has tables of electoral votes and electoral college votes for each state and the District of Columbia since 1964, including census population, country, total vote (Republican, Democratic, and other), plurality, and percentage, plus county outline maps. The final section concerns presidential primaries.

In general, votes for Republican, Democratic, and other parties are listed in three columns. A fourth column is added for those candidates who received an appreciable vote, such as in the 1992 election, when H. Ross Perot received 18.9 percent of the vote. The front section note presents votes for all candidates and other events, such as the resignation of Vice-President Agnew and President Nixon. The election notes for each state cover other votes and such information as canvass reports, creation of new counties, and the Twenty-Third Amendment to the Constitution, which entitles the District of Columbia to choose three electors.

American Votes has a much broader coverage, complementing *America at the Polls* on presidential elections. The biennial contains the most recent election results for senator, representative, and governor; state-by-state primary results; state-by-state presidential election totals since 1920; and presidential primary totals since 1972.

Gallup Poll is a collection of polls based mostly on telephone interviews. These polls and survey findings are arranged by date. Topics are broad, but most concern politics. Each poll includes a scope note (with or without selected national trends) followed by editorial comments. Opinions are classified, depending on the data, by sex, ethnic background, education, age, politics, household income, special status, and political ideology. In addition to the data, the book includes an introduction to sample surveys, a record of Gallup Poll accuracy from 1936, a chronology of specific events that may be related to poll results, and Gallup regions. For recent polls, refer to *Gallup Poll Monthly*, 1965–   (formerly *Gallup Report* and *Gallup Political Index*, ISSN 10512616).

POLL, provided by the Roper Center, a nonprofit research institution in the field of public opinion and policy, covers data from 1936 forward (with some earlier data). Since 1995, some data contain detailed breakdowns such as the race, gender, age, education, and geographic location of the people surveyed. It is marketed via Dialog (File 468).

Vital Statistics on American Politics is a collection of statistical data on various topics relating to American politics. Topics include, for instance, mass media, campaigns and elections, political parties, public opinion, interesting groups, the three branches of government, federalism, foreign and military policy, social policy, and economic policy. For each topic are provided a brief introduction, statistical data in either figures and/or tables, and a series of questions intended "to enhance the reader's understanding of how to make better use of tabular information" (Introduction). There are more than 200 figures and tables. There is a teacher's manual available that contains the answers to the questions.

Vital Statistics on Congress may be considered a companion to *Politics in America* or *Almanac of American Politics*. It consists of (1) members of Congress, (2) election, (3) campaign finance, (4) committees, (5) congressional staff and operating expenses, (6) activity, (7) budgeting, and (8) roll call voting. Some statistical data cover from 1910 to 1981.

Handbooks, Yearbooks, and the Like

United States

In the United States today, there are one federal government, 50 state governments, and over 78,000 local governments, which include counties, municipalities, townships, school districts, and special districts.

General

> *The United States Government Manual*, 1935–   . U.S. Office of the Federal Register, National Archives and Records Administration. Washington, DC: GOP. Annual. Print & digital. (Q114)

The *Government Manual* is an important reference to government agencies, their creation, authority, organization, organizational charts, activities, and chief officials. It is divided into three parts: the Legislative Branch, the Judicial Branch, and the Executive Branch. Also listed are selected multilateral and bilateral organizations. Appendixes are (A) Commonly Used Abbreviations and Acronyms, (B) Terminated and Transferred Agencies, and (C) Agencies Appearing in the Code of Federal Regulations. There are two indexes: Name and Agency/Subject. The *Manual* is also available on the Internet via *GPO Access*, noted in Chapter 7.

Executive Branch

> *Congressional Quarterly's Guide to the Presidency*. 2nd ed. Michael Nelson, ed. Washington, DC: Congressional Quarterly, 1996. 4 vols. ISBN 156802018X. (Q115)

The *Guide to the Presidency* describes "every president's accomplishments and failures, virtues and foibles" (Preface). It contains 37 chapters contributed by nineteen scholars. Chapters are grouped into seven parts as follows: Origins and Development of the Presidency; Selection and Removal of the President; Powers of the Presidency; The President, the Public, and the Parties; The White House and the Executive Branch; Chief Executive and Federal Government; and Biographies of the Presidents and Vice-Presidents. At the end are two appendixes providing reference materials. Appendix A contains 42 documents and texts including Declaration of Independence, Washington's Farewell address, the Monroe Doctrine, Franklin D. Roosevelt's "Four Freedoms" Speech, and Nixon's China Trip Announcement. Appendix B is Tabular and Graphical Data.

Legislative Branch

> Congress and the Nation, 1945/64–   : A Review of Government and Politics. Washington, DC: Congressional Quarterly Service, 1965– . Quadrennial. ISSN 10471324. (Q116)
>
> Congressional Quarterly Service Weekly Report, 1946– . Washington, DC: Congressional Quarterly Service. ISSN 00105910. (Q117)
>
> C Q Almanac, 1945– . Washington, DC: Congressional Quarterly Service, 1945– . Annual. ISSN 00956007. (Q118)

Congress and the Nation is one of the best works on the activities of the federal government. The first volume covers the period from 1945 to 1964. From Volume 2 on, each volume covers a four-year period. The sixth volume, 1981–1984 (1985, 1,162 p., ISBN 0871873346) is "a summary of major congressional action; budget and taxes; Central America; Lebanon; war power; elections and political activities; arms control; social security" (title page). It is divided into sixteen chapters on various topics, including agriculture, commerce, communications, defense, economics, education, energy, environment, health, housing, labor, transportation, urban aid, and welfare. The first chapter, forming a framework for the chapters that follow, gives a legislative summary of each session and a discussion of the 1980 and 1985 elections. Each of the other chapters begins with an introduction that gives an overview of the four-year period, followed by a chronology of legislative action from 1981 through 1984. Some entries have extensive coverage. The appendixes contain a glossary of congressional terms, the legislative processes in brief, key votes, Congress and its members, congressional reapportionment, the presidency, and political charts. For current information, refer to Weekly Report and C Q Almanac, both noted later.

The Weekly Report is a news service providing reports on the executive branch, major legislative action, court decisions, party politics, and on various subjects such as appropriations, banking, economic affairs, education, foreign policy, government operations, science/technology, and trade.

The C Q Almanac is a compendium of legislation for one session of Congress. It begins with a chapter of legislative overview of the 100th Congress, second session, followed by legislative actions under fifteen topics. At the end are three chapters dealing with political reports, special reports, and voting studies. It is an excellent reference work for the study of legislative actions and politics.

Judicial Branch

> *Congressional Quarterly's Guide to the U.S. Supreme Court.* 3rd ed. Joan Biskupic and Elder Witt, eds. Washington, DC: Congressional Quarterly, 1996. 2 vols. ISBN 1568021305. (Q119)
> *Supreme Court Yearbook*, 1990– . Washington, DC: Congressional Quarterly. Annual. ISSN 10542701. (Q120)

The guide contains seven parts: (1) origins and development of the court; (2) the court and the federal system; (3) the court and the individual; (4) pressures on the court; (5) the court at work; (6) members of the court, consisting of surveys of the characteristics of 101 justices and biographical sketches from John Jay to John Paul Stevens; and (7) major decisions of the court, a synopsis of court decisions from 1790 to the the 1970s.

The *Supreme Court Yearbook*, 1995–1996 (Kenneth Jost, 1996, 358 p., ISBN 0871878984) consists of four chapters: (1) The Center Reappears, analyzing justices' voting patterns and examining the possibility of an ideological shift on the court after the 1996 presidential election, (2) The 1995–1996 Terms, (3) Case Summaries, and (4) Preview of the 1996–1997 Term. Appendixes are Opinion Excerpts, How the Court Works, Brief Biographies, Glossary of Legal Terms, and the United States Constitution.

State and Local

> *The Book of the States*, 1935– . Lexington, KY: Council of State Governments. Biennial. ISSN 00680125. (Q121)
> *The Municipal Year Book*, 1934– . Washington, DC: International City-County Management Association. Annual. ISSN 00772186. (Q122)

The 1998/99 *Book of the States* (1998, 507 p., ISBN 0892929477) surveys the structure, working methods, financing, and functional activities of state governments. It is a combined handbook, compilation of statistical data, and directory covering such topics as state constitutions, state executive branch, the legislatures, the judiciary, elections, campaign finance, initiatives, management, regulations, personnel, programs and issues, intergovernmental affairs, and state pages. Statistical sources are substantial. Two supplements are published in the odd-numbered years, giving a complete listing of state officials and members of the legislatures: *State Administrative Officials Classified by Functions*, 1977– (Lexington, KY: Council of State Governments, ISSN 01919423) (Q123), and *State Elective Officials and the Legislatures*, 1977– (Lexington, KY: Council of State Governments, ISSN 01919431) (Q124). The Council of State Government also publishes state white pages for quick reference: *State Administrative Officials* (annual, ISSN 01919423) (Q125), *State Elective Officials* (annual, ISSN 01919466), and *State Legislative Leadership, Committees and Staff* (annual, ISSN 01956639) (Q126).

The Council of State Governments also maintains a Web site (http://www.csg.gov) (Q127) that enables a user to search for information on state and local government, state pages, law and justice, federal government, and news. Its State and Local Government category provides access to a number of agencies and organizations, biographies of candidates and elected officials, and U.S. State and Local Gateway. Over 13,000 biographies are compiled. "Your Government" provides information on the states, the three branches of the federal government, historical documents and resources, and links to other educational resources. In both Law and Justice and Federal Government, links to a number of agencies and organizations are provided. The Web site is good for ready reference on American government, identification of candidates and officials, and links to other resources.

At the local level, *The Municipal Year Book*, 1996 (Evelina Moulder, ed., 338 p., ISBN 0873269713), contains signed articles in five parts: (1) management issues and trends, (2) the intergovernmental dimension including a review of major judicial decisions, (3) staffing and compensation, (4) directories, and (5) references. Since the demise of *The County Year Book*, 1975–1978 (Washington, DC: International City Management Association and National Association of Counties, annual), an article, "County Government: A Century of Change," in part A of the *Year Book* is the best source available for counties.

International

> *Political Handbook of the World*, 1927– . Arthur S. Banks, ed. New York: McGraw-Hill. Annual. ISSN 0193175X. (Q128)
> *Yearbook of the United Nations*, 1946/47– . New York: United Nations Publications. Annual. ISSN 00828521. (Q129)
> *Yearbook of the United Nations Special Edition UN Fiftieth Anniversary, 1945–1995*. The Hague: Martinus Nijhoff, 1995. 443 p. ISBN 0792331125. (Q130)

Reference works on governments in the world are many. *Statesman's Year-book* and *Europa*, both mentioned in Chapter 4, are the best works of this kind. The *Political Handbook* listed here is one more good reference work on world governments. It is designed to furnish factual information on all countries and international organizations in two parts. Part 1 lists governments in alphabetical order by name of the country, but the Palestine

Liberation Organization is included. For each country, the book gives background information and information on government and politics, political parties, legislature, cabinet, news media, and diplomatic representation. Compared with *Statesman's Year-book* and *Europa*, the *Handbook* focuses on government and party officials. Part 2 is a listing of selected intergovernmental organizations. Two indexes are supplied: a geographical and organizational names index and a personal names index.

Yearbook of the United Nations consists of two parts: (1) the United Nations, including political and security questions, economic and social questions, questions relating to the declaration on granting independence and to the international trusteeship system, legal questions, and administrative and budgetary questions; and (2) the intergovernmental organizations related to the United Nations, including specialized agencies. The specialized agencies, such as the International Labor Organization and UNESCO, are largely self-governing bodies brought into relationship with the United Nations by agreements between the agencies and the Economic and Social Council of the United Nations.[7]

The *Yearbook* is the most complete work on the functions and organization of the United Nations and its related agencies. Appendixes give the roster of the United Nations, the United Nations Charter and the Statute of the International Court of Justice, structure of the United Nations, current agenda of United Nations principal organs, and United Nations Information Centers and Services. Names of officials of the United Nations and its related agencies are given in the *Yearbook*, but there are no biographical sketches. There are three indexes: (1) subject, (2) names, and (3) resolutions and decisions.

Less comprehensive in coverage of the United Nations is *Everyone's United Nations: A Complete Handbook of the Activities and Evolution of the United Nations* (10th ed., New York: United Nations, 1986, 484 p., ISBN 9211002737) (Q131), covering 40 years of the United Nations. It supplements the *Yearbook* for retrospective information. Another concise overview of the United Nations activities in the last four decades is *Basic Facts about the United Nations* (United Nations, Department of Public Information, New York, 1985, pagination varies, ISBN 9211002540) (Q132). It begins with the origin, purposes, principles, and structure of the United Nations, followed by activities divided into international peace and security, economic and social development, human rights, international law, and intergovernmental agencies related to the United Nations. Appendixes provide information on growth of membership (1945–1984), member states date of admission, scale of assessments, information centers and services, and a reading list. It is continued by the special edition, noted next.

The special edition of the *Yearbook of the United Nations* provides a narrative account of the achievements of the United Nations with key documents "over the past 50 years in the areas of international peace and security, development and strengthening of international law, disarmament, decolonization and the advancement of economic and social progress" (About the Special Edition of the Yearbook). It consists of five parts: (1) International Peace and Security, (2) International Law, (3) Emerging Nations, (4) Economic and Social Development, and (5) Human Rights Questions. It concludes with "Into the twenty-first century," "Who's who in the United Nations at the time of its founding," selected bibliography, and an index.

For current information on the activities of the United Nations, the *UN Chronicle*, noted earlier, should be consulted. The *Chronicle* consists of the news digest, a record of the month, and is divided along the line of the *Yearbook of the United Nations* into political and security, economic and social, administrative and budgetary, and legal topics. It also carries the meetings calendar, documents, publications, and resolutions.

NOTES

1. Jean M. Driscoll, "The Nature of Political Science," in Martin Feldman and Eli Seifman, eds., *The Social Studies* (Englewood Cliffs, NJ: Prentice-Hall, 1969), pp. 114–123.

2. *Contemporary Political Science* (Paris: UNESCO, 1950), p. 4.

3. Heinz Eulau and James G. March, eds., *Political Science* (Englewood Cliffs, NJ: Prentice-Hall, 1969), p. 13.

4. *Contemporary Political Science*, p. 4.

5. Charles E. Merriam, "Political Science in the United States," in *Contemporary Political Science*, pp. 233–248, 234ff.

6. Alfred de Grazia, "Continuity and Innovation in Reference Retrieval in the Social Sciences: Illustrations from the Universal Reference System," *American Behavioral Scientist* 10 (1967): 1.

7. Article 57, Charter of the United Nations.

Chapter 16

Psychology

Psychology studies the behavior of people and animals in all its manifestations. The study of human behavior dates back to as early as the time of Confucius and Plato. Not until the late nineteenth century did psychology detach itself from philosophy and become a distinct area that uses experimental and observational method to study psychological problems.

Psychology belongs to both the biological and the social sciences.[1] As a part of the biological sciences, psychology studies the lower organisms and the role of organs in mental processes. The social sciences–oriented psychology focuses attention on attitudes, opinion studies, and group dynamics. The inter-disciplinary approach is clearly reflected in the publications of the American Psychological Association.

There are, in general, two approaches to the study of psychology.[2] One, the humanistic approach, studies the inner aspects of mental life, such as feelings, motives, drives, and expectations of an individual person. The other, the behavioral approach, focuses attention on the externally observable aspects of mental life, such as the bodily response to environmental stimuli.

Josef Cohen has listed ten basic topics that constitute the subject matter of psychology: sensation-perception, motivation, motion, innate patterns, learning, thinking, intelligence, personality, group dynamics, and behavior pathology.[3] The present interest, according to Ernest R. Hilgard, lies in five topics: physiological processes, learning, motivation, cognitive processes, and clinical psychology.[4] Physiological processes deal with the role of organs of the body in mental processes and activities. They consist of such subfields as neuropsychology, the study of the brain, sensory, and motor; psychochemistry, the study of chemical influence on behavior; and psychopharmacology, the study of the effects of drugs on behavior.[5] Physiological processes cover the same areas as human and animal experimental psychology, including sensory processes, motor, motivation, learning, and thinking.[6] Learning studies relatively permanent change of behavior that occurs as a result of prior experience.[7] Instinct, drives, primitive motives, and secondary personal or social motives are the subject matter of motivation. Cognitive processes, the higher mental processes, include thinking, creating, and problem solving. The largest field of specialization is clinical psychology.[8] It is concerned with the diagnosis of mental or emotional disturbances and the treatment and prevention of illness with psychological causes.[9]

Whether one branch of psychology, social psychology, should be considered a branch of psychology or one of sociology remains to be determined. Social psychology studies the behavior or mental life of an individual or a group of individuals influenced by the social environment. Both sociology and social psychology deal with human social behavior, but with different purposes.[10] Sociology studies social structure, social groups, and social processes. The influence of social phenomena upon the behavior of society's members is the primary concern of social psychology.[11]

ACCESS TO SOURCES

Guides

Quite a few guides to help students in doing research have been published. Though in many respects out of date, *Professional Problems in Psychology* by Robert S. Daniel and C. M. Louttit (New York: Prentice-Hall, 1953, 416 p.) (R1) remains an important guide to the literature of psychology. The work covers three areas: literature search, scientific reports, and professionalization. Of particular importance to library users are the two chapters "A Survey of Psychological Literature" and "Bibliographical Problems in Psychology." These chapters discuss the scattered nature of the literature of psychology and evaluate bibliographic sources in psychology and its related fields. It has four appendixes: bibliographies of reference books; journals; sources for books, tests, apparatus, equipment and supplies; and a glossary of abbreviations.

Current guides include:

> *How to Find Out in Psychology: A Guide to the Literature and Methods of Research.* D. H. Borchardt and R. D. Francis. New York: Pergamon, 1984. 189 p. ISBN 0080312802. (R2)
> *Library Use: A Handbook for Psychology.* 2nd ed. Jeffrey B. Reed and Pam M. Baxter. Washington, DC: American Psychological Association, 1992. 177 p. ISBN 1557981442. (R3)
> *Psychology: A Guide to Reference and Information Sources.* Pam M. Baxter.

Englewood, CO: Libraries Unlimited, 1993. 219 p. ISBN 0872877086. Reference sources in the social sciences series, 6. (R4)
Research Guide for Psychology. Raymond G. McInnis. Westport, CT: Greenwood Press, 1982. 604 p. ISBN 0313213992. (R5)

The Borchardt and Francis book is a bibliographical review of 186 references in English and the languages of Western Europe. Its clarity and fine touch on historical perspectives make the work pleasant reading.

Library Use is intended "to bridge the gap between the need that a student embarking on a psychology research project has for information and the information that is available in the college library" (Introduction). It provides an introduction to getting started, selecting and defining the topic, and locating a book and presents with sample pages the use of abstracting, indexing, government documents, computer searching, and psychological tests and measures. There are three appendixes: (A) Additional Specialized Sources, (B) Brief Guide to Literature Searching, and (C) Exercises and Other Topics to Pursue. For a more detailed guide, refer to one of the books noted next.

Baxter's *Psychology* contains 667 annotated titles and agencies grouped into four sections: General Social Science Reference Sources, Social Science Disciplines, General Psychology Reference Sources, and Special Topics in Psychology. Titles and agencies in each section are arranged by either format or subjects followed by format. It covers also other subdisciplines of the social sciences, such as anthropology, criminal justice, economics, education, history, political science, and sociology. It has an author/title index and a subject index.

An extensive guide to reference sources is the McInnis *Research Guide*, consisting of seventeen parts. Part A deals with general works arranged by type. Parts B through Q are subfields of psychology, including experimental psychology, physiological psychology, physiological intervention, communications systems, developmental psychology, social processes and social issues, personality, physical and psychological disorders, treatment and prevention, educational psychology, applied psychology, and so on. Information sources in these parts are grouped in four broad categories: (1) research guides, (2) substantive information sources, (3) substantive-bibliographic information sources, and (4) bibliographic information sources. Length of parts varies depending upon the sources available. For instance, Part Q, Parapsychology, is covered in six pages, in contrast to the more than 70 pages in Part H, Social Processes and Social Issues. It is a valuable reference book.

Bibliographies

General

For retrospective bibliographies, reference may be made to Benjamin Rand's *Bibliography of Philosophy, Psychology and Cognate Subjects* (New York: Macmillan, 1905, 2 vols.) (R6), published as volumes 3 and 4 of James Mark Baldwin's *Dictionary of Philosophy and Psychology*. Psychology is presented in its Bibliography G in Part II (pp. 913–1,192). Rand covers books and articles in the various languages published before the twentieth century. It was continued by *Psychological Index*, noted later.

Some representative bibliographies are:

> *Bibliographic Guide to Psychology*, 1975– . Boston: G. K. Hall. Annual. ISSN 0360277X. (R7)
> *Eminent Contributors to Psychology*. Robert I. Watson, Sr., ed. New York: Springer, 1974. 2 vols. ISBN 0826114504. (R8)
> *PsycBooks: Books and Chapters in Psychology*, 1988–1990. Washington, DC: American Psychological Association. Annual. ISSN 10441514. (R9)

G. K. Hall's 1996 *Bibliographic Guide* (1997, 165 p., ISBN 0783817746), part of its *Bibliographic Guide Series*, lists publications catalogued by the Library of Congress and the Research Library of the New York Public Library. *Eminent Contributors in Psychology* lists primary and secondary references to 538 individuals living between 1600 and 1967. The 538 individuals include psychologists, philosophers, biologists, physiologists, anatomists, neurologists, ophthalmologists, geneticists, psychoanalysts, psychiatrists, hypnotists, anthropologists, sociologists, and others. The first volume is devoted to about 12,000 primary references, with an average of 23 references per person arranged in alphabetical order by individual. For each individual are given full name, dates of birth and death, the country (or countries) where the person's principal work was done, major field of endeavor and, in parentheses, the eminence rating score (explained later), followed by a list of the person's works. Volume 2 has the same arrangement, listing more than 55,000 selected secondary references to the works of the same contributors to psychology. The bibliography contains books and articles, in English and other languages, book reviews, and dissertations. Both volumes are also good sources of biographies and autobiographies.

In both volumes, contributors are listed alphabetically. The information for each contributor includes the full name, dates of birth and death, the country/countries where the principal work was done, major field of endeavor, and eminence rating score in parentheses, followed by a listing of bibliographical citations. The method of selecting contributors may be of interest: A list of 1,040 contributors to psychology who lived between 1600 and 1967 was compiled. These names were submitted to a panel of nine leading psychologists from the United States, France, Japan, and Belgium. The panel members rated the contributors by providing one check mark if he recognized the name; two check marks if he could identify the person's contribution to psychology; and three check marks if he considered the person important enough to be included among the 500 most distinguished psychologists since 1600 and not living. Contributors who received a score of 11 to 27 (highest) were selected for inclusion.

PsycBooks provides summaries of books sent to the American Psychological Association to be considered for review by *Contemporary Psychology*, noted later. It contains five volumes: (1) Experimental Psychology: Basic and Applied; (2) Developmental, Personality, and Social Psychology; (3) Professional Psychology: Disorders and Treatment; (4) Educational Psychology and Health Psychology; and (5) Author and Subject Indexes. The book records contain three main parts: a full bibliographical citation, the book's table of contents (in full or abbreviation), and content summary information quoted from the book. The chapter records include a bibliographical citation and content summary quoted from the chapter. It is no longer published. Its online version, PsycBooks, is limited to APA books, noted later.

Subfield

Attitudes and Behavior: An Annotated Bibliography. Daniel J. Canary and David R. Seibold. New York: Praeger, 1984. 221 p. ISBN 0030602939 paper. (R10)

Bibliography of Aggressive Behavior: A Reader's Guide to the Research Literature. Michael Crabtree and Kenneth E. Moyer. New York: Alan R. Liss, 1977. 416 p. ISBN 0845102001. (R11)

Bibliography of Aggressive Behavior: A Reader's Guide to the Research Literature. Kenneth E. Moyer and J. Michael Crabtree. New York: Alan R. Liss, 1981. 489 p. ISBN 0845102125. (R12)

Body Movement and Nonverbal Communication: An Annotated Bibliography, 1971–1981. Martha Davis and Janet Skupien, eds. Bloomington, IN: Indiana University Press, 1982. 294 p. ISBN 0253341019. (R13)

Female Psychology: An Annotated Psychoanalytic Bibliography. Elenor Schuker and Nadine A. Levinson. Hillside, NJ: Analytic Press, 1991. 678 p. ISBN 088163087X. (R14)

The Physical Environment and Behavior: An Annotated Bibliography and Guide to Literature. Joachim F. Wohlwill and Gerald D. Weisman. New York: Plenum Press, 1981. 474 p. ISBN 0306407396. (R15)

Attitudes and Behavior is a bibliography of published papers arranged alphabetically by author. It features description of type of study, procedure used, moderators, and attitude-behavior relation. It concludes with "The Specialized Reference" that provides thirteen content categories serving as a subject index to entries.

The two volumes of *Bibliography of Aggressive Behavior* provide approximately 7,500 entries. The first volume consists of two parts: human aggression and animal aggression, which are further divided into many subfields. The second volume simply arranges entries in alphabetical order by first author. The bibliography is not annotated, but each entry is assigned a code word or words, substituting for subjects. Also, *Aggressive Behavior*, a periodical, has as its regular feature "A Guide to the Literature on Aggressive Behavior."

Body Movement and Nonverbal Communication continues *Understanding Body Movement: An Annotated Bibliography* by Martha Davis (New York: Arno Press, 1972, 190 p. ISBN 0405002866) (R16). The 1972 bibliography provides 931 entries in alphabetical order by author. The present bibliography, also arranged alphabetically by author, lists 1,411 items— books, periodical articles, parts of books, and dissertations on psychology and anthropology of body movement.

Female Psychology is a classified listing in five sections: (1) Historical Views; (2) Developmental Perspective; (3) Female, Sexuality, Character, Psychopathology; (4) Clinical Concepts; and (5) Reading Lists. There are an author index and a subject index.

In environmental psychology, a good bibliography is *The Physical Environment and Behavior*. It contains 1,491 entries of books, articles, reports, and dissertations classified into sixteen chapters in four parts: (1) general materials, (2) psychological processes in the individual's response to the environment, (3) applied areas and special issues, and (4) cognate areas. Most entries are annotated, and for some books contents are given.

Theses and Dissertations

Doctoral dissertations used to be included in *Psychological Abstracts*. Since 1980, they have been contained in the database *PsycINFO*. A case study points out that the inclusion of dissertations in *PsycINFO* lags significantly behind *Dissertation Abstracts International*.[12] Dissertations are also published in journals as noted in Chapter 6.

Reviews

For a review of the literature in psychology, an indispensable source is:

Annual Review of Psychology, 1950–   . Palo Alto, CA: Annual Reviews. ISSN 00664308. (R17)

This is the earliest of four annual reviews in the social sciences. The other three are in the fields of anthropology, political science, and sociology. According to its master plan, the *Review* offers certain articles every year, other articles in alternate years, and still others every third or fourth year, under main headings. Each volume also includes special chapters on timely topics that are not among the main headings. All reviews have lengthy citations of significant works. The Table of Contents can also be viewed through the publisher's Web site (http://www.annualreviews.org).

There are two periodicals noted for their reviews:

Contemporary Psychology: A Journal Reviews, 1956– . Washington, DC: American Psychological Association. Monthly. ISSN 00107549. (R18)

Psychological Bulletin, 1904– . Washington, DC: American Psychological Association. Bimonthly. ISSN 00332909. (R19)

Contemporary Psychology reviews books, films, tapes, and other media relevant to psychology. It carries critical reviews of books, books briefly, preview, and "On the Other Hand," a good feature to present different views on the book reviews. The journal publishes a substantial number of reviews each year.

Reviews of literature in psychology are issued in *Psychological Bulletin*. The *Bulletin* publishes "evaluative and integrative reviews and interpretations of substantive and methodological issues in scientific psychology" (verso of the cover page). It is a major reviewing organ in psychology. The journal consists of three departments: review articles, quantitative methods in psychology, and other. In the abstracting service, *Psychological Bulletin* is the predecessor of *Psychological Abstracts*, noted later.

Indexes

Psychology is one of the fields in the social sciences that enjoys the best indexing and abstracting services. American Psychological Association (APA) dominates the indexing and abstracting services in psychology. *Psychological Index*, 1894–1935 (Princeton, NJ: Psychological Review, 1895–1936, 41 vols.) (R20), which continued Rand, noted earlier, is a classified bibliography of original publications with an average of 5,000 titles of books and periodical articles listed each year. It covers all aspects of psychology in various languages and is more complete than Rand. *Psychological Index (PI)* ceased publication in 1936, and its work has been carried on by *Psychological Abstracts*, noted next.

Abstracts

General

Psychological Abstracts, 1927– . Washington, DC: American Psychological Association. Monthly. ISSN 00332887. Print & digital. (R21)

PsycINFO, 1967–   . Washington, DC: American Psychological Association. Monthly. Digital. (R22)

Psychological Abstracts (*PA*) started in 1927 to take over the abstracting service of *Psychological Bulletin*. *Psychological Bulletin* included a few abstracts in its earlier issues and in 1921 began publication of a large number of them. Thus, Peter R. Lewis considers *PA* the oldest abstract in the social sciences, dating from 1904.[13]

Each issue consists of four parts: (1) Table of Contents, a list of seventeen classification categories and subcategories; (2) Abstracts, arranged in alphabetical order by author within the classification categories and subcategories; (3) Brief Subject Index, an alphabetical list of subject terms from the *Thesaurus of Psychological Index Terms* (8th ed., Alvin Walker, Jr., ed., Arlington, VA: American Psychological Association, 1997, 378 p., ISBN 1557984026) (R23) that contains postable and nonpostable index terms of 7,726; and (4) Author Index. The *Thesaurus* is a hierarchically structured vocabulary of 4,000 terms. The eighth edition has over 200 new standardized terms and 110 new scope notes. It consists of three sections: relationship, rotated, and term clusters. The *Thesaurus* is accessible as part of *PsycINFO*, marketed through Dialog (File 11).

PA contains abstracts and for some works mere citations of books, book chapters, reports, and periodical articles in English and other languages. A list of journals and serials scanned regularly and abstracted selectively is published in the annual author index.

A backward abstracting service is *Psychological Index Abstract References* edited by H. L. Ansbacher (Columbus, OH: American Psychological Association, 1940–1941, 2 vols.) (R24). It lists, by the *PI* serial number, the items in *PI* for which abstracts were located in periodicals, together with necessary references. The first volume covers the period from 1894 to 1918, and the second volume covers 1919–1928. As nearly 42 percent of the 107,000 titles in *PI* were covered in this way, it extends the coverage of *PA* backward to 1894.

PA is one of the Information Services in Psychology of the American Psychological Association. Information Services also provides *PA* on magnetic tape formerly known as *PATELL* (PA Tape Edition for Lease or License) (R25), online databases such as *PsycINFO*[14] marketed through Dialog (File 11), Ovid (File PSYC), DataStar (File PSYC), FirstSearch, and EBSCOhost, as well as on CD-ROM, called *PsycLIT* (R26), marketed by different vendors, such as EBSCO, Ovid, and SilverPlatter. *PsycLIT* corresponds in part to *Psychological Abstracts* and the online *PsycINFO* database.

PsycINFO, formerly *Psychabs*, adopted the present title in 1980 to distinguish it from the print product. The database provides access to 1,300 periodicals, dissertations, technical reports, and other sources. It contains

25 percent more citations in each update than the print counterpart. Tips for search and news on *PsycINFO* products are released in *PsycInfo News*, 1981– (quarterly, print & digital, http://www.apa.org/psycinfo/issues.html) (R27). A weekly update service is *PsycALERT* (http:// www.apa.org/psycalert.html) (R28), and updated records are transferred to *PsycINFO* monthly.

One good feature of using the database is its field search. The user may limit the search by fields to achieve relevant and precise results. Some enhancements may be noted. It expanded the Population Group field to include gender distinctions, inpatient/outpatient status, and new age group; revised the Document Type field to include empirical studies, case reports, longitudinal studies, literature reviews, bibliographies, and so on; and added the Population Location field to indicate geographical location by country name.

Besides *PI* and *PA*, *Social Sciences Index* and *Wilson Social Sciences Abstracts*, noted in Chapter 3, and *Child Development Abstracts and Bibliography*, noted later, all have good coverage of psychology periodical literature. Currently, *Social Sciences Index* and *Wilson Social Science Abstracts* index and abstract over 30 psychology periodicals, many of which are American Psychological Association publications.

Subfield

> *Child Development Abstracts and Bibliography*, 1927– . Chicago: University of Chicago Press for the Society for Research in Child Development. 3/year. ISSN 00093939. Print & digital. (R29)
>
> *Psychoanalytic Abstracts*, 1985– . Washington, DC: American Psychological Association. Quarterly. ISBN 10669884. (R30)
>
> *PsycSCAN: Applied Psychology*, 1980– . Washington, DC: American Psychological Association. Quarterly. ISSN 02717506. (R31)
>
> *PsycScan: Behavior Analysis and Therapy*, 1995– . Washington, DC: American Psychological Association. Quarterly. ISSN 10783946. (R32)
>
> *PsycScan: Clinical Psychology*, 1980– . Washington, DC: American Psychological Association. Quarterly. ISSN 01971484. (R33)
>
> *PsycScan: Developmental Psychology*, 1980– . Washington, DC: American Psychological Association. Quarterly. ISSN 01971492. (P34)
>
> *PsycScan: Learning and Communication Disorders and Mental Retardation*, 1982– . Washington, DC: American Psychological Association. Quarterly. ISSN 07301928. (R35)

The *Child Development Abstracts and Bibliography* "publishes abstracts from professional periodicals and reviews books related to the growth and development of children" (verso of the cover). It is classified into six headings: biology, health and medicine; cognition, learning, and perception; education; psychiatry and clinical psychology; social psychology and personality; and theory, methodology, and reviews. Each issue contains abstracts, book notices, a subject index, an author index, and author addresses. The 1998 volume lists more than 670 abstracts and some 26 book notices. It complements *PA*, particularly in the field of medical science. *Child Development Abstracts and Bibliography* is also available on the Internet (http://www.journals.uchicago.edu/CDAB/journal).

Beginning in 1980, *PA* launched *PsycScan*, which abstracts a limited number of periodicals in a particular field, tailored to the needs of the individual. Each publication contains more than 1,000 abstracts per year and features a scanning format for quick but thorough review of each journal issue. There were six *PsycScans*. Currently, APA publishes five *PsycScans* and *Psychoanalytic Abstracts*, listed above, formerly *PsycScan Psychoanalysis*.

Contents Reproduction

Contents reproduction of journals in psychology can be found in *Current Contents*, noted in Chapter 3, and *PsycNet* for APA's books and journals, noted next.

SOURCES OF INFORMATION

General

> *PsycNet*. Washington, DC: American Psychological Association. http://www.apa.org (R36)
>
> *Psych Web*. http://www.psywww.com (R37)
>
> *Psychology*. Harrisonburg, VA: James Madison University. http://library.jmu.edu/library/guides/psych/psychome.html (R38)
>
> *PsychCrawler*. Washington, DC: American Psychological Association. http://www.psychcrawler.com (R39)

PsycNet provides information on the American Psychological Association (APA). The APA is one of the largest professional associations, including more than 155,000 members with affiliations to 59 state, territorial, and Canadian provincial associations. The home page has five main categories for choosing: About APA, Public Area, Member Area, APA Publications, and Student Information. APA Publications consists of current APA books and journals. *PsycBooks*, different from its print version, noted earlier, is limited to APA books with annotations and table of contents (http://www.apa.org/books). Contents of current issues of journals can also be viewed on the Internet (http://www.apa.org/journals).

James Madison University hosts the *Psychology* Web site, containing Electronic Journals, Books, Test Information (Mental Measurements Yearbook, HAPI, Assessment), Style Guides (APA), Discussion Lists and News

Groups on Psychology Topics, Jobs, Government Information, Professional Organization Web Sites, Counseling, Neuropsychology, Good Web Sites for Psychology, and so on. It also includes a nine-page *Guide to Psychology Resources* compiled by Lynn Cameron (R40). The *Guide* lists resources by type into Dictionaries and Encyclopedias, Handbooks, Annual Reviews, Books, Periodicals Indexes, Citation Indexes, Test Information, Diagnosis and Treatment, and Style Manual, with links to some resources.

Psych Web contains psychology and psychology-related information grouped into the following categories: APA Style Resources, Books, Brochures, Careers in Psychology, Commerce, Departments, Discussion Pages, Find Anything, Journals, Megalists, and Mind Tools. Currently, Books on *Psych Web* contains *The Interpretation of Dreams* by Sigmund Freud and *The Varieties of Religious Experience* by William James. Departments of Psychology are listed in alphabetic order with links to their home pages in Psychology Departments on the Web.

PsychCrawler is designed to provide quick access to resources in Web sites. Currently, Web sites indexed on *PsychCrawler* include American Psychological Association (http://www.apa.org), APA Public Information (http://www.helping.apa.org), National Institute of Mental Health (http://www.nimh.nih.gov), The Substance Abuse and Mental Health Services Administration (http://www.samhsa.gov), and U.S. Department of Health and Human Services, Center for Mental Health Services (http://www.mentalhealth.org). Boolean, proximity, wildcard, exact match, thesaurus, and concept operators can be used for searching.

Encyclopedias

General

James Mark Baldwin's *Dictionary*, noted later, may be regarded as the earliest encyclopedia, though Baldwin preferred the label of dictionary in spite of the book's encyclopedic treatment of many topics. *Encyclopedia of Philosophy*, edited by Paul Edwards (New York: Macmillan, 1967, 8 vols.) (R41) is a comprehensive and authoritative work offering 1,500 articles of ample length on philosophy and other disciplines, including psychology. Its coverage of psychological topics is, however, limited. Other general encyclopedias in psychology include:

> *Companion Encyclopedia of Psychology.* Andrew M. Colman, ed. London: Routledge, 1994. 2 vols. ISBN 0415064465. (R42)
> *Concise Encyclopedia of Psychology.* 2nd ed. Raymond J. Corsini and Alan J. Auerbach, New York: Wiley, 1996. 1,035 p. ISBN 0471131598. (R43)
> *Encyclopedia of Psychology.* 2nd ed. Raymond J. Corsini. New York: Wiley, 1994. 4 vols. ISBN 0471558192. (R44)

Encyclopedia of Psychology. H. J. Eysenck, W. Arnold, and R. Meili, eds. New York: Herder and Herder, 1972. 3 vols. (R45)

The Gale Encyclopedia of Psychology. Susan Gall, ed. Detroit: Gale Research, 1996. 435 p. ISBN 0787603724. (R46)

International Encyclopedia of Psychiatry, Psychology, Psychoanalysis, and Neurology. Benjamin B. Wolman, ed. New York: Van Nostrand Reinhold, 1977. 12 vols. (R47)

International Encyclopedia of Psychiatry, Psychology, Psychoanalysis, and Neurology. Progress Volume I. New York: Aesculapius, 1983. (R48)

Survey of Social Science: Psychology Series. Frank N. Magill, ed. Pasadena, CA: Salem Press, 1993. 6 vols. ISBN 0893567329. (R49)

The *Companion Encyclopedia of Psychology* contains 68 articles organized in thirteen sections. Volume 1 consists of seven sections: (1) introduction; (2) biological aspects of behavior; (3) sensation and perception; (4) cognition; (5) learning and skills; (6) emotion and motivation; and (7) individual differences and personality. Other sections are in volume 2: (8) developmental psychology; (9) social psychology; (10) abnormal psychology; (11) special topics; (12) research methods and statistics; and (13) the profession of psychology. Each section has the editor's introduction, highlighting the the section theme and contents of the section articles. In section 1, "What is psychology?" by the editor is a fine introduction to psychology, presenting the origin of the word, historical background, related disciplines and practices, and key concepts. There are a glossary (pp. 1275–1307) and a general index.

The *Concise Encyclopedia* is an abbreviated version of most of the entries in the four-volume set of encyclopedia listed next. It "retained more than 95% of the entries and an estimated 80% of the contents" (Preface). There are two indexes: name and subject, but no bibliography.

The first three volumes of the Corsini *Encyclopedia of Psychology* contain the subject topics in alphabetical order. The fourth volume consists of biographies (pp. 1–180), a bibliography (pp. 181–516), a name index, a subject index, and appendixes. There are approximately 2,500 subject and biographical entries and close to 20,000 references. Each entry is signed and ends with cross-references. The length of entries ranges from 200 to 9,000 words. Both living and deceased psychologists are included. The bibliography has a substantial number of entries of 15,000 arranged by author, and by title if no author. It is neither classified nor annotated, and it cannot serve as a guide to literature. Appendixes are: (1) Ethical Principles of Psychologists and Code of Conduct; (2) Editor's Note on U.S. Trade Commission 1993 "Draft of Complaint"; and (3) Contracts for Practicing Psychologists. The *Encyclopedia*, except its bibliography, is condensed into the *Concise Encyclopedia*, noted above.

The *Encyclopedia of Psychology*, by Eysenck and others, claimed to be an international venture, is published in English, German, French, Spanish, Portuguese, and Italian. The work, contributed by over 250 specialists from 22 countries, contains short entries of one or two lines each and some 280 articles on important terms and concepts of various lengths, up to 4,000 words. It appears that its arrangement has been influenced by *A Comprehensive Dictionary* by English and English, noted later. Though its entries are fewer in number than English and English, Eysenck is more current and features inclusion of biographies and many articles that are fully treated with suitable bibliographies for further study.

Some 500 entries are included in *The Gale Encyclopedia*, accompanied with many illustrations in alphabetical order. The length of articles varies from one paragraph to several paragraphs. Each entry has a brief definition followed by explanation, ended with further reading. It covers key concepts, terms, and biographies. There are three appendixes (glossary, bibliography, and organizations) and two indexes (subfield and subject).

A monumental work is the *International Encyclopedia of Psychiatry, Psychology, Psychoanalysis, and Neurology*, an encyclopedia of 5 million words contributed by 1,500 specialists. It contains over 1,900 articles, including 300 biographies on the entire field of the disciplines, as indicated in its title, and related disciplines such as biochemistry, genetics, ergonomics, and psychosomatic medicine. The first eleven volumes include in alphabetical order all entries, most of which are appended with bibliographies. The twelfth volume is an index containing a complete list of articles, a name index, and a detailed subject index. The *Progress* Volume updates the encyclopedia.

The *Psychology Series* is one of the four sets in the *Survey of Social Science*. It contains 410 articles arranged in alphabetical order from "Ability Testing: Individual and Group" to "Work Motivation." All articles are signed. Each article, about six pages in length, begins with type of psychology and field of study, a brief summary, and principal terms, followed by the main text. The main text consists of overview, applications, and context. "Overview" introduces and explains the topic; "Applications" describes how the topic is put into practice; and "Context" deals with the subject within the context of psychology as a whole, its relevant historical or cultural currents, and implications (Publisher's note). Appended with each article are an annotated bibliography and cross-references.

The format well suits nonspecialists, at whom the series is aimed. Articles are written with clarity. Through cross-references, readers are introduced to related topics, and they may do further studies on the basis of bibliographies. There are no biographies. However, articles refer to numerous psychologists and their contributions.

The *Psychology Series* covers eighteen areas: biological bases of behavior, cognition, consciousness, developmental psychology, emotion, intelligence and intelligence testing, language, learning, memory, motivation, origin and definition of psychology, personality, psychological methodologies, psycho-pathology, psychotherapy, sensation and perception, social psychology, and stress. Each volume has an alphabetical list and a category list. The last volume provides a glossary and an index to all volumes. It appears that the *Survey* is published under a different title as *International Encyclopedia of Psychology* (Frank N. Magill, ed. London: Fitzroy Dearborn, 1996, 2 vols., ISBN 1884864583) (R50).

Subfield

> *Encyclopedia of Clinical Assessment*. Robert Henley Woody, ed. San Francisco: Jossey-Bass, 1980. 2 vols. ISBN 0875894461. (R51)
> *The Encyclopedia of Mental Health*. Ada P. Kuhn and Jan Fawcett. New York: Facts on File, 1993. 464 p. ISBN 0816026947. (R52)
> *Encyclopedia of Occultism and Parapsychology*. 3rd ed. Leslie Shepard, ed. Detroit: Gale Research, 1991. 2 vols. ISBN 0810349078. (R53)

Ninety-one articles contributed by 110 authors are contained in *Encyclopedia of Clinical Assessment*. The encyclopedia is divided into eleven parts, including individual development, contextual challenges, major disorders, personality development, sexuality, learning and education, social involvement, idiosyncratic considerations, and so on. Articles follow a uniform approach, that is, each article consists of opening paragraphs on the dimension of the topic, background and current status, critical discussion, application to particular variables, and references. In addition to the table of contents, it provides an alphabetical listing of articles.

Entries in *The Encyclopedia of Mental Health* are arranged in alphabetical order, some with references and *see* and *see also* references. It also contains an appendix of organizations arranged by subject and a classified, but not annotated, bibliography (pp. 401–444).

The *Encyclopedia of Occultism* is "a compendium of information on the occult sciences, magic, demonology, superstitions, spiritism, mysticism, metaphysics, psychical science, and parapsychology with biographical and bibliographical notes and comprehensive indexes" (title page). The term *occult* "has been interpreted in its widest sense of 'hidden, secret, beyond human understanding' as well as pertaining to magical spells, miracles, and witchcraft" (Introduction). The first edition was based on *Encyclopedia of Occultism* by Lewis Spence (1920) and *Encyclopedia of Psychic Science* by Nandor Fordor (1934), with updated and new entries. But the original subjects in its two predecessors were retained. Entries are arranged in alphabetical order with cross-references in boldface. There are two sets of indexes: general and topical. The topical indexes are organized in nine categories: animals, birds, insects; demons; gems; geographical (Places of phenomena); gods; paranormal phenomena; periodicals; plants and flowers; and societies and organizations. There are 37 topics in the paranormal phenomena index, such as animal magnetism, animals (psychic), automatic writing, card guessing, clairaudience, elongation, ESP, eyeless sight, glossolalia (or xenoglossis), haunting, telekinesis, telepathy, and teleportation.

Dictionaries

General

The earliest major work in the English language is the *Dictionary of Philosophy and Psychology* edited by James Mark Baldwin (New York: Macmillan, 1901, 2 vols. of text; 2 vols. of bibliography) (R54). Baldwin is an encyclopedic dictionary, "including many of the principal conceptions of ethics, logic, aesthetics, philosophy of religion, mental pathology, anthropology, biology, neurology, physiology, economics, political and social philosophy, philology, physical sciences, and education and giving a terminology in English, French, German and Italian" (title page). There are many biographical sketches and indexes of Greek, Latin, German, French, and Italian terms.

An earlier good dictionary may be mentioned: *A Comprehensive Dictionary of Psychological and Psychoanalytical Terms: A Guide to Usage* by Horace Bidwell English and Ava Champney English (New York: David McKay, 1958, 594 p.) (R55). Though antiquated, this dictionary of 1,300 defined terms is an outstanding work. There are some 280 articles of considerable length. It aims to include "all terms frequently used in a special or technical sense by psychologists" and "the terms which denote mental and behavioral phenomena, and the concepts and constructs used in ordering these phenomena," as noted in the preface. For current reference, dictionaries are listed here:

Dictionary of Concepts in General Psychology. John A. Popplestone and Marion White McPherson. New York: Greenwood Press, 1988. 380 p. ISBN 0313231907. (R56)

Dictionary of Key Words in Psychology. Frank Joe Bruno. London: Routledge and Kegan Paul, 1986. 275 p. ISBN 0710201907. (R57)

The Encyclopedic Dictionary of Psychology. Rom Harré and Roger Lamb, eds. Cambridge, MA: MIT Press, 1983. 718 p. ISBN 0262081350. (R58)

The International Dictionary of Psychology. 2nd ed. Stuart Sutherland. New York: Crossroad, 1996. 515 p. ISBN 0824525094. (R59)

Longman Dictionary of Psychology and Psychiatry. Robert M. Goldenson, ed. New York: Longman, 1984. 816 p. ISBN 0582282578. (R60)

The Penguin Dictionary of Psychology. 2nd ed. Arthur S. Reber. London: Penguin, 1998. 880 p. (R61)

Reference Handbook of Research and Statistical Methods in Psychology: For Students and Professionals. R. Yaremko and others. New York: Harper & Row, 1982. 335 p. ISBN 0060473320. (R62)

Dictionary of Concepts in Psychology consists of four parts for each entry: (1) current meaning and/or meanings, (2) concepts origins, (3) citations of references discussed in the preceding part, and (4) additional sources of information for further investigation.

Terms and biographies are included in the *Dictionary of Key Words in Psychology*. Each term consists of three sections: definition, example, and connections. The connections section "seeks to search term within a larger framework, pointing out associations and links to other aspects of psychological thought," according to its preface.

The Encyclopedic Dictionary of Psychology contains entries contributed by over 300 authors in alphabetical order on such areas as cognitive psychology, psycholinguistics, neuropsychology, developmental psychology, clinical psychology, and "unofficial" psychology that refers to the theories and practices of lay folk. Almost all entries are appended with a bibliography. There are an index and a glossary. Its by-products, including *The Dictionary of Developmental and Educational Psychology*, are noted later.

The new edition of *The International Dictionary of Psychology* includes a number of terms relating to computer programs and simulation and a few new terms from the fourth edition of the *Diagnostic and Statistical Manual (DSM-IV)*. Entries are arranged in alphabetical order, but headings with exceptions are not inverted. There are five appendixes: (1) Sulci and gyri of the lateral surface of the cerebral cortex; (2) Sulci and gyri of the medial surface of the cerebral cortex; (3) Brodmann's areas of the lateral surface of the cerebral cortex; (4) Brodmann's areas of the medial surface of the cerebral cortex; and (5) Medial view of the brain. The work is also published as *The MacMillan Dictionary of Psychology* (3rd ed., 1995, 515 p., ISBN 0333623231) (R63).

Longman Dictionary of Psychology and Psychiatry contains 21,000 entries, including over 1,000 biographical entries. Definitions are in general short, but they cover well the core areas of psychology and psychiatry, such as psychoanalytic theory and practice, physiological psychology, neuropsychology, psychopharmacology, cognitive psychology, psychotherapy, mental disorders, genetics, statistics, and so on. In addition, interface areas including neurology, biofeedback, anthropology, sociology, market research, and environmental psychology are also covered.

In *The Penguin Dictionary of Psychology*, definitions are brief. Longer definitions are provided to some 80 terms, a listing of which precedes the main entries. The new edition adds more terms in social psychology, terms from *Diagnostic and Statistical Manual* (1994) and the International Classification of Diseases (ICD), and tests and measurements. There are two appendixes, Simple Phobias and Authorities Cited.

The *Reference Handbook* defines with examples as needed terms on research and statistical methods and related topics. A categorical listing of entries at the beginning of the book provides an overview of categories that are covered by the entries. There are 23 statistical tables included in the appendixes.

Subfield

Abnormal Psychology

A Reference Companion to the History of Abnormal Psychology. John G. Howells and M. Livia Osborn. Westport, CT: Greenwood Press, 1984. 2 vols. ISBN 0313221839. (R64)

Terms, books, journals, institutions, and persons are provided in *A Reference Companion.* The book explains terms, provides biographies, and describes books, journals, and institutions. As the authors state, "The companion paints on a broad canvas packed with holy springs, sacred plants, old superstitions, ancient fears, amulets, potions, strange beliefs, madhouses, scientific ideas, instruments of therapy, legal edicts, famous books, poets, painters, politicians, kings, queens, humble folk, popes." Each entry is accompanied by a bibliography for further reading. Its broad coverage is reflected by its appendix, "List of Entries by Categories," which includes abnormal behavior shown by people; animals, animal studies, ethologists; art, music, painters, sculptors, architects, composers, actors, singers, musicians; body components and body conditions; caring professions and occupations; clinical states; and educators and writers.

Clinical Psychology

The Dictionary of Physiological and Clinical Psychology. Rom Harré and Roger Lamb. Cambridge, MA: MIT Press, 1986. 314 p. ISBN 0262580756. (R65)

This dictionary and the two dictionaries (development psychology and personality and social psychology) by the same authors listed later are adapted from the authors' *Encyclopedic Dictionary of Psychology*, noted earlier, with updated and supplemental material. Most entries in the *Encyclopedic Dictionary* are retained.

Developmental Psychology

> *The Dictionary of Developmental and Educational Psychology.* Rom Harré and Roger Lamb, eds. Cambridge, MA: MIT Press, 1986. 271 p. ISBN 0262580772. (R66)

This is one of the three dictionaries listed here that are adapted from the authors' *Encyclopedic Dictionary of Psychology*, noted earlier.

Mind

> *A Companion to the Philosophy of Mind.* Samuel Guttenplan. Oxford: Blackwell, 1994. 642 p. ISBN 0631179534. (R67)
> *The Oxford Companion to the Mind.* Richard L. Gregory, ed., with the assistance of O. L. Zangwill. New York: Oxford University Press, 1987. 856 p. ISBN 019866124X. (R68)

A Companion to the Philosophy of Mind contains two parts: part 1, An Essay on Mind, with cross-reference to entries in the second part, and part 2, a listing of approximately 100 entries in alphabetical order, including action, artificial intelligence, behaviorism, cognitive psychology, emotion, intention, memory, sensation, thought, and so on. Each entry is appended with *see also* references and a bibliography for sources of more detailed information. There is a subject and name index.

The *Oxford Companion to the Mind* has a much broader scope than its title suggests. It refers to the mind in its broadest sense including perception, thinking, consciousness, unconsciousness, behavior, brain, and nervous system and many other subjects relating to the mind and persons. Over 210 authors contributed to the work. Most entries are appended with a bibliography. Length of the entries varies from one paragraph to several pages, such as entries on "brain development" (ten pages) and "nervous system" (20 pages).

Psychiatry

> *American Psychiatric Glossary.* 7th ed. Jane E. Edgerton and Robert J. Campbell, eds. Washington, DC: American Psychiatric Press, 1994. 224 p. ISBN 0880485264. (R69)
> *Psychiatric Dictionary.* 7th ed. Robert Jean Campbell. New York: Oxford University Press, 1996. 840 p. ISBN 0195102592. (R70)

There are two good dictionaries in psychiatry: *American Psychiatric Glossary* and *Psychiatric Dictionary*. The former is a revised edition of the American Psychiatric Association's *Psychiatric Glossary* published in 1984. It contains entries of terms, concepts, institutions, journals, and persons.

The tables in the appendixes are a useful reference. They include commonly used drugs, drugs used in psychiatry, legal terms, neurologic deficits, psychological tests, research terms, and schools of psychiatry.

An extensive coverage of terms and persons in psychiatry is provided by *Psychiatric Dictionary*. It deleted some 600 entries from its earlier edition published in 1970 and added 800 more new entries. Arrangement is in alphabetical order with many cross-references. Definitions are generally brief, but there are entries of more than one page in length, such as the entries for "aphasia" and "ego." More than 210 kinds of fear are defined in the entry of "fear." Pronunciation is supplied for some terms.

Psychotherapy

> *Dictionary of Psychotherapy*. Sue Walrond-Skinner. New York: Routledge and Kegan, 1986. 379 p. ISBN 0710099789. (R71)

Dictionary of Psychotherapy contains terms, concepts, schools of thought, and persons, arranged in alphabetical order from "A-Historical" to "Zurich School." It features different usages of the concept and a short bibliography for most entries.

Social Psychology

> *The Blackwell Encyclopedia of Social Psychology*. Anthony S. R. Manstead, ed. Oxford: Blackwell, 1995. 694 p. ISBN 0631181466. (R72)
> *The Dictionary of Personality and Social Psychology*. Rom Harré and Roger Lamb, eds. Cambridge, MA.: MIT Press, 1986. 402 p. ISBN 0262580780. (R73)

Over 340 entries on four levels by the number of words are provided in *The Blackwell Encyclopedia*. The four levels of entries are (1) 93 feature items of 3,000 words each; (2) 101 major items of 1,000 words each; (3) 200 words each for 64 glossary items with brief explanations; and (4) 90 glossary items of 50 words each. Entries are arranged in alphabetical order. The entry in the first three levels has a bibliography for sources of more detailed information. There is a subject and name index.

As noted earlier, the dictionary by Rom Harré and Roger Lamb is adapted from the authors' *Encyclopedic Dictionary of Psychology*, and it retains most of the entries.

Others

> *Dictionary of Behavioral Assessment Techniques*. Michel Hersen and Alan S. Bellack, eds. New York: Pergamon Press, 1987. 519 p. ISBN 0080319750. (R74)

The Mental Retardation Dictionary. Alexander J. Tymchuk. Los Angeles: Western Psychological Services, 1980. 112 p. ISBN 0874241251. (R75)

Dictionary of Behavioral Assessment Technology lists entries in alphabetical order. Each entry consists of six sections: description, purpose, development, psychometric characteristics, clinical use, and future directions, with references for further reading. A convenient feature of the dictionary is its guide to the focus of assessment, such as acrophobia, aggression, anxiety, depression, and unassertiveness.

The Mental Retardation Dictionary contains entries of terms, tests, institutions, organizations, and persons primarily concerned with the exceptional child. Treatment of entries varies in length and appears to be unbalanced. The length of entries ranges from a few words to two or more paragraphs to two pages.

Directories

Directory of Public and Private Programs for Emotionally Disturbed Children and Youth. Ronald E. Fritsch. Phoenix, AZ: Oryx Press, 1985. 336 p. ISBN 0897741994. (R76)

Directory of Residential Centers for Adults with Developmental Disabilities. Phoenix, AZ: Oryx Press, 1989. 396 p. ISBN 0897745337. (R77)

Directory of Residential Centers for Adults with Mental Illnesses. Phoenix, AZ: Oryx Press, 1990. 328 p. ISBN 0897745639. (R78)

Directory of Residential Facilities for Emotionally Handicapped Children and Youth. 2nd ed. Barbara Smiley Sherman. Phoenix, AZ: Oryx Press, 1988. 284 p. ISBN 0897744071. (R79)

Mental Health Directory, 1995. Adele S. Fell, comp. Washington, DC: GPO, 1995. 559 p. ISBN 0160482550. (R80)

Graduate Study in Psychology, 1968/69– . Washington, DC: American Psychological Association. Annual. ISSN 00725277. (R81)

The International Directory of Psychology: A Guide to People, Places, and Policies. Benjamin B. Wolman. New York: Plenum Press, 1979. 279 p. ISBN 0306402092. (R82)

In the preceding list are four directories dealing with facilities and institutions. Entries provide adequate descriptions of facilities. These directories provide for each entry name, address, contact person, facility profile, client profile, and social, rehabilitative, educational, and vocational services. Entries are arranged by state.

The government publication *Mental Health Directory* lists names, addresses, and telephone numbers of institutions and agencies, arranged by state. The institutions and agencies include outpatient mental health clinics, psychiatric hospitals, residential treatment centers for emotionally disturbed children, mental health day/night facilities, and multiservice mental health organizations.

Information on graduate programs was a regular feature of *American Psychologist*, 1946–   (Washington, DC: American Psychological Association, monthly, ISSN 0003066X) from 1951 to 1966. Since 1967, information on graduate programs has been carried on by the annual listed earlier. *Graduate Study in Psychology* (formerly *Graduate Study in Psychology and Associated Fields*) profiles over 600 departments in four sections: (1) departments and schools of psychology offering the doctoral degree (APA-accredited programs included); (2) other departments offering the doctoral degree; (3) graduate departments of psychology offering less than the doctoral degree; and (4) other graduate departments offering less than the doctoral degree. One criterion for inclusion is that programs must be offered by institutions with full accreditation from one of the seven regional accrediting bodies recognized by the United States Department of Education through the Council on Post-Secondary Accreditation.

The International Directory of Psychology provides factual information on psychology in over 60 countries and territories. It highlights development and status of psychology in the country or territory and lists national organizations, structure, membership, divisions, activities, and so on. For current information, refer to *International Directory of Psychologists*, noted later.

Biographies

Some reference works mentioned in this chapter also provide biographical information on psychologists, such as *Eminent Contributors to Psychology, Encyclopedia of Psychology* (Corsini), and *International Encyclopedia of Psychology, Psychiatry, Psychoanalysis and Neurology*. The following are sources for psychologists:

The APA Membership Register, 1967–   . Washington, DC: American Psychological Association. ISSN 07371446. (R83)

Biographical Dictionary of Psychology. Noel Sheehy, Antony J. Chapman, and Wendy A. Conroy, eds. New York: Routledge, 1997. 675 p. ISBN 0415099978. (R84)

Directory of the American Psychological Association, 1916–   . Washington, DC: American Psychological Association. Quadrennial. ISSN 01966545. (R85)

Eponyms in Psychology: A Dictionary and Biographical Sourcebook. Leonard Zusne. New York: Greenwood Press, 1987. 339 p. ISBN 0313257507. (R86)

The Great Psychologists: A Historical Thought. 5th ed. Robert I. Watson, Sr., and Rand B. Evans. New York: HarperCollins, 1991. 658 p. ISBN 0060419199. (R87)

International Directory of Psychologists Exclusive of the U.S.A. 4th ed. K. Pawlik. Amsterdam: North-Holland, 1985. 1,181 p. ISBN 0444877746. (R88)

The *Membership Register* lists roster of fellows, members, and associate members, roster of international affiliates, divisional membership rosters, and diplomates of the American Board of Professional Psychology and the American Board of Psychological Hypnosis. The 1998 Register (976 p., ISBN 1557985022) contains a total of 82,938 names (4,409 fellows, 71,364 members, and 7,165 associate members). It provides names, mailing addresses, fax and telephone numbers, e-mail addresses, membership status, and divisional affiliation. It is appended with statistical data and acronyms. There are no biographical sketches. For biographical sketches, refer to the *Directory of the American Psychological Association*, noted next.

Biographical Dictionary was first published as *Names in the History of Psychology: A Biographical Sourcebook* by Leonard Zusne (Washington, DC: Hemisphere, 1975, 489 p., ISBN 047098676X) (R89). In the first edition, the names were selected from a list of psychologists, 1600–1967, compiled by E. L. Annin and others.[15] The current dictionary covers the period from the emergence of experimental psychology in the mid-nineteenth century through to the late twentieth century. Some 500 psychologists are included. Each entry contains name, date and place of birth and death as appropriate, nationality, main area of interest in psychology with reference to the Divisions of the American Psychological Association, education, principal appointments, honors and awards, principal publications, further reading, intellectual development and main ideas including an assessment of influence, and key terms against which the person's contributions should be indexed. There are four indexes: names, interests, institutions, and key terms. The earlier editions may be retained for psychologists not included in the new one.

For contemporary psychologists, two directories are invaluable: *Directory of the American Psychological Association* (formerly *Biographical Directory of the American Psychological Association*) and *International Directory of Psychologists*, which complement each other. The 1997 edition of the *Directory of the American Psychological Association* (2 vols., ISBN 1557984239) contains main alphabetic member roster, geographic index, divisional membership roster, diplomates roster, and international affiliates. Its main listing contains profiles of 82,387 American Psychological Association members (4,350 fellows, 70,587 members, and 7,450 associate members). For each entry are given name, address, office phone, home phone, fax, e-mail address, date of birth, higher degree, major field, psychological specialty areas, diplomates, licensure or certification as a psychologist, principal current employment, other current or past employment, APA and divisional membership status, and directory recency symbol. It also provides information about APA, including officers and by-laws. It has an appendix of abbreviations.

The *International Directory* consists of a brief description of psychological societies and institutions and biographies. Biographies are arranged by country or territory. As the title indicates, American psychologists are not listed, to avoid duplication with the *Directory of the American Psychological Association*, just noted. It concludes with a listing of psychologists from the membership files of the International Association for Cross-Cultural Psychology.

In *Eponyms in Psychology*, "an eponym is both the person after whom something is named and that which is named after the person" (Preface). It includes psychological eponyms as well as selected eponyms from related fields, arranged in alphabetical order. According to the author, an effort was made to locate English-language biographical information for all eponyms.

The Great Psychologists contains 27 chapters in four parts: (1) The Ancient World; (2) The Dark and Middle Ages; (3) The Renaissance and the Early Modern Period; and (4) The Modern Period. It covers from the earliest period of recorded psychological thought, from Thales, Hippocrates, Plato, and Aristotle before psychology to the modern period of Wilhelm Wundt, Herbert Spencer and to the American psychology of Thomas Uphain, William James, and James Watson. Each chapter presents psychologists in historical perspectives and their ideas, position, interpretation, and contributions. As compared with its earlier edition, the current edition has added chapter 1 on different views of historical progress, chapter 17 on American psychology before William James, and chapter 21 on applied psychology. There are two indexes: names and subjects.

Handbooks, Yearbooks, and the Like

Tests and Measurements

It is estimated that half of the tests currently on the market should never have been published. Listed here are works dealing with tests and measurements:

> *Directory of Unpublished Experimental Mental Measures*, 1974–1997. Washington, DC: American Psychological Association. Irregular. ISSN 07318081. (R90)
>
> *The Mental Measurements Yearbook*, 1938–   . Lincoln, NE: Buros Institute of Mental Measurements, University of Nebraska. Biennial. ISSN 00766461. (R91)
>
> *Tests in Print*, 1961–   . Linda L. Murphy, ed. Lincoln, NE: Buros Institute of Mental Measurements, University of Nebraska. Quinquennial. ISSN 0361025X. (R92)

Volume 7 of the *Directory* (Bert A. Goldman, David F. Mitchell, and Paula E. Egelson, eds., 1997, 501 p., ISBN 1557984492) lists over 2,000 mental measures drawn from 37 relevant professional journals organized by topics in alphabetical order from achievement, adjustment—educational, to values, vocational evaluation, and vocational interest. Each entry provides test name, purpose, description (number of items, time required, format), statistics (reliability, validity), source (author, title, journal), and related research. The seven volumes give a total of more than 7,400 items of mental measures.

The *Mental Measurement Yearbook (MMY)* is one of the series of publications initiated in 1935 designed to assist in selection of tests available for purchase in education, psychology, and industry. *MMY* and *Tests in Print (TIP)* are companions and are mutually related. As the introduction states, *MMY* consists of descriptive listings, references, and critical reviews of commercially published tests in English. *TIP* provides descriptive listings and references, without reviews, of commercially published tests that are in print and available for purchase. It also serves as a comprehensive index to the contents of all of the *Mental Measurements Yearbooks* published to date.

The thirteenth *Mental Measurements Yearbook (MMY)* (James C. Impara and Barbara S. Plake, eds., 1998, 1,322 p., ISBN 0910674442) contains Tests and Reviews, Index of Titles, Index of Acronyms, Classified Subject Index, Publishers Directory and Index, Index of Names, and Score Index. It lists 369 tests, 693 test reviews with 3,222 references in the professional literature, and 1,140 references supplied by reviewers. Tests are briefly described. Criteria for inclusion are "that the test be (a) new or revised since last reviewed in the MMY series, (b) commercially available, and (c) published in the English language" (Introduction). Included at the end is "Code of Professional Responsibilities in Educational Measurement." A Supplement is published between editions.

TIP is a comprehensive bibliography of 4,000 tests published as separates in print for use with English-speaking subjects. It is distinguished by the long references appended to many of its entries. Reviews in *MMY* are also indicated. There are three indexes: a classified subject index, a publishers directory and index, and a name index.

Handbooks

General

A *Chronology of Noteworthy Events in American Psychology* Warren R. Street. Washington, DC: American Psychological Association, 1994. 424 p. ISBN 1557982678. (R93)

A *Pictorial History of Psychology.* Wolfgang G. Bringmann and others, eds. Carol Stream, IL: Quinessence, 1997. 636 p. ISBN 0867152923. (R94)

A Chronology of Noteworthy Events in American Psychology contains 2,827 events, with an emphasis on American psychology and the American Psychological Association. "The collection includes dates of birth; publication of important books, articles, and mental tests; passage of influential legislation; events in the histories of psychological associations and institutions; court decisions, research announcements, and awards; and scores of other events not easily categorized" (Introduction). Arranged in chronological order from May 22, 427 B.C., to November 29, 1993, it is organized in seven periods: (1) before 1892: diverse traditions; (2) 1892–1919: the first generation; (3) 1920–1939: between the wars: consolidation as an independent science; (4) 1940–1949: postwar diversity and expansion; (5) 1950–1969: psychology comes of age; (6) 1970–1985: a partnership of science and practice; and (7) 1986–present: the second century. There are four indexes: name, subject, calendar, and APA division.

The *Pictorial History* is partially based on chapters translated from a German version: *Illustriert Geschichte der Psychologie (The Illustrated History of Psychology)*. There are 57 translations from the German edition and 50 new English-language essays by historians of psychology, grouped into seven sections: (I) The Beginnings; (II) From Psychophysics to Behaviorism; (III) Gestalt Psychology; (IV) Human Development and Personality; (V) Psychiatry; (VI) Growth of Branches; and (VII) International Developments. All articles are signed.

Subfield

Handbook of Child Psychology. 5th ed. William Damon, ed. New York: John Wiley, 1998. 4 vols. ISBN 0471178934. (R95)

Handbook of Clinical Behavior Therapy. Samuel M. Turner, Karen S. Calhoun, and Henry E. Adams, eds. New York: Wiley, 1981. 765 p. ISBN 0471041785. (R96)

Handbook of Cross-Cultural Psychology. 2nd ed. Harry C. Triandis and Richard W. Brislin, eds. Boston: Allyn, 1980. 6 vols. 1996– . (vol. 1, ISBN 0205160743; vol. 2, ISBN 0205160751) (R97).

Handbook of Environmental Psychology. Daniel Stokols and Irwin Altman, eds. New York: Wiley, 1987. 2 vols. ISBN 0471866318; reprint, Krieger, 1991. ISBN 0894646095. (R98)

Handbook of Interpersonal Communication. 2nd ed. Mark L. Knapp and Gerald R. Miller, eds. Beverly Hills, CA: Sage, 1994. 768 p. ISBN 0803948069. (R99)

Handbook of Learning and Cognitive Processes. W. K. Estes, ed. Hillsdale, NJ: Lawrence Erlbaum Associates, 1976–1978. 6 vols. ISBN 0470245859. (R100)

Handbook of Psychotherapy and Behavior Change: An Empirical Analysis. 4th ed. Allen E. Bergin, and Sol L. Garfield, eds. New York: John Wiley, 1993. 896 p. ISBN 0471545139. (R101)

Psychology is one of the fields in the social sciences that has a substantial number of handbooks. Handbooks in psychology are similar in format. Each handbook consists of a number of articles contributed by experts in the fields, and all articles are appended with references for further investigation.

Handbook of Child Psychology, formerly *Manual of Child Psychology*, provides an account of the state of knowledge of child psychology. Its four volumes are (1) Theoretical Models of Human Development, edited by Richard M. Lerner, in nineteen chapters; (2) Cognition, Perception, and Language, edited by Deanna Kuhn and Robert S. Siegler, in nineteen chapters; (3) Social, Emotional, and Personality Development, edited by Nancy Eisenberg, in sixteen chapters; and (4) Child Psychology in Practice, edited by Irvine E. Sigel and K. Ann Renninger, in seventeen chapters. The four volumes contain 71 chapters contributed by 112 authors. Each volume has an author and a subject index. The handbook presents the current state of developmental psychology, including theoretical models and approaches.

Handbook of Clinical Behavior Therapy contains 24 articles contributed by 46 authors. It is designed to deal with "how various clinical syndromes are handled with behavioral intervention strategies, empirical evidence of their efficacy, and knowledge of the theoretical foundation for the various techniques," as stated in the preface. Articles cover specific clinical syndromes, such as pervasive anxiety, substance abuse, disorders of eating, sleep disorders, sexual dysfunction, childhood behavior problems, mental retardation, and so on. Each article includes a discussion of behavioral strategies that are appropriate for each disorder or class of behavior.

Cross-cultural psychology, according to the *Handbook of Cross-Cultural Psychology*, is concerned with systematic study of behavior and experience in different cultures and is influenced by culture or results in changes in existing cultures.[16] The handbook consists of six volumes as follows: (1) perspectives, consisting of eight articles providing background and theory of cross-cultural psychology and its relationship with other related fields; (2) methodology, in twelve articles, dealing with methodological problems and difficulties; (3) basic processes in seven articles on perception, learning, emotion, motivation, and aesthetics; (4) developmental psychology, consisting of nine articles on such topics as language, schooling, personality, cognition, and so on; (5) social psychology, containing eight articles on such major topics as attitudes, beliefs, values, groups, cultural change, and organizational psychology; and (6) psychopathology, having seven articles on alienation, disorders, and methods of clinical work. It is in the process of revision, towards a second edition. Three volumes have been published: Volume 1, "Theory and Methods" (1996, 406 p., ISBN 0205160743); Volume 2, "Basic Process and Human Development" (1997, 416 p., ISBN 0205160751); Volume 3, Social Behavior and Application (1996, 544 p., ISBN 020516076X).

Handbook of Environmental Psychology consists of 43 articles grouped in six parts as follows: (1) an overview of the field with a focus on origins of environmental psychology; (2) processes of person-environment transaction intended "to highlight novel directions of inquiry and to identify recent and prospective linkages among diverse research paradigms" (Preface); (3) levels of environmental analysis, on the analysis and resolution of community problems; (4) applications of environmental psychology to community problems; (5) international perspectives on environmental psychology for an analysis and comparison of environmental psychology research in ten countries or geographical regions; and (6) environmental psychology prospects and potentials for further research.

Handbook of Interpersonal Communication focuses on five major themes: behavior, time, social cognition, aspects of culture, and individual differences. It consists of fifteen chapters arranged in four parts: (1) basic positions and issues, (2) fundamental units, (3) basic processes, and (4) contexts. Each chapter is provided with references for further investigation.

The six volumes of *Handbook of Learning and Cognitive Processes* consist of (1) introduction to concepts and issues, as an overview of the field and a review of the principal theoretical and methodological issues; (2) conditioning and behavior theory; (3) approaches to human learning and motivation; (4) attention and memory; (5) human information processing; and (6) cognitive theory.

Handbook of Psychotherapy and Behavior contains 33 chapters contributed by 39 experts grouped into six parts: (1) basic methodology and orientation; (2) evaluation of process and outcome in psychotherapy and behavior change; (3) analysis of developments in behavior therapies; (4) learning, cognitive, and self-control processes in psychotherapy and behavior change; (5) appraisals of group and innovative approaches in psychotherapy and behavior change; and (6) evaluation of the training of therapists.

NOTES

1. Ernest R. Hilgard, "Psychology: Its Present Interest," in Bernard Berelson, ed., *The Behavioral Sciences Today* (New York: Harper and Row, 1963), p. 40.

2. Clifford T. Morgan and Richard A. King, *Introduction to Psychology*, 5th ed. (New York: McGraw-Hill, 1975), p. 506; Z. Barbu, "Social Psychology," in Norman Mackenzie, ed., *A Guide to the Social Sciences* (New York: New American Library, 1966), pp. 151–52.

3. Josef Cohen, "Psychology," *Encyclopaedia Britannica Macropedia*, vol. 25 (1974), pp. 149–50.

4. Hilgard, "Psychology," pp. 43ff.

5. Clifford T. Morgan, "Physiological Psychology," in *International Encyclopedia of the Social Sciences*, vol. 13 (New York: Macmillan and Free Press, 1968–), p. 61.

6. Ibid., p. 62.

7. Gregory Kimble, "Learning: Introduction," in *International Encyclopedia of the Social Sciences*, vol. 13, p. 61.

8. Morgan and King, *Introduction to Psychology*, pp. 8–9.

9. Hilgard, "Psychology," p. 47.

10. Barbu, "Social Psychology," pp. 152–154.

11. Ibid.

12. E. Paige Weston and Diane S. Lauderdale, "How Do We Learn What a Database Includes? A Case Study Using Psychology Dissertations," *RQ* 28, no. 1 (1988): 35–41.

13. Peter R. Lewis, "The Present Range of Documentation Services in the Social Sciences," *Aslib Proceedings* 17 (1965): 45.

14. For *PsycINFO*, see the Association's *PsycINFO User Manual* (Arlington, VA, 1992, 251 p.).

15. "Important Psychologists, 1600–1967," *Journal of the History of the Behavioral Sciences* 4 (1968): 303–325.

16. Harry C. Trandis, "Introduction to *Handbook of Cross-Cultural Psychology*," *Handbook*, vol. 1 (Boston: Allyn, 1980), p. 1.

Chapter 17

Sociology

The study of society is as old as that of politics. The Greek philosophers studied society and social life for the purpose of creating an ideal state; their studies were a part of politics. The theory of social contracts as advocated by Thomas Hooker, Thomas Hobbes, John Locke, and Jean-Jacques Rousseau distinguished society from state. This distinction helped develop the study of society and social life into a new field. Sociology as a distinct discipline, however, is a product of the nineteenth century. It was Auguste Comte who gave sociology its name when he used the term "sociology" to distinguish the systematic empirical approach from metaphysical and theological speculations.

Sociology, as defined by Theodore Abel, is the study of the resultants of human activities, "the intention of which is the adjustment of individuals to each other necessitated by the exigencies of living together."[1] The primary resultants of human activities are social positions, social relationships, and social groups.[2]

Although sociology deals primarily with social positions, relationships, groups, institutions, and processes, sociologists differ in their classification of the subject fields of sociology. T. B. Bottomore classifies sociology into three main areas: (1) the conceptual and theoretical aspects, (2) the study of actual societies or social systems, and (3) the technique of inquiry.[3] Eight main fields of sociology are suggested by George Simpson: the nonsocial determinants, socialization of the individuals, sanctioned behavior, social structure, social processes, social ideology, sociology of thought systems, and methodology.[4] Alex Inkeles offers a detailed listing of 27 subject items in sociology grouped into four areas: (1) sociological analysis, (2) primary units of social life, (3) basic social institutions, and (4) fundamental social processes.[5] The present interest of sociologists focuses on three areas: the study of groups, institutional analysis, and the study of social structure in general.[6]

The study of groups deals with such problems as social groupings, structures, relations, and processes. Studies of social institutions such as marriage, family, law, property, religion, and science are the subjects of institutional analysis. Social structure is concerned with social bond, demographic composition, social cohesion, and social stratification.

In recent decades, sociology has made advances in mathematical sociology and in macrosociology.[7] The application of mathematical formulas to sociological research has been rapidly increased. Sociologists are also concerned with macrosociology, the study of sociology on a large scale, such as the social problems of a whole continent.

ACCESS TO SOURCES

Guides

> *The Student Sociologist's Handbook*. 4th ed. Pauline Bart and Linda Frankel. New York: Random House, 1986. 291 p. ISBN 0394351098 paper. (S1)
> *Sociology: A Guide to Reference and Information Sources*. 2nd ed. Stephen H. Aby. Littleton, CO: Libraries Unlimited, 1997. 227 p. ISBN 1563084228. (S2)

The handbook, designed primarily for undergraduate students in sociology, serves both as an introduction to the discipline and library research and a guide to periodicals, research and resource materials in sociology and related fields, and governmental and nongovernmental sources of data. A chapter on computers in sociological work briefly describes text editors and statistical packages. A few dated entries are still included, and there is no mention of online databases. The appendix includes, for library users, outlines of the Dewey and the Library of Congress classification schemes.

Sociology is an annotated listing of 576 entries of reference sources, periodicals, organizations, institutions, database vendors, and publishers. The book consists of four parts: Part 1, general social science reference sources; Part 2, broad social science disciplines; Part 3, sociology general reference sources; and Part 4, specific sociological fields. The second edition features a listing of Web-based reference sources. The Aby work is well compiled and useful for information sources not only in sociology, but also in the social sciences in general and in subfields.

Bibliographies

General

Finding the Source in Sociology and Anthropology: A Thesaurus-Index to the
    Reference Collection. Samuel R. Brown. New York: Greenwood Press,
    1987. 269 p. ISBN 0313252637. (S3)
International Bibliography of Sociology. Bibliographie Internationale de So-
    ciologie, 1951– . London: Routledge, 1952– . Annual. ISSN
    00852066. Print & digital. (S4)

Finding the Source in Sociology and Anthropology is a listing of 586
entries arranged by subjects into four broad areas: general sources, social
sciences, anthropology, and sociology. The areas are further divided. For
instance, the area of sociology consists of population and life cycle; racial,
ethnic, and social groups; sexuality; social issues; and social forces and
social welfare. Although not annotated, the book features a thesaurus-index
providing multisubject access points to the contents of the book cited.

The International Bibliography, formerly a part of Current Sociology,
published as alternative issues, became a separate publication in 1955. Current Sociology; La Sociologie Contemporaine, 1951– (Newbury Park,
CA: Sage, 1952– , 3/year. ISSN 00113921) (S5) is devoted, in each issue,
to a trend report, a sort of "state of the art" report on significant pieces of
work, significant trends or perspectives,[8] and a bibliography on a specific
topic. It is one of the four parts of International Bibliography of the Social
Sciences, noted in Chapter 3.

Subfield

Aging

A Guide to Research in Gerontology: Strategies and Resources. Dorothea R.
    Zito and George V. Zito. New York: Greenwood Press, 1988. 130 p.
    ISBN 0313259046. (S6)
Sociology of Aging: An Annotated Bibliography and Sourcebook. Diana K.
    Harris. New York: Garland, 1985. 463 p. ISBN 0395285283. (S7)

The Zito and Zito Guide provides resources on gerontology in eight
chapters. The first two chapters are an introduction to the gerontological
literature and research strategies. The remaining six chapters deal with resources including handbooks, directories, encyclopedias, indexes, abstracts,
agencies and other specialized sources, computerized information retrieval
systems, and community resources. Its four appendixes are useful bibliographies: (1) general reading list on aging, (2) selected list of indexes and

abstracts, (3) gerontology and geriatrics journals, and (4) selected computerized databases.

Sociology of Aging consists of eight parts: (1) introduction, (2) culture and society, (3) social inequality, (4) social institutions, (5) environment and aging, (6) periodicals, (7) research materials on aging, and (8) offices, associations, and centers on aging. Part 8 is a directory providing names and addresses of agencies and organizations.

Ethnic Studies

> *Afro-American Reference: An Annotated Bibliography of Selected Resources.* Nathaniel Davis, comp. and ed. Westport, CT: Greenwood Press, 1985. 288 p. ISBN 031324930X. (S8)
>
> *Asian American Studies: An Annotated Bibliography and Research Guide.* Hyung-chan Kim, ed. New York: Greenwood Press, 1989. 504 p. ISBN 0313260265. Bibliographies and Indexes in American History, number 11. (S9)
>
> *Bibliographic Guide to Black Studies, 1975–* . Thorndike, ME: G. K. Hall. Annual. ISSN 03602710. (S10)
>
> *Sourcebook of Hispanic Culture in the United States.* David William Foster, ed. Chicago: American Library Association, 1982. 352 p. ISBN 0838903541. (S11)

Afro-American Reference contains 642 entries focusing on Afro-American experience in the United States. It is a classified listing arranged by topic, including journal abstracts, indexes, guides, genealogy, history, slavery, social sciences, mass media, education and multimedia, family and related studies, psychology, and so on. There is a section devoted to the black experience in Latin America and the Caribbean.

The *Bibliographic Guide* is an extensive bibliography of non-serial materials in black studies. It is basically the holdings of the Schomburg Center for Research in Black Studies, New York Public Library, also noted later.

Asian American Studies lists 3,396 entries in 27 topics grouped in two parts: (1) historical perspectives and (2) contemporary perspectives. Topics include culture, justice, law, politics, immigration, acculturation, assimilation, identity, naturalization, autobiography, biography, and so on. Each topic classifies entries in general into books and monographs, periodicals, and theses and dissertations. Most entries are annotated.

Three groups of Hispanic Americans are identified in the *Sourcebook of Hispanic Culture*: Mexican Americans, Continental Puerto Ricans, and Cuban Americans. Under each group there is an essay discussing the problems and concerns of a specific discipline with a specific group, trends, and conclusions, followed by an annotated bibliography of monographs, essays, journals, and reports on the topic.

Marriage and Family

> *Childhood Information Resources.* Marda Woodbury. Arlington, VA: Information Resources, 1985. 593 p. ISBN 087815051X. (S12)
>
> *International Bibliography of Research in Marriage and the Family, 1900–1964.* Joan Aldous and Reuben Hill. Distributed by the University of Minnesota Press for the Minnesota Family Study Center and the Institute of Life Insurance, 1967. 508 p. (S13)
>
> *International Bibliography of Research in Marriage and the Family. Volume II, 1965–1972.* Joan Aldous and Nancy Dahl. Minneapolis: University of Minnesota Press in association with the Institute of Life Insurance for the Minnesota Family Study Center, 1974. 1,530 p. (S14)
>
> *Inventory of Marriage and Family Literature,* 1973–1993. St. Paul, MN: National Council on Family Relations, 1975–1995. Annual. ISSN 00947814. (S15)

Childhood Information Resources "concerns childhood as a whole, primarily emphasizing current information sources on American children from conception through age 12" (Preface). Some 1,000 items are included, with an additional 148 items in the appendix, "Multidisciplinary Handbooks and Compendiums." The book is arranged in four parts: (1) overview, explaining the book's organization; (2) printed reference works, including dictionaries, encyclopedias, thesauri, library catalogs, histories and concepts, ongoing annals, bibliographies, book reviews, mediaographies, indexes and abstracts, periodicals and newsletters, and directories; (3) nonprint sources on the child, devoted to computerized retrieval sources, child-related organizations, institutions, and so on; and (4) special subjects such as measurements, tests, and assessments; statistics; children and books; and parenting and parent education.

The *International Bibliography* by Aldous and Hill uses machine procedures for assembling and classifying the references. It consists of 11,850 items arranged in five sections: (1) the keyword-in-context (KWIC) index, based on permutations of reference titles; (2) the subject index; (3) the complete reference list; (4) the author list; and (5) the periodical list. The work is limited to research work, which means "any work which reported empirical data, whether a description of the family in another historical era or a single case history" (Introduction). Though international in coverage, English publications dominate, comprising 87.9 percent of the total. The second volume, by Aldous and Dahl, retains the same arrangement, except that it has omitted the "Complete Reference List." The work contains 12,870 items with an increased number of entries of foreign publications.

Inventory of Marriage and Family Literature continues the two bibliographies until volume 20 and is replaced by *Family Studies Database*, noted in Abstracts later.

Population

> *International Bibliography of Historical Demography; Bibliographie Internationale de la Demographie Historique*, 1978– . Paris: International Union for the Scientific Study of Population. Annual. ISSN 02550849. (S16)
> *Population Bulletin*, 1945– . Washington, DC: Population Reference Bureau. Quarterly. ISSN 0032468X. (S17)

International Bibliography is an unannotated listing of books and periodical articles in Dutch, English, French, German, Italian, Russian, and Spanish classified into ten areas: general; spatial distribution of population; population growth; mortality; fertility; nuptiality, families, households; structure of past populations or subpopulations; interrelations between economic and demographic variables; interrelations between demographic variables and other social factors; and methodology of historical demography. *Population Bulletin* carries theme articles containing references, suggested readings, tables, and figures.

Social Problems

> *Drug Use and Abuse: A Guide to Research Findings*. Gregory A. Austin and Michael L. Prendergast. Santa Barbara, CA: ABC-Clio, 1984. 2 vols. ISBN 0874364140. (S18)

Drug Use and Abuse contains summaries of the findings of 238 studies conducted between 1970 and 1980 on psychosocial aspects of drug use and abuse in two volumes: Volume 1, on adults, contains studies of adult populations mainly devoted to opiates. Volume 2, on adolescents, contains studies of adolescent and college-age populations devoted to marijuana and hallucinogens. "Each volume consists of two major parts: (1) lengthy abstracts listing the research findings themselves, and (2) a series of indexes that make it possible to locate specific findings of interest," as stated in its introduction. One criterion for inclusion is that the research has been funded at least partly by a federal grant since 1970. Each abstract includes six sections: citation, summary table, purpose, operational definitions, funding, and conclusion. Ten indexes are provided: author, topic, drug, sample type, sex, age, ethnicity, location, methodology, and instrument.

Social Services

> *Reference Sources in Social Work: An Annotated Bibliography*. James H. Conrad. Metuchen, NJ: Scarecrow Press, 1982. 201 p. ISBN 0810815036. (S19)

Reference Sources in Social Work is an annotated bibliography classified into six sections: (1) general, (2) history of social work, (3) allied fields, (4) fields of services, (5) service methods, and (6) the social work profession. Over 600 titles of reference sources and some monographs are represented in the book. Also of reference value are its three appendixes: social work journals, social service organizations, and social work libraries. Three indexes are provided: an author index, a title index, and a subject index.

Urban Affairs

Urban America: A Bibliography. Dale E. Casper. New York: Garland, 1985. 212 p. ISBN 0824088158 paper. (S20)

Casper's *Urban America* is primarily a bibliography that consists of three sections: abstracts and indexes, periodicals, and listings. The first two sections are annotated. The listings section contains 2,070 entries of journal articles and books classified into several units such as geographic, quintet (United States in general, the East, the South, the Midwest, and the West), ethnicity, "sewer" socialism, people, politics, schooling, and so on. Although this section is not annotated, each unit provides highlights of the contents of the unit. There are a geographic index and a topical index.

Women's Studies

The following are two bibliographies on women's studies. For current materials, refer to the databases in Abstracts (later in this chapter).

Women's Studies: A Recommended Core Bibliography. Ester F. Stineman with Catherine R. Loeb. Littleton, CO: Libraries Unlimited, 1979. 670 p. ISBN 0872871967. (S21)
Women's Studies: A Recommended Core Bibliography, 1980–1985. Catherine R. Loeb, Susan E. Searing, and Ester F. Stineman with the assistance of Meredith J. Ross. Littleton, CO: Libraries Unlimited, 1987. 538 p. ISBN 0872874729. (S22)

The two women's studies reference sources are extensively annotated bibliographies. The base volume lists 1,750 books and fifteen periodicals published through 1979, organized by discipline and genre. The five-year supplement gives a total of 1,211 items arranged by subject, including such topics in the social sciences as anthropology, business, economics, education, history, law, politics, psychology, and sociology. Also of reference value are two chapters on reference and periodicals. Both volumes provide author, title, and subject indexes. For current bibliographies, refer to *Family Studies Database*, noted later.

Theses and Dissertations

A retrospective bibliography of doctoral dissertations is *Sociology Dissertations in American Universities, 1893–1966*, by G. Albert Lunday (Commerce, TX: East Texas State University, 1969, 277 p.) (S23). The book gives approximately 4,000 dissertations classified into 26 subject areas, from alcohol, drugs and gambling, communications, and community, regional, and city planning, to social changes, social psychology and theory. There is an author index. In social work, doctoral dissertations were published in *Social Service Review* and have been carried on by *Social Work Abstracts*. Periodical listings of theses are noted in Chapter 6. Dissertations may also be found in databases noted elsewhere in this chapter.

Reviews

Good review publications include:

> *Annual Review of Sociology*, 1975–   . Palo Alto, CA: Annual Review. Annual. ISSN 03600572. Print & digital. (S24)
> *The Women's Review of Books*, 1983–   . Wellesley, MA: Wellesley College, Center for Research on Women. Monthly except August. ISSN 07381433. (S25)

Annual Review of Sociology is one of the reviews in the social sciences. The other three are mentioned in the chapters on anthropology, political science, and psychology. Each volume of the *Annual Review* contains some fifteen topics. Articles deal with timely topics with extensive citations of literature. Its table of contents can be viewed on the Internet (http://www.annualreview.org). Its database, *Annual Reviews: Sociology Online*, is available through *Social Science Ready Reference*.

Other review organs are many. "International Review of Publications in Sociology," a part of *Sociological Abstracts*, noted later, publishes book reviews and an extensive listing of citations to book reviews. *Women Studies Abstracts*, noted later, also publishes an extensive listing of media and book reviews. *Contemporary Sociology*, a periodical, carries a substantial number of book reviews.

The Women's Review of Books is another journal devoted to book reviews. It is "feminist but not restricted to any one conception of feminism" (editorial statement). According to its editorial policy, the periodical welcomes "all writing that is neither sexist, racist, hemophilic, nor otherwise discriminatory." It publishes book reviews, letters, poems, and books-received. The number of reviews varies. Some fifteen to 30 reviews were published in each issue. The books-received column lists books by and about women. It also carries advertisements of new books, job vacancies, program announcements, and so on.

Indexes

Both *International Bibliography of Sociology* and *Sociological Abstracts*, noted later, serve as indexes to periodical articles. Listed here are indexes in sociology:

General

> *Combined Retrospective Index to Journals in Sociology, 1895–1974*. Arlington, VA: Carrollton Press, 1978. 6 vols. ISBN 0840802189. (S26)
> *Index to Sociology Readers, 1960–1965*. Harold J. Albramson and Nicholas Sofios. Metuchen, NJ: Scarecrow Press, 1973. 2 vols. (S27)

CRIS and *Index to Sociology Readers* are two retrospective indexes. *CRIS*, one of the three parts of the Combined Retrospective Index Sets—the other two are mentioned in Chapters 15 and 17 respectively—lists some 110,000 articles in 118 English-language sociology journals.

An access to collections of essays is provided by *Index to Sociology Readers*. It indexes literature contained in 227 edited collections, anthologies, and readers of sociological studies published in the English language from 1960 to 1965. Though not annotated, the *Index* provides citations to periodicals and books if articles are not original publications.

Subfield

Ethnic Studies

> *Black Studies Database*, 1948–1986– . Baltimore: National Information Services Corporation. http://www.nisc.com (S28)
> *Chicano Index*, 1967– . Berkeley, CA: University of California at Berkeley, Ethnic Studies Library Publication Unit. Annual. ISSN 10443487. (S29)
> *Index to Afro-American Reference Resources*. Rosemary M. Stevenson, comp. Westport, CT: Greenwood Press, 1988. 315 p. ISBN 0313245800. (S30)
> *Index to Black Periodicals*, 1960– . Thorndike, ME: Macmillan Library Reference. Annual. ISSN 08996253. (S31)

Three sources listed here deal with Black studies. *Black Studies Database* currently covers literature from 1948 to 1986 of the print version of *The Kaiser Index to Black Periodicals* (S32) from the Schomburg Center for Research in Black Culture of the New York Public Library. It contains over 170,000 records from more than 150 journals and newspapers. The print version, *The Kaiser Index to Black Resources, 1948–1986*, was published in 1992 (New York: Carlson, 5 vols., ISBN 0926019600) (S33).

The Stevenson book is an index by subject to some 180 books that contain information on the black experience primarily in the United States, with selective coverage for Canada, the Caribbean, South America, Africa, Asia, and Europe. It is not annotated. An author index and a title index are given.

Index to Black Periodicals, formerly *Index to Periodicals by and about Blacks* (1972–1983), continues A. P. Marshall's *Guide to Negro Periodical Literature* (S34), published in 1941. It is a subject and author index in one alphabetical order.

Chicano Index (formerly *Chicano Periodical Index*) was first published in 1981 (Boston: G. K. Hall, 1981, 972 p., ISBN 0816103631) covering the period 1967–1978. The index consists of four parts: Chicano Thesaurus, fourth edition; subject index being the main part of the index; the supplementary author and title indexes; and a directory of Chicano periodicals. More than 12,000 entries are included.

Population

> *Population Index*, 1935– . Princeton, NJ: Office of Population Research, Princeton University and the Population Association of America. Quarterly. ISSN 00324701. Print & digital. (S35)

Population Index is not an index in the pure sense. It consists of two parts: (1) current items, containing articles, notes, and sometimes bibliographical essays; and (2) bibliography, a classified, annotated listing of international coverage on books, periodicals, periodical articles, statistical publications, professional meetings and conferences, working papers, doctoral dissertations, and machine-readable data files, with an author index and a geographical index in each issue. More than 400 titles of periodicals are regularly consulted.

Its annual index has seven indexes: index of current items, index of cover materials, index of indexes, index of bibliography, notes on sources, author index, and geographical index. The "Notes on Sources" section of the annual index gives a listing of current bibliographies, journals, and other serial publications reviewed for inclusion in *Population Index*.

Population Index is available on the Web (http://popindex. princeton.edu) as *Population Index on the Web* (S36). It contains abstracts from 1986. Over 40,000 records are included in the Web site.

Urban Affairs

> *Index to Current Urban Documents*, 1972/73– . Westport, CT: Greenwood Press. Quarterly with annual cumulation. ISSN 00468908. (S37)

Index to Current Urban Documents indexes documents issued by the largest cities and counties in the United States and Canada. It consists of two parts: geographic index and subject index. In the geographic index, entries are arranged alphabetically by place name, then by issuing agency and title. Each entry gives bibliographical description and microfiche order number and number of fiche. This microfiche information is for the full text of documents, most of which are filmed as the *Urban Documents Microfiche Collection*. The subject index section lists items by place name. The *Index* provides access to *Urban Documents Microfiche Collection*. The 1997–1998 cumulated volume 26 (ISBN 031330954X, 589 p.) contains 2,400 entries. It is appended with "Website Addresses for Contributors of Documents to This Edition," abbreviations, and information on microfiche collection.

Abstracts

General

> *Sociological Abstracts*, v. 1– , 1952– . San Diego, CA: Sociological Abstracts. 5/year. ISSN 00380202. Print & digital. (S38)
> *Human Resources Abstracts*, 1966– . Newbury Park, CA: Sage. Quarterly. ISSN 00992453. (S39)

Sociological Abstracts (*SA*) is one of the best abstracting services in the social sciences. It has grown from a mimeographed edition of 586 abstracts to over 14,000 abstracts in the 1998 volume. *SA* is classified into 29 main areas and 95 categories with subject, author, and periodical indexes. There are three sections in each issue: (1) the main section for abstracts of periodical articles, books, and book chapters and indexed listings of relevant dissertations drawn from *Dissertation Abstracts International*, A: The Humanities and Social Science and B: Worldwide; (2) International Review of Publications in Sociology, containing citations of selected book, film, and other media reviews; and (3) The index section, consisting of author index to main and International Review of Publications in Sociology sections and subject index. *SA* also includes a CAS (Conference Abstracts Supplement) issue. The 1998 Supplement 182 contains abstracts of papers presented at the 14th World Congress of Sociology and the 93rd Annual Meeting of the American Sociological Association.

The *SA* database incorporates *Social Planning, Policy and Development Abstracts* (print version ceased). It is marketed through Dialog (File 37), Ovid (File SOCA), DataStar (File SOCA), and EBSCOhost, as well as on CD-ROM as Sociofile (S40) marketed through other vendors, such as SilverPlatter and EBSCO.

For the convenience of use, particularly of online searching, Barbara Booth and others have edited *Thesaurus of Sociological Indexing Terms*

(4th ed., San Diego, CA: Sociological Abstracts, 1996, 344 p.) (S41). It adds 147 new entries and 50 scope notes.

As compared with *International Bibliography of Sociology*, *SA* has more extensive coverage of periodical articles and is published more frequently. Being interdisciplinary, *SA* is not limited to sociology per se; it includes political science, anthropology, education, psychology, history, and other disciplines of the social sciences.

A related work is *Human Resources Abstracts*, formerly *Poverty and Human Resources Abstracts* (vols. 1–9, 1966–1974). It covers "human, social, and manpower problems and solutions ranging from slum rehabilitation and job development training to compensatory education, minority group problems, and rural poverty," as stated on the verso of the title page. Each issue contains 250 abstracts with author and subject indexes. Annual cumulative author and subject indexes and a source list appear in Issue 4 of each volume.

Subfield

The following are abstracts that represent the subfields of aging, alcohol problems, child abuse, ethnic studies, marriage and family, social services, urban affairs, and women's studies.

Aging

> *Ageline*, 1978– . Washington, DC: American Association of Retired Persons, National Gerontology Resource Center. Bimonthly. Digital. (S42)

The *Ageline* database marketed through Dialog (File 163) and Ovid (File AARP) deals with social gerontology, the study of aging. According to the producer, the delivery of health care to the older population and its associated costs and policies are particularly well covered. Data are drawn from books, book chapters, journal articles, monographs, newsletter articles, and reports. Some 500 journals are regularly scanned for inclusion. It is good for locating publications on aging, but also for conference data and funding sources.

Child Abuse

> *Child Abuse and Neglect*, 1965– . Baltimore: National Information Services Corporation. http://www.nisc.com (S43)

The database offered in association with the National Clearinghouse on Child Abuse and Neglect Information, covers physical, sexual, emotional, and psychological abuse and child neglect. It consists of a number of subfiles: (1) Child Abuse and Neglect Documents Database with over 22,000 abstracts from books, journals, government documents, conference papers, and unpublished materials. (2) Audiovisual Database with 1,100 records, most with abstracts. (3) National Organization Database with 150 records of organization profiles. (4) Child Abuse and Neglect Thesaurus.

Ethnic Studies

> *Sage Race Relations Abstracts*, 1975– . Thousand Oaks, CA: Sage. Quarterly. ISSN 03079201. (S44)

Sage Race Relations Abstracts deals with European, Scandinavian, American, and Latin American materials. It contains bibliographical essays in addition to abstracts. The 1997 volume provides over 800 abstracts. Another useful feature is its regular listing of addresses of relevant organizations and publications.

Marriage and Family

> *Family Studies Database*. Baltimore: National Council on Family Relations. http://www.nisc.com. (S45)
> *Sage Family Studies Abstracts*, 1979– . Thousand Oaks, CA: Sage. Quarterly. ISSN 01640283. (S46)

Family Studies Database (FSD) continues the bibliographies, noted earlier, contains all records of *Inventory* (see S24), and incorporates *Australian Family and Society Abstracts*, 1980– , produced by the Australian Institute of Family Studies (S47). It contains over 180,000 abstracts and bibliographic records drawn from books, journals, conference papers, government documents, and other sources.

In general, all Sage publications have a similar pattern: they are classified bibliographies; each issue carries about the same number of abstracts; and cumulative author and subject indexes appear in the last issue of each volume. *Sage Family Studies Abstracts* provides in each issue some 250 abstracts with an author index and a subject index. Abstracts are classified by topic including trends in marriage, family, and society; sexual attitudes, behavior, and problems; gender roles, issues concerning reproduction; singlehood, mate selection, and marriage; child care; late socialization; adolescence; life cycle; divorce; minority and cross-cultural relations, and so on. Cumulative author and subject indexes and a source list appear in issue 4 of each volume.

Population

> *Popline*, 1827– . Baltimore: Johns Hopkins School of Hygiene and Public Health. Monthly. http://www.jhuccp.org/popline (S48)

Claimed to be the largest population database in the world, *Popline (POP-ulation information onLINE)* contains 250,000 citations with abstracts drawn from books, journals, monographs, reports, laws, bills, court decisions, government documents, theses, conference papers, newspaper articles, and unpublished reports worldwide. Subject coverage includes family planning technology, family planning programs, fertility, population law and policy, demography, maternal and child health, AIDS and other sexually transmitted diseases, related reproductive health programs, women in development, primary health care communication, and population and environment. The database is supported by the United States Agency for International Development and the United Nations Population Fund. Its compact disc form is free to qualified organizations in developing countries. *Popline* is also available on CD-ROM, updated every six months.

Social Problems

> *Alcohol and Alcohol Problems Science Database*, 1972–   . Rockville, MD: U.S. National Institute on Alcohol Abuse and Alcoholism. Monthly. Digital. (S49)

Alcohol and Alcohol Problems Science Database, marketed through Ovid (File ETOH), provides access to books, book chapters, journal articles, dissertations, papers, and other materials. It has an international coverage dealing with all aspects of alcoholism research, including psychology, psychiatry, epidemiology, biochemistry, sociology, treatment and prevention, and drinking and driving. It contains over 90,000 records.

Social Services

> *Mental Health Abstracts*, 1969–   . Wilmington, NC: IFI/Plenum Data Corp. Monthly. Digital. (S50)
> *Social Work Abstracts*, 1965–   . Washington, DC: National Association of Social Workers. Quarterly. ISSN 10705317. Print & digital. (S51)

An international database marketed through Dialog (File 86), *Mental Health Abstracts* covers aging, child development, crime and delinquency, mental health services, psychiatry, psychology, sexology, and social issues. It indexes and abstracts books, book chapters, book reviews, dissertations, letters, proceedings, research reports, program data, and over 1,000 periodicals.

Formerly *Abstracts for Social Workers* (1965–1977) and *Social Work Research and Abstracts* (1978–1994), *Social Work Abstracts* includes abstracts of periodical articles on all aspects of social work knowledge and other fields related to social work practice. Abstracts are arranged in four major categories and many subcategories. The four major categories include social work profession, theory and practice, areas of service, and social issues/social problems. Each issue has an author index and a subject index. The 1997 volume provides over 1,800 abstracts. From 1975 to 1987, abstracts of doctoral dissertations were separately listed in Number 3 of each volume, formerly a feature of *Social Service Review*, mentioned earlier. Beginning in 1988, doctoral dissertations are entered under their subject classifications and are no longer published as a separate listing. *Social Work Abstracts* is also available online, marketed through Ovid (File SWAB), on CD-ROM as SWAB-Plus (S52), marketed through SilverPlatter, and on the Internet (http://www.naswpress.org).

Urban Affairs

> *Sage Urban Studies Abstracts*, 1973–   . Thousand Oaks, CA: Sage. Quarterly. ISSN 00905747. (S53)
> *Urban Affairs Abstracts*, 1971–   . Louisville, KY: University of Louisville, Center for Urban and Economic Research. Monthly with annual cumulation. ISSN 03006859. (S54)

Literature on urban studies, including books, articles, pamphlets, government documents, significant speeches, and legislative research studies is covered in *Sage Urban Studies Abstracts*. The 1997 volume published 1,000 abstracts from more than 120 sources.

For current publications, the choice is the monthly *Urban Affairs Abstracts*. Its coverage includes such topics as agriculture, business, computers, crime, government, health, housing, land use, law, sociology, telecommunications, women, youth, and so on. There are three indexes: an author index, a geographical index, and an index to subject descriptors.

Women's Studies

> *Women's Resources International*, 1972–   . Baltimore: National Information Services Corporation. http://www.nisc.com (S55)
> *Women Studies Abstracts*, 1972–   . New Brunswick, NJ: Rutgers University, Transaction Periodicals Consortium. Quarterly. ISSN 00497835. (S56)

Women's Resources International contains over 200,000 records drawn from ten women's studies databases as follows: (1) *Women Studies Abstracts*, noted next, from 1984 with over 33,000 records; (2) *Women's Studies Database*, 1972–   (S57), with over 61,000 records drawn from 126 journals worldwide, and Women Studies Librarian consisting of four files from the University of Wisconsin; (3) *New Books on Women and Feminism* (S58); (4) *WAVE: Women's Audiovisuals in English: A Guide to Nonprint Resources in Women's Studies* (S59); (5) *Women, Race, and Ethnicity: A Bibliography* (S60); (6) *The History of Women and Science, Health, and Technology: A Bibliographic Guide to the Professions and the Disciplines* (S61); (7) *European Women from the Renaissance to Yesterday:*

A Bibliography, 1610– (S62), with over 11,000 records; (8) *Popline* (noted earlier), *Subset on Women,* 1964– , with nearly 40,000 abstracts; (9) *Women of Color and Southern Women: A Bibliography of Social Science Research,* 1975–1995 (S63), with over 7,000 records on eighteen different ethnic groups; (10) *Women's Health and Development: An Annotated Bibliography, 1995* (S64), with some 200 records drawn from English-language journals and other holdings of the World Health Organization Library in Geneva. The database covers such topics as child abuse, developing countries, domestic violence, employment, feminism, family, law, lesbianism, racial/ethnic studies, reproductive rights, and Victorian period.

Women Studies Abstracts is classified by nearly 30 subject headings, such as women studies, education and socialization, psychology of women, sex roles and characteristics, employment, sexuality, family, society, politics and government, science and technology, violence against women, finances, women's liberation movement, and biography and criticism. Each issue provides an index. The 1997 volume provides more than 2,500 items of abstracts, simple listings of resources, and media and book reviews.

Contents Reproduction

> *International Current Awareness Service: Sociology and Related Disciplines,* 1990– . London: Routledge. Monthly. ISSN 09601546. (S65)

ICAS is noted in Chapter 3.

SOURCES OF INFORMATION

General

> *WWW Virtual Library: Sociology.* Hamilton, Ontario, Canada: McMaster University. http://www.mcmaster.ca/socscidocs/w3virtsoclib/index.htm (S66)

WWW Virtual Library, constructed in 1995, contains resources grouped into twelve categories: Institutions—Departments; Associations and Organizations; Directories of Resources; Discussions: Newsgroups, Listservs, Chats, IRCs; Research Centres; Databases and Archives; Courses and Curricula Resources; Electronic Journals and Newsletters; Theories; Software Resources, Miscellaneous; and Related Fields. The category of Institutions is divided by continent and country. Over 40 countries are represented. In the United States, there are 415 departments of sociology. More than 30 associations and organizations, including sections of associations are listed in Associations and Organizations. Its Research Centers, Directories of Resources, Databases and Archives, and Other Resources are listings of sources. Some 25 electronic journals are listed. The category of Related Subjects is very broad, including aboriginal studies, African Studies, anthropology, Asian Studies, Latin American Studies, humanities, Internet Studies, men's issues, psychology, religion, and social sciences. The sites for area studies have been noted in Chapter 4.

Encyclopedias

General

> *Encyclopedia of Sociology*. New and updated. Guilford, CT: DPG Reference, 1981. 317 p. ISBN 087967329X. (S67)
>
> *Encyclopedia of Sociology*. Edgar F. Borgatta, ed. New York: Macmillan, 1992. 4 vols. ISBN 0028970519. (S68)
>
> *The International Encyclopedia of Sociology*. Michael Mann, ed. New York: Continuum, 1984. 534 p. ISBN 0826402380. (S69)

The *Encyclopedia of Sociology* from DPG Reference is a compact paperback prepared by more than a hundred contributors on "the language of sociology, the full range of its theories, the institutions of society, and the leading figures in both historical and contemporary sociology." It contains about 1,300 articles of various lengths from 25 to 2,500 words, arranged alphabetically and tied together with cross-references and item guides. Its subject maps are useful in that they outline the area of sociological study under fourteen headings. The work is replete with illustrations and includes at the end "Selected Readings in Sociology," a classified listing of books and periodical articles for the use of nonspecialist readers.

Encyclopedia of Sociology, edited by Borgatta, includes 370 articles arranged in alphabetic order, from adulthood, affirmative action, African studies, African-American studies, aggression, to work orientation and world religions. The encyclopedia has a broad coverage, including articles in business, economics, history, law, political science, and psychology as reflected by its entries on such topics as collective behavior, court systems of the United States, criminology, economic institutions, game theory, genocide, international law, money, peace, political party systems, science, voting behavior, and war. Each article is signed, with cross-references and reference notes. No biographies are included. There is a subject and name index.

Approximately 750 sociological terms, theories, and sociologists are briefly treated, with a few longer articles, in the *International Encyclopedia*. Forty-two experts contributed to the encyclopedia. Many cross-references and references to important books are good features. Its "List of Entries" serves as a table of contents.

Subfield

Aging

> *The Encyclopedia of Aging.* George L. Maddox, ed.-in-chief. New York: Springer, 1986. 890 p. ISBN 0826148409. (S70)

The Encyclopedia of Aging contains nearly 500 entries contributed by more than 200 experts. Its section on references (pp. 705–833) is an extensive bibliography of books, articles, and parts of books on aging.

Ethnic Studies

> *The African American Encyclopedia.* Michael W. Williams, ed. New York: Marshall Cavendish, 1993. 6 vols. ISBN 1854355457. (S71)
> *The African American Encyclopedia: Supplement.* Kibiki V. Mack, ed. New York: Marshall Cavendish, 1996. 2 vols. ISBN 0761405631. (S72)
> *The Asian American Encyclopedia.* Franklin Ng, ed. New York: Marshall Cavendish, 1995. 6 vols. ISBN 1854356771. (S73)
> *The Latino Encyclopedia.* Richard Chabrán and Rafael Chabrán, eds. New York: Facts on File, 1996. 6 vols. ISBN 0761401253. (S74)
> *Encyclopedia of African-American Culture and History.* Jack Salzman, David Lionel Smith, and Cornel West, eds. New York: Macmillan Library Reference, 1996. 5 vols. ISBN 0028973453. (S75)
> *Harvard Encyclopedia of American Ethnic Groups.* Stephan Thernstrom and others, eds. Cambridge, MA: Harvard University Press, 1980. 1,076 p. ISBN 0674375122. (S76)

In recent years, quite a few reference sources have been published in ethnic studies. The three encyclopedias on African Americans, Asian Americans, and Latino Americans are compiled in a similar pattern. *The African American Encyclopedia* and its *Supplement* cover concepts, events, organizations, people, and terms, with cross-references. Articles are arranged in alphabetic order. The length of articles varies, from 350 to 5,000 words. Some long articles "provide broad overviews of some twenty major aspects of African American life, showing the relationships between many of the topics addressed in shorter individual entries and interpreting the implications of central concepts and events." (Publisher's Note). There are plenty of photos. Some articles are appended with suggested readings.

The Asian American Encyclopedia contains more than 2,000 entries and more than 1,100 charts, tables, graphs, and maps. It covers Chinese Americans, Filipino Americans, Japanese Americans, Asian Indian Americans, Korean Americans, Vietnamese Americans, Hmong Americans, Pacific Islander Americans, and others. Its scope, however, is not limited to Asian Americans. The encyclopedia includes many foreign figures and entries on international relations, such as U.S. relations with India, Japan, Korea,

Laos, the Philippines, and Taiwan. The length of entries varies up to 4,000 words for long articles. It has a number of appendixes: Time Line; Organizations; Museums; Research Centers and Libraries; Asian American Studies Programs; Newspapers, Newsletters, Magazines, and Journals; Films and Videos; Bibliography; and Subject List. A general index is provided.

In *The Latino Encyclopedia*, the terms *Latino* and *Hispanic* are used interchangeably; both refer to Mexican, Puerto Rican, Cuban, Central or South American, or other Spanish culture or origin, regardless of race (publisher's note). It stresses Latino life, including concepts, terms, groups, events, people, organizations, and court cases, with rich illustrations. Articles are cross-referenced and long articles appended with bibliographical references to sources for further study. Foreign figures are also included. The length of articles varies up to 4,000 words each for long articles. Appendixes include Broadcast Media; Businesses Owned by Latinos, 1993; Educational Institutions and Programs; Filmography; Organizations; Time Line; Bibliography of Literature; Bibliography of Reference Works; Entries by Latino Subgroup or Region of Origin; and Entries by Subject. There is a general index.

Some 2,200 articles arranged in alphabetical order are contained in the *Encyclopedia of African American Culture and History*. It is not limited to African Americans. Several articles deal with Africa, West India, states, and cities. Two-thirds of the articles are biographies from the beginning of the seventeenth century to the end of the twentieth century. There are "a number of large essays by well-known scholars that examine the importance and legacy of such events as the Civil War and the various civil rights movements or discuss the role of religion in the lives of African Americans" (Preface). All articles are signed, with cross-references, and end with references. Volume 5 provides Appendix: Tables, Charts, and Other Statistical Data; Biographical Entries by Profession under 38 categories, such as actors, ambassadors, comedians, cowboys, filmmakers, librarians, military, scientists, singers, and writers; and an index.

Harvard Encyclopedia of American Ethnic Groups "contains 106 group entries, as well as 23 thematic essays, 87 maps, and other supplementary material," as stated in the introduction. Some 120 authors contributed articles to the work. The term "ethnic groups" is broadly interpreted to designate any group characterized by some of the fourteen features including common geographic origin; migratory status; race; language or dialect; religious faith or faiths; ties that transcend kinship, neighborhood, and community boundaries; literature, folklore, and music; food preferences; settlement and employment pattern; internal sense or external perception of distinctiveness; and so on. Entries on each ethnic group cover, in general, such topics as origins, migration, arrival, settlement, economic life, social structure, social organization, family and kinship, behavior and personal/individual characteristics, culture, religion, education, politics, intergroup relations, group maintenance, individual ethnic commitment, and a bibliography. There are two appendixes: (1) methods of estimating the size of groups and (2) 23 tables reproduced from examples of data provided by the U.S. Census Bureau.

Three types of entries are included in *Encyclopedia of Black America*: articles, biographies, and cross-references. The encyclopedia deals with the past and present life and culture of Afro-Americans. There are approximately 125 major articles, 200 minor ones, and 1,400 biographies. References are given in major articles.

Population

> *International Encyclopedia of Population*. John A. Ross, ed.-in-chief. New York: Free Press, 1982. 2 vols. ISBN 0029274303. (S77)

International Encyclopedia of Population contains 129 articles by 129 authors, all appended with bibliographies, and ten short entries by the editorial staff. It covers countries, population and related topics, and organizations. There are separate articles on the eleven largest countries. All other countries are grouped in regions. The "Outline of Contents" lists topical articles under eleven headings, a good approach for an overview of the contents. Serials, data, bibliographies, and reference sources are mentioned elsewhere in the articles. The following articles are particularly useful for these materials: "Publications" (vol. 2, pp. 558–574); "Directories" (vol. 1, pp. 148–150); "Machine-Readable Data Files" (vol. 2, pp. 427–629); "Organizations and Agencies" (vol. 2, p. 506); and "Data Collection" (vol. 1, pp. 127–145). No biographies are included. Readers are referred to *ESS* and *IESS*, both noted in Chapter 5.

Social Problems

> *The Encyclopedia of Alcoholism*. 2nd ed. Robert O'Brien and Morris Chafetz, eds. New York: Facts on File, 1991. 346 p. ISBN 081601955X. (S78)
> *The Encyclopedia of Drug Abuse*. 2nd ed. Robert O'Brien, Sidney Cohen, Glen Evans, and James Fine. New York: Facts on File, 1992. 500 p. ISBN 0816019568. (S79)

The Encyclopedia of Alcoholism and *The Encyclopedia of Drug Abuse* are companion volumes. The former begins with an introduction to the history of alcohol and people and concludes with a bibliography. Entries are arranged in alphabetical order from absenteeism, absinthe, absolute alcohol to Yale University Center of Alcohol Studies and zinc supplements. Appendixes contain (1) tables and figures, including 31 tables and sixteen figures on alcohol and treatment funding information, alcoholism treatment units, international alcohol consumption rate, United States consumption rate, adverse medical consequences, adverse social consequences, drinking patterns, and (2) sources of information, consisting of a directory of agencies in the United States and Canada, foreign sources, and selected English-language journals and periodicals.

The Encyclopedia of Drug Abuse, compiled on the same pattern, begins with an article on the history of drugs and people, Drug Classification Chart, and concludes with a bibliography. It is "designed to give an overview of the issue, with entries ranging from descriptions of the medical and physical effects of drugs, to psychological factors in drug abuse, to political and legal factors, and, since the problem is international, to how widespread drug abuse is around the world and how it is handled in different countries" (Preface to the first edition). Entries are arranged in alphabetical order, from absenteeism, absinthe, absolute alcohol, absorption to *yayin*, yerba mate, and youths. Although alcoholism and alcohol abuse are included, the other companion volume should be consulted for extensive coverage. About one-third of the volume is devoted to appendixes that include (1) street language, (2) slang synonyms for drugs, (3) tables and figures, and (4) sources of information—a listing of agencies and organizations in the United States and Canada and international and foreign agencies and organizations, major English-language journals, newspapers, and periodicals.

Social Services

> *Encyclopedia of Social Work*, 1929–   . Washington, DC: National Association of Social Workers. Irregular. ISSN 00710237. (S80)

Encyclopedia of Social Work (formerly *Social Work Year Book*, 1929–1960) is a reference of high quality. Its nineteenth edition (1995, 3 vols., ISBN 0871012553, also on CD-ROM), first time in three volumes, contains 290 entries with some longer "overview" articles. The new edition has some features: increased attention to diversity and the social work response to the "ugliness of racism, homophobia, sexism, and other 'isms' such as age discrimination" (Preface); adding entries on people of different national origins; increasing the diversity of authors; and doubling the number of entries from the previous edition related to women and aging. Biographies of deceased persons appear in a separate section in volume 3 (pp. 2569–2619) contain 142 profiles, including persons not in the field of social work, such as Martin Luther King, Jr., and Thurgood Marshall.

A full table of contents and an index to entries are provided in each volume. Entries are arranged in alphabetical order, and each entry contains cross-references at the end, references, further reading, cross-references for further information, and a box of keywords. Eighty Reader's Guides are interspersed with entries for locating entries and related topics. Ten appendixes include NASW Code of Ethics, Distinctive Dates in Social Welfare History, IFSW Code of Ethics, NASW and CSWE Presidents and Executive Directors, Acronyms, and Evolution of Selected Organizations.

Dictionaries

General

A still useful earlier work is *Dictionary of Sociology and Related Sciences* by Henry Pratt Fairchild (New York: Philosophical Library, 1944, 342 p.; reprint ed., New York: Rowman and Allenheld, 1984) (S81). The dictionary consists of some 500 entries completed with the aid of 93 specialists. Terms in economics, psychology, political science, statistics, and history are included, when they have "genuine sociological significance." Other dictionaries include:

> *A New Dictionary of the Social Sciences*. Geoffrey Duncan Mitchell. New York: Aldine, 1979. 244 p. ISBN 0202302857. (S82)
>
> *The Penguin Dictionary of Sociology*. 3rd ed. Nicholas Abercrombie, Stephen Hill, and Bryan S. Turner. Viking Penguin, 1995. 528 p. ISBN 0140512926. (S83)

Mitchell's *New Dictionary*, formerly *A Dictionary of Sociology* published in 1968, consists of about 300 terms not adequately covered by ordinary dictionaries. Forty-six experts contributed entries to the dictionary. The description of terms in general is short, followed by historical usage and citations for further reference. Several terms are given longer treatment, with one to three pages given to such terms as "authority" and "kinship." It features also biographies of deceased sociologists and entries on social movement.

The Penguin Dictionary of Sociology contains entries on concepts, debates, and schools, "not only technical definitions (like standard deviations), but also running debates (agency and structure, for example), type of argument (like organic analogy), major writers (for example, Durkheim), and whole schools (labour process approach, for instance)" (How to Use This Dictionary). Many entries are appended with references. At the end of the book is an extensive bibliography, which lists references cited in the text.

Subfield

Aging

> *Dictionary of Gerontology*. Diana K. Harris. New York: Greenwood Press, 1988. 208 p. ISBN 0313252874. (S84)

Dictionary of Gerontology serves as both a dictionary and a bibliography. Entries are arranged in alphabetical order, and each entry is appended with at least one reference. Terms within an entry that are themselves entries are followed by an asterisk, and related terms are listed at the end of most entries. It also features a timetable of important developments.

Population

> *The Dictionary of Demography* and Roland Pressat and Christopher Wilson, eds. New York: Blackwell, 1985. 243 p. ISBN 0631127461. (S85)
>
> *Dictionary of Demography: Multilingual Glossary*. William Petersen and Renee Petersen. Westport, CT: Greenwood Press, 1985. 259 p. ISBN 0313251398. (S86)
>
> *Dictionary of Demography: Terms, Concepts and Institutions*. William Petersen and Renee Petersen, with collaboration of an international panel of demographers. New York: Greenwood Press, 1986. 2 vols. ISBN 0313241341. (S87)

The Dictionary of Demography by Pressat was adapted from the French version of *Dictionnaire de Démographie*. It contains entries contributed by 31 authors on all aspects of demographic study and is particularly strong on technical concepts and measures. Many entries are appended with either reading or references or both.

The two works by Petersen and Petersen and the *Dictionary of Demography: Biography*, noted later, are companion volumes. The multilingual glossary dictionary consists of English to French, Spanish, Italian, and German; English to Japanese and Chinese (*pinyin* and Wade-Giles); English to Russian; and all these non-English languages to English. The other dictionary provides 1,484 entries in a single alphabetical order of terms, institutions, and countries. Many entries are appended with references. Its appendix includes a classified list of institutions, organizations, associations, and agencies; references; and an index.

Social Problems

> *A Dictionary of Drug Abuse Terms and Terminology*. Ernest L. Abel. Westport, CT: Greenwood Press, 1984. 187 p. ISBN 0313240957. (S88)

A Dictionary of Drug Abuse Terms and Terminology includes words and expressions relating to drug use and is particularly good in locating the meaning of jargon words, as for example, "atom bomb," "broccoli," and "junk man." Many terms were adapted from the author's earlier work, *A Marihuana Dictionary*. According to the author, terms on alcohol and tobacco are not included. The dictionary concludes with a glossary that serves as a table of contents and a bibliography.

Social Services

> *Dictionary of Social Welfare.* Noel Timms and Rita Timms. Boston: Routledge, Chapman and Hall, 1982. 217 p. ISBN 0710090846. (S89)
>
> *The Social Work Dictionary.* 3rd ed. Robert L. Barker. National Association of Social Workers, 1995. 448 p. ISBN 0871012537. (S90)

As indicated in the introduction, *Dictionary of Social Welfare* presents "the meaning or range of meanings of a word and then outlines its application in welfare, in legislation policy, controversy, and use by welfare practitioners." Most entries are accompanied with references.

Over 5,000 entries, including 1,500 new ones, of terms, concepts, organizations, trends, events, philosophies, legislation, and individuals are defined in *The Social Work Dictionary.* The new edition has an increased number of terms on cultural sensitivity.

Urban Affairs

> *The Language of Cities: A Glossary of Terms.* Charles Abrams. New York: Viking Press, 1971. 365 p. ISBN 0670417823. (S91)

The Language of Cities is intended to (1) "identify some of the most relevant urban terms for the expert and layman," (2) "define them simply and accurately, expanding on the definition where clarification is necessary," and (3) add some of the author's personal opinions, says the preface. The main feature of this work is its clarity. The simple definitions come from a man who is knowledgeable but witty. Definitions for terms such as "Mrs. Murphy," "Rachmanism," "Slurb," and "Trystorim," for example, reflect the author's deep grasp of urban life and his wit.

Directories

General

> *Guide to Graduate Departments of Sociology*, 1965– . Washington, DC: American Sociological Association. Annual. ISSN 00917052. (S92)

The 1997 *Guide to Graduate Departments of Sociology* (406 p.) profiles 248 graduate departments of sociology (206 U.S. departments and 42 international departments). Of the 248 departments, 152 offer both master's and doctorate programs, 83 offer a master's program only, and 13 offer the Ph.D. degree only. Arrangement is by countries: United States followed by foreign countries in alphabetical order. There are three indexes: faculty, special programs, and doctorates awarded.

Subfield

Ethnic Studies

> *Guide to Information Resources in Ethnic Museum, Library, and Archival Collections in the United States.* Lois J. Buttlar and Lubomyr R. Wynar. Westport, CT: Greenwood Press, 1996. 369 p. ISBN 0313298467. (S93)

Resources in the *Guide* represent 70 ethnic groups. They are arranged alphabetically in 68 categories, from Afghanistan American Resources, African American Resources to Welsh American Resources. Cross-references are provided in some categories. Each complete entry includes the name of cultural institution, type of institution (museum, library, archives, art gallery), address, telephone number, fax number, sponsoring organization, personnel, contact person, date founded, scope, availability, admission, visitors, staff, operating budget, publications, collection, and comments. A good feature is that each entry indicates the type of institution, such as museum, library, archives, and art gallery. Information contained in each entry is sufficient enough for quick reference. Many institutions listed in the *Guide* can be found in other reference sources, such as *Encyclopedia of Associations*, noted in Chapter 4, but the *Guide* focuses on museums, libraries, archives, and art galleries. In this respect, the information contained in the *Guide* is unique. There are two indexes: an institutional index and a geographic index.

Population

> *Guide to Demographic Data Sources, 1986/87.* Ithaca, NY: American Demographics, 1986. Pagination varies. (S94)

Although stressing demographic data sources, the *Guide to Demographic Data Sources* provides information on various sources of statistics divided into five chapters: federal agencies, state and local sources, private data companies, nonprofit organizations, and international sources.

Social Problems

> *National Directory of Drug Abuse and Alcoholism Treatment and Prevention Programs.* U.S. Department of Health and Human Services, Alcohol, Drug Abuse, and Mental Health Administration. Washington, DC: GPO, 1989. 370 p. DHHS Publications, no. 89–1603. (S95)
>
> *The Resource Book: Directory of Organizations, Associations, Self-Help Groups, and Hotlines for Mental Health Service Professionals and Their Clients.* Robert L. Barker. New York: Haworth Press, 1986. ISBN 0866566228. (S96)

The *National Directory of Drug Abuse and Alcoholism Treatment and Prevention Programs* lists 8,689 facilities. For each facility are given name, address, and telephone number.

The Resource Book is a simple listing of addresses and telephone numbers of the national offices with brief description of their functions. There are 25 categories in which offices are listed. They are, for example, children's services, civil rights and minority concerns, emergency assistance, environmental protection, family services, handicap services, hotline toll-free telephone numbers, mental health, self-help, U.S. government agencies and departments, and women's organizations.

Social Services

> *National Directory of Retirement Facilities, 1991.* 3rd ed. Baltimore: HCIA, 1990. 992 p. ISBN 0897745450. (S97)
> *Public Welfare Directory,* 1940–   . Washington, DC: American Public Welfare Association. Annual. ISSN 01638267. (S98)

More than 12,000 residential alternatives are listed in *National Directory of Retirement Facilities.* According to the publisher, all entries are taken from state licensing agencies, the rosters of advocacy groups for senior citizens, and the membership directories of religious and fraternal agencies. Arrangement is by state, then by city, and within city by facilities. Each facility gives address, telephone number, facility type, capacity, and contact. The Directory is also available on CD-ROM and diskette.

The 1997 *Public Welfare Directory* (vol. 58, 1997, 554 p. ISBN 0910106282) consists of four parts: state agencies, federal agencies, Canadian agencies, and international social services. It lists agencies, key staff, and description of public human services offered by federal, state, territorial, county, and major municipal agencies. Its seven appendixes include administration of human service programs, supplemental security income program, TRICARE managed health care program, state directors of research, and so on.

Urban Affairs

> *American Community Organizations: A Historical Dictionary.* Westport, CT: Greenwood Press, 1986. 286 p. ISBN 0313240531. (S99)

The term *community organization* in *American Community Organizations,* as defined by the author, "refers to organizing efforts designed to facilitate the development of local constituencies and to formulate strategies for action in specific geographic areas or cities" (Preface). This is a dictionary of organizations, legislation, and individuals, concluded with

"The History of Community Organization: A Bibliographic Review." Entries are historical in nature and signed, all appended with a bibliography. There are three appendixes: (1) Chronological List of Organizations, (2) Legislation Affecting Community Organization, and (3) Key Figures in the Community Organization Movement. A name index and a subject index are supplied.

Biographies

There is no major biography especially devoted to sociologists. Biographical information on sociologists, however, may be found in many other reference works, such as dictionaries and encyclopedias, already mentioned, and almanacs, handbooks, and yearbooks, to be noted next. A good source is membership directories of professional associations, such as the *Directory of Members of the American Sociological Association*, 1950– (Washington, DC: The Association, biennial, ISSN 10527184) (S100). The 1997 *Directory* (576 p.) lists 13,000 members. The other professional directory is *NASW Register of Clinical Social Workers*, 7th ed. (Silver Spring, MD: National Association of Social Workers, 1993. 1,197 p., ISBN 0871011476) (S101). It is a listing of qualified clinical social workers arranged alphabetically by state and by city within state, followed by foreign countries. Each entry provides name, address, registration number, education, description of practice, and experience.

Subfield

Biographical Dictionary of Social Welfare in America. Walter I. Trattner, ed. New York: Greenwood Press, 1986. 897 p. ISBN 0313230013. (S102)

Contemporary Black Biography: Profiles from the International Community, v. 1– . Detroit: Gale, 1992– . ISSN 10581316. Print & digital. (S103)

Dictionary of Demography: Biography. William Petersen and Renee Petersen, with the collaboration of an international panel of demographers. Westport, CT: Greenwood Press, 1985. 2 vols. ISBN 0313214109. (S104)

Notable Latino-Americans: A Biographical Dictionary. Matt S. Meier. Westport, CT: Greenwood Press, 1997. 431 p. ISBN 0313291055. (S105)

Social welfare is defined in the *Biographical Dictionary* to denote "preventive and ameliorative efforts by private individuals . . . and paid personnel . . . to improve communities or promote the financial, physical, and emotional well-being of individuals or groups that needed such assistance" (Preface). The dictionary contains more than 300 articles contributed by approximately 200 authors. Each article provides a summary of the biographee's life, career, and significance for American social welfare history, and concludes with a bibliographical essay for additional research. There are three appendixes: (1) a brief chronology of significant events in American social welfare history, (2) a listing of subjects by year of birth, and (3) a listing of subjects by place of birth.

Contemporary Black Biography "covers persons of various nationality in a wide range of fields, including architecture, art, business, dance, education, fashion, film, industry, journalism, law, literature, medicine, music, politics and government, publishing, religion, science and technology, social issues, sports, television, theater, and others" (Introduction). Each biographical profile has a box of "At a Glance" that highlights the individual's accomplishments and a photo and ends with Sources. The latest volume, 19 (1998, 293 p., ISBN 0787612758) contains some 64 profiles. There are four cumulative indexes: nationality, occupation, subject, and name. It is also available on CD-ROM and is accessible through *Lexis-Nexis* and *GaleNet*.

Dictionary of Demography, a companion to the two works by Petersen and Petersen mentioned earlier, has an international coverage of demographers whose works are related in some way to population analysis. A complete listing for each person provides full name, sex, dates of birth and death, nationality, principal career, positions, main publications, and references for additional information. The appendix is a listing of biographees classified by nationality. It concludes with references and an index.

Biographies of 127 U.S. Latinos are given in *Notable Latino-Americans*. "The biographees range widely from distinguished scientists to champion tennis players, from actors to activists, from business women to political personalities, from literary luminaries to labor leaders" (Introduction). There are two appendixes: Fields of Professional Activity and Ethnic Subgroups, followed by further reading.

Statistical Sources

United States

The Official Guide to Racial and Ethnic Diversity: Asians, Blacks, Hispanics, Native Americans, and Whites. Cheryl Russell. Ithaca, NY: New Strategist Publications, 1996. 634 p. ISBN 0885070039. (S106)

Population Demographics, 1990– . New York: Market Statistics. Annual. Digital. (S107)

The Population of the United States: Historical Trends and Future Projections. Donald J. Bogue. New York: Free Press, 1985. 728 p. ISBN 0029047005. (S108)

Social Indicators, 1977– . Palo Alto, CA: American Institutes for Research, Social Indicators Research Program. Bimonthly. Looseleaf. (S109)

The Official Guide to Racial and Ethnic Diversity is a compendium of statistical data on Asians (Asians and Pacific Islanders) and other racial and ethnic groups, covering the total population and attitudes. For racial groups, statistical data consists of education, health, households and living arrangements, housing, income, labor force, population, and for Asians, wealth and spending. There is a glossary.

Population Demographics, marketed through Dialog (File 581), is based on the 1990 U.S. census data, with current-year estimate and five-year projections. A user may search for a geographic name such as state, county, city or numeric information for total population, total households, total household population, average household size, average household income, per capita income, buying power index, population by age, current year estimate, population by race (White, Black, Other, and Hispanic), industry and occupation, marital status, and so on. For instance, under population by age and sex, it breaks down by sex (female and male), age group (0–5, 6–11, and so on), number and percentage for each group, population number and percentage estimate, and population number and percentage projection.

The Bogue work is an explanatory text of population statistical data. It consists of 20 chapters grouped into five sections. Section 1 is an overview of the United States population growth, composition, and spatial distribution. Section 2 studies population change by marriage, divorce, mortality, and so on. Sections 3–4 deal with social and economic aspects of population composition. The final section focuses on special topics such as poverty, housing, and religion. There are three appendixes: (1) population of the United States by age and sex, 1940–1980, in four tables: total population, white population, black population, and Spanish-origin population; (2) population growth in individual Standard Metropolitan Statistical Areas (SMSAs), 1960–1980; and (3) demographic characteristics of central cities and metropolitan areas.

Social Indicators contains "selected data on social conditions and trends in the United States" (subtitle). It is arranged in eleven chapters by subject such as population and the family, health and nutrition, housing and the environment, education and training, social security and welfare, income and productivity, and leisure and use of time. Each chapter consists of text, color charts, and statistical tables. A number of interpretative essays based on this book were published in the *Annals of the American Academy of Political and Social Science* (number 453).

International

Demography Yearbook; Annuaire Démographique, 1948–   . United Nations
Statistical Office. New York: United Nations. Annual. ISSN
00828041. (S110)

Demographic Yearbook: Special Issue: Historical Supplement, 1948–1978.
    30th ed. United Nations, 1979. 1,171 p. ISBN 0800210530. (S111)
World Population Projections: Estimates and Projections with Related Dem-
    ographic Statistics. Philadelphia: World Bank. Biennial. ISSN
    02574403. Print & digital. (S112)

Demographic Yearbook is a compendium of statistical data for about
220 countries and areas in the world. It consists of two parts. The first part
contains tables on world summary, population, infant and maternal mortality, nuptiality, and divorce. The second part deals with special topics
tables on natality, foetal mortality, legally induced abortion, and female
population by children ever born and children surviving and live births to
women under 20. As usual, technical notes on statistical tables precede the
two parts. However, the current volume does not include special articles
of interest to the users.

The *Historical Supplement* to the foregoing is a 30-year time series on
population, urban/rural residence, mortality and nuptiality, and selected
derived measures of these components of population changes in the past.
It may be noted that the 1948 *Yearbook* carries statistical tables for the
period 1932 to 1947. The volume together with the *Historical Supplement*
provide fifty years of demographic data.

World Population Projections was first published in summary form in
the World Bank's *World Development Report* and in greater detail in the
World Population Projections, a biennial. The latest edition, *World Population Projections, 1994–95* (Eduard Bos, My T. Vu, Ernest Massiah, and
Rodolfo A. Bulatao, Washington, DC: World Bank, 1994, 532 p., ISBN
0801849470) consists of an introduction and detailed population projections, further divided by world, regions, and country. The introduction
presents a brief history of the bank's projections, sources of data used, the
methodology, and assumptions.

Handbooks, Yearbooks, and the Like

Handbook on the Aged in the United States. Erdman B. Palmore, ed. West-
    port, CT: Greenwood Press, 1984. 458 p. ISBN 0313237212. (S113)
The Hispanic Almanac. Washington, DC: Hispanic Policy Development Pro-
    ject, 1984. 164 p. ISBN 0918911001. (S114)

The *Handbook* contains 24 articles grouped into four parts: (1) Demographic Groups, (2) Religious Groups, (3) Ethnic Groups, and (4) Groups
Presenting Special Concerns. In each group, articles are arranged in alphabetical order by topic. It is a well-written overview of the aged with substantial statistical data. Some articles provide directory information, such
as the one on retiree organizations (pp. 74–75) and organizations relating

to nursing homes and care institutions (p. 350). Each article gives references for further investigation. The article on famous aged is an interesting reference.

There are quite a few works on ethnic groups. Oceana Publications published, beginning in 1971, a series of handbooks on ethnic groups in America entitled *The Ethnic Chronology Series* (Dobbs Ferry, NY: Oceana) (S115). The series provides a quick reference to dates, source materials, and bibliographies on such ethnic groups as blacks, British, Chinese, Dutch, Estonians, French, Germans, Hungarians, Irish, Italians, Japanese, Jews, Koreans, Latvians, Poles, and Puerto Ricans, to name just some. The series was updated by *Ethnic America, 1978–1980,* by George H. Lankevich (Dobbs Ferry, NY: Oceana, 1981, 434 p., ISBN 0379007118) (S116).

The Hispanic Almanac is a collection of data about Hispanics in the United States classified in five parts: (1) U.S. Hispanics: who they are, whence they came, and why; (2) the national socioeconomic profiles of Hispanics; (3) the top 20 Hispanic market profiles; (4) the Hispanic electorates; and (5) "For Further Information"—sources and resources, a listing of materials and organizations and research institutions. It is replete with statistical data.

NOTES

1. Andres W. Thompson, *Gateway to the Social Sciences*, rev. ed. (New York: Holt, Rinehart and Winston, 1965), p. 97.

2. Ibid.

3. T. B. Bottomore, "Sociology," in Norman Mackenzie, ed., *A Guide to the Social Sciences* (New York: New American Library, 1966), p. 86.

4. George Simpson, *Man in Society* (New York: Random House, 1954), pp. 62–72.

5. Alex Inkeles, *What Is Sociology?* (Englewood Cliffs, NJ: Prentice-Hall, 1964), p. 12.

6. Harry Alpert, "Sociology: Its Present Interests," in Bernard Berelson, ed., *The Behavioral Sciences Today* (New York: Harper and Row, 1963), p. 63ff.

7. Emory S. Bogardus, "Twenty-Five Years of *American Sociology*: 1947–1972," *Sociology and Social Research* 57, no. 2 (1973): 146.

8. L. E. Watson et al., "Sociology and Information Science," *Journal of Librarianship* 5, no. 4 (1973): 74.

Appendix: Cited URLS

African Studies WWW Virtual Library, http://www.vibe.com/history/africanstudies/africanwww.html

African Studies, 19th century, http://www.nisc.com

AgEcon Search, http://agecon.lib.umn.edu

Agricultural Economics Virtual Library, http://www.aeco.ttu.edu/aecovl

American Anthropological Association, http://www.ameranthassn.org

American Libraries, http://www.ala.org/alonline

American Memory, http://memory.loc.gov/ammem/amhome.html

Americana, http://go.grolier.com

Annual Reviews, http://www.annualreviews.org

Anthropological Index Online, The, http://lucy.ukc.ac.uk/AIO.html

Anthropology Resources on the Internet, http://www.nitehawk.com/alleycat

APA Public Information, http://www.apa.org/pubinfo

ArchivesUSA, http://archives.chadwyck.com

ASDP Syllabus and Bibliography Collection Online, http://lama.kcc.hawaii.edu/asdp/index.html

Asian Studies WWW Virtual Library, http://coombs.anu.edu.au/wwwvl-asianstudies.html

AskERIC, http://www.askeric.org

Association of American Geographers, http://www.aag.org

Background Notes, http://www.state.gov/www/background_notes

Baron's, http://www.barons.com

Bibliography of Native North Americans, http://www.yale.edu/hraf/home.htm

BIDS-IBSS, http://libwww.essex.ac.uk

Black Studies Database, http://www.nisc.com

Blaise Web, http://www.bl.uk/services/bsds/nbs/blaise

Bloomberg Online, http://www.Bloomberg.com

Booklist, http://www.ala.org/booklist

Books & Periodicals Online, http://www.periodicals.net

Britannica Online, http://www.eb.com

British Library's OPAC, http://opac97.bl.uk

BUBL (BUlletin Board for Libraries), http://www.bubl.ac.uk/BUBL

Bureau of the Census, http://www.census.gov

Bureau of Labor Statistics, http://www.bls.gov

Business & Industry, http://www.rdsinc.com

ByteSearch, http://www.bytesearch.com

Carroll's Government Personnel Charts and Directories, http://www.carrollpub.com

CenStats, http://www.census.gov

Child Development Abstracts and Bibliography, http://www.journals.uchicago.edu/CDAB/journal

Choice, http://www.ala.org/acrl/choice/home.html

Chronicle of Higher Education History Section, http://chronicle.com/free/history

Chronicle of Higher Education, http://chronicle.com

CollegeSource Online, http://www.cgf.org

Columbia International Affairs Online, http://www.ciaonet.org

CompaniesOnline, http://www.companiesonline.com

Congressional Universe, http://web.lexis-nexis.com/cis or http://www.cispubs.com/conguniv

Consular Affairs Home Page, http://travel.state.org

Contents Pages from Law Reviews . . . , http://tarlton.law.utexas.edu/tallons/content_search.html

COPAC, http://www.copac.ac.uk/copac

Council of State Government, http://www.csg.org

Country Studies/Area Handbook Series, http://lcweb2.loc.gov/frd/cs/cshome.html

CPI, http://www.stats.bls.gov/cpihome.htm

CRB/Market Center, http://crbindex.com

Democratic National Committee, http://www.democrats.org

Directory of History Departments and Organizations, http://chnm.gmu.edu/aha/pubs/directories.htm

Dow Jones Interactive, http://www.djinteractive.com

EBSCOhost, http://www.ebscohost.com

EconData, http://www.inform.umd.edu/EdRes/Topic/Economics/EconData/Econdata.html

Economic Departments with Ph.D. Programs, http://www.albany.edu/econ/eco_phds.html

Economic History Services, http://www.eh.net

Economic Research Service, http://www.econ.ag.gov

Economic Working Paper Archives (EconWPA), http://econwpa.wustl.edu

EdgarPlus, http://www.disclosure-investor.com

EDRS, http://www.edrs.com

Educational Resource Organizations Directory, http://oeri.ed.gov/BASISDB/EROD/direct/SF

ERIC, http://www.accesseric.org

ERIC Information and Technology, http://ericir.syr.edu/ithome

ERIC Reading, English, and Communication, http://www.indiana.edu/~eric_rec

ERIC Systemwide, http://www.aspensys.com/eric

ERIC Urban Education, http://eric-web.tc.columbia.edu

Eureka, http://eureka.rlg.org

Family Studies Database, http://www.nisc.com

Federal Judiciary, http://www.uscourts.gov

Federal Web Locator, http://www.law.vill.edu/Fed-Agency/fedwebloc.html

FedLaw, http://www.legal.gsa.gov

Fedstats, http://www.fedstats.gov

FedWorld Information Network, http://www.fedworld.gov

FinWeb, http://www.finweb.com

Franchise Handbook: Online, http://www.franchisel.com

Gabriel Web, http://www.bl.uk/gabriel

Gateway to Educational Materials, http://www.thegateway.org

Geospatial and Statistical (GeoStat) Data Center, http://fisher.virginia.edu

GISLinx, http://www.gislinx.com

Government on the WWW, http://www.gksoft.com/govt

GPO Access, http://www.access.gpo.gov/su_docs

GrantsSelect, http://www.oryxpress.com

Great GIS Net Sites, http://www.hdm.com

Guide to the National Archives of the United States, http://www.nara.gov

Handbook of Labor Statistics, http://www.bls.gov

Handbook of Occupational Outlook, http://www.bls.gov

Hieros Gamos, http://www.hg.org

HLAS Online, http://lcweb.loc.gov/hlas

Hoover's Online, http://www.hoovers.com

House of Representatives, http://www.house.gov

IAC Incite, http://www.iac-insite.com

ICPSR, http://www.icpsr.umich.edu

ILLINET Online, http://pac.ilcso.uiuc.edu

Inside, http://www.bl.uk/online/inside

Internet Public Library, The, http://www.ipl.org

Internet Resources for GIS, http://perseus.holycross.edu/PAP/General/Res.Starting.html

Jurist: The Law Professors' Network, http://jurist.law.pitt.edu

Latin American Studies, http://www.nisc.com

Latin American Studies WWW Virtual Library, http://www.lanic.utexas.edu/las.html

Legal Information Institute, http://www.law.cornell.edu

Lexis-Nexis, http://www.lexis-nexis.com

Lexis-Nexis Academic Universe, http://web.lexis-nexis.com/universe

Library Journal, http://www.ljdigital.com

Library of Congress Catalog, http://lcweb.loc.gov

Library of Congress Information Bulletin, http://www.loc.gov/loc/lcib

Mamma, http://www.mamma.com

Map Collections (Library of Congress), http://memory.loc.gov/ammen/gmd.html/gmdhome.html

Mapquest, http://www.mapquest.com

Martindale-Hubbell Law Directory, http://www.martindale.com

MetaCrawler, http://www.go2net.com/search.html

Middle East Network Information Center, http://menic.utexas.edu/mes.html

Million Dollar Directory, http://www.dnbmdd.com

Monthly Bulletin of Statistics On-line, http://www.un.org

Moody's, http://www.moodys.com

Moody's FIS Online, http://www.fisonline.com

Multilateral Project, http://www.tufts.edu/fletcher/multilaterals.html

National Agricultural Statistics Service, http://www.usda.gov/nass

National Atlas of the United States of America, http://www-atlas.usgs.gov

National Center for Education Statistics, http://nces.ed.gov

National Center for Health Statistics, http://cdc.gov/nchswww/default.htm

National Institute of Mental Health, http://www.nimh.nih.gov

National Referral Center, http://www.roster.com

NCJRS Abstracts Database, http://www.ncjrs.org

NetEc, http://netec.wustl.edu/netEc.html

NICEM Net, http://www.nicem.com

NUCMC Cataloging, http://lcweb.loc.gov/coll/nucmc/nucmc.html

OCLC, http://www.oclc.org

Office of Management and Budget, http://www.whitehouse.gov/WH/EOP.OMB/html/OMBhome.html

Outstanding Reference Sources, http://www.ala.org/rusa/bestbooks.html

Periodical Contents Index, http://pci.chadwyck.com

Personal Journal, http://www.wsj.com

Petersons.Com: The Education & Career Center, http://www.petersons.com

Political Science Virtual library, http://www.lib.uconn.edu/PoliSci

Popline, http://www.nisc.com

Population Index on the Web, http://popindex.princeton.edu

Profound, http://www.profound.com

ProFusion, http://www.profusion.com

Psych Web, http://www.psywww.com

PsycBooks, http://www.apa.org/books

PsychCrawler, http://www.psychcrawler.com

Psychological Association, http://www.apa.org

Psychology, http://library.jmu.edu/library/guides/psych/psychome.htm

PsycNet, http://www.apa.org

Republican National Committee, http://www.rnc.org

Resources for Economists on the Internet, http://econwpa.wustl.edu/EconFAQ/EconFAQ.html

Rettig on Reference, http://www.hwwilson.com and http://www.Thomas.com/gale/rettig/rettig.html

RLIN, http://www.rlg.org

SavvySearch, http://www.savvysearch.com

Schomburg Center, New York Public Library, http://www.nypl.org/research/sc

SEC Filings Guide, http://www.disclosure-investor.com/retail/helps/sec_guide.cgi?Vendor=Internet

Senate, http://www.senate.gov

Social Science Information Gateway (SOSIG), http://sosig.ac.uk

Social Science Ready Reference, http://www.mnsfld.edu/~library/mu-scref.html

Social Work Research and Abstracts, http://www.naswpress.org

SSRN, http://www.ssrn.com

Standard & Poor's Investor Center, http://www.stockinfo.standardpoor.com/mks.htm

STAT-USA, http://www.stat-usa.gov

Statistical Abstract of the United States, http://www.census.gov/stat_abstract

Statistical Universe, http://www.lexis-nexis.com/universe

Substance Abuse and Mental Health Services Administration, http://www.samhsa.gov

Survey of Current Business, http://www.bea.doc.gov/bea.pubs.htm

Thomas, http://thomas.loc.gov

Thomas Register, http://thomasregister.com

TIGER Mapping Service, http://tiger.census.gov

Time Warner's Pathfinder, http://www.pathfinder.com

U.S. Department of Health and Human Services, Center for Mental Health Services, http://www.mentalhealth.org

U.S. Network for Educational Information, http://ed.gov/NLE/usnei.html

UnCover, http://uncweb.carl.org

UnCover/Reveal, http://uncweb.carl.org/reveal

United Nations, http://www.un.org

United States Law Week, http://subscript.bna.com

Universal Application (Peterson's), http://CollegeQuest.com

US News.edu, http://usnews.com

USGS Geographic Names Information System, http://www-nmd.usgs.gov/www/gnis-ofrm.html

Value Line, http://www.valueline.com

Wall Street Journal, http://www.wsj.com

WESTLAW, http://www.westlaw.com.

White House, http://www.whitehouse.gov

White House Briefing Room, http://www.whitehouse.gov/WH/html/briefroom.html

WLN, http://www.wln.org

Women's Resources International, http://www.nisc.com

World Biographical Index, http://www.saur.de

World Economic Outlook, http://www.imf.org

World Factbook, http://www.odci.gov/cia/publications/factbook

WWW Virtual Library: Anthropology, http://anthrotech.com/resources/

WWW Virtual Library: Sociology, http://www.mcmaster.ca/socscidocs/w3virtsoclib/index.htm

WWW-VL-History, http://history.cc.ukans.edu/history/WWW_history_main.html

Name and Title Index

Subject Index

About the Author

TZE-CHUNG LI is Professor in the Graduate School of Library and Information Science at Dominican University. He was formerly National Librarian for the Republic of China and is the author of numerous articles and several books, including *An Introduction to Online Searching* (Greenwood, 1985).

ISBN 0-313-30483-1

90000>

EAN

9 780313 304835

HARDCOVER BAR CODE